Politics, Power, Common *and the* *Good*

An *Introduction* *to Political* *Science*

Politics, Power, *and the* Common Good

An Introduction to Political Science

Eric Mintz
Grenfell Campus, Memorial University of Newfoundland

David Close
Memorial University of Newfoundland

Osvaldo Croci
Memorial University of Newfoundland

Fifth Edition

Editorial Director: Claudine O'Donnell
Acquisitions Editor: Darcey Pepper
Marketing Manager: Christine Cozens
Program Manager: Madhu Ranadive
Project Manager: Colleen Wormald
Manager of Content Development: Suzanne Schaan
Developmental Editor: Jennifer Murray

Production Services: iEnergizer Aptara®, Ltd.
Permissions Project Manager: Shruti Jamadagni
Photo and Text Permissions Research: Integra Publishing Services
Interior and Cover Designer: Anthony Leung
Cover Image: Dizain/Fotolia
Vice-President, Cross Media and Publishing Services: Gary Bennett

Pearson Canada Inc., 26 Prince Andrew Place, Don Mills, Ontario M3C 2T8.

ISBN: 978-0-13428688-4

2   17

Library and Archives Canada Cataloguing in Publication

Mintz, Eric, author

Politics, power and the common good : an introduction to political science / Eric Mintz (Grenfell Campus, Memorial University of Newfoundland), David Close (Memorial University of Newfoundland), Osvaldo Croci (Memorial University of Newfoundland).—Fifth edition.

Includes bibliographical references and index.
ISBN 978-0-13-428688-4 (softcover)

1. Political science—Textbooks.   I. Close, David, 1945-, author
II. Croci, Osvaldo, author   III. Title.

JA66.M56 2017   320   C2016-907658-X

BRIEF CONTENTS

CONTENTS

Politics is a fascinating subject and one that affects all of our lives. Unfortunately, some students are turned off by politics because they see it as an activity involving people who seek personal benefits or glory. The overblown rhetoric, distortions, and lies of some government leaders, the exaggerations and unfulfilled promises of the politicians who seek our votes, and the violence and wars that have been justified by dubious political ideals are sufficient to lead us to adopt a skeptical view of politics.

However, there is another side to the story. Politics can and should be about how we might best achieve what is good for our communities and for the world as a whole. Humanity faces many important challenges—for example, how to establish and expand human rights, protect the environment, reduce poverty, and create a more peaceful world. Political actions and decisions are very important in dealing with such challenges. In order to act effectively in political life, it is essential to understand how the political world works. We need to examine different views about how political communities should be organized and the values they should pursue.

A number of years ago, we decided to write a textbook that would provide students with an interesting, easy-to-read, and straightforward introduction to the discipline. With this fifth edition of *Politics, Power, and the Common Good,* we continue to endeavour to present a clear explanation of the basics of politics, while at the same time raising challenging questions that will encourage students to think deeply about the contemporary political world.

In this book, we provide the basic knowledge that every citizen (or potential citizen) should have, from understanding the political parties that seek our votes to understanding the way that Canada's parliamentary system works. While readers need to understand the politics and political structure of our own country, politics is about more than the institutions of government. Globalization makes it important to understand what is happening in the world at large and how this affects our lives in Canada. Readers will learn about the contending perspectives that are used to understand the world, the problems of the nearly one billion people who live in extreme poverty, the global political systems of the twenty-first century, and much more.

As the authors of this book, we do not claim to have all of the answers to political problems, nor do we want to promote a particular political perspective. Instead, our goal is to introduce our readers to the analysis of politics and government and to raise important political questions to ponder and discuss.

HALLMARK FEATURES

Chapter-Opening Vignettes

An interesting and often provocative story introduces each chapter and its content. Among the book's vignettes are the controversies surrounding new petroleum pipelines, the retreat from democracy in several countries, the citizen initiatives that resulted in legalizing marijuana in several American states, and the surprising election of an NDP government in Alberta.

Chapter Objectives

Each chapter's learning objectives situate the material and help students to structure their reading effectively.

Boxes

Appearing in every chapter, the boxed material emphasizes important political issues. These boxes deal with such topics as climate change, the welfare state, national security and WikiLeaks, American gun culture, Britain's vote to leave the European Union, and terrorism and the Islamic State.

Key Terms

Important terms are set in boldface in the narrative, appear in the margin for instant reference, are listed at the end of each chapter, and can be found in the end-of-book Glossary.

Summary and Conclusion

Every chapter ends with a summary and conclusion, providing a quick recap of the chapter's contents.

Discussion Questions

Questions located at the end of each chapter spark critical thought and conversation.

Further Reading

This section steers students toward references that will expand their understanding of the chapter's topics.

Weblinks

Web addresses found in the margins provide additional research resources.

Text Design

The text's colour design showcases photos, figures, tables, and cartoons to illuminate concepts discussed in the text and to capture students' interest.

NEW TO THIS EDITION

This fifth edition of *Politics, Power, and the Common Good* provided us with an opportunity not only to update the textbook but also to make a number of additions and changes to improve the book, including:

- A new section on fundamentalism, Islamism, and radical Islamism (Chapter 4)
- Increased political involvement by Canadian youth (Chapter 5)
- The 2016 race for US presidential nomination (Chapter 6)
- The election of the Alberta NDP government and the Canadian Liberal government in 2015 (Chapter 7)
- The retreat from democracy in Hungary, Poland, and Nicaragua (Chapter 11)
- A new section on international law (Chapter 12)
- The 2016 United Kingdom referendum vote to leave the European Union (Chapter 13)
- New sections on inequality in wealth and income, free trade and investment protection agreements, and social policy (Chapter 16)

SUPPLEMENTS

The supplements package for this book has been carefully created to enhance the topics discussed in the text. These instructor supplements are available for download from a password-protected section of Pearson Canada's online catalogue (www.pearsoncanada.ca/highered). Navigate to your book's catalogue page to view a list of those supplements that are available. Speak to your local Pearson sales representative for details and access.

- **Instructor's Manual:** For each chapter of the text, this manual provides sample lecture outlines, clarification of potentially confusing terms and ideas, and a description of the major themes. In addition, it includes sample course outlines and lecture schedules.
- **PowerPoint Presentations:** This instructor resource contains key points and lecture notes to accompany each chapter in the text.
- **Test Bank:** This test bank in Microsoft Word contains more than nine hundred multiple choice, true/false, short answer, and essay questions.

ACKNOWLEDGMENTS

We would like to thank the many people at Pearson Canada whose professional expertise and enthusiasm have been essential in developing this text. In particular, we would like to thank Jennifer Murray, Developmental Editor; Darcey Pepper, Acquisitions Editor; Madhu Ranadive, Program Manager; Colleen Wormald, Project Manager; Susan Bindernagel, Copy Editor; and Meera Menon, Proofreader.

Eric Mintz would like to thank Diane Mintz for her continuing support and willingness to put up with the many long hours involved in writing this textbook. David Close and Osvaldo Croci would like to acknowledge the support of the colleagues and staff of the Political Science Department at Memorial University of Newfoundland.

Finally, we would like to thank Tami Thirlwell (tthirlwell14@gmail.com), whose original cartoons were especially designed for this book.

We look forward to receiving comments and suggestions from students, teaching assistants, professors, and other readers to help us in writing the next edition. Please send comments to emintz@grenfell.mun.ca with the subject line "PPCG5."

1 Understanding Politics

Many people gathered in Paris at the 2015 international conference on climate change to encourage world leaders to limit the increase in global warming caused by greenhouse gases. 95 countries signed a legally binding commitment to reduce the increase in global temperature. However in 2016, president-elect Donald Trump (who claims that global warming is a hoax) said he would cancel the US commitment to the Paris Agreement.   epa european pressphoto agency b.v./Alamy Stock Photo

After reading this chapter, you should be able to:

1. discuss the importance of politics
2. define the concepts of power, authority, and legitimacy
3. discuss whether seeking the common good is a meaningful goal of political life
4. explain the difference between the empirical and normative analyses of politics

Climate change, the biggest threat to the world, is a critical political issue. If effective action is not taken, the effects could be horrific. A huge decline in the ability to grow food could lead to mass starvation, riots, wars, flooding of large areas, and massive population migrations (Dyer, 2008). Ultimately, climate change could result in the extinction of most species, including human beings.

Carbon dioxide, a greenhouse gas (GHG) that is the leading cause of human-induced warming, stays in the atmosphere for a very long time. It has increased from 280 parts per million (ppm) in the atmosphere prior to the Industrial Revolution to over 400 ppm in 2015 (National Oceanic and Atmospheric Administration, 2015), particularly through the burning of fossil fuels (coal, oil, and natural gas). Already the average global temperature has increased by about one degree Celsius over the average in the twentieth century, and the negative effects of climate change are being felt, particularly in tropical areas and in the Arctic. When CO_2 concentration in the atmosphere reaches 450–600 ppm, accelerating temperatures will likely be irreversible. (Solomon, Plattner, Knutti, & Frielingstein, 2009).

There is a strong scientific consensus that urgent action is needed to limit climate change, but substantial change has been difficult to achieve. The very large corporations that extract, process, and sell fossil fuels have been able to exert powerful influence on governments to continue to support their activities. They have also devoted considerable efforts to try to persuade the public that they are committed to environmental protection while supporting groups that question the need for action. Some governments have been reluctant to take decisive action on climate change because of the revenues, jobs, and economic growth associated with fossil fuel exploration, production, and transportation. Developing and poor countries point out that most of the increase in CO_2 in the atmosphere has been released by industrialized countries over the past few centuries, and are concerned that global measures to reduce GHG emissions will affect their ability to develop their economies.

In 1997, the Kyoto Protocol was adopted, committing the industrialized countries to an overall reduction of GHG emissions by 5.2%. However, the United States refused to sign the Protocol, and Canada withdrew from the Protocol in 2011 after having increased its emissions.

At the twenty-first international conference on climate change in Paris, 2015, an agreement was reached by 195 countries that included a commitment to keep the global average temperature increase "well below" 2°C compared with pre-industrial levels and to make efforts to limit the increase to 1.5°C. Each country would determine its own contribution to this worldwide goal and the developed countries made a non-binding commitment to provide $100 billion a year to help the developing countries. Although the Paris Agreement was hailed as a major breakthrough, critics pointed out that there is no enforcement mechanism, reductions in GHG do not come into effect until 2020, and $100 billion is insufficient to help poorer countries deal with climate change. Further, although US President Obama and Hillary Clinton endorsed the agreement, Republican presidential candidate Donald Trump and a number of Republican members of Congress were critical of efforts to deal with climate change.

The common good of humanity requires a very great reduction in the use of fossil fuels. However, this would involve major challenges to political and economic power and the lifestyles of individuals. Difficult questions exist about how the costs of addressing the problem should be distributed and how a coordinated response can be achieved in a world characterized by power conflicts and a highly unequal distribution of wealth.

WHY IS POLITICS IMPORTANT?

Politics sometimes seems to be a trivial or undesirable activity. When we see political party advertisements that are devoted to personal attacks on leaders of other parties, politics may seem like a game played by those seeking to gain or maintain power. When we hear about politicians defrauding governments of millions of dollars, we may view politics as characterized by corruption. When politicians avoid fulfilling their promises and seem to spout empty rhetoric, we may wonder why anyone would bother to spend time following politics.

Ancient Greek philosophers viewed politics as the "master science." This depiction of politics may seem strange, but it reflects an important reality. The laws and policies of government can affect all aspects of our lives and our society. The opportunity of many students to receive a higher education is affected by the funding of educational institutions, the availability of loans and grants to students, and the tuition fees (directly or indirectly set by government) that students must pay. If you are unable to find work or become disabled, your ability to live a decent life may depend on the level of support that governments have provided. Political decisions affect the economy, the quality of the environment, the freedoms you enjoy, and whether your country will send troops to fight in another part of the world.

BASIC CONCEPTS

It is important to recognize that there are no universally accepted definitions for many of the concepts used in analyzing politics. Those with different perspectives about politics will often define concepts in different ways. For example, while democracy is often defined primarily in terms of the procedures for holding elections to choose among competing parties and candidates, others define democracy as involving direct control of governing decisions by the people, or even "government that is by or for the common people" whether or not that government is chosen by a competitive election (Macpherson, 1965, p. 5). Similarly, there are no generally accepted definitions for the concepts of politics, power, and the common good, which are discussed in this chapter. Nevertheless, clear definitions of basic concepts are important if we are to analyze, understand, and discuss politics in a meaningful way.

Politics

Politics can be viewed as a feature of all organized human activity (Leftwich, 1983). Whether in a family, a business, or a sports group, decisions about what the group should do need to be made. Different members of the group will often have different views, and efforts may be made by members of the group to try to persuade others about a particular course of action. Power relationships will likely have an effect on what the group does. Thus we can analyze the politics of any group to assess how decisions are made, which people tend to get their way, and whose ideas, interests, and values the group's decisions tend to reflect.

Some political scientists view the study of politics as including all relationships that involve power (Hay, 2002). Generally, however, political science focuses primarily on the making of decisions that relate to the governing of a political community. David Easton's definition of politics as the "authoritative allocation of values for a society" (1953, p. 129) is used by many political scientists. The "allocation of values" refers to how the limited resources of a society (more generally, those things that are desired or valued) are allocated (distributed). By referring to the *authoritative* allocation of values, Easton suggests that what is distinctive about the allocation of values through governmental institutions is that this allocation is generally accepted as binding on all persons in the community. Politics, in this view, "concerns all those varieties of activity that influence significantly the kind of authoritative policy adopted for a society and the way it is put into practice" (Easton, 1953, p. 128). However, while many government decisions are authoritative, governments also take actions that are not considered binding on the members of the political community. For example, governments may try to persuade us to adopt healthier lifestyles.

politics

Activity related to influencing, making, or implementing collective decisions for a political community.

For the purposes of this book, we define **politics** as activity related to influencing, making, or implementing collective decisions for a political community (whether a country, a local community, or the loosely organized global community). Political activity includes individuals and groups trying to influence the collective decisions and policies of governments and mobilizing support for political parties seeking to gain or maintain control of the government, as well as the interactions among various governing institutions in developing and implementing public policies. Raising awareness of problems affecting the political community and efforts to change political values, attitudes, and opinions can also be viewed as political. In addition, collective action concerning problems that affect society or the world as a whole might also be considered political regardless of whether the action is directed at influencing government (as discussed in Box 1-1 A Broader View of Politics).

Discussion and analysis of politics often focuses on power. Statements such as "the prime minister is very powerful," "big business is more powerful than ordinary citizens," and "the United States is the most powerful country in the world" are frequently made. Determining the validity of such statements,

BOX 1-1   A Broader View of Politics

We often think of political activity as involving the struggle for political power and the attempts to influence the decisions of government. But this may be too limited a focus. Consider the following examples.

Various environmental groups have sought to end the clear-cutting practices of forest companies in British Columbia. Having had limited success in persuading the B.C. government to pass stricter logging regulations, they turned to other methods to achieve their objective. Europeans were encouraged to participate in a boycott of products made with B.C. lumber, and pressure was put on retail businesses such as Home Depot to sell only lumber produced in an environmentally friendly manner. These activities had considerable success, and a number of B.C. forest companies began to change their logging practices.

In 2010, environmental groups, including Greenpeace and Forest Ethics, reached an agreement with the Forest Products Association of Canada. The major forestry companies agreed to stop logging about 30 million hectares of boreal forest, which is the prime habitat of endangered caribou herds, to reduce GHG emissions to become carbon neutral, and to meet or exceed the high sustainability standards set by the independent Forest Stewardship Council. In return, environmental groups promised to suspend their boycott campaigns and help the industry market itself as "green" (Mittelstaedt, 2010); however, two environmental groups later withdrew from the agreement claiming that too little was being done to protect the ecosystem. As well, Aboriginal First Nations opposed the agreement viewing it as an attack on their treaty rights that had been negotiated without their knowledge or participation.

In many ways, these activities by environmental groups are similar to what we normally consider political. People were mobilized to try to achieve an objective that was viewed as being in the public interest. Rather than influencing government to adopt a policy that might change the actions of forestry companies, environmental groups directly pressured some of the companies to change their actions to deal with a public problem. The activities of environmental groups, therefore, could be considered political, even though the groups decided to try to affect the decisions of private businesses rather than the decisions of government.

however, can be difficult and controversial. Nevertheless, power is important in affecting political decisions.

Power is often defined as the ability to achieve an objective by influencing the behaviour of others (Nye, 2004), particularly to get them to do what they would not have otherwise done.[1] Power, in this definition, is a relationship among different individuals and groups. As such, it is not easily quantifiable and changes depending on the objective being pursued and the circumstances involved. For example, the president of the United States may be very powerful in decisions concerning the deployment of armed forces, but less powerful when trying to persuade the American Congress concerning agricultural or housing policies.

power

The ability to achieve an objective by influencing the behaviour of others, particularly to get them to do what they would not have otherwise done.

---

[1]Some political scientists prefer to use the term *influence* for the general ability to affect behaviour, leaving the term *power* to refer to the use of coercion, inducements, or manipulation to get people to act against their own desires or interests (Dahl, 1984).

Political power can be exerted in several different ways.[2] *Coercion* involves using fear or threats of harmful consequences to achieve an outcome. For example, Nazi Germany's threat to invade Czechoslovakia in 1938 was successful in convincing the Czech government to allow Germany to annex part of its territory. If your employer threatens to fire you unless you work on behalf of a certain candidate in an election, coercive power has been used to intimidate you. *Inducements* involve achieving an outcome by offering a reward or bribe. For example, if your employer promises to give you a promotion should you decide to support a particular candidate, power has been exercised in the form of an inducement. *Persuasion* is a very important aspect of political life, as people are often involved in trying to persuade other people to think and act in particular ways. Persuasion may involve the use of truthful information to encourage people to act in accordance with their own interests or values, or the use of misleading information to manipulate people. In practice, it is often difficult to distinguish between persuasion based on truthful information and persuasion involving manipulation, as exaggeration

"Don't they understand that politics is about power?"
Tami Thirlwell

---

[2]Power can be significant even when there is no intentional exercise of power. Political actors may change their behaviour because they *anticipate* that there will be negative consequences from those with greater power if they act in a particular way, even if no direct threat has been made.

and selective presentation of the facts are often used to make a persuasive argument. Power can also be exercised through *leadership*. For example, a country that is successful in providing wealth and harmony to its population may be able to convince other countries to follow its example (Nye, 2004).

Power does not necessarily mean that one actor controls or dominates others, although the term is generally used to refer to situations where one person or group is in a stronger position than others. Politics often involves considerable bargaining and negotiating among different political actors. Although bargaining sometimes involves exchange among equals (as when two legislators agree to support each other's proposals for new legislation), the type of bargain achieved often reflects differences in power among the parties to the bargain. For example, rich countries may be in a better position than poor countries to negotiate an international trade agreement favourable to the rich countries' interests because of their greater power, even if some concessions are made to poorer countries to win their support or to legitimate the agreement.

It is difficult and often contentious to determine who is powerful in any political community and whether power is concentrated in a small number of hands or widely dispersed. Even if through careful analysis we were able to determine who influenced various decisions that we considered important, this would not necessarily give us a full picture of who is powerful. If those who are powerful are able to prevent important issues from being raised, then power has been exercised through "non-decisions" (Bachrach & Baratz, 1962). For example, the owner of a polluting factory may be said to be powerful if discussion of the pollution problem is deliberately avoided by the political leaders of the community or by the media. In other words, power can be exercised through control of the **political agenda**, that is, the issues that are considered important and are given priority in political deliberations.

In addition, those who are able to shape the dominant ideas in a society may have a general, long-term effect on the politics of that society and the decisions that are made. If those dominant ideas work against the interests of the weaker groups in society and result in the weaker groups acting against their own "true" interests, then it could be argued that power has been exercised in an indirect manner (Lukes, 1974). Take, for example, societies where women are expected to confine themselves to domestic responsibilities such as cooking, cleaning, and raising children, while men are involved in public activities, including politics. Ideas that these "separate spheres" are "natural" or that women do not have the qualities necessary to participate in public life might lead many women to believe that their proper role is different from that of men, and thus avoid challenging a patriarchal system. In this case, power has been exerted through the dominant ideas that favour the interests of men, rather than through deliberate efforts to affect specific decisions.

This "third face" of power (see Table 1-1) moves us away from power being defined solely in terms of a relationship in which a person or group directly influences another person or group. Instead, this approach assumes

political agenda

The issues that are considered important and given priority in political deliberations.

TABLE 1-1
The Three Faces of Power

First face	Ability to affect decisions
Second face	Ability to ensure that issues are not raised
Third face	Ability to affect the dominant ideas of society

that decisions will reflect the interests of the dominant groups because of their ability to shape the ideas of the political community. Subordinate groups may be unlikely to act in their own interests because they have accepted the ideas that benefit the dominant groups. However, determining what is in the "true interests" of an individual or group is often contentious, because it assumes that the preferences of an individual (for example, which party a person votes for) are not necessarily the same as what is good for that person.

THE DISTRIBUTION OF POWER   In any society, the resources that give individuals and groups the potential to exert political power are unequally distributed. Wealth, control of important aspects of the economy, social status and prestige, official position, control of information and expertise, the ability to mobilize supporters, control of the means of force, and the ability to influence people are some of the resources that can be used for advantage in politics. Although all citizens in a democracy have some potential power through their right to vote, other resources are less equally distributed.

Analyzing the distribution of power involves more than adding up the resources available to different groups. Groups differ in how effectively they use their power resources. Some groups are more successful than others in mobilizing potential supporters, forming alliances with other groups, and appealing to the values and beliefs of the community to achieve their objectives. As Box 1-2 People Power, illustrates, mobilizing ordinary citizens around a popular cause can sometimes bring about fundamental changes.

The political power of different individuals and groups is not only a product of their skill in mobilizing resources. Political institutions may be organized and operate in ways that advantage or disadvantage certain groups. For example, the US Senate, which contains two senators elected from each state, gives the representatives of small states the power to reject proposals favoured by those representing a substantial majority of the American population. This has, for example, been the case for attempts to pass gun control legislation.

Overall, different analysts come up with different depictions of how power is distributed in particular countries. When considering democratic countries like Canada and the United States, some see power as highly concentrated, particularly because decisions tend to reflect the interests and involvement of a small number of persons, such as government and business elites (Domhoff, 2009; Rothkopf, 2008, 2012). Others note the influence of a wide variety of groups that promote many different interests and argue that power is quite dispersed throughout society, with no group or interest dominant (Dahl, 1961).

BOX 1-2   People Power

Those who control large corporations, occupy top government positions, or head major social organizations clearly have many resources that can be used to affect governing and collective decisions. Occasionally, however, groups and individuals with seemingly few resources are able to bring about major changes in the way the political community is governed.

Peaceful demonstrations by ever-larger numbers of people in Eastern Europe helped to bring down communist regimes in 1989. Black South Africans, by engaging in a determined struggle against the white minority-controlled government and organizing international support for their cause, were eventually successful in challenging the oppressive system of apartheid. Large-scale protests brought down the dictatorial governments of Tunisia and Egypt in 2011 (although the military overthrew Egypt's elected president in 2013 and many opponents of the new regime were arrested). Canadian Aboriginals, who in the past were ignored by the political system, have been able to make their voices heard through successful legal cases in the courts, confrontation with Canadian authorities, and building a strong moral case that they have been treated unjustly. In each case, ordinary or disadvantaged people were able to challenge the powerful through determined and skilful action, even though serious personal risks and sacrifices were involved.

"People power" is not always successful. For example, student-led actions to support demands for democracy in the People's Republic of China were brutally suppressed by the army on orders from the Communist party leadership in 1989. Despite the outrage in many parts of the world when news coverage revealed the suppression of peaceful protest, the Chinese government did not back away from its hardline stance.

People power. Citizens of Prague, Czechoslovakia, turned out by the hundreds of thousands in November 1989 to protest the communist regime led by General Secretary Milos Jakes. Just one month later, the regime toppled peacefully, and the formerly communist Assembly elected Václav Havel, leader of the pro-democracy Civic Forum, as the country's president.
David Turnley/Corbis Premium Historical/Getty images

Similarly some view political power as widely dispersed in a democracy because voters can affect the general direction of government through their choice among the political parties that compete for their support.

THE POSITIVE AND NEGATIVE SIDES OF POWER   Power is often viewed negatively because of its association with efforts to dominate or exploit others. Governments, at times, have used the power they wield to establish, promote, or defend systems of economic, social, and military domination and exploitation. As well, there are tendencies for individuals with political power to use their power for their own benefit rather than for the good of the political community. In addition, those in powerful positions may become arrogant and unresponsive to the needs and desires of the population. As former US senator William Fulbright put it, "power has a way of undermining judgment, of planting delusions of grandeur in the minds of otherwise sensible people and otherwise sensible nations" (cited in Lobe, 2002, p. 3).

Power is often thought of in terms of some people, groups, or countries having *power over* others, which is then used to the benefit of those holding the power. However, we can also think about power (particularly in the form of authority, discussed below) in a more positive way as the *power to* achieve worthwhile collective goals. Power is often necessary to induce people to cooperate in order to achieve objectives that benefit themselves and the political community as a whole, such as developing the economy, providing security, and protecting the environment. Such objectives may not be easily achieved by individuals, but might be achievable by using the collective power of the community organized by government. This can be illustrated by what is known as the **free-rider problem**. Imagine that there was agreement in a community that each person would contribute to building a road that would benefit everyone. One miserly individual might decide not to contribute, knowing that the road would still be built with the contributions of others. However, if enough people followed this self-interested logic, the road might never be built and everyone would suffer. The use of the coercive power of government (for example, to enforce the payment of taxes) is often useful or necessary to achieve goals that benefit the community as a whole. However, as Box 1-3 The Tragedy of the Commons illustrates, sometimes there are alternatives to the use of coercive action by government to achieve the common good.

free-rider problem

A problem with voluntary collective action that results because an individual can enjoy the benefits of group action without contributing.

Authority and Legitimacy

Authority, the right to exercise power, is of special importance in understanding politics. Those with political authority claim that they have been *authorized* (whether by God, tradition, legal rules, election, or some other source) to govern. If the right to make governing decisions is generally accepted by those being governed, then that authority can be viewed as having **legitimacy**. More generally, we can assess the extent to which a system of governing is accepted by the population as being legitimate.

authority

The right to exercise power.

legitimacy

Acceptance by the members of a political community that those in positions of authority have the right to govern.

ESTABLISHING AND MAINTAINING LEGITIMACY How is the legitimacy of a system of governing established and maintained? Why do most Canadians accept the right of a few people in government to make decisions for the political community, even though they may not agree with the decisions that are being made? German sociologist Max Weber (1864–1920)

BOX 1-3 The Tragedy of the Commons

In a famous article, Garrett Hardin (1968) asks us to imagine a situation where herders allow their flocks to graze on a common pasture (that is, a pasture available freely to all members of the community). To make more money, each herder may find it profitable to purchase more cattle to graze on the common land. Eventually, the pasture will be overgrazed, and all will suffer. One solution would be to privatize the commons, with the owner then charging a fee to allow each head of cattle to graze there. This would not necessarily lead to the common good, however, as only those who could afford the fee could then graze their cattle. It might also result in the owner converting the pasture to another, more profitable endeavour, thereby depriving herders of their livelihood. The alternative that Hardin favours involves a coercive government ensuring that the commons is not overused.

However, American political scientist and Nobel economics prize winner Elinor Ostrom (2000), looking at a variety of real-world situations, points out that under the right circumstances co-operation among the users of a common resource, such as water or pastures, can result in the proper management of that resource. These conditions include the development of a sense of community, shared values, and mechanisms to monitor and enforce the use of the resource to ensure that no cheating occurs. In contrast to Hardin's bleak outlook, which included the idea that a dictatorial, overbearing global government might be needed to solve global environmental problems such as overpopulation, Ostrom's analysis points to the possibility that co-operation to achieve solutions potentially can be achieved even when individuals are concerned with their own interests, provided that there is trust and discussion among the members of the community. To what extent this can apply to global problems remains an open question, although Ostrom suggests that co-operative institutions in combination with governments and markets can be useful in dealing with global environmental problems (Dietz, Ostrom, & Stern, 2003).

described three basic types of authority, each of which could try to establish its legitimacy in its own way:

- charismatic authority
- traditional authority
- legal–rational authority

In practice, there are often combinations of these types of authority.

Charismatic authority is based on the personal qualities of the leader. These qualities might include exhibiting extraordinary or supernatural qualities through such means as performing miracles, issuing prophecies, or leading a military victory (Weber, 1958). Charismatic leaders, such as Mao Zedong, leader of the Chinese communist revolution, have inspired intense devotion in their followers. Some democratic leaders such as John F. Kennedy, Winston Churchill, Charles de Gaulle, and Justin Trudeau have been described as charismatic, although this has not been the basis of their authority. Indeed, in democratic countries with media freedom, opposition parties, and active social groups, it would be difficult for a leader to maintain a charismatic image.

Traditional authority, whether exercised through the elders of a tribe or a ruling family, is based on customs that establish the right of certain persons to

charismatic authority

Authority based on the perception that a leader has extraordinary or supernatural qualities.

traditional authority

Authority based on customs that establish the right of certain persons to rule.

rule. The traditional authority of monarchs who inherited their position was often buttressed with the idea that rulers had a divinely created right to rule that was sanctified by religious authorities. Japanese emperors, for example, claimed to be descended from the sun goddess. The legitimacy of traditional authority can be based on beliefs that a certain family has always ruled and that customs are sacred practices that will bring evil consequences if violated (Weber, 1958). Queen Elizabeth II exercises traditional authority, although her authority is very limited. As the saying goes, "The monarch reigns, but does not rule."

Modern societies, in Weber's view, are characterized by efficient management and bureaucratic organization. Their **legal–rational authority** is based on legal rules and procedures rather than on the personal qualities or characteristics of the rulers. Authority is impersonal in the sense that it rests in official positions such as prime minister or president, rather than in the individuals holding such positions. The right of those in governing positions to rule is based on being chosen by a set of established and accepted legal procedures. Those holding official positions are expected to act in accordance with legal rules and procedures. Thus, their authority is limited. The legitimacy of the system of governing is based on a general belief in the legality of the procedures for selecting those who have official duties and the legal "correctness" of the procedures that are used in governing (Weber, 1958). This type of authority is "rational" in that it is logically connected to what Weber saw as the goal of governing: maintaining public order (Nelson, 2006).

legal–rational authority

The right to rule based on legal rules and procedures rather than on the personal qualities or characteristics of the rulers.

Charismatic leaders, such as Mao Zedong, leader of the Chinese communist revolution, inspire intense devotion in their followers. Charismatic authority rests upon the belief of followers in magical powers, revelations, and hero worship. The Chinese media depicted an elderly Mao supposedly performing the heroic feat of swimming across the Yangtze River to maintain his charismatic image.
AP Images

Holding free and fair elections involving all adult citizens using procedures established by law to select those authorized to make governing decisions is often considered to be the most effective way of establishing the legitimacy of government. Nevertheless, a "legitimacy crisis" can occur even in democratic systems (Habermas, 1975). Although an unpopular government in a democracy can be voted out, if governments are persistently ineffective in dealing with serious problems or are seen as corrupt, citizens might question the legitimacy of the democratic institutions and processes in their country. For example, if the policies of successive governments led to widespread poverty and unemployment or to a collapse in the value of the currency, then the legitimacy of the system of governing might be challenged. Legitimacy can also be reduced if some groups feel that there is a long-term pattern of mistreatment by the government. In other words, the legitimacy of a democratic government not only may require an acceptance of the procedures by which governing authorities are chosen and actions are taken, but also may depend on the perceived rightfulness of how government (or, more generally, the system of governing) exercises its authority (Barnard, 2001). In particular, the governing authorities will have a higher level of legitimacy if their actions are perceived as being consistent with the general principles and values of the political community (Gilley, 2006).

In addition, a system of governing that is imposed on a country or on a part of the population without its consent might be viewed as illegitimate, even if it establishes democratic procedures. For example, when a democratic system of governing was established in Germany after World War I, some Germans doubted its legitimacy, partly because they viewed it as being imposed on the country by the victors in that war. The problem of legitimacy, combined with the failure of German governments to deal effectively with the problems the country faced, eventually contributed to the demise of the democratic system and the takeover by Adolf Hitler and the Nazi party. Likewise, conquered peoples are often unwilling to accept the legitimacy of the governing authorities imposed by the foreign rulers.

THE SIGNIFICANCE OF LEGITIMATE AUTHORITY   Effective governing depends not only on governing institutions having the power to force people to act in certain ways, but also on their ability to establish and maintain legitimate authority. A government that is not accepted as legitimate by a significant proportion of the population will have to devote much of its energy and resources to persuading or coercing the population to obey its laws and maintain order. All governments rely on coercion and other forms of power to some extent, but generally most people feel an obligation to obey a legitimate government. Thus, a government whose rule is considered legitimate can rely more on authority than on coercion to get people to obey the laws it adopts.

Having legitimate authority gives government a powerful resource to achieve its goals. People usually obey laws, even when they find those laws to be against their interests or values, because they view the source of those laws as legitimate. This can potentially allow the government to act for the good of the community as a whole, even when some may object to the policies adopted. However, even though most people would agree that political authority is a necessary and desirable feature of an orderly society, questions can arise concerning whether there are circumstances in which authority should be resisted or disobeyed. What would you do if you were drafted to fight in a war that you considered unjust? Would you resist the authority of a democratically elected government that was persecuting an unpopular minority, even if that persecution were done in a legal manner?

The Common Good

common good

What is good for the entire political community.

Political philosophers have often viewed politics as different from other activities in that it should be concerned with the **common good** of the community as a whole. Ensuring the good functioning of governing—such as maintaining order and security, providing for a just settlement of disputes, helping to develop a prosperous, sustainable economy, providing quality education, protecting the environment, and working toward a peaceful world—potentially benefits all members of the political community (Wolin, 1960).

On the surface, the concept of the common good seems uncontroversial. Who would not agree that political activity should be directed toward the common good of the political community? However, in practice, determining and achieving the common good can be contentious as members of a political community have different interests and values. Not every individual and group in the community will agree on what is good for the community as a whole.

individualist perspective

A perspective that views human beings as acting primarily in accordance with their own interests.

Those who have an **individualist perspective** on politics assume that human beings act primarily in accordance with their own interests—in other words, selfishly. In this perspective, a political community is basically a collection of individuals each pursuing his or her own interests. Thus, it is naive or hopelessly idealistic to expect people (whether as voters, politicians, or government officials) to deliberately act for the common good, particularly when that involves sacrificing their own interests.

Those who hold the individualist perspective often argue that if every person is free to pursue his or her own interests, the result will lead to the best overall result for the members of the community. For example, Scottish philosopher Adam Smith (1723–1790) suggested that if individuals pursue their own economic self-interest in a competitive free-market system, the result will be maximization of the wealth of society. For many of Smith's contemporary followers, the implication is that government should be restricted to the minimum needed to provide security and protection for individuals and the free market.

Are we concerned only with our own good? If individuals pursue their own interests, will the good of the entire community be served? Are the communities that we live in no more than a collection of independent individuals? Critics of the individualist perspective argue that humans are social beings who flourish through harmonious interaction with others. Connected to our social nature is the capability to care about others. This capability initially develops within our own family, but can extend to the social groups to which we belong, to citizens of our country, and potentially to the world as a whole. The outpouring of assistance by people around the world to Haiti following the devastating earthquake there in January 2010 suggests that individuals exhibit a concern for the well-being of others that is not motivated solely by self-interest. Indeed, although Adam Smith is often associated with the idea of the importance of self-interest, in *The Theory of Moral Sentiments* (1759/2010) he emphasized that individuals have an interest in the happiness of others.

Further, the communities to which we belong—including political communities—help to shape our sense of ourselves, that is, our identity. A sense of belonging to and participating in a political community could be considered an important part of a fulfilling and meaningful life. People have an interest not only in their own material well-being, but also in the quality of their community and the social relations that are a part of that community (Lutz, 1999). Individuals engage in political activity not only to advance their own interests, but also to pursue the values they think should guide the actions of government (Lewin, 1991).

Contemporary political communities often feature considerable diversity such that a consensus on what is the common good may be difficult or impossible to achieve. The values of a particular religion in many countries no longer provide a widely accepted guide as to what constitutes a good life and a good society. Even if a number of general values such as freedom, equality, order, and justice are shared by people within the community, these values may be thought of in different ways, and different people or groups may give these values different priorities.

As well, the costs and benefits of actions to achieve the common good are often unequally distributed. For example, most people would agree that reducing air pollution would be for the common good of the political community. However, the costs of reducing pollution to achieve this objective may fall more heavily on some, such as factory owners and automobile users, than on others. Likewise, a free school breakfast program primarily benefits those whose parents are very poor. Nevertheless, we might view such a program as being for the common good if we assume that being part of a community involves caring about others in that community and supporting policies that help all people enjoy the benefits of the community. However, in countries where there are sharp divisions (based, for example, on economic inequality, religion, region, or cultural identities), the sense of being members of a shared political community and a willingness to be concerned about others may be weak or non-existent. In such political communities, the notion of the common good may not be very meaningful.

ACHIEVING THE COMMON GOOD?   We often look to government to achieve the common good. But how can we be assured that government will pursue the common good rather than the particular interests of those in government? In *The Republic*, the ancient Greek philosopher Plato (c. 429–347 BCE) sketched out an ideal of how the common good might be achieved. This involved placing political authority in the hands of a wise philosopher–king who had been thoroughly educated in the art of governing. To ensure that such a leader would rule for the common good rather than out of personal interest, leaders would be prevented from having a family or owning property.

What might this suggest for governments and their citizens operating in the real world and not in a great thinker's utopia?

In the contemporary world, democracy is often seen as the form of government most likely to actually pursue the common good. Ideally, through discussion among citizens, an informed consensus can be reached about the policies that are desirable for the common good. However, meaningful discussion is often difficult to achieve outside of small groups and small communities. Instead, there is often an expectation that decisions in a democracy will tend to reflect the opinions of the majority of the population. Even if this is the case, it does not ensure that the common good of the community will be achieved. The majority is not necessarily oriented toward the common good of all members of the community, and at various times majorities have supported policies that oppress minorities. Furthermore, governments in some countries can be elected with the support of only a minority of voters, and thus may be inclined to adopt policies favoured by their supporters rather than a majority of the population.

pluralist system

A political system in which a large number of groups representing a wide variety of interests are able to influence the decisions of government. Government tries to satisfy as many groups as possible, and no group has a dominant influence on government.

Some suggest that a **pluralist system**, one in which a large number of groups put forward the demands of a wide variety of people and interests and government tries to satisfy as many groups as possible, will result in the common good. A potential problem is that, even if government is responsive to groups representing a wide variety of interests, this does not necessarily result in the common good. Providing particular benefits to various groups that are able to exert effective pressure may not be the same as acting for the common good. If each group pursues its own interests, the good of the entire community may be ignored.

Although seeking the common good may be a worthwhile objective for political life, it should be kept in mind that the claim to be acting for the common good (or other ideals) can be deceptive. Ruthless leaders have tried to justify brutal actions in the name of the long-term good of the political community. For example, the Soviet leader Joseph Stalin tried to justify his actions, which resulted in the starvation of millions of peasants, with the ideal of creating a "classless society." Fascist leaders such as Adolf Hitler and Benito Mussolini used the appeal of the good of the nation to suppress dissent and justify wars of aggression. Even in those democratic countries where individual rights are valued, appeals to the common good are sometimes made to justify repressive government actions in order to fight terrorism, subversion, and crime. In general, there is a real danger that government leaders claiming to pursue the common good of the political community as a whole will act in ways that are oppressive to some members of that community.

A QUESTION OF COMMUNITIES AND THE FUTURE   The common good is often thought of in terms of the country in which we live. But the common good of the country may not necessarily be the same as the common good of the other political communities to which we belong, such as provincial or local communities. Indeed, some argue that we should be concerned about the common good of humanity. The processes of globalization have increased interaction and interdependence among the peoples of the world. However, despite greater awareness of and concern for what happens in other parts of the world, for most of us our sense of being part of a global political community is much weaker than our sense of being Canadian. Major differences among the peoples of the world in culture and circumstances mean that there are fewer shared interests and values upon which a consensus about the common good of humanity could be based.

In addition, the common good is often thought of in terms of the quality of life and the community in the present. However, should the quality of life of future generations be taken into account in seeking the common good, even though they have no voice? Pursuing rapid economic growth may be in the common good of people today, but what if global climate change leaves humanity 50 years from now with a devastated environment?

WHAT IS POLITICAL SCIENCE?

The term **political science** may sound confusing, as politics and science seem to be very different. Indeed, some universities and colleges prefer to use terms such as *political studies*, *politics*, or *government* rather than political science. However, keeping in mind that the word *science* is derived from a Latin word meaning knowledge, we could define political science simply as the systematic study of politics. As Box 1-4 The Development of Political Science, indicates, political science includes a diverse set of ways to approach the study of politics.

A distinction is often made between empirical analysis and normative analysis (see Table 1-2). **Empirical analysis** involves explaining various aspects of politics, particularly by using careful observation and comparison to develop generalizations. The goal of empirical analysis is not simply to gather data to describe various features of politics and government, but also to develop testable theories that will help us to understand how politics

political science

The systematic study of politics.

empirical analysis

Analysis that involves explaining various aspects of politics, particularly by using careful observation and comparison to develop generalizations and testable theories.

BOX 1-4   The Development of Political Science

The origins of political science are often traced back about 2400 years to the works of ancient Greek philosophers Plato and Aristotle.[*] Building on the works of many classic thinkers, political philosophy examines important normative questions: Who should rule? Are we obligated to obey the decisions of those in positions of political authority? What values, such as freedom and equality, should be pursued in politics?

Political science as an academic discipline distinct from economics, philosophy, and law developed in the late nineteenth century and often focused on the analysis of governmental institutions and constitutional law. Beginning in the 1950s, behaviouralism focused on systematic observation of the attitudes and behaviour of political actors such as voters and legislators using quantitative methods such as survey research. It sought to apply a value-free scientific approach to the study of politics. Subsequently, a deductive approach, rational choice theory, based on the assumption that individuals will act rationally to maximize their interests, has also been widely used to try to explain political behaviour. The behavioural emphasis on rigorous scientific testing of hypotheses with empirical data has also been complemented by an interest in a broader understanding and theorizing about politics and its relationship with society, the economy, and historical development. The systematic study of politics often takes a comparative approach of explaining political phenomena through a detailed analysis of similarities and differences in the politics of different countries.

Political philosophy has been reinvigorated in recent decades by major works on topics such as justice, the accommodation of diversity, and deliberative democracy. Critical theories including Marxism, feminism, and postmodernism have stimulated much debate within political science (and the other social sciences).

*In addition, about 2500 years ago, Confucius developed political ideas that are still influential, particularly in China and East Asia.

TABLE 1-2
Empirical, Normative, and Policy Analysis: An Example

Empirical analysis	Why are women less likely than men to run for Parliament?
Normative analysis	Should legislatures be a microcosm of society?
Policy analysis	What is the best way of increasing the proportion of women in Parliament?

normative analysis

Analysis that includes examining ideas about how the community should be governed and what values should be pursued through politics.

works. **Normative analysis** includes examining ideas about how the community should be governed and what values should be pursued through politics.

In practice, the distinction between empirical and normative analysis is not as clear-cut as it seems. Political scientists are part of the world they study; the empirical questions they choose to study and the way they go about researching those questions will be affected by their values and perspectives. Likewise, normative analyses are based on understandings of human nature and how the political world works. The combination of empirical and normative analysis is often evident in policy analysis, which may involve evaluating existing policies and assessing possible alternatives to deal with particular problems. Policy analysts have to consider what is feasible rather than ideal, which calls for an understanding of political realities; that is, they need to consider how best to achieve desired values under particular circumstances.

Why Study Politics?

Understanding politics is essential in order to take effective action to achieve our goals and ideals. Imagine that you are concerned about global climate change and would like governments to take actions to reduce the use of fossil fuels. Or perhaps you think that university tuition fees are too high and should be lowered or eliminated to allow greater accessibility to higher education. Or you heard that a friend has been killed by someone who was drinking and driving, and you decide that stricter laws are needed. How would you go about trying to achieve your goals? Would you email the prime minister, your member of Parliament, your member of the provincial legislature, or your local municipal council? Join a group that is taking up your cause? Organize a protest demonstration? Sign an on-line petition? Vote for a party that appears sympathetic to your concerns? Run for public office? Sit back and hope that decision makers in government make the right decision?

Understanding politics can help you to think about the issues that arise in politics, and how to pursue what is best for your community, country, and the world. Studying political science is also interesting and challenging because of the wide variety of perspectives and approaches used to analyze politics.

CAREER TIES Students often ask how taking political science courses or getting a degree in political science will help them to find employment and pursue a career. Political science would obviously be useful for anyone contemplating a career in politics, but most of those who study politics are not budding politicians. Nevertheless, about one-fifth of Canadians work for government or its agencies. Those who work for business or non-profit organizations often interact with government and governmental agencies. Knowledge of government policies and regulations and the operations of the political system are useful in almost every field of endeavour. And, in an increasingly globalized world, knowledge of foreign political systems and international organizations and agreements is very important for doing business. Taking political science courses or a degree in political science provides a good background to a wide variety of career choices.

Political science courses can also be helpful in developing general intellectual skills that are useful in one's personal development and eventual career. Such skills include developing the ability to communicate effectively, read carefully, research thoroughly, and think critically.

Canadian Political Science Association
www.cpsa-acsp.ca

Political Science Resources
www.psr.keele.ac.uk

✓• SUMMARY AND CONCLUSION

Politics plays a vital role in our lives, our communities, and the world as a whole. Whether or not we are interested in politics, we are affected by political decisions.

Because of disagreements about what governments should do, political activity involves mobilizing people to advance their interests and values. As well, politics involves trying to resolve conflicts in order to achieve the co-operation needed to achieve collective goals.

Politics is a complex activity. To understand what goes on in political life and the decisions and policies that result from political activity, it is necessary to examine the interests that people and groups pursue, the ideas and values that affect their activities and decisions, the identities that are important to them, and the institutions, rules, and processes that shape political activities and lead to the actions and policies of government. As well, politics in any particular political community is affected by the economic, social, and historical context and the international system in which it operates (with government policies, in turn, affecting economic and social systems as well as individual behaviour). Of particular importance in determining the actions that governments take is the distribution of political power.

People often have a negative view of politics because of its association with unscrupulous efforts to gain or maintain power. Governments are often criticized for being inefficient, wasteful, and prone to corruption. Some governments have supported or acquiesced in the domination and exploitation of the weak within the society that they govern. The laws and policies adopted by governments may reflect the interests and values of the dominant groups in society, resulting in the harassment, persecution, or neglect of the less powerful. As well, some governments have pursued the conquest, control, and exploitation of other countries. Because power and authority are easily abused, it is important to ensure that those in governing positions are held accountable for their actions and that excessive concentration of power

is resisted. As the famous saying of nineteenth-century British historian Lord Acton warns, "Power tends to corrupt and absolute power corrupts absolutely."

There is, however, a positive side to politics. Many people engage in political activity not only to advance their own interests or to pursue power for its own sake, but also with the hope of advancing the common good of the political community. For example, through political action by many people, including many young persons, governments have been pressured to deal with global climate change.

Many governments have been able to work toward the common good by such measures as establishing peace and security within the political community, creating a fair and impartial system of justice, helping to develop their country's economy and infrastructure, and providing accessible education and health care. Governments can also promote the common good by regulating and checking the power wielded by various social and economic institutions, and thus help to protect and assist the weaker or disadvantaged members of society.

Political science, the systematic study of politics, has its roots in thousands of years of discussion and analysis about what is good for the communities we live in and how this good can best be achieved. Contemporary political science is building a systematic, theoretically based understanding of politics while continuing to examine fundamental questions about the values upon which governing should be based. Many political scientists also use their research to provide practical advice about the political processes and public policies that are for the common good.

✔• KEY TERMS

DISCUSSION QUESTIONS

1. What are the major political issues in your local, provincial, and national communities? What about in the global community? Do the most talked-about issues reflect the most serious problems that each of these communities faces? Are any important issues ignored?

2. Should we be concerned if political power is highly concentrated? Can we trust government to look after the common good?

3. Is it meaningful to talk about the common good in a diverse society?

4. How important is the study of politics? Is it an essential component of a good education?

5. Do all citizens have a responsibility to keep themselves informed about politics?

FURTHER READING

Aristotle. (1973). *Politics of Aristotle* (E. Barker, Trans.). New York: Oxford University Press.

Dahl, R.A., & Stinebrickner, B. (2002). *Modern political analysis* (6th ed.). Upper Saddle River, NJ: Prentice Hall.

Etzioni, A. (2004). *The common good*. Oxford: Polity Press.

Leftwich, A. (1983). *Redefining politics: People, resources and power*. London and New York: Methuen.

Marsh, D., & Stoker, G. (Eds.). (2010). *Theory and methods in political science* (3rd ed.). New York: Palgrave Macmillan.

Menzies, H. (2014). *Reclaiming the commons for the common good*. Gabriola Island, BC: New Society Publishers.

Pyrcz, G. (2011). *The study of politics. A short survey of core approaches*. Toronto: University of Toronto Press.

Theodoulou, S.Z., & O'Brien, R. (Eds.). (1999). *Methods for political inquiry: The discipline, philosophy, and analysis of politics*. Upper Saddle River, NJ: Prentice Hall.

A number of *novels* provide interesting and provocative descriptions of politics in the past, present, and possible future:

Atwood, M. (1985). *The handmaid's tale*. Toronto: McClelland & Stewart.

Bradbury, R. (2012/1951). *Fahrenheit 451*. New York: Simon & Schuster.

Follett, K. (2010, 2012, 2015). *The century trilogy*. New York, NY: Penguin.

Koestler, A. (2011). *Darkness at noon*. New York: Random House.

LeGuin, U.K. (1974). *The dispossessed*. New York: Avon Books.

Orwell, G. (1948). *1984*. New York: New American Library.

2 The Nation-State and Globalization

More than a million Catalans march in Barcelona demanding that the Spanish government recognize Catalonia as a nation.　epa european pressphoto agency b.v./Alamy Stock Photo

After reading this chapter, you should be able to:

1. discuss the nature of the modern state
2. explain the difference between a nation and a state
3. discuss the significance of nationalism and national self-determination
4. examine the meaning of citizenship
5. outline the nature and significance of globalization

On June 18, 2006, 74 percent of Catalans voting in a binding referendum supported the adoption of a revised Statute of Autonomy of Catalonia (a region of northeastern Spain with 7.2 million people who have a distinct language, history, and culture). The revised statute recognized the Catalan nationality and expanded the self-governing powers of Catalonia's government. Recognizing this distinct nationality came after an intense debate within Spain and a close vote in the Spanish legislature.

A few days later, Canadian Prime Minister Stephen Harper and his Cabinet attended the *Fête Nationale* celebrations in Quebec City. When reporters asked Harper if he would describe Quebec as a nation, he evaded the question. However, in December 2006, Harper introduced a motion that the Canadian House of Commons "recognize that the Québécois form a nation within a united Canada" (*Globe and Mail* Online, December 19, 2006). Although the motion, which passed by a 266–16 margin, has no legal significance, it stirred up considerable controversy. Michael Chong resigned from the Cabinet, stating that he believed that Canada is one nation—a view widely shared by English-speaking Canadians. Other Cabinet ministers differed on the meaning of recognizing the Québécois as a nation: did it refer only to French-speaking Quebecers, most of whom share a common culture, or did it refer to all residents of Quebec?

In June 2010, Spain's constitutional court struck down provisions of the Autonomy Statute that gave preferential status to the Catalan language and declared that there was no legal basis to recognize Catalonia as a nation. In response, more than one million Catalans marched in protest in Barcelona chanting the slogan: "We are a nation." In January 2013, the parliament of Catalonia passed a Declaration of Sovereignty of the Catalan people proclaiming that "the people of Catalonia have—by reason of democratic legitimacy—the character of a sovereign political and legal entity." In the September 2015 Catalan election, parties supporting independence

for Catalonia won a majority of seats (but slightly less than a majority of votes). The Catalan legislature passed a "roadmap" to Catalan independence; however, the Spanish government said that it would not allow any steps to be taken toward Catalan independence, and the Spanish Constitutional Court ruled that the Catalan legislation violated the Spanish constitution. Nevertheless, the Catalan government continued to proceed with its plans to "disconnect" from Spain. (*The Guardian*, 2016, January 10 and July 27).

Disputes about whether Catalonia and Quebec are nations are not simply about the extent to which these regions are different than other parts of their countries in history, language, and culture. Rather, the term *nation* is a highly charged political term because the major form of political community in the modern world is the nation-state. Declaring a region or a group within a country to be a nation is viewed by some as undermining efforts to build a strong national identity in the country as a whole and leading eventually to the breakup of the country. Others argue that recognition that countries like Canada and Spain contain different nations that should have considerable self-governing powers enhances the stability of those countries and the legitimacy of the state.

A basic political question is whether the world should be divided into self-governing countries, each based upon a people that consider themselves a nation. Or can stable and well-governed countries be built on the recognition and political accommodation of different peoples?

INTRODUCTION

If you look at a map of the contemporary world, you will see that all of the land mass (except Antarctica) is divided into about 200 countries. Almost all of these countries consider themselves to be independent or sovereign, meaning that they are not controlled by another country and thus are self-governing within their borders. There are some anomalies. Borders and control of certain areas are disputed. For example, India and Pakistan each lay claim to Kashmir, and Israel controls the West Bank and East Jerusalem that it captured in a 1967 war. There are also a number of territories that are controlled by another country and thus are not fully self-governing, including Bermuda by the United Kingdom, Puerto Rico by the United States, and New Caledonia by France.

Although the contemporary world is basically one of self-governing states, if you looked at a map of the world in 1913, you would see quite a different pattern of political organization. Empires including the French, Austro-Hungarian, Ottoman, and Russian controlled and dominated many subject peoples. The British Empire, in particular, controlled a sizable proportion of the world and its population.

We begin this chapter by examining the nature of the modern state. Then we look at the concept of nation, which is often viewed as the basis of the modern state, thus making the nation-state the leading form of political organization. Finally, we discuss the processes of globalization, which some observers believe is eroding the significance of nation-states.

THE STATE

state

An independent, self-governing political community whose governing institutions have the capability to make rules that are binding on the population residing within a particular territory.

A **state** is an independent, self-governing political community whose governing institutions have the capability to make rules that are binding on the population residing within a particular territory.[1] In Max Weber's classic definition, the state successfully claims "the monopoly of the legitimate use of physical force within a given territory" (Weber, 1970, p. 78).

government

The set of institutions that makes decisions and oversees their implementation on behalf of the state for a particular period of time.

The state can be viewed as a more extensive and permanent expression of the political community than the **government**, the set of institutions that makes decisions and oversees their implementation on behalf of the state for a particular period of time (Heywood, 2002).[2] The Canadian state, for example, includes not only the Canadian government and the governments of the provinces and territories, but also the military and police forces, the employees of the various levels of government, and state-owned corporations (termed

---

[1]The term *state* as used in political science is often misunderstood because regional political units within some countries (including the United States, Australia, and India) are called states.

[2]The term *government* refers, in the Canadian context, particularly to the prime minister and the Cabinet at the national level, although the public service that works under their direction could also be considered part of the Canadian government.

Crown corporations in Canada). Some state institutions (such as the courts and the Bank of Canada) are autonomous in the sense of being free (or largely free) of direct government control.

Overall, states play a major role in modern societies. In addition to their traditional functions of providing law, order, and security, modern states are very involved in activities such as regulating business activity; fostering economic development; stabilizing the economy; providing health, education, and social services to the public; assisting the disadvantaged; and protecting the environment. Indeed, the institutions of modern states deeply affect all aspects of our lives from birth to death. As Table 2-1 indicates, government spending (including transfers to individuals, businesses, and other organizations) accounts for a substantial proportion of a country's gross domestic product (GDP)—the total monetary value of all goods and services produced within the country usually calculated on an annual basis. Generally, government spending as a proportion of GDP is higher in the richer countries than in the poorer countries, although some exceptions to that pattern exist. As countries become more prosperous, the state is able to provide a higher level of services to its population. Indeed, governments in most countries have substantially increased their spending on such matters as education, health care, social services, research, and business subsidies and regulation since World War II.

TABLE 2-1

Total Government Spending in Selected Countries as a Percentage of Annual GDP

COUNTRY	GOVERNMENT EXPENDITURE AS % OF GDP	COUNTRY	GOVERNMENT EXPENDITURE AS % OF GDP
Cuba	60.2	United States	40.1
Greece	58.5	Turkey	37.6
Denmark	57.2	Russia	37.5
France	57.0	Australia	35.7
Sweden	51.9	Switzerland	34.1
Italy	50.6	Egypt	32.7
Netherlands	50.4	South Africa	32.6
United Kingdom	48.2	Nigeria	28.2
Spain	44.8	Vietnam	27.6
Germany	44.7	Mexico	27.1
Argentina	44.3	India	26.9
New Zealand	43.6	China	24.8
Poland	42.0	Chile	23.6
Japan	42.0	Pakistan	21.5
Canada	41.5	Indonesia	19.7
Brazil	40.4	Bangladesh	16.3

Notes: *GDP* is gross domestic product. *Government expenditure* includes direct government spending and transfers to individuals.

Source: Compiled from the 2015 Index of Economic Freedom by The Heritage Foundation, 2015; retrieved from www.heritage.org/research/features/index. Reprinted with permission of The Heritage Foundation

Sovereignty and the State

sovereignty

The principle that states are the highest authority for their population and territory and are not subject to any external authority.

States are often described as being sovereign. The **sovereignty** of states has two basic related dimensions. First, states claim to be the highest authority for their population and their territory. Second, states are not subject to any external authority, but rather are able to act independently in the world. As such, they are viewed as legally equal to other states regardless of differences in power. They may make agreements with other states for various purposes, but they remain sovereign because they can cancel those agreements.

Although some forms of political organization resembling the state have existed in different times and places, the modern state is generally viewed as developing in Europe over the past several centuries and spreading to other parts of the world in more recent times. In particular, as the feudal system declined in Europe, various monarchs strove to establish themselves as the highest authority in the territory that they controlled by limiting the authority of lords and nobles and challenging the authority of the Catholic Church. The treaties comprising the Peace of Westphalia (1648), which ended the devastating Thirty Years War (based, in part, on conflicts between Protestant and Catholic rulers), established the idea that states and their rulers were the supreme authority in their territory. Devastating civil wars led to the idea that a single absolute power with the means of coercion was needed to maintain order.

The development of bodies (such as Parliament) that represent different parts of the country and important elements of the population provided rulers with a means to levy and collect the taxes needed to wage wars and to develop an administrative structure (McGovern, 2007). The development of the capitalist economic system and the Industrial Revolution also were important in the development of the modern state. Costly infrastructure (such as canals, roads, railways, and ports) needed to be built by, or with the financial support of, the state. Markets needed to be created by removing internal barriers to trade within a country. A common language, an educational system, and an extensive array of laws governing business activities were needed to service the needs of business and industry.

Prior to the development of the modern state, the territories controlled by European monarchs were often viewed as their own property to be disposed of as they saw fit. Territory sometimes passed from one set of rulers to another as a result of royal marriages or conquest. Although the term *sovereign* referred to a monarch with absolute authority, legislatures and the people challenged the absolute power claimed by monarchs. In England, the Glorious Revolution (1688) resulted in Parliament's removal and replacement of a monarch and established the idea that Parliament is the supreme authority. The leaders of the French Revolution (1789) proclaimed that sovereignty rested with the people. Regardless of whether sovereignty is viewed as resting in the hands of a single individual, Parliament, the constitution, the people as a whole, or some combination of these, the modern state itself is viewed as sovereign. Thus, the idea developed that the state is an impersonal authority separate from particular individuals and from society; that is, "an independent structure of laws and institutions which rulers are trusted to administer on behalf of the community" (McGovern, 2007, p. 23).

Although the state is sometimes depicted as a powerful, unified body with a particular purpose, the various institutions that make up a state do not necessarily work co-operatively in pursuit of a common interest or goal. For example, in Canada's federal political system, the national and provincial governments each have their own important legislative (law-making) powers entrenched in the constitution and substantial financial and administrative capabilities to implement their own policies. Even in basically unitary political systems in which authority rests with the central government (such as the United Kingdom, Spain, and France), there has been movement away from a highly centralized state. In addition, binding, collective decisions have increasingly been made and implemented through negotiations and agreements between state and societal agencies (Pierson, 2011). The term **governance** is often used to describe this broader collaboration in making and implementing decisions.

governance

The making and implementing of decisions often with the involvement of state and non-state organizations.

The concept of state sovereignty is particularly important when we look at the relationship among states. A central principle of international law is that the states of the world are the legal equals of one another, and thus states should not interfere in the affairs of other states unless invited to do so. In other words, states are expected to respect each other's sovereignty. States, whether large or small, powerful or weak, rich or poor, are viewed as being self-governing.

Overall, the number of sovereign states has increased substantially. As of 2016, 193 states are members of the United Nations (see Figure 2-1), ranging from China[3] with a population of about 1.375 billion to the island of Tuvalu with a population of 10 837.

Civil wars, extreme corruption, uncontrolled violence, and economic collapse have occasionally shattered states, resulting in no effective governing authority. In these countries, often referred to as **failed states**[4], governments cannot enforce laws, maintain order, protect the lives of citizens, or provide basic services. For example, Somalia in east Africa lacked an effective government beginning in 1991; instead, the means of coercion were held by warlords,

failed state

A state that is unable to enforce laws, maintain order, protect the lives of citizens, and provide basic services.

---

[3]The Republic of China (Taiwan) was removed from the United Nations upon the admission of the People's Republic of China. Palestine was given non-member state observer status by a vote of the UN General Assembly in 2012. The Holy See (ruled by the Pope) has had this status since 1964. Several territories that have declared themselves independent including South Ossetia (from Georgia) and Somaliland (from Somalia) have not gained widespread recognition by other countries as sovereign states and are not members of the United Nations.

[4]The Fund for Peace that has tracked failed states for many years renamed their index "fragile states" in 2015, and listed 16 countries as on "high" or "very high" alert for failure.

FIGURE 2-1

The Increasing Number of Sovereign States: Membership in the United Nations

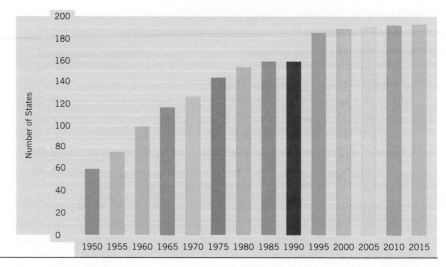

Note: Almost all recognized sovereign states are members of the United Nations.

Source: From The Increasing Number of Sovereign States: Membership in the United Nations, United Nations. Reprinted with the permission of the United Nations.

The Fragile States Index
http://fsi.fundforpeace.org/rankings-2015

clans, militias, and a variety of armed groups. Although a recognized government was established in 2012 after intervention by African Union troops, one region, Somaliland, declared itself a sovereign state and Al-Shabaab, an al-Qaeda affiliated militant group, continued to control some areas of the countryside and launch attacks on government forces. In a number of other countries, state institutions only have a weak governing capacity.

Although there is widespread acceptance of the principle that states are sovereign, in reality because of the great disparities in power among the states of the world, some of the weaker countries have found their sovereignty limited at times. The United States, for example, has a long history of involving itself in the affairs of Caribbean and Latin American countries, including invading and overthrowing the governments of Grenada (1983) and Panama (1989). The former Soviet Union exercised tight control over the countries of Eastern Europe, and its successor, Russia, used its special forces to take Crimea from Ukraine in 2014.

At times, various elements of the international community have intervened in sovereign states to protect human rights. For example, the North Atlantic Treaty Organization (NATO), which includes Canada, bombed Serbia (then known as Yugoslavia) in 1999 to end Serb mistreatment of ethnic Albanians in the province of Kosovo. Such actions are often controversial because of differences of opinion about whether the actions are justified and whether they will have the desired effects.

In 2001, the Canadian-sponsored International Commission on Intervention and State Sovereignty (ICISS) concluded that in certain circumstances, the responsibility to protect the people of a country justified international action, particularly through the Security Council of the United Nations, despite the principle of state sovereignty:

With no effective government from 1991 to 2012 to maintain order, militants with guns rode freely through Mogadishu, the capital of the failed African state of Somalia.

epa european pressphoto agency b.v./Alamy Stock Photo

State sovereignty implies responsibility, and the primary responsibility for the protection of its people lies with the state itself. Where a population is suffering serious harm, as a result of internal war, insurgency, repression or state failure, and the state in question is unwilling or unable to halt or avert it, the principle of non-intervention yields to the international responsibility to protect. (ICISS, 2001, p. xi)

At the UN World Summit in 2005, it was agreed (and reaffirmed by the UN Security Council in 2006) that there is a collective international responsibility to protect if genocide, war crimes, ethnic cleansing, and crimes against humanity are involved. In 2011, the Security Council agreed (with five countries abstaining) to authorize action to enforce a "no fly zone" over Libya to protect civilian protestors against the brutal dictatorial regime of Colonel Muammar Gaddafi. Critics argued that the NATO-led coalition (including Canada) went beyond the UN mandate, in effect supporting the rebels in their successful effort to overthrow the regime.[5] In 2012, the Security Council unanimously backed international military intervention to Mali (a former West African French colony) to stop humanitarian violations particularly by jihadist insurgents in northern Mali. In 2013, France used this authority to attack the insurgents who were advancing towards Mali's capital, and the Security Council approved the deployment of a peacekeeping force to support the

---

[5]This led to a lengthy civil war with contending militias each setting up their own government. Extremist Islamic fighters affiliated with terrorist groups temporarily captured some towns.

Malian armed forces. French-backed peacekeepers authorized by a Security Council resolution became involved in the Central African Republic in 2013 where there have been serious conflicts between Christians and the Muslim minority with hundreds of thousands people fleeing to neighbouring countries. Subsequently the UN took over this mission in 2014 with a large multinational peacekeeping force. However, UN peacekeepers have been accused of sexual exploitation and abuse in several countries, and were at least partly responsible for the widespread cholera outbreak in Haiti in 2010 that killed at least 10 000 persons.

THE NATION-STATE

The basis for dividing the world into about two hundred states is that each state claims to represent a particular nation. By having its own state, a nation can be self-governing rather than being controlled by a foreign power. Thus modern states are often referred to as **nation-states**; that is, sovereign states based on people living in a country who share a sense of being a member of a particular nation. In reality, however, many states are not based on a single nation. To understand the nation-state, we need to examine the meaning of the term of "nation."

nation-state

A sovereign state based on people living in a country who share a sense of common identity as members of a particular nation.

Nation

The term *nation* is often confused with that of the *state*, but the two terms have different meanings. A **nation** can be defined as a group of people who share a sense of common identity and who typically believe they should be self-governing within their homeland (Suny, 2006).[6] Unlike other social groupings to which people belong or with which they identify, members of the nation usually have a collective desire to have at least a substantial degree of self-government.

nation

A group of people who share a sense of common identity and who typically believe they should be self-governing within their homeland.

A sense of national identity often exists among people with ties to a particular territory who share common characteristics such as ethnicity (that is, a belief in a common ancestry), language, culture, and religion. There are a few countries (for example, Japan and Iceland) in which a high proportion of the population have common characteristics. However, most countries feature a diverse population, to varying extents.

A feeling of belonging to a nation can also develop over time from the shared experiences of living in a particular region or country and from sharing the values, including the basic political values, common to the people of that area.

---

[6]A distinction is sometimes made between a nation in a sociological sense (that is, a people having shared characteristics and culture) and a nation in a political sense of a people in a geographical area that has or wants self-government or their own sovereign state. See, for example, Trudeau (1993).

The Development of National Identities

Benedict Anderson (2001) describes a nation as an "imagined community" in that people in a nation will never meet or know most of the other people in their nation. How does a sense of national identity develop among a large group of people who do not know each other? In Europe, the development of the printing press helped to promote national languages (rather than Latin) and, along with mass circulation newspapers, spread national languages to the general public who spoke a variety of local dialects (Anderson, 2001). Challenges to the Catholic Church created divisions within Europe; the growth of national economies, trade, transportation links, the Industrial Revolution, and the development of the capitalist system contributed to a weakening of ties to local communities and regions.

To promote a national identity, governments have often made deliberate efforts to replace local and regional dialects, cultures, and identities with a national culture, language, and identity. For example, in the latter part of the nineteenth century the government of France created a French identity in the country's rural areas by instilling patriotism through the educational system and encouraging the use of Parisian French throughout the country instead of the very distinct dialects that were spoken in various parts of France (Weber, 1976).

National myths have been created and histories written to celebrate heroes of the country's past and support claims that the state was built upon an ancient people. In reality, in many countries, Indigenous peoples who were the original inhabitants had their land taken from them, were excluded from the settler society and political institutions, and pressured or forced to give up their much of their culture. In the United States, where persons from a variety of countries settled, American governments devoted considerable effort to the creation of a common sense of American identity, although blacks and Native Americans were largely excluded from the American "melting pot." Creating a national identity has often involved trying to persuade different people to adopt the culture, language, and values of the dominant group.

Nationalism

Connected to the development of national identities is the perspective of nationalism and associated nationalist movements. **Nationalism** is based on the view that the nation-state is the best form of political community, that a nation should have its own self-governing state, and that the interests, culture, and values of the nation should be promoted. Nationalism has been one of the most influential political ideas of recent centuries and has inspired important political movements and actions.

Nationalists view their nation as having a distinctive and positive character, and typically believe that people's primary loyalty should be to their nation. Many nationalists seek to limit foreign cultural influences and protect domestic businesses from foreign investment, products, and services. As

nationalism

The idea that the nation-state is the best form of political community, that a nation should have its own self-governing state, and that the interests, culture, and values of the nation should be promoted.

The Nationalism Project
www.nationalismproject.org

Internet Modern History Sourcebook:
Nationalism
www.fordham.edu/halsall/mod/
modsbook17.html

millions of people fled from the violence in Syria and Iraq in 2015 and 2016, many nationalists in European countries sought to strictly limit the number of refugees admitted to their country.

In some cases, nationalists have sought to expand the boundaries of their country (by force if necessary) to include areas deemed to be a historical part of their nation or simply to enhance the power of their country. In other cases, nationalists seek independence so as to form their own nation-state or, at least, to achieve autonomy.

TYPES OF NATIONALISM   A distinction is often made between ethnic nationalism and civic nationalism. **Ethnic nationalism** views common ancestry along with the cultural traditions and language associated with a particular ethnic group as the proper basis for a nation-state. By attempting to base a state on a particular ethnic group, ethnic nationalism can result in harassment, discrimination, and the oppression of those who do not share the characteristics of the dominant group. In some cases, as in the former Yugoslavia, Rwanda, and Burundi, it can lead to "ethnic cleansing," the forcible removal and even the massacre of people whose ethnicity differs from that of the dominant ethnic group. Ethnic nationalism can also result in war if attempts are made to seize areas in other countries where members of the ethnic group live or areas that are considered part of the traditional homeland of the ethnic group.

ethnic nationalism

Nationalism based on common ancestry along with the cultural traditions and language associated with a particular ethnic group.

civic nationalism

Nationalism based on the shared political values and political history of those who are citizens of a country.

Civic nationalism views shared political values and political history as the basis of a nation-state. Civic nationalism tends to be more inclusive than ethnic nationalism as it treats all permanent residents of a state as equal citizens regardless of their characteristics. Civic nationalists often want to create a sense of nationhood among citizens by encouraging the adoption of a common set of political values and beliefs and promoting loyalty to the nation-state through patriotic rituals.

In practice, nationalism often involves a combination, to varying extents, of civic and ethnic nationalism. For example, contemporary Quebec nationalists often claim that their nationalism includes all residents of Quebec and is therefore civic nationalism. However, comments by some Quebec nationalists implying that only those descended from the original French settlers are "true" Quebecers suggests that there is also an element of ethnic nationalism.

The Development of Nation-States

The French Revolution of 1789 was based on the idea that the state is an instrument of the people (that is, the nation), rather than the king, with the people having the right to overthrow rulers who do not reflect the will of the people.[7] The subsequent Napoleonic Wars helped to create a sense of unity

---

[7]Likewise, the idea that the state is based on the people was reflected in the American Declaration of Independence (1776) which refers to "one people" and the American Constitution (1789) that begins "We the people."

and pride in the French nation and its citizen army (which replaced reliance on foreign mercenaries). In the nineteenth century, the concept of popular sovereignty (that the people should be able to govern themselves) often became transformed into the idea that nations, defined particularly in ethnic and cultural terms, should be self-governing. Throughout the nineteenth and early twentieth centuries, nationalist movements developed throughout Europe seeking independence. Some revolts were successful in creating new nation-states including Greece, Belgium, Serbia, Romania, and Bulgaria. As well, a variety of small states and principalities were united into new countries: Germany and Italy. However, many European countries aggressively pursued the acquisition of colonies in Africa and elsewhere. Nationalist sentiment at home supported the conquest and domination of people abroad.

In 1915, American president Woodrow Wilson declared that "every people has a right to choose the sovereignty under which they shall live" (Ferguson & Mansbach, 2012). Wilson argued that the League of Nations, formed in the aftermath of World War I, should not only guarantee the territorial integrity of its member states but should also be empowered to accommodate future territorial adjustments based on the principle of self-determination. There was, however, no mention of this principle in the League's Covenant (Charter).

The Treaty of Versailles (1919) that was imposed by the victors in World War I created the new states of Poland, Czechoslovakia, Hungary, and Yugoslavia.[8] It was recognized, however, that it would be unrealistic to establish states strictly on the basis of the location of national cultures. Thus, attempts were made to persuade new states to protect minority nationalities that resided in their territory (Harty & Murphy, 2005). Although the governments of these new states (based in part on a particular nationality) were supposed to protect the rights of the often substantial national minorities within their state, some of the new regimes turned out to be oppressive of their minority peoples as they built their state upon the dominant nationality. Further, some of the victors in World War I drew boundaries to add territory to their own states and divided the colonies of the German empire among themselves. Much of the Middle East that had been part of the defeated Ottoman Empire was put under British and French "mandates." This division of the Ottoman Empire did not take into account ethnic, cultural, and religious differences and could be viewed as contributing to the enduring conflicts in the Middle East.

After World War I, a substantial nationalist movement developed in the Indian subcontinent to seek independence from British rule (achieved in 1947). After World War II, national liberation movements throughout the "Third World" were eventually successful (often after lengthy conflicts) to gain their independence from European empires. The United Nations International

---

[8]Lithuania, Latvia, Estonia, and Finland declared their independence from Russia after the Bolshevik Revolution of 1917.

Covenant on Economic, Social, and Cultural Rights, which came into force in 1976, established that "all peoples have the right to self-determination," which involves the right to "freely determine their political status and freely pursue their economic, social, and cultural development" (Article 1). This is sometimes described as the principle of **national self-determination**.

Whether a result of ethnic, racial, linguistic, religious, cultural, historic, or regional differences, there are many countries where substantial numbers of people view themselves as having a different national identity than their fellow citizens. Dividing the world into states based on where people with a particular national identity reside is hard to achieve. In many parts of Eastern Europe and the Balkans, for example, different nationalities are so highly interspersed that it would be very difficult to draw boundaries that would include each nationality within its own state. Indeed, in some cases, the creation of a homogeneous nation-state has only been achieved by the traumatic expulsion of those of different nationalities—as occurred during and after World War II.

Even in Western Europe, there are countries (for example, Belgium, Spain, Switzerland, and the United Kingdom) that could be considered **binational or multinational states**. Many countries in Europe and elsewhere have become more diverse in ethnicity, language, culture, and religion as a result of immigration from various parts of the world. However, integrating immigrants that differ substantially in culture and religion has proven difficult in a number of European countries.

The attempt to create a single national identity within a diverse country has not been very successful in many parts of the world. Most African countries, for example, have retained the boundaries that resulted from conquest by various European empires. These political boundaries generally bear little relationship to the geographical location of peoples, languages, cultures, and religions. In other words, the boundaries are artificial, often combining very dissimilar peoples into the same country. Despite efforts by the leaders of independence movements and post-independence governments to create new national political identities, severe tensions often exist among peoples sharing the same country. This has helped to fuel the civil wars that have plagued a number of African countries.

Because there are different bases for a sense of national identity (that sometimes change over time) and because there are important implications for the governing of a country, the question of whether a country is a nation-state can be the subject of serious political controversy, as discussed in Box 2-1, Is Canada a Nation-State?

MULTICULTURAL STATES   Instead of encouraging or persuading different ethnic, cultural, and linguistic groups to give up their distinctiveness and assimilate into the dominant group, Canada and some other countries in recent times have adopted

national self-determination

The idea that nations should have the right to determine their political status, including choosing to have their own sovereign state.

binational or multinational states

States whose populations are composed of two or more nations.

In recent decades, Canada's multicultural policy has encouraged persons of different cultures to retain their culture and traditions. Pictured here is a performer at Toronto's Caribana festival, which is enjoyed by over one million people each year.

Adrien Veczan/The Canadian Press

BOX 2-1   Is Canada a Nation-State?

Canada was largely built on the foundations laid by three peoples: Aboriginal (Indigenous) peoples (who are themselves very diverse in language and culture), the French colonists of the seventeenth and eighteenth centuries, and persons of English, Scottish, Welsh, and Irish ancestry, many of whom came to Canada from the United States after the American War of Independence. Added to this diverse foundation are large numbers of persons from various countries in Europe, Asia, Africa, and Latin America, particularly since the late nineteenth century. Because of Canada's lingering ties to Britain, a sense of Canadian national identity was slow to develop. Indeed, for a very long time Canada lacked specifically Canadian symbols of identity including citizenship (adopted in 1947), a Canadian flag (1965), and an official Canadian national anthem (1980).

Most English-speaking Canadians view Canada as a nation-state, based on each resident of Canada having the same rights. With only about one-half of Canadians tracing their ancestry to either the British Isles or France, Canadian governments since the early 1970s have promoted the view that Canada is a multicultural nation (that is, one nation composed of a variety of different cultural groupings) with two official languages. However, many francophone Quebecers view Quebec as a distinct nation, with a substantial minority favouring the establishment of an independent Quebec nation-state. Aboriginal peoples resent the privileging of those of British and French ancestry in such ideas as "two founding peoples" and "two

nations." Instead, many First Nations assert that Canada should be considered as a partnership between indigenous sovereign nations and the descendants of subsequent settlers.

Thus, Canada can be considered a nation-state, a multicultural nation-state, a nation-state with one or more minority nationalities, a binational state, or a multinational state, depending on one's perspective. The complexity of the concept of *nation* is illustrated by the fact that many Quebecers view themselves as both Québécois and Canadian without necessarily seeing one national identity as subordinate to the other.

The question of whether Canada is a nation-state is not only a definitional argument, but also a political dispute of potentially great significance. If, for example, Quebecers are officially recognized as members of a distinct nation, this suggests that the Quebec government may need greater powers to act on behalf of the Quebec nation. Proposals in the 1980s and 1990s that the Canadian constitution recognize Quebec as a distinct society met with vigorous opposition from those who view Canada as one nation with all provincial governments having the same powers. Likewise, recognition of Aboriginal nations can lead to expectations that Aboriginal governments should be treated as equals to other governments in Canada, that they should control their own territory and the protection and development of its resources, and that they should be responsible for providing most government services, including their own legal system, to their people.

a policy of **official multiculturalism.** This involves recognizing the cultural diversity of the country and providing encouragement and support for those of different cultures to retain and foster their cultures and traditions.

Advocates of multiculturalism view diversity as desirable and argue that tolerating and accommodating differences strengthens national unity. Critics argue that multiculturalism could conflict with individual rights (for example, by protecting cultural traditions that discriminate against women) and interfere with the integration of immigrants into society.

official multiculturalism

The policy of recognizing the cultural diversity of the country and providing encouragement and support for those of different cultures to help them retain and foster their cultures and traditions.

BOX 2-2 Multiculturalism and the Niqab

Multiculturalism is viewed by many Canadians as enriching the country with the ideas, cuisine, music, dance, dress, and customs of peoples from around the world. However, there has been increasing criticism of multiculturalism in many countries by those who argue that it interferes with the integration of immigrants into society.

Although only a very small number of Muslim women in North America and Europe wear a niqab (face covering), the Netherlands, Belgium, and France have made covering one's face in public illegal. Indeed, in 2016, a number of French municipalities banned the wearing of the burkini (a swimsuit for women that covers most of their body other than face, hands, and feet in accordance with the Islamic requirement that women wear modest attire). Although the ban was supported by national political leaders, it was overturned by France's top administrative court.

In 2011, Canada's immigration minister issued a directive that women had to show their face when taking the citizenship oath. However, both the Federal Court and Federal Court of Appeal rejected the niqab ban. Subsequently, the Conservative government launched an appeal of the ruling to the Supreme Court of Canada and campaigned on the issue in the 2015 Canadian election. Although there was strong public support for the ban, the Liberal party and the NDP opposed the ban, and the newly elected Liberal government removed the requirement and cancelled the appeal to the Supreme Court.

Those who supported banning the niqab in public places argued that this garment symbolizes the subservience of women and undermines gender equality. Opponents of the ban viewed it as a means to single out Muslims for discrimination, a threat to multiculturalism, and an unnecessary restriction on rights and freedoms.

Multiculturalism has been challenged in a number of countries. For example, Germany requires that immigrants seeking to become citizens take classes in German language and culture, and German Chancellor Angela Merkel has stated that multiculturalism has "utterly failed" (quoted in Sutherland, 2012, p. 137). Multiculturalism has been particularly controversial in a number of European countries where some view the immigration of substantial numbers of Muslims as a threat to the values and culture of the society (see Box 2-2 Multiculturalism and the Niqab).

Is the Nation-State the Most Desirable Form of Political Community?

In a nation-state, people have a bond with each other and may be more likely to feel a commitment to advancing the good of the political community. A sense of trust in government and other institutions may also be easier to develop. Political compromises that are acceptable to different social groups may be easier to achieve because an appeal can be made to a common national interest (Keating, 1996). In a nation-state, rule is by members of the nation who can claim to have the good of the nation at heart and to share the basic values of the other members of the nation. The legitimacy of the state and governing authorities is less likely to be questioned when the state is based on people who consider themselves part of a common nation. A stable democratic system may be more likely to be sustained in a nation-state. Democratic dialogue is facilitated by having a common language, culture, and basic political values. Deep divisions and the lack of a common sense of nationhood can hinder efforts to develop or maintain democracy. Nevertheless, some democratic countries such as Canada that might be considered binational or multinational have survived and flourished despite occasional "national unity" crises and the presence of separatist movements.

The development of separatist movements seeking to create a new nation-state out of a region of an existing state raises questions about whether it is desirable that nations with small populations and located in small geographical areas have their own self-governing state. Certainly, larger states have advantages in terms of having large internal markets, spreading the costs of government services over a large population, and being able to defend the country militarily. However, some small states such as Singapore and Luxembourg have been very successful economically and able to maintain their sovereignty. The development of economic agreements and military alliances composed of a number of countries has helped to offset some of the problems that might otherwise face small nation-states. Nevertheless, some nations are so small and lacking in economic capabilities that establishing a sovereign state for each group that considers itself a nation is unrealistic.

CITIZENSHIP

Connected to the development of the modern nation-state is the idea of **citizenship**—that a country's permanent residents are full members of the political community with certain duties and rights. A citizen is not only subject to the laws passed by the governing institutions of that state, but also shares in the power of the sovereign state (Rousseau, 1762/1968).

Those who are born in a particular country with at least one parent who is a citizen are usually considered citizens automatically. In many cases, a person does not have to be born in the country as long as at least one parent (or in some countries a grandparent) is a citizen. In many countries, the spouse of a citizen is granted citizenship (although in some countries this depends on gender). Most countries have a naturalization process by which those resident in a country for a period of time and able to demonstrate knowledge of the country and its official language (English or French in Canada) can become citizens upon taking an oath of allegiance.[9] A number of countries (including Germany, Russia, and China) have special procedures to facilitate the granting

citizenship

The idea that a country's permanent residents are full members of the political community with certain duties and rights.

---

[9]Some countries, including Saudi Arabia, Kuwait, and the Gulf States, make it virtually impossible for foreigners (and their children) to obtain citizenship. In a few countries this has resulted in only a minority of residents having citizenship and the majority of workers having no rights.

BOX 2-3   Dual Citizenship

Should individuals be required to have citizenship status in only one country or is dual citizenship (as allowed by Canada's Citizenship Act, 1977) an appropriate response to increased migration and the reality of globalization?

At times, questions of conflicting loyalties have arisen when governmental or military leaders have retained dual citizenship. For example, when Michaëlle Jean (who came to Canada from Haiti as a child) was appointed Canada's governor general in 2005, controversy erupted when it was revealed that she was a citizen of both France and Canada. Although France requires that foreign leaders give up their French citizenship, this was not required because the French government considered Jean's position to be ceremonial. Nevertheless, to avoid controversy within Canada, Jean voluntarily gave up her French citizenship. Subsequently, controversy arose when Stéphane Dion was elected as Liberal Party leader in 2006. Although born in Canada, Dion retained French citizenship based on his mother's nationality. NDP leader Thomas Mulcair, born in Canada, decided to also be a citizen of France like his wife who was born in France but became a dual citizen of Canada and France. Little notice was taken of Liberal leader (and, briefly, prime minister in 1984) John Turner's dual British and Canadian citizenship.

The Australian Constitution prohibits those holding a foreign citizenship from being a member of Parliament. The American Constitution requires that the president be a "natural born citizen" of the United States. Despite having a birth certificate from the state of Hawaii, some critics claimed that Obama had been born in Kenya and so should be removed from the presidency. Senator Ted Cruz (born in Calgary to an American citizen) faced allegations from Donald Trump that he was not a "natural born citizen" as he sought to be the Republican Party's 2016 presidential candidate.

of citizenship to those having an ethnic (or in Israel, an ethnic or religious) relationship to the country.

Although we often think of citizenship as involving an exclusive loyalty to one country, a number of countries, including Canada, allow persons to hold citizenship in two (or, in a few cases, more) countries. This raises questions as to whether those holding dual citizenship should be able to hold top political office and whether dual citizens should have the same rights as those who are only a citizen of the country they live in (see Box 2-3).

In most countries citizenship is a right that cannot be revoked unless it was obtained under false pretences. However some countries have adopted provisions that allow dual citizens to lose their citizenship in certain circumstances. The Strengthening Canadian Citizenship Act, 2015, allowed the government to revoke the Canadian citizenship of dual citizens convicted of crimes against Canadian security such as treason, espionage, and terrorism. The ringleader of the Toronto 18 bomb plot who was born in Jordan but came to Canada at an early age was the first to have his Canadian citizenship revoked. Critics argued that this was discriminatory in that his punishment was more severe than that for other Canadians involved in similar activities. Justin Trudeau promised to introduce legislation to remove the provision.

Does citizenship involve only individual rights or does it also involve obligations to the political community? For example, citizens may be expected to defend their country in times of war. Many governments have used this argument to justify compulsory military service (usually for men, but in a few countries, including Israel, Norway, North Korea, and Eritrea, also women) to train for and potentially fight in wars, even those that are not strictly defensive in nature. As well, since citizenship is associated with being a member of the political community, some have argued that citizens have an obligation to become informed participants in politics. For example, several countries (including Australia and Italy) require that all citizens vote in elections and penalize those who do not. Immigrants seeking to become Canadian citizens must demonstrate knowledge of Canada and the rights and responsibilities of citizens (including voting in elections, serving on a jury, obeying the law, taking responsibility for oneself and one's family, and helping others).

The concept of citizenship is generally based on the view that all citizens should be equal members of the political community regardless of social status, ethnicity, gender, wealth, or other characteristics. In the past, citizenship was limited to a small segment of the population, such as males, property owners, and those born in the country. The struggles for equal political rights in the past century-and-a-half have been successful in most countries in expanding citizenship to include most of the population. There has been increasing discussion about whether members of certain groups should have different citizenship rights because of their particular circumstances (termed "differentiated citizenship") such as historic rights, a legacy of oppression and discrimination, or exclusion of the group from the mainstream of society. For example, many Aboriginal First Nations in Canada have various rights established by treaties and other agreements between Aboriginal chiefs and the British Crown or the Canadian government, rights that are now recognized in the Canadian Constitution.

Some have argued that the special rights of Aboriginals eventually should be extinguished so that they can be treated in the same manner as other Canadian citizens (as was proposed by the Canadian government in 1969). Political scientist Alan Cairns (2000) argues that Aboriginals should be considered "citizens plus," with Aboriginal differences recognized, but not at the expense of a strong common citizenship that would bind Canadians together. A few First Nations have adopted procedures in which their members can be citizens of their Aboriginal First Nation in addition to being citizens of Canada (Harty & Murphy, 2005). For example, in accordance with the Nisga'a Treaty (2000), the Citizenship Act of the Nisga'a Lisims government in British Columbia established criteria by which Canadian citizens (and permanent residents of Canada) can also become Nisga'a citizens.

On February 15, 1996, Federal Minister of Indian Affairs Ron Irwin, Nisga'a Tribal Council President Joseph Gosnell, Sr., and B.C. Minister of Aboriginal Affairs John Cashore signed a treaty with the Nisga'a First Nation that includes recognition of Nisga'a citizenship.
H. Ruckemann/UPI Photo Service/ Newscom

GLOBALIZATION

Global Policy Forum
www.globalpolicy.org

The Globalist
www.theglobalist.com

globalization

The processes that are increasing the interconnectedness of the world.

Some analysts claim that the modern state is declining in significance. Globalization is making the boundaries of states less relevant, eroding state sovereignty, and reducing the ability of governments to determine the direction of their countries.

Globalization is often described in terms of the processes that are, in effect, shrinking the world. The obstacles of space and time are being rapidly overcome by contemporary technology, such as high-speed, low-cost communications. This is increasing the interconnectedness of the world and creating a greater awareness of the world as a whole. American journalist Tom Friedman (2005, p. 9) describes globalization as

> the inexorable integration of markets, nation-states and technologies to a degree never witnessed before—in a way that is enabling individuals, corporations and nation-states to reach around the world farther, faster, deeper and cheaper than ever before, and in a way that is enabling the world to reach into individuals, corporations and nations farther, faster, deeper, and cheaper than ever before.

Globalization is often seen as an inevitable process. However, various circumstances, including the policies adopted by governments, can accelerate, slow down, or even reverse the trend. For example, the economic globalization that developed in the late nineteenth and early twentieth centuries was reversed by World War I and later by the rise of economic and political nationalism during the Great Depression of the 1930s. On the other hand, globalization accelerated beginning in the 1980s as many governments adopted policies aimed at promoting free trade, free markets, the free flow of capital, and a reduction in the role of government.

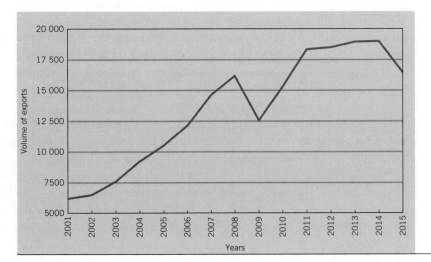

FIGURE 2-2
Volume of World
Merchandise Exports,
2001–2015

Note: Total Merchandise Trade,
World, Exports, US Dollars
(Trillions)

Source: World Trade Organization, Statistics, Database http://stat.wto.org/StatisticalProgram/
WSDBViewData.aspx?Language=E

Economic Globalization

A key aspect of globalization that has important political implications
is the development of a global economic system in terms of production,
trade, and finance. Many business corporations have become global in
their activities; they move or contract out their production facilities to
wherever goods and services can be produced at the lowest cost and sell
their products and services in a variety of countries. Global trade has
increased greatly since 1950, although dropping in 2009 as a result of a
global financial crisis and increasing at a slower rate since then as can be
seen in Figure 2-2.

Globalization has been most pronounced in the international financial
markets that provide a substantial proportion of the money and credit needed
by business and government. Approximately $5.3 trillion is traded daily on the
currency markets, much of it speculatively (McLeod, 2014). Large amounts
of capital can flow instantaneously in and out of countries that do not have
restrictions on currency movements.

However, there is no global free market in labour, as most workers in the
poorer countries cannot easily move to countries that offer high wages and
employment opportunities. In addition, despite general commitments to global
free trade, most countries provide some protection of certain domestically produced goods and services from foreign competition. For example, Canada protects its cultural industries and dairy producers. The United States has various
protections against what it considers to be unfair foreign competition and has
also adopted "Buy American" policies.

Globalization potentially can increase overall economic efficiency by increasing competition, allowing countries to focus on the products and services they can produce at the lowest cost, and using trade to obtain products and services that can be obtained more cheaply elsewhere. Consumers can benefit from lower prices and a wider selection of goods, and businesses and governments have broader sources of finance.

Globalization has important risks as economic problems in one country can quickly spread around the world. For example, a serious global economic crisis began in 1997 when financial capital fled from a number of Asian countries, beginning with Thailand, even though their economies were relatively strong. The contagion quickly spread to other parts of the world. The removal of controls of the flow of speculative capital looking for short-term profits and the ending of stable currency exchange rates are often blamed for the financial crises that have become quite frequent occurrences (Rodrick, 2011; Veseth, 2010).

An even more serious global economic crisis began in the United States in 2007 as leading financial institutions that held mortgage-backed securities and complex derivative instruments based on those securities faced bankruptcy as many American homeowners were unable to make mortgage payments. Stock markets crashed, governments bailed out some major corporations, and many economies around the world went into recession.

Overall, economic globalization tends to reduce the ability of national governments to manage their own economies. Large multinational corporations have been able to gain considerable influence as governments seek to attract businesses or discourage them from withdrawing their investments. Multinational corporations are able to pressure governments to provide them with a variety of benefits and to adopt policies that are to their own advantage. The ability of many multinational corporations to move their operations to low-wage counties can lead to pressures on workers in the richer countries to accept lower wages and benefits to maintain their jobs. Globalization thus has tended to result in increased inequalities in income, wealth, and power within many countries.

It is often argued that globalization represents the triumph of free-market capitalism. In recent decades many Western governments have privatized various state-owned enterprises, lowered business taxes, and reduced their regulation of business activity. With the collapse of communism in the Soviet Union and Eastern Europe (1989–1991), most of their state-owned enterprises were privatized. However, particularly in Russia, privatization was often associated with corruption and the concentration of wealth in the hands of a small elite (referred to as "oligarchs") who had connections to the government.

Yet despite the participation of most countries in global trade and investment, there has not been a complete adoption of free-market capitalism throughout the world. Many countries (such as China, the world's leading exporter of goods) have maintained substantial state direction of their major businesses. Government-owned sovereign wealth funds control large foreign investments in many countries. For example, the China Investment Corporation has $US 746.7 billion of investments in developed and developing countries, including Canada. Sovereign wealth funds in Norway, $873 billion; the United Arab Emirates, $773 billion; Saudi Arabia, $685 billion; and Kuwait, $592 billion have been based on government's oil and gas revenues (Sovereign Wealth Fund Institute, 2016). World-wide, sovereign wealth funds hold assets estimated at $US 7.1 trillion (CNBC, 2015).

Cultural Globalization

Globalization also involves spreading cultural products and values around the world. Advances in communications, such as the Internet, have greatly increased the interaction of individuals, businesses, and political groups worldwide. Leading brands such as Coke, Pepsi, McDonald's, Taco Bell, and Nike have become familiar to people around the world. American movies, television shows, and music videos are the leading sources of entertainment in many parts of the world. CNN and BBC World are major sources of news in many countries.

Cultural globalization is often viewed as a process in which Western (and particularly American) culture is spread globally. Although the transformation of communications has given us increased access to cultures in other parts of the world, the flow of cultural communication outward from Western countries is substantially greater than the flow in the reverse direction. English has become the leading language of international communication (although many more people speak Mandarin as their first language).

In the past, European colonization helped to spread Western ideas and practices around the world. In turn, global dominance and exploitation contributed to Western prosperity and power. The United States as the leading contemporary military, economic, and cultural power continues to have a major influence in the world. The democratic ideas that developed in the West have been adopted, to varying extents, by many countries.

Is globalization creating a "McDonaldization" of societies (Ritzer, 2012) or a "McWorld" (Barber, 1995)? Although McDonald's and other Western fast-food restaurants have opened in many parts of the world (sometimes with local menu variations), they have not fundamentally changed the eating habits of people outside the West. Despite the popularity of sushi and curry restaurants, few would suggest that their popularity involves an "Easternization" of the West. The more profound aspects of culture in many non-Western societies continue to differ in important ways from that of the Western world (Jacques, 2012).

"Somehow this curry doesn't seem authentic."
Tami Thirlwell

Political Globalization

Many contemporary problems, including the regulation of global business and finance, global climate change, international crime and terrorism, and the spread of diseases, cannot be dealt with effectively by individual states alone. A variety of institutions have developed to try to coordinate the actions of states, promote trade and investment, and deal with global problems. The European Union has created a level of governing above that of the state. In other cases, including the North American Free Trade Agreement (involving Canada, the United States, and Mexico), countries have negotiated agreements that affect the policies they adopt without establishing a political union. With the development of a number of regional economic, political, and military agreements, the interconnectedness of the world involves a substantial degree of regionalization.

At the global level, the United Nations and its agencies have had some success in dealing with global issues including promoting human rights, international law, humanitarian aid, and sustainable development as well as involvement in peacekeeping and peace building. Three major international financial institutions are of considerable importance in regulating the global economy and promoting global free market policies. The World Trade Organization, with 162 member states, is dedicated to pursuing free trade, resolving trade disputes, and overseeing trade agreements. The International Monetary

Fund, with 188 member states, oversees the global financial system and provides loans to countries facing financial crises. The World Bank, which also has 188 member states, focuses on providing assistance to developing countries through its five organizations. In addition, annual summits of the leaders of countries with some of the largest national economies (the G7/G8, and the G20) provide a forum for discussion of the global economy and other important international issues.[10]

Global Policy Forum
www.globalpolicy.org

Many non-governmental organizations operate on a global scale seeking to influence policies in such areas as human rights, the environment, the status of women, and peace, as well as being directly involved in projects to aid developing countries. Greenpeace, for example, grew from a small Vancouver organization concerned with nuclear weapons testing in Alaska to a large international organization involved in environmental causes around the world. A concerned American, Jody Williams, made extensive use of email to mobilize a wide variety of groups and individuals around the world that successfully pressed for an international treaty (the Landmines Ban Convention, 1997, also known as the Ottawa Treaty) banning anti-personnel land mines.[11] International business, labour, and religious groups are also important actors on the global political stage.

International Forum on Globalization
www.ifg.org

Landmines Ban Convention
www.apminebanconvention.org/

Globalization and the State

Is globalization seriously eroding the power of states? The heightened pressures of economic competition has encouraged many countries to adopt policies that focus on removing barriers to international markets, reducing the role of government in regulating the economy, and cutting the taxes that are needed to provide social benefits. The rules of trade adopted by bodies such as the World Trade Organization are aimed at trying to establish a "level playing field" in which government policies that protect domestic products and services and place barriers to trade and investment are expected to be eliminated.

Nevertheless, different countries have adapted in different ways to globalization reflecting continuing differences in cultures, histories, politics, and circumstances. Economic and social policies can differ in major ways even among

---

[10]The G7, established in 1975, includes Canada, France, Germany, Italy, Japan, the United Kingdom, and the United States along with a representative of the European Union. Russia was invited to join in 1997, creating the G8. However Russia's membership in the G8 was suspended in 2014 after Russia seized Crimea from Ukraine. The G20 consists of countries responsible for about 85 percent of the global economy, including major developing countries such as China, India, Brazil, Indonesia, and South Africa. None of these groups has a permanent staff.

[11]Although 162 countries have agreed to be bound by the convention, some countries continue to develop and use landmines (including the United States, Russia, China, India, Pakistan, Iran, Syria, and Saudi Arabia).

countries that have prosperous, developed economies. For example, Sweden, with an export-oriented economy, has maintained an extensive system of social benefits paid for by high taxes, while Japan, whose developed economy is also export-oriented, provides a very low level of social benefits to its citizens (Steinmo, 2010). Likewise, the governments of the newly industrialized countries of East Asia are more heavily involved in directing their economies than is the case in the United States and Canada.

Despite some downsizing of government, reduction of business regulation, and privatization of some government services in a number of countries beginning in the 1980s, governments are still far more active than they were in the past. Indeed, concerns about security and terrorism have increased the role of the state in some areas, including increased surveillance of the population. Some developing countries have had to reduce state control of imports and investment in order to gain access to the global economy. However, they have needed greater state action to provide better education and training, a stronger framework of laws concerning property rights and business activities, various public services, and a competent administrative structure (Wolf, 2001). Therefore, although globalization creates new challenges, the state remains strong in developed countries, while many countries in the developing world have been strengthening their state apparatus.

Globalization can lead to a strengthening of national identities as people look for stability in a changing world. Relatively few people have developed a cosmopolitan or global sense of identity, and international institutions have not developed a significant degree of legitimacy among the general population. Most people continue to expect their own state to deal with the issues and problems that are of greatest concern to them. Even the European Union, which establishes a high level of integration among its member states, has been unable to establish a strong sense of legitimacy among European people. In a June 2016 British referendum, 52% of voters chose the option of their country leaving the European Union. Similarly there has been growing criticism of the European Union in a number of member countries. In other countries, notably the United States, there has been growing criticism of free-trade agreements.

Finally, it has been argued that globalization is eroding the power of the nation-state not only by shifting power upward to global institutions, global markets, and global corporations, but also by indirectly challenging the nation-state from below. If states are less able to provide for the well-being of their people, this may stimulate separatist movements. The development of organizations such as the European Union makes it possible for some people in smaller areas, such as Scotland and Catalonia, to think that membership in such organizations will offset the disadvantages they would face by separating from a larger country. Likewise, trade and security agreements may be seen as reducing the risks and costs of separation.

✔• SUMMARY AND CONCLUSION

The nation-state is often considered to be the primary basis for the way the modern world is organized. Modern states claim to be the highest authority within a particular, well-defined territory. State sovereignty is the legal principle that states have the right to govern their populations and territories without outside interference and that they should be treated as equals on the world stage. Questions have been raised, however, as to whether outside intervention is justified in some instances, such as when state authorities violate or are unable to protect the basic human rights of the people they govern.

The rationale often given for state sovereignty is that states are the political expression of a nation and that nations should have the right to govern themselves. However, not all nations have their own state, and many states are not based on a single nation. The determination of what constitutes a particular nation can be controversial. Nations are often thought of in terms of the common ancestry, language, culture, and other characteristics of a people. However, a sense of belonging to a nation can also develop among people of diverse backgrounds and characteristics living in a particular country. Governments, along with intellectuals and artists, have often developed myths of nationhood to try to unify the people of their country and create a common culture. However the large influx of refugees, particularly from the Middle East in recent years, has resulted in serious tensions in a number of European nation-states.

The political doctrine of nationalism—with its goals of trying to establish or maintain a self-governing state based on a particular nation and promoting the interests and values of that nation-state—continues to have great significance for the politics of the modern world. However, many states are not based on a people with a single, common identity or set of characteristics. Although some binational and multinational states are stable and successful, the determination of the common good in these states can be difficult because the good of each nation needs to be taken into account to maintain the legitimacy of the state.

Associated with the development of the nation-state is the concept of citizenship. The idea that all permanent members of a political community should be equal citizens with the same rights and responsibilities has been challenged, particularly by minority nationalities that wish to have a different relationship to the state than other citizens.

The contemporary state faces challenges from globalization as well as from regions and groups within the state that would like to gain greater autonomy or independence. Economic globalization reduces the ability of states to manage their economies for the good of all their people, cultural globalization may reduce the significance of national cultural differences, and political globalization can limit state sovereignty. However, although a variety of organizations beyond the state have increased in importance, states are still the most important political units. States continue to play a crucial role in providing order and security; economic development and regulation; justice, social, health, and educational services; environmental protection; and other highly important aspects of our lives.

Globalization presents important political challenges—in particular, how to establish effective global institutions that can work for the common good of the world rather than concentrating power in the hands of large multinational corporations, unaccountable international organizations, and certain powerful states. To make progress toward achieving the common good of humanity, the development of a consciousness of being part of a global community as well as citizens of a particular state may be necessary.

KEY TERMS

Binational or multinational states 34	Globalization 40	National self-determination 34
Citizenship 37	Government 24	Nationalism 31
Civic nationalism 32	Governance 27	Official multiculturalism 35
Ethnic nationalism 32	Nation 30	Sovereignty 26
Failed state 27	Nation-state 30	State 24

DISCUSSION QUESTIONS

1. Should each nation be self-governing?

2. Is Canada a nation-state?

3. What should be the rights and obligations of citizens? How should citizenship be determined? Should a person be allowed to be a citizen of more than one country?

4. Is multiculturalism a positive feature of countries such as Canada?

5. Is globalization reducing the importance of the state?

FURTHER READING

Bosworth, R.J.B. (2007). *Nationalism*. Harlow, UK: Pearson.

Ferguson, Y.H., & Mansbach, R.W. (2012). *Globalization. The return of borders to a borderless world?* New York: Routledge.

Friedman, T. (2005). *The world is flat: A brief history of the twenty-first century.* New York: Farrar, Straus and Giroux.

Giddens, A. (2000). *Runaway world: How globalization is reshaping our lives.* New York: Routledge.

Harty, S., & Murphy, M. (2005). *In defence of multinational citizenship.* Vancouver and Toronto: UBC Press.

Hirst, P., Thompson, G., & Bromley, S. (2009). *Globalization in question: The international economy and the possibilities of governance* (3rd ed.). Cambridge, UK: Polity Press.

Pierson, C. (2011). *The modern state* (3rd ed.). New York: Routledge.

Rodrick, D. (2011). *The globalization paradox. Democracy and the future of the world economy.* New York: W.W. Norton.

Smith, A.D. (2010). *Nationalism. Theory, ideology, history* (2nd ed.). Cambridge, UK: Polity Press.

Sutherland, C. (2012). *Nationalism in the twenty-first century. Challenges and responses.* Houndmills, UK: Palgrave Macmillan.

3 Liberalism, Conservatism, Socialism, and Fascism

Vladimir Lenin's brother was arrested and then hanged for plotting to assassinate Tsar
Alexander III. On learning of the execution, Vladimir promised to "make them pay for this!"
Soon thereafter, he began studying the works of revolutionary thinkers Karl Marx and Frederick
Engels and later, as the leader of the Bolsheviks, advocated revolutionary action.
Thinkstock/Photos.com/Getty Images

After reading this chapter you should be able to:

1. explain the meaning and significance of political ideology
2. discuss the ideas of liberalism, conservatism, socialism, and fascism
3. outline the development and major variations of each ideology
4. apply the terms "left" and "right" to the analysis of political perspectives

After his brother was arrested for concealing a bomb in a medical encyclopedia, Vladimir Ilyich Ulyanov—and ultimately world politics—underwent a profound change. Vladimir was still a teenager when his older brother Alexander was hanged for planning to assassinate Russia's Tsar Alexander III. On learning of the execution, Vladimir reportedly proclaimed, "I'll make them pay for this! I swear it!" (Shub, 1966, p. 16).

Expelled from university for supporting student demands, Vladimir began studying the works of revolutionary thinkers Karl Marx and Frederick Engels and passed the examinations needed to become a lawyer. Later, in exile in Switzerland, he adopted the name Lenin. He became the leader of the Bolshevik Party (later known as the Communist Party), which advocated revolutionary action.

With Russia suffering extreme hardships and military defeats in World War I, Tsar Nicholas II was forced to abdicate in March 1917. A provisional government continued the devastating war and did little to alleviate the dire circumstances faced by much of the population. Using the slogan "peace, bread, land," the Bolsheviks led a successful attack on the seat of government in Petrograd (now St. Petersburg). After a bitter civil war (in which foreign countries, including Canada, intervened to try to defeat the communists), Lenin was able to gain control of Russia, which was renamed the Union of Soviet Socialist Republics.

In many ways, the communist regimes of Lenin and his successor Stalin were even more oppressive than the tsarist governments that had ruled Russia for centuries. Dissent of any kind was brutally repressed. Forced labour camps were set up in remote regions of Russia. Whole populations were exiled from their homelands. And exceptionally tight control was exerted over all aspects of the economy and society by the Communist Party. Despite becoming a major power as a result of World War II, the Soviet Union could not match the economic strength of the advanced Western countries. Attempts to reform the economic system under President Gorbachev failed, and the Soviet Union collapsed in 1991.

Strongly held ideas and beliefs, whether religious or political, can have a profound effect on the world and on our lives as well as shaping the way that we understand the world. In this chapter, we examine four important ideological perspectives.

POLITICAL IDEOLOGIES

A **political ideology** is a package of interrelated ideas and beliefs about government, society, the economy, and human nature that inspire and affect political action. Each ideology provides a different perspective that is used to understand and evaluate how the world actually works (Sunderlin, 2003). Marxism, for example, looks at the world through the lens of class conflict, liberalism views historical development as involving the struggle for individual freedom, and conservatism sees order in society as maintained by following traditional values.

Most political ideologies also provide a vision of what the world should be like and propose a means of political action to achieve their objectives. Some ideologies challenge and seek to transform the existing basic power arrangements; other ideologies provide justifications for the existing political, social and economic order. Ideologies are often associated with social movements and political parties. For example, democratic socialism (or social democracy) has usually been associated with the labour movement and with political parties including the New Democratic Party in Canada, the Labour Party in the UK and Australia, and Social Democratic parties in Europe.

The development of political ideologies is associated with the ideas of the European **Enlightenment** and with the economic and social upheavals that accompanied the development of capitalism and the Industrial Revolution. The mid eighteenth century Enlightenment involved a major shift from traditional religious beliefs toward an optimistic belief in the power of human reason to make the world better. Setting the tone for the modern world, Enlightenment thinkers argued that, through reason and science, people could understand the world. Progress could be achieved by consciously shaping the world and its institutions. Human beings could create a better society on Earth, rather than waiting for the life after death promised by religion. The French Revolution of 1789, influenced in part by Enlightenment ideas, involved a fundamental challenge to the traditional bases of authority: the monarchy, the aristocracy, and the Catholic Church. New and competing sets of ideas developed about how society and the state should be organized and run. Likewise, the rise of capitalism and the Industrial Revolution disrupted previous patterns of economic and social life, leading to intense disputes over the desirability of the capitalist system. The political ideologies that developed in Europe spread to the rest of the world, although they have often been modified by different cultures and circumstances.

Ideological conflict has been an important feature of politics for more than three centuries. Intellectuals, politicians, and political activists often have a particular ideological perspective. Controversies over a variety of public policy issues often reflect the views of those who have different ideological perspectives. Many people do not consciously hold an ideological perspective, but nonetheless are affected in their thinking by elements of one or more ideologies. Whether in a subtle or explicit manner, ideological perspectives are often

political ideology

A package of interrelated ideas and beliefs about government, society, the economy, and human nature that inspire and affect political action. Each ideology provides a different perspective that is used to understand and evaluate how the world actually works. Most ideologies also provide a vision of what the world should be like and propose a means of political action to achieve their objectives.

Enlightenment

An intellectual movement that developed in the mid eighteenth century, emphasizing the power of human reason to understand and improve the world.

conveyed to the public by governments, various political and social groups, the educational system, and the mass media. Ideas related to particular ideologies are often used in political life to mobilize support for particular causes, movements, parties, policies, and governments.

The Negative Side of Ideology

The term *ideology* originated to describe efforts to develop a science of ideas. However, the term is often used to describe certain sets of ideas and ways of thinking in a negative way. For Karl Marx, the key developer of communism, ideology was the instrument of the ruling class used to justify the harsh realities of the capitalist system. Others use the term to describe what are viewed as extremist perspectives such as communism and fascism. Politicians often describe themselves as "pragmatic" (that is, practical and relying on common sense) and characterize their opponents as "ideologues."

There is some validity to the negative characterizations of ideology. Some people treat the leading texts of their ideology as if they were the absolute truth and refuse to consider seriously any criticisms of their perspective. Further, ideological thinking can be simplistic, and ideological adherents may provide distorted depictions of reality to fit their mental model of the world. More importantly, ideologies have been used to justify the unjustifiable, such as the extermination of the European Jewish population by the Nazis and the mass murder of educated city residents in Cambodia in the 1970s.

However, ideologies are not only the belief systems of fanatics, extremists, and simplistic thinkers. Some of those whose ideas reflect the mainstream ideologies of liberalism or conservatism are dogmatic in their thinking. As well, those who view themselves as practical or pragmatic may, often unknowingly, be influenced by an ideological perspective. In particular, the leading or dominant ideology in a community will often seem to be "common sense."

On the positive side, an ideology can provide some coherence, consistency, and direction to a person's political thinking and actions. As Boris DeWeil (2000) argues, the ongoing debate among different ideologies is an inherent and desirable aspect of democratic politics, resulting from the fact that people have different value priorities (for example, whether equality or freedom is more important). Ideologies provide us with different ideas about the common good and how it may be achieved.

Ideologies have been used to justify the unjustifiable, such as the death of about one-fifth of the population of Cambodia from 1975 to 1979. In an attempt to create an agrarian communist utopia, Pol Pot's Khmer Rouge regime evacuated the cities and undertook a deliberate campaign of destroying the educated part of the population through starvation, slave labour, and executions. Some Western intellectuals, blinded by the regime's ideology, tried to deny the reality of the Cambodian "killing fields."

Rachel Stuckey

LIBERALISM	CONSERVATISM	SOCIALISM	FASCISM
Human nature			
Individuals able to think and act according to reason	Humans imperfect with capacity for evil	Humans co-operative and social	People motivated by emotion rather than reason
Key value			
Individual freedom	Order, stability, social harmony	Equality	Loyalty to the nation-state
Political system			
Liberal, representative democracy	Traditional institutions	Egalitarian democracy	Totalitarian leader
Rights			
Protect individual rights	Rights balanced by duties	Provide universal social and economic rights	Subordinate individual to the state
Morality			
State should not impose morality	Maintain traditional moral values	Promote equalitarianism	Duty to obey the state and its heroic leader
Economy			
Free market with equality of opportunity	Free market with social harmony	Planned economy	Corporate state
Political analysis			
Struggle for freedom	Radical changes undesirable	Struggle for equality	Racial or national conflict inevitable

TABLE 3-1
Ideologies: Key Themes

Note: These are only broad characterizations that do not capture the diversity and evolution of each ideology. Nazism can be distinguished from fascism in several ways including the importance of race rather than nation (Gibbins and Youngman, 1996).

Examining Ideologies

When examining ideologies, we should keep in mind that each ideology is a broad perspective containing many variations that evolves over time. It is not always easy to distinguish clearly between one ideology and another because differences between them may be subtle. However, each of the major ideologies has some distinguishing themes (see Table 3-1).

Political parties with ideological names, such as Liberal or Conservative parties, do not *necessarily* reflect the ideology corresponding to their name. Political parties are often, but not always, founded on a set of ideological principles. However, in the pursuit of electoral success, they may find it desirable to modify or ignore those principles.

Left and Right

A simple way of depicting ideological positions is in terms of left and right, as illustrated in Figure 3-1. The terms *left* and *right* originated in the seating

arrangements of the French National Assembly established after the French Revolution of 1789. Those who favoured the old order sat to the right of the chairman of the Assembly. Those who opposed the absolute authority of the monarch, demanded that the power and privileges of the Catholic Church be reduced or eliminated, and favoured redistributing the property and wealth of the nobility sat to the left (Needler, 1996; Grant, 2001). The seating arrangement of parties of the left and right continues to this day in the semi-circular French National Assembly and in the European Parliament.

In contemporary usage, the **left** is associated with the pursuit of greater social and economic equality, while those on the **right** generally see inequality as a natural feature of human society. A secondary meaning is that those on the right believe that traditional (usually religious-based) moral values should be reflected in laws and supported by community institutions, while those on the left generally oppose state support for religious institutions and favour laws based on universal human rights rather than traditional morality. In other words, equality and human rights are often associated with the left while traditional morality and elite authority tend to be associated with the right.

While liberalism is typically depicted as being in the centre of the ideological spectrum, we need to be careful about the meaning of the centre. Because being in the centre is often viewed positively, assessing what is the centre can often be controversial. Fascists often claimed that they represent a middle way between communism and capitalism. Conservatives often suggest that liberals in North America are left wing rather than centrist, while liberals often view conservatives as being far to the right.

Although the terms *left* and *right* are often used in political discussion, portraying political perspectives along a single dimension can be misleading, as the differences among the ideologies are multi-dimensional. For example, although communism and fascism are very different in their views on equality, communist and fascist states have exhibited some similarities in their efforts to exert tight control over their societies. Furthermore, some perspectives such as nationalism and environmentalism do not fit easily on the left–right dimension because their focus is on different sets of concerns.

left

The general ideological position associated with advocacy of greater social and economic equality, laws based on universal human rights rather than traditional morality, and opposition to state support for religious institutions.

right

The general ideological position associated with opposition to imposing greater social and economic equality and with maintaining traditional (usually religious-based) moral values and institutions.

LIBERALISM

Your ideological position: an easy, anonymous, five-minute quiz
www.politicalcompass.org

The ideology of liberalism emphasizes the desirability of a high level of individual freedom, based on a belief in the inherent dignity and worth of each individual. Individuals are assumed to be capable of using reason and taking rational actions in pursuit of their interests. Thus individuals should take responsibility for their own lives with as little interference by government as possible (see Box 3-1 John Stuart Mill: A Liberal Defence of Freedom).

BOX 3-1 John Stuart Mill: A Liberal Defence of Freedom

In his influential essay *On Liberty*, John Stuart Mill (1806–1873) made the case that individuals should be free to pursue their own good in their own way:

> The only purpose for which power can be right-fully exercised over any member of a civilized community, against his will, is to prevent harm to others. His own good, either physical or moral, is not a sufficient warrant . . . . Over himself, over his own body and mind, the individual is sovereign (Mill, 1859/1912, p. 15).

Liberty does not simply allow individuals to satisfy their desires; rather it is necessary for the development of each individual's capabilities: *Developing one's perceptions, judgments, discriminative feeling, mental activity, and even moral preferences are only exercised in making a choice* (Mill, 1859/1912, p. 72). In addition, the free competition and interplay of different ideas allows the more valid ideas to show their worth.

Suppressing false opinions cannot be justified because they may contain an element of truth. The expression of false opinions helps the holders of true opinions to understand the basis for holding their opinions. Further, being challenged by different ideas helps society avoid stagnation and helps individuals to exercise their capacity for reason.

Mill's defence of liberty raises some controversial issues. Should individuals be free to promote hatred against particular races, ethnic groups, religions, or genders? Should behaviours that may not cause direct harm to others, such as prostitution, using marijuana, or practising polygamy, be illegal? Although Mill suggested that a person should be warned against but not prevented from crossing an unsafe bridge, laws in Canada require the wearing of seatbelts and motorcycle helmets both to protect individuals and to reduce government spending on those who might be injured and hospitalized.

Historically, liberalism developed out of the struggles against the arbitrary power of absolute monarchs, restrictions on free business activity, the imposition of one set of religious values on the population of a country, and the granting of special privileges to particular groups—such as churches, aristocrats, and business monopolies.

Although liberals see a need for government, they are concerned that those in governing positions will abuse their power to pursue their own interests. Therefore, a central goal of liberalism is to ensure that the rights of individuals are firmly protected so they cannot be taken away by government. Liberals advocate the **rule of law**; that is, government should act only in accordance with established laws rather than in an arbitrary fashion, and all persons should be equally subject to the law. Liberals also believe that the scope of government activity should be limited. This involves distinguishing a substantial area of private activity, where government should not be involved, from matters of public concern, in which government may be involved. As former Canadian Liberal Prime Minister Pierre Trudeau argued, "The state has no place in the nation's bedrooms." What goes on between consenting adults, in this perspective, should be left to their own moral judgment.

rule of law

The idea that people should be subject to known, predictable, and impartial rules of conduct, rather than to the arbitrary orders of particular individuals. Both the rulers and the ruled should be equally subject to the law.

Religious belief, in the liberal view, is a private matter based on the conscience of the individual. A policy of tolerance should be adopted concerning those holding different beliefs. Government should not require or promote adherence to any particular religion, and laws should not be based on any particular religious perspective. Government is not a creation of God to promote or enforce moral values, but rather a human creation for more limited purposes, specifically to provide the rules and procedures under which individuals can enjoy freedom.

Liberalism is also associated with the view that government should be based on the consent of the governed. In particular, **liberal democracy** combines the liberal ideas of limited government, individual rights and freedoms, and the rule of law with a democratic system of governing based on the election of representatives.

Classical Liberalism

Classical liberalism emphasizes the importance of limited government and a free market economy. John Locke (1632–1704), a key figure in the development of classical liberalism, argued that individuals had been free and equal in the state of nature (that is, before the establishment of government), but lacked the means to settle disputes fairly. Therefore, through a "social contract," people agreed to establish government for limited purposes—namely, the protection of life, liberty, and property. Government should be limited in its powers, acting as a trustee to protect the rights of the people, and removable by the people if it infringes on the liberties that it was established to protect.

Classical liberals favour a **laissez-faire economic system**, in which workers, consumers, and privately owned businesses freely interact in the marketplace without government interference. Economic freedom, including the freedom to produce and trade, to sell one's labour, and to enjoy one's property is, in this perspective, a basic human right. Property rights protect individual liberty against the power of the state by dispersing power and resources among the population. The proper economic role for government is only to protect property, prevent fraud, and impartially settle disputes.

Reform Liberalism

Reform liberalism (also referred to as social liberalism, welfare liberalism, or modern liberalism) combines support for individual freedom with a belief that government action may be needed to help remove obstacles to individual development. Reform liberalism developed in the latter part of the nineteenth century as many liberals became concerned that the laissez-faire system established in countries such as Britain seemed to offer little to develop the capabilities of workers and disadvantaged sectors of society.

liberal democracy

A political system that combines the liberal ideas of limited government, individual freedom, and the rule of law with a democratic system of governing based on the election of representatives.

classical liberalism

A form of liberalism that views government has having the limited purposes of protecting life, liberty, and property.

laissez-faire economic system

A system in which privately owned businesses, workers, and consumers freely interact in the marketplace without government interference.

reform liberalism

A version of liberalism that combines support for individual freedom with a belief that government action may be needed to help remove obstacles to individual development.

Life was harsh for the majority of the population, who worked long hours in unsafe conditions to eke out a living with no protection against sickness, disability, unemployment, or old age.

Reform liberals argue that government should play a role in assisting the disadvantaged through such measures as employment insurance, old-age pensions, health care, and subsidized education. This creates a more meaningful freedom for the less fortunate members of society by ensuring that a basic standard of living is available to all. In other words, reform liberals have viewed freedom as a matter of not simply limiting government interference in people's lives. For example, philosopher John Rawls (1999) states that the first principle of justice is that "each person is to have an equal right to the most extensive basic liberty compatible with a similar liberty for others." This is modified by his second principle that "social and economic inequalities are to be arranged so that they are to be of greatest benefits to the least advantaged members of society."

Some contemporary reform liberals argue that preferential treatment (e.g., affirmative action programs) should be given to members of disadvantaged groups (such as racial minorities and women) to overcome discrimination and achieve greater equality in education, employment, and leadership positions (Gibbins & Youngman, 1996).

Liberal International
www.liberal-international.org

Reform liberals generally share with classical liberals a belief in the virtues of a free-enterprise system. However, reform liberals argue that government regulations of business are needed for a variety of purposes, such as protecting workers from unsafe working conditions, consumers from harmful products, and the environment from the discharge of pollutants. Further, Liberal British economist John Maynard Keynes (1883–1946) argued that a laissez-faire economic system does not necessarily lead to the common good. Government spending is needed, particularly during economic downturns, to foster full employment and maintain demand for the products that business produced, even if it means that government would be running a deficit.

Neo-Liberalism

The growth of government combined with economic globalization has led to a reinvigoration of some of the ideas of classical liberalism, often labelled **neo-liberalism.**

neo-liberalism

A perspective based on a strong belief in the free marketplace and opposition to government intervention in the economy.

The perspective of neo-liberalism is based on a strong belief in the values of competition, entrepreneurship, and individual responsibility. Applying the free market to most areas of human activity, neo-liberals favour privatizing government services wherever possible with individuals free to choose and pay for the services they wish to receive. Taxes should be substantially reduced to encourage entrepreneurship and investment. Removal of all barriers to trade and investment is seen as maximizing efficiency on a global scale. Although labelled "neo-liberal," this strong belief in the free-market system and limited government is often associated with contemporary conservatism, particularly in the United States and Canada.[1]

CONSERVATISM

Conservatism emphasizes the values of order and stability in the community. Viewing humans as being imperfect, conservatism is critical of those who advocate rapid and fundamental change. Thus conservatism lacks "a vision of another, different and better world" and "prefers the familiar to the unknown" (Oakeshott, 1991: 428, 408). Although conservatism has been described as "the ideological justification of actual social and political institutions" (Huntington, 1957: 459), this definition applies to long-standing institutions rather than those established by radical or revolutionary changes.

Conservatism as a distinctive perspective or ideology developed particularly in response to the French Revolution (1789), which challenged the privileges of elites, promoted equality and popular sovereignty, proclaimed the "Rights of Man," and sought to reorganize society along rational principles. Some conservatives (labelled **reactionaries**) responded to the failures of the French Revolution by advocating a return to the values and institutions of the old order. Other conservatives,[2] such as British Member of Parliament Edmund Burke (1729–1797), took a more moderate position, arguing that change, when necessary, should be slow, gradual, and consistent with the particular traditions of a country.

To maintain civilized values that have gradually developed, laws need to be respected and vigorously enforced by government, and respect for those in positions of authority maintained. Therefore, conservatives have generally favoured a strong government with strong leadership that is able to protect order and stability and to pursue national interests. As well, many conservatives argue that traditional, religion-based moral values need to be maintained in order to prevent the collapse of civilized society.

Because of the individual's limited capabilities to reason and because of the complexity of society, conservatives argue that we should respect the wisdom that has slowly built up over the ages. This wisdom, they argue, is reflected in traditional customs and practices. Conservatives tend to be critical of attempts to improve society by deliberate political effort.

Conservatives view the institutions of private property, religion, marriage, and the family as the bulwarks of the social order. They generally oppose government policies designed to move society in the direction of greater equality

---

[1]In continental Europe, the term "liberal" generally refers to a belief in a free-market economy, limited government, individual freedom, and a separation of religion from laws and governing.

[2]Burke was a Whig (although part of the conservative faction of the liberal–conservative Whigs) rather than a Tory (a grouping that became the Conservative Party). Nevertheless, he is regarded as the founder of modern conservatism in the English-speaking world.

(for example, by redistributing income, wealth, and property from the rich to the poor) based on the view that people are naturally unequal. Attempts to impose equality are disruptive and undermine the natural leadership of elite groups. Instead, conservatives have traditionally looked to the upper classes to help, protect, and provide moral guidance to the poor.

Conservatism, particularly in its traditional versions, tends to differ from liberalism in being less concerned with the rights of individuals. Instead, as Edmund Burke put it, society should be viewed as a living organism in which the well-being of the individual is dependent on the well-being of the whole, or as a tapestry composed of interwoven threads. Society and the state are not simply based on a temporary contract among individuals, but rather are a permanent partnership "between those who are living, those who are dead, and those who are to be born" (Burke, 1790/1955, p. 110). Governments, along with religious organizations, are important features of human society that are needed to restrain the passions of individuals. Instead of proclaiming the universal rights of all humanity, Burke argued that the traditional liberties of particular countries should be defended. Nevertheless, conservatives tend to place a higher priority on law and order than on individual freedom and often stress the responsibilities of individuals to society.

The Canadian Conservative Forum
www.conservativeforum.org

Historically, British conservatism was associated with the landowning, hereditary aristocracy, which viewed itself as preserving civilized values and having an obligation to lead society. The relentless pursuit of profit by entrepreneurs in the growing industrial and commercial sector of the economy was viewed with disdain. Some conservatives worried that the revolutionary impact of the modern free-market economy and associated global free trade could undermine the local values and particularisms that conservatives cherish. Some conservatives (such as British Prime Minister Benjamin Disraeli) were concerned that a pure free-market capitalist system created deep social divisions between capitalists and workers that could threaten national unity and social order.

In the United States that lacked an aristocracy, conservatism developed in association with the values and interests of the business community, supported the free-market capitalist system, and tended to be individualistic rather than favouring collective action to pursue the common good. Thus American conservatives have been critical of the growth of government and opposed to the development of the **welfare state**. Likewise in Canada, the National Citizens Coalition (once led by former Canadian Prime Minister Stephen Harper) seeks "more freedom through less government."

welfare state

A state in which government ensures that all people have a decent standard of living and are provided protection from hardships resulting from circumstances such as unemployment, sickness, disability, and old age.

The New Right

An influential contemporary version of conservatism, termed the **New Right**, developed in the 1970s combining, in various ways, the promotion of free-market capitalism, limited government, and traditional cultural and moral values, as discussed in Box 3-2 The "Iron Lady."

New Right

A perspective that combines, in various ways, the promotion of free-market capitalism and limited government and traditional cultural and moral values.

BOX 3-2 The "Iron Lady": Margaret Thatcher (1925–2013)

In 1984, the National Union of Mineworkers began a year-long strike in Britain to protest the closure of twenty state-owned coal mines and the loss of twenty thousand jobs. Conservative Prime Minister Margaret Thatcher took a tough stance against the strike. Strikers on the picket line were subject to attacks by police, and thousands of picketers were arrested; laws were passed to curb strikes and end "closed shops" (mandatory union membership); and welfare benefits were denied to the spouses and children of strikers. This led to accusations that Thatcher wanted to starve strikers back to work. In the end, the dejected and divided miners returned to work with no concessions.

Margaret Thatcher received a degree in chemistry from Oxford, practised law, and was elected to Parliament in 1959. She gained notoriety as Minister of Education for eliminating free milk for schoolchildren. After defeating former Conservative Prime Minister Edward Heath to become Conservative Party leader, she led her party to electoral victory in 1979. She served as prime minister until forced out by her party caucus in 1990. She was known as the "Iron Lady" (a term a Russian military journalist used to describe her) for her toughness and determination. Under her direction, the British government greatly reduced the regulation of business, privatized state-owned industries and public housing, and reformed education, health, and welfare systems. In addition, Thatcher was an advocate of traditional moral values, hard work, and individual responsibility; introduced legislation to prevent the promotion of homosexuality; and took tough measures against criminal behaviour. In international affairs, she was a strong ally of American President Ronald Reagan in the fight against communism and ordered British troops to retake the disputed Falkland Islands (Malvinas) in the South Atlantic that had been captured by Argentina.

Thatcher changed the course of British politics and revitalized the conservative ideology throughout the world by adopting a strong free-enterprise orientation. Indeed, Labour Prime Minister Tony Blair did not try to reverse Thatcher's policies, but rather turned his party

British Prime Minister Margaret Thatcher meeting with US President Jimmy Carter in 1977.
Trikosko, Marion S/Library of Congress Prints and Photographs Division [LC-DIG-ppmsca-09786]

away from socialism and, to some extent, followed in her footsteps.

Unlike traditional conservatives, Thatcher had a strongly individualistic perspective, claiming that "there is no such thing as society." Instead of the moderate, consensus-oriented approach favoured by many Conservative politicians, Thatcher forcefully pursued a new direction, for better or worse. While many conservative thinkers claim that conservatism is not an ideology, being pragmatic rather than pursuing a vision of society, few would doubt that Thatcher's tough-minded conservatism was ideological in nature.

Some contemporary conservatives focus primarily on limiting the activities of government, promoting a purer free market economy, and protecting property rights.[3] Other conservatives (termed social conservatives) focus on restoring traditional moral values arguing that liberal social values have fostered a permissive society in which "anything goes." In particular, social conservatives are opposed to abortion, same-sex marriage, pre-marital sex, and sexually explicit television, movies, and music. **Social conservatism** (also referred to as the Religious Right or the Christian Right) in the US is associated with the growth of fundamentalist and evangelical Christianity including the view that the Bible is the literal truth. Social conservatives generally criticize the individualism and materialism of modern society and support laws and government action to help create a moral community.

The New Right has opposed affirmative action programs that give preferential treatment for minorities and women in employment and education, arguing that legal equality and laws preventing discrimination are sufficient to provide equal opportunities for all. In addition, government encouragement for groups to develop their distinctive cultures and identities is viewed by the New Right as weakening the nation-state by undermining the common interests and values of the nation (Whitaker, 1997).

The New Right (particularly the element labelled "neo-conservative") is also associated with advocating a hardline approach in international relations. The United States should exercise global leadership and use its strength to promote Western values—including democracy, freedom, and the free-market capitalist system—worldwide. This involves ensuring that the United States has overwhelming military superiority and a willingness to take military action against "rogue regimes" and those who support terrorism.

social conservatism

A version of conservatism that advocates public policies based on traditional moral and religious values including opposition to abortion, same-sex marriage, pre-marital sex, and euthanasia.

Traditional Conservatism and the New Right

In some ways, the New Right is not entirely new. Conservatives have always been defenders of property rights and have supported the idea of limited

---

[3]An extreme version adopted by some conservatives (and classical liberals) is libertarianism, which argues that the role of government should be strictly limited to the protection of liberty, property, and contract (Nozick, 1974).

government while favouring laws to punish "immoral" behaviour. Both traditional conservatives and the New Right have been strongly critical of socialism and the redistribution of wealth by government. Many traditional conservatives, however, do not accept the pure free-market and minimal-government perspective associated with some elements of the New Right.[4] In addition, the activist approach of neo-conservatives to foreign policy, particularly in exporting democratic values, tends to differ from traditional conservatism, which was often concerned with maintaining a stable "balance of power" in international politics and, in the United States, sought to limit foreign involvements.

Traditional conservatism emphasizes the need to respect authority and thus, in modern times, tends to favour limited forms of democracy. In contrast, the New Right has a substantial element of populism that is critical of government and believes that the common people should be in more direct control of decision making through such devices as referendums, initiatives, and recall. New Right populists claim that politicians, government officials, and judges have undermined traditional values, have catered to what the New Right considers to be "special interests" (such as various equality-seeking groups), and do not reflect the views of the "silent majority" that holds traditional or conventional moral values.

More generally, many traditional conservatives preach the virtues of moderation and gradual change. The New Right, by contrast, has tended to pursue its convictions with greater ideological zeal.

SOCIALISM

socialism

An ideological perspective based on the view that human beings are basically social in nature and that the capitalist system undermines the cooperative and community-oriented nature of humanity. Socialism advocates the establishment of an egalitarian society.

Socialist International
www.socialistinternational.org

Socialism developed as an important political ideology in reaction to the exploitation of workers in the developing capitalist system. Socialists view human beings as basically social and thus tend to be critical of the capitalist system for its emphasis on competition, which undermines the cooperative and community-oriented nature of humanity. Inequality is viewed as largely the result of the power relations in society and the capitalist economic system rather than of the inherent differences in the capabilities of individuals. A more equal society in terms of the distribution of wealth, income, and power will lead to a greater sense of community and solidarity and will facilitate co-operation rather than conflict (Heywood, 2003). Social justice can be achieved by reducing inequalities and ensuring that all persons have the rights and resources needed for a life of dignity.

Within the socialist ideology, there are a variety of views as to what an ideal society would be like and how such a society could be achieved. Traditionally, socialists have advocated some form of social (collective) rather than private

---

[4]The strong anti-government perspective is particularly characteristic of contemporary American conservatism.

BOX 3-3   Utopian Socialism

In his classic book *Utopia*, English writer Thomas More (1478–1535) condemned the evils of pride, envy, and greed that result "wherever men have private property and money is the measure of everything" (1516/2004, p. 198).

In existing societies, More asserted, the rich "serve their own interests under the name of the common good" while in reality they look after only their private good. Instead of only a few being prosperous and happy "while all the rest live in misery and wretchedness," More imagined a society in which all things are owned in common, money is no longer used, and everyone is free to take from the common storehouses all the necessities that are needed to live a meaningful life. In such a society, people would be concerned with the "common affairs" of the society, rather than worry about earning a livelihood (More, 1516/2004, pp. 198–202).

More did not intend *Utopia*, which literally means "nowhere," to be a blueprint for society. However, a number of socialists, particularly in the nineteenth century, developed elaborate models of an ideal communal society. These "utopian socialists" were criticized by other socialists, including Marx and Engels, for having the naive view that fundamental changes could occur by developing visionary schemes or establishing model communities instead of taking political action to transform the capitalist system.

Nevertheless, a number of small-scale communes have been established at various times. Israel's kibbutzim, although involving only a very small proportion of the country's population, are one of the few successful secular communal societies. Various religious sects, such as the Hutterites, have maintained a communal lifestyle that they view as following the teachings of Jesus Christ.

ownership of the major means of production so that many of the decisions that affect the life of the community are no longer in the hands of large corporations. Some have envisaged the establishment of small, self-sufficient communes in which property would be collectively owned, all would work co-operatively, and material goods would be shared equally (see Box 3-3 Utopian Socialism). Others have looked to the state to own the major means of production and operate them for the good of society as a whole. Still others envision a system of worker-run co-operative enterprises. Many contemporary socialists look to some form of mixed economy where government plays a substantial role in planning and regulating the economy as well as providing various free or low-cost public services (such as health care, education, and child care).

Marxism and Communism

The ideology of socialism developed from a variety of sources and has numerous variations. The ideas of Karl Marx (1818–1883) and Frederick Engels (1820–1895), often termed Marxism, were adopted by the revolutionary movements that established communist regimes and had an influence, to some extent, on democratic socialist parties. Their analysis, termed **historical materialism**, starts with the assumption that historical development can be understood in terms of the way society is organized to produce material goods. In every society except the most primitive ones, production involves the exploitation of a subordinate

historical materialism

The view that historical development and the dynamics of society and politics can be understood in terms of the way society is organized to produce material goods.

class by a smaller, dominant class. The leading ideas, beliefs, and morals of a society serve the interests of the dominant class by limiting awareness of their exploitation among the subordinate class. However, each of the major systems of production—slave-owning, feudal, and capitalist—has internal tensions ("contradictions") that eventually become irresolvable. This eventually leads to an overthrow of that system and its replacement by a new system of production.

In their examination of the capitalist system of production, Marx and Engels argued that the profits obtained by the owners of capital (the bourgeoisie) were based on the exploitation of the workers (the proletariat). The capitalist system appeared to be free, as goods and labour could be freely bought and sold in the marketplace. It was, however, only the appearance of freedom. Workers, in reality, had little choice but to sell their labour power to survive. In addition, the emphasis on competition, profit, and selfishness in the capitalist free-market system violated what Marx and Engels viewed as the essentially social and creative nature of humanity.

The capitalist system in the Marxist view is an important, but not the final, stage of historical development. Conflict between the working class and the bourgeoisie will intensify because the two classes have incompatible interests. The large working class that was developing in Marx and Engels's time as a result of industrialization would eventually organize itself into a revolutionary force. This class would overturn the capitalist system and replace it with a system based on social, rather than private, ownership of the means of production. Although the capitalist system was much more productive than

This statue of Marx and Engels in the former East Berlin is a reminder of the importance of the communist ideology in the past century.
Eric Mintz

earlier systems of production, its unplanned nature meant that it could not fully unleash the power of human productivity. In particular, capitalism, Marx and Engels believed, was prone to ever-increasing crises of severe unemployment and depression. In addition, free competition among capitalists would be undermined as weaker capitalists were forced out of business, leaving the remaining capitalists with monopoly control of the marketplace.

Marxists Internet Archive
www.marxists.org

Because the state generally acts in the interests of the capitalist class, the working class would have to capture control of the state and then use the state apparatus to transform the capitalist system into a socialist system. This would likely necessitate a revolution, as capitalists will be unlikely to give up their control voluntarily or peacefully. However, as workers in Europe began to gain the right to vote in the late nineteenth century, Marx and Engels saw a possibility that, in some countries, working-class control of state power *might* be achieved through the election of socialist political parties, provided that police and military forces were not used to suppress the socialist movement.

After the revolution, the workers would control the state in the interests of the working class ("the dictatorship of the proletariat") and would use the state to expropriate the property of the capitalists. *Eventually*, Marx and Engels argued, the selfishness that is characteristic of economic systems based on private ownership would disappear. The increased production of an economy devoted to human needs rather than private profit would lead to material abundance that could fulfill the basic needs of everyone. A further transition from socialism to **communism** would then occur. In a communist society, everyone would be free to take from society what they need. Although production would be highly organized, the need for a coercive state would diminish or disappear because, in the Marxist perspective, the need for a coercive state arises out of the need to use coercion to maintain private property and the inequality that it entails.

communism

A system in which private property has been replaced by collective or communal ownership and everyone is free to take from society what they need.

LENINISM Vladimir Lenin (1870–1924), the Russian Communist leader, modified the ideas of Marx and Engels into a viewpoint known as **Leninism**. In Lenin's view, the capitalist system could be overthrown only by force—but the workers themselves could not spontaneously overthrow the system. What was needed was a tightly disciplined party firmly controlled by a revolutionary vanguard.

Leninism

The version of Marxism that includes the belief that the capitalist system can be overthrown only by force, by means of a tightly disciplined party controlled by a revolutionary vanguard.

Because nineteenth-century Russia was largely a peasant society with a relatively small working class, the Communist Party that was in the vanguard of the proletariat was particularly important in leading the revolution and directing the subsequent course of revolutionary change. Instead of putting power in the hands of councils of workers and peasants, as many of those involved in the Russian Revolution had hoped, Lenin, and even more so his successor, Joseph Stalin (1877–1953), established a tight grip on Soviet society and established a totalitarian regime dedicated to rapidly building an industrialized economy. Similarly, tight party control was also characteristic of government in China, where the Communist Party under Mao Zedong (1893–1976) was successful in capturing power in 1949 after a lengthy guerrilla war.

THE COMMUNIST SYSTEM COLLAPSES   Communist Party control of the Soviet Union and Eastern Europe collapsed at the end of the 1980s. A loosening of the tight control exercised by Communist leaders allowed the people to overthrow their governments with a minimum of violence. China is still controlled by the Communist Party; however, it has abandoned efforts to create an egalitarian communist society and instead has developed an export-oriented state-directed economy that has become a major force in the global economic system.

Democratic Socialism

democratic socialism

The perspective that socialism should be achieved by democratic rather than revolutionary means and that a socialist society should be democratic in nature with political rights and freedoms respected.

Democratic socialism is based on the belief that only democratic methods should be used to work toward a socialist society. Democratic socialists reject the notion of the dictatorship of the proletariat, arguing instead that political rights and freedoms should be respected. Likewise, although they believe that an active government is needed to provide for the well-being of the citizenry, they argue that governments should abide by the rule of law, protect civil liberties, and not act in an arbitrary manner.

Rather than complete state ownership of the means of production, democratic socialists have favoured measures such as public ownership of some key industries, encouragement for co-operative enterprises, requirements that workers have a voice in the decisions of the businesses that employ them, the right of workers to unionize and bargain collectively, and government planning and regulation of the economy. To achieve greater equality, democratic socialists advocate government provision and subsidization of various services, along with some redistribution of income and wealth from the rich to the poor, particularly through the tax system.

Social Democracy

Over time, ideas about nationalizing (having the government take over) the "commanding heights" of the economy, or about replacing the capitalist system, have generally moved to the fringes of democratic socialist parties. Indeed, many leading figures within democratic socialist parties prefer to call themselves social democrats[5] to indicate that they no longer believe in a socialist economic system (that is, one with a high level of state ownership or control).

---

[5]The term *social democracy* has had different meanings. In the nineteenth century, a number of European Social Democratic parties adopted a Marxist perspective. After the establishment of the Soviet Union, there was a split between Marxist-Leninists, who called themselves communists, and social democrats, who rejected the revolutionary path to socialism. In recent decades, the term *social democracy* has often been applied to those who no longer advocate the goal of a socialist economy.

Instead, contemporary social democrats generally believe that the capitalist economy can be reformed to ensure that it works for the common good. Social democrats also advocate greater social and economic equality to achieve a meaningful democracy. As Ed Broadbent (2001), a former leader of Canada's New Democratic Party, put it, market economies have "generated the wealth needed to provide effective social rights," but its unequal distribution of income and power "runs counter to the democratic goal of equal citizens." For Broadbent, democracy involves not only political and civil rights, but also entitlements that ensure that various social and economic rights such as health, education, employment, and child care are available to all persons. In other words, social democrats believe that the excesses of the free-market capitalist system can be curtailed by government action to provide a welfare state, greater equality, and regulation of the market economy.

Social democratic ideas provided much of the basis for the consensus concerning the welfare state and the relations between business and labour that developed in many of the countries of the Western world after World War II. However, globalization and neo-liberalism have created challenges for social democrats, who have generally looked to a strong state to provide a variety of public services and a substantial degree of control of the market. In Western Europe, some social democrats played a key role in developing the European Union and ensuring that its free-market policies were combined with guarantees of human rights and environmental protection. In the United Kingdom, former Labour Party Prime Minister Tony Blair sought to modernize social democracy through the "Third Way," which involved greater acceptance of the free market, globalization, individualism, and personal responsibility. Other social democrats, while favouring global social justice and the development of democratic global institutions, are critical of economic globalization, emphasize the importance of social solidarity rather than individualism, and see a continuing need for the market economy to be controlled for the common good (Leggett, 2007).

Anarchism

Anarchism, which literally means "without rule," seeks to eliminate the state, which it views as a key source of oppression. Socialist anarchism (or anarcho-communism) advocates the elimination of both the state and private property. In its place, socialist anarchists advocate a cooperative or communal society based on what they see as the natural principle of mutual assistance. Instead of large and powerful states, they envision a world based on voluntary cooperation among a network of local communities.

Anarchists generally favour "direct action" such as demonstrations, civil disobedience, street theatre, and general strikes, rather than establishing political parties (which they view as an instrument of power) and voting to achieve their objectives. Although many anarchists oppose all forms of violence, some

anarchism

An ideology that views the state as the key source of oppression and seeks to replace the state with a system based on voluntary co-operation.

Anarchy Archives
http://dwardmac.pitzer.edu/ Anarchist_Archives/

anarchists have used violence (and, historically, selected assassination of business and government leaders) in the hope of encouraging a popular uprising. Whether members of the "Black Bloc," who have clashed with police and smashed windows at various protests (such as the G20 summit in Toronto in June 2010), are truly anarchists or simply "hooligans" is a matter of debate.

Various forms of socialist anarchism were important in the international socialist movement in the latter part of the nineteenth century and early twentieth century as well as in the Spanish Civil War (1936–1939). Anarchism continues to have some significance; for example, as an element of the anti-globalization movement.[6]

FASCISM

fascism

An ideology that combines an aggressive form of nationalism with a strong belief in the naturalness of inequality and opposition to both liberal democracy and communism.

The ideology of **fascism** developed in the period between World War I and World War II based in part on the views of various thinkers who were critical of the ideas of the Enlightenment. Fascism combines an aggressive form of nationalism with a strong belief in the naturalness of inequality and opposition to both liberal democracy and communism.

Nationalism and Racism

Loyalty to the nation-state is extremely important in fascist thought. In the fascist view, the well-being of the individual is based on the well-being of the nation-state to which the individual belongs. Individuals owe absolute loyalty to the state, and the state has the right to control all activities in order to promote its interests. Further, the nation is seen by fascists as an organic entity in which each member of the nation is part of the collective organism rather than an individual with particular rights (Griffin, 2010). Foreigners and those of minority cultures are viewed as a threat to the creation of a homogenous society based on the dominant nationality.

Related to the extreme nationalism of fascist ideology is a belief in the superiority of particular nationalities and races. This superiority is exhibited not only in cultural achievements, but also in such characteristics as bravery and heroism. War allows that superiority to be realized, and the conquest and subordination of "inferior" nations and races is justified.

Nazism

A version of fascism associated with Adolf Hitler, the Nazi leader of Germany, emphasizing racial conflict and the superiority of the "Aryan race."

NAZISM The ideas of racial superiority and racial conflict were particularly evident in **Nazism**. Building on some European nineteenth-century theories that viewed racial differences as profound, the Nazis proclaimed their belief that the Germans and some related Nordic peoples were the heirs of an "Aryan master race" that could be restored through careful breeding. As a

---

[6]There is also anarcho-capitalism that advocates replacing the state with voluntary agreements among individuals.

BOX 3-4 The Holocaust

The racist ideology of the Nazis that viewed Jews as "subhuman" had horrific consequences.

In the 1920s and 1930s, stirring up anti-Semitic prejudices was an important part of the Nazi appeal. After gaining power, the Nazis began taking away the rights of Jews, including their citizenship, and encouraged attacks on Jewish businesses and individuals. As the German armies conquered Eastern Europe in World War II, they began rounding up Jews and shooting them in mass pits or gassing them in mobile gas chambers. Eventually, Adolf Hitler and his top officials decided on what they termed the "final solution" to the "Jewish problem" (that is, the total elimination of the Jewish people). Persons of Jewish ancestry were transported to massive concentration camps for slave labour and systematic, industrial-style extermination.

In all, the Nazis organized the deliberate murder of about six million persons of Jewish ancestry, including about one-and-a-half million children. In addition, about five million other persons were killed, deemed "unfit" because of their nationality (particularly the Roma [gypsies]), disabilities, sexual orientation, or political views. The Holocaust is particularly horrifying because of the systematic, determined, and state-directed nature of the "extermination." Further, it occurred in modern and so-called civilized societies, often with the acquiescence and involvement of people throughout Europe, despite some heroic exceptions.

The Holocaust should not be viewed as a single, isolated event. The persecution of Jews had a very lengthy history throughout Europe. Likewise, racist views that some peoples are inferior or not fully human were used to justify massacres of the Indigenous population in many parts of the Americas after the European conquest, the massive slave trade in various parts of the world, and the murder of hundreds of thousands of Tutsis in Rwanda in 1994.

"culture-creating" master race, a revived Aryan race would exert dominance over other "inferior" races. The Nazis viewed the Jews as their key racial enemy and sought to rid Europe of the Jews. This resulted in the systematic genocide known as the **Holocaust** (see Box 3-4 The Holocaust).

Belief in a Natural Inequality

Fascists also believe that there is a natural inequality within society between the masses and their natural leaders. The masses can be mobilized by skilful leaders through the use of slogans and symbols. Democratic leaders are seen as weak because they pander to the masses to gain their support. Instead, fascists often argue that a heroic leader with a creative "will to power" will arise above the masses in exceptional circumstances. Such an exceptional leader, fascists believe, embodies the will of the people. Fascism favours strong, authoritarian leadership, arguing that natural leaders should be allowed free rein to rule in the interests of the nation-state, enhancing its unity, culture, and power.

Rejection of the Enlightenment

Underlying fascist ideology is a rejection of Enlightenment thought. Fascists assume that human beings are motivated by emotion rather than by reason.

Holocaust

The systematic extermination of six million European Jews by the Nazis during World War II.

The Holocaust History Project
www.holocaust-history.org

People are rooted in their ancestry and their territory, and can be mobilized into action through myths and propaganda. As well, fascism rejects the idea that we are all part of a common humanity (Eatwell, 1995). Instead of the liberal and socialist belief that a peaceful world can be created, fascism sees struggle and the use of force as inevitable.

Because fascists see the world as based on a struggle for dominance, they argue that constant preparation for war is necessary. The strength of one's nation-state must be developed to ensure its dominance. Divisions or disagreements within the nation-state cannot be tolerated because they lead to weakness. Fascists believe that it is right and natural that the strong should dominate and subjugate the weak, and that humanitarian policies directed at aiding the disadvantaged lead to weakness. Adapting the **social Darwinist** ideas of English social theorist Herbert Spencer (1820–1903), fascists see war and conflict as a natural process that allows humanity to evolve through the "survival of the fittest."

social Darwinism

The use of Darwin's theory of evolution to argue that competition and conflict allow humanity to evolve through the "survival of the fittest."

Corporate State

corporate state

A system associated with fascist Italy in which business and labour work harmoniously to achieve goals established by the state to advance the good of the nation.

Benito Mussolini's Italian fascist regime adopted the idea of the **corporate state**, in which business and labour would work harmoniously to achieve goals established by the state to advance the good of the nation (Heywood, 2003). In practice, this involved the subordination of labour and business to the fascist regime and the suppression of the labour movement.

A New Order

Fascism is often depicted as a reactionary ideology. To some extent this is valid, as fascism rejects many aspects of modern society and politics, including individualism and materialism, which fascism views as a cause of moral decay. However, German Nazism and Italian fascism embraced only selected myths from the past, such as the ideal of the heroic Teutonic warrior or the glories of the Roman Empire. The Nazis glorified the ethnically homogenous rural communities of the past, but also celebrated modern technology with a vision of a technological future (Neocleous, 1997). Unlike reactionary conservatives, fascists described their goal in terms of creating a new order rather than restoring the old order in Europe.

Fascism can be described as a radical right-wing ideology. The interwar fascist movement gained considerable support from nationalistic, authoritarian conservatives and other right-wing forces who shared with fascists a belief in order, leadership, and authority and who were anti-Semitic and anti-democratic. Nevertheless, fascism tends to be distinct in its emphasis on conflict, militarism, total control of society, mobilization of the people behind a populist leader, and its rejection of most moral principles (Mann, 2004).

The Continuing Significance of Fascism and the Radical Right

Fascism is often associated with the dictatorial regimes of the Italian fascist leader Benito Mussolini (from 1922 to 1943) and the German Nazi leader Adolf Hitler (from 1933 to 1945). However, fascist movements had substantial followings in a variety of countries in the 1930s, and some non-fascist political leaders privately expressed admiration for Mussolini and Hitler. The decisive defeat of the militarist fascist regimes in World War II and the revelation of the horrors they perpetrated resulted in the discrediting of the fascist ideology. Nevertheless, semi-fascist regimes remained in power in Spain and Portugal until the early 1970s, and a number of countries, including Greece, Guatemala, Argentina, Bolivia, Chile, and Paraguay, at various times came under the control of authoritarian right-wing regimes that reflected some elements of fascism.

A number of radical right-wing movements and far right and **neo-fascist** political parties (including the Front National in France, Austria's Freedom Party, the Dutch Party for Freedom, and the Slovak National Party) have developed in many European countries. In particular, various parties have adopted racist policies, including encouraging or requiring those of non-European ancestry to return to their homelands. The Jobbik Party, which campaigns for Hungarian racial "purity" and is connected to an illegal paramilitary group that uses symbols similar to those used by the Hungarian Nazis, won 20.2 percent of the vote in Hungary's 2014 parliamentary election. The Danish People's Party, strongly opposed to immigrants, received the second largest number of votes and seats in the 2015 election, giving it an important influence on the governing Venstre (conservative-liberal) party that relies to a considerable extent on its support. At the time of writing, the presidential candidate for Austria's Freedom Party had the support of about one-half of the electorate while the Front National's leader, Marine Le Pen, was expected to be a serious contender in the 2017 French presidential election. In the United States, 2016 Republican presidential candidate Donald Trump used similar appeals to that of some radical nationalist, anti-immigrant, far-right European parties.

In Greece, the extreme right-wing Golden Dawn Party won 18 seats in Parliament in 2012 and 2015. Although its leader claims the party is nationalist rather than neo-Nazi, its website calls for an ethnically pure Greece, its campaign slogan was "rid this country of filth" (Dale, 2012), it uses Nazi-like symbols and salutes, its black-shirted "storm troopers" march through immigrant neighbourhoods singing Nazi chants and beating up immigrants, and one of its MPs elected in 2012 was the lead singer of the white power rock group Pogrom that sings the praises of Auschwitz, the infamous Nazi death camp.

neo-fascism

A revival of some of the characteristics of fascism in contemporary times including ethnic nationalism, opposition to immigrants who have different racial or religious characteristics, and support for a populist leader who will take decisive action to strengthen the nation.

Neo-nazism in contemporary
Greece
Tami Thirlwell

In addition, there has been increasing violence by extreme European right-wing groups directed at Muslims, Roma, Jews, immigrants, and various other racial, religious, and ethnic minorities. In particular, as large numbers of Muslim refugees fled Syria and other war-torn countries in 2015 and 2016, participation in militant right-wing extremist groups that sought to expel Muslim refugees increased in many European countries. In the United States, groups like the Aryan Nation promote racism and the ideal of an all-white America, and some militia groups train for armed resistance to what they believe is a new world order conspiracy to take over the United States. Individuals influenced by militia groups carried out the bombing that killed 168 people at the U.S. government building in Oklahoma City in 1995.

✔• SUMMARY AND CONCLUSION

Political ideologies have had a major impact on politics in the modern era. Political ideologies provide not only basic sets of values and goals to those who engage in political activity, but also differing ways of analyzing and understanding the world.

Liberalism focuses on the ideal of individual freedom. The coercion of individuals should be minimized, and the common good is best achieved by allowing individuals to pursue their own interests, develop their own capabilities and morality, and act on their own values. Because those with power are likely to use that power for their own interests, protecting individual rights and freedoms and establishing the rule of law are important means to achieve the objectives of liberalism. A peaceful and prosperous world can be developed through the promotion of tolerance, adherence to laws, and the facilitation of global interactions through free trade and the free interaction of ideas. For classical liberals, the free market, equal legal rights, and limited government ensure that individuals are not subject to the arbitrary and oppressive power of government and other institutions. Reform liberals seek meaningful freedom for all and believe that government can play a useful role by removing the obstacles to individual development and promoting equality of opportunity.

Conservatism, because of its pessimistic view of human capabilities, does not generally present an ideal of a better world that can be achieved through conscious political action. The common good is best obtained in an orderly community in which traditional moral values and institutions are maintained. The limitations of human reason suggest that change should be gradual. Traditional conservatives believe that respect for those in positions of authority should be promoted, and those with wealth and privilege should be encouraged to look after the well-being of society. Because of human frailties and the human capacity for evil, restraints on individual actions are necessary to ensure the common good of the community. The New Right version of conservatism views the welfare state and the undermining of traditional Western values as the cause of many contemporary problems. The New Right generally favours strengthening the state's ability to fight criminal and immoral behaviour and to promote Western values at home and abroad. As well, New Right conservatives and neo-liberals generally favour a global laissez-faire capitalist system with minimal government involvement in the economy.

Socialism promotes the ideal of a society based on co-operation and equality. The focus of the capitalist system on the pursuit of profit and individual wealth hinders the achievement of the common good. Eliminating oppression and inequalities and ensuring that the needs of all are fulfilled would allow humans, as social and cooperative beings, to pursue the common good of humanity. For communists, a revolution based on the working class is needed to destroy the oppressive power of capitalism and the capitalist-based state. This will allow for the creation of a classless socialist—and eventually communist—society. Democratic socialists, on the other hand, argue that socialism can be achieved through the election of a socialist party and the gradual evolution of society toward socialism. Contemporary social democrats suggest that the major ideals of socialism can be achieved by reforming capitalism, reducing inequalities, and guaranteeing social and economic rights to all.

Fascism seeks to build a powerful, united, militaristic nation-state that will provide strong leadership and direction to the masses. Order, leadership, and discipline need to be strong in a world characterized by conflict and the struggle for dominance. Fascists view the idea of the common good of humanity as a whole as unrealistic. Instead, the collective good of the state, nation, or race is emphasized in fascist thought.

✓• KEY TERMS

Anarchism 67

Classical liberalism 56

Communism 65

Conservatism 58

Corporate state 70

Democratic socialism 66

Enlightenment 51

Fascism 68

Historical materialism 63

Holocaust 69

Laissez-faire economic system 56

Left 54

Leninism 65

Liberal democracy 56

Nazism 68

Neo-fascism 71

Neo-liberalism 57

New Right 59

Political ideology 51

Reactionary 58

Reform liberalism 56

Right 54

Rule of law 55

Social conservatism 61

Social Darwinism 70

Socialism 62

Welfare state 59

DISCUSSION QUESTIONS

1. How important are political ideologies in contemporary political life? Do national and provincial political parties in Canada tend to reflect different ideological perspectives?

2. Is a particular ideological perspective prevalent in your community, among your friends, or at your university or college?

3. Which ideological perspective do you think provides the best perspective on basic political values?

4. Are socialism and communism still relevant in the contemporary world?

5. What are the views of the different ideologies on the common good?

FURTHER READING

Ball, T., Dagger, R., Christian, W., & Campbell, C. (2012). *Political ideologies and the democratic ideal* (3rd Canadian ed.). Toronto: Pearson Canada.

Griffin, R. (1993). *The nature of fascism.* London: Routledge.

Harrington, M. (1989). *Socialism.* New York: Penguin.

Kelly, P. (2005). *Liberalism.* Cambridge, UK: Polity Press.

Mann, M. (2004). *Fascists.* New York: Cambridge University Press.

Nisbet, R. (1986). *Conservatism: Dream and reality.* Milton Keynes, UK: Open University Press.

Paxton, R.O. (2004). *The anatomy of fascism.* New York: Vintage Books

Pierson, C. (2001). *Hard choices: Social democracy in the twenty-first century.* Cambridge, UK: Polity Press.

Ryan, A. (2012). *The making of modern liberalism.* Princeton, NJ: Princeton University Press.

Scruton, R. (2014). *The meaning of conservatism* (3rd ed.). South Bend In: St. Augustine's Press.

Segal, H. (1997). *Beyond greed: A traditional conservative confronts neo-conservative excess.* Toronto: Stoddart.

Singer, P. (1980). *Marx.* Oxford: Oxford University Press.

4 Other Perspectives

Malala Yousafzai, the sixteen-year-old advocate for girls' education who was shot in the head by the Pakistani Taliban, attends the United Nations Youth Assembly on "Malala Day," July 12, 2013. Dpa picture alliance/Alamy Stock Photo

After reading this chapter, you should be able to:

1. describe and discuss the feminist perspective
2. compare the different versions of feminism
3. describe and discuss the distinctive features of environmentalism
4. compare the different versions of environmentalism
5. discuss the significance of fundamentalism and radical Islamism

On October 9, 2012, 15-year-old Malala Yousafzaj was going home on a school bus when she was shot in the head by two Taliban militants. Malala lived in the Swat Valley, a border area of Pakistan that had been controlled by the Pakistani Taliban, who opposed education for women and shut down girls' schools.

Malala was flown to England where surgery saved her life. Although the Taliban threatened to attack her again, Malala emerged from surgery saying "I want every girl, every child, to be educated." She continued to be an outspoken advocate for girls' education and along with her father established the Malala Fund to achieve this objective. In 2014 she received the Nobel Peace Prize and used the $1.1 million prize to finance a secondary school for girls in Pakistan.

Although girls and women no longer face limitations in their educational opportunities in Canada, this is not the case in many parts of the world. Nevertheless, Canadian women are still much less likely than men to be elected to Parliament or sit on the board of directors of corporations. Women are more likely to work in low-paying jobs. The United States has no legal requirement for paid maternity leave, and Canadian women often find it difficult to obtain affordable, good quality child care. In addition, sexual abuse is a problem faced by women in all countries.

The long struggle of women to achieve equality has stimulated the development of the influential perspective of feminism. Feminism raises basic questions about the position of women that were often given very limited attention in the past.

This chapter also examines environmentalism, which presents fundamental challenges to our ways of thinking about our relationship to nature, the way our economic system and our institutions operate, and how we should live. Both feminism and environmentalism seek fundamental changes in the values, institutions, and policies of the political community. These perspectives also provide challenges to our behaviour and attitudes in our daily lives.

The attack by the Taliban on Malala is one example of the significance of extremist religious-based ideologies in contemporary politics. In the Middle East, and parts of Asia and Africa, a radical form of Islamism has become a powerful political force.

Some prominent political commentators have argued that the age of ideologies has ended (Bell, 1998; Fukuyama, 1992). With the collapse of communism and the differences between liberals, conservatives, and social democrats appearing to diminish, political controversy, they say, will involve the details of policy rather than the clash of sharply different perspectives. However, the perspectives of feminism, environmentalism, and fundamentalism raise important issues and controversies as this chapter will illustrate.

FEMINISM

Feminism is often thought of in terms of achieving equality for women. This involves not only establishing equal rights and opportunities for women and eliminating discriminatory practices, but also challenging the traditional views about women that have often had the effect of confining women to domestic life and restricting their freedom. Beyond seeking to achieve equality with men, many feminists argue that political decisions should give greater emphasis to the different experiences and values of women instead of being based primarily on male values.

In the perspective of feminism, all societies are, to varying extents, characterized by **patriarchy**. As explained by Lorraine Code (1988, p. 18), "patriarchal societies are those in which men have more power than women, readier access than women to what is valued in the society and, in consequence, are in control over many, if not most aspects of women's lives." Changing the patriarchal nature of society is a basic goal of feminism.

feminism

A perspective that views society as patriarchal and seeks to achieve full independence and equality for women.

patriarchy

A system in which power is in the hands of men and many aspects of women's lives are controlled by men.

The Development of Feminism

A sexual division of labour in which women are seen as suited for household duties, including the raising of children, and men are seen as best suited for politics, ruling, and other public activities has often been viewed as natural. Some argued that women needed to be protected from the harsh realities of politics, while others viewed women as more prone to emotion than reason. Even the ancient Greek philosopher Aristotle, who viewed females as equal to males with the capacity for reason and deliberation, asserted that "the male, unless constituted in some respect contrary to nature, is by nature more adept in leading than the female" (*The Politics*, quoted by Bradshaw, 1991, p. 563). Therefore, he argued, men should rule in both the household and the political community. This view of women has persisted despite occasional examples of strong, powerful, and tough-minded female rulers such as Queen Elizabeth I of England (1533–1603) and Catherine the Great, Empress of Russia (1729–1762). In more recent times, there have been a number of influential women prime ministers and presidents, including Michelle Bachelet, Benazir Bhutto, Indira Gandhi, Ellen Johnson-Sirleaf, Golda Meir, Angela Merkel, Margaret Thatcher, and Sheikh Hasina Wajed. Canada has only briefly had a female prime minister, Kim Campbell; at the time of writing there were three female provincial premiers (Christy Clark, Rachel Notley, and Kathleen Wynne).

Worldwide Guide to Women in Leadership
www.guide2womenleaders.com/ Current-Women-Leaders.htm

The *Declaration of the Rights of Man*, a product of the French Revolution of 1789, inspired one of the first statements of feminist ideas. In *A Vindication of the Rights of Woman* (1792), Mary Wollstonecraft rejected the common notion that women's natural role was to please men and to bear and raise children. Wollstonecraft argued that women are human beings with

German Chancellor Angela Merkel proved that women can be successful in politics by leading her party to victory for the third time in September 2013 with an increased share of the vote. She is Germany's first female Chancellor.

epa european pressphoto agency b.v./Alamy Stock Photo

the same capacity for rational thinking as men and should therefore have the same rights as men. If women appeared more emotional and less concerned about the good of the political community, it was a result of being deprived of adequate education and the opportunities to develop themselves, rather than being an inevitable product of their nature (Adams, 2001). Likewise, John Stuart Mill argued in *The Subjection of Women* (1869) that freeing women from being subordinate to men, providing equal educational opportunities, and establishing a full set of civil and political rights for women were justified because women had the same capacity for rational thought and action as men.

Although both Wollstonecraft and Mill advocated equal rights and education for women, they assumed that women were more likely to choose domestic life rather than paid employment. By being educated and equal, women would be better equipped to raise their children, and marriages would be happier if wives could interact intelligently with their husbands. Other early feminists, particularly those involved in the revolutionary politics of Marxism and anarchism in the late nineteenth and early twentieth centuries (for example, Emma Goldman), went further by advocating the liberation of women from their domestic roles and from traditional sexual constraints.

In the nineteenth and early twentieth centuries, women played a major role in various political activities including anti-slavery campaigns, the temperance movement, and the struggle for the right to vote. In addition, in the first wave of the women's movement, various groups challenged a variety of laws that

BOX 4-1   Betty Friedan: "The Problem That Has No Name"

The 1950s and early 1960s seemed to be a good time for white, middle-class women in North America. Comfortable houses were built in the suburbs. Labour-saving devices like washing machines became widely used. Middle-class women increasingly obtained a university education. And life as depicted on such popular television shows as *Father Knows Best* appeared satisfying for mothers, fathers, and their children.

However, in *The Feminine Mystique* (1963), Betty Friedan depicted life in the suburbs as one of frustration and boredom. Women suffered a "problem that has no name": "a sense of dissatisfaction . . . that each suburban wife struggles with alone. As she makes the beds, shopped for groceries . . . she was afraid to

ask even of herself the silent question—'Is that all?'" (Friedan, 1963, p. 15). Friedan founded the National Organization for Women in 1966, which sought to create a fully equal partnership between women and men, including the adoption of the Equal Rights Amendment to the American constitution. Although Congress passed the amendment by large margins in 1972, it failed to gain the necessary ratification by three-quarters of the state legislatures, particularly due to the conservative opposition mobilized by Phyllis Schlafly. In contrast, women's groups were successful in pressuring governments to include gender equality in Canada's constitutional Charter of Rights and Freedoms in 1982.

gave men legal control of women, their property, and even their children—laws that in some jurisdictions were not repealed until recent decades.

Legal equality and the rights of citizenship did not, however, create full equality. Women continued to be expected to be homemakers, carrying out domestic duties, raising children, and arranging social functions, while paid employment, business, and politics were considered male activities. Challenging these "separate spheres" of male and female activity led to the second wave of the women's movement (see Box 4-1 Betty Friedan: "The Problem That Has No Name"). Nevertheless, in Canada and other countries, women are still more likely than men to have lower earnings, spend more time in household work, and are much less likely to hold top management positions. However, differences between men and women in hours spent on household and paid work have decreased substantially among those aged 20–29 (Marshall, 2011). Further, Canadian women are now more likely than men to be enrolled in university degree programs and to have a professional occupation.

Equality and Difference

Feminism is usually associated with the struggle for equality for women. Most feminists reject the traditional view that biological differences make women more suitable for domestic rather than public activities. However, to varying degrees, many feminists also assert that the social roles typically assigned to women have resulted in different female values that can make an important contribution to the political community. Based on their experiences, women are more likely to have attributes such as nurturing, caring, cooperation, emotion, and spirituality. These attributes are under-valued in male-dominated societies, which instead emphasize competition, aggression, and rationality. In this perspective, society needs to be trans-formed so that female values are given greater importance, because female and male values are either complementary (if given equal weight) or even superior to male values (for example, more likely to lead to a peaceful and harmonious world). Indeed, Barbara Ehrenreich and Deidre English (1979, p. 292) argue that

> *The human values that women were assigned to preserve [must] expand out of the confines of private life and become the organizing principle of society. The market [. . .] must be pushed back to the margins. And the "womanly" values of community and caring must rise to the centre as the only human principle.*

As with other perspectives, there is a variety of different versions of con-temporary feminism. This diversity is often discussed in terms of three basic categories:

1. liberal feminism
2. socialist feminism
3. radical feminism

Liberal Feminism

Liberal feminism extends the struggle of women in the latter part of the nine-teenth century and the first decades of the twentieth century for equal legal and political rights to the advocacy of equal opportunities for women in such areas as education and employment.

For liberal feminists, the key problem is the discrimination against women that limits their opportunities. Ending unjust laws and adopting affirmative action programs would allow women to participate fully in the mainstream of society. Liberal feminism thus focuses on ensuring that women have the freedom and opportunity to engage in politics, business, careers, and employment on the same basis as men. Liberal feminism has been successful to some degree: the laws and policies that discriminated against women have been eliminated in many countries, and many women have taken the opportunity to obtain higher education and pursue pro-fessional careers. However, women comprise only 18.1 percent of senior officers and top earners at Canada's largest companies (McFarland, 2013). Likewise, although politics used to be almost entirely a male domain, women are still substantially under-represented in legislative bodies in many countries.

Feminist Collections
http://womenst.library.wisc.edu/
publications/feminist-coll.html

liberal feminism

A version of feminism that advocates equal opportunities for women in such areas as education and employment as well as equal legal and political rights.

Is there still a "glass ceiling" (invisible barrier) that makes it very difficult for women to obtain top positions in business and government?
Tami Thirlwell

Socialist Feminism

Socialist feminism views women as oppressed by both the male-dominated character of society and the capitalist system. Women's housework and child care are unpaid labour essential for the profitability of capitalism and ensuring there is a supply of labour for the future. Women also provide the capitalist system with a "reserve army" of low-cost labour that can be mobilized when needed to maintain the profitability of capitalist enterprises. Socialist feminists argue that male–female relations reflect the exploitative relationships of capitalists to workers. Just as the capitalist boss dominates and exploits workers, so, too, husbands are dominant in the home and exploit the domestic labour of their wives.

Socialist feminists argue that the liberation of women involves both a struggle against patriarchy and the transformation of capitalism into a more cooperative and egalitarian socialist society. The free, public provision of child care and possibly other domestic services would help to create the conditions for the liberation of women. Overcoming the sexual division of labour, in which women have primary responsibility for most domestic duties, along with transforming the division of labour in the capitalist system, would also enable everyone to live more creative, fulfilling lives.

socialist feminism

A version of feminism that views women as oppressed by both the male-dominated character of society and the capitalist system. The liberation of women is connected to the transformation of capitalism into a more cooperative and egalitarian socialist system.

For some of those influenced by the Marxist version of socialism, the struggle of working-class women and men to overturn capitalism is needed to achieve women's liberation. However, most other socialist feminists do not accept the idea that the struggle of women should be subordinated to the struggle of the working class. In their view, overturning capitalism would not necessarily liberate women and end the sexual division of labour. For example, the Soviet Union initially exhibited a strong commitment to the liberation of women, but never achieved this ideal in practice.

Radical Feminism

radical feminism

A version of feminism that views society as based on the oppression of women and seeks to liberate women through the fundamental transformation of social institutions, values, and personal relationships.

In the perspective of **radical feminism**, patriarchal values are deeply embedded in culture and affect the way that women, as well as men, see themselves (Millett, 1985). Institutions such as the state, the family, and schools perpetuate male dominance and the subjugation of women. Male supremacy is maintained through the dominant values, ideas, and practices of society, which encourage women to be dependent upon and subservient to men. Further, in a male-dominated society, women are dehumanized by treating them as sexual objects, for example, by beauty contests. Male supremacy is also maintained, according to radical feminists, by the use of force in the form of violence against women, including the threat of rape, to keep women under control and subordinate (Brownmiller, 1975). Overall, radical feminists argue that society is still patriarchal and in need of collective action to achieve social, political, and cultural change.

Radical feminism views the oppression of women as the oldest, most pervasive, and most deeply entrenched form of oppression. As Robin Morgan (1997) asserted, "Sexism is the root oppression, the one which, until and unless we uproot it, will continue to put forth the branches of racism, class hatred, ageism, competition, ecological disaster, and economic exploitation" (p. 9). The implication is that the struggle of women against oppression is fundamentally revolutionary because it has the potential to end various forms of domination and subordination.

Feminist Theory Website
www.cddc.vt.edu/feminism/enin. html

liberation

Freeing the human potential that has been stifled by the organization and values of society.

The goal of radical feminism is **liberation**. Liberation, whether used in feminist theory, Marxism, or the theories developed by those challenging imperialist power in the colonized Third World, goes beyond the concept of individual freedom that is at the core of the liberal ideology. Liberation involves freeing the human potential that has been stifled by the organization and values of society. Oppression warps the personality of the oppressed, particularly by forcing them to adopt the values of the oppressor. Indeed, from this point of view, those in the oppressor groups are also deprived of an authentic human existence by being expected to take the dominant role. In other words, it is argued that the way society defines what it is to be female and male is restrictive to both women and men.

Liberation, therefore, is not simply a matter of ending male domination of positions of governing authority or of limiting the power of the state over women. Rather, radical feminism seeks a fundamental transformation of social institutions, values, and personal relationships. In particular, male dominance in the family is often viewed as the root of male social, political, and economic domination. By making the personal political, radical feminists hope to expose and challenge what they view as a major basis of male power (Bryson, 2003). To initiate this process, the women's liberation movement (based in part on radical feminism) has sought to raise women's consciousness (awareness) of their oppression and to encourage women to take pride in their distinct gender identity.

ENVIRONMENTALISM

The world faces numerous serious environmental problems. These include the following:

- Increasing emissions of greenhouse gases, such as carbon dioxide and methane, resulting from fossil fuel production and burning, deforestation, and various industrial and agricultural processes. The resulting global climate changes will likely have profound consequences for all life forms.
- Contamination of air, water, and soil. For example, a substantial proportion of the world's population lacks access to clean water, and water shortages may reduce food production in the future.
- Devastation of tropical rainforests, which contain much of the Earth's biological diversity, and the extinction of an unprecedented number of species of animals and plants. The decline in biodiversity may hamper the search for new medicines and hinder the world's capability to maintain agricultural production.
- Pollution of various forms, which is degrading the environment and harming the health of humans and other species.

In 1962, American biologist Rachel Carson's *Silent Spring* eloquently made the case that synthetic pesticides were silencing the voices of birds that heralded the coming of spring. More generally, Carson pointed out that the fragile ecology of the earth was threatened by the large-scale production and use of dangerous chemicals. A series of environmental disasters, including massive oil spills, further increased concern about environmental problems and led to the development of a large environmental movement. In conjunction with this movement, the perspective of **environmentalism** developed.

Environmentalism is not simply an expression of concern about various environmental problems and support for efforts to clean up the environment and reduce pollution. Rather, environmentalism provides a distinctive

environmentalism

A perspective based on the idea that humanity needs to change its relationship to nature so as to protect the natural environment and ensure that it can sustain all forms of life.

Climate change in the Arctic.
Tami Thirlwell

perspective on the fundamental causes of environmental problems and a vision of an environmentally sustainable world.[1]

Environmentalism is based on the belief that humanity needs to fundamentally change its relationship with nature. Influenced by the science of ecology, which emphasizes the complex interrelatedness of the natural world, environmentalists argue that we need to view ourselves as part of the intricate and fragile web of nature. Understanding our dependence on nature is necessary to living in harmony with it. Instead of viewing humanity as being outside of nature with the right to control and dominate it, we need to think of ourselves as part of nature and limit our impact on the Earth (Schumacher, 1973).

As Petra Kelly, a founder of the German Green Party, stated,

> *We must learn to think and act from our hearts, to recognize the interconnectedness of all living creatures, and to respect the value of each thread in the vast web of life . . . . We have borrowed the Earth from our children. Green politics is about having just "enough" and not "more," and this runs counter to all of the economic assumptions of industrial*

---

[1]Because those who believe that fundamental changes are needed in our relationship with the environment differ considerably from those who think that environmental problems can be handled without major changes, the term *ecologism* is sometimes used to describe the stronger, more distinctive forms of environmentalism (Dobson [2007]).

society . . . . The industrialized countries must move from growth-oriented to sustainable economies, with conservation replacing consumption as the driving force (quoted in Ball & Dagger, 2004, pp. 442, 445).

Many of those who hold an environmentalist perspective argue that one of the basic causes of environmental problems is the idea that we can control nature and use it for our benefit without concern for the consequences. Instead of a focus on human well-being (termed **anthropocentrism**), environmentalism (particularly in its stronger versions) advocates the adoption of a more **ecocentric** philosophy that views nature as having its own intrinsic value; that is, value in and of itself rather than its value for human use (Eckersley, 1992). In addition, those who hold the stronger versions of environmentalism argue that dealing with environmental problems is not simply a matter of developing better technologies, such as pollution-abatement equipment and fuel-efficient automobiles, or applying better techniques for managing natural resources. Instead, fundamental economic, social, and political changes along with changes in the relationship of human beings to the natural world are needed to limit economic growth and achieve a sustainable world (Dobson, 2007).

anthropocentrism

The focus on human well-being that is at the centre of most political thought.

ecocentrism

The view that nature has intrinsic value and should not be valued only in terms of its use for human beings.

Limits to Growth

Environmentalism views our obsession with economic growth as an important cause of environmental problems. Since the Industrial Revolution, there has been a massive increase in the production, transportation, and consumption of material goods. People in the developed countries have come to enjoy high levels of consumption, while the production and consumption of goods is increasing rapidly in newly industrialized countries such as China, India, and Brazil. Governments have made the pursuit of economic growth their primary objective, and the success of different countries is usually measured in terms of their annual increase in gross national product (the monetary value of the goods and services produced).

The environmentalist perspective emphasizes that there are limits to growth. The Earth has a limited carrying capacity; that is, there are inherent limits to the capacity of Earth's ecosystems to support increasing levels of consumption while absorbing waste (Rees & Wackernagel, 1996). As of 2015, it was estimated that humanity uses the equivalent of 1.6 Earths to provide the resources we use and to absorb our wastes[2] (Global Footprint Network, n.d.). Growth in human use of the Earth's resources cannot continue endlessly. At some point, the Earth will reach the limit of its ability to absorb our effluents and provide the accessible resources and energy for our ever-increasing production of material goods.

Ecological Footprint Quiz
www.myfootprint.org

---

[2]It would take approximately 3.7 Earths if all counties in the world had the same ecological footprint as Canada (World Wildlife Fund, 2014).

A Sustainable Society

sustainability

Maintaining the integrity of ecosystems by ensuring that renewable resources are not being used at a rate that exceeds the ability of ecosystems to regenerate them, developing renewable substitutes to replace the consumption of non-renewable resources, and ensuring that the emission of pollutants does not exceed the ability of the ecosystem to handle them without damage.

A basic goal of environmentalism is **sustainability**, particularly in terms of maintaining the integrity of ecosystems. Specifically, renewable resources should not be used at a rate that exceeds the ability of ecosystems to regenerate them. Renewable substitutes should be developed to replace the consumption of non-renewable resources. The emission of pollutants should not exceed the ability of the ecosystem to handle them without damage (Korten, 1996). Instead of continual growth of production and consumption, some of those who hold the environmentalist perspective favour a steady-state (no-growth) economy so as to live within the capacities of the Earth. This would ensure that future generations have the same enjoyment and benefit of the environment that we do. However, with the world's population continuing to grow, a no-growth strategy would likely mean a declining material standard of living.

How can a sustainable society be achieved? Some thinkers have argued that centralized, authoritarian governments are needed to take the strict and unpopular measures needed to protect the environment (Hardin, 1974; Heilbroner, 1974). However, the environmental record of many authoritarian governments provides little support for this position. Instead, some environmentalists look to self-governing and largely self-sufficient local communities in which all citizens would be able to participate directly in the decisions that affect their lives. Local communities with local-focused production are seen as more natural than nation-states and large corporations and more likely to undertake sustainable management of their environment. Critics argue, however, that the vision of a global network of cooperating local communities is unrealistic in a world dominated by large cities, powerful nation-states, and a global population that is projected to increase from 7.4 billion in January 2016 to 10 billion by 2056 (World Population Clock, n.d.).

Charter of the Global Greens
**www.globalgreens.org/
globalcharter-english**

An open pit coal mine in Colombia. Large-scale mining creates difficult challenges in terms of achieving a sustainable society.
Jose Miguel Gomez/Reuters

Sustainable Development

A major problem for environmentalism is that limiting economic growth on a global basis could deprive persons in the poorer countries of the opportunity to try to catch up to the standard of living enjoyed in the richer countries or even to ensure that their basic needs are satisfied. Thus it is often argued that the objective of sustainability needs to be combined with global social justice involving a more equitable distribution of the world's wealth and a concerted effort to reduce global poverty.

Discussions of how to take action to deal with both environmental problems and global poverty have often focused on the concept of **sustainable development**. The World Commission on Environment and Development (1987, p. 8), which popularized this concept, defined sustainable development as ensuring that development meets "the needs of the present without compromising the ability of future generations to meet their own needs." There are two elements to this definition:

- First, development is needed to ensure that the needs of the poor are fulfilled.
- Second, the sustainability of the environment needs to be protected for the well-being of future generations.

Although the Commission's report highlighted a number of serious environmental challenges and noted the necessity of maintaining the carrying capacity of the Earth, it did not accept the limits-to-growth argument. Instead, the Commission noted that economic growth was needed for much of the world to overcome poverty. However, the Commission argued that the quality of growth should be changed so as to put less stress on the environment. Economic growth should be more equitable, extreme rates of population growth limited, and the resource base of economies conserved and enhanced. Hope was placed on reorienting technology to deal with environmental problems, integrating environmental and economic objectives in political decision-making, and increasing public participation in the decisions that affect their communities.

Discussions of the popular idea of sustainable development have often been vague, allowing many businesses, governments, and environmentalists to adopt the general goal of sustainable development while differing on the meaning of that goal and the actions needed to achieve it. Further, as discussed in Box 4-2 Development and Sustainability, it can be difficult to achieve both economic development and environmental sustainability.

Varieties of Environmentalism

REFORM ENVIRONMENTALISM The idea of sustainable development as expressed, for example, by the World Commission on Environment and Development could be considered a version of **reform environmentalism**.

sustainable development

Meeting the needs of the present without compromising the ability of future generations to meet their own needs; it involves development to ensure that the needs of the poor are fulfilled and protecting the environment for the well-being of future generations.

reform environmentalism

A perspective that views the solution to environmental problems primarily in terms of better science, technology, and environmental management.

BOX 4-2   Development and Sustainability

The relationship between economic development and environmental sustainability is complex. The ecological footprint of individuals in the poorest countries is very small compared to that of individuals in the rich developed countries. Nevertheless, poor countries have experienced a reduction of their natural resources through deforestation, desertification, overfishing, and changes in agricultural practices. In poorer countries that are successfully growing their economies (such as China and India), there is a huge negative impact on the environment as polluting industries are set up, often with inadequate government regulation. Many millions of persons in the developing countries are now able to purchase consumer products such as cars and refrigerators and have changed their eating habits to include regular meals of meat and fish rather than depending on grains, which generally have a lower environmental impact.

Economic growth may allow countries to afford to invest in less-polluting technologies (Beckerman, 1992). However, rapid economic growth can cause irreparable harm to the environment (for example, by degrading soils or by polluting the water supply). Indeed, this harm may eventually inhibit a country's economic growth (Arrow et al., 1995; Stern, 2004).

Overall, the sustainability of a world in which people in the poorer and developing countries would enjoy an equivalent level of wealth and consumption to that of people in the richer countries is questionable. Although the rich countries have been responsible for many of current problems of environmental degradation, the newly industrialized countries are quickly adding to global environmental problems. China, for example, has become a world leader in developing renewable energy. However, this hardly offsets the environmental impact of its rapid industrialization that has resulted in China becoming the leading annual emitter of carbon dioxide, in part a result of its continued use of coal. Nevertheless, since carbon dioxide lasts in the atmosphere for centuries, most of the CO_2 currently in the atmosphere was produced in Britain, the United States, and some European countries. Those in developing countries argue that it is these countries that should be primarily responsible for reducing emissions.

Is there a sustainable model for development that will improve the lives of the people in the poorer countries without unduly adding to the environmental burden on their countries and the Earth as a whole? Focusing on policies that improve the quality of life rather than increasing gross national product in both developing and rich countries could be helpful. Nevertheless, as various newly industrialized countries along with some of the less developed countries follow the path of the rich industrialized countries, the question of global sustainability becomes more urgent.

Reform environmentalism is less distinctive than stronger versions of environmentalism and can be found in combination with other ideological perspectives including liberalism, conservatism, and socialism. Unlike stronger versions of environmentalism that advocate fundamental changes, this perspective views the solution to environmental problems primarily in terms of better science, technology, and environmental management. Developing and using better pollution-control technology, encouraging more recycling efforts, promoting measures to assess and mitigate the negative potential effects of new developments, and taking more care to conserve natural resources are seen as resulting in environmental improvement.

Reform environmentalism does not view economic growth and environmental protection as necessarily incompatible. Industry, it is argued, can become more efficient and profitable by incorporating environmental considerations into the production process and adopting more sophisticated, less-polluting technologies (Weale, 1992). Indeed, in a number of countries, considerable progress has been made since the 1970s in adopting a variety of environmental policies, reducing some types of pollution, and using energy more efficiently.

FREE-MARKET ENVIRONMENTALISM In the perspective of **free-market environmentalism**, guarantees of the rights of private property and a free-market economy are crucial to environmental protection (Anderson & Leal, 2015). The argument is that the private owners of farms, forests, or fishing areas are more likely to manage the resources they own in a sustainable fashion than if government owns those resources or imposes strict regulations on their use. However, while this may be valid for some small farmers and private woodlot owners who wish to see the land they own be sustainable for their own children and grandchildren, it is less convincing with regards to large multinational corporations that often seek short-term profitability with no particular commitment to any particular location.

Supporters of free-market environmentalism also point out that competition encourages businesses to produce goods in the most efficient manner. However, the pursuit of profits may encourage companies to ignore the environmental effects of their actions if the costs of environmental damage are borne by the communities in which they operate. Despite attempts to create a green image, corporations are in business to sell their products and, through their advertising, seek to encourage increased consumption while pressuring government to avoid strict environmental regulations.

To make the market effective in reducing the environmental impact of business activity, the full environmental costs of production should be included in the price of goods. Likewise, government subsidies, incentives, and tax breaks for polluting industries need to be ended for the free market to operate in a more environmentally friendly manner.

DEEP ECOLOGY, SOCIAL ECOLOGY, AND ECOFEMINISM
Among the stronger and more distinctive versions of environmentalism are deep ecology, social ecology, and ecofeminism. **Deep ecology** views the anthropocentric beliefs that have been at the centre of Western thinking as the fundamental cause of environmental degradation and advocates the cultivation of an environmental consciousness and a sense of oneness with the world that recognizes the unity of humans, plants, animals, and the Earth (Devall & Sessions, 1998). Deep ecology views all forms of life as being of intrinsic value, with humans having no right to reduce the richness and diversity of life forms except to satisfy vital needs. As well, deep ecology advocates a substantial decrease in the human population, the return to a simpler lifestyle in which human impact on the environment is greatly reduced, and the protection and

free-market environmentalism

The perspective that holds that guarantees of the rights of private property and a free-market economy are crucial to environmental protection.

deep ecology

An environmentalist perspective that views anthropocentrism as the fundamental cause of environmental degradation and advocates the cultivation of an environmental consciousness and a sense of oneness with the world that recognizes the unity of humans, plants, animals, and the Earth.

Foundation for Deep Ecology
www.deepecology.org

social ecology

A perspective that views social, economic, and political relationships of hierarchy and domination as the cause of both human and environmental problems.

Institute for Social Ecology
www.social-ecology.org

ecofeminism

A combination of environmentalism and feminism that views male dominance as the basic cause of the degradation of the Earth.

What is ecofeminism anyway?
http://eve.enviroweb.org/what_is/main.html

fundamentalism

The revival of strict religious beliefs seeking to promote the fundamental principles of the faith, including the belief that sacred scriptures are the word of God, and should be strictly followed in all areas of life.

expansion of areas of wilderness to allow other species to flourish (Naess & Sessions, 1993).

Social ecology views social, economic, and political relationships of hierarchy and domination as the cause of both human and environmental problems. An egalitarian and cooperative society is needed to end domination within human societies and the exploitation of nature. Both social ecology and deep ecology favour small-scale, self-sufficient communities in a world in which political power rests primarily with local communities. Social ecology, however, views humans as active and creative stewards of the natural world (Bookchin, 1980), while deep ecology promotes a view of humans as being just one of numerous life forms and advocates that humans return to a more natural lifestyle.

Ecofeminism, a combination of environmentalism and feminism, views male dominance as the basic cause of the degradation of the Earth. Male domination and exploitation of nature is an extension of male domination of women; the "rape" of nature arises out of male desires for control and mastery in a patriarchal society. Women, it is argued, are more closely related to nature and are more likely to understand the world in terms of a network of interrelationships (that is, an ecological way of thinking). Thus, giving greater importance to women's values, perspectives, and experiences is needed to restore harmony with nature. As well, ecofeminists suggest that greater educational and employment opportunities for women, making contraceptive information and choices readily available, and challenging patriarchal traditions tends to slow population growth, thereby reducing pressure on the environment.

FUNDAMENTALISM

The term **fundamentalism** originated in the United States in the early twentieth century to describe Protestants who wanted "to preserve the 'fundamentals' of the Christian faith" from biblical critics and proponents of the theory of evolution (Almond, Appleby, & Sivan, 2003, pp. 1–2). Fundamentalists of various religions view their sacred scriptures (such as the Bible and the Qur'an) as the literal word of God, reject analyses that find inconsistencies in the scriptures, and are critical of efforts to interpret sacred scriptures in light of modern realities.

Fundamentalism is not simply a return to orthodox or traditional versions of religion. In an effort to create or revive a "purer" form of their religion, fundamentalists typically interpret or emphasize certain aspects of sacred texts in ways that differ from established religious institutions and religious authorities (Almond, Appleby, & Sivan, 2003). Because they believe that they have the only legitimate interpretation of the word of God, they reject some of the traditional interpretations of sacred texts and religious customs. As well, they contend that God-given laws are more important than laws adopted by legislatures (Koopmans, 2015).

Fundamentalists often view religion as way of life for the individual and the community as a whole, not simply a matter of private belief. Thus, fundamentalists are critical of the separation of church and state that has become a basic principle in many Western societies. Fundamentalists are particularly critical of **secular humanism**, the view that ethical principles and moral standards can be developed through human reason. This, they argue, has resulted in a decline in morality. Immoral behaviour should be suppressed and religious belief promoted throughout society.

secular humanism

The view that ethical principles and moral standards can be developed through human reason.

The concern of fundamentalists with morality is evident in their views on sexual behaviour and the family. Fundamentalists view homosexuality, abortion, and sex outside marriage as evils. Likewise, they object to the portrayal of sexuality and nudity in the media and seek to encourage modesty in dress and behaviour. Most fundamentalists uphold a patriarchal vision of the family, viewing the husband as the head of the household and provider for the family and the wife as being responsible for the raising of children and other household duties. Islamic fundamentalists seek to prevent immoral behaviour by such measures as avoiding the mixing of sexes in schools and other public places and forbidding the use of alcohol. In the strongest versions, women are required to cover their faces as well as their bodies and be chaperoned by a male family member when venturing outside of their home.

Fundamentalists generally view the world in terms of the struggle between good and evil. This struggle against evil is both an internal personal struggle against sin and temptation and, for many fundamentalists, an external struggle against the forces of evil in the world. Some fundamentalists seek to build an enclave that strictly follows the laws of their religion and shields the community of believers from the temptations of the outside world (Almond, Appleby, & Sivan, 2003). Others believe that they have a duty to spread God's message throughout the world by converting non-believers as well as persuading those of their own faith to return to the path of righteousness.

Fundamentalism has become an important political as well as religious doctrine. In the United States, fundamentalists associated with the Christian Right (through organizations such as the Christian Coalition of America) have been very active in the Republican Party. Various groups associated with the Christian Right were also successful in preventing the Equal Rights Amendment that would have entrenched male–female equality in the American constitution from gaining the necessary approval. Prominent American fundamentalist preachers Jerry Falwell and Pat Robertson claimed that the terrorist attacks on the United States in 2001 were God's punishment because America had strayed from the path of Christian morality.

Islamism

Islam is a monotheistic religion followed by more than 1.5 billion people that views the prophet Mohammed as completing Allah's (God's) revelations that had been made to earlier Jewish and Christian prophets including Moses and Jesus.

Terms such as **Islamism** and *political Islam* are often used to refer to the perspective or ideology that seeks to implement Islamic beliefs and values in all spheres of life, including politics. In particular, Islamism is based on a strict, literal reading of the Qur'an which it believes contains the exact words of Allah, and the hadith[3] – the words and actions of Mohammad (the messenger of Allah). Islamists believe that all aspects of life, both public and private, should be governed by the sharia (Islamic law based on the Qur'an). Generally, Islamism seeks to politically unify the Islamic community (ummah). However Sunni Muslim leaders often assert that Shiite, Sufi, and other Muslims are not true followers of Islam and there is a lengthy history of conflict between Sunni and Shiite Muslims.

A particularly strong version of Sunni Islamism, Salafism, seeks to go back to the seventh-century origins of Islam, purify Islam from later practices, and follow the path set out by Mohammed and his early followers. While many Salafists are focused on the revival of their version of Islam, others sometimes termed "Salafist jihadists" take a more extreme approach including the use of violence to achieve their objective by defeating (and even killing) those they consider non-believers and creating an ummah based on their interpretation of the Qur'an.

Islamism

The revival of Islam based on a strict, literal interpretation of the Qur'an and a belief that public and private life should be governed by the sharia (Islamic law).

Radical Islamism

Militant versions of Islamic fundamentalism (including that of Salafist jihadists), termed **radical Islamism**, advocate strong action to purge "degenerate" foreign elements from Muslim society and establish a "pure" Islamic state based on the sharia. The revolution in Iran in 1979 against the Western-oriented Shah (monarch) resulted in the establishment of a Shiite Islamic Republic in which clerics play a leading role. In Afghanistan, the Taliban applied an extremely harsh version of Islamic fundamentalism from 1996 to 2001. Various radical Islamic movements and political parties continue to challenge and seek to overthrow governments throughout the Middle East, parts of Africa, and central Asia that are viewed as not strictly conforming to their interpretation of Islamic law.

The development of various forms of radical Islamism is sometimes explained in terms of the sense of humiliation experienced as parts of the once powerful and culturally advanced Islamic world came under the control of Western powers in the late nineteenth century and the first half of the twentieth century. Direct foreign control of a number of Muslim countries ended

radical Islamism

The perspective often associated with those seeking to purge "degenerate" foreign elements from Muslim society and establish a "pure" Islamic state based strictly on the sharia (Islamic law).

---

[3]There are different versions of the hadith used by Sunni, Shiite and other branches of Islam.

in the period after the Second World War, although some Western powers continued at times to involve themselves in the affairs of Muslim countries (for example, British and American involvement in the overthrow of an elected government in Iran in 1953).

The adoption, to some extent, of Western ideas by the autocratic rulers of many Muslim countries that sought to modernize and develop their countries was often unsuccessful and unpopular. This encouraged some to look to the creation of a religiously based political community (uniting all Muslims rather than dividing into nation-states) as an alternative to governments that were often corrupt. A return to the "straight path" of Islam in accordance with their interpretation of the Qur'an was seen not only as a solution to the problems faced by many Muslim countries, but also as a way of creating a positive sense of identity. By rejecting Western practices and lifestyles, a purer Islamic identity could be reasserted (Milton-Edwards, 2005).

QUTB AND BIN LADEN   During his stay in the United States in the late 1940s, Sayyid Qutb, a key figure in the development of the ideology of radical Islamism, was shocked by the American way of life, which he viewed as sinful, degenerate, sexually promiscuous, and materialistic (Lewis, 2004). This contributed to his hatred of Western societies. Qutb argued that Muslims needed to fight to revive Islam, which had been abandoned by the Westernizing rulers and elites of the Muslim world. Through a militant jihad, Muslims could ensure that the message of Allah would be heard throughout the world (Cook, 2005). This included using physical force to overthrow Muslim rulers who had departed from the ways of Islam. Qutb, an active member of the Muslim Brotherhood, was executed for alleged involvement in an attempted assassination of Egyptian President Nasser in 1966.

In some versions of radical Islamism, such as that espoused by al-Qaeda leader Osama bin Laden, Western "Crusaders" and Jews are viewed as conspiring to destroy Islam. Violence and self-sacrifice ("martyrdom") are required to defeat the enemy (including "infidel" Muslims). For bin Laden and some other radical Islamists, the global Islamic community they seek to create is based on the austere community led by Mohammed in Medina (Saudi Arabia) in the seventh century CE. Nevertheless, they have become adept at using modern technology such as social media and online videos to spread their message and mobilize their followers.

Those committed to a violent global jihad constitute a small minority of Islamic fundamentalists. Indeed, questions have been raised as to whether the radical philosophy espoused by Qutb and bin Laden reflects the fundamentals of Islam. Nevertheless, small numbers of committed believers can have major political effects, particularly when large numbers of persons might be influenced in certain circumstances (see Box 4-3 Radical Islamism: The Taliban and the Islamic State).

BOX 4-3 Radical Islamism: The Taliban and the Islamic State

In 1979, the Soviet Union invaded Afghanistan to support a Soviet-backed regime. Subsequently, Islamic Afghan fighters with covert support from the United States, Pakistan, Saudi Arabia, and other countries fought the Soviet army. After the Soviet troops withdrew in 1989, civil war broke out among the Afghan factions. The Taliban, with support from Pakistan and students indoctrinated in schools funded by Saudi Arabia, took control of Afghanistan in 1996. They imposed a severe regime based, in part, on their interpretation of the Qur'an. Public executions were held in stadiums, women were banned from most employment and had to wear a full covering burka in public, education for most girls was suspended, and men were required to grow beards. Almost all forms of entertainment were banned. In 2001 al-Qaeda, led by bin Laden, launched a terrorist attack on the UnitedStates from its base in Afghanistan, The United States and its allies (along with the Afghan Northern Alliance) quickly defeated the Taliban government. However the Taliban recovered and fought against a large international force and the Afghan army. In 2015, the Afghan army took over most of the continuing fight against the Taliban.

In 2003 the United States and some of its allies invaded Iraq in 2003 and overthrew the dictatorial regime of Saddam Hussein, leader of the secular Ba'ath party. After the withdrawal of foreign forces, the Iraq government came to be dominated by Shiite Muslims. This facilitated the development of ISIS (originally an offshoot of al-Qaeda) among Sunni Muslims. As Iraqi soldiers fled from the much smaller number of ISIS soldiers, ISIS captured large quantities of American-supplied armaments. As well, ISIS seized large amounts of money from banks and took over oil wells to finance their activities.

In Syria the dictatorial government of Bashar-al Assad (based on the Alawite minority, a Shiite sect) tried to crush opposition (inspired by the "Arab Spring")

in 2011. This resulted in a devastating conflict between the Syrian military and a variety of rebel forces (who often fought with each other). This led to nearly six million refugees leaving Syria by 2016, over seven million persons displaced within Syria, and at least 400 000 deaths. It also became an international conflict as Iran, the Hezbollah, and Russia assisted the Syrian regime while the United States and some of its allies provided support to certain anti-Assad rebel groups (although Turkey attacked some Kurdish forces that fought both Syrian and ISIS forces).

ISIS (also known as ISIL and Daesh) conquered substantial portions of Syria and Iraq in 2014 and declared the establishment of a worldwide Islamic caliphate, the Islamic State. Abu Bakr al-Bagdadi, the self-appointed calif (leader), claimed to be a successor to the Prophet Mohammed and, as such, declared that all Muslims must pledge allegiance to him. Almost all Islamic scholars criticized this declaration, and no Islamic country recognized the Islamic State. Nevertheless, through the use of social media (including gruesome videos of masked Islamic State soldiers beheading "infidels"), the Islamic State enticed tens of thousands of men and women from both Muslim and Western countries to come to the Islamic State to join the jihadi struggle.

The Islamic State created an extremely brutal and repressive regime. As they conquered various territories, they imposed their very strict version of Islam. Males belonging to minority groups were executed and girls were forced into sexual slavery. Groups claiming to be supporters of ISIS developed in a number of other countries. On November 13, 2015, ISIS claimed responsibility for the terrorist attack in Paris in which 130 were killed and several hundred injured, while in 2016 attacks in Brussels killed 32 and in Nice killed 84. Most of the terrorists were citizens of France or Belgium. In 2016, ISIS lost much of the territory and cities they had captured in Syria and Iraq. Nevertheless, radical Islamism will likely continue to be a threat to peace and tolerance around the world.

✔• SUMMARY AND CONCLUSION

The goal of feminism is to achieve a society in which women enjoy independence and equality, with full control over their own lives and bodies. In addition to working toward removing obstacles to the full and equal participation of women in social, economic, and political life, many feminists have sought to affirm the distinct identity of women. Achieving equality and giving greater significance to female values are seen as being not only desirable for women, but also for the common good of humanity.

The ideology of environmentalism raises important questions about the relationship between human beings and the environment. Environmentalism views human dominance and exploitation of nature as leading to disastrous consequences for the world. Humans need to recognize that they are a part of nature and should learn to live in harmony with it. This involves treading lightly on the Earth and ending the exponential growth in production, consumption, population, and waste. From an environmentalist point of view, the common good should refer not only to the good of human beings, but also to the good of the world as a whole, of which we are an integral part. An important challenge facing environmentalism is the question of how to achieve sustainability while improving the circumstances of people in less developed countries.

Religious beliefs have always been an important force in political life affecting a variety of political ideas and ideologies. Religious fundamentalists promote a traditional interpretation of their faith's scriptures, and some seek to impose a strict moral code on society. Religious fundamentalism challenges the liberal, secular views of modern Western political thinking. Many fundamentalists seek to undo the separation between religion and the state as religion is seen as necessary for a good society. The laws laid out in sacred scriptures are of enduring importance and should be the basis for any human created laws. For some religious fundamentalists, a total belief in the righteousness of their cause serves to justify extreme actions to achieve their objectives. In particular, groups associated with radical jihadist versions of Islamism have had profound effects on contemporary politics.

The perspectives examined in this chapter provide different ways of understanding the world and advocate fundamental changes in society, politics, and our lives. The intensity of the political controversies generated by the stronger versions of these perspectives suggests that the clash of different political ideologies and perspectives continues to be an important feature of political life.

✔• KEY TERMS

Anthropocentrism   85
Deep ecology   89
Ecocentrism   85
Ecofeminism   90
Environmentalism   83
Feminism   77
Free-market environmentalism   89

Fundamentalism   90
Islamism   92
Liberal feminism   80
Liberation   82
Patriarchy   77
Radical feminism   82
Radical Islamism   92

Reform environmentalism   87
Secular humanism   91
Social ecology   90
Socialist feminism   81
Sustainability   86
Sustainable development   87

◆ DISCUSSION QUESTIONS

1. Why do some feminists view women as oppressed? Is this a valid depiction of the position of women in Canada?

2. Are fundamental changes needed to improve the position of women?

3. Would a government that had a female majority and female leadership act differently than governments dominated by men?

4. How can an environmentally sustainable society best be achieved?

5. Do the stronger versions of environmentalism provide a desirable and practical vision for the world? Does reform or free-market environmentalism provide a suitable response to environmental problems?

6. Why have significant numbers of young people been attracted to radical Islamism?

FURTHER READING

Bromley, V.L. (2012). *Feminisms matter: Debates, theories, activism*. Toronto: University of Toronto Press.

Carter, N. (2007). *The politics of the environment: Ideas, activism, policy* (2nd ed.). Cambridge, UK: Cambridge University Press.

Dobson, A. (2007). *Green political thought* (4th ed.). New York: Routledge.

Donovan, J. (2012). *Feminist theory: The intellectual traditions* (4th ed.). New York: Continuum.

Dryzek, J.S. (2012). *The politics of the earth*. Oxford: Oxford University Press.

Dryzek, J.S., & Schlosberg, D. (Eds.) (2005). *Debating the earth. The environmental politics reader* (2nd ed.). Oxford: Oxford University Press.

Dyer, G. (2015). *Don't panic: ISIS, terror and today's Middle East*. Toronto: Random House Canada.

Hannam, J. (2007). *Feminism*. Harlow, UK: Pearson Longman.

Osman, T. (2016). *Islamism. What it means for the Middle East and the world*. New Haven, CT: Yale University Press.

Rashid, A. (2010). *Taliban: Militant Islam, Oil and Fundamentalism in Central Asia* (2nd ed.). New Haven, CT: Yale University Press.

Tong, R. (2013). *Feminist thought: A comprehensive introduction* (4th ed.). Boulder, CO: Westview Press.

5 Political Culture, Political Participation, and Political Socialization

Some people saw the destruction of New York's World Trade Center by al-Qaeda terrorists in 2001 as evidence that there was a "clash of civilizations" between Islam and the West.   Chris Collins Studio, Inc./Corbis Historical/Getty images

After reading this chapter, you should be able to:

1. explain the meaning and significance of political culture
2. discuss the differences between the Canadian and American political cultures
3. outline the level of political interest, knowledge, and participation
4. examine the decline of confidence and trust in politicians and governments
5. define political socialization and discuss the agents of political socialization
6. explain the postmaterialist theory of change in political culture

The image of the twin towers of New York's World Trade Center collapsing after they were struck by jets hijacked by al-Qaeda terrorists is one that few people will forget.

The horrific events of September 11, 2001, seemed to confirm the argument of Harvard University political scientist Samuel P. Huntington (1993, 1996) that a "clash of civilizations," such as the clash between Islam and the West, will become the leading source of international conflict. Cultural conflicts, he suggests, have replaced the ideological conflict between communism and capitalism as the major potential source of world war. Huntington (1993) views the world as increasingly divided into seven or eight major civilizations—broad cultural groupings based on differences in history, language, traditions, and particularly religion (Western, Confucian, Japanese, Islamic, Hindu, Slavic-Orthodox, Latin American, and possibly African). In contrast to those who view globalization and modernization as resulting in increased homogenization or Westernization of the cultures of the world, Huntington argues that non-Western peoples are rejecting Western values and building on their own indigenous cultures. "The Western ideas of individualism, liberalism, constitutionalism, human rights, equality, liberty, the rule of law, free markets, the separation of church and state," he writes, "have little resonance in other cultures" (Huntington, 1993, p. 40).

Huntington's analysis has been criticized on a number of grounds. Norris and Inglehart (2002) provide evidence that the people of Western and Islamic countries do not generally differ greatly on democratic political values, although people in the West have become more favourable to gender equality and sexual liberation than people in the Islamic world. The adoption of tolerant liberal values by Western societies on such issues is a relatively recent phenomenon; thus differences between Western and Islamic countries might diminish over time as countries modernize. Huntington has also been criticized for exaggerating the similarities among the cultures within each broad civilization. For example, although there are broad similarities among the cultures of the Western world, there are also important differences in political culture both between and within particular countries.

The "Arab Spring" uprisings that began in 2010 demonstrated that large numbers of people were willing to take concerted action to challenge dictatorial regimes (some of which had been supported by the United States) and press for democracy. In the end, however, most of the uprisings were suppressed. Nevertheless, the extreme al-Qaeda and ISIS zealots who seek to impose a very strict interpretation of Islamic law and who use terrorism are supported by only a small proportion of people in the Islamic world.

Overall, Huntington's prediction that conflict between different civilizations will become more frequent and deadly is questionable. Civil wars within countries are much more common. Although tensions exist between Western countries and China, war between these two leading civilizations seems unlikely, particularly given their level of economic interdependence (Ferguson, 2011). Terrorism by Islamic extremists has continued to be a serious problem, and the Islamic State (ISIS) views itself as leading a clash of civilizations. However, the level of conflict within some Islamic countries is higher than between Islamic countries and the West.

INTRODUCTION

The fundamental political values, beliefs, and orientations that are widely held within a political community are often referred to as its **political culture**. In this chapter, we focus particularly on the political cultures of Western democracies including examining the extent to which Canada and the United States have different political cultures. We also examine political participation, because a vibrant democratic political culture is often thought to be one in which citizens are actively involved in political life. Finally, we consider whether important changes are occurring in the political values of contemporary societies.

political culture

The fundamental political values, beliefs, and orientations that are widely held within a political community.

EXAMINING AND EXPLAINING POLITICAL CULTURE

One way that political scientists examine political culture is through sample surveys that indicate what proportion of the public has various politically relevant attitudes. Others examine the literature, popular culture, symbols, myths, political institutions, constitution, and policies of a country to gain an understanding of its collective political culture (Bell, 2004). As well, political culture can be analyzed by looking at the nature of political discourse—that is, the language, meanings, and interpretations that are used in political life to discuss and make use of key terms such as democracy, freedom, and equality (Benedicto, 2004).

It is often assumed that each country has a particular political culture based on such factors as the characteristics of the population, its history, and its political experiences. However, in many countries there are different sub-cultures based on particular class, ethnic, linguistic, religious, regional, gender, or generational groupings. In Canada, for example, not only are there differ-ences between the political culture of the French-speaking people of Quebec and that of the rest of the country, but also the political cultures of Indigenous peoples are substantially different from that of the rest of the Canadian popu-lation. In the United States, there are important regional differences in political culture, with the southern states, in particular, having a somewhat different political culture than the rest of the country (Grabb & Curtis, 2005). Further, in every country, a distinction can be made between elite political culture—that is, the values and beliefs of those most influential in political life—and mass political culture.

Huntington's analysis suggests that there are general similarities among groupings of nations ("civilizations") with similar backgrounds, traditions, and religious beliefs. Others explain the general differences in political culture among different countries more in terms of different levels of socio-economic development, with more prosperous regions of the world developing the cultural values that emphasize such values as individual autonomy, self-expression, political freedom, and gender equality (Inglehart & Welzel, 2005).

Shanghai is a major business centre and a showcase for the Chinese economy that has rapidly grown in recent decades.

kalafoto/Fotolia

Thus, it is argued, economic development (along with globalization) will reduce the differences in political culture among different countries, peoples, and regions.

Will the political cultures of the industrializing countries of East Asia and elsewhere become more similar to that of the Western democracies? Certainly, the West has provided an influential model for many developing countries. However, some assert that the 5000-year-old Chinese civilization has continued to influence the basic values of the Chinese people (for example, more collectivist and accepting of hierarchy and authority) despite the political upheavals China has faced. Indeed, some argue that a prosperous and powerful China could provide an influential alternative model in developing countries to that of the liberal democratic culture of the Western world (Jacques, 2012). Others suggest that modernization and economic development is gradually shifting the political culture of East Asian countries towards a more individualistic and liberal democratic political culture (Welzel, 2011).

Ideological Perspectives

One way to describe the political culture of a political community is in terms of its dominant ideological perspective and fundamental politically relevant values. For example, the political culture of the United States is often described as basically classical liberal (that is, combining protection for the rights and freedoms of individuals with support for a free-market capitalist economy and limited government). The political culture of Sweden differs somewhat from that of the United States in its support of a high level of socio-economic equality and a wide range of government social programs benefitting all citizens combined with a globally competitive economy featuring cooperative relationships between large corporations and labour unions (Steinmo, 2010).

Louis Hartz (1964) argued that, as the societies of Western Europe developed from feudalism to capitalism, traditional conservative perspectives clashed with the liberal perspectives that arose among those seeking a freer society and a free-market economy. This clash between conservative and liberal views led to a synthesis in the form of socialism. The outcome, Hartz concluded, is that Western European political cultures are diverse, with conservative, liberal, and socialist perspectives all important elements of their political cultures. In countries colonized by European settlers, however, only the leading part of the mother country's political culture was carried to the new lands. In Hartz's view, the United States and English Canada are basically liberal "fragments" where such values as individual freedom are predominant.

Others suggest that the United Empire Loyalists (Americans who left the United States after its War of Independence because of their loyalty to the British Crown) brought to Canada some traditional conservative values (sometimes referred to as a "Tory touch") along with the liberal values characteristic of the American political culture. This in turn made possible the later development and acceptance of an element of socialist values, which in Hartz's theory require the presence of both liberal and conservative orientations (Horowitz, 1966). Thus, even though the individualistic values of liberalism are important in both Canada and the United States, liberalism is not the only significant ideological perspective in Canada.

Seymour Martin Lipset (1990) also viewed Canada and the United States as having somewhat different political cultures, which he explained in terms of their different historical experiences. The United States was founded through revolution, while Canada's historical experience was counter-revolutionary, as Canadians did not join Americans in overthrowing British rule. This resulted in a more conservative political culture in Canada with a greater concern about maintaining law and order.

Canadians, Lipset argued, are more deferential toward those in positions of authority and more willing to support collective action for the common good. Americans are more individualistic and distrustful of government (see Box 5-1 American Gun Culture and the Sandy Hook Massacre). The Canadian political culture also is characterized by a greater acceptance and tolerance of differences and diversity in society than the American political culture. For example, in 2015 65% of Canadians supported the Liberal government's promise to bring 25 000 Syrian refugees to Canada while only 28% of Americans supported President Obama's plan to accept 10 000 Syrian refugees (Adams, 2015).

Although Lipset viewed the Canadian political culture as generally more conservative than the American one, he noted that Canadians had become more liberal than Americans in their views on social and moral issues such as abortion and homosexual rights. Lipset attributed this to the growing strength of conservative fundamentalist religious groups in the United States as compared to the more liberal direction taken by the major Canadian religions. Further, although he viewed the American political culture as including a strong belief in equality of opportunity so that individuals could advance based on their own merit, he noted that Canadians had become more willing than Americans to support government action to pursue egalitarian policies that redistribute wealth and income to the poor and disadvantaged (Lipset, 1990). Nevertheless, democratic socialist Bernie Sanders gained considerable support in the 2016 Democratic party presidential nomination campaign for his strong advocacy of measures to reduce inequality (including free tuition for students at public universities and colleges).

Although some aspects of Lipset's depiction of the differences between the two political cultures are valid, it is questionable whether the Canadian political culture is still more conservative than the American one. Canadians have

BOX 5-1   American Gun Culture and the Sandy Hook Massacre

On December 14, 2012, twenty-year-old Adam Lanza took a Bushmaster Assault Rifle (with several magazines that each held 30 rounds) and two high-quality handguns from the arsenal in his mother's unlocked closet. He killed his mother and then entered the Sandy Hook Elementary School in Newtown, Connecticut. His shooting spree killed 20 six- and seven-year-old pupils and 6 staff members.

It is sometimes asserted that the United States has a gun culture that reflects its political culture of individualism and distrust of government. Indeed, the United States has by far the highest proportion (88.8 per 100 persons) of privately owned civilian firearms in the world (Small Arms Survey, 2007). Between 1986 and 2010 nearly 150 million small arms were produced or imported for the US market (Brauer, 2013). The widely supported right to keep and bear arms is entrenched in the American constitution.[*] Some U.S. states allow people to carry concealed weapons. Many weapons are purchased over the Internet or at gun shows without the checks for mental illness or prior convictions that are normally required before a purchase. Politicians who advocate some restrictions on the most deadly weapons have faced severe criticism organized by one of the largest and most powerful interest groups in the United States, the National Rifle Association.

The United States is not the only country that has experienced serious massacres. In 2011, Andreas Beivik, a right-wing extremist, bombed a government building in Norway, after which he carried out a mass shooting at a Labour Party youth camp that killed 77 persons, mainly teenagers. In 1989 Marc Lépine entered the École Polytechnique de Montréal and shot and killed fourteen women, and wounded ten women and four men before committing suicide. Nevertheless, there have been a particularly large number of massacres in the United States (including the killing of 49 people and wounding 53 by Omar Mateen at a gay nightclub in Orlando, Florida in 2016) as well as a very high incidence of the use of guns in murders. Most other countries have adopted strict controls on assault weapons and handguns.

In Canada, those seeking to purchase a firearm legally must obtain a firearms acquisition certificate, undergo a criminal record check, and take a safety program. There are restrictions concerning handguns and fully automatic weapons. Intense controversy surrounded the adoption of the Firearms Act, 1995 that required all firearms to be registered by 2003. Opponents raised concerns about privacy and complained about the high cost of the registry. In 2011, the Conservative government obtained parliamentary approval to abolish the Firearms Registry and destroy its records. Although Canadians were divided on the issue of ending the long-gun registry, the right to own and carry all kinds of firearms with few restrictions could be viewed as reflecting basic differences in the political cultures of the two countries.

---

[*]The right to keep and bear arms is part of the Second Amendment to the Constitution that enables states to establish a militia. Having state militias (rather than a national professional standing army) was viewed as protecting liberty against a tyrannical government. However, the US Supreme Court interpreted the provision as an individual right and struck down attempts to place restrictions on gun ownership.

Is the right to bear arms
an important and distinctive
feature of the American
political culture?

Tami Thirlwell

become less deferential to authority than Americans (Nevitte, 1996). As well, the level of trust and confidence in government tends to be low in both Canada and the United States.

Democratic Political Culture

Democracy involves various processes and institutions such as elections, political parties, and governments that are accountable for their actions. However, since democracy is ultimately based on the citizenry, it is often suggested that a democratic political culture is needed if democracy is to be sustained and meaningful.

In a classic study based on sample surveys of the population in five countries, Gabriel Almond and Sidney Verba (1963) classified political culture in terms of three basic types. In *parochial cultures*, characteristic of underdeveloped countries, most people are largely unaware of the political system, do not have much in the way of expectations about what government should do, and do not participate in politics. In *subject political cultures*, characteristic of countries that are non-democratic or only recently have emerged from an authoritarian system, citizens exhibit an awareness of the political system and the policies that government adopts, but they are not oriented to trying to affect those policies. In *participant political cultures*, citizens are both aware of the political system and have an activist orientation in seeking to affect what government does.

Although one might think that a participant political culture would be the most suitable basis for a democracy, Almond and Verba argued that a participant political culture could lead to instability if citizens put forward too many demands that governments would be unable to fulfill. In their view, the political culture that works best in a democracy (which they termed a **civic culture**) features a mixture of subject and participant political roles. Citizens in a civic culture respect legitimate government authority and have a positive view of the political system. Most citizens involve themselves in politics through voting, while a highly educated minority of citizens participate more actively in politics and policy making (Dalton & Welzel, 2014). The assumption is that this provides a balance in democracy between the power of government to govern and the responsiveness of government to the people. Almond and Verba's view of democracy has been echoed by those who argue that excessive demands have "overloaded" government (Crozier, Huntington, & Watanuki, 1975). By responding to the demands of the people, governments, it is argued, have been pressured to take actions that do not take into account the long-term well-being of the country.

A different viewpoint is expressed by those who view active citizen participation as an essential feature of democracy:

> An active citizenry is required because it is through discussion, popular interest and involvement in politics that societal goals should be defined and carried out. Without public involvement in the process, democracy loses both its legitimacy and its guiding force (Dalton, 2006, p. 35).

While the civic culture model provided a good description of the political culture in Great Britain, the United States, and Canada in 1963, citizens in many countries have become more assertive, more critical of government, and more likely to participate in more active forms of political participation. Public satisfaction with governments has generally declined, and challenges to government policies and the power of elite groups has grown.

A more politically active and assertive citizenry is evident not only in well-established democracies, but also many people in undemocratic countries have challenged the ruling elites. In some cases, established governments have been overthrown through widespread popular protest (for example, Czechoslovakia, 1989; the Philippines, 1986; and Tunisia, 2011) and in other places repressed by force (eg. China, 1989).

SUPPORT FOR DEMOCRACY The World Values Survey conducted in 51 countries between 2010 and 2014 found that most people agreed that having a democratic system of governing was very good or fairly good. This included those surveyed in non-democratic countries such as China. However in a number of countries (including Russia, India, Brazil, and Mexico) a

civic culture

A mixture of subject and participant political roles among the general population.

majority of people thought it was very or fairly good to "have a strong leader who does not have to bother with parliament and elections." As well, in a number of countries (including the United States, Germany, and Australia) one-half or more of those surveyed agreed that "having experts, not government, make decisions according what they think is best for this country" was very good or fairly good.[1]

Like other advanced democracies, Canada's political culture is based to a considerable extent on liberal democratic values. Most Canadians share a belief in the desirability of political freedom, individual rights, political equality, and government based on the rule of law. A consensus about general political values is, however, not always matched by a high level of support for the application of these values in practice. For example, although most Canadians support the principle of protecting civil liberties, the majority of people favour suspending civil liberties if there is a national emergency (Sniderman, Fletcher, Russell, & Tetlock, 1996). Likewise, despite a political culture based on individual rights and freedoms, few Americans opposed the stricter measures limiting rights and freedoms that were adopted after the 2001 terrorist attacks on the United States.

World Values Survey
www.worldvaluessurvey.org

ATTITUDES CONCERNING GOVERNMENT AND POLITICIANS

Public confidence and trust in government, elected representatives, political leaders, and political parties has declined in almost all of the advanced democratic countries in recent decades (Dalton, 2006). As Figure 5-1 indicates, only a small proportion of people in the advanced democracies said that they had "a great deal of confidence" in government. Only 3.7 percent of Canadians said they had a "great deal" of confidence in the government and 34.5 percent said they had "quite a lot" of confidence in the government with similar proportions having confidence in Parliament. Confidence in political parties was even lower with 2.1 % of Canadians having a great deal of confidence and 21.3% "quite a lot of confidence" (World Values Survey, 2005–2008). A more recent survey found that a higher proportion of Canadians had a lot of trust in the Supreme Court, the justice system, and municipal government than had little or no trust in those institutions. Conversely, more people had little or no trust in Parliament, the prime minister, the mass media, and political parties than had a lot of trust (Americas Barometer, 2014).[2]

Political efficacy, the attitude that individuals think that they can have an impact on political decisions and that government is responsive to what

Canadian Opinion Research Archive
www.queensu.ca/cora

political efficacy

The attitude that individuals think that they can have an impact on political decisions and that government is responsive to what people want.

---

[1]Canada did not participate in this survey. In the fifth wave of the survey, 2005–2008, 22.3% of Canadians thought it was very good or fairly good to "have a strong leader who doesn't bother with parliament and elections" and 41.5% thought it was very good or fairly good to "have experts, not government, make decisions according to what they think is best for Canada."

[2]A majority of those surveyed took an intermediate position between a lot of trust and little or no trust (3 to 5 on a seven-point scale) for each of these institutions.

FIGURE 5-1

Confidence in the Government, Selected Countries

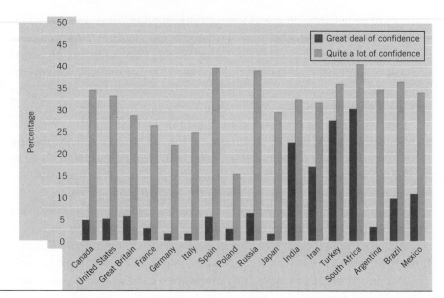

Notes: Studies conducted between 2005 and 2008. Those not answering the question or answering "don't know" were excluded from the calculation.

Source: Compiled from World Values Survey, Fifth Wave, 2005–2008. Variable V138. www.worldvaluessurvey.org

people want, is also quite low in the advanced democracies. For example, the 2011 Canadian Election Study found that 70 percent of Canadians agreed or somewhat agreed with the statement that "once elected to Parliament, MPs soon lose touch," and 66 percent agreed or strongly agreed that "government doesn't care much about what people like me think" (Canadian Opinion Research Archive, n.d.). Another study found that 52 percent agreed that "people like me don't have any say in what government does" (Clarke, Kornberg, & Scotto, 2009b). Somewhat similarly, the 2012 American National Election Study found that 61 percent of Americans in 2008 agreed and 18 percent disagreed that "public officials don't care what people think"; 48 percent agreed and 15 percent disagreed that people don't have a say in what government does; and only 19% agreed that government is run for the benefit of all" (The ANES Guide to Public Opinion and Electoral Behavior, n.d.).

What explains the general distrust of government and politicians? In some cases, political scandals and broken promises have created distrust. However, the fact that increasing distrust is a feature of most advanced democracies suggests that other factors are involved. Citizens have become better informed about the failures of government through the mass and online media. A more educated public has higher expectations of government, which leads to disappointment when those expectations are not fulfilled. Dissatisfaction may also be a result of the declining capacity of governments to satisfy the needs and desires of the citizenry because of the impact of globalization (Pharr, Putnam, & Dalton, 2000). In addition, the decline in trust and confidence in politicians and political institutions may be part of a general decline in deference toward authority in various forms.

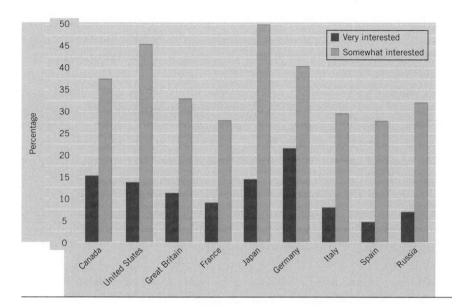

FIGURE 5-2

Interest in Politics, Selected Countries

Notes: Studies conducted between 2005 and 2008. Those not answering the question or answering "don't know" were excluded from the calculation.

Source: Compiled from World Values Survey, Fifth Wave, 2005–2008. Variable V39. Retrieved from www.worldvaluessurvey.org

Overall, although citizens have become more critical of government, political parties, and politicians, this does not indicate dissatisfaction with democracy. Instead it helps to explain the increase in protest activity and an increased desire for a greater voice for citizens in decision making.

POLITICAL INTEREST AND KNOWLEDGE   As Figure 5-2 indicates, only a fairly small minority of the population is very interested in politics. Similarly, the World Values Survey (2010–2014), conducted in 51 countries, found that 12.3% of those surveyed said they were "very interested in politics," 34.3% "somewhat interested," 30.5% "not very interested," and 22.9% "not at all interested." The Americas Barometer survey (2014) found that 16% of Canadians said that they had a lot of interest in politics, 39% had some interest, 31% little interest, and 13% no interest. Nevertheless, most citizens pay some attention to politics, particularly during election campaigns. For example, 38.1 percent of Canadians said they paid "a lot" of attention to the 2011 federal election campaign and 46.5 percent paid "some attention." Similarly, 38.8 percent said they watched the English-language debate on TV while 20.0 percent said they watched the French-language debate in 2011 (Fournier, Cutler, Soroka, & Stolle, 2011).

As an example of how knowledgeable people are about politics, consider that 84 percent of Canadians polled in 2004 could name Canada's prime minister, and 97 percent of Canadians knew who was president of the United States. However, only 33 percent knew who the leader of the official opposition was and only 10 percent could name the minister of finance (Canadian Broadcasting Corporation, 2004). Sixty percent of Canadians would fail the test of basic knowledge about Canada that immigrants need to pass to become citizens, although 70 percent of a sample of first-generation Canadians passed (IPSOS Reid/Dominion Institute, 2007). The majority of Canadian voters do not know which party has taken a particular stand on most of the important issues during election campaigns (Fournier, 2002). Likewise, only one-third of Americans knew who was their representative in the House of Representatives, and slightly more than one-half knew which of the two major parties was more conservative (Milner, 2002).

Although the general level of political knowledge (and sophistication in understanding politics) may be low, most people are knowledgeable (and have a reasonably sophisticated understanding) about those political issues that they consider important to themselves personally (Elkins, 1993). Many citizens are not knowledgeable about the major political issues as defined by politicians, journalists, or academics, but rather focus on understanding the particular issues that interest or concern them.

POLITICAL PARTICIPATION

Even though there has been increasing dissatisfaction with politicians and political parties, the majority of people in most countries participate in political life at least to the extent of voting in elections.

Voting

Election turnouts have generally declined to varying extents in many democratic countries. In parliamentary elections in Europe, for example, voter turnout declined from an average of 82.2 percent in the 1970s and 82.0 percent in the 1980s to 70.9 percent in the first eight years of the twenty-first century (Siaroff, 2009a). Turnout in Canada ranged between 70 and 80 percent in the 1960s, 1970s, and 1980s, but was substantially lower in subsequent elections. In the 2008 Canadian election, turnout was only 58.8 percent of registered voters, the lowest in the country's history, rising only slightly to 61.1 percent in the 2011 election. However turnout in the 2015 election increased to 68.5%. probably because a substantial proportion of the electorate was determined to oust Stephen Harper's Conservative government (see Figure 5-3). The increase in turnout was particularly strong among younger people whose turnout had been quite low in previous elections.

As Table 5-1 indicates, there is considerable variation among democratic countries in turnout for elections. The variation in turnout rates not only suggests that some countries have a more participatory democratic political culture, but also reflects differences in the rules governing elections and the nature of political party competition in particular countries.

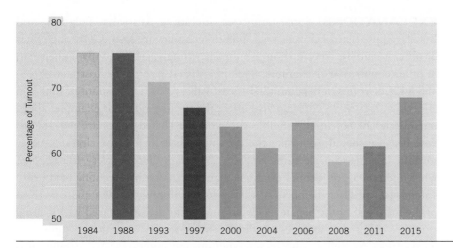

FIGURE 5-3
Turnout in Recent Canadian National Elections

Notes: Turnout figures represent the total ballots cast as a percentage of electors on the voters list. Changes in the way the voters list is prepared and the conduct of elections make comparisons imprecise.

Source: This reproduction is a copy of the version available at www.elections.ca. Reproduced with the permission of Elections Canada.

TABLE 5-1   Turnout in Recent Elections, Selected Countries

Note: Turnout is for parliamentary elections, except for countries marked with an asterisk (*), where turnout is for presidential elections (first round where applicable). Turnout is generally calculated in terms of the proportion of registered voters casting valid votes. In the United States, the calculation is based on potentially eligible voters. Some figures are unofficial.

COUNTRY	YEAR	% VOTER TURNOUT	COUNTRY	YEAR	% VOTER TURNOUT
Argentina*	2015	78.7	New Zealand	2014	70.3
Canada	2015	68.5	Nigeria*	2015	42.4
Czech Republic	2013	59.4	Pakistan	2013	53.9
Denmark	2015	85.9	Poland	2015	50.9
Egypt*	2014	47.4	Russia*	2012	65.3
France*	2012	79.5	South Africa	2011	60.1
Germany	2013	71.5	South Korea	2016	62.9
Greece	2015 (second election)	56.7	Spain	2016	69.2
Hungary	2014	53.8	Sweden	2014	82.5
India	2014	66.8	Switzerland	2015	48.0
Iran*	2013	72.7	Tanzania	2015	65.3
Japan	2014	56.8	Turkey	2015	85.2
Mexico*	2012	57.6	United Kingdom	2015	66.1
Netherlands	2012	74.6	United States*	2012	60.4

Source: International Foundation for Electoral Systems *Election Guide.* Retrieved from www.electionguide.org.

EXPLANATIONS Some countries, including Australia, Belgium, and Brazil, require that all citizens vote. Where such rules are enforced through fines or other penalties, voter turnout is, not surprisingly, substantially higher than in other countries. For example, 86% of registered voters in Australia (2016) and 84% of voters in Belgium (2014) cast valid votes. The amount of time and effort that it takes to vote can also affect the turnout rate. For example, about one-quarter of potentially eligible voters in the United States are not able to vote because they do not take the time to register before the election. Voter turnout in American elections is also substantially higher every fourth year, when there is a presidential election, than in "midterm" elections held every second year to elect members of the House of Representatives and one-third of the members of the Senate. As well, Americans are often faced with a long, complex ballot that includes candidates for a variety of national, state, and local offices, as well as various referendums and initiatives. Accessibility also affects voting rates: countries that make voting possible by mail or Internet and provide alternatives for those who will be absent on election day have substantially higher voter turnout (Blais, Massicotte, & Dobrzynska, 2003). Long line-ups at polling stations (as is common in American cities) can discourage voting.

International Institute for Democracy
and Electoral Assistance
www.idea.int

Countries using proportional representation systems of election (see Chapter 7) tend to have higher voter turnout in part because every vote counts in determining how many representatives each party has in the legislature. As well, countries using a proportional representation system tend to have more political parties likely to gain seats in their legislative body, thus offering more significant choices to voters. In countries that use a single-member plurality system, many votes could be considered irrelevant, as it does not matter whether a candidate wins by one vote or twenty thousand votes. Thus, some people may not bother to vote if they think that their preferred candidate is well ahead of the other candidates or, alternatively, if they think that the candidate or party they support has no chance of winning.

Countries with well-organized political parties that can mobilize people to vote are also more likely to have high turnout rates. Being contacted by a party worker and persuaded to vote on election day by the party or candidate that you support increases the likelihood that you will cast a ballot. Likewise, countries where a high proportion of people have a strong attachment to a political party are more likely to have high turnout rates. The nature of party competition can also affect the level of voter turnout. If the major parties differ significantly in ideology or on policy issues that are important to voters, a higher proportion of citizens will likely vote. As well, voter turnout tends to be higher in elections that feature a close race among the leading parties or candidates.

Other Types of Political Participation

Only a small proportion of the public is actively involved in politics through working for a party or candidate during an election. For example, 6.3 percent

TABLE 5-2   Political Participation, Selected Countries

Notes: Surveys conducted between 2010 and 2014. Those not answering the question or answering "don't know" were excluded from the calculation. Many respondents indicated more than in boycott, and peaceful demonstration.

COUNTRY	ACTIVE MEMBER POLITICAL PARTY	ACTIVE MEMBER ENVIRONMENTAL ORGANIZATION	POLITICAL ACTION: RECENTLY SIGNED PETITION	POLITICAL ACTION: RECENTLY JOINED IN BOYCOTT	POLITICAL ACTION: RECENTLY ATTENDED PEACEFUL DEMONSTRATION
Australia	1.9%	4.3%	80.3%	60.9%	54.8%
Brazil	2.5	2.4	63.4	66.4	76.0
Germany	2.8	2.4	67.7	50.2	37.9
Japan	1.2	1.0	54.6	44.8	25.6
Mexico	8.2	7.1	83.6	67.3	76.5
Russia	0.5	0.4	68.3	48.5	47.1
Spain	0.8	0.3	75.6	56.9	66.3
Sweden	3.0	1.5	65.2	48.4	34.3
United States	14.7	4.7	68.4	57.4	14.7

Source: Compiled from World Values Survey, Sixth Wave, 2010–2014. Variables V29, V30, V90, V91, V92. Retrieved from www.worldvaluessurvey.org

of Canadians said they volunteered for a party or candidate in the previous 12 months that included the 2011 federal election (Fournier et al., 2011). As well, membership in political parties has been declining in many countries. However, citizen involvement in a wide variety of issue-oriented public interest groups has been increasing. By participating in public interest groups and social movements, citizens can try to affect government policies and promote social change. Various forms of protest activity have also become more common in contemporary political life (see Table 5-2). An online survey of Canadians conducted in 2014 found that in the previous 12 months 64% said that had signed a petition; 34% boycotted or bought a product for an ethical, environmental, or political reason; and 22% had participated in a protest or demonstration (Samara Canada, 2015).

Who Participates?

AGE   A particularly striking feature of political participation is that young adults are much less likely to vote and participate in election campaign activity than are middle-aged and older voters. For example, estimates of turnout by 18–24 year olds in the 2011 Canadian election ranged from 38.8 percent to about 50 percent compared to the 61.1 percent turnout for the electorate as a whole (Elections Canada, 2012; Statistics Canada, 2011). As Box 5-2 Why Do So Few Young People Vote? explains, both the **life-cycle effect** and the **generational effect** contribute to this low level of voting.

Younger people are more likely than older people to engage in some protest activities, and they participate in issue-oriented groups at almost the same

life-cycle effect

The effect of one's age on one's attitudes and behaviour. As people grow older, their attitudes and behaviours may change due to changing circumstances (such as education, marriage, employment, and retirement) related to age.

generational effect

The effect on attitudes and behaviour of the views of different generations that persist throughout the life cycle.

BOX 5-2   Why Do So Few Young People Vote?

Studies of voting behaviour in a variety of countries have found that younger people are much less likely to vote than middle-aged and older people.

Canadian surveys have indicated that most middle-aged and older people feel that they have a moral obligation to vote. This sense of duty tends to be somewhat weaker among younger voters. For example, 48% of Canadians 18–29 years old agreed that voting is a duty compared to 83% of those 60 or older (Americas Barometer, 2014). Younger persons tend to pay less attention to elections, have less interest in politics, and have less political knowledge (Blais et al., 2002, 2004; Pammett & LeDuc, 2003). The lower level of youth voting is *not* a result of a more cynical outlook on politics or a higher level of negative feelings concerning all of the political parties (Blais et al., 2002).

A survey conducted after the 2011 Canadian election found that both motivational and access factors were significant in explaining non-voting by younger persons. Specifically, a lower level of political interest and knowledge, a belief that all parties are the same, and a lesser sense of civic duty reduced the level of voting participation by younger persons. As well, insufficient knowledge that there were options for voting other than at the polling station on election day, the requirement

that proof of identity and address be provided, and difficulty getting to the polling station were cited by many youthful non-voters (Elections Canada, n.d.). However in the 2015 Canadian election there was a substantial increase in voting by younger persons that was likely a result of discussion of the election on social media, Liberal and NDP policy proposals directed at young persons, the popularity of Justin Trudeau, and dissatisfaction with the Harper government. The location of advance voting booths on 39 campuses facilitated student voting.

To some extent, there is a tendency for people to be more likely to vote as they get older. Termed a life-cycle effect, this could be a result of becoming more connected to one's community through work, involvement in community organizations, raising a family, and home ownership as well as increased interest and knowledge of politics. Nevertheless persons reaching voting age in recent times generally have been less likely to vote than those reaching voting age in the past. This generational effect suggests that overall voting turnout rates will continue to decline in most elections (Blais et al., 2004). Whether the upsurge in youth voting in the 2015 Canadian election is a temporary exception to the decline in voting or the start of a new trend remains to be seen.

rate as older persons (Dalton, 2006). As well, 18- to 34-year-old Canadians are more likely to discuss politics online and offline, work with others on a community issue, be active in protests, and about as likely to be involved in civic engagement activities such as volunteering, donating to a cause, and participating in various groups and organizations (Samara, 2014).

EDUCATION AND SOCIAL CLASS   Political participation is also related to education and other indicators of social class such as income, occupation, and social status. Those with higher levels of education, higher incomes, and professional or managerial occupations are more likely to engage in various forms of political participation, including both electoral and protest activity (Dalton, 2006). However, in countries where there is a major party that represents the working class, differences in voting participation among those in different class positions are small (Verba, Nie, & Kim, 1978). One might expect that the large increase in post-secondary education enrolment in recent decades would have the effect of increasing the turnout in elections. However voting by those with less education, has declined sharply, thus usually offsetting the increase that could be expected from the growth in post-secondary education (Blais et al., 2004).

GENDER   Although politics has traditionally been thought of as a male activity, in recent Canadian elections women have been slightly more likely to vote than men (Elections Canada Online, n.d.). It is in higher-level political activities, such as seeking and holding national or provincial political office or a top position in a political party or interest group, in which women are less likely to be involved than men.

POLITICAL ATTITUDES, INTEREST, AND KNOWLEDGE   Political participation is also affected by various individual political attitudes. Those with a strong sense of attachment to a political party are more likely to vote and be involved in election campaign activities (Dalton, 2006). Likewise, those with a high level of political efficacy, political interest, and political knowledge are more likely to be active participants in politics.

CIVIC ENGAGEMENT   Participation in groups such as community choirs, bowling leagues, and service organizations can help to develop trust in others, mutual co-operation in pursuit of common goals, tolerance, and leadership skills. According to Robert Putnam (2000), a democratic political culture and effective democratic governing rest on a citizenry that is not only politically active, but also active in the non-political associations within the community. Putnam has expressed a concern about the decline of citizen engagement in the organizational life of communities. However, membership in most types of voluntary organizations has increased in Canada (Baer, Curtis, & Grabb, 2001). Just over one-half of Canadians say that they volunteered for a community group or non-profit organization in the last 12 months (Fournier et al., 2011).

POLITICAL SOCIALIZATION AND CHANGING VALUES

Opinions about specific political issues and personalities can often change quickly. However, a person's basic political values, beliefs, and orientations are usually more resistant to change. Therefore, **political socialization**, the processes by which the values, attitudes, and beliefs of the political culture are transmitted to members of the political community, is important. Socialization can provide for continuity as the values and beliefs of older generations are passed on to newer generations. As well, immigrants may want or be encouraged to adopt some of the political values and beliefs that are prevalent in their new country.

political socialization

The processes by which the values, attitudes, and beliefs of the political culture are transmitted to members of the political community.

Political socialization does not always ensure continuity in political thinking. Governments or other powerful forces may attempt to modify the political culture through deliberate socialization efforts so as to promote the legitimacy of government and other social and political institutions, develop a sense of national pride, or achieve other objectives. However, political socialization does not involve only deliberate efforts to indoctrinate people with particular values and beliefs. It often occurs in a more haphazard fashion; for example, when young people observe the discussions and actions of adults.

There are a variety of different agents of political socialization, including the family, peer groups, the educational system, the communications media, religious organizations, the military, unions, and the workplace. Although socialization is a lifelong process, it has often been assumed that many basic values and orientations are acquired at an early age, making the family a major agent of political socialization. In particular, parents are very important in shaping the religious, ethnic, and other group identities of their children. American studies in the 1950s and 1960s also found that children and young adults have a strong tendency to adopt the party identification (sense of attachment to a political party) of their parents, although later studies did not find as strong a tendency (Jennings & Niemi, 1968, 1981). Not surprisingly, children are more likely to adopt the party identification of their parents if politics is frequently discussed at home. However, once these young people become adults they are more likely than those raised in less politicized families to change their party identification presumably because they are more likely to pay attention to politics than those raised in less politicized homes (Dinas, 2014). The correspondence between parents and young adults in other political attitudes—such as political trust, political efficacy, orientations toward political participation, and opinions on public policy issues—is not particularly strong (Jennings, 1984; Jennings & Niemi, 1981; Mintz, 1993).

Thinking about political socialization as the transmission of political attitudes and values, particularly from parents to their children, can be misleading. Young persons develop their political ideas and orientations from a variety of sources including discussion with their peers. Social media have become for young people a major forum of discussion and source of information and views on a wide variety of topics, including politics. As well, a variety of websites provide a diversity of views. Thus there is much less reliance on the newspaper delivered to the home and television news broadcasts that were once the primary source of political information and opinions in many families. Further, young persons may be active participants in a family's discussion of politics rather than passive recipients of their parents' views. Where discussion of politics is encouraged or mandated in schools, young persons may bring ideas and information that differ from that of their parents to family discussions of politics. Indeed, the political ideas of young people may "trickle-up" to have an influence on the political views of their parents (McDevitt & Chaffee, 2002; Niemi & Hepburn, 1995).

Tami Thirlwell

State-Directed Socialization

Countries vary in the extent to which state institutions make deliberate and vigorous efforts to promote particular political values. Revolutionary regimes such as the Soviet Union, the People's Republic of China, and Nazi Germany devoted great efforts to socializing the young, as well as the population as a whole, into the new values associated with the revolutionary ideology. Schools, the media, youth groups, and various organizations were required to promote "correct" values and criticize traditional values.

In liberal democracies, educational systems are often less explicitly political in terms of promoting a particular ideological perspective. Indeed, schools in many Canadian provinces provide only a limited amount of education concerning the political system. Nevertheless, schools often promote various politically relevant values and ideas.

The establishment of public educational systems in the nineteenth century was associated, in many countries, with the goal of creating a unified nation-state (Weber, 1976). In the United States, the school system has been seen as a means of creating a common sense of being American among a diverse immigrant population. American values were promoted (and often continue to be promoted) through required courses in "civics." Public education systems also served the needs of the emerging industrial system for a disciplined workforce through the practices enforced in the classroom.

In the 1960s and 1970s, a more child-centred educational approach was adopted in many Western democracies. This approach focused on developing the potential of each individual in a less structured environment. Values such as respect for differences and cultural diversity were promoted, thus coinciding with the political trend in some countries to recognize and promote multiculturalism.

In recent years, this "liberal" approach to education has been challenged. Concerns about preparing for the challenges of a competitive global economy have often led to a renewed emphasis on standards, testing, and basic skills such as mathematics and literacy. Worries about "homegrown" terrorism and the integration of immigrant families with different cultural practices have led some countries such as the United Kingdom, the United States, and France to consider, and in some cases implement, educational policies that reverse the tolerant, multicultural approach of previous decades and instead promote dominant national values and patriotism (Mitchell, 2003). For example, some American states have reinstituted school requirements concerning patriotic rituals such as reciting the pledge of allegiance. France, in a move directed at its large Muslim minority, has banned the wearing of religious symbols and clothing, including the hijab (head scarf) in schools.

The success of government-directed socialization efforts in many countries should not be exaggerated. Teachers do not necessarily follow the government-prescribed curriculum. Religious groups and the Western media brought Eastern Europeans messages that contradicted the socializing messages conveyed by the Communist Party. The Internet is bringing Western views about freedom and liberal democracy to countries like China and Iran despite efforts by authoritarian governments to try to block these views. As well, young people do not passively accept what they are told. When different socializing agencies provide different perspectives, young people may develop values, attitudes, and beliefs in their own ways. Thus, new generations are not copies of older generations in their political thinking, nor do their ideas necessarily reflect the ideas of the dominant ruling groups.

Changing Value Priorities

Ronald Inglehart (1977, 1990) has suggested that modern societies are undergoing a fundamental change in value priorities. According to his **postmaterialist theory**, political socialization is affected by the conditions present when a person is young. The generations that grew up in the relative security and affluence of the Western world since World War II are more likely to give priority to **postmaterialist values** such as freedom of expression, participation, concern about the quality of life, and appreciation of a more beautiful environment. Earlier generations are more likely to have materialistic values such as a concern for economic growth, order, and physical security (see Box 5-3 Are You Materialist or Postmaterialist?). This is not simply a matter of being more concerned with material and security needs as one grows older. Rather, studies conducted by Inglehart and his

postmaterialist theory

A theory that modern societies are undergoing a fundamental change in value priorities because generations that grew up in the relative security and affluence of the Western world since World War II are more likely to give priority to postmaterialist values than to materialist values.

postmaterialist values

Non-materialist values such as freedom of expression, participation, concern about the quality of life, and appreciation of a more beautiful environment.

BOX 5-3 Are You Materialist or Postmaterialist?

Read the following statement and answer the two questions to determine if you would be considered materialist or postmaterialist.

There is a lot of talk these days about what the aims of this country should be for the next ten years. Listed below are some of the goals to which different people would give top priority. If you had to choose, which one of these things would you say is the most important? Which would be the next most important?

1. Maintaining order in the nation
2. Giving people more say in important government decisions
3. Fighting rising prices
4. Protecting freedom of speech

If you chose items 1 and 3, you would be considered materialist; if you chose items 2 and 4, you would be considered postmaterialist; and if you chose a different combination, you would be categorized as mixed.

The four items on this quiz do not fully reflect all of the values associated with materialism and postmaterialism, but are often used instead of a twelve-item scale. The other postmaterialist values used in the twelve-item scale include more say in work/community; more humane society; make cities/country more beautiful; and ideas count more than money. The other materialist values include a high level of economic growth; a stable economy; fight against crime; and a strong defence.

Source: Adapted from the World Values Survey, www.worldvaluessurvey.org with permission.

associates have found that the increased tendency to give priority to postmaterialist values has persisted among recent generations as they grow older.

Postmaterialism—in combination with the development of a post-industrial, knowledge-based economy, greater access to higher education, and new means of communications—may be creating major changes in the political culture of the advanced democracies. These changes, argues Russell Dalton (2006), have resulted in a **new style of citizen politics**. This includes greater citizen activism, the questioning of authority, the development of new political parties and new social movements, the raising of new types of issues (such as issues related to the environment and gender equality), and the development of more liberal social values (for example, greater acceptance of same-sex marriage). As well, the significance of traditional political divisions ("cleavages") based on such group characteristics as class, religion, and ethnicity has been declining to some extent. Likewise, the strength of individual and group attachments to particular political parties has generally tended to diminish.

The extent of value change should not be exaggerated. The trend toward greater postmaterialism found in surveys from the 1980s and 1990s was reversed to some extent in some countries in subsequent surveys. In most countries, the majority of the population has a mixture of materialist and postmaterialist values, and in many countries there are more people with materialist than postmaterialist values. Interestingly, Canada had the highest proportion of postmaterialists among the fifty-six countries surveyed in 2005 to 2008.

new style of citizen politics

A set of changes including greater citizen activism, the questioning of authority, the development of new political parties and new social movements, the raising of new types of issues, and the development of more liberal social values.

TABLE 5-3   Materialist and Postmaterialist Values, Canada and the United States

	CANADA			UNITED STATES			
	1990	2000	2006	1990	1999	2006	2011
Materialist	11.9%	8.6%	10.3%	16.4%	9.5%	21.5%	23.8%
Mixed	62.5%	62.0%	58.5%	61.2%	64.9%	60.7%	59.1%
Postmaterialist	25.6%	29.4%	31.2%	22.5%	25.6%	17.8%	16.7%
N (of respondents)	1647	1882	2143	1839	1179	1222	2232

Note: Canada did not participate in the most recent survey.

Source: Reprinted with permission from World Values Survey Association - WVSA.

Materialist concerns about unemployment, economic prosperity, health care, security, and taxes are still often the leading political issues. Postmaterialist issues (such as concern for the environment) have been added to the political agenda, but have not transformed the conflicts and social divisions that typically affect political life.

✓• SUMMARY AND CONCLUSION

Examining the political culture of a country can be helpful in understanding the politics and governing of a country. The dominant political values will likely affect how people think and act in political life and, to some extent, what kinds of policies its governments adopt. However, there are often substantial differences in the political values, beliefs, and political orientations of different groups (such as those based on religion, ethnicity, region, age, gender, and class) as well as differences between political elites and the rest of the population.

The political cultures of the Western democracies are often viewed as more liberal and individualistic than other political cultures that are more collectivist and deferential to authority. Whether this is a persistent feature based on differences related to religious values, historical circumstances, or the level of socio-economic development is unclear. Within Western democracies, there are significant differences—for example, the political cultures of Canada and a number of Western European countries tend to be somewhat less individualistic and more liberal and secular in social and moral values than the United States. However, there are important differences in political

culture within Canada, the United States, and Western European countries.

The democratic ideal of an interested, active, and well-informed citizenry is far from realization even in countries where democratic values and institutions have become solidly entrenched. A relatively small proportion of the population is highly interested in and knowledgeable about politics. Voting participation and membership in political parties has declined in many countries with younger people, in particular, generally having a low level of voting. However participation in citizens' groups and protest activities has tended to increase.

A high proportion of citizens in many countries say that they favour democracy (although what they think democracy means may differ). However, the levels of trust and confidence in government and politicians in democratic countries have become rather low in in recent times. Some analysts have argued that this indicates that there is a "crisis in democracy." Increasing demands from citizens have "overloaded" governments, in the sense that governments do not have the resources to meet all of the demands being placed on them by citizens. Dissatisfaction with government has grown, creating a potential problem of legitimacy for democratic governments. Others argue that a more educated, postmaterialist citizenry has higher expectations of government. With increased information, citizens are more aware of what goes on in government. Citizens have often become dissatisfied because of the slowness of governments to respond to their desire for more effective participation.

Research concerning political culture and political participation raises some important issues concerning the ability of democratic countries to pursue the common good. On the one hand, the development of a more critical citizenry can be helpful in making government more responsive to the needs and preferences of citizens and in holding government accountable for its actions. The increase in active participation, particularly in citizens groups that seek the common good (or at least their version of the common good), can be viewed as a positive feature of modern, democratic politics. On the other hand, the rather low level of political knowledge among the citizenry raises questions about whether the common good can be effectively pursued through active citizen participation in politics. Declining voting turnout increases the likelihood that governments will be based on the electoral support of a minority of citizens. This may encourage politicians to be concerned with the good of only a limited part of society.

✔• KEY TERMS

Civic culture 104	New style of citizen politics 117	Political socialization 113
Generational effect 111	Political culture 99	Postmaterialist theory 116
Life-cycle effect 111	Political efficacy 105	Postmaterialist values 116

DISCUSSION QUESTIONS

1. Do you think that a "clash of civilizations" is inevitable?

2. Is a particular kind of political culture needed to develop and sustain a democratic political system?

3. Does Canada have a distinctive political culture?

4. Do you think you will vote in the next national, provincial, and local elections? Why do you think that younger voters are less likely to vote than older voters? Is voting a civic duty that all citizens have a responsibility to perform?

5. Do you have the same basic political values, beliefs, and orientations as your parents, other family members, or your friends? How would you explain the similarities and differences?

6. Is a postmaterialist political culture developing? What would be its implications for political life?

FURTHER READING

Adams, M. (2003). *Fire and ice: The United States, Canada and the myth of converging values*. Toronto: Penguin.

Almond, G.A., & Verba, S. (1963). *The civic culture: Political attitudes and democracy in five nations*. Princeton, NJ: Princeton University Press.

Dalton, R.J. (2014). *Citizen politics: Public opinion and political parties in advanced industrial democracies* (6th ed.). Washington, DC: CQ Press.

Dalton, R.J. & Welzel, C. (Eds.) (2014). *The civic culture transformed. From allegiant to assertive citizens*. New York: Cambridge University Press.

DeBardeleben, J., & Pammett, J.H. (Eds.). (2009). *Activating the citizen: Dilemmas of participation in Europe and Canada.* New York: Palgrave Macmillan.

Huntington, S.P. (1996). *The clash of civilizations and the remaking of world order.* New York: Simon & Schuster.

Lipset, S.M. (1990). *Continental divide.* New York: Routledge.

Milner, H. (2002). *Civic literacy: How informed citizens make democracy work.* Hanover, NH: University Press of New England.

Putnam, R. (2000). *Bowling alone: The collapse and revival of American community.* New York: Simon & Schuster.

Wiardia, H. J. (2014). *Political culture, political science, and identity politics.* Burlington, VT: Ashgate Publishing.

6 Political Parties

Justin Trudeau delivers his acceptance speech after winning the leadership of the Liberal Party of Canada on April 14, 2013. Adrian Wyld/The Canadian Press

After reading this chapter, you should be able to:

1. explain the significance of parties
2. distinguish among different types of political parties
3. evaluate the methods used for choosing party leaders
4. outline the characteristics of the major Canadian parties and the nature of the Canadian party system
5. discuss the financing of political parties and election campaigns

Choosing a Leader: The Liberal Party of Canada

After the defeat of the Liberal Party in the 2006 Canadian election and the resignation of its leader, Paul Martin, the Liberal Party selected Stéphane Dion as leader, even though he was the first choice of only 17.8 percent of those voting at a party convention. As successive ballots were held and other candidates dropped out of the race, Dion came out ahead of the initial front-runners, Michael Ignatieff and Bob Rae.

The Liberal Party under Dion's leadership did poorly in the 2008 election. Under pressure from his party's caucus, Dion agreed that he would resign after a new leader was chosen at the party's convention in May 2009. With the three opposition parties angered by the minority Conservative government's budget in December 2008, the Liberals and NDP agreed to form a coalition government with the support of the Bloc Québécois to replace the Conservative minority government. Dion would temporarily become prime minister until a new Liberal leader was chosen. Prime Minister Stephen Harper asked the governor general to prorogue Parliament (ending a session of Parliament) rather than face certain defeat in the House of Commons. The Conservatives then mounted a strong attack on the plan for a coalition government. Faced with public opposition to the idea that Dion might become temporary prime minister, the Liberal caucus pressured him to resign immediately as party leader and chose Michael Ignatieff as interim leader. At the 2009 Liberal Party convention, Ignatieff was confirmed as leader since no other candidates decided to seek the leadership.

When the Liberal Party suffered their worst result ever in the 2011 election, Ignatieff resigned and Bob Rae (Liberal MP and former NDP premier of Ontario) was chosen interim leader. Instead of holding a party convention to choose a leader as the party had done since 1919, Liberals decided to conduct a direct vote for the choice of leader by all party members and those who declared themselves to be supporters of the party. No fee was charged for supporters to register and vote. Members and supporters, who had to register at least 41 days in advance, voted online or by telephone between April 6 and 13, 2013 by listing candidates in their order of preference.[*] Justin Trudeau easily won on the first ballot with 78.7 percent of the 104 552 votes cast, defeating five other candidates. However, the 127 261 eligible voters were far less than the nearly 300 000 party members and supporters that the party claimed to have signed up.

In May 2016, the convention of the Liberal party of Canada followed Justin Trudeau's desire to promote a wide-open Liberal party that would be more of a movement than a political party. Rather than party membership, anyone could register online with the Liberal party for free and would be able to participate in the nomination of candidates for election, the selection of the Liberal leader, policy development , and Liberal conventions. Opening the party has the potential to increase participation in the party, provide greater diversity in party activists, and identify a substantial number of people to volunteer to work in election campaigns. However, it could result in the choice of a party leader, candidates, and executive officials who are not committed to the party and its basic principles.

INTRODUCTION

Political parties can provide an important link between citizens and their government. In democratic countries, parties compete to mobilize voters to elect their candidates to public office and to control the government. To achieve this goal, parties present a platform of what they intend to do if elected based, in part, on what they think will appeal to voters. Parties also try to influence the opinions of the public to gain or maintain their support.

Despite their importance in the political process, the membership of political parties in many of the advanced democracies has dropped substantially since the 1960s (Siaroff, 2009b). In Canada, only about 2 percent of adult Canadians are regular members of a political party (Cross, 2004), although party membership often increases substantially when leaders or candidates are being selected.

Political parties are viewed negatively by a substantial majority of the population in many countries (Dalton, 2006). Members of a political party are often dissatisfied with their limited influence on the development of party policy positions (Cross, 2004). Although the theory of liberal democracy contends that competition among political parties allows citizens to influence the policies adopted by government, the link between citizens and government provided by political parties is often weak. The decisions of government do not necessarily reflect the policy positions presented by the party (or parties, in a coalition government) that has been elected to govern.

Because most major parties are focused on gaining and maintaining political power, they may compromise their principles in order to gain support from voters or from their financial backers. Instead of stimulating policy discussion among their members and among the public, parties are often more concerned with their image and that of their leader, along with discrediting their opponents.

Nevertheless, political parties are important. They play a dominant role in elections by recruiting candidates, running election campaigns, and presenting policy platforms to the public. The governing party (or parties) in a parliamentary system determines the agenda of government, oversees the development of public policies, and is usually able to obtain the support of Parliament needed to pass laws and approve the spending and taxing measures of the government. The opposition parties also play an important role in trying to hold government accountable for its actions and raising issues that have not been dealt with adequately by government. In most democratic countries, parties act as disciplined, united teams in Parliament, thereby simplifying the choice voters make in an election. Through debate among parties, voters may be able to obtain an understanding of the issues facing their country and the strengths and weaknesses of alternative approaches to handling important problems. Political parties can be important instruments of change by publicizing problems and taking decisive action when governing. However, the intense partisanship that often goes along with party politics may lead parties to misinform and mislead voters, and governing parties may fail to take into account the differing viewpoints held by the public and other parties.

THE ORIGINS AND DEVELOPMENT OF POLITICAL PARTIES

Legislative bodies have always had factions composed of individual members with similar interests and perspectives. As legislative bodies, such as the British Parliament, took the power to choose a government (prime minister and cabinet) away from the monarch, these factions transformed themselves into **political parties**. The parties that developed in the second half of the nineteenth century (including the Conservative and Liberal parties in Canada and the United Kingdom and the Democratic and Republican parties in the United States) are often referred to as **cadre parties**. In general, cadre parties had little in the way of formal organizational structures or membership outside of Parliament. They looked instead to local "notables" (that is, the local elites) who had the prestige and financial resources to support the party's candidates in elections (Duverger, 1964). This left the members of the party in Parliament and its leadership generally free to take positions in Parliament and government as they saw fit (or in accordance with the views of their financial backers and elite supporters). Cadre parties thus provided a limited link between the people and the government.

Mass parties developed in the latter part of the nineteenth century and the start of the twentieth century to challenge the elite domination of politics and organize the mass of the population. Socialist and Labour parties were formed out of working-class movements and pressed to gain the right to vote for all adults. Other mass parties were formed in some countries on the basis of nationalist, farmers', and religious movements. Unlike the cadre parties, which usually were created internally within legislatures, the mass parties generally were externally created to represent major sections of the newly enfranchised population, particularly the working class. Because many of these parties did not have the support of the wealthy, they generally tried to develop a large membership base that supported the party by regularly paying a small membership fee.

Collecting fees from large numbers of people required a large organization based on a network of local branches with a central office. Democratic procedures, including **party conventions** (regular meetings of elected delegates of the membership), were adopted to approve party positions and to choose members for various positions in the party. Because mass parties generally developed outside of the legislature, members elected to the legislature were expected to follow the wishes of the party membership as expressed by policy resolutions adopted at party conventions. As well, mass parties typically sought to penetrate and associate with various social groups such as unions and religious organizations (Gunther & Diamond, 2001). Generally, mass parties attempted to involve their members on a regular basis and to educate their members concerning their party's perspective (Ware, 1987). In some countries, this involved publishing newspapers, sponsoring sports teams, and organizing the lives of their members through recreational and social activities.

Mass parties also tend to be more disciplined than cadre parties. Bound by a common ideological perspective, a strong organizational structure, and a commitment to a particular platform, the parliamentary representatives of mass parties tend to act in a more united fashion than the more independent-minded elite MPs of cadre parties.

Mass parties generally have a stronger link between citizens and political leaders than cadre parties. However, power tended to be concentrated in the hands of party officials (those with paid positions within the party organization) rather than in the mass membership of the party. Based on his observation in the early twentieth century of the German Social Democratic party (a classic example of a mass party), Robert Michels developed what he termed the **iron law of oligarchy**. This generalization claims that all organizations, even those that appear democratic, inevitably become dominated by a small group of leaders.

iron law of oligarchy

A generalization that claims that all organizations, even those that appear democratic, inevitably become dominated by a small group of leaders.

As mass parties in a number of countries succeeded in developing large, membership-based organizations, cadre parties eventually found it necessary to respond to this challenge by developing regular membership-based organizations and adopting some of the democratic procedures pioneered by mass parties. Nevertheless, traces of the difference still remain. For example, parties with cadre origins often consider the party leadership as the final determinant of party positions and tend to rely more than other parties on financing from business and the wealthy. In contrast, parties with mass origins typically place the authority to approve policy positions in the hands of a party convention and make greater efforts to involve their members in policy development.

The development of modern election campaign techniques, such as the use of television advertising and social media, and the solicitation of funds through direct mail and the Internet, has reduced the necessity of building and maintaining a large membership organization. In many countries, parties are now funded to a considerable extent by the state. Professionals skilled in the techniques of advertising, public relations, fundraising, campaign management, and public opinion research have become very important to parties in their efforts to gain political power. Mass parties, like parties with cadre origins, have found it necessary to make use of campaign professionals to try to appeal to the electorate. Cadre parties have found it useful to adopt the mass party characteristic of a disciplined parliamentary party (Budge, Keman, McDonald, & Pennings, 2012), often under tight control by the party leader, in order to carry a uniform and consistent appeal to the public. With the development of the "permanent campaign" (see Chapter 7), party discipline and message management has become a key goal of many contemporary party leaders.

CONTEMPORARY POLITICAL PARTIES

Most major political parties today can be described as **electoral–professional parties** (Panebianco, 1988). Such parties are *electoral* in that their dominant concern is winning elections and *professional* in their reliance on experts to market them to the electorate. These parties may mobilize substantial numbers of supporters during an election campaign (and when leaders and candidates are being chosen), but will tend to shrink to a small number of active members at other times. Electoral–professional parties may attempt to appeal to all or most of the electorate by avoiding clear ideological positions, shifting their policy positions in response to public opinion, and focusing on the personal qualities of the party's leaders and candidates (Gunther & Diamond, 2001). This tendency to move away from ideological positions and develop broad, middle-of-the-road positions was particularly evident in Social Democratic parties and Labour parties that became described as "catch-all parties" (Kirchheimer, 1966). While initially successful in gaining support, some of these parties have suffered declining membership and electoral support. In some countries this has led catch-all parties to return to some aspects of their traditional ideological positions. It has also led to the formation of new parties with a more critical orientation to mainstream politics (Poguntke, 2014; Karreth, Polk, & Allen, 2013). This includes the development of a number of populist and far right political parties as well as new left-wing parties.

The term **brokerage party** has often been used to describe the leading Canadian parties (particularly the Liberal Party) that have attempted to find compromises to accommodate a variety of interests (particularly regional and ethnic/cultural interests) so as to try to build broad support across the country in a non-ideological manner. The focus of a brokerage party is on winning elections rather than promoting an ideological program (Carty, 2013). However, despite their efforts to appear broad-based and non-ideological, the policies in government of brokerage parties may tend to reflect business interests and the country's dominant ideological perspective (Brodie & Jenson, 1988). As well, even though major political parties try to maintain an image of appealing to the electorate as a whole, they often actually target their appeals to gain the support of those groups and individuals needed to gain a majority of legislative seats.

Programmatic parties tend to devote greater attention to the development of a coherent party program and view themselves as more principled than brokerage parties. Nevertheless, to remain competitive, programmatic parties have often adopted some of the techniques and strategies of electoral–professional parties. In Canada, the former Reform Party, the Co-operative Commonwealth Federation (forerunner to the NDP), and the Green Party might be described as programmatic parties.

BOX 6-1   Running to Make a Point: Minor Political Parties

In the 2008 Canadian election campaign, the leader of the Marijuana Party said that there was no reason to vote for his party. The party was not seeking to elect any members to the House of Commons; rather, he said, the party wanted to put the issue of legalizing cannabis a little higher on the political agenda.

In most democratic countries there are a large number of political parties, many of which have little expectation of electing representatives or even gaining more than an insignificant number of votes. Although the media generally pay little attention to these parties, election campaigns do provide an opportunity to try to get their message across. Some of these parties (such as communist, libertarian, and fundamentalist Christian parties) represent distinctive political perspectives that are strongly held by their members but not reflected in the "mainstream" parties. Others have a particular cause. For example, the Pirate Party that participates in elections in many countries (and topped the public opinion polls in Iceland in 2016) on a platform that includes

greater protection for Internet privacy, open government, and reform of patent and copyright laws, including the legalization of non-commercial Internet file sharing. Although some minor parties have only a short-lived existence on the political landscape, others have exhibited considerable staying power. Most notably, the Prohibition Party in the United States, which seeks to ban the production and sale of alcohol, has run a candidate for president in every election since 1872 (although it gained only 519 votes in the 2012 election).

There have also been parties that seek to make fun of parties and politicians. Poland's Beer-Lovers Party managed to elect sixteen members to the Sejm (lower chamber of Parliament) in 2001 before splitting into large-beer and small-beer parties. The Official Monster Raving Loony Party has been a satirical feature of British elections since 1983. Canada's Rhinoceros Party, led originally by a thick-skinned resident of the Granby Zoo, managed to win 110 000 votes in the 1980 election. One of its key promises is to keep none of its promises!

Not all significant political parties have developed a reliance on professional expertise and a heavy focus on winning elections. Some newer parties that have developed out of social movements (such as Green parties) continue to rely to a considerable extent on amateur activists to carry their message to the public and retain some elements of "grassroots democracy" even as they become more professional and election oriented (Rihoux & Frankland, 2008). Rather than trying to appeal to the electorate as a whole, some parties focus on representing the interests of a particular ethnic, religious, or cultural group, nationality, or region. For example, the Scottish Nationalist Party (which favours independence for Scotland) participates in elections for the United Kingdom Parliament (winning 56 of Scotland's 59 seats in the 2015 UK election). Other examples include the Bloc Québécois and Finland's Swedish People's Party. There are also political parties that put forward candidates in elections primarily in order to promote a particular interest or cause rather than to obtain seats in a legislative body (see Box 6-1 Running to Make a Point).

Finally, personalistic parties are dominated by a powerful leader combined with a weak party organization that follows the wishes of the leader

personalistic party

A party dominated by a powerful leader combined with a weak party organization that follows the wishes of the leader.

(Kostadinova & Levitt, 2014). The classic case of a **personalistic party** is the Union pour la Nouvelle République (often referred to as the "Gaullist party") formed in 1958 to support General Charles de Gaulle, who led the "Free French" government-in-exile during World War II. Likewise, in Argentina, the Partido Justicialiste was formed in 1945 to support the presidential candidacy of Juan Perón. In 1993, billionaire Italian media tycoon and football club owner Silvio Berlusconi created his own party, Forza Italia, which successfully supported his ambition to become prime minister.

CANADIAN POLITICAL PARTIES

The Conservative Party

Canada's first organized political party, the Conservatives, originated as a cadre party based on the coalition of factions that supported the union of the British North American colonies in 1867. The party had close relations with elite groups, including big business. The Conservative Party—which adopted the name Progressive Conservative (PC) in 1942—was traditionally associated with tariff protection for manufacturing industries and a strong central government. However, in the 1980s, the PC government reached a free-trade agreement with the United States and advocated greater provincial government powers. Support for the party collapsed in the early 1990s, with the party winning only two seats in the 1993 election. The Reform party (established in 1987) promoted the populist New Right vision of a greatly reduced role for government and appealed particularly to Western Canadians who were distrustful of the PC government's efforts to satisfy Quebec's demands for constitutional change.

Conservative Party of Canada
www.conservative.ca

With the conservative or right-wing vote outside Quebec split between the PCs and the Reform party, the Reform party tried to convince the PCs to merge with them. The first attempt—the Canadian Reform Conservative Alliance (commonly known as the Canadian Alliance), established in 2000 with Reformer Stephen Harper as its leader—had limited success since many national PCs were opposed to the strongly ideological views of the party. Nevertheless, in 2003 (over the objections of some of its prominent members), the PC party agreed to merge with the Canadian Alliance to form a new Conservative Party, with Stephen Harper subsequently chosen as its leader. The new version of the Conservative Party generally favours smaller government, lower taxes, less regulation of business, free trade, increased provincial government autonomy, and mandatory minimum sentences for criminal offences.

The Liberal Party

The Liberal Party developed out of a diverse set of factions, including those who supported the establishment of a democratic system of government in which power ultimately rested on the support of the elected representatives of the people; those opposed to the power and privileges of elites, including the established religions (particularly the Catholic Church in Quebec); and Maritimers who had opposed joining Canada. By the 1880s, the Liberal Party had become a unified party in Parliament, but like the Conservative party its extraparliamentary party organization was slow to develop.

Liberal Party of Canada
www.liberal.ca

The early Liberal Party generally adopted the positions of classic liberalism favouring free trade and limited government, as well as supporting provincial rights rather than a dominant central government. As with the early Conservative Party, it moderated its ideological perspective to gain support. In particular, it became associated with national unity as it gained the support of French-speaking Quebecers as well as English-speaking Canadians. Beginning in the early 1940s, the Liberal Party oversaw the gradual development of the welfare state and, particularly when Pierre Trudeau was prime minister (1968–1979 and 1980–1984), supported a strong national government in the face of the growing assertiveness of provincial governments. The party views the adoption of the Charter of Rights and Freedoms (1982) as one of its key accomplishments.

The New Democratic Party

The New Democratic Party (NDP) has its roots in the Co-operative Commonwealth Federation (CCF), which was established in 1932 by delegates from various farmer, labour, and socialist groups during the height of the Great Depression. Its limited support at the national level and weak finances led the CCF to join with the Canadian Labour Congress (the largest umbrella organization of labour unions) to form the NDP in 1961.

New Democratic Party of Canada
www.ndp.ca

The NDP supports welfare state measures and greater social and economic equality. As well, it favours an active role for government in managing the economy, stronger environmental regulations, and liberal social policies. It has generally opposed greater military involvement with the United States and has been critical of free trade and investment agreements that don't protect Canadian jobs.

The Bloc Québécois

The Bloc Québécois was founded in 1990 by members of Parliament (mainly PC but also Liberal) who were upset that the PC government was considering modifying a proposed constitutional agreement (the Meech Lake Accord) that would have recognized Quebec as a distinct society. The Bloc, which favours Quebec independence, contests seats only in Quebec and is primarily concerned with representing Quebec's interests in the Canadian House of Commons. Like the NDP, it tends to favour social democratic policies and stronger environmental measures.

Bloc Québécois
www.blocquebecois.org

Environmentalist Elizabeth May, executive director of the Sierra Club of Canada from 1989 to 2006, was elected leader of the Green Party of Canada in 2006 and became the first elected Green Party MP in 2011.

Andrew Vaughan/The Canadian Press

Green Party of Canada
http://greenparty.ca

cleavage

A social division that involves those associated with each grouping having a distinct collective identity and distinct interests that can lead to the development of organizations such as political parties that reflect the different sides of the social division.

The Green Party

There are more than a dozen smaller parties that regularly contest Canadian elections. However, only the Green Party has, since 2004, become a significant part of the Canadian party system. Although distinctive in its focus on environmental issues, the Green Party has also developed positions on a variety of issues, including human rights, poverty, health care, electoral system reform, and foreign policy. Its leader, Elizabeth May, became the first elected Green Party MP in 2011.

PARTY SYSTEMS

A party system refers to the basic pattern of relationships among political parties (Sartori, 1976). In an influential analysis, Seymour Martin Lipset and Stein Rokkan (1967) argued that the party systems of Western countries developed in response to two major historical turning points. First, the development of the modern nation-state in the eighteenth and nineteenth centuries often involved conflict between the dominant national culture and various minority cultures, particularly in the more remote regions, creating a centre–periphery **cleavage**. As well, conflicts between the developing state and the Catholic Church, which wanted to preserve its privileges and power, sometimes created a cleavage between Catholics and Protestants or between those with a religious orientation to politics and those with a secular orientation. Second, the Industrial Revolution of the nineteenth century created a cleavage between agricultural interests and the new industrialists and later a cleavage between the owners of industries and industrial workers (a class cleavage).

Although the national and industrial revolutions affected all Western societies, the specific historical circumstances of each country affected the manner in which the party system developed in that country. For example, the modern British party system was strongly affected by the class cleavage, while the German party system was affected by a combination of class and religious cleavages. In Lipset and Rokkan's view, the basic pattern of connections between the major interests in society and the party system had become firmly established by the 1960s.

Subsequently, the raising of new issues such as concern about the environment and women's rights, along with the development of postmaterialist values, the creation of new political parties, and the weakening of the relationship between social group membership and voting choice, led some analysts to

COUNTRY	BASIC IDEOLOGICAL PERSPECTIVE
Canada	**Liberal**; **Conservative**; **NDP** (social democratic); Bloc Québécois (Quebec nationalist); Green
United States	**Democratic** (liberal); **Republican** (conservative)
United Kingdom	**Conservative**; **Labour** (social democratic); United Kingdom Independence (populist right/anti EU); Liberal Democrats (liberal); Scottish National
Australia	**Liberal** (centre-right); **Labour** (social democratic); National (rural conservative); Green
France	**Socialist Party**; **Republicans** (conservative); **Front National** (far right); Greens; Left Front; UDI (centrist)
Germany	**Christian Democratic Union**/Christian Social Union (conservative); **Social Democratic**; The Left (socialist); Greens; Free Democratic (liberal)
Sweden	**Social Democratic**; **Moderate** (liberal-conservative); Sweden Democracy (far right); Green; Centre (agrarian-liberal); Left party (socialist); Liberal; Christian Democrats
Spain	**People's Party** (conservative/Christian democracy); **Socialist Workers Party** (social democratic); **Podemos** (left-populist); Citizen (liberal)

TABLE 6-1

Party Ideologies in Selected Western Democracies

Notes: Leading parties are in bold; parties with less than 4 percent of the vote in the most recent election have generally been excluded. Parties are listed in order of popular vote in latest election. Some of the ideological depictions are imprecise and in some counties (such as Sweden) alliances of parties have been formed.

argue that Western party systems were changing, with the alignments between social groups and political parties becoming less important (Dalton, 2006). Nevertheless, the party systems in many Western countries still reflect, to varying extents, the continuing significance of their cleavage structures.

Ideology and the Party System

Although electoral–professional parties generally tend to downplay their ideological positioning, most party systems do feature at least some degree of ideological competition. As indicated in Table 6-1, many countries feature competition between social democratic parties on the left and conservative or Christian Democratic parties[1] on the right.

It is often argued that political parties will tend to adopt similar positions as they seek to win elections (as discussed in Box 6-2 Do Parties Tend to Converge in Their Basic Positions?). Some researchers have found a tendency for the leading parties to become less ideological as time passes and to drift to the centre of the ideological spectrum (Caul & Gray, 2000). As well, there has been a tendency for parties established to represent particular segments of society to move

---

[1]Christian Democratic parties generally combine traditional Christian social and moral views with notions of social solidarity and the common good that reject the individualism of laissez-faire capitalism as well as opposing the ideas of class struggle and state planning of classical socialism. Although arising out of Catholic social movements, Christian Democratic parties have also found support among conservative Protestants in some continental European countries.

BOX 6-2   Do Parties Tend to Converge in Their Basic Positions?

In *An Economic Theory of Democracy* (1957), Anthony Downs argued that in a two-party system, parties will converge in the ideological centre, defined in terms of the ideological position held by the largest number of voters. Assuming that voters are aware of the positioning of the parties and will vote for the party that is closest to their own position, a left-wing party will find that it gains more votes as it moves toward the centre. Likewise, there is a strong electoral incentive for a right-wing party to move to the centre such that the two parties become virtually indistinguishable in ideological terms. It should be noted that Downs's theory does not apply fully to situations where there are more than two parties. If, for example, there is a far-left party as well as a moderate leftist party, the moderate leftist party may lose votes to the far-left party if it moves too close to the centre.

Although Downs's theory provides a simple model of the dynamics of party competition, it has also been subject to criticism. Party members may choose leaders and candidates whose policy positions most closely resemble their own position rather than that of the average voter, thus leading parties to move away from

the ideological centre (Adams & Merrill, 2005). Many of those active in a political party are concerned not only with winning elections, but also with implementing their views about what is best for the political community. Thus, party activists who are committed to a particular perspective may seek to move their party in a more distinctive ideological direction. Furthermore, parties need to distinguish themselves from their opponents in order to appeal to voters, supporters, and financial backers. In particular, opposition parties need to distinguish themselves from the governing party in order to make their case for a change in government. Overall, there is a strong relationship between the ideological position taken by a political party and those who vote for that party (Dalton, Farrell, & McAllister, 2011). Furthermore, a vigorous appeal to right-wing or left-wing themes may, at times, have a greater appeal to voters than a bland centrist appeal. For example, the Conservative Party led by Margaret Thatcher and the Republican Party led by Ronald Reagan were successful with their right-wing ideological appeal to voters.

toward a broader appeal. For example, the British Labour party, under the leadership of Tony Blair (prime minister from 1997–2007), dropped its commitment to public ownership of industry and moved away from a focus on the interests of the working class. This was not simply a successful electoral strategy; it also reflected the moderate ideological vision (termed the "Third Way") of Blair and his supporters. However, the election of Jeremy Corbyn as Labour Party leader in 2015 indicated that the majority of ordinary party members preferred to return to the party's democratic socialist ideological roots. Similarly, New Right, Christian Right, and right-wing populist ideologies have become more influential within the U.S. Republican party than moderate versions of conservatism. In Canada, the centrist Liberal party has often been described as non-ideological. Nevertheless, there have been substantial ideological differences among the major Canadian parties since 1980 (Cochrane, 2010). Although the NDP has moved somewhat towards the ideological centre, the Conservative Party has moved to the right (Bittner & Koop, 2013). The Liberal Party moved toward the left in the 2015 election campaign taking votes away from the NDP. At the time of writing it was not clear to what extent this would be reflected in Liberal government policies and whether the NDP would return to a more leftist position.

NEW PARTIES The establishment of new parties can also contribute to making the party system more ideological. In recent decades, Green parties promoting an environmentalist perspective along with advocacy concerning social justice, feminism, grassroots democracy, and peace have been established in about seventy countries.

Likewise, in recent decades, new right-wing populist parties generally favouring major tax cuts, substantial reductions in government, and having strong nationalist and anti-immigrant appeals (including the United Kingdom Independence Party, the Swiss People's Party, France's Front National, Denmark's People's Party, Norway's Progress Party, Hungary's Jobbik Party, the Slovak National Party, and Alternative for Germany) have at times been able to gain significant support in several countries, as have a few extreme right-wing or neo-fascist parties (such as Greece's Golden Dawn Party and Slovakia's People's Party). The influx of millions of refugees from Syria and other Muslim countries in 2015 and 2016 generally increased support for radical right-wing populist parties. Thus, even if competition among the leading parties often tends to be more about gaining power than debating different ideological perspectives, new parties may inject different basic points of view into the party system. In some cases, this has encouraged other parties to adopt positions advocated by newer parties in order to avoid losing some of their supporters.

Two-Party, Multiparty, and One-Party Dominant Systems

In addition to characterizing party systems in terms of cleavages and ideological competition, party systems are often analyzed in terms of the number of significant political parties. The number of parties varies considerably. In the United States, there are only two significant parties (the Democratic and Republican parties). In contrast, at the time of writing, Italy had ten parties represented in its Chamber of Deputies (organized into 4 groupings), and Israel had ten parties or groupings represented in its legislative body, the Knesset.

A distinction is often made between two-party, multiparty, and one-party dominant systems. In a **two-party system** (as, for example, in the United States, Malta, and Jamaica), the two leading parties typically win the vast majority of seats in the legislature.[2] This usually results in the formation of a majority government (that is, one in which the governing party has a majority of the

two-party system

A party system in which two major parties contend to control the government.

---

[2] Some political scientists prefer to characterize party systems in terms of the proportion of votes parties receive rather than in terms of the proportion of seats.

FIGURE 6-1   Party Representation in the Canadian House of Commons, 1953–2015

Notes: Progressive Conservative (PC) Party 1953–2000; Conservative Party, 2004–2015; CCF 1953–1958; NDP 1962–2015; Social Credit (and Ralliement Créditiste) 1953–1980; Reform Party 1988–1997; Canadian Alliance, 2000. Independents and Green Party not shown.

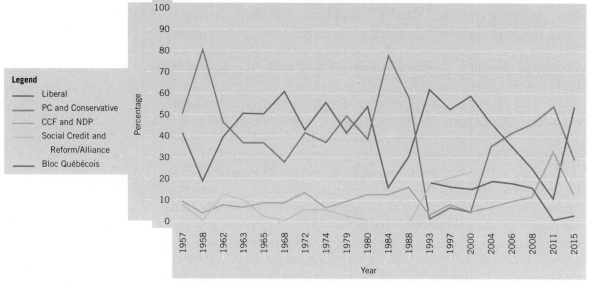

Sources: Calculated from H.G. Thorburn & A. Whitehorn (Eds.), *Party politics in Canada* (8th ed.), Toronto: Prentice-Hall, 2001; and Elections Canada (2004, 2006, 2008, 2011, and 2015), retrieved from www.elections.ca

members in its legislature. Two-party systems are competitive in the sense that a single party does not usually govern for a lengthy period of time.

multiparty system

A political party system featuring several parties that are significant actors in the competition for political power.

Multiparty systems, the most common democratic party system, feature three or more parties with significant legislative representation. In a *two-plus party system* (also called a two-and-a-half party system), the two leading parties usually win at least 75 or 80 percent of the seats, but one or more of the smaller parties has sufficient support to prevent, from time to time, either of the leading parties from gaining a majority of seats. From 1921 to 1993, Canada could be characterized as having a two-plus party system (see Figure 6-1). In a *moderate multiparty system*, there are three to five significant parties, with the two leading parties usually having less than four-fifths of the seats. Many countries could be characterized as having a moderate multiparty system, including contemporary Canada[3], Germany, and Austria. Finally, in *fragmented multiparty systems* (such as in Italy, Netherlands,

---

[3]Although the two leading parties gained 87% of the vote in the 2011 election and 83% in the 2015 election, the two leading parties were the Conservative party and the NDP in 2011 and the Liberal and Conservative parties in 2015. Thus Canada is best described as currently having a moderate multiparty system at the national level because there have been three parties that have had a large proportion of seats in at least one of the past two elections. This may change if a more consistent pattern develops in future elections.

Belgium, and Israel) there are five or more significant parties, with typically no single party having a large number of seats (Siaroff, 2009a). Multiparty systems are often governed by a coalition of political parties.

In a few cases, liberal democracies have had a **one-party dominant system** in which a predominant party governs for a lengthy period of time because the opposition is divided among a number of parties, none of which has the support needed to mount an effective challenge to the governing party. This has been the case in some Canadian provinces (notably Alberta until recently) and American states (particularly in the south) as well as in Botswana and South Africa. Japan is often described as having a one-party dominant system as the Liberal Democratic Party (LDP) has formed the government almost exclusively since a democratic system was imposed after World War II. However, the LDP consists of a number of shifting factions resulting in thirty-five changes in prime ministers from 1945 to 2009 (Steinmo, 2010). Competition often exists within parties as well as between parties.

Many contemporary non-democratic countries are one-party systems in which only one party is allowed or in which opposition parties are prevented from mounting an effective challenge to the governing party (for example, by harassment or imprisonment of opposition party members, lack of access to the media, or by the falsification of election results).

The number of significant political parties is affected, in part, by the electoral system. Countries with proportional representation systems generally have more significant parties in their legislatures than countries that have a single member plurality electoral system (which usually gives a boost in representation to the largest parties). In Canada, which has used the single member plurality electoral system, only the Liberal and Conservative parties have ever formed the government at the national level (except for a coalition government formed during World War I). Nevertheless, Canada has had a number of minority governments (that is, one in which the governing party has less than half of the seats in the House of Commons). Elections from 1957 to 2015 resulted in nine minority and twelve majority governments. The 2011 and 2015 elections produced majority governments even though the party that won a majority of seats obtained slightly less than two-fifths of the popular vote.

one-party dominant system

A party system in which a single party rules for long periods of time and the opposition parties are not likely to gain the support needed to successfully challenge the dominant party for control of the government.

PARTY ORGANIZATION

Imagine that you decide to join a political party. Undoubtedly you would be asked to help the party elect its candidate in your district in the next election. In addition to paying a very small membership fee (depending on the party), you would likely be encouraged to make a regular donation to the party. But would your opinions and the opinions of other "ordinary" members of the party have a substantial effect on how the political community is governed? To discuss this question, we need to examine the organization and operations of political parties. In particular, we need to look at the extent to which ordinary party members (those not sitting as part of a legislative body) are influential in selecting the party leader and the candidates that represent the party in an election and in developing and deciding on the policy positions that the party takes.

Selecting the Party Leader

Choosing a party leader is a very important task for political parties. Not only is the leader the chief spokesperson for the party but, more importantly in a parliamentary system, the leader whose party gains the most representatives in an election usually (but not always) becomes the head of government. In effect, parties choose the most powerful person in government as well as the leaders of the opposition parties.

There are several different methods that parties use to choose their leaders:

- *Selection by parliamentary party.* The parliamentary party selects the leader in some countries, such as Australia. Such a system, unlike other alternatives below, ensures that leaders have the support of their colleagues so that they can lead their party effectively in Parliament. Leaders chosen by the parliamentary party are likely to have considerable parliamentary experience, and candidates do not need financial backing to seek the leadership. Selection exclusively by the parliamentary party, however, does not provide a voice for ordinary citizens who are party members.
- *Selection at party conventions.* Party conventions allow various components of the party to participate in the election of the leader. Typically, delegates elected from each electoral district, along with the party's legislators, party officials, candidates, and representatives of different associations within the party (such as those representing women, youth, or students), choose among leadership candidates at a party convention. The standard procedure in Canada has been to hold successive ballots. The candidate with the least number of votes or any candidate not receiving a certain number of votes is dropped from the ballot, and new votes are held until one candidate has a majority of the votes cast. For example, following the resignation of Dalton McGuinty, the Liberal Party of Ontario held a convention in January 2013 at which about three-quarters of the delegates were elected by party members. Six candidates were on the first ballot but none gained a majority of votes. Kathleen Wynne defeated Sandra Pupatello on the third ballot.

  While party conventions are more representative of the party as a whole than is the parliamentary party, the choice of the convention will not necessarily reflect the choice of all party members. Delegates tend to have a higher socio-economic position than the general membership (in part because of the costs of attending a convention) and the presence of substantial numbers of non-elected delegates may give party elites some ability to influence the results. On the other hand, delegates to a party convention are likely to be committed party members, and party conventions allow those choosing the leader to meet the candidates, hear their speeches, and discuss the merits of the candidates with other delegates.

- *Selection by direct membership vote.* In recent times, some parties have decided to choose their leader by a direct membership vote through the use of mail-in ballots, telephone, or the Internet. That is, all party members have the opportunity to choose among the leadership candidates. In some ways, the direct membership vote is the most democratic way of choosing a leader. It not only allows each party member a direct voice in choosing a leader, but also makes it easier for party members who cannot spend the money or devote the time to attend a leadership convention to participate in the choice. As well, the ability of candidates to perform well in an election campaign can be tested by their campaign for party leadership. However, direct membership vote systems can place the power to select a leader in the hands of those with little or no involvement or attachment to the party.

Canadian parties adopted the party convention method of choosing a party leader in the first decades of the twentieth century. In recent years, the major national parties (as well as many provincial parties) have adopted direct membership vote systems. Both the Liberal and Conservative parties use a system in which each electoral district is given an equal number of points regardless of the number of persons voting. The winning candidate needs to receive a majority of points. The NDP uses a one-member, one-vote system.

Removing a Party Leader

Removing a party leader can be highly contentious. Although some leaders voluntarily resign after their party performs poorly in an election, a few leaders have been reluctant to resign even when it is apparent they are a liability to their party. In other situations, unhappiness about the prime minister's policies or the ambitions of a potential leader has resulted in the removal or resignation of a leader who is prime minister. For example, Paul Martin was able to mobilize Liberal Party members to challenge Prime Minister Jean Chrétien's leadership. Chrétien decided to retire earlier than planned in 2003 rather than be humiliated by a party leadership review vote. Prime Minister Margaret Thatcher resigned in 1990 despite winning three UK elections when it appeared certain that an opponent within the party would be selected leader. Likewise, pressure from his party led to the resignation of three-term Labour prime minister Tony Blair in 2007.

The Canadian Conservative Party's constitution requires that a vote be held at a party convention after an election loss to determine if the leadership selection process should be initiated. Similarly, after an election defeat the Liberal Party holds a party membership vote on whether to endorse their leader. These parties thus prevent a prime minister from facing a challenge from party members. However, legislation passed in 2014 allows each party's parliamentary caucus, after a general election, to decide if they want to adopt a process to conduct a leadership review and elect an interim leader. At every biennial party convention, the NDP holds a vote concerning whether a leadership contest should be conducted.

In Australia the parliamentary caucus of a party can vote to oust their leader at any time (termed leadership "spill"). In 2010, Kevin Rudd, who had led the Australian Labour party to victory in 2007, resigned after it became apparent that he no longer had the support of his party's parliamentary caucus. His successor, Julia Gillard, was defeated in 2013 by a caucus vote, and Rudd was elected as party leader (and became prime minister). In 2015, Liberal leader and prime minister, Tony Abbott, was ousted by a majority of his party's parliamentary caucus. Malcolm Turnbull was elected as party leader who then took over as prime minister.

Candidate Selection

Political parties are very important in the selection of candidates for election. Very few candidates are successful in being elected unless they represent a political party. In Canada, party members usually vote to choose their party's candidate, although the Liberal Party gives its leader the right to appoint a number of candidates without a vote of the party members in the district. Canadian parties have sometimes automatically renominated all their sitting members of Parliament. In addition, parties vet potential candidates to try to ensure that there is nothing in their background that could be embarrassing to the party. Indeed, a number of candidates in the 2015 Canadian election were forced to withdraw when their party found embarrassing postings on Facebook or other social media from years prior to their nomination.

In some countries, party members select delegates to make the candidate selection. Still others rely on local or regional party officials or a candidate selection committee. Generally, most of the advanced democracies involve the local or regional party organization in the selection process, with the party leader or party executive having the ability to veto the choice of candidates (Scarrow, Webb, & Farrell, 2000). In 2011, the French Socialist Party held a direct election of their presidential candidate by all registered voters who said they supported the values of the Left. Nearly 8 million votes were cast and the winner, François Hollande, was elected president of France in 2012. A similar process open to anyone

International Institute for Democracy and Electoral Assistance, Quota Project
www.quotaproject.org/aboutQuotas. cfm

GONNA BE GREEAAAAAAAT!!!

Many Republican politicians feared that Donald Trump's racist, misogynist, deceitful, fear-mongering speeches would lead to a disaster for the party in the 2016 presidential election. However, Trump won the election (although receiving about 2 1/2 million fewer votes than Hillary Clinton because of the workings of the Electoral College system discussed in Chapter 7).

Tami Thirlwell

who identified themselves as centrist or centre-right was used by, the parti Républicain (formerly UMP), to choose its presidential candidate in 2016. The Democratic and Republican parties in the United States use a complex system for choosing their presidential candidate (as discussed in Box 6-3 The Amazing Races: Seeking the Republican and Democratic Presidential Nominations, 2016).

Gender Quotas

The constitutions or laws of a considerable number of countries (for example, France, Belgium, Argentina, and Mexico) require that parties nominate a certain proportion of women as candidates. Parties failing to nominate the required proportion of female candidates may have the public subsidy for their operations reduced or even have their slate of candidates rejected by election officials. A few countries reserve a certain proportion of seats in their legislative body for women. Rwanda, which reserves 24 of the 80 seats in its Chamber of Deputies, is the country with the highest proportion of women (63.75%) in its

BOX 6-3　The Amazing Races: Seeking the Republican and Democratic Presidential Nomination, 2016

The presidential candidates for the Democratic and Republican parties in the United States are selected by a vote of each party's national convention usually held about two months before the November presidential election. However, the choice of who will be each party's presidential candidate is normally decided by primary elections and party caucuses held in each of the country's states and territories on various dates in the first half of the election year. **Primary elections**, conducted by state governments in a large majority of states, allow registered supporters of a party (including, in some states, those not affiliated to a party) to vote for their preferred candidate. A much smaller number of states (including U.S. territories) use a unique American party caucus system in which registered party supporters meet in each community, may discuss the candidates, and select delegates pledged to vote for a candidate.[4] In addition, about 15% of the voting delegates at the Democratic national convention are "super-delegates" (officeholders and party officials).

The 2016 race for the presidential nomination was unusual in that prominent contenders for the parties were party "outsiders." Donald J. Trump, the successful Republican candidate, had no political experience and had at one time been a member of the Democratic party. His unusual campaign involved blistering attacks on his Republican opponents and included promising to build a wall to keep out Mexicans and make Mexico pay for it, a temporary ban on Muslims entering the United States, deporting 11 million illegal immigrants, and opposing free trade (including withdrawing from the North American Free Trade Agreement). Indeed, the positions he took were often different from positions associated with the Republican party. His personal attacks on individuals, negative comments about women and various minorities, and many contradictory, crude, and inflammatory statements gained him extensive free media coverage that far exceeded media coverage of the other candidates. Despite being a billionaire, Trump tapped into the anger of many ordinary Americans against politicians and the direction of the country.

The Democratic race was expected to be a shoo-in for Hillary Clinton who had considerable political experience, substantial financial support, took positions that fit the mainstream of the Democratic party, and had overwhelming support from the party establishment. She had come close to winning the Democratic presidential nomination in 2008, and the idea of electing the first female president appealed to many. Her main opponent, Bernie Sanders, identified himself as a democratic socialist, had been involved in protest movements, and sat in the US Senate as an independent. His campaign focused heavily on reversing the increasingly high level of inequality of wealth and income in the United States, and promises of universal health care, child care, and free post-secondary education. Strongly critical of Clinton's ability to raise campaign funds from the wealthy, the Sanders campaign raised even more money from millions of small donations. Seventy-four year-old Sanders drew strong support from young Americans, and made the contest for delegates (other than super-delegates) a close race. Unlike the 16 candidates for the Republican nomination who dropped out during the race, Sanders fought to the end to promote his ideas even when it became obvious he could not win.

---

[4]The Democratic party divides state delegates committed to a candidate in proportion to the votes cast for each candidate that received at least 15% of the vote. Some Republican primaries use a proportional system while others use a "winner take all" system based either on winning more votes than the other candidates or winning at least 50% of the vote. In some states, delegates go to a county and/or a state convention where they vote for delegates to the national convention.

The adoption of primary elections in the early twentieth century reflected a distrust of parties and concern about the corrupt practices often associated with party "bosses" and party "machines." However, the primary system weakens political parties since they do not have much control over the selection of party candidates, and reinforces the tendency in American politics for legislators of each party to act independently rather than as members of a group.

Primary elections provide an opportunity for those with little or no political experience (such as Donald Trump) to win a party's nomination if they can mount a strong public campaign. Potential candidates have to raise very large sums of money to win a nomination, thus making successful candidates dependent on the support of wealthy backers, a large personal fortune, or in unusual cases, the ability to appeal to millions of people to make small donations.

legislature (Interparliamentary Union, 2016).[5] Voluntary gender quotas have been adopted by at least 168 political parties in 69 countries (International Institute for Democracy and Electoral Assistance, 2007a). Quotas, if substantial, may compensate for the obstacles that many women face in seeking public office. As well, it gives women a greater voice in making laws and public policies. The use of quotas, however, may reduce the ability of party members and voters to select their preferred candidate and will not necessarily result in the election of candidates committed to improving the position of women.

In Canada, there are no legally established quotas for female candidates and the proportion of female candidates is fairly low (see Table 6-2). Some political parties, however, have undertaken to try to nominate more female candidates. The NDP has set an objective of having 60 percent female candidates in "winnable" constituencies (excluding those where the incumbent is seeking re-election) and requires that constituencies prove that they have searched for one or more potential candidates who are female or from other under-represented groups before selecting a candidate. Liberal party rules for the 2015 election required each electoral district to "provide documented evidence of a thorough search for potential candidates who are female and who are a reflection of the demographic and linguistic of the local electorate" although a provincial or territorial committee could waive this requirement (Liberal Party of Canada, 2013, Rule 1.7). Unlike several previous elections the Liberal party did not set a specific target of at least one-third female candidates. The Conservative party has, thus far, not adopted measures to encourage a representative slate of candidates.

As Table 6-2 indicates the Liberal party was not particularly successful in nominating female candidates in the 2015 election. Nevertheless, Prime Minister Trudeau decided to appoint equal numbers of women and men to his cabinet. When asked why having a cabinet with an equal number of men and women is important to him, he famously replied "because it's 2015."

primary election

A state-run election in which citizens vote for the candidate of their preferred party that they want to be chosen to run in the general election.

---

[5]Some countries also reserve a certain number of seats for ethnic, linguistic, or religious minorities.

TABLE 6-2

Percentage and Number of Female Candidates and Elected Members of Parliament by Party, 2015 Canadian Election

PARTY	% (NUMBER) OF PARTY'S CANDIDATES	% (NUMBER) OF PARTY'S ELECTED MEMBERS
Liberal	31.1% (105)	27.2% (50)
Conservative	19.2 (65)	17.2 (17)
NDP	42.9 (145)	40.1 (18)
Bloc Québécois	28.2 (21)	20.0 (2)
Green	40.2 (135)	100.0 (1)
Total (5 parties)	33.0% (471)	26.0% (88)

Source: Calculated and adapted from *History of Federal Ridings since 1867, Women Candidates in General Elections - 1921 to Date,* Library of Parliament, data retrieved from www.parl.gc.ca/About/Parliament/FederalRidingsHistory/hfer.asp?Language=E&Search=WomenElection. Reproduced with the permission of the Library of Parliament, 2015.

Party Policy

Parties with mass origins generally give formal authority to a party convention to approve the policy positions that the party is supposed to pursue, while parties with cadre origins typically view policies adopted at party conventions as only one source of advice for the leader and the party's parliamentary members. Indeed, until the 1960s, the Liberal and PC parties of Canada did not hold regular party conventions to discuss policy. Policy resolutions proposed at leadership conventions were not always thoroughly discussed, formally voted upon, carefully recorded, or made accessible.

In some parties, there is vigorous debate over policy resolutions at party conventions, providing an opportunity for active party members to be involved in the discussion of party policy positions. However, the party leader and key party officials often exercise a considerable degree of control over the process of discussing and adopting resolutions at a party convention. Efforts may be made to modify or avoid a vote on resolutions that could harm a party in its attempts to gain public support. Furthermore, the election platforms of parties are typically developed by the party leader, the leader's advisers, and campaign experts concerned with successfully marketing the party to the electorate. In the legislature, the party leader and parliamentary party members often feel free to interpret party resolutions as they see fit. After their party is elected, the prime minister and Cabinet typically argue that they have to make decisions that are for the good of the country as a whole, or to carry out election campaign promises, rather than acting in accordance with their party's policy resolutions.

Overall, then, party members are more likely to have an effective voice in candidate and leadership selection than in determining the policies that their party will pursue. Nevertheless, modern political parties do, to varying extents, involve their ordinary members in policy discussion even if control of party policy decisions rests largely in the hands of the party leadership (Scarrow, Webb, & Farrell, 2000).

Party Caucus and Party Government

Parliamentary parties are generally tightly organized. There is a strong expectation that each party's members of Parliament will support the positions that the **party caucus** (a closed-door meeting of the party's parliamentary members) has decided to take. In particular, party leaders typically exercise considerable influence and control over their party's members of Parliament. Party discipline is weaker in the United States, and presidents do not control their party's members of Congress.

Political parties play a crucial role in governing especially in parliamentary systems. The prime minister and Cabinet are almost always members of a particular parliamentary party (or, in the case of coalition governments, members of the parties forming the coalition) and rely on the support of their parliamentary party to maintain their positions and to approve their legislative and budgetary proposals. However, this does not necessarily mean that the governing party as a whole has a high level of influence on the decisions of the government, as the prime minister and Cabinet (along with various advisers) are crucial in making policy decisions.

party caucus

A closed-door meeting of the party's parliamentary members.

PARTY FINANCE

Parties need considerable amounts of money to finance their operations and conduct expensive election campaigns. The financing of political parties and candidates has often been considered a major political problem (see Box 6-4 "Granny D"). Those whose make large donations often seek to influence government policies or gain specific benefits through their financial support. Politicians may be more concerned about maintaining the support of their financial backers—often large corporations and wealthy individuals—than about acting for the common good.

Many countries establish limits on election expenses, put restrictions on campaign advertising, provide public subsidies to parties and campaigns, and require public disclosure of the names of donors. Generally, this allows for fairer competition among political parties, reduces the likelihood that undue influence will be placed on politicians, and limits the taint of scandal and corruption that has often been associated with money in politics. However, government financing of political parties can be used to discriminate against smaller or new political parties and thus maintain the dominance of the larger, established parties. As well, the dependence of parties on public funds may reduce their incentive to maintain strong ties with their supporters (Katz & Mair, 1995).

In the United States, there are no limits on campaign spending for Congressional elections and no public subsidies for these campaigns. Candidates in presidential primaries and presidential elections can receive public money to match individual donations (if they raise money in at least twenty states) provided they are willing to limit their total campaign expenses. In the 2012 election, neither

BOX 6-4   "Granny D": Raise a Little Hell

On January 1, 1999, 89-year-old Doris "Granny D" Haddock began a walk across the United States to publicize the need for campaign finance reform. For 14 months, the great-grandmother slogged through deserts, climbed mountain ranges, braved blizzards, and even skied 62 kilometres when the roads were impassable before reaching Washington, DC.

Haddock argued that the American political system had been corrupted by the huge amounts of money corporations give to candidates in return for grants and legislation that make these corporations highly profitable at the expense of ordinary citizens. After her trek, she continued to actively participate in rallies and demonstrations despite being jailed twice. Finally, in 2002, Congress passed a campaign reform bill banning corporations and labour unions from broadcast advertising that explicitly promoted the election or defeat of specific candidates sixty days before an election. Relying on small donations, Haddock ran for the U.S. Senate in 2004, saying, "You're never too old to raise a little hell." She received about one-third of the votes cast.

In January 2010, the U.S. Supreme Court in a five-to-four vote supported a challenge by "Citizens United" (a political action committee promoting the interests of large corporations and conservative causes) to election financing restrictions. The majority ruled that the protection of free speech in the Constitution meant that limits on corporations and unions seeking to influence elections were unconstitutional. This resulted in the formation of "Super PACs" (political action committees) that can raise and spend unlimited amounts of money

"Granny D" fought tirelessly against the corruption of American politics caused by large corporate campaign contributions.
Jim Cole/AP Images

from any source and run campaign advertising provided they do not act in concert with a party or candidate. Indeed, non-profit PACs do not have to reveal the names of those who donated money. President Barack Obama called the decision "a major victory for big oil, Wall Street banks, health insurance companies and other powerful interests that marshal their power every day in Washington to drown out the voices of everyday Americans" (quoted by Liptak, 2010).

Haddock's voice was silenced on March 12, 2010, when she died at age 100. Undoubtedly, she would have been outraged to learn that the two Koch brothers (major funders of Citizens United) were planning to spend up to one billion dollars to support right-wing Republican candidates in the 2016 election (Meyer, 2016).

Barack Obama nor Mitt Romney were willing to accept limits to their campaign expenses, which amounted to about US$1 billion each, including spending by Super PACs, in support of their candidacy (Braun & Gillum, 2012).

Until 2004, there were no limits on contributions to political parties and candidates at the national level in Canada. The Liberal and PC parties relied heavily on contributions from large corporations to fund their parties and their election campaigns. The NDP derived a significant proportion of its funding from unions. Beginning in 2004, contributions by businesses and labour unions were banned. Individuals are now limited to contributing a maximum of about $1500 (indexed to inflation) per year to each of the following: registered political parties, other party entities (district associations, nomination contestants, and candidates), leadership contestants, and independent candidates. There are also spending limits on election-oriented advertising by groups or individuals that are not parties or candidates.

The restrictions on contributions are offset, to some extent, by payments to Canadian parties from public funds. Parties are reimbursed for 50 percent of their eligible campaign expenses.[6] Candidates are reimbursed for 60 percent of their expenses if they obtain at least 10 percent of the vote in their electoral district. There are also limits on the spending of candidates and parties in elections and nomination contests, public disclosure of contributors and expenditures, and generous tax credits for individuals who make relatively small contributions to parties and candidates.

---

[6]This is provided only to parties that receive at least 2 percent of the valid vote nationally or at least 5 percent in all the electoral districts in which the party ran candidates.

✓• SUMMARY AND CONCLUSION

Political parties play a central role in the competition for political power and in the governing of modern democratic states. Political parties have been criticized for being organizations dominated by the party leader and a small number of party insiders. The involvement of people who join political parties is often limited to canvassing on behalf of the party's candidates during election campaigns. However, political parties generally have become more democratic in the processes they use to select their leaders and candidates and in the holding of regular party policy conventions. Changes in the regulation of party finance in Canada and a number of other countries (with the exception of the United States) have helped to reduce the influence on political parties of big business and wealthy donors.

The intense partisanship and the view that "winning is all that matters" in the competitive struggle for power has alienated many people from party politics (Obama, 2006, p. 51). Instead of debating possible solutions to problems, political parties often focus on trivial issues,

mislead the public about the positions taken by the contending parties, and turn rational discussion into emotional arguments.

Nevertheless, political parties are a crucial element of democracy. As E. E. Schattschneider (1942/1977) asserted, "political parties created democracy, and modern democracy is unthinkable save in terms of the parties" (p. 1). A competitive party system allows voters to choose which set of politicians should be responsible for governing and which party's platform and perspective they prefer. Parties are also important in aggregating (putting together) the interests and perspectives of different sectors of society and trying to develop a coherent program for governing that will have wide support. Thus, it has been argued that parties are essential "to bring interests together for the common good" (Dalton & Wattenburg, 2000, pp. 283–284). Indeed, by mobilizing people who might otherwise be ignored in political life, strong political parties potentially can be important instruments of change and social justice.

✓• KEY TERMS

Brokerage party   126
Cadre party   124
Cleavage   130
Electoral–professional party   126
Iron law of oligarchy   125

Mass party   124
Multiparty system   134
One-party dominant system   135
Party caucus   143
Party convention   124

Personalistic party   128
Political party   124
Primary election   141
Programmatic party   126
Two-party system   133

◆ DISCUSSION QUESTIONS

1. Is there a particular party (or more than one party) that reflects your viewpoints, interests, or identity, or do you feel that none of the major parties really represents you?

2. Are all of the major interests and viewpoints in Canada adequately represented by the major Canadian parties?

3. Is it important for political parties to be democratic in their organization?

4. How should parties choose their leaders?

5. Is the common good better served by two parties with a broad appeal or by a multiparty system in which a variety of different societal interests and ideological perspectives are represented?

6. Are political parties a necessary and desirable feature of democratic politics?

FURTHER READING

Bittner, A. & Koop, R. (Eds.). (2013). *Parties, elections and the future of Canadian politics.* Vancouver: UBC Press.

Cross, W. (2004). *Political parties.* Vancouver: UBC Press.

Cross, W.P. & Blais, A. (2012). *Politics at the centre: The selection and removal of party leaders in the Anglo parliamentary democracies.* Oxford, UK: Oxford University Press.

Dalton, R.J., Farrell, D., & McAllister, I. (2011). *Political parties and democratic linkage: How parties organize democracy.* Oxford, UK: Oxford University Press.

Gagnon, A.-G., & Tanguay, A.B. (Eds.). (2007). *Canadian parties in transition* (3rd ed.). Peterborough, ON: Broadview Press.

Gunther, R., Montero, J.R., & Linz, J.J. (Eds.). (2002). *Political parties: Old concepts and new challenges.* Oxford: Oxford University Press.

Johnston, R.; Sharman, C. (Eds.). (2015). *Parties and Party Systems: Structure and Context.* Vancouver, B.C.: UBC Press.

Katz, R.S., & Crotty, W. (Eds.). (2006). *Handbook of party politics.* London, UK: Sage.

Stonecash, J.M. (2013). *Understanding American political parties. Democratic ideals, political uncertainty, and strategic positioning.* New York: Routledge.

7 Elections, Electoral Systems, and Voting Behaviour

On May 5, 2015, Rachel Notley led the NDP to its first victory in an Alberta provincial election. The NDP increased its representation in the legislature from 4 to 54 and more than quadrupled its share of the vote compared to the previous election.   Felix Choo/Alamy Stock Photo

After reading this chapter, you should be able to:

1. discuss what is needed for elections to be considered free and fair
2. explain and evaluate the different types of electoral systems
3. evaluate the usefulness of election campaigns in helping people decide how to vote
4. outline the different factors that explain voting behaviour

On May 5, 2015, Rachel Notley led the NDP to a stunning victory in the Alberta provincial election winning 54 of the province's 87 legislative seats. In the previous election (2012), the NDP won only 4 seats. The NDP's share of the vote increased from 9.9 percent to 40.6 percent. The NDP victory was particularly surprising because Alberta has the reputation of being Canada's most conservative province: the Progressive Conservative (PC) party governed from 1971–2015 and the right-wing Social Credit party from 1935–1971.

Rachel Notley, the daughter of a former Alberta NDP leader who died in a plane crash while campaigning, graduated with degrees in political science and law. Prior to being elected to the Alberta legislature in 2008, she was employed as an occupational health and safety officer, was an assistant to the B.C. attorney general, and worked with public service unions. Notley was elected NDP leader on October 18, 2014.

In 2015, Progressive Conservative (PC) premier Jim Prentice (a former minister in Stephen Harper's federal cabinet) presented a budget that included severe cuts to social programs, and higher taxes (except corporate taxes) and fees because of a large provincial deficit. Despite the province's election law that established a fixed four-year term, Prentice asked the lieutenant governor to call an election a year earlier. With nine members of the official opposition Wildrose party (including its leader) defecting to the PCs, Prentice thought the time was right for an election that his party could win. Despite his extensive political experience, Prentice performed poorly in the campaign. In particular, his comment in the televised leader's debate that "math is difficult" in a response to Notley was seen by many as patronizing or sexist. The PCs won only 10 seats and Prentice resigned as leader and legislative member.

The Alberta election illustrates two important points. First, elections can bring dramatic changes. The NDP victory was completely unexpected—far beyond the NDP's hopes. Second, the election result showed that the electoral system used in Canada, the single-member plurality system, provides a distorted reflection of the votes for each party. With 40.6 percent of the vote, the NDP received 62.1 percent of the seats in the Alberta legislature. This creation of an artificial majority is not unusual. In the 2011 Canadian election, the Conservatives won 53.9 percent of the seats based on 39.6 percent of the vote. Likewise, in the 2015 Canadian election, the Liberals won 54.4 percent of the seats based on 39.5 percent of the vote. Based on a minority of votes, a party can govern as if they had majority support.

DEMOCRATIC ELECTIONS

Nearly all countries now hold elections. However, elections vary greatly, from those that can be considered democratic in terms of ensuring that voters have a free and fair choice to those that coerce or manipulate voters into endorsing a dictatorial ruler. The practice of elections in many countries, particularly newer democracies, falls between these two extremes. Even long-established democracies do not necessarily provide a completely fair election process.

Meaningful Elections

Elections are only meaningful if those elected have real power. Voters should be able to choose freely among candidates and parties seeking office. To protect voters from intimidation and to discourage bribery, a secret ballot should be used. To ensure meaningful competition, all citizens should have the right to run in elections, and all political parties should have the right to nominate candidates and campaign on their behalf.

In other words, an election is not democratic if only those candidates authorized by the state or other institutions are allowed to run or if some parties are prevented from participating in an election campaign. Sometimes, however, even liberal democracies have banned extremist political parties that are viewed as a threat to the democratic system. For example, in the past, Canada banned the Communist party and Germany continues to ban neo-Nazi parties.

UNIVERSAL SUFFRAGE   Democratic elections are based on the principle of "one person, one vote," with each vote having the same value. Thus, we usually only consider a system of elections fully democratic if there is **universal suffrage**; that is, all adult citizens have an equal right to vote regardless of such characteristics as gender, ethnicity, wealth, or education. Further, it should be easy for citizens to exercise their right to vote. For example, provisions should be made for students and others who are away from home on election day to vote, and the use of difficult voter registration requirements should be avoided. Ensuring that each vote has the same value can be controversial, as persons in rural and remote areas worry that their interests will not be given due attention because of the large numbers of voters in the major cities. As well, elected representatives will have a more difficult task in meeting their constituents in large, sparsely populated electoral districts (such as those in northern Canada).

INFORMATION   Voters need to be provided with useful information if their vote is to be meaningful. Parties and candidates must have the opportunity to get their message to voters. This may involve putting some limits on spending to ensure that one party or candidate does not dominate the campaign, and providing some subsidies to help parties and candidates that do not

universal suffrage

The right of all adult citizens to vote regardless of such characteristics as gender, ethnicity, wealth, or education.

have the support of wealthy contributors. Extensive government advertising during an election campaign should be avoided, as it could give the governing party an unfair advantage. The media should provide fair and extensive coverage of the contending parties and candidates.

INDEPENDENT COMMISSIONS   To ensure that elections are conducted fairly, it is important that the process be overseen by an independent commission. The contending parties and candidates should be able to observe the casting and counting of votes. Foreign observers have played a role in ascertaining whether elections have been properly conducted in many countries that have recently become democratic. If there is evidence that the election rules have not been properly followed, losing candidates should have the right to request a recount and to appeal to the courts or an independent body. The adoption of electronic voting systems and Internet voting has raised concerns about electoral fraud. Without physical ballots, recounts may be impossible, and the accuracy of vote tabulations might be questioned.

Similarly, the drawing of electoral district boundaries should be done by an independent body. In 1812, the term **gerrymander** was coined to describe a sprawling electoral district established by Governor Gerry of Massachusetts for partisan advantage that looked like a salamander. Gerrymandering continues to be practised in many countries including the United States, where electoral districts for the US House of Representatives are drawn by the majority party in most state legislatures. In Canada, independent boundary readjustment commissions, usually headed by a judge, have been used since 1964 to readjust federal electoral district boundaries after the decennial census.

A REGULAR VOTE   To ensure that those elected to office are held accountable to the people, it is important that elections be held on a fairly regular basis. In most democratic countries, the election of representatives occurs at least once every four or five years. A small number of countries, including Australia and New Zealand, require that elections be held within a three-year period. In some countries, the dates for elections are fixed by law. For example, the election of the U.S. president is always held on the Tuesday following the first Monday in November every fourth year.

In parliamentary systems, the prime minister and Cabinet have to retain the support of the majority of members of the elected legislature. Failure to maintain that support (as exhibited in a vote of non-confidence in the government or the defeat of a crucial aspect of the government's agenda such as the budget) usually results in an election. In the past, Canadian elections were also held when requested by the prime minister, within a five-year period. The Canada Elections Act was amended in 2007 to require that national elections be held on the third Monday in

Elections Canada
www.elections.ca

ACE Electoral Knowledge Network
www.aceproject.org

International Institute for Democracy and Electoral Assistance
www.idea.int

gerrymander

The manipulation of the division of the country into electoral districts so as to benefit a particular party.

October every four years starting in 2009, although the governor general retains the discretionary power to dissolve Parliament and call an election earlier.[1] Amid considerable controversy, Prime Minister Stephen Harper (who had promoted the adoption of fixed election dates) requested and received permission for an election to be held on October 14, 2008, even though his government (elected in 2006) had not been defeated in the House of Commons. In 2011, the House of Commons passed a motion of non-confidence in the government based on a Commons committee report that the government had been in contempt of Parliament. The governor general then accepted the prime minister's request for an early election on May 2, 2011.

A number of other countries with parliamentary systems have also adopted fixed election dates. For example, in 2001 the United Kingdom adopted legislation requiring that elections be held in May every five years. An election can be held earlier with the agreement of at least two-thirds of the members of the House of Commons or if the government is defeated on a confidence vote and no other parties are able to form a government capable of having the confidence of the House.

ELECTORAL SYSTEMS

There are a variety of **electoral systems** that are used to translate the votes that people cast into the composition of the legislature and the selection of the government. Electoral systems differ in the extent to which they accurately represent the votes cast for each party, provide a close link between representatives and voters, facilitate the accountability of government, and enable governments and representatives to claim that they have the support of the majority of voters. Because none of the electoral systems is best on every one of these criteria, there has been considerable discussion about which electoral system is most desirable.

There are three major types of electoral systems used to elect members to legislative bodies:

- plurality/majoritarian (including single member plurality, runoff elections, and preferential ballot)
- proportional representation
- mixed member proportional

As Table 7-1 indicates, the single member plurality (SMP) and the proportional representation (PR) systems are most common, although the mixed member proportional (MMP) system has also become quite common.

electoral system

The system used to translate the votes that people cast into the composition of the legislature and the selection of the government.

---

[1]Almost all provinces have also adopted legislation establishing that elections normally be held on fixed dates every four years.

TABLE 7-1   Electoral Systems Used to Elect Members of the National Legislature, Selected Countries.

Note: Elections to a lower or single legislative chamber.

SINGLE MEMBER PLURALITY	RUNOFF	PREFERENTIAL BALLOT	PROPORTIONAL REPRESENTATION	MIXED MEMBER PROPORTIONAL	SINGLE TRANSFERABLE VOTE
Bahamas	Central African Republic	Australia	Argentina	Bolivia	Ireland
Bangladesh	France	Fiji	Austria	Germany	Malta
Bermuda	Haiti	Papua New Guinea	Belgium	Hungary	
Botswana	Iran		Brazil	Japan	
Canada	Mali		Czech Republic	Mexico	
Ethiopia	Uzbekistan		Denmark	New Zealand	
Ghana	Vietnam		Finland	Pakistan	
India			Greece	Philippines	
Jamaica			Indonesia	South Korea	
Kenya			Israel	Taiwan	
Liberia			Netherlands	Thailand	
Malaysia			Poland	Tunisia	
Nigeria			Romania	Ukraine	
Tanzania			Russia		
UK			South Africa		
USA			Spain		
			Sweden		
			Switzerland		
			Turkey		

Sources: Compiled from International Institute for Democracy and Electoral Assistance, retrieved from; ACE: The Electoral Knowledge Network, retrieved from www.aceproject.org/ace-en/comparative-data; International Foundation for Electoral Systems Election Guide, retrieved from www.electionguide.org

Plurality and Majoritarian Electoral Systems

Plurality and majoritarian systems typically involve electing a single representative based on which candidate has more votes than any other candidate. In the majoritarian version, the electoral system is designed to try to ensure that the winning candidate has the support of a majority of those voting. Plurality and majoritarian systems often result in a party gaining a majority of legislative seats even if that party did not win a majority of votes.

SINGLE MEMBER PLURALITY   In a **single member plurality (SMP) system** (also known as "first past the post" or "FPTP"), voters in each electoral district elect a single representative to the legislature. The candidate with the most votes is elected, even if that candidate did not receive the majority of votes.

single member plurality (SMP) system

An electoral system in which voters in each electoral district elect a single representative to the legislature. The candidate with the most votes is elected, even if that candidate did not receive the majority of votes.

BOX 7-1   Distortion in the Single Member Plurality System

Imagine a very small legislature consisting of five seats. The hypothetical results of voting in each of the five electoral districts are as follows:

Party A would win all of the seats despite having the support of only 40 percent of the voters, while the substantial proportion of the population who voted for parties B or C would be unrepresented.

	District #1	District #2	District #3	District #4	District #5
Party A	40%	40%	40%	40%	40%
Party B	39%	39%	39%	39%	39%
Party C	21%	21%	21%	21%	21%

Canada, like the United Kingdom and many former British colonies,[2] uses the SMP system. This system provides a simple method for a representative to be chosen from a particular area. However, elections involve more than choosing a representative for a legislative body; they are also very important for choosing a party to form a government for the country and thus involve choices among competing parties. The SMP system tends to inaccurately translate the votes that a party receives across the country into the seats that it receives in the legislature (see Box 7-1 Distortion in the Single Member Plurality System). In particular, the SMP system usually gives an added boost in representation to the leading party (see Table 7-2). The distorting effects of the SMP system are stronger in some elections than others and affect the representation of some parties more than others.

In some cases, the SMP system allows the governing party to completely dominate the legislature, thus hindering the provision of effective opposition to the governing party. For example, the 1987 New Brunswick provincial election resulted in the Liberal Party winning all of the seats based on its 60 percent share of the vote. Similarly, in the 2001 British Columbia provincial election, the Liberals won seventy-seven of the seventy-nine seats based on 57.6 percent of the vote.

The SMP system generally favours the most popular party at the expense of smaller parties. However, parties that have their support concentrated in particular geographical areas tend to do much better than parties with modest support spread across the country. For example, the Bloc Québécois has

---

[2]The United Kingdom used proportional representation to elect members to the European Parliament and mixed member proportional systems are used to elect members to the Scottish Parliament and Welsh Assembly. New Zealand switched from an SMP to a MMP system in 1993 after two consecutive elections in which the party with the most votes did not win the election. In a 2011 referendum, New Zealanders voted to keep the MMP system.

TABLE 7-2   The Impact of the SMP Electoral System: Canada, 2008, 2011, and 2015

Note: "Others" includes independents.

PARTY	2008 ELECTION			2011 ELECTION			2015 ELECTION		
	VOTES	SEATS	DIFFERENCE	VOTES	SEATS	DIFFERENCE	VOTES	SEATS	DIFFERENCE
Conservative	37.7%	46.4%	+8.7	39.6%	53.9%	+14.3	31.9%	29.3%	−2.6
Liberal	26.3%	25.0%	−1.3	18.9%	11.0%	−7.9	39.5%	54.4%	+14.9
NDP	18.2%	12.0%	−6.2	30.6%	33.4%	+2.8	19.7%	13.0%	−6.7
Bloc	10.0%	15.9%	+5.9	6.1%	1.3%	−4.8	4.7%	3.0%	−1.7
Green	6.8%	0.0%	−6.8	3.9%	0.3%	−3.6	3.4%	0.3%	−3.1
Others	1.0%	0.6%	−0.4	1.0%	0.0%	−1.0	0.8%	0.0%	−0.8

Source: Official Election Results, Elections Canada. This reproduction is a copy of the version available at www.elections.ca. Reproduced with the permission of Elections Canada.

Electoral College

A body that elects the president of the United States. Members of the Electoral College from each state are expected to vote for the presidential candidate who has won the most votes in their state.

usually benefited from the workings of the SMP system, while the NDP has received a substantially smaller proportion of seats than votes in every national election except in 2011. Parties with relatively low levels of support are generally unable to gain representation in the legislature. The SMP system tends to exaggerate the regional character of the parties in Parliament. For example, the Conservative Party has appeared more Western-Canadian based in terms of their representation in the House of Commons than in terms of the votes they received. The distorting effects of the electoral system occasionally results in the most popular party losing the election. The 2000 American presidential election illustrates the same basic principle: Republican George W. Bush barely won the presidency, even though the Democratic candidate, Al Gore, gained nearly one-half million more votes, because the candidate winning the most votes in a state receives all of the **Electoral College** votes for that state regardless of the margin of victory.[3]

During the 2015 Canadian election campaign, Justin Trudeau promised that there would not be another federal election under the SMP system. Trudeau seemed to favour a preferential ballot (which might work to the advantage of the Liberal party).

An all-party House of Commons committee was established in June 2016 to consider alternative voting systems to replace the SMP system as well as examining mandatory and online voting. After widespread consultations, the committee was to report by December 1, 2016 with legislation to establish a new electoral system to be passed by Parliament by August 2017 (a deadline

---

[3]In Maine and Nebraska, two electors are selected on a state-wide basis and the remainder are based on the vote in each Congressional district. The Electoral College does not actually meet and has no function other than selecting the president and vice president. Their members, who are selected by each political party, almost always vote for the candidate who received the most votes in their state. If no candidate receives a majority of Electoral College votes, the House of Representatives chooses among the three candidates who received the most Electoral College votes.

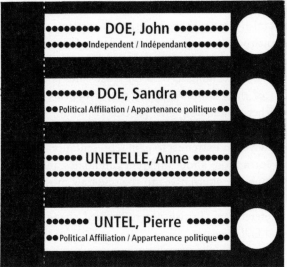

Canadian voters cast a ballot that contains the names and party affiliations of the candidates in their electoral district.
Elections Canada.

needed to put in place a new electoral system in time for the 2019 election). The Conservative party's demand that changes to the electoral system should only be adopted if approved by a national referendum was rejected by the Liberal government. As well, critics argued that there was insufficient time to thoroughly consider and implement fundamental changes to the electoral system.

RUNOFF ELECTIONS Many countries, including France, Russia, Brazil, Argentina, Indonesia, and Chile, use a system of **runoff elections** (also known as two-round elections) for the election of a president. If no candidate receives a majority of votes, another election is held in which only the top two candidates appear on the ballot.[4] A few countries use runoff elections to elect representatives to a legislative body. For example, if no candidate to represent a district in the French Assembly obtains a majority of votes, a second election is held. Only the candidates who received at least one-eighth of the votes of the total electorate on the first ballot can remain on the second ballot. The candidate with the most votes on the second ballot wins. The winning candidate often obtains a majority as a result of deals made among parties of the left and among parties of the right so that only the top candidate of the left and right appear on the second ballot. The two-round system was designed to reduce the fragmentation of the French party system by leaving smaller parties without legislative representation (Baldini & Pappalardo, 2009).

Canadian Electoral Reform:
**policyoptions.irpp.org/magazines/
June-2016/electoral reform**

runoff election

An election held if no candidate receives a majority of votes; generally, only the top two candidates appear on the ballot to ensure that the winning candidate has a majority of the votes cast.

---

[4]In some countries, including Mexico, South Korea, the Philippines, and Taiwan, the candidate with the most votes in a single election is elected as president regardless of whether that candidate received a majority of votes.

preferential ballot

An electoral system in which voters
rank candidates in order of preference.
If no candidate has a majority of first
preferences, the candidate with the
least votes is dropped, and the second
preferences of those who voted for that
candidate are added to the votes of
other candidates. This process continues until one candidate has a majority.

PREFERENTIAL BALLOT   Another type of majoritarian electoral system is the **preferential ballot** (also known as preferential voting, ranked ballots, the alternative vote, or instant-runoff voting). Instead of voting for a particular candidate, voters rank candidates in order of preference. If no candidate has a majority of first preferences, the candidate with the least votes is dropped, and the second preferences of those who voted for that dropped candidate are added to the votes of other candidates. This process continues until one candidate has a majority. The effect of the preferential ballot is generally to make it difficult for parties viewed as extremist to gain representation. As well, it may encourage voters to learn more about different candidates and parties so as to decide on how to rank the alternatives to the one they most favour. Australia uses this system to elect candidates to the House of Representatives (lower house). In a 2011 referendum, British voters rejected changing their SMP system to a preferential ballot system.

Proportional Representation

The single member plurality, runoff election, and preferential ballot electoral systems result in legislatures that do not reflect the overall distribution of support for political parties. To deal with this issue, many countries have adopted some form of **proportional representation (PR) system,** in which the proportion of seats a party receives in the legislature reflects the proportion of votes it has obtained. If, for example, 40 percent of voters supported party A, 39 percent supported party B, and 21 percent supported party C, this would result (in a pure PR system) in 40 percent of the seats going to party A, 39 percent to party B, and 21 percent to party C.

**proportional
representation
(PR) system**

An electoral system in which the proportion of seats a party receives in the
legislature reflects the proportion of
votes it has obtained.

A PR system requires that several representatives be elected from each electoral district. The larger the number of representatives for each district, the more closely the representation of the parties in the legislature will reflect the support each party has in the electorate. In a few cases—the Netherlands, Israel, and Slovakia—the country as a whole is treated as a single district, such that representatives do not represent a particular geographical area.

In some countries (for example, Spain and Norway), a closed-list PR system is used in which individual legislators are selected based on the order of their placement on a list of candidates drawn up by each party. In our hypothetical five-member legislature, the top two names on party A's list of five candidates would become legislators. Other countries with PR systems (for example, Sweden, Poland, and Brazil) use some form of an open-list system that allows voters to indicate which candidate they prefer from the party they have chosen to vote for. Popular candidates who receive a sufficient proportion of votes can be elected even if low on their party's list.

By quite accurately reflecting the support for parties by voters, a PR system almost always results in a situation where no single party has a majority of seats in the legislature.[5] Thus, PR systems typically involve **coalition government**, where two or more parties share in governing. PR systems also often result in a substantial number of parties being represented in the legislature. To try to prevent an overly complex party system in the legislature and keep small extremist parties or parties representing very narrow interests from gaining a voice in legislature, many countries with a PR system require that parties obtain a certain percentage of the popular vote as a prerequisite for gaining legislative seats. For example, the minimum threshold to gain representation is 4 percent in Austria, 3 percent in Greece, and 5 percent in Poland.

Although a PR system provides for more accurate representation of voter support for political parties than other electoral systems, it may reduce the strength of the link between a legislator and his or her district. Multimember districts are much larger than single-member districts, and PR systems tend to focus on representation by party rather than by individual legislators.

Proportional representation systems (including MMP) tend to result in greater representation for women and minority groups. This is particularly the case where a closed-list system is used. Parties are more likely to make their candidate lists more representative of different characteristics than in those countries with SMP and preferential ballot systems, where district party associations often have the primary responsibility for choosing candidates.

Mixed Member Proportional

To try to combine the benefits of a single member representing a particular electoral district with an accurate translation of votes into seats, some countries have adopted a mixture of SMP and PR systems, termed a **mixed member proportional (MMP) system.**

In the MMP system used, for example, in Germany and New Zealand, voters cast one vote for the party they prefer and one vote for the candidate they prefer. Some legislators are elected to represent particular districts, based on gaining the most votes in that district. Others (about one-half of the legislators in the case of Germany) are selected so the overall representation of the parties in the legislature is proportional to the votes received by each party in the election. In effect, the selection of representatives by PR in this system is used to compensate parties that were hurt by the workings of SMP (thus termed a *compensatory MMP system*).[6]

coalition government

A form of government in which two or more parties jointly govern, sharing the Cabinet positions.

Fair Vote Canada
www.fairvotecanada.org

mixed member proportional (MMP) system

An electoral system in which some legislators are elected to represent particular electoral districts based on gaining the most votes in that district, while others are elected based on the popular vote received by their party.

---

[5]In 2005, Italy adopted a PR system in which the coalition of parties that wins the most votes is guaranteed to receive at least 54 percent of the seats in the Chamber of Deputies while the other coalitions and individual parties obtain the remaining seats in proportion to the votes they received provided they have received a certain minimum proportion of votes. In the 2013 election, the Common Good coalition with 29.54 percent of the vote received 55 percent of the seats.

[6]In elections for the Scottish Parliament, this system is called the additional member system. Voters chose their preferred candidate in each of the 73 single member districts elected by FPTP, voters' second vote for their preferred party results in seven members in each of eight regions based on the lists compiled by each party.

In another type of MMP system (termed a *parallel MMP system*), part of the legislative body is elected by SMP and the other part by PR without using the PR seats to compensate for the distortions in party representation resulting from the election of representatives for the SMP seats. The parallel system tends to give a boost in representation to the most popular party. For example, in the 2012 Japanese election, the Liberal Democratic Party won 61.3 percent of the total legislative seats based on only 35.4 percent of the party vote. Its decisive victory was a result of winning 79 percent of the single-member districts based on 43 percent of the district candidate vote.

Single Transferable Vote System

single transferable vote (STV) system

An electoral system in which voters rank order their preferences for candidates in a multimember electoral district. Candidates who receive a certain proportion of the vote are declared elected. The second preference of a voter that is surplus to what that winning candidate needs is then transferred to that voter's second preference candidate. The process is continued until all seats in the district are filled.

The **single transferable vote (STV) system** used in Ireland could be viewed as a variation on the PR system. Voters rank order their preferences for candidates in a multimember electoral district. Candidates who receive a certain proportion of first preference votes are declared elected. Normally an insufficient number of candidates receive the required number of first preference votes to be elected. If a voter's preferred candidate has been elected, then the voter's second preference will be given that vote. The process is continued using third and subsequent preferences if necessary until all seats in the district are filled (Blais & Massicotte, 2002). Unlike PR systems, STV focuses on the choice of candidates rather than parties. Indeed, it encourages competition for votes among the candidates of the same party, thus potentially contributing to tensions within a party. STV does not generally produce as accurate a translation of party votes into party representation as PR systems, although the distorting effects are usually not large. The B.C. Citizen's Assembly on Electoral Reform established by the B.C. government recommended the use of STV for B.C. elections. However, referendums to support the adoption of this system did not obtain the required 60 percent approval of voters (57.69 percent in 2005 and 39.09 percent in 2009) and majority support in 60 percent of electoral districts.

ELECTION CAMPAIGNS

Parties, leaders, and candidates have many potential ways of appealing to voters for support. Pippa Norris (2002) distinguishes between three basic types of campaigns:

- premodern campaigns
- modern campaigns
- postmodern campaigns

Premodern Campaigns

Premodern campaigns were characteristic of many countries until the 1960s. These campaigns involved considerable personal contact with the voters, and campaigning was largely localized. Party volunteers canvassed their neigh-bourhoods, seeking to determine who supported their candidate so they could ensure that their supporters voted on election day. Leaflets were dropped in mailboxes, supporters were encouraged to put up signs, and all-candidates meetings were often held. National leaders traversed the country by train, greeting supporters at the railway stations in small communities and holding rallies in the larger centres. National campaign organizations were small, with the leader and some experienced party advisers establishing the general direc-tion of the campaign, which often involved appealing to members of groups that supported that party.

Modern Election Campaigns

Modern election campaigns are more sophisticated. Public opinion polling is used to provide the basic information needed to develop campaign strate-gies. Professional consultants, including experts in advertising and market-ing, largely determine how the campaign will be conducted and the kinds of appeals that will be made to the voters. Modern campaigns are more centrally coordinated or controlled than premodern campaigns.

The development of television contributed to the emphasis in modern campaigns on managing the image of the party leader (or, in the United States, candidate). Creating favourable "photo ops" of the leader that will be picked up by the national television news broadcasts is of great importance. As well, short attention-getting television advertisements are a central feature of mod-ern election campaigns. The typical campaign strategy is to focus on simple, basic themes (Plasser & Plasser, 2002).

Modern campaigns often tend to downplay political party affiliations. Instead of appealing primarily to the party faithful to mobilize them to vote on election day, the goal of the modern campaign is to appeal to a broader, national audience, particularly by focusing on the party leader. The more localized and personalized techniques of the premodern campaign con-tinue to be used, but are not of central importance in the modern campaign (Norris, 2002).

Waging a modern election campaign requires substantial amounts of money and access to professional expertise. American-based campaign pro-fessionals have been hired by parties in many countries to assist in running their campaigns. However, in some countries, legal regulations prevent the full adoption of modern campaign techniques. For example, a number of Euro-pean countries do not allow paid political advertising on television; instead, longer free-time television broadcasts are provided to the parties. In addition, various institutional characteristics (including the nature of the electoral, party, media, and governing systems) and cultural factors affect the ways in which American-developed modern campaign techniques have been applied in other countries.

Postmodern Campaigns

New forms of communication allow a return to more interactive and personalized styles of political communication. Specialized television channels, computerized direct mail and telemarketing techniques, and email and social media allow campaigners to direct specific messages to targeted groups and individuals. In addition to public opinion surveys, postmodern campaigns make extensive use of focus groups to develop their messages to targeted voters and to design effective television commercials. Even more than in the modern campaign, there is a focus on strictly controlling the message and developing the capability to instantly rebut the arguments of opponents (Plasser & Plasser, 2002).

Televised commercials continue to be the leading means of campaign persuasion in the United States and Canada. For example, over one million ads were aired in the 2012 American presidential election (Baum, 2012a). However, the Internet has become increasingly important as a means to mobilize supporters and potential supporters in election campaigns. Barack Obama's 2008 campaign was particularly effective in using the Internet for fundraising; a substantial proportion of the $656.6 million raised in individual donations (many in small amounts) were obtained through Internet appeals (Boatright, 2009). Further, through websites, blogs, and social media, supporters were encouraged to volunteer for Obama's campaign and to spread his message. However, the ability of campaigns to control online messages is limited: for example, 104 456 videos related to Obama and 64 092 related to McCain were placed online during the campaign by individuals and groups not controlled by the 2008 presidential candidates' campaigns (Owen, 2009).

Although the Internet has become an important aspect of campaigning, its effect in enhancing democracy may be limited. Political parties and candidates generally use the various new media to disseminate their message, often one that is centrally controlled. Many of those who read the messages and view the campaign videos are already committed to supporting the party or candidate. Thus, to some extent, the interaction between a party and its supporters could be described as an "echo chamber" in which the party message reinforces the commitment of party supporters rather than encouraging interaction between the party and citizens (Lilleker & Jackson, 2011). Nevertheless, some parties do encourage active engagement on their sites. Social media have been particularly important in reaching young people.

Norris (2000, p. 147) also pointed out that we are moving toward "the permanent campaign, in which the techniques of electioneering become intertwined with those of governing." The techniques developed to market the party during an election campaign may also be used by the governing party to try to control the message the government presents to the public. In addition, parties are increasingly using campaign-style advertising, even if an election is not imminent. For example, when Dion, Ignatieff, and Justin Trudeau each became Liberal leader, the Conservative Party quickly ran campaign-style ads to promote a negative image of the new leader.

Election Campaigns and Informed Choice

Ideally, elections allow people to choose among parties offering different platforms or directions for the country, and thus affect the way the country is governed. Candidates try to meet as many of their constituents as possible during the election campaign. The mass media provide extensive coverage of election campaigns. Parties carry their basic message to the public through extensive advertising and party platforms, leaders' speeches, and other campaign materials are easily accessible online.

However, political parties do not always clearly state their views on major issues during election campaigns. Because parties usually want to appeal to a diverse set of voters, they are often reluctant to take clear positions that might be viewed negatively by a significant group of voters. Instead, vague

Do campaigning politicians tell us what they will really do if elected?

Tami Thirlwell

Donald Trump performed poorly compared to Hillary Clinton in all three U.S. presidential debates that were viewed on television and on-line by a record number of voters.
Drew Angerer/Getty Images News/ Getty Images

statements about how they are going to make the country great are often combined with sharp attacks on their opponents. Nevertheless, those who follow an election campaign closely may find differences on important issues. For example, in the 2012 US presidential election campaign, Obama and Romney took opposing views on whether taxes on the wealthy should be raised, health care reform repealed, the military budget increased, carbon dioxide emissions regulated, subsidies to big oil companies reduced, same-sex marriage legalized, and abortion made illegal.

PROMISES   Parties usually make a variety of specific promises during an election campaign, such as spending money on particular programs and cutting taxes. However, voters cannot be certain that the promises will actually be carried out. Interestingly, when former Ontario premier Dalton McGuinty was sued for not fulfilling an election promise that he had made that taxes would not be raised, Judge Paul Rouleau dismissed the case noting that "anyone who believes a campaign promise is naive about the democratic system" (Makin, 2005). Nevertheless, governing parties try to fulfil, at least in part, many of their campaign promises, although changing circumstances may hinder their adoption.

ADVERTISING   The short (fifteen- or thirty-second) television advertisements that have become a major feature of election campaigns do not provide detailed information. Rather, they often rely on repeating a simple slogan or playing on people's fears (see Box 7-2 Negative Campaign Ads). The emphasis on the party leaders in modern campaigns can mean that consideration of the policy directions proposed by the parties is limited. The televised leaders' debates that have become a regular feature of election campaigns in most coun-

BOX 7-2   Negative Campaign Ads

Negative and misleading advertising is a key feature of election campaigns.

One of Republican candidate Mitt Romney's television ads in the 2012 presidential campaign featured a clip from Obama's 2008 campaign ad in which he said, "If we keep talking about the economy, we're going to lose." In fact, the full quote referred to John McCain, the 2008 Republican presidential candidate: "Senator McCain's campaign advertisements said, and I quote, "If we keep talking about the economy, we're going to lose" (Krasny, 2011).

An analysis of television commercials in the 2012 American presidential election found that 58.5 percent of the ads authorized by the Obama campaign were negative, 27 percent contrasted the views of the two leading candidates, and 14.5 percent were positive. Of the Romney campaign's ads, 49.2 percent were negative, 30 percent contrasted the candidates, and 21.8 percent were positive. In addition, 78 percent of the ads run by groups supporting Obama were negative, as were 89 percent of ads by groups supporting Romney (Baum, 2012b).

Negative ads have also been a feature of Canadian campaigns. For example, Liberal ads in 2006 claimed that Harper had a hidden agenda to dismantle the public health care system. For the 2011 campaign, one Conservative ad falsely claimed that Ignatieff would try to form another "ruthless coalition" with the NDP and Bloc Québécois as "he did before" (Jeffrey, 2011, p. 56). A 2011 Liberal ad listed government scandals and ended with: "Deceit, abuse, contempt for Canadians. Harper thinks he's above the law. Is this your Canada or Harper's?" In the 2015 campaigns, the Conservatives devoted many of their ads to the slogan" "Justin, just not ready" with one ad showing Trudeau walking the wrong way up escalating stairs. The Liberal ads criticized Harper politics of "fear and division" while using the theme "ready for real change." Some of the NDP ads contrasted Harper's "politics of fear" with the "politics of hope and optimism." The BQ attacked the NDP (NPD in French) on the niqab issue by posting a Facebook image of the House of Commons as seen through a niqab with the message: "Faut-il se cacher le visage pour voter NPD."

A distinction should be made between negative ads that critically assess the promises or performance of another party and those that engage in mudslinging, deception, or unjustified fear mongering (Jamieson, 1992). Negative ads that show the flaws and inconsistencies in another party's positions and performance may be more helpful to voters than ads that rely on platitudes, vague slogans, or general promises.

Overall, negative campaign advertising, along with the frequent use of personal attacks on those in opposing parties, has become a major feature of election campaigns in many countries. Negative advertising is not necessarily more effective in persuading voters than positive ads that focus on the reasons to vote for a particular party or candidate (Lau, Sigelman, Heldman, & Babbitt, 1999). Indeed, negative advertising can backfire if voters view the ads as unfair. However, viewers are more likely to remember an attack ad than a positive one, and the media are more likely to comment on negative than on positive ads. Researchers have also found that negative attack ads reduce voting turnout, while positive ads slightly increase turnout (Ansolabehere, Iyengar, Simon, & Valentino, 1997). The increasing use of negative advertising may also be a contributing factor to the increasing distrust of politicians and political parties.

tries potentially provide an opportunity for the voters to compare the arguments of the different parties as well as some of the qualities of the leaders. However, coverage of election campaigns in the mass media has often been criticized for avoiding serious discussion of the issues and focusing more on the "horse-race" aspect of the election and the personalities (and gaffes) of the party leaders.

GLEANING USEFUL INFORMATION Although election campaigns can be criticized for being exercises in manipulation, obfuscation, and dishonesty, those who follow a campaign carefully can often gain useful information about the parties' positions on specific issues and their general values and priorities. Of course, we have to be careful in interpreting the meaningfulness of the parties' campaign rhetoric. Although parties that are elected to govern may feel it necessary to fulfill or partly fulfill many of their specific promises, the general impression given by vague statements may be misleading. Promises to fix the health care system, reduce pollution, or operate government more efficiently are not very helpful unless there are clear indications as to how such objectives are to be achieved. Likewise, attacks on another party for its proposals, actions, or inactions are not very meaningful unless alternative approaches and policies are presented.

VOTING BEHAVIOUR

Canadian Election Studies
www.ces-eec.umontreal.ca

American National Election Studies
www.electionstudies.org

The British Election Study
www.britishelectionstudy.com

Why do people vote the way they do? Who tends to vote for each party? What affects the outcome of elections? Political scientists have devoted much research effort to such questions, particularly by using survey research techniques. However, the answers tend to be complex because a large number of factors can affect voting behaviour. These factors can be divided into two basic categories (Miller & Niemi, 2002):

- long-term predispositions of voters based on their social characteristics, values and ideology, and sense of identification with a particular political party
- short-term factors related to the circumstances of a particular election such as the leaders, candidates, and campaign issues

Long-Term Predispositions

SOCIAL CHARACTERISTICS Members of a social grouping based on such characteristics as class, religion, ethnicity and race, region, and gender may tend to support a particular party that they associate with the interests or the identity of their group. Thus, one or more major social cleavages (divisions) often affect the long-term patterns of voter support for different political parties. Although social divisions have generally been of declining importance in affecting voting choice in the advanced democracies, there are still some important differences in the voting patterns of different social groupings. In Canada, region and culture (including ethnicity and language) continue to be related to voters' party choices. In the United States, racial and ethnic, urban/rural, and, to some extent, religious differences are of continuing significance (see Figure 7-1). These differences have been quite consistent over the past few decades. Gender, education, and age were particularly important in the 2016 U.S. presidential election with women, those with higher education, and younger persons much more likely to support Democratic candidate Clinton than Republican candidate Trump.

FIGURE 7-1   Vote for Obama (Democratic Party), US Presidential Election, 2012

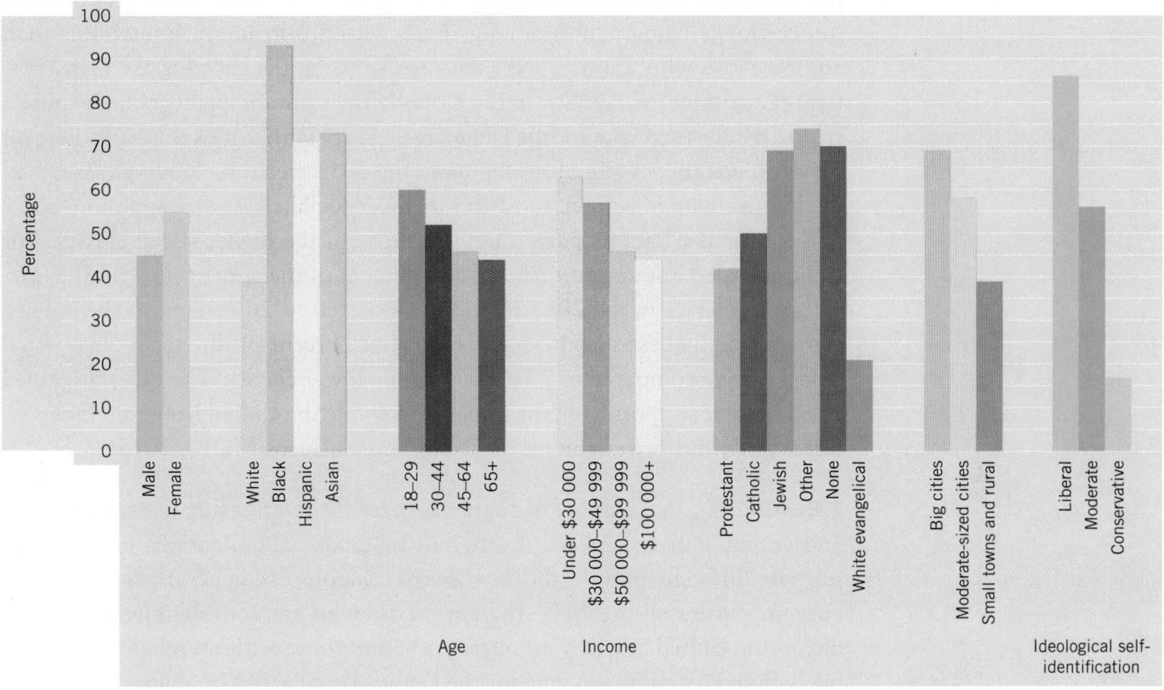

Source: Edison Research in *Washington Post* (2012). Exit polls 2012: How the vote has shifted. Retrieved from www.washingtonpost.com/wp-srv/special/politics/2012-exit-polls/table.html

CLASS   In most countries, there is a tendency for class divisions (divisions based on position in the economy or a combination of income, education, and social status) to affect voting behaviour. Most democratic countries have a social democratic party, allied formally or informally with the labour movement, which is able to gain the votes of a substantial proportion of unionized workers. As well, most democratic countries have one or more conservative parties, often informally allied with business interests, which are able to gain the votes of a substantial proportion of the more affluent and business-oriented segments of society. However, there has been a tendency for such differences in voting by class to decline over time as class distinctions have become blurred and the traditional industrial working class has shrunk. Nevertheless, issues regarding income inequality (such as the concentration of wealth among the top 1 percent) and employment have been increasingly important in politics in recent years

Class voting has not been strong at the national level in Canada, although class differences are significant in affecting voting behaviour in some provincial elections. Many Canadians think of themselves more in terms of provincial, ethnic, and cultural identities than in class terms. Political parties (except, to some extent, the NDP) have not been viewed by the majority of voters as connected to particular classes. Differences in voter support for different parties based on income level are fairly small. The NDP tends to do better (other things being equal) among those who are in union households than among those who are not, with the reverse being the case for the Conservatives (Gidengil et al., 2012). In the United States, union members have quite a strong tendency to vote for the Democratic Party with, for example, 65 percent of union members voting for Obama in the 2012 election. Although class voting has declined in Britain, those in the lower social classes are still more likely to vote for the Labour party than are those in the higher social classes. For example, the Labour party received 41 percent of the vote of those in the lowest social classes in the 2015 election, compared to 26 percent of the vote of those in the highest social classes. Forty-five percent of the upper class voted Conservative compared to 27 percent of the lower classes. The Liberals gained more of their support from the upper class while the United Kingdom Independence party did better among the lower classes (Ipsos MORI, 2015).

RELIGION   In a number of countries there is a relationship between religion and voting choice. Persons of different religious denominations may tend to support different parties; those who are religious are generally less likely to vote for parties on the "left" than are those who are not religious. For example, in the United States, Catholics, Jews, and those with no religion are more likely than Protestants to vote for the Democratic Party (see Figure 7-1). Those who attend church regularly are somewhat more likely to vote Republican. In Britain, Catholics are more likely than Presbyterians and Anglicans to vote for the Labour party. In France, those who are not religious are more likely than those who are religious to vote for one of the parties of the left (Dalton, 2006). In some countries, religious divisions in voting patterns have increased when parties have taken different positions on controversial moral issues such as abortion and same-sex marriage.

In Canada, Catholics (along with those who are not Christian) are generally more likely than Protestants to vote Liberal. Although this religious difference has generally weakened, the Conservative Party developed strong support from fundamentalist and evangelical Christians (Gidengil et. al., 2009). The NDP tends to do better among secular than among religious voters (Gidengil et al., 2012).

ETHNIC, RACIAL, AND CULTURAL GROUPS   Differences in voting behaviour are often apparent in countries that have ethnic, racial, and cultural minority groups with distinctive identities. The extremely high support among African-Americans for Democratic candidate Barack Obama not only reflected their support for the country's black presidential candidate, but also was consistent with very strong African-American support for the Democratic Party over the past several decades. Indeed, Obama was able to win in 2008 and 2012 with strong support from minority voters even though the Republican presidential candidate received about 60 percent of the vote from the white majority. Similarly in Canada, the Liberal Party has generally enjoyed a large lead among visible minorities and recent immigrants. Racial and ethnic differences are apparent in British voting. For example, in the 2015 British election 65 percent of black and minority ethnic voters chose Labour compared to only 23 percent of whites (Ipsos MORI, 2015).

REGION   In some countries, there are important regional differences in voting behaviour. For example, support for different parties often varies substantially across Canada, reflecting not only differences in the political culture and economy of different parts of the country, but also a tendency to evaluate governments and political parties in terms of perceptions of how good or bad they are for the interests of one's province or region. Voters in the prairie provinces have given strong support to conservative parties since 1958. In the 2015 election, the Liberals gained the majority of votes (and all the seats) in Atlantic Canada while the Conservatives won almost three-fifths of the votes in Alberta. However Quebec voters have not given much support to conservative parties for the last century (except in 1984 and 1988). The British Labour party has drawn its strongest support from Scotland (although in 2015 it lost much of that support to the Scottish National Party), the north of England, and Wales, while the Conservative Party is particularly strong in the south. In the United States, in recent decades the Democratic Party has been generally strong in the northeast and the west coast while the Republican Party has been generally strong in the south, plains, and Rocky Mountain states.

GENDER   Some political scientists have forecast that the gender gap in support for different parties will widen, in part because of the tendency of women in recent times to hold more liberal or leftist views, including a more favourable view of social welfare programs and a less favourable view of pure free-market policies, aggressive military action, and harsh treatment of criminals (Gidengil et al., 2003; O'Neill, 2002). However, gender differences in voting behaviour are generally quite small.

In the United States, women are more likely to vote for the Democratic Party than the Republican Party. For example, 55 percent of women compared to 45 percent of men voted for Obama (Democratic party) in 2012. In the 2015 British election, 38 percent of men and 37 percent of women voted Conservative, while 33 percent of women and 30 percent of men voted Labour (Ipsos MORI, 2015). In Canada, the NDP has gained slightly more support from women than men, while the Conservatives have done slightly better among men than women (Gidengil et. al., 2012). This gender gap is more evident among younger than older persons. In the 2011 Canadian election, the female–male gender gap was either small or insignificant (Soroka et al., 2011; LeDuc & Pammett, 2011). In the 2015 election, men were more likely than women to vote for the Conservative party, the NDP was slightly more likely to gain votes from women than men, and there was little difference between men and women in support for the Liberal party (O'Neill & Thomas, 2016).

AGE Green parties in many countries (including Canada) tend to receive greater support from younger than older voters. The NDP has also tended to do better among younger voters than among older ones. This was particularly evident in the 2011 election where the NDP was the leading party among younger voters, while the Conservatives had a strong lead among older voters (LeDuc & Pammett, 2011). In the 2015 election, the Liberals gained support from both older voters who had voted Conservative and younger voters who had voted NDP in the previous election. Nevertheless the Conservatives had stronger support among seniors than among young voters with the reverse the case for the NDP (Ekospolitics.com, 2015). In the 2008 and 2012 US presidential elections, Barack Obama drew strong support from younger voters. However, age differences were fairly small in most previous American presidential elections (*The New York Times*, 2008). In the 2015 British election (as in earlier elections) the Conservatives did much better among older than younger voters gaining 47 percent of the vote among those sixty-five and older, but only 23 percent among those 18–24. In contrast, Labour received 43 percent of the vote among the youngest voters (who were much less likely to vote) but only 23 percent among the oldest group (Ipsos MORI, 2015). Support for the United Kingdom Independence party was much higher among elderly than young persons with the opposite the case for Green party support.

OTHER CHARACTERISTICS Various other social characteristics are related to differences in voting behaviour in some countries. Voters in rural areas, small towns, and suburban areas tend to be more supportive of conservative parties than are big city voters. For example, in the 2004, 2006, and 2008 Canadian elections, the Conservative Party did not win a single seat in Canada's three largest cities (other than in surrounding suburban areas). Although the Conservatives made gains in urban areas in the 2011 election, almost all of the urban gains were lost in 2015. In the United States, the Republican Party has tended to draw stronger support from rural areas and small towns than from big cities.

IDEOLOGY AND VALUES Studies in many countries have found that how people view themselves in ideological terms is related to their voting choices (Miller & Niemi, 2002). That is, there is generally a strong tendency for voters who view themselves as leftist to vote for a left-wing party and those on the right to vote for a right-wing party. This relationship is stronger in countries where the major parties take distinctly different ideological positions. Overall, the relationship between left/right ideology and the vote tends to be stronger than the relationship between social characteristics and the vote (Dalton, Farrell, & McAllister, 2011).

The relationship between ideology and vote is not as strong in Canada as in some European countries. Nevertheless, Canadian voters who are skeptical about the capitalist system and favour greater economic equality and social welfare programs are more likely to vote for the NDP, while those who believe in the free market with a limited role for government are more likely to vote for the Conservative Party. Those who favour closer ties to the United States and those who hold traditional moral values (such as being critical of same-sex marriage and feminism) are also more likely to vote Conservative (Gidengil et al., 2012). In Quebec, support for Quebec sovereignty has clearly distinguished those who vote for the Bloc Québécois from those who vote for the Liberal party (Blais et al., 2002). In the United States, voters who considered themselves "liberal" voted overwhelmingly for the Democratic Party candidate for president in 2012, while most "conservatives" voted for the Republican Party candidate.

PARTY IDENTIFICATION   Political scientists often use party identification as a major explanation for why people vote the way that they do. **Party identification** can be thought of as a long-term attachment to a particular political party. It is not simply an agreement with the issue positions that a party is currently taking, or a preference for a particular leader or candidate representing the party. Rather, it is a long-term feeling of closeness to a party that may be the result of political socialization, one's social group identity, or one's ideological perspective (Abramowitz & Saunders, 2006).

party identification

A long-term attachment to a particular political party.

Those that identify with a particular political party tend to develop a positive view of the party's leader and candidates, prefer that party's position on the issues of the day, and believe that their party is the most competent to handle the tasks of governing. Therefore, even though voters typically vote in accordance with their evaluation of the leaders, candidates, and issue positions of the parties, the long-term influence of party identification may lie behind voters' evaluations of the particular features of an election.

The theory of party identification does not mean that an individual's vote is completely determined by long-term party ties. Voters with weak or nonexistent ties to a party will frequently shift their votes from election to election, resulting in changing election outcomes. An unpopular party leader or party issue position may lead a party identifier to vote for a different party. However, the theory suggests that deviations from voting for one's party usually will be only temporary. Party identifiers may vote for another party while still retaining their long-term party identification.

Although the theory of party identification is useful in understanding voting behaviour and long-term patterns of support for different parties, party identification has tended to decline in importance in many countries. Fewer people now view themselves as strong party identifiers, and the proportion of people who view themselves as independent or without a party identification has been increasing in recent decades in the advanced democracies (Dalton,

2000, 2006). For example, in 2012, 33 percent of registered Americans voters viewed themselves as "independent" (Pew Research Centre for the People and the Press, 2012), a substantially higher proportion than in the 1950s and 1960s. In Canada there are differences among researchers concerning the proportion of Canadians who do not have a party identification and the extent to which party identification is flexible (Gigengil et al., 2012; Clarke, Kornberg, & Scotto, 2009a). A considerable proportion of party identifiers do vote for different parties particularly when their party has an unpopular leader or is not seen as competent while still retaining their party identification (Gidengil et al., 2012). Nevertheless, the Liberal Party's proportion of party identifiers at the national level declined from 40 percent in 2000 to 18 percent in 2011, matching its decline in voting support (Clarke et al., 2011). At the time of the 2015 election, the proportion of Liberal party identifiers increased from 18 percent in 2012 to 26 percent, Conservative identifiers dropped from 30 percent to 26 percent, and NDP identifiers dropped from 17 percent to 14 percent (Clarke, Reiffler, Scotto, & Stewart, 2016).

Short-Term Influences

Although long-term factors continue to be important in affecting voting, short-term factors such as leader preferences and campaign issues have increased in significance. Many voters decide how to vote during the election campaign, with some even deciding on election day (Clarke, Kornberg, & Scotto, 2009a). Support for the NDP nearly doubled during the course of the 2011 campaign, fueled in part by the party's strong campaign and the weakness of the Liberal campaign (Clarke et al., 2011). However in 2015, NDP support during the election campaign dropped from 33.2 percent to 19.7 percent while Liberal support increased from 25.9 percent to 39.5 percent (Grenier, 2015).

It is not easy to determine the relative importance of such factors as the quality of leaders and candidates, the issue positions of the parties, and general perceptions of the quality, competence, and performance of the parties, as each factor will tend to influence the others. For example, those who trust a particular party leader may come to agree with the positions that leader's party takes on certain issues, while those who agree with a party's positions may be more inclined to develop a favourable impression of that party's leader and candidates. As well, the importance of various short-term factors may differ from election to election and from country to country, depending on how the parties appeal to the voters and what the media emphasize in their coverage of a particular election.

LEADERS   With the general decline of partisanship in many countries and the focus of television on the leaders and their personal qualities, it is not surprising that the party leaders have become increasingly important in affecting voting. This is particularly the case for political parties that are viewed as basically non-ideological (Blais, 2011). An analysis of data from 35 elections in seven Western countries including Canada found that the personality traits of the party leaders had a significant effect on voters. Although voter's evaluation of leaders was quite strongly affected by the voter's partisanship and ideology (and to a lesser extent their social characteristics), evaluation of the character and competence of the leaders had a significant effect independent of partisanship and ideology. This does not mean that the party whose leader is viewed as the best will necessarily win an election. However, in some cases the evaluation of the leaders' personalities did make a decisive difference in the outcome of an election. Further, this study found that voter's evaluations of the leaders had a greater influence on the vote than the election platforms of the political parties (Bittner, 2011).

In the 2011 Canadian election, NDP leader Jack Layton's positive rating was an important factor in the NDP's major increase in vote, particularly since Liberal leader Michael Ignatieff was rated very poorly by the voters. Although Stephen Harper's average score was slightly negative on a "like–dislike" scale (although improved from 2008), he tended to be viewed as more competent to handle the economy than the other leaders (Clarke et al., 2011). The positive image of Justin Trudeau undoubtedly helped the Liberals in the 2015 election.

CANDIDATES   Candidates in an electoral district tend to be less important than party leaders in affecting voting behaviour and election outcomes. Nevertheless, one study found that local candidate preference was a decisive factor for 5 percent of Canadian voters independent of their feelings about the parties and their leaders (Blais, 2003). In a closely contested electoral district, a strong candidate can make a difference. In American elections, candidates can have very important effects because they often distance themselves from their party. In doing so, they gain or lose support based, to a considerable extent, on their own characteristics, campaigns, and positions. Incumbent members of the US Congress usually have a strong ability to win re-election.

ISSUES   Although many voters cite issues as the most important reason for their vote choice, the leading parties do not always stake out clearly different positions on what should be done about important problems. Instead, **valence issues**—those on which the contending parties differ as to which party is most competent to deal with the problem area—have been important in many elections (Clarke, Kornberg, & Scotto, 2009a). For example, in the 2011 Canadian election, issues on which the parties had different positions, including same-sex marriage, the war in Afghanistan, the gun registry, and Quebec sovereignty, were each cited as most important by no more than 1 percent of the voters. The top-ranked issues, the economy and health care, were basically valence issues as the major parties did not take distinctly different positions (Clarke et al., 2011).

valence issues

Issues on which the contending parties differ as to which party is most competent to deal with a problem rather than clearly taking different positions as to what should be done.

Valence issues can have an impact on the outcome of an election if voters feel that one party is more competent to handle the problem or if they assign blame or credit for the handling of the problem in the past. However, in many cases (such as the economic problems of unemployment and inflation), voters may feel that "their" party is best able to handle the problem, thus reducing the impact of the issue on the election outcome.

ACCOUNTABILITY   Do voters hold the governing party accountable for its actions in office? An analysis of the 2000 Canadian election found that voters' evaluations of the Liberal government's performance generally had a significant effect on their electoral choice. (In Quebec, however, voters made their choice primarily based on their views about Quebec sovereignty.) Interestingly, the Liberal Party was re-elected despite considerable voter dissatisfaction with its record on such key issues as health care, taxes, and corruption. Those who were dissatisfied with the Liberal government's record divided their votes among the various opposition parties, thereby limiting the negative impact of their dissatisfaction. A complicating factor was the tendency of many voters to blame their provincial government as well as the federal government for problems with the health care system (Blais et al., 2002). Holding a governing party accountable for its actions may be difficult if voters are not comfortable voting for an alternative party.

STRATEGIC VOTING   Generally, people tend to vote for the candidate of the party that they prefer. However in the 2015 Canadian election, considerable attention was given to strategic voting. With many Canadians upset with the policies of Harper's Conservative government, various efforts were made to encourage people to vote for whichever candidate of another party in their district had the best chance of defeating the Conservative MP. The advocacy group Leadnow commissioned polls to determine which candidate was most likely to defeat the Conservative candidate (including many NDP candidates), especially in 72 Conservative districts. 90 000 persons pledged to vote strategically for the candidate that was most likely to defeat a Conservative candidate. However, it is not clear how effective these campaigns were at the constituency level. With the Liberals gaining support across the country at the expense of the NDP during the election campaign, many anti-Conservative voters apparently switched from NDP to Liberal regardless of Leadnow's recommendation in their district.

A study of strategic voting in the 2015 election looked at voters in Ontario, Quebec, and British Columbia whose preferred party was not one of the perceived top two contenders in their constituency. Nearly one-half of this group in Ontario and British Columbia and just over one-third of this group in Quebec voted for one of the leading contenders rather than their preferred party's candidate (Doust & Bol, 2016).

ECONOMIC CONDITIONS   Voters are concerned about the state of the economy, not only in terms of their own economic well-being, but also in terms of the overall economic condition of the country. Researchers have found that economic conditions can have an effect on the outcome of an election (Lewis-Beck & Whiffen, 2013). The incumbent party generally tends to do well when the economy is performing well and tends to do poorly when the economy is faltering. Some studies found that Barack Obama's presidential election victory in November 2008 was predictable based on the declining economic situation and the unfavourable rating of the outgoing Republican president.[7] Although some political scientists predicted that Obama would lose in 2012 because of the continuing weakness in the economy (Berry & Bickers, 2013), Obama was not blamed by a majority of voters for economic problems. The very wealthy Republican candidate Romney, who paid a low rate of taxes, was viewed by many voters as being unconcerned with those who were struggling economically. A secretly recorded video of Romney's speech to a wealthy private audience in which he declared that "47 percent of Americans pay no income tax . . . My job is not to worry about these people" was particularly damaging. Among those who viewed the economy as the top issue, Romney had only a very slight advantage, while Obama held a sizable lead among those who ranked health care as the top issue.

Although the majority of Canadian voters thought the economy was worsening at the time of the October 2008 election (Clarke, Kornberg, & Scotto, 2009b), the governing Conservatives managed to increase their popular vote and number of parliamentary seats, falling just short of gaining a majority in the House of Commons. In this case, the opposition Liberal Party was burdened with an unpopular leader who had trouble explaining and defending his proposed carbon tax. Further, although their leader was not rated positively by voters, the Conservatives were somewhat more likely to be viewed as the party best able to handle the economy—an issue that was, by far, the most important to voters (Clarke, Kornberg, & Scotto, 2009b). In the 2011 election, the Conservatives benefited from growing optimism about improvement in the economy. The economy was the single most important issue to voters, and 58 percent of those who cited this issue as most important ranked the Conservatives as the best able to handle the economy (Clarke et al., 2011).

Overall, although economic conditions have an effect on voters and the outcome of elections, an analysis of voting behaviour in eleven elections in Canada, the United States, and Britain found that that the issue positions adopted by the parties or presidential candidates were a decisive consideration for about twice as many voters than economic conditions (Blais et al., 2004). The significance of economic conditions for election outcomes depends, at least in part, on how voters perceive the capabilities of parties to manage the economy and deal with economic problems. As well, other important concerns (such as war or terrorism) may be more important to voters in certain elections.

---

[7]See PS: *Political Science and Politics*, vol. 42, no. 1 (2009) for differing analyses.

✓• SUMMARY AND CONCLUSION

Elections are often viewed as the central feature of democratic politics. Elections determine legislative representation and which party or parties will form the government (or who will be president). If parties take different ideological positions, voters can shift the general direction of the government by their choice of which party to support. Although election campaigns feature manipulation of the voters by the competing parties and politicians, election campaigns bring politicians into closer contact with voters. In anticipation of an election, parties and politicians ask themselves, "What do voters want?" Appealing to the public may have to be modified, however, to ensure the support of the party's activists, core supporters, and financial backers.

A basic problem with elections is that we are asked to convey a lot of information by our vote. We may use our vote to express which of the competing platforms we prefer, which candidates and leaders we think are most competent, which party we think is best, what our evaluation is of the current governing party, and so on. However, placing a single X on a ballot cannot really convey our views on a variety of matters.

Voters often express a variety of different attitudes, values, preferences, and judgments when they cast their vote. This can make the interpretation of the result of a particular election difficult and controversial. The messages being sent by voters to politicians through an election are often unclear. Thus, statements by a governing party that it has a mandate to carry out particular policies because it won an election can be misleading.

The single member plurality (SMP) electoral system tends to distort the choices made by voters. By giving a boost to the leading party at the expense of the smaller parties, the governing party often does not have the support of the majority of the voters for the direction in which it plans to take the political community, even if it has the majority of elected representatives on its side. Likewise, although the SMP system provides a single representative for each electoral district, many representatives are elected by less than a majority of those voting in their district. Representation of diverse viewpoints and interests tends to be inhibited because of the discrimination

suffered by smaller parties in SMP systems. Systems of proportional representation (PR), although providing fairer representation, typically result in coalition governments that may be difficult to hold accountable for their actions. Elections using PR systems often result in only small changes in party representation, and major changes in government are less common than in SMP systems. Furthermore, some PR and mixed member proportional (MMP) systems do not give voters the opportunity to get rid of undesirable representatives. Overall, the choice of electoral system is controversial because it affects the power of different political parties, the basic nature of the government (for example, the likelihood of coalition government), and the way the public is represented.

When we consider whether elections serve the common good, we should remember that elections are the culmination of the struggle for political power within a democracy. The contending parties in an election are not engaged in deliberation about what is best for the community, but rather are engaged in a competitive struggle for votes. So it should not be surprising that election campaigns often manipulate rather than enlighten voters. Nevertheless, election campaigns can serve to mobilize those who support a particular party or candidate to vote and stimulate discussion of political issues even among many who do not ordinarily follow politics. Political campaigns may not live up to the ideal of deliberative democracy, but then neither does political discussion in other forums such as political websites, radio talk shows, or Question Period in the Canadian House of Commons.

In societies with deep social divisions, election campaigns can inflame those divisions, and thus violence sometimes accompanies elections. This is particularly the case for elections that are conducted on a winner-takes-all basis (for example, elections using the SMP system and in presidential elections) in countries where some groups fear serious consequences if a party representing an opposing section of society wins.

Despite their limitations, elections can be important in enabling voters to hold a government accountable for its actions and to have some ability to affect the direction taken by the political community. In democratic systems, voters do sometimes use the opportunity provided by elections to remove governing parties that have become corrupt, incompetent, unresponsive, or lacking in new ideas. If elections are viewed by citizens as free and fair, those elected to govern normally will be viewed as having legitimate authority. Transitions of political power from one group to another can be accomplished smoothly. Overall, then, the common good is served by a system of free and fair elections. Establishing a legitimate government, providing an incentive for governments to be responsive to those they govern, and providing a peaceful mechanism to remove governments that do not deserve to continue to be in power is good for all members of the political community.

✔• KEY TERMS

Coalition government   157
Electoral College   154
Electoral system   151
Gerrymander   150
Mixed member proportional
   (MMP) system   157

Party identification   169
Preferential ballot   156
Proportional representation
   (PR) system   156
Runoff election   155

Single member plurality
   (SMP) system   152
Single transferable vote (STV)
   system   158
Universal suffrage   149
Valence issues   171

◆• DISCUSSION QUESTIONS

1. Are Canadian elections free and fair? Should voting be modernized by the adoption of electronic or Internet voting?

2. Should Canada change its single member plurality electoral system? If so, what is the best alternative?

3. Should politicians be expected to keep the promises they make in an election campaign? What should happen if they do not?

4. How would you interpret the outcome of the last national, provincial, or local election? Did voters send a clear message about the direction they want their government to follow?

5. What criteria have you used, or do you think you should use, in deciding how to vote? Should you vote for the best leader, the best party, or the best local candidate?

FURTHER READING

Anderson, C.D., & Stephenson, L.B. (Eds.). (2010). *Voting behaviour in Canada.* Vancouver: UBC Press.

Aarts, K., Blais, A., & Schmitt, H. (Eds.). (2011). *Political leaders and democratic elections.* Oxford, UK: Oxford University Press.

Baldini, G., & Pappalardo, A. (2009). *Elections, electoral systems and volatile voters.* New York: Palgrave Macmillan.

Bittner, A. (2011). *Platform or personality. The role of party leaders in elections.* Oxford: Oxford University Press.

Clarke, H.D., Kornberg, A., & Scotto, T.S. (2009). *Making political choices: Canada and the United States.* Toronto: University of Toronto Press.

Courtney, J.C. (2004). *Elections.* Vancouver: UBC Press.

Gidengil, E., Nevitte, N., Blais, A., Everitt, J., & Fournier, P. (2012). *Dominance & decline: Making sense of recent Canadian elections.* Toronto: University of Toronto Press.

Lilleker, D.G. & Jackson, N.A. (2011). *Political campaigning, elections and the internet: Comparing the US, UK, France and Germany.* London: Routledge.

Pammett, J.H., & Dornan, C. (Eds.). (2016). *The Canadian federal election of 2015.* Toronto: Dundurn Press.

Pilon, D. (2007). *The politics of voting: Reforming Canada's electoral system.* Toronto: Edmond Montgomery.

West, D.M. (2013). *Air wars: Television advertising and social media in election campaigns, 1952–2012* (6th ed.). Washington, DC: CQ Press.

8 Political Influence and Political Communication

Lois Gibbs turned political activist extraordinaire when her children fell seriously ill and she realized that the Love Canal toxic dump she lived on top of was to blame. Joe Traver/Hulton Archive/Getty Images

After reading this chapter, you should be able to:

1. examine the characteristics, organization, and significance of interest groups and social movements
2. discuss the extent to which interest groups and social movements help or hinder the achievement of the common good of the political community
3. assess the relative importance of corporations and interest groups in influencing government
4. evaluate the effectiveness of the mass media, online and social media in facilitating the achievement of democratic ideals

Lois Gibbs was a housewife who became a political activist when her children fell ill. In 1976, Gibbs learned that the blue-collar subdivision in Niagara Falls, New York, where she lived with her husband and two small children, was built on the Love Canal, an unfinished canal that had been used as a chemical disposal site. Over the years, the Hooker Chemical Company, later bought by oil giant Occidental Petroleum, had dumped twenty thousand tonnes (more than eighteen thousand kilograms) of highly toxic chemical waste into the never-completed canal. It was covered over and the land was sold to the municipality of Niagara Falls for one dollar.

In 1978, Gibbs's children became very sick. Her son developed epilepsy and her daughter almost died of a rare blood disease. Talking to other parents in the subdivision, Gibbs found that many children had birth defects, miscarriages were very common, and children often came home from the playground with burns on their hands and faces. Gibbs went around to her neighbours with a petition, asking them if they were as upset as she was. They were, and soon they had formed the Love Canal Homeowners Association. Over the next two years, Gibbs led the association in legal and political battle against Occidental Petroleum and all three levels of government: city, state, and federal. Although the company and the governments all argued that the Love Canal's toxic wastes did not cause the residents' health problems, the community eventually won a settlement of US$120 million and more than eight hundred families were relocated to safe, healthy homes. President Jimmy Carter later declared the Love Canal a national disaster area.

The protest that Lois Gibbs organized and led has left two important legacies: the Environmental Protection Agency's multibillion-dollar Superfund, used to find and clean up toxic sites throughout the United States, and the Center for Health, Environment, and Justice (CHEJ), which Gibbs founded. The CHEJ works with community groups across the United States to protect neighbourhoods from the hazards of toxic wastes.

The Love Canal incident sparked thousands of other grassroots organizations to campaign against toxic sites. By being brave enough to stand up to the powerful and resourceful enough to found and lead a successful political protest, Lois Gibbs showed that even ordinary people can wield a lot of political power when they organize and refuse to take no for an answer.

After an extensive cleanup and secured sealing of toxic chemicals, the Love Canal was declared completely safe in 2004 and a new community was established on the site. However, in 2011 the Herr family who had moved to the community heard "weird popping and hissing sounds" in their basement, a foul chemical smell burned their eyes and nostrils, and the family pets started vomiting. Melanie Herr and her children experienced various health problems and some children in the area suffered birth defects that were attributed to chemicals from the Love Canal. The Herrs and other residents launched a $113 million lawsuit claiming the Love Canal is leaking and causing a variety of serious illnesses to many people who moved to the area (Specht, 2013; Herbert, 2013). Lawsuits involving about 1000 plaintiffs were still outstanding in 2016.

INTRODUCTION

An important element of political analysis is determining the relative ability of different groups and individuals to influence those in governing positions and the laws and policies that are adopted. Although voters play an important role in deciding which political party and which individuals will be in governing and legislative positions, elections are infrequent events. Voters may have some effect on the general direction taken by government through their choice among parties. However, citizens usually do not have much influence through their vote over the specific policies adopted by governments and legislatures.

In liberal democracies, people are free to voice their opinions and organize into groups in order to try to exert political influence over the public policies that affect their lives. In the liberal democratic ideal, government does not control society and individuals; rather, government is expected to listen to and be responsive to the views of the people in making decisions. In reality, however, questions are often raised about the extent to which government is responsive to the people. Undoubtedly some individuals and groups are more influential than others.

There are a variety of sources of political influence in any political community. In this chapter we will focus on interest groups, social movements, and the media.

INTEREST GROUPS

interest group

An organization that pursues the common interests of groups of people, particularly by trying to influence the development, adoption, and implementation of public policies.

Interest groups[1] are organizations that pursue the common interests of groups of people, particularly by trying to influence the development, adoption, and implementation of public policies. Since the early 1960s, there has been a great growth in the number of interest groups, the size of their membership, and the diversity of interests that are represented. The growth of interest groups reflects, to a considerable extent, the growth of the activities of government. As governments have become more heavily involved in health care, education, social programs, business regulation, gender issues, and environmental protection, a variety of groups have been formed to promote, modify, or challenge further government actions in such areas (Mahoney & Baumgartner, 2008).

Many interest groups do not exist exclusively or primarily for political purposes. However, in representing the interests of a particular segment of society, interest groups often find political action necessary or desirable to

---

[1] Interest groups are sometimes referred to as pressure groups, particularly to refer to their involvement in influencing government. Young and Everitt (2004) suggest that the term *advocacy groups* is preferable to *interest groups* because many groups are not concerned primarily with gaining benefits for their members but rather promoting their view about issues that may not affect them directly. The term *non-governmental organization* (NGO) is also widely used to include non-profit groups involved in advocacy and in providing services such as humanitarian relief and international development programs.

protect or promote the interests of the group. For example, the major activities of the Canadian Medical Association include the exchange of medical information and the certification of doctors. Nevertheless, because the interests of doctors are strongly affected by government policy, the Canadian Medical Association is also active in developing and promoting a variety of policy positions concerning the health care system.

Self-Interest and Public Interest Groups

The term *interest group* refers to a wide variety of different types of groups. Many groups have been formed by specific economic and occupational interests. Groups to promote various business, agricultural, and labour interests were among the first to be established in many countries. Most professions have also developed well-organized interest groups. Groups based on economic and occupational interests primarily pursue a material interest in the government policies that affect the wages, jobs, or profits of their members. Generally, groups that represent economic and occupational interests as well as groups that want a benefit from government for its members (such as a softball organization that wants to persuade a city council to improve the condition of ball fields) can be considered to be **self-interest groups**.

Public interest groups (also known as citizens' groups) are not primarily concerned with gaining specific benefits for their members, but rather have been formed to promote a position on certain issues or a particular cause that they believe to be in the public interest. For example, in many countries, pro-choice and pro-life groups are active in promoting their viewpoints on whether abortions should be legal. Likewise, Amnesty International mounts public pressure to try to prevent human rights abuses around the world. A variety of interest groups have also been formed to develop, express, and promote the identity, rights, and interests of a particular segment of society. For example the Canadian Ethnocultural Council, which promotes the vision of a multicultural country and the elimination of discrimination and racism, represents a number of different ethnic interest groups.

The distinction between self-interest groups and public interest groups is often not clear. Self-interest groups usually argue that the policies they hope to obtain will benefit the whole community. For example, business groups seeking lower taxes claim that such policies will help to create jobs and prosperity for the country as a whole. On the other hand, some public interest groups have been accused of raising funds for a popular cause primarily to provide generous salaries and benefits to the leaders and staff of the organization. Furthermore, some groups combine activities to benefit their members with support for broader public causes. For example, the Canadian Federation of Students not only has involved itself in pursuing lower tuition fees and more government support for higher education, but also has pursued various national and international causes not directly related to the self-interest of students.

self-interest group

An interest group whose primary objective is to promote the interests of the group and its members and to seek benefits that are primarily or exclusively for its members.

public interest group

A group that seeks to achieve goals that the group views as being for the good of the community as a whole rather than providing specific benefits for its members.

Amnesty International Canada
www.amnesty.ca

Canadian Ethnocultural Council
www.ethnocultural.ca

Canadian Federation of Students
www.cfs-fcee.ca

Supporters of Amnesty
International participate
in the Europride march
in Marseille, France.
Gay Pride Parade/Alamy

Issue-Oriented and Institutionalized Interest Groups

There is a great deal of variation in interest groups, not only in their goals and whom they represent, but also in their organizational development. A distinction is often made between issue-oriented interest groups and institutionalized interest groups (Pross, 1993).

Issue-oriented interest groups often spontaneously develop to express the views of people on a particular issue, concern, or grievance. For example, a concerned citizens group, the North Dufferin Agricultural and Community Taskforce, successfully pressured the Ontario government to conduct a full environmental assessment of an application to build a massive limestone and aggregate quarry that would not only destroy a large area of prime Ontario farmland, but could affect the water supply of over one million people. This led Highland (an American hedge fund) to withdraw its application in 2012.

Some issue-oriented groups have only a temporary existence and are not concerned about developing a formal organization. When the issue is resolved or passions concerning the issue dissipate, such groups may fold or fade away.

Many other interest groups, particularly those representing economic or professional interests or a major sector of society, have developed a formal organization, including such features as a well-established membership base, paid professional staff, permanent offices, and a capability to keep their members, government, and the public aware of their views and activities. Such groups, termed **institutionalized interest groups**, typically develop and promote positions on a variety of issues, monitor the activities of government,

**issue-oriented
interest group**

An interest group that spontaneously
develops to express the views of people
on a particular issue, concern, or
grievance.

**institutionalized
interest group**

A group that has developed a formal
organization, including such features
as a well-established membership
base, paid professional staff, permanent offices, and the capability to keep
its members and the public aware of its
views and activities.

and try to develop close working relationships with key government officials (Pross, 1993). For example, the Canadian Chamber of Commerce, the Canadian Federation of Agriculture, and the Assembly of First Nations are regular and long-lasting organizations that are important features of political life. They are generally recognized by government as being the legitimate representatives of particular segments of society that expect to be consulted when proposed policies affect their interests.

Issue-oriented interest groups and institutionalized interest groups could be considered as extremes on a continuum of organizational development, with many groups falling somewhere between these two types. Some interest groups concerned with a single issue (such as Mothers Against Drunk Driving) have developed a professional, structured organization so as to have a more permanent and effective vehicle for their concerns.

Assembly of First Nations
www.afn.ca

Canadian Chamber of Commerce
www.chamber.ca

Canadian Federation of Agriculture
www.cfa-fca.ca

Mothers Against Drunk Driving Canada
www.madd.ca

Membership in Interest Groups

Organized collective action gives individuals a chance to be influential, which is usually why people join and support interest groups. Modern governments are large, and the policy-making process is complex. Few individuals have the contacts and expertise needed to influence decisions. Although your member of Parliament may be willing to listen to your request and a letter or email to a Cabinet minister or the prime minister may result in a computer-generated response, it is highly unlikely that one individual's demands or opinions will affect government decisions. Most individuals are much more likely to be able to influence political decisions through involvement in an organization than by trying to influence politicians and government officials themselves.

THE FREE-RIDER PROBLEM   Mancur Olson (1965) raised the following question: Under what conditions is it rational for individuals to join and support groups to pursue their political interests? In what Olson describes as the *free-rider problem*, an individual can often enjoy the benefits of the successes of an interest group whether or not that individual is a member or financial supporter. If, for example, an environmental group is successful in a campaign to reduce air pollution, we all benefit from that action whether or not we supported the group. Rational, calculating individuals may figure that it is to their advantage to let others contribute time and money to the campaign. Of course, if enough people think this way, an interest group will not be able to survive.

The free-rider problem is particularly serious for public interest groups because their goals can benefit the political community as a whole. Self-interest groups that seek a specific benefit exclusively for their members find it easier to gain and maintain the support of those who will potentially benefit. Individual companies can anticipate a direct and substantial impact on their profitability if the business association that represents them is successful in persuading government to adopt certain policies that benefit their sector of the economy.

In some cases, the free-rider problem is largely irrelevant because membership in a group is compulsory. For example, in unionized workplaces, union dues are automatically deducted from paycheques. Likewise, student unions (many of which are members of the Canadian Federation of Students), after obtaining a majority vote of students, have convinced university administrations to require that all students pay union dues. Similarly, to practise a profession (such as a doctor, engineer, or pharmacist) a person is required to be a member of the appropriate professional association.

Further, individuals do not necessarily join an organization for its political activities or its stance on political issues. For example, those who are members of a Canadian church may not even be aware that the Canadian Council of Churches, which represents most Christian denominations, has been critical of free-trade agreements and founded Project Ploughshares, a group that promotes peace with justice.

REASONS FOR JOINING To some degree, public interest groups can try to avoid the free-rider problem by offering particular benefits (termed **selective incentives**) to their members. Some groups provide a glossy magazine, offer merchandise at reduced rates, and arrange for reduced insurance rates and discounts on car rentals and hotel accommodations. However, many public interest groups that provide few selective incentives have developed in recent decades, with some (such as environmental and conservation groups) attracting very large numbers of members. People often join or support public interest groups because of the satisfaction that can be achieved by expressing one's values and contributing to the good of their community, community, or the world. Some people also join interest groups for social reasons, that is, because they enjoy interacting and working with like-minded persons.

More generally, an increasingly educated population with greater skills and more leisure time is more likely to pursue various causes through involvement in public interest groups. Nevertheless, many public interest groups experience a high turnover in membership and face large swings in membership and financial support as different causes become more popular. Therefore, they often must devote considerable effort and resources to motivating volunteers and maintaining financial solvency.

Democratic Organizations?

Many interest groups have democratic organizational structures. Institutionalized interest groups usually have some regular method for electing their chairperson and board of directors, who oversee the operations of staff members and set the direction for the organization.

The Canadian Council of Churches
www.councilofchurches.ca/en/

Project Ploughshares
www.ploughshares.ca

selective incentive

A particular benefit that is made available to members of an interest group but is not available to the public as a whole.

However, the "iron law of oligarchy" (the claim that all organizations become dominated by a small group of leaders) applies to many interest group organizations. Although some interest groups do provide for active participation by their members in the group's decision making (for example, by establishing local chapters), there is often not a strong relationship between the members of an interest group and those who act on its behalf. Some of the large national interest groups devote most of their energies to influencing government policy makers, leaving the "grassroots" members largely uninvolved in the organization (Shaiko, 1999).

Even though many interest groups do not provide a strong vehicle for the voices of their members, there will usually be some shared perspectives between the spokespersons for the group and its members. A group that deviates strongly from the views of its grassroots supporters or members may find that its funds, membership, and ability to mobilize members in support of its cause fade. However, some groups, such as those based on cultural, ethnic, and religious interests, may be able to retain their members even if the political positions they pursue are not fully in tune with the views of the membership.

Government Support for Interest Groups

Government organizations have, at times, provided some financial support and encouragement for the formation and development of interest groups. Beginning in the 1960s, some Canadian governments have encouraged and helped to finance the development of groups representing segments of the population that were largely unrepresented by well-organized interest groups, including Aboriginals, women, and poor people (Pal, 1993).

Why would governments fund groups that represent disadvantaged segments of the population when such groups are often critical of government policies and government's lack of action to deal with their problems? Governments may seek to offset the influence that groups representing business and other privileged elements of society are often able to exert on government. This could give government greater flexibility to act as it sees fit. Particular government departments and agencies may find it useful to have active and vocal interest groups in their policy area to assist their competition with other departments or agencies of government for more funds or new programs.

FUNDING AND CRITICISM   It is sometimes thought that interest groups that receive assistance from government will become tame supporters of government. However, feminist, Aboriginal, environmental, and poor people's groups that have received funding from the Canadian government have, at times, been sharply critical of the policies of the governments that helped to fund them. In response, governments have sometimes reduced or eliminated funding for such groups. For example, the Harper Conservative government sharply reduced or eliminated the funding of a number of organizations that provided independent policy analysis and advocacy.

Government funding of public interest groups has been criticized particularly by those who feel that some of the groups are too radical or represent only "special interests." Often ignored is that the promotion of business interests is, in effect, subsidized by government. In calculating their taxes, businesses can deduct contributions to interest groups and other expenses they incur in trying to influence government. In contrast, individuals can only receive a tax credit for contributing to organizations that are deemed to be charitable, which in Canada and the United States generally excludes organizations that devote more than 10 percent of their revenues to political action.

Interest Group Activities

In analyzing how interest groups try to influence public policy, a distinction may be made between inside and outside strategies (Walker, 1991). **Inside strategies** involve interest group leaders developing close contacts with key decision makers in government and the public service. Presenting briefs to government based on the group's research and participating in advisory bodies also allow influence to be exerted in a quiet fashion. **Outside strategies** involve appealing to the public for support (for example, through the communications media and advertising) and mobilizing members and supporters to put pressure on decision makers (for example, through petitions, emails, social media, and demonstrations).

Inside strategies have the advantage of directly influencing those responsible for developing government policies. However, developing a very close relationship with the government may result in interest group leaders becoming influenced by and associated with the policy direction and concerns of the government. Outside strategies, if successful in mobilizing the support of the public, may be useful in pressuring politicians who are worried about their chances for re-election. Outside strategies may also be useful in building and maintaining an active membership-based organization. However, governments are often reluctant to be seen as backing down under pressure, and therefore groups using outside strategies can have difficulty exerting influence once government has publicly committed to a particular course of action.

CHOICE OF STRATEGIES Different types of interest groups tend to use different mixtures of strategies. Business and professional associations are more likely to use inside strategies, although they may devote some attention to outside strategies if they find government unsympathetic to their concerns. Unions, public interest groups, issue-oriented groups, and groups that have developed out of social movements are more likely to use outside strategies. However, combining outside and inside strategies may be useful in persuading government to adopt specific policies (see Box 8-1 Campaigning for a Clean Harbour).

inside strategies

Strategies in which interest group leaders develop close contacts with key decision makers in government and the public service in order to influence public policies.

outside strategies

Strategies in which interest group leaders appeal to the public for support and mobilize members in order to put pressure on decision makers concerning public policies.

BOX 8-1   Campaigning for a Clean Harbour

Trying to clean up the St. John's harbour has meant dredging up support from far and wide.

The Newfoundland capital was just one of a number of Canadian cities that dump untreated sewage into their harbours. Not only is raw sewage toxic to marine life, it also interferes with the development of the tourist industry and the enjoyment of the harbour. But in the case of St. John's, the substantial cost of building sewage treatment facilities, estimated at $93 million in 1997, was beyond the capability of the city government.

An arrangement to share the costs among the national, provincial, and local governments was worked out in the early 1980s. However, a dispute between the Canadian and Newfoundland governments in 1982 over an unrelated issue (the control of offshore oil) led to the suspension of plans to build a sewage treatment facility. The St. John's city government was subsequently unable to persuade the senior levels of government to carry out their commitments to provide funding.

In 1991, the Canadian government established the Atlantic Canada Action Program (ACAP) to encourage community initiatives, particularly those that would deal with the environmental problems of harbours and coastlines. Based on this, the St. John's Harbour ACAP organization was formed by a group of local citizens. It built on a citizens' group, the Friends of St. John's Harbour, and included representatives of the three levels of government. Partial funding for the organization was provided by Environment Canada.

In addition to carrying out scientific research to document the environmental problems of the harbour, St. John's Harbour ACAP decided that it needed to take political action to clean up the harbour. Its approach involved an outside strategy of mobilizing public support and an inside strategy of collaborating with governments to design the appropriate facilities and negotiate suitable financial arrangements. The group raised the issue in federal, provincial, and municipal elections and kept the public informed of the issue. It lobbied governments and gained the support of local businesses, especially the tourist and convention industries, for its goal.

In 1996, pressure from the St. John's Harbour ACAP helped persuade the three municipal governments in the St. John's area to commit to the project and begin some preliminary work. It was another four years before the provincial government, worried that the Canadian government would not contribute, was persuaded to commit to sharing the costs of the project. The Canadian government was reluctant to commit to the project, fearing that it would be seen as a special handout to one area of the country. Finally, in 2002, as part of a national infrastructure-building program, the Canadian government agreed to provide one-third of the funding.

Although the experience of the St. John's Harbour ACAP suggests that a combined inside/outside strategy is desirable, it has its difficulties. Putting outside pressure on government may result in an antagonistic relationship that can impede efforts to collaborate with government. Although the Canadian government (through Environment Canada) was involved with the formation and activities of St. John's Harbour ACAP, the group had a difficult time persuading the Canadian government to act. On the other hand, an inside strategy of collaborating with government may detract from efforts to mobilize the public support that is often needed to convince governments to act. In this case, over time the two dedicated part-time staff members of the St. John's Harbour ACAP were able to learn the skills of successful interest group activity. They patiently pursued their goal despite years of frustration (Close & Mintz, 2005). In the end they were successful: the primary sewage treatment plant began operations in 2009!

The political activities and strategies of interest groups are also affected by the organization and operations of the system of government. Interest groups in the United States devote considerable effort in trying to influence individual elected representatives in Congress because of the substantial involvement of Congress in the development of public policies. Canadian interest groups, particularly institutionalized interest groups, tend to direct much of their activity toward influencing those public servants who are important in developing public policy and the particular Cabinet minister whose government department is most relevant to the concerns of the interest group. For example, interest groups representing farmers devote much of their efforts to trying to influence those involved in policy development within the Department of Agriculture and meet regularly with the minister to discuss their concerns and proposals.

In several Western European countries (including, to varying extents, Austria, Germany, Sweden, and the Netherlands), the state actively collaborates with selected major interests (particularly the national organizations of business and labour) to seek a consensus concerning the country's major economic and social policies. State officials guide or facilitate the development of a consensus among the leading interests. In turn, the leaders of these interests persuade those they represent to accept the agreements that have been reached (such as agreements concerning wage and price increases). In such systems (termed **neo-corporatism**[2]), the activities of the leading interest groups and their relationship to government tends to be quite different than in Canada, the United States, and the United Kingdom.

LOBBYING   The inside strategy is often associated with the activity of lobbying. The term **lobbying** arose from the practice, by those seeking favours from government or seeking to influence the passage of legislation, of congregating in the lobby of the British House of Commons to make their case to members of Parliament. In contemporary usage, lobbying refers to efforts to influence not only legislators, but also those involved in the executive and administrative aspects of government. Regulatory agencies such as the Canadian Radio-television Telecommunications Commission (CRTC) are also an important target for lobbyists particularly because their decisions often affect the profitability of particular corporations. Specifically, lobbying refers to efforts to persuade those involved in making and implementing public policies to adopt and implement certain policies or decisions, particularly through direct personal contact.

Lobbying has increasingly become a professionalized activity. In addition to individuals within corporations and interest groups who have developed expertise in lobbying government, a number of consulting firms specialize

---

neo-corporatism

A political system in which the state actively collaborates with selected major interests (particularly the national organizations of business and labour) to seek a consensus concerning the country's major economic and social policies.

lobbying

An effort to persuade those involved in making and implementing public policies to adopt and implement policies or decisions favoured by an individual, business, or group particularly through direct personal contact.

---

[2]Neo-corporatism should be distinguished from the fascist corporate state, which involved authoritarian direction and control of business and labour.

in lobbying on behalf of a variety of clients, particularly corporations. As of 2015, there were 8425 active lobbyists registered at the national level in Canada (Office of the Commissioner of Lobbying Canada, 2014–15). In the United States, 3587 corporations reported spending $1.84 billion on lobbying expenses in 2012 while trade associations (such as the American Petroleum Institute) spent $553 million and business-wide associations (such as the American Chamber of Commerce) spent $175 million. Overall, US business related lobbying groups spent 34 times that of unions and public interest groups (Drutman, 2015). Many professional lobbyists are persons who have had high-level experience in government. Their inside knowledge of the workings of government and the thinking of policy makers, as well as their extensive contacts within government and administration, can make them valuable assets to their clients. However, the revolving door between working in government and working as a lobbyist, as well as the government's hiring of lobbying firms for research and public relations, often leads to ethical questions being raised about whether the relationship between government and lobbyists is too close.

Lobbying often has a very negative image, as it raises the possibility of special deals being worked out in secret to provide benefits, at public expense, to particular individuals, businesses, or groups. Governments in Canada, the United States, and elsewhere have adopted legislation to regulate the activities of lobbyists and to require that lobbyists be registered and publicly disclose some of their activities. It is difficult, however, to ensure that particular interests do not receive special benefits due to influence exerted behind closed doors. For example, former Canadian Prime Minister Brian Mulroney secretly received envelopes containing several hundred thousand dollars from a notorious influence-peddling lobbyist shortly after leaving office.

INVOLVEMENT IN THE POLICY PROCESS In their interactions with government, many institutionalized interest groups do not simply put forward their demands and pressure government to give them what they want. Interest groups often supply information that government policy makers need and work with policy makers to try to find effective solutions to problems (Montpetit, 2004). The development of government policies is often a product of the discussions among networks of government officials, various interest groups, and experts in a particular policy field. In this situation, interest groups will represent the interest of their members, but as well they will often be involved in trying to find solutions that are acceptable to other interests and to government.

The involvement of interest groups in the policy process is often facilitated through the use of "think tanks," non-profit organizations that do policy research and develop policy proposals. The United States has a vast array of think tanks that provide influential policy advice. In Canada, the C.D. Howe Institute and the Fraser Institute have considerable influence on policy

C.D. Howe Institute
www.cdhowe.org

Fraser Institute
www.fraserinstitute.ca

Canadian Centre for Policy
Alternatives
www.policyalternatives.ca

discussion and development. Many think tanks are financed by contributions from the business community. A few, such as the Canadian Centre for Policy Alternatives, are supported by labour unions and individual members.

MOBILIZING PUBLIC SUPPORT   Most interest groups pay some attention to gaining support from the public for their concerns and proposals. For issue-oriented interest groups that have not developed close connections with policy makers, the "outside" strategy of taking their case to the public may be the only way of effectively influencing public policy. Institutionalized interest groups and individual corporations increasingly seek to create or maintain a good public image to counteract potential public campaigns that might harm their interests. For example, the Canadian Association of Petroleum Producers spends large amounts of money on advertising and public relations to try to clean up the negative image of their industry.

Mobilizing public support may involve getting the group's message to the public in the hope that a change in public opinion will affect the thinking of policy makers. In a more active way, interest groups may encourage their members to sign petitions, email their elected representatives, vote for candidates and parties that support their cause, and participate in public demonstrations.

As well, interest groups often try to build coalitions with other interest groups in order to add weight to their claim to speak on behalf of a large number of people on a particular issue. Although some coalitions of groups are only temporary alliances to pursue a particular issue, more permanent organizations are often formed to represent the interests of their member groups. For example, the Canadian Council for International Co-operation with nine staff members is a coalition of about 75 non-profit organizations that seeks to "end global poverty and to promote social justice and human dignity for all."

Canadian Council for International
Co-operation
www.ccic.ca

LEGAL ACTION   Interest groups often make use of the judicial system to advance their interests. For example, environmental groups have had some successes in the courts in forcing the Canadian government to undertake environmental assessments of proposed projects that have potentially negative effects on fish habitats. However, using the court system to pursue interests can be costly. The Canadian government has financed the Court Challenges program (a national non-profit organization) to assist equality-seeking groups, particularly women's groups and groups representing linguistic minorities, in challenging laws and policies that are viewed as discriminatory under the provisions of the Canadian Charter of Rights and Freedoms. Although this program was cancelled by the Conservative government in 2006, the Liberal government reinstated the Court Challenges Program in 2016 with a $5 million budget.

The use of the legal system to pursue interest group objectives is particularly common in the United States, where laws often contain specific obligations for government action and thus provide scope for legal action if the obligations are not fulfilled. In contrast, laws in Canada typically provide considerable discretion to government and administrators in determining when and how to carry out the general objectives contained in the law. For example, most environmental laws in Canada enable governments to take action to protect the environment, but do not require that they do so (Boyd, 2003).

Legal actions can also be used to intimidate interest groups. Some corporations have sued public interest groups for millions of dollars based on claims that their reputation has been harmed. Even if the corporation does not have a strong case, the public interest group may not be able to bear the cost of a defence in court.

Influence Potential

Interest groups vary in their capabilities to influence public policy. Several factors contribute to the amount of influence a group can exert:

- The size and cohesiveness of the group's membership
- The ability of a group to mobilize its members and supporters and its ability to establish coalitions with other groups to advance its causes
- The financial resources to maintain an effective organization, hire professional lobbyists and political consultants, and conduct research and advertising on behalf of the group's concerns.
- The ability to develop close ties with key government policy makers and have allies within government
- The perception by government, the media, and the public that the group has expertise and credibility
- Having ideas and proposals coincide with the general thinking of government, the media, and the public
- The ability to make credible threats about the adverse consequences of failing to act as the group recommends

In addition, a group is more likely to be influential if it does not face powerful competing interest groups in a particular policy area. Groups seeking to maintain the status quo are more likely to be successful than those seeking change (Mahoney, 2008).

Although a large number of interest groups have been established in modern liberal democracies, some groups are more influential than others. One study that examined 47 different issues in the United States found that trade or business associations and corporations were more likely to have some success in attaining their goals than citizen groups. However, in the very different context of the European Union, the study found that citizen groups were almost as likely as business groups and corporations to have some success (Mahoney, 2008).

It is often argued that business interests have a privileged position from which to influence many aspects of government policy (see Box 8-2 The Financial Crisis of 2007–2009). Business groups and individual large corporations possess

BOX 8-2   The Financial Crisis of 2007–2009

Between 2007 and 2009, many of the largest banks and other financial institutions in the United States and Europe faced bankruptcy, resulting in the worst economic crisis since the Great Depression of the 1930s. Governments felt that these corporations were too big to fail; that is, that their failure could lead to the collapse of the national and global economies. The American government, through various programs (including the US$700 billion Troubled Asset Relief Program), bailed out some leading financial institutions (along with GM and Chrysler). Governments around the world also initiated major government spending programs (estimated to total $5 trillion) to stimulate failing economies. While successful in preventing a serious economic depression, these efforts resulted in large government deficits and debts.

One of the leading causes of the financial crisis was the deregulation of the large financial industry that is the cornerstone of modern economies. Over the past several decades, banks and other financial institutions in the United States were allowed to hide money-losing assets on their financial statements; invest trillions of dollars in complex, highly speculative derivatives rather than in real assets such as houses and manufacturing plants; decide for themselves how much of their depositors' savings they needed to hold in reserve; and engage in a wave of mergers that created massive financial institutions. From 1998 to 2008, American financial institutions spent more than US$5 billion on political influence, including $1.7 billion in election campaign contributions and $3.4 billion on lobbying federal officials. As of 2007, there were nearly three thousand registered lobbyists working for financial institutions in the United States (Consumer Education Foundation, 2009). Influence was also exerted by the two-way flow of top personnel between the leading financial institutions and the American government, which facilitated the easy access of financial institutions to key policy makers and regulators (Rothkopf, 2009).

Simon Johnson, the former chief economist of the International Monetary Fund, suggests that the influence of the largest financial institutions was not simply a result of lobbying and campaign contributions. Their influence was particularly effective because "the American financial industry gained political power by amassing a kind of cultural capital—a belief system . . . that what was good for Wall Street was good for the country" (Johnson, 2009, p. 2).

considerable financial resources, sources of information, and expertise, and often have close relationships with government that give them considerable influence potential. More fundamentally, the government's desire to retain the confidence of the business community in order to maintain the material well-being of the community means that the interests and policy preferences of business are likely to be highly influential in the development of a wide variety of government policies that affect the activities and profitability of business (Lindblom, 1977). By contrast, the poor and various disadvantaged groups in society often do not have strong and effective interest groups to represent their interests, and their concerns may not be taken as seriously by policy makers as the interests of business.

social movement

A network of groups and individuals that seeks major social and political changes, particularly by acting outside of established political institutions.

Social Movements

Social movements seek major social and political changes, particularly by collective action outside of established political institutions (Martell, 1994).

Groups based on social movements may, like interest groups, seek to change various laws and public policies. However, social movements also have broader goals, including challenging and transforming the values, power relationships, and institutions of society and politics. A social movement can be thought of as a network of groups and individuals who share a common cause. As well, social movements are often based on, or seek to develop, a sense of collective identity among a substantial segment of society and seek to inspire collective action by this segment of society. For example, the women's movement has sought to raise the consciousness of women not only to increase awareness of the problems women face and challenge male dominance, but also to create a sense of solidarity among women and to encourage collective action to promote women's values and identity in politics and society.

The distinction between social movements and interest groups is not always clear because many public interest groups originated in and are associated with social movements. For example, some environmental interest groups are concerned primarily with remedying a specific environmental problem; other groups view themselves as part of a broader environmental movement that believes that major social, economic, and political changes are needed to deal with environmental problems.

Social Movements & Culture: A Resource Site
http://culturalpolitics.net/social_movements

Old and New Social Movements

Social movements have a lengthy political history going back at least to the beginning of the industrial age in Europe (Heberle, 1951). One of the earliest movements was for the abolition of slavery in Britain in the late eighteenth century (Coupland, 1964). Another early British movement, the Chartists, pressed for the expansion of democratic rights in the 1830s, including the right to vote for all men (Thompson, 1984). Other nineteenth-century movements in various countries sought basic democratic rights for ordinary people (especially the emerging industrial working class), national independence, and voting and legal rights for women (the suffragette movement).

A wave of protest and discontent that reached its peak in the late 1960s was associated with the development of a variety of new social movements, including the American civil rights movement, the women's movement, the environmental movement, Aboriginal movements, the gay and lesbian movement, the anti-war movement, and various new nationalist movements (including a Quebec nationalist movement). Later, the global social justice movement (often referred to as the anti-globalization movement) developed in the 1990s while the Occupy movement began in 2011.

Many of those involved in these movements shared the view that the elites (and large corporations) that dominated society and politics needed to be challenged and that major changes in values and institutions were needed to liberate oppressed groups. However, some contemporary movements have a different perspective (see Box 8-3 The Tea Party Movement). As well, movements that

BOX 8-3   The Tea Party Movement

Social movements are often thought of as "progressive" challenges to the existing political and social order including networks of groups and individuals seeking democracy and promoting the rights of disadvantaged or oppressed groups. But some important movements such as the Tea Party movement in the United States do not fit into this conception of a social movement. Indeed, the origins of the Tea Party apparently lie in the decision of tobacco companies to set up "third-party" interest groups to counter anti-tobacco taxes and regulations. Some of the groups that helped to form the Tea Party movement were supported by major corporate interests including the oil, pharmaceutical, and food and beverage industries (Fallin, Grana, & Glantz, 2013).

The Tea Party movement is named after the Boston Tea Party (1773) in which American colonists challenging British "taxation without representation" boarded British ships and dumped their cargo of tea into Boston's harbour, an action that helped to inspire the American Revolution. The Tea Party movement that burst onto the political scene in 2009 in opposition to government stimulus spending, bailouts, and takeovers of private industries is a radical conservative movement based on what it views as the founding principles of the United States. Their goals include limited government based on a free-market economy and an end to government deficit spending along with protecting the right to gun ownership, ensuring that government cannot expropriate private property, reducing personal and business income taxes, ending compulsory health insurance, and promoting traditional family and religious values.

The Tea Party movement, which claims tens of millions of supporters, has been active within the Republican Party, defeating moderate Republican representatives. However, the 2016 Republican presidential nomination campaign divided the Tea Party. Some Tea Party supporters, including Sarah Palin, supported Donald Trump who shares their angry anti-establishment feelings. However other Tea Party supporters opposed Trump's protectionist, anti-free trade positions and his reluctance to slash government "entitlements" such as spending on medicare and social security for seniors (Mascaro, 2016). For many Tea Party supporters, Ted Cruz (who fought vigorously against government spending in Congress) was their preferred presidential candidate.

seek to maintain traditional national ethnic, racial, and religious values and identity particularly by restricting immigration and expelling refugees have developed in a number of European countries.

Some of those active in the new social movements have been critical of the hierarchy and power politics of conventional political organizations and seek to create informal unstructured organizations or networks based on grassroots participation. Likewise, direct action by participants (such as demonstrations, sit-ins, and blockades) is seen as more effective in bringing about substantial change than working through existing political parties and interest groups. By using dramatic actions, activists in the new social movements have been able to gain media coverage for their causes.

The more flexible structures adopted by the new social movements give them real advantages because a broad framework allows a movement to grow and encompass as many people as possible who share its broad objectives. However, this very breadth can harm movements by presenting a confused picture of who they are and what they want.

The Tea Party
www.teaparty.org
www.teapartypatriots.org

Changes in Movements

Over time, there is often a tendency for organizations based on social movements to become more conventional in nature. The labour and socialist movements that developed in the latter part of the nineteenth century are no longer seen as unconventional forces in many countries. Likewise, many of the organizations that developed out of the women's and environmental movements have, to a considerable extent, become conventional in their structures and activities. When this happens we speak of the *demobilization, routinization,* or *institutionalization* of a movement (Wilson, 2002). It loses some of its spontaneity and becomes less confrontational in its relations with government. For example, a number of the large environmental organizations in the United States (sometimes referred to as the "Big Ten") became highly institutionalized organizations concerned primarily with fundraising and lobbying government officials. Foundations set up by wealthy business people and, in some cases, individual corporations have provided an important base of financial support, allowing these organizations to hire professional managers to play leading roles in the organizations. For example, over the years the Nature Conservancy has received $10 million from BP (infamous for causing the massive oil spill in the Gulf of Mexico in 2010) and has invested in oil, gas, and coal corporations. Indeed, the Nature Conservancy participated in fossil fuel extraction that contributed to the extinction of an endangered species on a Texas nature preserve donated to it by Mobil Oil (Klein, 2015). Conservation International received $2 million from BP and in the past included BP's CEO on its board of directors (*The Economist*, 2010)). The leaders of some of the large conservation and environmental organizations have come to prefer

Arab Spring supporters in Tahrir Square, Cairo, Egypt celebrate the resignation of President Hosni Mubarak on February 11, 2011. However the success of the movement in overthrowing the military-backed dictator was only temporary.

George Henton/Alamy Stock Photo

working with government and corporations, leaving grassroots activists and local organizations to take a tougher stance in defence of the environment

Some view the adoption of conventional interest group strategies as the "selling out" of a movement and its ideals. Others argue that it has increased the possibility of achieving success by influencing the policies of government or business through realistic proposals and by becoming an accepted participant in policy discussions. For example, nine major environmental groups worked with the twenty-one companies that are members of the Forest Products Association of Canada to reach the Canadian Boreal Forest Agreement in 2010 to protect one of the world's largest forest and wetlands ecosystems and the single largest terrestrial carbon storehouse. While scientists called for the protection of at least one-half of the 1.4 billion acres of this crucial ecosystem, thus far only a relatively small part of the ecosystem and caribou habitat has been protected. Two environmental groups withdrew from the agreement when talks with Resolute Forest Products to protect the forests were unsuccessful (Jang & Marotte, 2013). [3]

In some cases, those dissatisfied with the transformation of a movement into more conventional interest groups have established new groups that focus on grassroots mobilization and confrontation. For example, the Sea Shepherd Conservation Society was started by a founder of Greenpeace who favoured more vigorous direct action (such as attacking whaling vessels) and the radical group Earth First! was started by a former Sierra Club employee.

Overall, the continued existence of more "radical" elements within a movement can be useful in preventing the more moderate institutionalized groups from making excessive compromises of the movement's goals and principles. While institutionalized groups may become effective in the policy making process, it is the more militant thinkers and activists who usually "generate the ideas that ultimately shape political discourse and shift the tides of history" (Bosso, 2005, p. 154). As well, the existence of groups that can mobilize activists in support of a cause can help to provide leverage for the more conventional groups to persuade government to accept their moderate proposals so as to avoid being confronted with more extreme demands and disruptive actions.

Canadian Boreal Forest Agreement
www.canadianborealforestagreement. com

Transnational Social Movements

Social movements often migrate across borders and thus can be considered transnational. Older political movements such as the anti-slavery and labour movements were influential in many countries. Some newer social movements such as the women's and environmental movements have global reach, influencing politics in varying ways in many countries in almost all parts of the

---

[3]The Assembly of First Nations did not sign the Boreal Forest Agreement. In their view it did not reflect First Nations title, treaty rights, traditions, and practices on their lands.

world as well as seeking to influence various international institutions. For example, organizations associated with the environmental movement such as Greenpeace International, Friends of the Earth International, and the World Wide Fund for Nature have offices and undertake activities in many countries. Although based in the richer countries, they also have a substantial presence in a number of less developed countries.[4] The processes of globalization, particularly advances in communications and transportation, have facilitated the global reach of a number of social movements.

Activities

Those active in social movements often are involved in protest activities because their group has not been successful in achieving its goals through more conventional forms of political activity. Nevertheless, those associated with a social movement often establish public interest groups to pursue particular policy objectives related to the vision and perspective of the movement. In addition, some movements have led to the establishment of political parties, including social democratic and labour parties, nationalist and separatist parties, and green parties. Political parties based on the women's movement have been established in several countries, but with little electoral success.[5] Connections of movement activists to different mainstream political parties, beliefs that movement objectives might be better achieved through non-partisan action, a reluctance to expend a movement's energies on electoral politics, and a belief that engagement in party politics will lead to a compromise of the movement's principles can contribute to a reluctance to form a movement-based political party.

THE COMMUNICATIONS MEDIA

The communications media can be considered a major source of political influence. The media not only are important in communicating the concerns and views of various groups and individuals to government, but also have an ability to raise issues, influence both the public and politicians, and help shape political debate.

Ownership and Regulation

In liberal democracies, newspapers and other print media have usually been privately owned and free of government regulation, except for wartime censorship and the protection of national security. In many countries, there is a

---

[4]However, some countries have restricted the activities of international NGOs. For example, Ethiopia bans NGOs from promoting human and democratic rights, promoting equality, and campaigning for children's rights (*BBC News*, 2009).

[5]In Iceland, the Women's Alliance elected several female representatives. It later joined with three other leftist parties to form the Social Democratic Alliance, which formed the government in 2009 but was defeated in the 2013 election.

mixture of private and public ownership of the broadcast media (radio and television). Fears that privately owned American broadcast networks would move into Canada led to the establishment in 1936 of the Canadian Broadcasting Corporation (CBC), a Crown corporation that is expected to be non-partisan and independent of government control. In many European countries broadcasting was initially deemed a public service, but was opened to privately owned commercial television in the 1980s (Curran & Alberg, 2012). Many countries (other than the United States)[6] have retained a significant element of public broadcasting paid for by government subsidies and/or public fees.

CORPORATE OWNERSHIP In many countries, large corporations now own the majority of mass media outlets. There has been a trend toward concentration and cross-media ownership, in which a few large multinational corporations own a variety of different media and related entertainment industries. As a result, the diversity of the mass media has been reduced. Media outlets that are part of large corporate empires may be less likely to report on problems occurring with other branches of the corporation.

The ownership of much of the mass media by large corporations may result in a bias toward defending and promoting the interests of big business and the values of the capitalist system. Media owners tend to be conservative and oriented to the dominant interests in society. Their choice of executives to run their media outlets will likely reflect, at least to some extent, their ideological orientation. As well, their dependence on advertising revenues may lead to pressure to avoid or downplay certain stories. However, as profit-oriented enterprises, media corporations may want to attract as large an audience as possible by including different viewpoints. In addition, journalists and reporters tend to be less conservative than many mass media owners and executives (Alterman, 2003; Croteau, 1998; Miljan & Cooper, 2003).

There has been a tendency, particularly in the United States, for the mass media to become more ideological and partisan. Fox News has a strongly right-wing orientation and is favourable to the Republican Party, while MSNBC is clearly liberal and favourable to the Democratic Party. Newspaper editorial endorsements of political parties have been common in Canada and many other countries. In the 2015 Canadian election, *The Globe and Mail* editorially endorsed the Conservative party, but not its leader, Stephen Harper. The *National Post* and the *Sun* newspapers that take right-wing ideological positions endorsed the Conservative party, while the *Toronto Star*, the *Montreal Gazette*, and *La Presse* endorsed the Liberal party. *Le Devoir* endorsed the Bloc. As well, two of the major newspapers carried full front-page ads for the Conservative Party just before election day in 2015.

The Campaign for Press and
Broadcasting Freedom
www.cpbf.org.uk

Fairness & Accuracy in Reporting
www.fair.org

Freedom Forum
www.freedomforum.org

Electronic Frontier Foundation
www.eff.org

---

[6]The non-profit, non-governmental Corporation for Public Broadcasting is responsible for the Public Broadcasting Service (PBS) and National Public Radio (NPR), both of which are small networks that rely primarily on private and corporate donations for their funding.

REGULATION The broadcast media are regulated, to varying extents in different countries, by government or a government-appointed agency to try to ensure that they act in the public interest. In some countries this has involved requirements that a certain amount of time be devoted to news and public affairs programming. Canadian broadcast regulations require that radio and television stations carry a substantial proportion of Canadian content.

The broadcast media in many countries are required to be non-partisan and to provide balanced coverage of politics particularly during election campaigns. Radio and television stations in Canada are required to provide parties with advertising time at their lowest rate during election campaigns. This is divided among the parties based on each party's percentage of seats, votes, and candidates in the previous election. The United States requires that broadcasters sell advertising space to candidates at their lowest rate. However, with few effective limits on fundraising and spending because advertising considered constitutionally protected free speech, American television is dominated by political advertising during election years. During the 2012 presidential election $US1.4 billion was spent on campaign advertising with 950 million television spot ads aired (Fowler, Franz, & Ridout, 2016). In contrast, many European countries strictly limit campaign advertising. For example, in the United Kingdom no paid political ads on radio or television are allowed. Instead, free time for each party's political broadcasts—usually lasting five minutes—during the election campaign are provided.

Objectivity

When an independent commercial press that appealed to the mass public developed in North America in the late nineteenth century, journalists began to view themselves as professionals conveying the objective truth to the public. Editors expected writers to report only the facts without exaggeration, interpretation, or opinion (Hackett & Zhao, 1998). A sharp distinction was made between fact and opinion, with opinions relegated to the editorial page. However, the "facts" do not necessarily speak for themselves. Without background and interpretation, the facts may be largely meaningless for much of the public. Indeed, since the "facts" often come from official sources, the attempt to appear objective has been viewed by some analysts as reflecting a bias in favour of the dominant political forces (Hackett & Zhao, 1998). As well, since reporting inevitably involves selectivity in deciding what to report, objectivity may be impossible to achieve fully.

The ideal of objectivity has not disappeared, but it has tended to be treated in the broader sense of allowing background and interpretation, provided that reporters attempt to be impartial, fair, and balanced (Hackett & Zhao, 1998). This may involve presenting both sides of a controversial issue.

However, the interpretation of a news story often involves a subtle form of selectivity known as **framing**: "selecting and highlighting some facets of events or

framing

Selecting and highlighting some facets of events or issues, and making connections among them so as to promote a particular interpretation, evaluation, and/or solution.

issues, and making connections among them so as to promote a particular inter-pretation, evaluation, and/or solution" (Entman, 2004, p. 5). For example, the American media framed the story of the invasion of Iraq in 2003 by the United States and its allies in terms of an effort to liberate Iraqis from an evil dictator who possessed weapons of mass destruction. While Iraqi president Saddam Hussein certainly was a brutal dictator, there were no weapons of mass destruction, and the invasion directly or indirectly caused hundreds of thousands of civilian deaths.

The Media as Watchdogs?

The mass media are often expected to play a watchdog role. By bringing to public attention abuses of power or the failure of governments to deal with important problems, the media can help to check the power of government and assist citizens in pressuring government to correct problems.

Center for Investigative Reporting
https://www.revealnews.org/

Critics of the mass media argue that the mass media have often turned from watchdogs into attack dogs by mounting sharp personal attacks on politicians and other prominent persons. Political scientist Larry Sabato (1992) described American journalists as being like sharks engaging in a "feeding frenzy" when they publicize rumours and gossip about politicians and celebrities. The preva-lence of critical and negative journalism should not be exaggerated. The media can also be seen, to some extent, as lapdogs. There is often a cozy relation-ship between government and journalists, and much of what constitutes news originates from official sources. Journalists who are viewed as sympathetic to the government are more likely to be given the inside story, an exclusive inter-view with a leading political figure, or a "leak" about an impending govern-ment announcement. Even though contemporary journalists generally prefer to avoid too close a relationship with politicians, they rely on politicians and government officials for information to make sense of what is happening within government and to provide anecdotes for an interesting story. With pressure to report the news as quickly as possible and with media owners trying to pro-duce news at the lowest possible cost, journalists often lack the capability and resources to properly research the news stories they are presenting.

Project Censored
www.projectcensored.org

Furthermore, media watchdogs are sometimes asleep or muzzled. For example, the pattern of systematic physical, sexual, and cultural abuse of gen-erations of Aboriginals forced to attend residential schools across Canada did not receive media scrutiny until long after the schools were closed.

Walking the Dog: News Management

news management

The controlling and shaping of the pre-sentation of news in order to affect the public's evaluation of news stories.

Governments and politicians often try to manage the news so as to avoid gain-ing negative treatment. **News management**—controlling and shaping the presen-tation of information—includes such techniques as issuing news releases close to news deadlines so that journalists cannot check the facts or obtain critical comments. Information that reflects negatively on government is often released when a more dramatic news event is occurring or during the summer and on weekends when many journalists are not working and audiences are small.

Politicians and their media advisers are very concerned with controlling the "spin" put on what they have said—that is, trying to ensure that a favourable interpretation is placed on information. For example, during a leaders' debate, "spin doctors" for each party will try to persuade journalists that their leader has won the debate and explain away any mistakes that their leader has made. Prime Minister Harper's Conservative government was particularly concerned with news management, often requiring that every government event, press release, and speech by ministers, Conservative MPs, and senior public servants be scripted to present a consistent, positive image and be approved by the Prime Minister's Office or the Privy Council Office.

To avoid unfavourable framing of their proposals and actions, governments spend large sums of money on advertising to carry their message directly to the public. Although some government advertising is designed to increase awareness of government services and programs, governments have also mounted substantial advertising campaigns to promote their perspective on particular issues, boast about their accomplishments, and present themselves in a positive light.[7]

News management by government is most clearly seen in times of war and more generally in much of the coverage of international affairs. The mass media often consider it unpatriotic to question their government's decision to go to war or engage in foreign conflicts. Government officials and military leaders usually try to control the media tightly during a foreign conflict and may plant false or exaggerated stories about enemy atrocities.

The Media and Democracy

Debate exists about whether the mass media provide the political information that is needed for people to participate meaningfully in political life, make intelligent choices among parties and candidates, and hold those in public office accountable for their actions. Citizens require not only a set of facts, but also sufficient background and explanations and diverse opinions about what should be done in order to make sense of political issues. Although a large amount of political information is potentially available to the public, criticisms are often raised about the quality of information that the ordinary person obtains from the media. Because the mass media need to attract large audiences to be profitable, they tend to focus on providing entertainment to their audiences. Not only may this mean that news and public affairs programming is

---

[7]The Ontario's Government Advertising Act prohibits government advertising that promotes partisan interests and requires that provincial government ads be approved by the independent Office of the Auditor General of Ontario. However, online advertising is not covered by the act. The Trudeau Liberal government has promised to adopt legislation to restrict partisan government advertising.

In April 2004, investigative reporter Seymour Hersh published articles in *The New Yorker* magazine that included pictures illustrating the abuse and torture of Iraqis in the Abu Ghraib prison. This brought to public attention the evidence of abuse that had been largely ignored by the mainstream media.

AP Images

infotainment

The merging of information and entertainment in news and public affairs programming of the mass media, particularly television.

given limited resources, it can also result in the merging of information with entertainment. This combination, labelled **infotainment**, is particularly evident in the focus of television newscasts on stories that can be portrayed with dramatic images. As the cynical saying puts it, "If it bleeds, it leads."

For example, Arthur Kent, the Canadian-born journalist who reported on the 1991 Gulf War for American television network NBC, was critical of NBC and other networks for refusing to run serious stories about foreign affairs. Kent was fired as a result of his outspoken criticisms. However, during his successful lawsuit against NBC, network executives testified that news coverage was affected by a concern to broadcast entertaining stories (Kent, 1996).

Stories that can be portrayed in terms of conflict and controversy receive the most attention. News items have become increasingly short to discourage bored viewers from switching to a different channel. Statements and comments by politicians, experts, or ordinary people are edited to a single, snappy sound bite lasting only a few seconds. It is difficult, if not impossible, to explain an issue meaningfully in the sixty seconds that may be allotted to a television news story. Television news thus tends to be simplistic and does not generally provide the context or historical background needed to understand the events that it portrays. Further, "shock talk" radio programs that feature inflammatory and misleading diatribes that are often racist, homophobic, and misogynist are popular, particularly in the United States.

Tami Thirlwell

Online Media

Online media (including social media, blogs, and websites) are transforming political communications. The use of online media for political news and opinions is tending to surpass newspapers, television, and radio in importance, particularly among younger persons.

To some extent, online media have democratized political communications as social media involve large numbers of people communicating their views to many other people in an unmediated forum. Politicians and party spokespersons have found it useful to go online to communicate directly with the public (particularly their followers through Twitter, Facebook, and blogs). The Internet also provides the potential for campaign professionals to precisely target their messages to specific groups of people using the surveillance techniques that have been developed for consumer products. Not only do online media provide a large quantity of user-generated material that can potentially be viewed by large numbers of people, they have also made it easy to view a diversity of websites produced by the traditional media around the world (although full free access to many newspapers is restricted through pay walls). Online media have added to the diversity of media with news aggregators reducing reliance on a single news source. The easy availability of diverse sources of information and opinions can provide a broader perspective on politics. However, the new media can also reinforce and strengthen an individual's established perspective when that person only follows news sources with a similar perspective.

From the protests that shut down the Seattle meetings of the World Trade Organization in 1999 to the massive 2012 online protests against proposed American antipiracy laws that would limit Internet freedom, online media have been important in mobilizing very large numbers of people. Progressive activists using online media had an important part in mobilizing support to elect Barack Obama in 2008. Social media played an important role in the "Arab Spring" protests that brought down dictatorial regimes in Tunisia and (temporarily) Egypt.

Activists have also sought to exert political influence through the use of online petitions. For example, Avaaz, which describes itself as "a global web movement to bring people-powered politics to decision-making everywhere," has demonstrated an ability to quickly mobilize many of the over 44 million people who have joined the group to add their names to petitions to government leaders around the world on a variety of issues particularly related to human rights, environmental issues, and corruption. Likewise the petition site Care2, which focuses on animal rights, environmental issues, healthy living, and human rights, claims over 34 million members. Change. org claims that over 151 million persons view its petitions that can be started by anyone, anywhere.

Avaaz
www.avaaz.org

Care2
www.care2.com

Change.org
www.change.org

Online media do not always have positive effects. Jihadi groups (including ISIS) have used social media to recruit substantial numbers of volunteers from many countries to engage in war and terrorism. Security forces in Iran identified and punished those involved in the protests against electoral fraud in the Iran's 2009 presidential election by monitoring social media (Morozov, 2011). In 2016, China announced a ban on online media from foreign companies, and introduced a requirement that Chinese companies seek official approval of online content. As well, Wi-Fi access providers have to install tracking devices and a number of Chinese bloggers have been jailed.

Those who are skeptical about the ability of the new media to enhance political participation and democracy note that the digital media (such as YouTube) have been primarily used as a form of entertainment. As well, there has been a decline in the quality of traditional sources of political information as newspapers and the broadcast media often seek to deliver news quickly in order to remain relevant without necessarily doing adequate fact-checking. Further, with their revenues declining, newspapers have reduced their staff of reporters and some have closed.

Although those who use a diversity of sources of political information tend to have a higher level of political knowledge, the increased availability of political news (such as 24-hour news TV and online media) has not resulted in a more knowledgeable public according to American studies (Oxley, 2012).

Indeed, those who rely on online political blogs (as well as those who rely on Fox News) tend to be less knowledgeable about politics than those who use other sources. In addition to a declining level of political knowledge, the level of misinformation among the American public may have increased from 2003 to 2010 (Oxley, 2012).

Overall, online and digital media have not only increased the availability of political information, but also have greatly increased the availability of various sources of entertainment. This may have the effect of increasing the political knowledge gap between those who are more interested in politics and those who are less interested (Oxley, 2012).

✔• SUMMARY AND CONCLUSION

The freedom to organize into groups to express one's views and try to affect governing is a crucial element of liberal democracy. Interest groups potentially allow people to try to influence what government does on a day-to-day basis, not just on the infrequent occasions when elections occur. They convey the views, opinions, and problems of various elements of society to government and to other citizens on a regular basis. As well, interest groups often supply government with useful information, research, and advice, and some interest groups are directly involved with government in developing public policies. To some extent, the development of a large number of public interest groups has challenged the dominance of business influence. Nevertheless large corporations and business associations have a considerable ability to influence government to advance their own interests.

Social movements have often developed among segments of society that have been treated unfairly and ignored by government and conventional political institutions, and among those who believe that major changes in society and politics are needed. Even in democratic countries, the conventional channels for achieving desired goals are not always effective. Thus social movements often use unconventional means to carry their message to the public and to government.

The communications media are also very important in the processes of political influence. Not only can they affect the political agenda of government by raising or highlighting issues, but they may affect the general political values and beliefs that are present in a political community. Although the media are often viewed as important in holding the government accountable for its actions, they can also be a vehicle for government to try to influence the public. The concentration of mass media ownership in the hands of large corporations raises concerns about whether this leads to a bias in favour of corporate interests. Online and social media have increased the ability to access political information and opinions from a variety of sources. They can also facilitate the sharing of ideas and the mobilization of like-minded persons for political action.

✔• KEY TERMS

Framing   197
Infotainment   200
Inside strategies   184
Institutionalized interest group   180
Interest group   178

Issue-oriented interest group   180
Lobbying   186
Neo-corporatism   186
News management   198
Outside strategies   184

Public interest group   179
Selective incentive   182
Self-interest group   179
Social movement   190

DISCUSSION QUESTIONS

1. What interest groups are you a member of? Do you think that they reflect your views? Can they be considered democratic in the way they operate?

2. Are interest groups a threat to democracy and the common good?

3. What are the most important factors affecting the success or failure of interest groups and social movements?

4. Do the mass media provide you with a good, unbiased understanding of political issues?

5. What are the strengths and weaknesses of online and social media?

FURTHER READING

Berry, J.M., & Wilcox, C. (2016). *The interest group society* (6th ed.). New York: Routledge.

Carty, V. (2011), *Wired and mobilizing. Social movements, new technology, and electoral politics.* New York: Routledge.

Cigler, A., Loomis, B.A., & Nownes, A.J. (Eds.) (2016). *Interest group politics.* (9th ed.). Washington, D.C.: CQ Press.

Curran, J. & Aalberg, T. (Eds.) (2012). *How media informs democracy: A comparative approach.* New York: Routledge.

Drutman, L. (2015). *The business of America is lobbying: How corporations became politicized and politics became more corporate.* New York: Oxford University Press.

Godwin, K., Ainsworth, S.H., & Godwin, E. (2013). *Lobbying and policymaking: The public pursuit of private interests.* Washington, D.C: CQ Press

Grossman, M. (2012). *The not-so-special interests: Interest groups, public representation, and American governance.* Stanford, CA: Stanford University Press.

Schlozman, K.L., Verba, S., & Brady, H.E. (2012). *The unheavenly chorus. Unequal political voice and the broken promise of American democracy.* Princeton, NJ: Princeton University Press.

Smith, M. (2005). *A civil society? Collective actors in Canadian political life.* Peterborough, ON: Broadview Press.

Young, L., & Everitt, J. (2004). *Advocacy groups.* Vancouver: UBC Press.

9 Unconventional and Highly Conflictive Politics

From Protest to Revolution

Protestors seek to stop the construction of the Northern Gateway pipeline that would carry diluted bitumen from Alberta's oil (tar) sands to Kitimat, British Columbia for shipment through dangerous B.C. waters to Asia.   ZUMA Press, Inc./Alamy Stock Photo

After reading this chapter, you should be able to:

1. describe what political protest is and why people use protest as a political tool
2. discuss why not all political protest is democratic
3. understand why protest is an integral part of democratic politics
4. distinguish between insurgency and counter-insurgency
5. describe the characteristics of terrorism
6. discuss whether political violence is ever justifiable

In 2010 a pipeline operated by the Canadian firm Enbridge, carrying diluted heavy oil (bitumen) from the Alberta oil (tar) sands, ruptured in southwestern Michigan, spilling a million gallons of crude, diluted bitumen into the Kalamazoo River. Cleaning up the mess took four years and cost over $US 750 million. More importantly, pipelines became a political issue with important consequences for Canada.

Two major pipeline projects that have met great opposition are TransCanada's Keystone XL and Enbridge's Northern Gateway. The former was part of a four-part plan by TransCanada to move diluted bitumen from the Alberta oil sands to refineries in Texas. The latter would carry the same material from Alberta to Kitimat, British Columbia, for shipment to Asia. Although each originally received official approval, both failed in the face of protest.

TransCanada's problems began when residents of Nebraska protested that Keystone XL would cross the Nebraska Sand Hills, a designated National Natural Landmark that sits atop the Ogallala Aquifer, the source of water for 2 million people. This led the US State Department to reject TransCanada's proposal until alternative routes were considered. TransCanada then suggested a route that avoided the Sand Hills, but larger protests, these aimed at the carbon-intensive oil sands and their impact on climate change, followed. It was this final issue that led President Obama to reject Keystone XL in 2015.

Enbridge encountered resistance from environmentalists concerned not just about a pipeline leak but also oil spills from tankers; several First Nations, who cited both cultural and environmental threats; and from the British Columbia government, which saw Alberta reaping the project's benefits while British Columbia ran the risks. Further, there had been an unofficial ban on large tanker traffic along much of British Columbia's rugged coast since 1972. Although the project got conditional approval from the National Energy Board (NEB) in 2014, Justin Trudeau supported a ban on tanker traffic on B.C.'s north coast and placed a moratorium on the development of the Northern Gateway pipeline. A plan by Kinder Morgan to triple the bitumen capacity of their Trans Mountain pipeline from Alberta to Burnaby, B.C. was approved by the NEB, but faced opposition by First Nations and Vancouver's mayor.

Protest worked in affecting government decisions in the Keystone and Northern Gateway pipeline decisions for two reasons. First, protest generates publicity, turning low-key affairs into major issues. Second, when protest comes from sectors important to a party or leader, its impact is multiplied. These were plainly democratic protests, peacefully conducted. Yet they were examples of political conflict and, because they worked outside official channels, they involved political protest.

POLITICAL CONFLICT: PROTEST TO REVOLUTION

To many Canadians, political conflict suggests Question Period in the House of Commons or an election campaign debate. More broadly, **political conflict** refers to a state of opposition: someone objects to what someone else is doing or proposes to do. The "someone else" is often the government but could be groups or individuals with positions on public issues different from one's own. Political conflict in Canada frequently takes place within formal governmental institutions, staying within the limits of the law, and is usually peaceful. However, in other settings political conflict can be violent, involving resort to arms. This chapter discusses political conflict that goes on outside formal governmental institutions. That conflict is often disruptive and sometimes violent, but it is a form of political participation. We will examine several types of political conflict: political protest, insurgency and guerrilla war, terrorism, and revolution.

The term *political protest* may suggest helmeted police and rock-throwing demonstrators, but it also can be people picketing peacefully in front of city hall or organizing a petition. **Political protest** can be defined as oppositional political action that takes place outside formal channels, generally seeking to have government make significant changes in its policies. Political protest takes many forms (see Figure 9-1). The mildest of these include petitions, legally approved demonstrations, and voluntary boycotts of products or firms. Non-violent direct action—for example, civil disobedience, illegal demonstrations, or peaceful occupation of a building or office—is a stronger form. It involves illegal activities but is not violent, as is exemplified by **civil disobedience**: deliberate lawbreaking that accepts punishment by state authorities as part of the action. This strategy was chosen by Mahatma Gandhi in India from the 1920s to the 1940s to gain independence from Britain, and by Martin Luther King in the United States in the 1950s and 1960s (discussed in Box 9-1, The Civil Rights Movement).

Very different is protest that involves violence. Sometimes violence is an unintended consequence of a march or boycott, but it can also be used intentionally as a provocation. In other instances, violence is chosen as the best way to secure a political objective. Assassinations, **guerrilla warfare**, **insurgencies**, **revolutions**, and **terrorism** fall into this category.

political conflict

A state of opposition, usually involving groups and the state, over something government is doing or proposes to do.

political protest

Oppositional political action that takes place outside formal channels, generally seeking to have government make significant changes in its policies.

civil disobedience

Deliberate lawbreaking that accepts punishment by state authorities as part of the action.

guerrilla warfare

A form of highly political warfare built around lightly armed irregulars who oppose a government and use hit-and-run tactics and political work to take power.

insurgency

A rebellion or revolt, especially one employing the tools of guerrilla warfare.

revolution

The use of violence to overthrow a government, especially when the overthrow is followed by rapid, thoroughgoing social, economic, and political restructuring.

terrorism

The deliberate use of violence designed to induce fear in a population in order to achieve a political objective.

FIGURE 9-1
The Continuum of Protest

INSTITUTIONAL	MODERATE PROTEST	DIRECT ACTION	VIOLENCE
Voting	Petitions	Unofficial strikes	Unintentional
Lobbying	Legal demonstrations	Illegal demonstrations	Throw rocks and break windows
Interest groups	Boycotts	Peaceful occupations	Guerrilla warfare
		Civil disobedience	Assassination
			Terrorism

Source: Adapted with modifications from Dalton (2006, p. 65).

BOX 9-1   The Civil Rights Movement

The American civil rights movement is one of the most famous examples of how people without power, for whom the democratic process did not work, used protest to win their rights.

Although President Abraham Lincoln abolished slavery in 1863, for the next century African-Americans suffered systemic discrimination. Conditions were worst in the southern states where segregation, the legal separation of races, was in force. This meant that black children and white children went to different schools, that blacks and whites could not use the same restrooms or drinking fountains, and that blacks even had to give up their seats on buses to whites.

Throughout the first half of the twentieth century, African-Americans worked patiently through their country's courts to have segregation legislation declared

The greatest American proponent of civil disobedience was Dr. Martin Luther King, Jr. (1929–1968), a Baptist minister who lived in the South.
Bettmann/Getty images

unconstitutional. Although they had some significant victories, such as *Brown v. Board of Education* (1954), which declared segregated education unconstitutional, actually getting states to change their laws proved difficult. Despite a constitutional provision adopted in 1870 establishing that the right to vote cannot be denied on account of race or colour, various means such as literacy tests were used to prevent most African-Americans from voting.

Clearly, the normal channels of influence were of little use in trying to change discriminatory laws and policies. Protest action by the civil rights movement was needed to pressure governments to treat African-Americans fairly.

Sit-ins were one of the most effective tactics used by the civil rights movement. Black students would sit in the section of a restaurant or lunch counter that was reserved for whites. They would be refused service and told to leave, but would stay until arrested. They then would appeal their convictions for violating discriminatory laws, arguing that the law they broke violated the constitution and should have no force. Eventually this practice mobilized public opinion in the United States behind the civil rights movement, and legislation outlawing segregation followed.

Had African-Americans kept working within the rules, as they had for many years, segregation might have continued much longer. Politicians were hesitant to change the law, fearing that white voters would not re-elect them. Dramatic action like sit-ins focused the country's attention on the abuses of segregation and hastened that system's demise.

Seeking Change

People do not protest, let alone turn to political violence, for no reason. Protest is a means to seek political change. It usually is employed only after conventional approaches, such as lobbying, have failed. In non-democratic systems, though, it may be the only way to get change. This does not mean that everyone involved in a protest or who has joined a protest movement has personally tried other means or would even support trying them. Rather, it points to the most common sequence of events.

ANALYZING CONTENTIOUS POLITICS

To most people, seeking the common good suggests reasoned deliberation and debate, which are hallmarks of democratic politics. However, democracy did not grow just through the use of reason and polite persuasion. Those who hold power, the elite, are rarely keen to see their power diminished. Thus logic has often needed to be supplemented by more **contentious politics**—the usually disruptive, direct, and highly conflictive ways that people advance their claims on elites, authorities, and opponents, ranging from peaceful political protest to wars and other lethal conflicts (Tilly & Tarrow, 2007).

Political protest is political action because it aims to affect how public issues are treated. It is oppositional political action because those who protest want government to change its policies. This can mean demanding that a government do something it does not do now, stop doing something it now does, or take action instead of doing nothing. However, oppositional activity is immensely varied and does not always include protest. We reserve the label *protest* for political actions with the following characteristics:

1. Actions take place outside of formal channels.
2. They are usually carried out by individuals or groups that are not ordinarily important political actors.
3. Protest politics generally aims to have government make significant changes in the policies it pursues.

We will look at each of these three traits separately.

contentious politics

The usually disruptive, direct, and highly conflictive ways that people advance their claims on elites, authorities, and opponents, ranging from peaceful political protest to wars and other lethal conflicts.

Politics outside Formal Channels

Whether in dictatorships or democracies, politics works in set patterns. There are rules you are expected to follow to get something done. They may not always be formal written rules, but rather norms or unofficial standards. In either case, being politically effective and getting what you want usually requires following those rules and working within channels.

Playing by the rules benefits both governments and the groups and individuals that regularly deal with government. It obviously helps governments because they set the rules. However, keeping within channels also works well for those who deal regularly with government because they master the rules and can use them to their own benefit. But what if going through channels does not produce any results? In that case, there are two options: accept your fate or go outside channels.

When people have an issue that is very important to them, they are not likely to be satisfied with accepting defeat graciously. This is true even when the defeat comes as a result of a democratic process and reflects the will of the majority. Such an outcome is especially likely where the claimants belong to some permanent minority (for example, an ethnic or religious group) that the majority or government has consciously marginalized. Ordinary democracy may not work for those who can never become a majority.

"Unimportant" Actors or Issues

Protest is sometimes called the tool of the marginalized—people without the resources needed to gain political influence. We usually think of political influence as the ability to shape decisions, the ability to control large blocks of votes, or the possession of a lot of money or particularly valuable information. Having these resources makes an individual or group valuable to government, and governments often accommodate those who are valuable to them. Prospects are bleak for those groups or individuals with scarce resources unless they too make themselves important to government.

In the 1960s, political scientists began seeing protest as a political resource (Lipsky, 1968). Protest disrupts government's routines, making the authorities aware that something is happening. Although governments often characterize protest as lawlessness, they still know that part of their community feels strongly enough about an issue to take to the streets. In reality, the marginalized may have little option but to use protest. Largely invisible to those in power before beginning to protest, those on the outside frequently find that the rules of the game do not work for them. However, once a protest movement catches the authorities' attention, perhaps through media coverage, it can mobilize other resources, including the support of politicians, and further enhance its status.

marginalization

Exclusion from the mainstream.

Marginalization does not refer only to the dispossessed and disenfranchised. Issues, too, can be marginalized and only appear on the government's agenda after supporters take extraordinary measures. This explains the apparently contradictory phenomenon of the well-educated, middle-class-or-higher protester (Dalton, 2006) whose activity has been notable from the anti-Vietnam War movement of the 1960s to today's demonstrations favouring green energy. Although these individuals may have other resources that they can use to influence government, those resources may not work for a given issue. Therefore protest is another resource that the politically active can add to their arsenals (Opp, 1989). So even if protest is often the only tool of the marginalized, the well placed, too, can use it to get what they want.

CHALLENGES AND BENEFITS OF ORGANIZING Organizing people to act collectively and become involved in political protest can be difficult. It may be rational for a person not to participate in a protest, but rather to wait on the sidelines to see what it accomplishes. These *free riders* share the benefits of others' labour without having to do any work or take any risks.

Beyond the matter of getting people to join, movements engaged in protest cannot know how government will respond to their demands. There is no guarantee that time and energy invested in building a movement and organizing protest actions will change the status quo and advance a group's vision of the common good. Nevertheless, over the years, Canadians have seen workers, farmers, women, fishers, Quebec nationalists, Aboriginals, gays and lesbians, and anti-abortion activists use political protest to put themselves and their causes on the public agenda. Many of these groups became regular parts of the political process, and today governments in Canada generally do not question the right of these groups to have a voice in policy making. Whether events would have turned out this way had the groups not protested is impossible to determine. What we do know is that protest advanced their causes.

Riseup.net (Contemporary Progressive Movements)
http://lists.riseup.net

Seeking Significant Change

Protesters usually believe that there is something wrong that only government action can correct. Yet they also believe that the ordinary mechanisms of political pressure have failed, leaving protest as their last chance to be heard. This is why protest has been used to gain political rights for the excluded, to try to end wars, and to make absolutely clear the opposition of some part of the citizenry to some government policy. Protest is about changing what government does, and people have taken action to seek political change for a very long time.

PROTEST AND POLITICAL CHANGE

In general, then, people protest because they perceive what Clark, Grayson, & Grayson call "institutional deficiencies" (1976, p. 3)—they think that something is not working right and has to be fixed. Those who decide to protest may risk imprisonment and still not gain their objective. Nevertheless, political protest has secured some dramatic results and contributed greatly to strengthening democracy. In Canada, for example:

- *Women's right to vote*. Until the late 1800s, women everywhere were denied basic political rights. It was only in the twentieth century that political equality between men and women became a generally accepted principle of democratic life. The first step toward equality for women was winning the right to vote. Although we now find it unthinkable that women did not have the same political rights as men, Canadian women did not gain the right to vote in every provincial election until 1940. The proponents of women's suffrage (women's right to vote) lobbied governments and used various forms of protest, such as staging mock parliamentary debates, to demonstrate that they could argue as persuasively and as rationally as men (Cleverdon, 1974).

- *Making farmers' voices heard.* Farmers in Canada in the late nineteenth and early twentieth centuries felt excluded from power and sought to change the political system to better reflect their needs (Lipset, 1950; Macpherson, 1954; Morton, 1950). Unlike the movement for women's suffrage, farmers' movements decided that they needed to form new political parties. Although farmers were then the largest occupational group in the country, they had little influence. Farmers felt that the parties that then existed, the Conservatives and Liberals, ignored their views and listened only to big business. The parties the farmers' movements founded (United Farmers, Progressives, Co-operative Commonwealth Federation [CCF]) sought to represent the views of not just farmers, but all ordinary working people against the power of corporate interests. Although none of these parties ever won power federally, several of them governed provinces. Moreover, a number of them created Crown corporations (government-owned enterprises) that brought electricity and telephone service to many parts of rural Canada. One, the CCF, set up the country's first Medicare system in Saskatchewan.

Votes for women and more political power for farmers were issues that Canada's political establishment of a century past would not put on the public agenda. For these two marginalized groups to have their demands heard, they had to move outside the usual political channels. The mechanisms of ordinary democracy had served them badly, but political protest benefited both them and democracy. Yet we should recall that it took women decades of hard work to win the vote and the CCF's election as Saskatchewan's government in 1944 came 12 years after the party's founding. Protest is not a magic potion that brings immediate success to those who use it.

In fact, there are many cases where protest fails. Canada's peace movement has been active for years but it could not halt the testing of cruise missiles in Alberta in the 1980s and had little impact on decisions to send troops to Afghanistan. Outside Canada, the record is similar. A study of attempts by poor black citizens of Newark, New Jersey, to use protest to claim their rights and gain power showed how those in power frustrated the protesters at every turn (Parenti, 1970). Similarly, women fighting for the vote in Britain in the early 1900s turned to violence after being consistently rebuffed by government. They smashed the windows of elegant shops along London's Regent Street and, when arrested, they began hunger strikes. The authorities responded with force feeding and, eventually, used the "Cat and Mouse Law": a woman was allowed to starve herself until her health deteriorated. She was then released but would be jailed again once well. In the end, British women won the vote not due to their protest, but rather for their contribution to Britain's efforts in World War I. Even then they did not have the same voting rights as men until 1928 (Castle, 1987).

PROTEST IN DEMOCRACY

Some argue that political protest does not have a place in a democracy. They hold that people have the right to make their feelings known in elections, to work through their elected representatives, and to pressure government. Not everyone gets what they want, but that is not cause to go outside fair, well-known rules and procedures. If you fail to get what you want by working through regular democratic processes, it indicates that you are simply too weak or are pursuing goals that the majority rejects. Rather than protest, you should change your objectives and build a broader base.

The crux of this argument is that conventional democratic politics works. Although this view underlies our most basic beliefs about democracy, it is not entirely accurate. There are many instances in which following established democratic procedures did not help the weak and marginalized. This was the case for African-Americans who turned to protest to challenge the discriminatory system of **segregation** (see Box 9-1 The Civil Rights Movement).

Opportunity Structures

Protest movements have sometimes been able to use more conventional political actions because of the opportunities offered by their political systems. **Political opportunity structures (POS)** are the openings that political institutions and processes offer to or withhold from movements (Kitschelt, 1986; Tarrow, 1999). For example, the farmers' movement in Canada was able to build political parties and win power because our electoral system and system of parliamentary government, as well as the fact that farmers formed a majority of voters in several provinces, made this a workable option. **Secessionists** in Quebec have used the same strategy with some success because the supporters of Quebec's independence could unite behind a separatist party and, at times, gain control of the Quebec government.

Unconventional Protest

In 2011, young cyber activists in Spain organized their first demonstrations on May 15, 2011. The Indignados (also known as the M-15 movement) used sit-ins at the main squares of many cities and extensive use of social media to criticize government's austerity programs that caused high levels of youth unemployment. They promoted the ideas of participatory democracy and social justice while avoiding connections to a political party, ideology, or specific policies (Martinez-Arboleda, 2015).

The Indignados inspired the Occupy Wall Street movement[1]. Its hallmark slogan, "We are the 99%" became famous, and the movement's occupation of

segregation

The legal separation of blacks and whites, particularly in the southern United States.

political opportunity structures (POS)

The openings that political institutions and processes offer to or withhold from movements.

secessionist

A person who favours separation of a territory from an existing state.

---

[1]The idea of occupying Wall Street (the financial district where the New York Stock Exchange is located) came from the Vancouver-based magazine *Adbusters* in a poster that included the hashtag #OCCUPYWALLSTREET.

About 1000 persons in Tucson, Arizona participate in the Occupy movement that inspired hundreds of occupations around the world.
Norma Jean Gargasz/Alamy Stock Photo

Zuccatti Park in New York's Wall Street financial district from September 17 to November 15, 2011 received worldwide attention and sparked occupations in many communities.

The Occupy movement was about equality. Thus it protested inequality: economic, social, and political. It targeted corporate power, financial corporations, and the very rich: the 1 percent minority. Occupy was distinguished by its very open and democratic decision-making process. Although this kept the movement from formulating precise demands, it encouraged extensive participation and let people develop democratic skills. The Occupy movement had a clear political message—democracy needs more economic and social equality to work properly. However, its structure and mode of operation meant that it left formulating policy alternatives to others. Nevertheless, the movement was successful in making the increasing wealth and power of the very rich an important political issue in many countries.

Occupy Wall Street
www.occupywallst.org

Occupy
www.occupy.com

TRANSNATIONAL POLITICAL PROTEST

Social movements and political protest often cross borders. Nineteenth-century examples of transnational movements include the anti-slavery and labour movements. Later, the student movement of the 1960s and the women's rights movement of the 1970s were also international in scope. As well, protestors in one country, such as the Zapatistas in Mexico, gained support for their cause from sympathizers around the world. The anti-globalization movement is another example of contentious politics on a transnational scale.

Peoples' Global Action
www.nadir.org/nadir/initiativ/agp/en/index.htm

The anti-globalization movement, very active particularly from 1998 to 2010, emphasizes international finance and its effects on the world's economy. The movement targets meetings of the World Trade Organization (WTO), the G7/G8 and G20 summits of leaders of the world's largest economies, meetings of the International Monetary Fund and World Bank, and the European Union summits for its protests. Since its first protest in 1998, the movement has adopted increasingly contentious direct actions. Many of its demonstrations (see Table 9-1) have involved clashes with police. One, in Genoa, Italy, saw a demonstrator killed, several hundred injured, and charges of torture levelled against the Italian police. Protests decreased after 2003 but began again in 2007. Protests at the G20 summit in Toronto in June 2010 were generally peaceful, but produced some confrontations between security forces and protestors, damage to businesses, the torching of three police cars, and more than nine hundred arrests. In 2016, the movement mobilized opposition to the Transatlantic Trade and Investment Partnership (TTIP).

Though not specifically anti-globalization protests, riots in Iceland in January 2009 brought about the fall of a pro-globalization government, while Greece has been shaken repeatedly by violent demonstrations protesting austerity measures since 2009. The largest global-scale demonstrations, however, were held in March 2003 to protest the invasion of Iraq, attracting more than ten million protesters worldwide, including one million or more in London, Rome, Madrid, and Barcelona.

The anti-globalization movement was the first to use social media (initially email) widely, which let it organize effectively without complex permanent structures. However, this flexibility brought costs, too. Without a coordinating central institution, any group can join the movement and participate in its demonstrations. Thus violent anti-capitalist groups who wished to destroy the capitalist system mixed with protesters concerned about social justice on a global

TABLE 9-1
Participation in Anti-Globalization Protest Actions

PLACE	DATE	ESTIMATED NUMBER OF PARTICIPANTS
Seattle	September 1999	100 000
Washington	April 2000	10 000
Prague, Czech Republic	September 2000	12 000
Quebec City	April 2001	30 000
Genoa, Italy	September 2001	100 000
Barcelona, Spain	March 2002	250 000
Miami	November 2003	10 000
Heilingendam, Germany	June 2007	80 000
London	March 2009	35 000
Pittsburgh	September 2009	5 000
Toronto	June 2010	20 000

Note: Estimates of the number of demonstrators varies widely.

Source: Compiled by authors from press estimates, 1999–2010.

BOX 9-2 Protest in Dictatorships: Argentina and Cuba

Argentina has had many dictatorships but few as violent as the military regime that ruled from 1976 to 1983. Seizing power after an elected government that failed to contain a wave of urban guerrilla violence, the military waged a "Dirty War" against those it considered subversives and dissidents. Suspects were swept from the streets, taken to interrogation centres, and never heard from again. These were the Disappeared, and there were between ten thousand and thirty thousand of them.

Protest in Argentina began in 1977, when the mothers, wives, sisters, and other family members of the Disappeared, frustrated by government refusals to release any information regarding the whereabouts of their family members, took action. Every Thursday they walked around the Plaza de Mayo, a park in downtown Buenos Aires that faces the presidential residence on one side and the Ministry of Defence on another. The women faced severe repression by the military regime, but did not stop. Although the military regime ended in 1983, the women are still in the Plaza every Thursday in

2016; and have extended their search to include their stolen grandchildren, who were born in captivity and turned over to the families of military officers. Two ex-presidents, Reynaldo Bignone and Rafael Videla, were imprisoned in 2012 for these crimes.

Cuba too has had many dictatorships; its current one dates from 1959. Headed until 2008 by Fidel Castro and since then by his brother Raúl, the dictatorship tolerates neither dissent nor opposition. However, as in any political system, some people are dissatisfied enough to protest, a dangerous choice in a dictatorship.

The experience of the Ladies in White in Cuba has been similar to that of the Mothers of the Plaza de Mayo. Formed in 2003 by the female relatives of political prisoners, the Ladies attend Sunday mass together and then hold a procession to a local park. The Cuban authorities have often arrested the Ladies, whom they label "subversives," even allowing mobs to attack them. Because the Cuban authoritarian regime continues in power, the Ladies in White continue their protest, facing the same obstacles.

scale who were far less confrontational. The radical fringe sought violent clashes with police, which sometimes overshadowed the democratic reforms supported by the movement's majority.

PROTEST IN AUTHORITARIAN REGIMES

Authoritarian Regimes

Unlike democracies, authoritarian regimes do not tolerate dissent. This means that there is no legal way for citizens to voice their grievances. Thus protest is the only option. Sometimes the protest is low key, as with the Mothers of the Plaza de Mayo in Argentina and the Ladies in White in Cuba (see Box 9-2 Protest in Dictatorships: Argentina and Cuba), but it can also be as dramatic as the Arab Spring of 2011.

ARAB SPRING For decades the Arab world, stretching from Morocco to Iraq, knew only dictatorships or absolute monarchies. However, a wave of protests that began in Tunisia in December 2010 led to the overthrow of authoritarian rulers in that country, as well as in Egypt, Libya, and Yemen. A serious insurrection in Bahrain in 2014 was suppressed with help from forces from Saudi Arabia and the Gulf States. In 2011, the Syrian regime fired on peaceful protestors sparking a lengthy, bloody civil war in which many foreign countries and groups became involved. Protests also occurred in Algeria, Iraq, Jordan, Kuwait, and Morocco. These protests became known as the Arab Spring.

The Arab Spring was marked by the widespread use of social media, especially Twitter and Facebook, to mobilize supporters and coordinate actions. Further, all of the protest movements began peacefully, using strikes, demonstrations, marches, and rallies. However, violent government repression was common and was fiercest in Libya, Syria, and Yemen, where civil wars ensued, and Bahrain, where the state (assisted by Saudi Arabia and the United Arab Emirates) used violence to defeat the protesters. Finally, all the movements protested the concentration of power and wealth in the hands of autocrats, the lack of jobs for increasingly well-educated young people, and the routine abuse of human rights by the authoritarian regimes.

Six years after the start of the Arab Spring, it is clear that, except in Tunisia, the movements did not produce the intended results. Civil wars continue in Libya, Syria, and Yemen. In Egypt, the original protesters were pushed aside by the Muslim Brotherhood, which won legislative elections in 2011–12 and saw its leader Mohamed Morsi elected president. However, in 2013 the Egyptian military overthrew Morsi's government, violently suppressing any who protested the coup. Morsi was sentenced to death in 2015 for his alleged role in abetting a prison break. Protest may be the only way to secure change, but victory is never sure.

Project Disappeared
www.desaparecidos.org/arg/ eng.html

POLITICAL VIOLENCE

Political violence can be defined as the use of physical force with a political objective. Violence can enter politics in several different ways (see Box 9-3 Violence and Politics):

1. *Violence can be a tactic chosen by an organization, whether a protest movement or a guerrilla army, to advance its aims.* Although this is more common in countries that are not democracies and do not allow an open political opposition, even long-established constitutional democracies such as Canada and the United States have harboured groups that use violence to achieve their goals.

2. *Governments can also use violence against their citizens.* Sometimes they do so in response to a specific situation. For example, even democratic governments might order the police or military to use force against a demonstration. Far less common among democratic governments, though unfortunately not unknown, is using violence systematically as a regular instrument to repress dissent and maintain order. This is called **regime violence**.

political violence

The use of physical force with a political objective.

The American Political Science Association, Task Force on Political Violence and Terrorism
http://www.apsanet.org/ politicalviolence

regime violence

Political violence used by a government against its citizens, generally as a way to repress dissent and keep order.

BOX 9-3   Violence and Politics

British political scientist Bernard Crick argued that politics, which he termed "the political method of rule," is built on negotiation and the reconciliation of differences. As such, it excludes the use of violence as a governing instrument (Crick, 1993).

Nonetheless, violence is used for political ends every day, both by governments and by groups challenging government. But why use violence for political ends? And how does political violence differ from criminal violence?

States may use violence legitimately, either to defend themselves and their citizens or to preserve order. Sometimes, however, authoritarian governments use violence to suppress their opponents and repress dissent. Democratic governments may do the same, but

far less commonly than in dictatorships. Where states use violence, citizens may decide that violence is the only way they can protect themselves. Many would consider this a legitimate use of political violence.

Violence becomes explicitly political when it is used to influence, defend, or oppose government. However, revolutionaries committed to toppling a government through violence often resort to criminal methods such as robbery or kidnapping to finance their operations or show their strength. In these cases, political and criminal actions are joined. A further complication arises when peaceful protest turns violent, or when violent elements, even criminal ones, use ordinary protest as a cover for their illegitimate intentions.

3. *Finally, violence can be an unplanned and undesired side effect of an otherwise peaceful political action, such as a protest march.* Due to some unpredictable event, protestors and police clash.

Canadians generally abhor political violence. A movement that regularly uses violence, as did the Front de libération du Québec (FLQ), a revolutionary separatist group that kidnapped and murdered a Quebec Cabinet minister in 1970 (as discussed later in this chapter), is likely to lose public support. This revulsion also occurs when the police use excessive force, as happened at the 1997 Asia-Pacific Economic Cooperation (APEC) summit in Vancouver.[2] Canadians, like people in most democratic countries, usually draw the line at premeditated violence.

Although violent, even lethal, political contention has been rare in Canada's past, it is not unknown. The earliest significant cases occurred in what are now Quebec and Ontario during the Rebellions of 1837–1838. These democratic revolts challenged elite domination of politics and sought to give more power to the people's elected representatives, but were crushed by British troops.

After Confederation came the Red River Rebellion (1869–1870) and the North-West Rebellion (1885). Both were headed by Louis Riel, a leader of the Métis (Roman Catholics of mixed Aboriginal and European ancestry who

---

[2]RCMP officers and Vancouver riot police used violence against students who were peacefully protesting the presence of the Indonesian dictator Suharto at a meeting of APEC held at the University of British Columbia in 1997. Although there were suspicions that the prime minister's office had ordered the demonstrators to be forcefully dispersed, a later inquiry found no direct links.

lived an essentially Aboriginal lifestyle), in what is now Manitoba. The Métis were concerned that they had not been consulted about the transfer of the Red River colony, now a part of Manitoba, from the Hudson's Bay Company to be administered as a territory by a governor (notorious for his dislike of French-speaking Catholics) appointed by the Government of Canada. They feared that white Protestant settlers would overwhelm them, take their land, and destroy their way of life.

The Red River Rebellion was successful. The Canadian government agreed to establish a provincial government in Manitoba in 1870, with guarantees (overturned two decades later) for a Roman Catholic school system and the establishment of official status for both French and English languages. However, the North-West Rebellion, centred in what would become Saskatchewan and which tried to get Ottawa to pay attention to the needs of all residents of that region (Aboriginal, Métis, and European) failed. Violence ensued and the Métis forces were routed by Canadian troops. Riel was captured, tried for treason, and hanged.

We must remember that lethal contention in Canada in the 1800s grew from unfulfilled democratic demands. In the Red River Rebellion, the use of force led to talks with the government. In the other three rebellions, it was the failure of regular political processes that resulted in the use of violence.

This pattern of failure to address grievances underlies political scientist Ted Robert Gurr's frustration–aggression hypothesis (Gurr, 1970), which seeks to explain what triggers violent protest. Gurr argued that where levels of frustration are high within a population and have lasted for a long time, these feelings can readily find violent expression. This certainly seems to be what occurred at both Oka and Burnt Church (see Box 9-4 Violent Aboriginal Protest in Canada). However, this theory does not actually explain why people sometimes direct their energies into highly contentious, even violent, politics instead of ordinary political action, such as electoral campaigning, or even ignoring politics altogether.

The frustration–aggression hypothesis also does not address why governments use violence against their own citizens. When we think of regime violence what comes to mind is a police state where the security forces—police, military, secret police, intelligence services—have free rein to harass citizens. There are too many examples of political systems that have used violence systematically against their own people to treat here, but examples include Saddam Hussein's Iraq, the Assad family in Syria, the Taliban in Afghanistan, the Soviet Union under Stalin, and Hitler's Germany.

These examples come from dictatorships, but democracies also use regime violence when faced with political protest. For example, in the 1960s, police forces in American states where racial segregation was legal used violence against citizens engaged in peaceful protests demanding that African-Americans receive their full constitutional rights. Similarly, authorities can turn a blind eye to private citizens who use violence against protesters or other dissidents. Again, the American South offers an example: for many years, the

BOX 9-4   Violent Aboriginal Protest in Canada

In recent years, some of Canada's 1.4 million Indigenous peoples have made important gains in negotiations over land claims, and Aboriginal rights have been enshrined in the constitution. Yet there have also been violent confrontations between Aboriginal communities and federal or provincial authorities. Three of these were especially important:

- *Oka.* In 1990, plans by the town of Oka, Quebec to expand a golf course involved expropriating land that held a local Mohawk cemetery. An armed standoff between Quebec Provincial Police (QPP) and the Mohawk Warriors' Society led to the shooting of a QPP officer. A 78-day standoff with the Canadian army then followed.
- *Ipperwash.* In 1995, Ojibway from the Stony Point First Nation claimed that Ipperwash Provincial Park in Ontario belonged to them. A violent confrontation between the Aboriginals and the Ontario Provincial Police resulted in the death of protester

Dudley George. The government of the day refused to order an inquiry into George's death, but after a change of government in 2003, a commission of inquiry was established. The inquiry uncovered evidence of racist and culturally insensitive behaviour by the authorities. Based on its 2007 report, the land was turned over to its original owners.

- *Burnt Church.* In 1999, a confrontation at Burnt Church, New Brunswick, brought Aboriginal and non-Aboriginal fishermen into conflict. A month before this episode, a Supreme Court decision held that treaties from the 1760s exempted Aboriginals in the Maritimes and eastern Quebec from current fisheries regulations. Non-Aboriginal fishermen objected, fearing that uncontrolled fishing would destroy the resource. The two sides clashed violently at Burnt Church, leading to the destruction of much of the Aboriginals' gear and the burning of three fish-processing plants.

Ku Klux Klan terrorized black citizens who sought to exercise their legal rights while the authorities often refused to act against the Klan violence.

States might use violence against their own citizens for several reasons. One is to make the population so fearful that it will not dare to act against the government. Another is to maintain in power an individual or group (defined by class, colour, religion, ethnicity, or ideology) that would otherwise be thrown out. In fact, the two often go together.

TYPES OF POLITICAL VIOLENCE

We will analyze three types of political violence. The first is guerrilla warfare (and its counterpart, counter-insurgency). The second is terrorism, and the third is revolution.

Guerrilla Warfare or Guerrilla Insurgency

Like political protest, guerrilla warfare is principally an instrument of the weak. Also called guerrilla insurgency, it has been practised from time immemorial; we find references to it that date back 3500 years, and it is mentioned in the Bible. Nevertheless, it only received its current name in the nineteenth century,

BOX 9-5 Urban Guerrillas

When we think of guerrillas, we imagine soldiers in camouflage trekking through a jungle. We do so for two reasons. One is that the successes of rural guerrillas, such as Mao Zedong in China in the 1930s and 1940s and Fidel Castro in Cuba in the 1950s, have shaped our image of insurgent warfare. The other is that most guerrillas have operated mainly in rural areas. This puts distance between them and the government troops that they fight, gives them the advantage of operating in difficult terrain that they know better than their enemy, and puts them in touch with the rural poor, who are often among those guerrillas claim to defend. However, guerrillas can also operate effectively in urban areas.

In general, operating in urban areas benefits guerrillas. They have access to a large base of potential recruits, supplies are easier to obtain, urban home turf can be just as difficult for a counter-insurgent to penetrate as any jungle, and the counter-insurgent runs a very high risk of killing civilians, which raises the insurgents' legitimacy.

This sort of urban warfare causes many deaths, however. In 2016, the website Iraq Body Count (www.iraqbodycount.org) estimated that civilian fatalities in Iraq since the US-led invasion in 2003 totalled 174 000. Including military fatalities raises the number to 242 000.

Iraq is not the first case of urban guerrilla struggle. In the late 1960s and early 1970s, such groups were active in Uruguay and Argentina. They were violent, and used robbery and kidnapping to finance themselves. This provoked military coups in both countries, creating governments that eventually destroyed the guerrillas.

---

when it was applied to the Spanish resistance to Napoleon's invasion and occupation (*guerrilla* is Spanish for "little war"). Anthony Joes, an expert on guerrilla warfare, holds that "guerrilla insurgency is quintessentially a *political* phenomenon" (Joes, 2004, 7; emphasis in original), even if those who fight guerrillas often portray them as bandits.

All guerrilla insurgencies share five traits (Beckett, 2001; Joes, 1992, 2004; Laquer, 1977). First, the guerrillas are highly mobile and use hit-and-run tactics rather than set-piece battles. Second, they are fewer in number and less well armed than their adversaries. Third, guerrillas operate in familiar, often difficult terrain, which can be rural or urban (see Box 9-5 Urban Guerrillas), where their enemy loses its edge in technology and numbers. Fourth, the guerrillas know their locale and often have local support, which facilitates gathering intelligence and securing supplies. Finally, guerrilla war is usually protracted; if it ends quickly, the guerrillas have probably lost.

Although guerrilla warfare has existed for a long time, it became especially well-known in the twentieth century (see Table 9-2). Not only did a great number of exceptional guerrilla commanders emerge—for example, Mao Zedong of China, Augusto César Sandino in Nicaragua (discussed in Box 9-6 Guerrilla Violence), Ho Chi Minh in Vietnam, and Fidel Castro in Cuba—but guerrilla insurgency also came to be identified with revolutionary struggle. But why would revolutionaries use guerrilla warfare? Although all of the characteristics of guerrilla operations noted previously apply, there are two additional reasons that apply with special force to revolutionaries.

TABLE 9-2
Some Guerrilla Movements of the Twentieth and Twenty-First Centuries

WHERE	WHEN	LEADER OR COMBATANTS
China	1920s–1949	Mao Zedong
Nicaragua	1927–1934	Augusto César Sandino
Various	1939–1945	World War II partisans
Algeria	1940s–1958	Independence fighters
Vietnam	1940s–1975	Ho Chi Minh
Malaya	1946–1954	Communists
Mozambique and Angola	1950s–1974	Independence fighters
Cuba	1956–1959	Fidel Castro
Afghanistan	1979–1989	Mujahedeen
Afghanistan	2002–present	Taliban and others
Iraq	2003–present	Insurgents
Syria	2011–present	ISIS and other insurgent groups

One is that revolutionaries—who could be Marxists, independence fighters, or motivated by religion—generally are persecuted by governments. To survive, they must find ways to mount a successful resistance and be able to win adherents. Guerrilla operations do both. By emphasizing the use of small units, light arms, and brief engagements, guerrilla tactics allow insurgents to turn their usual liabilities—small size and poor equipment—into advantages. Further, having to operate clandestinely means that the insurgents must mix with the ordinary people for whom they claim to fight. This allows the revolutionaries to do the slow, painstaking work of convincing people to turn against the government (always a dangerous choice) and back the guerrillas. The guerrillas can fail militarily and still continue to exist if their political work succeeds. If they fail politically, though, military success will not suffice.

Just how do guerrilla revolutionaries do their political work? One way is to show people that the government is not all-powerful, so the guerrillas attack government installations, blow up power lines and bridges, and often kill government officials—police, military, mayors, etc. In general, guerrillas seek to

BOX 9-6 Guerrilla Violence

Because they fight foreign occupiers or domestic dictators, we often lionize guerrillas, treating them as ideal democratic heroes. However, they are waging a struggle that has a brutal side and sometimes use brutality.

Augusto César Sandino became famous for leading a guerrilla war against the US troops who occupied Nicaragua in the late 1920s. His Ejército Defensor de la Soberanía Nacional (Defending Army of National Sovereignty) worked patiently with peasants to win their allegiance but administered rough justice to those who took the government's side. Using machetes, the guerrillas would lop off an offender's head, or slice off his arms, causing him to bleed to death. These methods were used because, as Sandino said, "Liberty is not won with flowers" (Gambone, 2001).

limit the violence used against ordinary citizens, because the insurgents need their aid and these are the people the revolutionaries claim to defend. Some groups, however, have chosen to terrorize civilian populations. Among these are the Shining Path (Sendero Luminoso) guerrillas of Peru (Palmer, 1994; Rochlin, 2003), the Khmer Rouge in Cambodia (Kiernan, 2008), and ISIS in Iraq and Syria (Cockburn, 2015; Stern and Berger, 2015).

COUNTER-INSURGENCY C.E. Callwell, a nineteenth-century student of guerrilla warfare, said that "when [guerrilla warfare] is directed by a leader with a genius for war, an effective [**counter-insurgency**] campaign becomes well-nigh impossible" (quoted in Joes, 2004, p. 1). Yet guerrillas do not always win. Among the more famous counter-insurgent victories are two by the United States in the Philippines (1899–1902 and 1946–1954), one by the British in Malaya (1948–1960), and one by the democratic Venezuelan government against communist insurgents (1960–1964). On the other hand, even more famous losses were suffered by the United States in Vietnam and by the Soviet Union in Afghanistan. What does it take to make counter-insurgency work?

counter-insurgency

A blend of military and political action taken by a government to defeat an insurgency. The tactics are usually described as a mixture of repression and reform.

The answer seems simple: repress and reform. Government must control the guerrillas militarily at the same time that it addresses the complaints of those who support the insurgents. Counter-insurgency has a political dimension just as insurgency does. This political dimension also affects the military side, because government forces have to find a level of violence that defeats the guerrillas while minimizing harm to the general population.

Despite the centrality of politics in counter-insurgency, governments fighting guerrillas often overlook this element, preferring to rely on their superiority of force (Beckett, 2001; Hoffman, 2004; Joes, 2004). The US Army field manual on counter-insurgency (US Army, 2006) stresses political operations. Yet American experience since the 1960s suggests how difficult this is to achieve.

Terrorism

What sets terrorism apart from other forms of political violence is its deliberate targeting of the innocent. Terrorists use this tactic to sow fear among the population, either to demonstrate their power or to get citizens to press their governments to meet the terrorists' demands.

Even before al-Qaeda's terrorist attacks on the United States on September 11, 2001, democracies had faced terrorism:

- North Americans have witnessed domestic terrorist attacks by those who bomb abortion clinics, and right-wing extremists who blew up the Murrah Building in Oklahoma City in 1995 killing 168 persons and injuring more than 680 others. More recently, the two Tsarnaev brothers set off explosives at the 2013 Boston Marathon (claiming it was "payback" for US military actions in Afghanistan and Iraq).

BOX 9-7 Religion and Political Violence

"Kill them all; let God sort them out!" comes not from an ISIS video but rather from an abbot during the Albigensian Crusade waged by papal forces against heretics in thirteenth century France. There were also the murderous European religious wars of the sixteenth and seventeenth centuries that pitted Catholics against Protestants. More recently, the Lord's Resistance Army, operating in Uganda and elsewhere in East Africa since the 1980s, claims to be biblically inspired, and Hindu radicals in India, such as Rashtriya Swayamsevak Sangh, are alleged to have slaughtered Christians and Muslims.

- In Ireland and Britain, the Irish Republican Army (IRA) and its various factions used violence in their unsuccessful quest to bring Northern Ireland (Ulster) into the Irish Republic. The same applies to Spain, where the ETA (Euzkadi Ta Askatasuna, Basque Homeland and Freedom) waged a decades-long armed struggle to separate the Basque provinces from Spain.
- In the 1970s and 1980s, Germany faced serious episodes of terror by the Baader–Meinhoff Gang (which called itself the Red Army Faction), while Italy suffered terrorist attacks from both the Red Brigades on the extreme left and fascists on the extreme right.

ISIS (the Islamic State in Syria and Iraq) is an example of radical Islamic ideology, but it is also a violent, terrorist insurgency. Looking at ISIS in this way stresses how it resembles other groups that use terror (Huang, 2015; Pischedda, 2015). Most reports about ISIS stress its uniqueness; yet its behaviour is hardly uncommon. As noted in this chapter, extreme violence was used by the Khmer Rouge in Cambodia in the 1970s and the Shining Path guerrillas in Peru in the 1980s and 1990s. Further, like ISIS, other insurgents, including Mao Zedong's Chinese Communists in the 1930s and 1940s and the Faribundo Martí National Liberation Front in El Salvador in the 1980s and 1990s, have occupied territory and set up de facto governments that provided a range of social services. Further, existing theories of political terrorism and insurgency explain quite well the military tactics ISIS employs and how it uses violence. Even the Islamic State's focus on religion is unexceptional (see Box 9-7 Religion and Political Violence).

Those who defend the use of terror claim that when fighting the strong, the weak must use any instrument that advances their cause, including the use of violence against any target. This is the logic of total war. Thus terrorists also contend that there are no innocent victims. Everyone who is not on the terrorists' side, fully supporting their cause, is an enemy and must be destroyed.

suicide terrorism

A form of terrorist violence in which the attacker's object is to kill herself or himself as well as the target.

Of particular concern today is **suicide terrorism**, an attack in which the attacker's object is to kill herself or himself as well as the target. Nearly every day, there is news of suicide attacks in Iraq, Afghanistan, Syria, and Pakistan. Although these are now identified with Muslim extremists, until suicide bombings began in Iraq in 2003 it was the Tamil Tigers of Sri Lanka, Marxist guerrillas (active from 1974 until defeated in 2009) seeking an independent Tamil state in the country's north, that had claimed the greatest number of victims. Political scientist Robert Pape (2005) concluded that the best predictor of a country having suicide terrorists was not religion but the presence of an outside force the terrorists could paint as an occupier.

Terrorism is a form of violence used not only by insurgents.[3] Some states also use terror against their own citizens. Campaigns of ethnic cleansing—systematic attempts to remove all people of a particular ethnicity from a region, often by killing them (for example, as carried out in Rwanda and in the former Yugoslavia in the 1990s)—qualify as terror.

Authoritarian regimes often employ indiscriminate arrests, torture, and even murder to intimidate the population they govern. In several Latin American countries in the 1980s, "death squads" associated with repressive governments terrorized the population. As well, states sometimes sponsor terrorism to achieve international objectives. For example, Libyan intelligence agents were involved in the bombing of Pan-Am Flight 103 over Lockerbie, Scotland, in 1988, killing all on board (Coombes, 2003)—presumably as retaliation for an American attack against Libya's leader.

Terrorism is not unknown in Canada. Between 1963 and 1970, members of the Front de libération du Québec (FLQ) planted bombs, held up banks, and caused at least five deaths by bombs and gunfire. In October 1970, the FLQ kidnapped James Cross, the British trade commissioner in Montreal, and Pierre Laporte, labour minister in the Quebec government. Although Cross was released, Laporte was murdered by the terrorists. However, Canada's worst terrorist attack occurred on June 22, 1985, when bombs were planted by terrorists on board Air India Flight 182 before it left Vancouver. The bombing apparently was in retaliation for the Indian government's attack on the Golden Temple at Amritsar, the most important Sikh shrine. The bombs exploded while the 747 was over the North Atlantic and killed all 329 passengers and crew, most of whom were Canadians.

Is terror a political instrument because people believe their cause justifies using the most extreme measures? Or is it because terror works? In either case, terrorism is an ever-present concern.

Revolution

Revolution implies radical, far-reaching change. Political scientists want to know why revolutions happen, why they succeed or fail, and what revolutionaries do

---

[3]The designation of actions as terrorism is often controversial. For example, the Russian government condemns Chechen separatists who have bombed buildings and subway stations and have taken hostages as terrorists. Supporters of the Chechen rebels view the Russian government and military as terrorists for their brutal suppression of the breakaway Chechen Republic.

social revolution

A revolution that changes not just who governs but also how a state is organized and how its society and economy are structured.

once in power. Political science identifies two forms of revolution. The first classifies any armed overthrow of a government as a revolution. These are *political revolutions* that change rulers but need not affect the basic organization of society. They are the more common form of revolution. The second class brings fundamental economic, political, and social changes. These are **social revolutions** and are very rare.

We find the best examples of social revolutions among the great revolutions of the modern age, an era that reaches back to the latter part of the eighteenth century. These events defined new ways to govern, opened new political horizons for previously excluded sectors of society, and recast hierarchies of power and prestige. We usually encounter the following in this pantheon of revolutions:

1. The American, 1776–1783, with its entirely new model of government
2. The French, 1789, the first serious blow against aristocratic rule in Europe
3. The Haitian, 1791–1804, the first successful slave revolt in the New World
4. The Mexican, 1910–1920, a major social revolution
5. The Russian or Bolshevik, 1917, the first communist revolution
6. The Chinese, 1949, a guerrilla-led communist revolution in the world's most populous country
7. The Cuban, 1959, a guerrilla-led communist revolution in the Americas
8. The Iranian, 1979, a revolution linked to religion
9. The Eastern European, 1989, revolutions against communism

Other revolutions had important consequences for their countries but were of less historic significance. Some were wars of independence, as in Greece (1829). Others emerged from systematic restructurings of state and society following military coups, for example, Chile between 1973 and 1989.[4] Even failed revolutions, like those that swept Europe in 1848, can be important because they open the way to later reforms. Finally, there have been revolutions that were nearly non-violent, such as the 1989 Velvet Revolution in Czechoslovakia that brought the downfall of the country's communist regime (Wheaton & Kavan, 1992).

THEORIES OF REVOLUTION   In everyday language we often separate fact from theory, but in political science we use facts to build theories that we then use to interpret other facts. More formally, a "theory is a systematic explanation for observations that refer to a particular aspect of life" (Babbie, 1995, p. 49). Thus, a theory of revolution takes empirical observations about

---

[4]Although the political, economic, and social changes in Chilean society were brought about by the political right, they can still be classed as revolutionary. There is no reason why revolutions have to bring greater liberty and equality.

specific revolutions and derives from them an explanation about revolution in general. It considers why revolutions occur, what influences their evolution, and what results they produce.

The most famous theory of revolution comes from Karl Marx. Marx argued that fundamental changes in the structure of a country's economy, the means of production, lead to class conflict. Concretely, he predicted that capitalism would generate conflict between the capitalists (the bourgeoisie) who owned and directed the economy and the working class (the proletariat) whose labour made the economy function. The outcome he foresaw had the proletariat winning and setting humanity on the road to communism, a society without systematic conflicts because it would abolish classes.

More recent theorists have taken a more modest tack. Some have described specific revolutions in detail, searching for general patterns (Brinton, 1965). Others have hypothesized that key structural elements—such as changed relations among classes, an economic collapse, or a crisis of the state—exist in all successful revolutions, and have examined the record of revolutions to test their hypotheses (Skocpol, 1979). All search for a general theory of revolutions that will let us predict where a revolution will happen and how it will develop. Some theorists argue that prediction is impossible. Focusing on the Iranian revolution of 1979, Keddie (1995) notes that the structural characteristics visible in Iran before the revolution also existed in other countries where no upheaval occurred. Goldstone (1995), however, believes that attention to trends as well as structures should let us identify situations that can produce revolutions unless countermeasures are taken. We know that there will be more revolutions, but not necessarily where and when they will occur.

✓• SUMMARY AND CONCLUSION

Political protest attempts to influence government—it is a form of political participation. It can be the best, even the only, political tool available to the excluded. Even in democracies, normal channels can prove ineffective for the weak and marginalized. Yet political protest poses difficult questions for democratic citizens. Most of us usually play by the established rules of politics. We believe that they are basically fair or, if not, that they can be changed by normally available methods. However, we also know that some of our fellow citizens cannot make those rules work for them. We may or may not endorse their aims, but we wonder why our democratic rules make effective political action impossible for some people. We are witnessing a perennial problem of democratic politics.

Very few who live in democratic states accept violence for political ends. At times we may sympathize with guerrilla rebels who wage wars to overthrow brutal dictators and revolutions that promise people a better future. Where reasonable channels of political expression exist, though, it is hard to justify the use of force. It is even harder for citizens of Canada or other well-functioning democracies to countenance the use of terror as a means of protest. While terror occurs in war (including the indiscriminate killing of civilians and the use of chemical, biological, and nuclear weapons), we are loath to consider it a legitimate instrument of politics. Likewise, we find it troubling that some democratic states have supported and provided assistance to those who use terrorist tactics.

✔• KEY TERMS

DISCUSSION QUESTIONS

1. Have you ever been involved in a political protest? In what circumstances do you think that you would participate in one? Would you engage in civil disobedience?

2. Is terrorism ever justified? Are terrorists rational?

3. What are political opportunity structures and why are they important in understanding political protest?

4. Why do you think political violence has had a relatively limited role in Canadian protest politics?

5. What contemporary cases of political protest can you name? How are they different from older instances? How are they the same?

6. Why do revolutions occur? Why do you think Canada has never had a revolution?

FURTHER READING

Conable, B. & Libicki, M. (2010). *How insurgencies end.* Santa Monica, CA: Rand Corporation.

Cronin, A. (2009). *How terrorism ends: Understanding the decline and demise of terrorist campaigns.* Princeton, NJ: Princeton University Press.

Davis, M. (2007). *Buda's wagon: A brief history of the car bomb.* London: Verso.

Debray, R. (1967). *Revolution in the revolution.* New York: Grove Press.

Gitlin, T. (2012). *Occupy nation: The roots, the spirit, and the promise of Occupy Wall Street.* New York: !t Books.

Goldstone, J. (Ed.). (2003). *Revolutions: Theoretical, comparative, and historical studies* (3rd ed.). Belmont, CA: Wadsworth/Thompson Learning.

Guevara, C. (1967). *Guerrilla warfare.* Wilmington, DE: SR Books.

Irvin, C. (1999). *Militant nationalism.* Minneapolis, MN: University of Minnesota Press.

Kilkullen, D. (2010). *Counterinsurgency.* New York: Oxford University Press.

Mao Zedong. (1961). *On guerrilla warfare.* New York: Praeger.

Noueihed, L., & Warren, A. (2012). *The battle for the Arab spring: Revolution, counter-revolution, and the making of a new era.* New Haven, CT; Yale University Press.

O'Kane, R.H.T. (2012). *Terrorism* (2nd. ed.). Harlow, UK: Pearson Longman.

Sanderson, S. (2005). *Revolutions: A worldwide introduction to political and social change.* Boulder, CO: Paradigm Publishers.

Smith, J., & Johnston, H. (Eds.). (2002). *Globalization and resistance: Transnational dimensions of social movements.* Lanham, MD: Rowman & Littlefield.

Staggenborg, S. (2008). *Social movements.* Don Mills, ON: Oxford University Press.

Tilly, C., & Tarrow, S. (2007). *Contentious politics.* Boulder, CO: Paradigm Publishers.

10 Democracy and Democratic Government

A man smokes marijuana at the Seattle Center in Seattle, Washington on December 6, 2012 after voters in that state passed an initiative to legalize marijuana.   ZUMA Press, Inc./Alamy Stock Photo

After reading this chapter, you should be able to:

1. examine the development of democracy
2. discuss the advantages and disadvantages of democratic government
3. explain the differences between direct democracy and representative democracy
4. define liberal democracy
5. evaluate plebiscitary and deliberative democracy

On November 6, 2012, voters in Washington and Colorado voted to legalize marijuana. In 2014 voters in Alaska, Oregon, and Washington, D.C. voted for legalization* In these four states, those over 21 years old can possess a small amount of marijuana for recreational use. The state governments license and regulate the production, distribution, and sale of marijuana products, determine where cannabis can be used and whether a small number of plants can be grown for personal use. Nevertheless, the possession of marijuana remains illegal under US federal law. The Obama Administration decided not to challenge state laws legalizing marijuana provided that strict rules were maintained concerning sale and distribution.

The vote to legalize marijuana came about through a process known as *the initiative*. This allows laws proposed by citizens to be placed on the ballot after gathering a sufficient number of valid signatures on a petition within a certain time frame. Generally, the proposition in the initiative becomes law if passed by a majority of voters, even if it is not supported by a majority in the legislature.

Initiatives and other ballot questions have become a significant part of the political process in a number of American states. (There is no provision allowing initiatives at the national level.) In the 2014 election, 35 initiatives were on the ballot in various states. In addition, there were 101 laws and constitutional amendments referred from state legislatures to a vote by citizens (Initiative and Referendum Institute, 2014).

In Canada, only the province of British Columbia has provisions to allow initiatives. On July 1, 2010, the Harmonized Sales Tax (HST) that combined the federal goods and services tax (GST) with the provincial sales tax came into effect in British Columbia. Many people were upset that the B.C. Liberals had said in the 2009 election campaign that they did not contemplate adopting the unpopular HST (Spector, 2009), but nevertheless passed legislation implementing the HST a year later. Opponents to the HST then launched the only successful initiative in British Columbia, easily surpassing the requirement that at least 10 percent of registered voters in each of the province's 83 electoral districts sign the petition within a 90-day period. This was followed by a mail-in referendum ballot in which 57.43 percent of those voting supported rescinding B.C.'s adoption of the HST. Subsequently, the B.C. legislature passed legislation to end the HST. As of October 2016, four other initiatives had failed to obtain a sufficient number of signatures including one that would prohibit the use of provincial police resources to enforce laws concerning simple possession and use of marijuana by adults.

We usually think of democracy in terms of the election of representatives to make laws on our behalf. However, representative democracy might be viewed as a limited form of democracy as governments do not necessarily act in accordance with the wishes of the majority of citizens. Thus, some have argued that to be fully democratic, the people should have a more direct say in the laws and policies of democratic governments.

---

*In 2016, an additional 5 states held votes regarding whether to legalize recreational use of marijuana. A number of other states and D.C. allow the use of marijuana for medical purposes or have decriminalized possession. Marijuana is legal in Indiana only for members of the First Church of Cannabis.

INTRODUCTION

The term **democracy** comes from ancient Greek words that can be translated as "rule by the people." The democratic ideal is that all adult citizens should have an equal and effective voice in the decisions of the political communities to which they belong. Like all ideals, it may be impossible to fully realize the democratic ideal. Nevertheless, by analyzing the political systems of different countries, we can examine the extent to which they are democratic and the different ways in which the democratic ideal is pursued. In addition, because the idea of democracy is popular, there are many countries that claim to be democratic but that we would consider as having authoritarian or hybrid regimes (a mixture of democratic and non-democratic rule). This chapter will focus on the liberal democracies that developed in the Western world and have been adopted to varying extents in many other parts of the world.

democracy

Rule by the people.

DIRECT DEMOCRACY

About 2500 years ago, the important Greek city state of Athens adopted a system of **direct democracy**, that is, a system in which citizens themselves make the governing decisions. The citizens of Athens (which did not include women, slaves, and the foreign born) met in an open assembly about ten times a year. After a discussion in which all citizens could participate, the decisions governing this powerful political community were made through a vote by those present.[1] The Athenian statesman Pericles defended this system, saying that "instead of looking on discussion as a stumbling-block in the way of action, we think it an indispensable preliminary to any wise action at all" (Thucydides quoted in Warren, 2002, p. 174).

direct democracy

A system in which citizens themselves make the governing decisions.

In contrast, the Greek philosopher Plato (ca. 428–347 BCE) viewed democracy as involving leaders of the mass of people plundering the rich and distributing some of their wealth. Democracy, he argued, would degenerate into tyranny, as the mass would give up its freedom to a popular leader who would become a despotic tyrant. Plato's student Aristotle (384–322 BCE) examined 158 political communities and classified them in terms of whether there was rule by a single person, rule by a few, or rule by the many. Rule by one, a few, or many were good forms of government if the rulers worked toward the common good and governed in a lawful manner. Alternatively, if the ruling individual or group acted arbitrarily for its own interests, rule by one, a few, or the many could be considered a bad or "perverted" form of government. Aristotle's analysis is often summarized using a table that depicts six types of government (see Table 10-1).

---

[1]Many officials were randomly selected for short terms in office through a lottery system (as were juries).

TABLE 10-1
Aristotle's Basic Classification of Types of Rule

RULE BY	LAWFUL RULE FOR THE COMMON GOOD	ARBITRARY RULE FOR THE RULERS' OWN INTERESTS
One	Kingship	Tyranny
Few	Aristocracy	Oligarchy
Many	Polity	Democracy

Aristotle viewed democracy as a perverted form of government in which the poor, being the majority, governed in their own interests by taking away the property of the rich. Therefore, democratic government did not work for the common good. Aristotle was also concerned that the masses could be swayed by passion and demagogic speakers rather than by reason and might not act in accordance with established laws. However, he viewed citizen participation in politics as desirable and suggested that rule by the many could be a good form of government (which he termed "polity," or constitutional government) if it abided by the laws and governed for the good of all. Although rule by a virtuous few (aristocracy) would be best, in most cases he thought that it was not practical because of the small number of virtuous men. Instead, the best form of governing that could be established in most cases would be a combination of democracy and oligarchy (rule by the wealthy), particularly if there were a large middle class that could moderate the tensions between the rich and the poor. With a large middle class, the polity form of governing would reflect neither the arrogance of the rich nor the enviousness of the poor (Hallowell & Porter, 1997).

The idea of direct democracy has not completely disappeared. Citizen meetings make decisions in a few New England towns and small Swiss cantons (provinces). As well, the random selection of citizens to serve on juries bears a resemblance to the practices of ancient Athens. However, the idea of citizens assembling to make governing decisions became impractical as larger states developed. Thus, democracy in the modern era is generally associated with the concept of elected representation of the citizenry. Nevertheless, the use of instruments such as citizens' initiatives and citizen forums (discussed later in this chapter) could be considered to some extent as modern applications of direct democracy.

THE DEVELOPMENT OF DEMOCRACY

Athenian democracy lasted from about 510 BCE until Greece was conquered by Macedonia in 322 BCE. Several other ancient Greek cities also were influenced by the Athenian model in this time period. The Roman Republic (509–27 BCE) maintained some elements of direct democracy in its assemblies, but the significance of the assemblies was eclipsed as the aristocratic Senate became more powerful. In turn, as the Roman Empire replaced the Republic, power became highly concentrated in the hands of the emperor (Dryzek & Dunleavy, 2009). The ideal of democracy was revived in the 1640s by the Levellers in England, who demanded that all males be able to vote for the English parliament and that government be based on the free assent of the people (Birch, 1971). In the eighteenth century, philosopher Jean-Jacques Rousseau argued people are only truly free when government decisions are based on the general will of the people. This, he thought, could best be achieved in small communities through direct democracy in which all would participate (Birch, 1971).

The French Revolution (1789–99) challenged the "divine right" of kings and brought the idea of rule by the people and the human right to freedom and equality to the forefront of political discussion. The principle of universal male suffrage was established in the constitutions adopted by the revolutionary assemblies.[2] For the more radical individuals and factions that adopted some of the ideas of Rousseau, democratic government involved putting the will of the people directly into effect regardless of whether the rights of individuals were protected (Dryzek & Dunleavy, 2009). The mass executions by the revolutionary government's "Reign of Terror" served to discredit the idea of democracy, and universal male suffrage in France ended with the coming to power of the emperor Napoleon. Nevertheless, uprisings throughout Europe in 1848 indicated that there was a popular desire for democracy.

The French Revolution provided inspiration for those who viewed revolutionary action as necessary for a successful struggle by the mass of people against the rich and powerful and for the creation of a more equal society. However, an alternative route to a democratic political system has been through the development of legislative institutions, in which voters elect representatives to act on their behalf. For example, after the American Revolution (1775–1783), the founders of the United States established a republic in which the different branches of government (legislative, executive, and judicial) would each check the powers of the other branches. To some extent, this could be considered an application of Aristotle's ideal of a mixed form of government. Election to the House of Representatives was by male property owners, thus excluding women, the poor, and slaves. State legislatures selected members of the Senate as well as the Electoral College, which chooses the president and the vice-president.[3] Over time, this system gradually became more democratic.

Representative legislatures in England originated in meetings called by monarchs when they needed to gain the support of persons from different parts of their realm for new taxes. England's first parliament was summoned in 1275. However, until the Reform Acts of 1832 and 1867, it represented only a very small proportion of the population. Further, although the House

---

[2]There were certain qualifications to the principle. See Przeworski (2009).

[3]By 1824 almost all states used elections to choose members of the Electoral College. The practice of electing senators developed in the nineteenth century and was officially adopted in 1913.

of Commons was able eventually to put some limits on the power of the monarch, it was not until the middle of the nineteenth century that the executive became responsible to the House of Commons in the United Kingdom (and Canada). In addition, until 1911 the unelected House of Lords had the power to reject legislation passed by the House of Commons. Likewise, Canada's Senate, appointed on the recommendation of the prime minister, was active in rejecting House of Commons legislation in Canada's first half-century. It continues to have and occasionally use that power, as well as the authority to propose non-financial legislation.

The transition to a representative *democracy* in which all persons had a right to vote was often controversial. British parliamentarian Edmund Burke (1729–1797) argued that ordinary people did not know what was in the interests of the nation. Therefore, political power should be exercised by the "natural aristocracy" (including the nobility, who had inherited substantial property, as well as men of law, science, and the arts, and "rich traders") who had the education and leisure time to discern what was in the true interests of the nation and could represent the people as a whole (Macpherson, 1980, p. 47). Many nineteenth-century liberal political thinkers favoured equal political rights in principle, but worried about the consequences of granting equal voting rights to all persons. Some believed that the poor would use their voting power to elect those committed to taking away the wealth of the middle and upper classes. Others feared that the less educated would be intolerant and therefore their voting strength would be a threat to individual liberty.

Overall, representative democracy has become the leading form of democracy in the contemporary world. The development of working-class and socialist movements pressured governments to adopt universal adult suffrage. Indeed, the elites of society feared that the failure to include the growing working class could result in revolution. In addition, determined action by the suffragette movement led to the extension of the right of women to vote and hold office, although a number of countries were slow to respond (see Table 10-2).

In Canada, provincial governments were generally responsible for determining who had the right to vote both in provincial and federal elections until 1920. The property requirements that some provinces adopted excluded many persons from voting. In 1916 and 1917, the four western provinces and Ontario granted women the right to vote. In 1917, at the national level, the Union government, hoping to gain more votes in support of the war effort, extended the right to vote to women serving or who had relatives serving or who had served in the Armed Forces. In 1918, women were given the right to vote on the same basis as men, and in 1920, the property qualification for voting that still existed in two provinces was eliminated for federal elections (Elections Canada, 1997)[4]. However, at various times, those of certain races

---

[4]Women did not gain the right to vote in provincial elections in Quebec until 1940.

TABLE 10-2   Women's Right to Vote on the Same Basis as Men in National Elections, Selected Countries

Notes: In some cases, certain categories of women had the right to vote before these dates. The right to seek and hold public office occurred later than the right to vote in a number of countries. Women in some countries were able to vote in local and regional elections either earlier or later than in national elections. Saudi Arabia gave women the right to vote in 2015 (although they cannot drive themselves to a voting station).

New Zealand 1893	Austria 1918	France 1944	Pakistan 1956
Australia 1901	Sweden 1919	Japan 1945	Egypt 1956
Finland 1906	United States 1920	Argentina 1947	Iran 1963
Norway 1913	Italy 1925	Belgium 1948	Switzerland 1971
Denmark 1915	United Kingdom 1928	Greece 1952	Bangladesh 1972
Russia 1917	Chile 1931	Mexico 1953	Bahrain 2002
Canada 1918	Brazil 1932	Indonesia 1955	Kuwait 2005
Germany 1918	Turkey 1934	Ethiopia 1955	UA Emirates 2006

and religious groups were not allowed to vote, and voting rights for Aboriginals were not fully established until 1960.

The United States established voting rights for women through a constitutional amendment in 1920. Although the 15th Amendment to the US constitution (1870) had declared that voting rights could not be denied on the basis of "race, color, or previous condition of servitude," most black Americans in the southern states were effectively prevented from voting in national and state elections through literacy tests, poll taxes, and intimidation including threats of violence. The Voting Rights Act, 1965, enhanced the ability of the American government to ensure that voting rights were protected (although some states still try to make it difficult for poor blacks to vote).

REPRESENTATIVE DEMOCRACY

Representative democracy involves citizens electing representatives to the **legislature**, a body that is responsible for the formal approval of legislation and the raising and spending of funds by the government. Representative democracy is an indirect form of democracy in the sense that the people do not directly make the governing decisions, but rather determine, through an election, who makes such decisions on their behalf.

Extending the rights to vote and hold office to all citizens does not ensure that legislatures will be representative in the sense of accurately reflecting all characteristics of the population. For example, although the proportion of women in legislatures has been gradually increasing in many countries, women are underrepresented to varying extents in almost all legislatures, as Table 10-3 indicates.[5]

representative democracy

A form of democracy in which citizens elect representatives to the legislature to make decisions on their behalf.

legislature

An institution whose responsibilities include the approval of legislation and the raising and spending of funds by the government.

---

[5]Although only 27 percent of Liberal MPs elected in the 2015 Canadian election were women, Prime Minister Trudeau deliberately chose an equal number of women and men for his cabinet.

TABLE 10-3
Women in National
Legislatures

COUNTRY	% WOMEN IN LEGISLATURE	COUNTRY	% WOMEN IN LEGISLATURE
Rwanda	63.8%	China	23.6%
Sweden	43.6%	United States	19.4%
Mexico	42.4%	Indonesia	17.1%
South Africa	42.0%	Turkey	14.9%
Spain	40.0%	Russia	13.6%
Germany	36.5%	India	12.0%
Argentina	35.8%	Hungary	10.1%
Italy	31.0%	Brazil	9.9%
United Kingdom	29.4%	Japan	9.5%
Poland	27.4%	Nigeria	5.6%
Australia	26.7%	Iran	3.1%
France	26.2%	Qatar	0.0%
Canada	26.0%	**World Average**	**22.7%**

Note: Figures are for the lower house (such as the Canadian House of Commons) in countries with two legislative chambers. Data as of February, 2016.

Source: Adapted from Women in National Parliaments by Inter-Parliamentary Union (IPU) (2016): www.ipu.org/wne-e/classif.htm.

In most contemporary parliamentary democracies, elected representatives, other than those who are in the Cabinet, usually have a limited involvement in developing governing decisions. It is the political executive (in Canada, the prime minister and Cabinet), along with the leading advisors to the political executive, who have a key role in the development of laws and policies. The general role of Parliament is to debate and approve proposed laws that are presented to it by the prime minister and Cabinet. Representatives are almost always members of a political party, and elections focus on the competition among political parties to determine which party (or parties) will form the government. Elected representatives are generally expected to vote along party lines. This means that they do not necessarily vote in accordance with the views of those who elected them. Representation is more by party than by individual representatives.

Democracy Watch
www.dwatch.ca

LIBERAL DEMOCRACY

liberal democracy

A political system that combines the liberal ideas of limited government, individual freedom, and the rule of law with a democratic system of governing based on the election of representatives.

civil society

The voluntary groups and organizations that are not controlled by the state.

The version of representative democracy that developed in modern Western societies is often described as **liberal democracy**. Liberal democracy, as the term suggests, combines the ideology of liberalism, which advocates a high level of individual freedom, with a democratic system of governing based on the election of representatives. The power and scope of government should be limited, government should abide by the rule of law, and the rights of the people should be protected. In this view, democracy should be based on a vibrant **civil society** in which citizens are free to discuss, organize, and act, particularly through a diversity of voluntary groups and organizations that are not controlled by the state. Because it is based on the rule of law, it is sometimes called constitutional democracy. Liberal democracy is generally accepted not only by liberals, but also (sometimes with qualifications) by contemporary conservatives and democratic socialists.

Liberal democracy is based on the belief that power, even the power of a government that is supported by the majority of the people, is liable to be abused. Liberal democracy includes the following principles:

- Limits should be placed on what governments can do. Those in positions of political authority should not be able to rule in an arbitrary manner; rather, decisions should be taken according to established laws and procedures.
- All persons should have the freedom to express their views, including the freedom to criticize government and the freedom to organize themselves for political action.
- The communications media should be free of government control so that diverse sources of information and ideas are easily available to the public.
- Candidates and political parties should be able to freely compete for political power.

Political Pluralism

For a liberal democracy to function properly, there must be centres of power that are independent of government, including businesses, unions, educational institutions, interest groups, political parties, social movements, and the media. They are able to question what government does and compete to influence government. Nevertheless, some argue that political pluralism in democratic countries such as the United States and the United Kingdom is limited and that powerful forces are able to make some important key decisions (see Box 10-1 The Deep State).

The Rule of Law

John Adams, a leading figure in the American Revolution and the second president of the United States, coined the phrase "a government of law and not of men" to describe his view that government should be based on the rule of law. The rule of law places limits on government, as it is required to act in accordance with the law. Thus the rule of law is the keystone of a system that protects the people of a community against the arbitrary and abusive use of government power.

The rule of law exists where three conditions are met. First, the law is known, or at least knowable, to all. Second, in principle, the law applies equally to all. Third, even the government that makes the law can be made to obey the law by having an independent court system that is free from political pressure. However some argue that the ability and increased willingness of the

BOX 10-1 The Deep State

Many people are fascinated by conspiracy theories. Stories about an alien spaceship crashing at Roswell, New Mexico in 1947, the assassination of President John F. Kennedy in 1963, and the collapse of New York's World Trade Center on September 11, 2011, have led to claims about what really happened and why high-level politicians and officials supposedly hid the truth. Many conspiracy theories are clearly false. However, for some there may be a grain of truth.

Mike Lofgren (2016), a long-time Republican Congressional staffer, claims that there is in the United States "a hybrid association of key elements of government and parts of top-level finance and industry." This "deep state" in effect governs the country with "only limited reference to the consent of the governed as normally expressed through elections" (p. 6). Likewise, others have written about "the rise of America's secret government" (Talbot, 2015) and a

"shadow government" (Engelhardt & Greenwald, 2014). Indeed, American president Dwight Eisenhower in his Farewell Address (1961) warned about the power of "the military–industrial complex . . . the conjunction of an immense military establishment and a large arms industry."

Rather than a conspiracy, the "deep state" could be viewed as the efforts of the governments to guard against the threat of terrorism, to protect the "free world", and deal with problems of international peace and security. However, the increasing surveillance of the population, the power of large multinational corporations, the growth of the military establishment, and, at times, the brutal suppression of liberation movements in foreign countries has raised concerns about whether the public is fully informed and able to effectively influence the actions of their government and government agencies.

courts in many countries (including Canada and the United States) to strike down laws passed by elected legislative bodies has made unelected judges powerful and resulted in a decline of democracy (Allan, 2014).

DEMOCRATIC GOVERNMENT

Democratic government can take on various different forms. Parliamentary government involves a close interrelation between the executive (the prime minister and Cabinet) and Parliament (the legislative body). In the Canadian parliamentary system, the prime minister and Cabinet ministers are normally elected members of the House of Commons. They must retain the support of a majority of representatives in the Commons. However, despite the responsibility of the prime minister and Cabinet to the House of Commons, power tends to be concentrated in the hands of the executive (particularly the prime minister) who can usually control the Commons.

In the American presidential system, power is divided between Congress (composed of representatives elected to the House of Representatives and the Senate) and the executive branch headed by the elected president. The president is powerful in some respects including the conduct of foreign policy and the use of the military. However, the president's power is checked by a powerful, independent-minded Congress that exercises considerable control over legislation and the budget. Generally, parliamentary systems in which one political party commands a majority of elected members of Parliament has a greater potential to take concerted and coordinated action than the American presidential system.

In most liberal democratic countries, an independent court system provides a check on government by ensuring that it abides by the rule of law and the provisions of the constitution. In the United States, the Supreme Court plays an important role in the system of checks and balances that limits the power of each of the three branches of government.

Accountability

Perhaps the greatest advantage of democracy is that democratic governments can be held accountable for their actions and inactions. Citizens can assess the performance of their elected representatives and vote whether or not to allow them to continue to hold office. Citizens can also contribute to the re-election or defeat of the government by choosing whether or not to vote for a candidate representing the governing party.[6] At every election, those chosen by citizens to direct the government have to ask anew for our support. They are accountable to us and need our approval to continue in office.[7]

In addition to elections, ongoing accountability in liberal democracies is provided by the media and civil society organizations that inform the public about what the government is doing and provide assessments of government action and inactions. In parliamentary systems, the government (prime minister and Cabinet) is expected to be accountable to the elected legislative body whose support it requires to stay in office. In reality, when one party holds a majority of seats in the legislature, it is very unlikely that the legislative body (the House of Commons in Canada) will withdraw its support of the government and force an election. However, opposition parties provide criticism of the government's performance in the hope that this will affect the result of the next election.

As well, independent agencies and officials (such as the Office of the Auditor General, the Access to Information Officer, and the Parliamentary Budget Officer[8] in Canada) make public their reports assessing various aspects of the governing process and act as watchdogs that can hold government accountable. To counter criticism, the governing party will try to provide a defence for

---

[6]In countries with a proportional representation system, accountability by citizens involves political parties rather than individual candidates.

[7]Accountability is problematic in countries with a presidential system if the president is not allowed to serve more than one term (e.g., Mexico) or during the final second term in office (e.g., the United States).

[8]The Parliamentary Budget Officer in Canada is not fully independent. The Conservative government that established the office did not provide the mandate, information, or sufficient budget to carry out its task in analyzing government's spending plans (Page, 2015).

their policies. If the criticism of government policies resonates with the public, the government may decide to change its policies. For example, when faced with extensive criticism of the escalating costs of its proposed purchase of F-35 fighter jets, the Canadian government under Prime Minister Stephen Harper ordered a reassessment of the purchase in December 2012.

Transparency

transparency

Government's obligation to provide timely access to information and to operate visibly so that it can be held accountable for its actions.

An important corollary of accountability is **transparency**. Citizens, the media, citizen groups, political parties, and independent agencies need access to a great deal of information if they are to hold government accountable. Governments now provide a considerable amount of information through their websites and have adopted access to information (also known as freedom of information) laws, and many proclaim a commitment to "open government." Nevertheless, many governments charge fees to access information and make it difficult to analyze the mass of information that is available. Furthermore, governments often try to limit timely access to information that might reflect negatively on the government.

Although some government information may need to be kept secret if it threatens national security, infringes upon individual privacy, or undermines Cabinet solidarity, it can be very controversial when information is leaked by those who believe that the public should be made aware of wrongdoing (see Box 10-2 Daniel Ellsberg and Bradley Manning: The Pentagon Papers and WikiLeaks).

Transparency is also crucial in avoiding the taint of corruption and undue influence. Democratic governments are generally freer from corruption than non-democratic governments. Nevertheless, the Charbonneau inquiry (2011–2015) revealed a widespread system of kickbacks to politicians and union leaders by companies (some with connections to the Mafia) awarded government construction contracts in Quebec. Information about the corruption had been suppressed for many years and resulted in shoddy and expensive infrastructure. Several politicians and corporate executives resigned as a result of the inquiry.

Popular Participation

Informed public participation from all sectors of society is important to ensure that governments are responsive to the needs and wishes of the people. Without substantial popular participation, governments are more likely to act in the interests of powerful special interests.

Democratic Audit UK
www.democraticaudit.com

Participation in the form of voting has generally declined in many liberal democracies in recent decades while participation through various other forms of citizen participation has been increasing. Nevertheless, there is a significant segment of the public that is not involved politically through voting or other forms of participation, and thus may be largely ignored by politicians, parties, and governments.

BOX 10-2 Daniel Ellsberg and Bradley Manning: The Pentagon Papers and WikiLeaks

In 1969, Daniel Ellsberg, who had served in the Pentagon and in Vietnam, photocopied 7000 top-secret documents (the Pentagon Papers) commissioned by the US Defense Secretary. These papers showed that the US Administration had systematically lied to Congress and the public concerning the Vietnam War. Although the US government obtained a restraining order to prevent the *New York Times* from publishing excerpts of the papers, the Supreme Court ruled that that publication could continue. Subsequently, presidential aides arranged for a burglary of the office of Ellsberg's psychiatrist to try to find information to discredit Ellsberg and even plotted to drug him with LSD. Because of gross government misconduct and illegal wiretapping, a judge dismissed all charges against Ellsberg.

In 2010, Bradley Manning, a US army private, was arrested in Iraq for "aiding the enemy." He had downloaded hundreds of thousands of US diplomatic cables and army reports on the wars in Iraq and Afghanistan (including videos of American airstrikes that killed civilians and journalists). This classified material was sent to and posted on the website WikiLeaks. The publicity garnered by the diplomatic cables discussing the extreme corruption and extravagance of various dictators may have contributed to the "Arab Spring" uprisings that began in December 2010 in Tunisia (Dickinson, 2011).

Manning pleaded guilty to the charge of misusing classified material that he thought should be made public. A military court acquitted Manning on the charge of aiding the enemy, but convicted him of espionage, theft, and computer fraud. Julian Assange, the founder and editor-in-chief of WikiLeaks, took refuge in the London embassy of Ecuador, fearing extradition to face possible conspiracy charges in the United States related to the Manning case (as well as a sex-related charge in Sweden).

The Ellsberg and Manning cases pose difficult questions for liberal democracies. To what extent does the state need to protect information that it deems vital to national security and the conduct of war and foreign affairs? Should those who publicly release classified government documents that they believe the public needs to know be prosecuted and face lengthy prison sentences?

PFC Bradley [now Chelsea] Manning appears in military court at Fort Meade on March 15, 2013. Manning's leak of classified information to WikiLeaks resulted in a 35-year sentence.
BRENDAN SMIALOWSKI/AFP/Getty Images/Newscom

Government Responsiveness

To what extent are governments responsive to the interests, needs, and opinions of the public? To some extent, holding regular free and fair elections provides an important incentive for the governing party to be responsive to the electorate. In addition, governments today regularly engage in public opinion polling to find out the views of the public on a variety of issues. Public consultations allow for some dialogue between government and interested members of the public, although public consultations often only elicit limited participation from the general public unless the topic is highly controversial. Elected representatives also meet with many of their constituents and receive considerable communication from people concerned about particular issues or facing problems with government services. And the traditional practice of petitioning government to take action on particular matters has become more widespread as various groups are able to collect large numbers of signatures using websites and social media.

However, governments also try to shape the opinions and priorities of the public. Governments spend large amounts of money on advertising, not just to inform the public about programs and services, but also to promote a favourable image of the government. Governments often devote considerable attention to message management such as ensuring that all speeches and press

Welcome to the Northern
Gateway Public Hearings

Tami Thirlwell

releases by Cabinet ministers, governing party MPs, and public officials conform to the positive themes that the government wants to present to the public. As well, some government leaders strictly limit questions from the media and grant interviews only to those in the media that have a favourable view of the government. Of course, the opposition parties and those dissatisfied with government policies will try to present a more critical perspective and raise issues that government would prefer to ignore.

Overall, governments often prefer to govern rather than to engage in a meaningful dialogue with the public. Governing parties fear that changing their positions in response to public criticism will be viewed as a sign of weakness, and they typically only back down in response to public pressure when it is apparent that opposition to a particular policy is widespread and would reduce their chances of being re-elected. Further, governments often try to limit scrutiny of their proposals and actions. For example, Canadian governments in recent decades have made extensive use of "omnibus bills" containing a large number of often unrelated legislative proposals that do not receive adequate scrutiny by parliamentary committees as they are rushed through Parliament. Likewise, there have been efforts to limit public participation in hearings on controversial issues. For example, critics argued that public participation was deliberately restricted on hearings in 2012 and 2013 concerning the proposed Northern Gateway oil pipeline.

EXTENDING DEMOCRACY?

Liberal, representative democracy is sometimes viewed as a limited form of democracy. Citizens are free to vote for their representatives and directly (in a presidential system) or indirectly (in a parliamentary system) determine who will lead the government. However, they are usually not directly involved in the processes of making governing decisions. Instead, through the competition of political parties, voters collectively have the ability at an election to remove a government whose performance they view as unsatisfactory and replace it with a party whose platform, perspective, and politicians they prefer.

The political freedoms of liberal democracies allow people to try to influence the decisions made by their representatives and governments through various forms of independent political organization and expression. However, governments and representatives do not necessarily follow the wishes of the people. The often substantial level of public dissatisfaction with the performance of governments and politicians even in well-established democracies including Canada, the United States, and the United Kingdom suggests that there is a **democratic deficit**. Norris (2011) relates the rising expectations of the public, due in part to increased education, to a perceived shortfall in government performance. This democratic deficit is often exhibited in declining levels of voter turnout, low levels of trust and confidence in government and politicians, increased protest activity, and a feeling that ordinary people have

democratic deficit

The substantial level of public dissatisfaction with the performance of democratic governments and politicians exhibited in declining levels of voter turnout,

little influence on government. Advocates of plebiscitary democracy and deliberative democracy seek to modify liberal, representative democracy to provide for greater direct citizen involvement in the making of governing decisions.

Plebiscitary Democracy

plebiscitary democracy

A form of democracy in which citizens have greater control than in representative democracy through the use of such devices as referendums, citizens' initiatives, and recall elections.

populism

A perspective that advocates putting power in the hands of the people rather than the elites who control politics and society.

Plebiscitary democracy involves giving citizens greater control of public policies and representatives through the use of such devices as referendums, citizens' initiatives, and recall elections. This version of democracy is often associated with the perspective of **populism**, which is based on the idea that fundamental differences exist between ordinary people and the elites who control politics and society (Laycock, 2002). Ordinary people, in the populist perspective, possess common sense. Politicians, government bureaucrats, political parties, intellectuals, leading cultural figures, and the owners of banks and other big businesses are often viewed by populists as immoral, corrupt, or out of touch with common people. Elites and "special interests" strongly influence what public policies are adopted and take advantage of the hard-working majority. Representative democracy, populists argue, places power in the hands of politicians who are more interested in their own political careers, in acting in accordance with the views of their party, and in promoting special interests than in taking direction from the people whom they are supposed to represent. In practice, however, populist political parties that have been elected to govern have often concentrated power in the hands of a persuasive leader who claims to speak for ordinary people.

referendum

A vote by citizens on a particular issue or law.

REFERENDUMS   A **referendum** gives people the opportunity to vote on a particular issue or proposed law. A number of countries require that changes to their constitution be approved by a referendum. Referendums can also be used in some countries to repeal a law that has been passed by a legislative body. Many American states and municipalities make frequent use of referendums, although there has never been a national referendum in the United States. In Canada, there have been only three referendums at the national level. They concerned the prohibition of liquor (1898), conscription during World War II (1942), and the constitutional changes known as the Charlottetown Accord (1992).

Referendums have been somewhat more common at the provincial and local levels in Canada. Of particular importance were referendums concerning Quebec sovereignty. In 1980, 40.5 percent of Quebecers voted in favour of giving the Quebec government a mandate to negotiate "sovereignty-association" (a politically independent Quebec in an economic association with Canada) with the Canadian government. In 1995, 49.3 percent of Quebec voters supported giving the Quebec government a mandate to negotiate Quebec sovereignty. In response to a challenge to the 1995 referendum, the Supreme Court of Canada provided an opinion in 1998 that only if there was a clear majority on a clear question in a referendum could a province negotiate its independence with the other Canadian governments. The Canadian Parliament reinforced this ruling by passing the Clarity Act (2000). This Act states that the Canadian government will only enter into negotiations regarding the secession (separation) of a province if the Canadian House of Commons determines that a clear majority of the population of that province has voted in favour of secession on the basis of a clear question.

Although referendums involve a vote by the people, the decision to hold a referendum and the wording of a referendum are generally set by those in control of the government or the legislature. Thus, there is a possibility that a referendum can be used to manipulate the people through misleading wording. Indeed, many non-democratic governments have used referendums to try to legitimate their rule. For example, some dictators have held referendums asking for approval of their continued rule without allowing a choice among alternative candidates while suppressing criticism of the ruler.

CITIZENS' INITIATIVES   A stronger means of giving the public a direct voice in decision making is the initiative discussed in the opening vignette. In a few countries, including Switzerland, New Zealand, the Philippines, and Taiwan, citizens have the right, by obtaining a sizable number of signatures on a petition, to have a proposition that they have drafted put to a vote by the electorate for approval.[9] Likewise, 24 American states and British Columbia have established legal procedures for initiatives. Some countries (for example, Italy) allow **citizens' initiatives** on whether to repeal a law that has been passed by a legislative body. Other countries provide that citizens, through a petition process, can introduce bills for a legislative body to consider although the legislature is not obliged to pass the bill or hold a referendum. The European Union allows initiatives to call on the European Commission to prepare a law on matters that the EU can legislate provided they are signed by at least one million EU citizens coming from at least one-quarter of the member states (as of 2016, seven of 28 countries).

RECALL OF ELECTED REPRESENTATIVES   Recall procedures allow citizens to remove representatives from office before the end of their term of office. As with the initiative, most recall procedures involve gathering a sufficient number of names on a petition and then holding an election to determine whether the majority of voters wish to remove their representative and hold a new election.[10] Recall procedures are available in 19 American states, some Swiss cantons, Venezuela, the Philippines, and British Columbia. A recall election in 2003 saw Arnold Schwarzenegger replace Gray Davis as governor of California—only the second time that a governor in the United States has ever

citizens' initiatives

A procedure that gives citizens the right, by obtaining a sizable number of signatures on a petition, to have a proposition that they have drafted put to a vote by the electorate for approval.

Initiative & Referendum Institute
www.iandrinstitute.org

The Initiative & Referendum Institute Europe
www.iri-europe.org

recall

A procedure that allows citizens to remove representatives from office. By gaining a sufficient number of signatures on a petition, citizens can require that their representative seek re-election before the representative's term is over.

---

[9]In Switzerland and New Zealand, the initiative is not legally binding.

[10]California includes the choice of a new representative on the same ballot as the question about whether the current representative should be recalled.

been removed by a recall vote. In British Columbia, no recall attempts have been successful since recall procedures were adopted in 1991, although one provincial legislator resigned rather than suffer a likely defeat in a recall election. The adoption of recall elections might be viewed as incompatible with the Canadian system of government, since the recall of representatives from a small number of districts could result in the defeat of the governing party regardless of the wishes of people in the majority of districts.

PROBLEMS WITH PLEBISCITARY DEMOCRACY   There are some practical problems with referendums, initiatives, and recall elections. Citizens are not always prepared to vote on long and difficult proposals. When faced with a number of complex referendum and initiative questions on the ballot, voters may find it difficult to make informed decisions. This is particularly true if referendums or initiatives are worded in a manipulative fashion. Concerns have been expressed that voters may be swayed by the expensive advertising efforts of interest groups that present the issues simplistically or unfairly, or by businesses that may stand to profit by the vote.

For example, in California, more than $100 million was spent on the 2006 campaign for Proposition 87, which would tax the producers of oil extracted in that state to fund programs to reduce oil consumption and provide incentives for alternative energy. The large oil companies that spent the majority of funds were successful in defeating the initiative by a 55 to 45 percent margin. As in regular elections, it takes money and organization to win votes.

Referendums, initiatives, and recall may stimulate some public discussion of important issues, encourage representatives to be more responsive to voters, and result in laws that reflect the wishes of the majority. However, with the possibility for manipulation and the exertion of one-sided influence, voting is not necessarily the product of informed discussion and deliberation. As well, although some referendums have had a high rate of turnout, such as when 93.5 percent of Quebecers voted in the 1995 referendum, frequent use of referendums, initiatives, and recall can result in low turnout rates. This is particularly the case when voters have to deal with multiple, complex questions.

Deliberative Democracy

deliberative democracy

A political system in which decisions are made based on discussion by citizens rather than by elected representatives alone.

There has been considerable discussion among political theorists about the idea of **deliberative democracy** in which decisions are made based on discussion by free and equal citizens (Elster, 1998). Through involvement in deliberative processes, it is hoped that people will become better informed, more active citizens. Through dialogue, people will come to understand the viewpoints of others and then, ideally, work together constructively to propose policies that are in the common good. Unlike representative and plebiscitary versions of democracy, deliberative democracy brings citizens into decision making through discussion, rather than primarily through voting.

In theory, representative democracy involves thorough discussion and deliberation about political issues by the elected representatives who have the time, knowledge, and experience to devote to this important task. However, the reality is that thorough discussion and deliberation does not often occur in elected bodies such as the Canadian House of Commons. Instead, it is behind the closed doors of Cabinet and among senior government officials and advisors that most laws and policies are developed. Debate in the House of Commons often involves the governing party defending its actions and the opposition parties criticizing the government. The struggle for political advantage among parties is typically more important than an effort to seek the common good through discussion.

To some extent, contemporary governments have been encouraging increased public participation in the decision-making process through various forms of public consultation, such as public hearings. Although this is useful in allowing a variety of viewpoints to be heard, there is a tendency for public hearings to be dominated by spokespersons for particular interests. Further, governments often do not feel obliged to explain and justify why they are not following the advice given to them.

Advocates of deliberative democracy often envision it as operating primarily among citizens at the local level, where face-to-face dialogue is possible and the issues being discussed may have direct relevance for the lives of those involved. Giving people in local communities responsibility for the management of their resources, such as rivers, forests, and coastal fisheries, or establishing community Parliaments (Resnick, 1997) may encourage deliberative decision making.

Citizens' juries are another way to involve ordinary citizens in deliberation and decision making. They have been used in a variety of countries (including the United Kingdom, the United States, Germany, Spain, Australia, India, Bulgaria, and Brazil) in recent years. The citizens' jury brings together a group of randomly selected citizens. Like the juries used to determine the outcome of some court trials, citizens' juries are composed of persons without any special knowledge of the topic under consideration. Trained facilitators are used to guide the deliberation, jurors are provided with information, and witnesses are called to explain and justify different viewpoints. The jurors then make recommendations that are passed on to a governmental body (or, put to all citizens in a referendum as discussed in Box 10-3 Deliberative Democracy in Action) for possible action.

Citizens' juries directly involve only a tiny proportion of the public in deliberation. However, if combined with public hearings or referendums, they may stimulate broader public discussion of particular issues. For such a process to be meaningful, the recommendations of the citizens' jury must have some significance in the policy-making process (Smith & Wales, 2000).

citizens' jury

A group of randomly selected persons that deliberate about and make recommendations concerning particular issues.

The Participatory Budgeting Project
www.participatorybudgeting.org

BOX 10-3 Deliberative Democracy in Action

In 2003, British Columbia's government introduced a Citizens' Assembly to make a recommendation as to whether a new system should be used to elect provincial legislators. Two citizens were randomly selected from each provincial district to form, along with an appointed chair (a former university president), an assembly of 159 members. The random selection procedure was adjusted to ensure that equal numbers of males and females were chosen. Service on the assembly was voluntary, and members received $150 a day. In addition to obtaining expert advice on different electoral systems, the Assembly was required to hold public hearings across the province before making its recommendations. According to the participants, the deliberations were serious and meaningful. The recommendation for a new system of elections (the single-transferable vote) was put to the voters of the province in a binding 2005 referendum. Although 57.7 percent voted in favour of the new system, this was short of the approval by 60 percent of voters and by majorities in 60 percent of the province's electoral districts that was required for the adoption of the new system. In 2009, only 37 percent of those voting in a second referendum supported the

proposal. A similar process used in Ontario resulted in a referendum defeat for a proposal to adopt a mixed-member proportional electoral system.

A study of a citizens' jury in Denmark (termed a *deliberative poll*) found that ordinary citizens were willing to engage in reasoned deliberation about the complex issue of whether Denmark should adopt the common European currency (the euro). Participants not only increased their knowledge of the issue, but also gained a better understanding of different viewpoints as well as becoming more interested in the issue. In the deliberations, participants mainly used arguments involving general principles and appeals to the common good, although self-interested arguments were also used and some participants tended to dominate the discussion. The deliberations in 2000 were televised and extensively reported in the mass media. In the end, however, voters in Denmark rejected the adoption of the euro even though a majority of those involved in the deliberations favoured it (Andersen & Hansen, 2007).

At the municipal level, in Porto Alegre, Brazil (a city of about 1.5 million people), between 15 and

The British Columbia Citizens' Assembly discusses its recommendations for changing the province's electoral system.

25 percent of the city's budget is set aside for municipal projects, with the rest of the money going to pay salaries and other bills. The investment budget, as it is often called, is set after citizens meet to identify needs, discuss options for meeting them, select projects, and set the order in which they will be carried out. The process takes several months and involves large-scale citizen assemblies in each of Porto Alegre's sixteen wards. Since 1989, this system has produced major improvements in the quality of basic services provided to the city's citizens (Gret, 2005). Because of its success in Brazil, more than 1500 cities around the world have adopted their own variants of participatory budgeting (Ganuza & Baiocchi, 2012).

CHALLENGES FOR DEMOCRATIC GOVERNMENT

Democracy and Equality

Democracy is closely associated with the ideal of equality. Almost all countries with democratic governments have established the equal right of all adult citizens to vote. Exclusions based on gender, ethnicity, race, religion, and other characteristics have generally been eliminated.[11] Having an equal right to vote does not ensure that legislative bodies are representative of the characteristics of the citizenry. Some countries have adopted measures to increase the proportion of women in legislatures, such as reserving seats for women and encouraging or requiring political parties to select a certain proportion of female candidates. A few countries do the same for disadvantaged minority groups; for example, New Zealand reserves 7 of its 70 legislative seats for its Indigenous Maori people.

Democracy is also associated with the idea that all residents of a country should have equal legal rights. For example, the Canadian Constitution, 1982 (section 15) states: "Every individual is equal before the and under the law and has the right to the equal protection and equal benefit of the law without discrimination and, in particular, without discrimination based on race, national or ethnic origin, colour, religion, sex, age, or mental or physical disability."

The adoption of democratic procedures and institutions does not necessarily result in greater social or economic equality. Indeed, the power of big business in the United States has led to the claim that it is the "world's most advanced oligarchy" (Johnson, 2009). Nevertheless, democracy has the potential to give some influence to those who would otherwise be powerless. This influence may encourage elected politicians to develop policies that benefit all members of society.

However, there is often some tension between the liberal and democratic aspects of liberal democracy. From the perspective of classical liberalism

---

[11]Some countries, including the United Kingdom and the United States, deprive most prisoners of the right to vote (including, in a few US states, those who have ever been jailed for a felony even after their release).

governments should have a limited role in society and the economy. Pursuing substantially greater social and economic equality can limit individual and business freedoms. On the other hand, substantial social and economic inequality can limit the capability of many people to influence the decisions of government. Thus while social democrats share with liberal democrats a belief in equal political and legal rights, social democrats also believe that governments should pursue greater social and economic equality.

Democracy and the Nation-State

Democracy is often thought to work best in a political community where there is a common identity, common culture, and common values and ideals. When one has a sense of partnership with other citizens, it is easier to consider the common good of the community. It is not surprising, therefore, that modern democracy often developed alongside the development of the nation-state.

In countries that are divided by language, it may be difficult for a common dialogue about political issues to develop among those speaking different languages. In countries with sharp cultural, regional, class, religious, or other divisions, there may be insufficient trust and respect to sustain a dialogue about the good of the community as a whole. Nevertheless, viable democracies have been built in countries such as Canada, Belgium, and Switzerland despite the challenges posed by linguistic, cultural, and regional divisions. Indeed, some argue that diversity helps to create a more vibrant democracy because a variety of different perspectives can be brought into political discussion.

One way that democracy can be sustained in countries with sharp divisions is by avoiding a strict application of the principle of majority rule. By trying to ensure that there is a broad consensus among different groups about major issues and that different groups are represented in government, minority groups are less likely to feel dominated by the majority. Indeed, politics in some Western European democracies lean in the direction of finding a consensus rather than majority rule (Lijphart, 2012). Another way to try to accommodate different cultural groups that are geographically concentrated is to adopt a **federal system** of government, in which some important decisions are made at the provincial level, such as in Canada. In this way, different groups can have a degree of democratic self-government.

federal system

A system of governing in which sovereign authority is divided or shared between the central government and regional governments, with each deriving its authority from the constitution.

✓• SUMMARY AND CONCLUSION

Democracy is based on the idea that all adult citizens should have an equal and effective voice in the decisions of their political community. By involving the population as a whole, better policies may result because more views (including the views of those who would otherwise be powerless) can be taken into account. By guaranteeing political rights and freedoms, liberal democracy ensures that individuals can express their views, organize to influence the laws and policies of government, and have a free and informed choice in elections.

Holding elections is not sufficient to ensure that democratic governments pursue the common good. Without limits on election spending and effective regulation of lobbying activity, the wealthy and powerful may be able to exert undue influence on democratic governments. A high level of government accountability and transparency along with an independent and active media are needed to help voters make intelligent choices. As well, to pursue the common good, government needs to make use of various sources of independent expertise (including a non-partisan public service) in the development and implementation of its policies.

A government that only acts on the views and interests of those who vote for it may not act for the common good. Indeed, some electoral systems usually result in the governing party controlling the legislature based on less than a majority of votes. While governments based on a coalition of parties (typical in countries with a proportional representation electoral system) tend to be more inclusive of different interests and perspectives, they may have to accept some of the demands of parties in the coalition that represent special interests or minority views to stay in office.

Overall, democratic governments may be far from perfect, but they are generally much better than non-democratic governments. Government decisions can benefit from the ability of persons and groups to freely discuss and promote a wide variety of viewpoints. Governments that have been chosen by a free election are more likely to be accepted as legitimate by their populations. Because the people have a role in the political process, they are more likely to accept what government does, even if they disagree with particular decisions. Democracies also have the positive feature of allowing for a peaceful transition of power; citizens can remove a government with which they are dissatisfied without having to resort to violence. Democracy may also encourage people to be more civic minded. Through involvement in politics, people may feel a greater attachment to the political community and be more likely to assume a sense of responsibility to their fellow citizens.

✓• KEY TERMS

DISCUSSION QUESTIONS

1. Is democratic government the best form of government?

2. Should extremist political parties be prevented from contesting elections?

3. Should each electoral district elect one male and one female candidate to create gender equality in Canada's House of Commons and provincial legislatures?

4. Should greater participation of the people be encouraged in democratic countries such as Canada? If so, how should this be achieved?

5. Does liberal democracy provide an appropriate combination of freedom and equality?

FURTHER READING

Achen, C.H., & Bartels, L.M. (2016). *Democracy for realists. Why elections do not produce responsive government*. Princeton, NJ: Princeton University Press.

Cross, W. (Ed.). (2010). *Auditing Canadian democracy*. Vancouver: UBC Press.

Dahl, R.A. & Shapiro, I. (2015). *On democracy* (2nd ed.). New Haven, CT: Yale University Press.

Dryzek, J.S. & Dunleavy, P. (2009). *Theories of the democratic state*. Houndmills, UK: Palgrave Macmillan.

Fournier, P., Van Der Kok, H., Carty, R.K., Blais, A., & Rose, J. (2011). *When citizens decide: Lessons from citizen assemblies on electoral reform*. Oxford: Oxford University Press.

Held, D. (2006). *Models of democracy* (3rd ed.). Cambridge, UK: Polity Press.

Lenard, P.T. & Simeon, R. (2012). *Imperfect democracies: The democratic deficit in Canada and the United States*. Vancouver: UBC Press.

Lijphart, A. (2012). *Patterns of democracy: Government forms and performance in thirty-six countries* (2nd ed.). New Haven, CT: Yale University Press.

Norris, P. (2011). *Democratic deficit: Critical citizens revisited*. Cambridge: Cambridge University Press.

Przeworski, A. (2010). *Democracy and the limits of self-government*. Cambridge, UK: Cambridge University Press.

11 Non-Democratic Government: Hybrid and Authoritarian Regimes

Although Hungary is no longer a communist dictatorship, its prime minister, Viktor Orbán, wants to move his country away from liberal democracy.   Cylonphoto/Alamy Stock Photo

After reading this chapter, you should be able to:

1. distinguish among the various forms of non-democratic governments
2. understand why and how non-democratic governments use such democratic institutions as elections
3. explain what a political regime is
4. describe what distinguishes democratic from non-democratic regimes

Besides democracies and authoritarian systems, political science also studies hybrid regimes: political systems that have both democratic and authoritarian features. Some these hold elections but go no further toward democratic government. Others do not hold free elections, but respect some political rights and liberties. Hybrid regimes are neither new nor temporary phenomena: one governed Mexico from 1929 to 2000 and they were common in Europe and Latin America in the nineteenth century. Some of today's hybrids, however, were emerging democracies before a freely elected leader changed their direction.

One case is Hungary. From 1989, the end of Hungary's Communist era, to 2010 the country was unquestionably democratic. Elections in 2010, though, brought the Fidesz party and its leader Viktor Orbán to power. Both leader and party appeared democratic, but Orbán used his parliamentary majority to amend the constitution and leave Fidesz appointees in control of the courts and the electoral authority. Fidesz (with its loyal subsidiary, the KDNP) won the 2014 election retaining just over two-thirds of the seats based on 44.9 percent of the vote. This gave Orbán the power to make further constitutional changes.

Orbán has described himself as a builder of "illiberal democracy," meaning the holding of elections, but with limited freedom. Although Fidesz could still lose elections, the reforms Orbán made will be hard to change and will leave Fidesz with great power, even out of office.

A second case is Poland, where Jarosław Kaczyński has orchestrated a turn from democracy. Unlike Orbán, Kaczyński, a former prime minister, now holds no elected office but does head the governing Peace and Justice Party. This government has forbidden Poland's constitutional court from reviewing the constitutionality of legislation unless it has parliamentary approval. It also now also appoints the managers of TV stations, endangering media freedom.

Nicaragua is a third example. It differs from the other two because the fairness of its elections is questioned. Daniel Ortega, Nicaragua's president from 1984 to 1990, and again since 2007, controls the courts and the elections office, and both the military and the national police report directly to him. His party, the Sandinista National Liberation Front, dominates the legislature and controls the bulk of the country's municipalities. But independent media still exist and opposition parties, though weak, have room to operate.

What all three cases share is determined leaders who halted democratic progress, opting instead to retreat from democracy.

NON-DEMOCRATIC GOVERNMENT IN THE WORLD TODAY

For most Canadians, like the citizens of other democracies, democracy is the best option for any political system. We assume that democracy means free and fair elections, accountable and transparent government, and guaranteed protection of personal freedoms. However, the historical record reveals that, for most of human history, democracy either did not exist or was deemed undesirable. Even today, more than half the world's population lives in regimes that do not meet Canadians' definition of what a democratic **regime** is and does.

Freedom House, an American organization dedicated to the promotion of liberal democracy, charts the state of personal freedom around the globe. Its measure of political rights and civil liberties is derived, to some extent, from the Universal Declaration of Human Rights, which was adopted by the United Nations in 1948.[1] Its classification of countries as free, partly free, and not free is based on an assessment of the extent to which the political and civil rights necessary for a country to be considered a liberal democracy are protected in each country. Table 11-1 shows that regimes classed as not free have declined dramatically since 1972, but the proportion of countries rated free has declined slightly since the early 2000s.

Currently, only 86 of 195 countries are fully free and unquestionably democratic; 51 have no claim to be democratic; 58 show a mix of democratic and non-democratic elements. Political scientists generally recognize that it is impossible to clearly demarcate the frontier between democracies and non-democracies. Therefore, it is better to array countries along a continuum running from the most to the least democratic. In the 1960s, the list of regimes went from democratic to authoritarian to totalitarian. In 2016, the concept is the same, but we now speak of democracies, hybrids, and authoritarians (see Box 11-1 Classifying Regimes).

regime

The broadest class of political system, it encompasses the bases of the system's legitimacy; how and to whom government is accountable; who has access to and influence with government; how government, civil society, and private citizens interact; and what its governmental institutions are. Examples include democracy, dictatorship, and monarchy.

Freedom House
www.freedomhouse.org

Economist Intelligence Unit (EIU) Democracy Index
www.eiu.com/democracy2015

Bertelsmann Transformation Index
www.bertelsmann-stiftung.de/en

Universal Declaration of Human Rights
www.un.org/en/documents/udhr/

Polity IV Project
www.systemicpeace.org

YEAR	FREE	PARTLY FREE	NOT FREE
2015**	44%	30%	26%
2002	46%	29%	25%
1992	40%	30%	30%
1982	33%	28%	39%
1972*	29%	25%	46%

*First year; **Latest year available

Source: Compiled by the authors from Freedom House (2016).

TABLE 11-1

Free, Partly Free, and Not Free Countries, 1972–2012

---

[1]The principal drafter of the document was John Humphrey, a Canadian international lawyer who taught at McGill University.

BOX 11-1 **Classifying Regimes**

There are four publications that classify the world's political regimes: The *Bertelsmann Transformation Index* (2016); Economist Intelligence Unit, *Democracy Index* (2016); Freedom House, *Freedom in the World* (2016); and Polity IV, *Global Report* (2014).

Each uses a slightly different set of indicators, which is interpreted by different sets of experts to produce a score for each country, which is the basis for the rankings. Further, each publication uses different terminology. However, the rankings are very similar across all four, although different cut-off points put some countries in different classes in each study. Thus, anyone consulting these sources needs to exercise care in interpreting their findings, especially in comparing the four indices.

The Bertelsmann Transformation Index, published in Germany, uses eighteen variables to rank 129 countries and has five classes of regime: two clearly democratic, two mixed systems, and one plainly autocratic. The Economist Intelligence Unit's Democracy Index is the newest of the four; dating from 2007, it employs 60 variables and classifies 165 nations as either democracies, flawed democracies, hybrids, or authoritarians. Freedom House gives special weight to political rights and civil liberties, and states are ranked as free, partly free, or unfree, depending on the scores they receive on its seven-point checklist. Results are available since 1972. Polity IV includes 167 countries, uses 36 variables, and has three categories, democratic, anocratic (mixed democratic and autocratic), and autocratic, producing a "governance scale" based on political institutions and processes. Each has its strengths, but the Freedom House rankings are the most widely used.

NON-DEMOCRATIC VS. DEMOCRATIC REGIMES

authoritarian regimes

Non-democratic governing systems that feature absolute rule over the population. People are prevented from choosing their government and influencing its decisions.

hybrid regimes

Governing systems that are a mixture of democratic and non-democratic rule. Hybrid governments typically gain and keep power through electoral fraud, corruption, and legal manoeuvres.

Since there are so many **authoritarian regimes** and **hybrid regimes** in the world, we need to understand how they work. The best way is through a two-step process, where the starting point is a comparison of the two regimes. We can then move on to examine the forms and operational styles of the wide variety of non-democratic political systems.

To Adam Przeworski (1991, p. 10) "(d)emocracy is a system in which parties lose elections . . . (a)nd there are periodic winners and losers." In democracies, nobody wins all the time. Even parties with a long string of victories, like the Alberta Progressive Conservatives (12 straight wins, from 1971 to 2012, but defeated by the NDP in 2015), never know when voters will choose a new governing party. All this really says is that democracies hold elections freely and fairly enough that an incumbent can lose power and that citizens can change their governors without violence. However, holding free and fair elections presupposes that there is universal suffrage and freedom of association, expression, and information; that is, all adults can vote, have access to information, and meet with others and discuss public affairs, if they so wish. It also means that votes are counted and reported accurately and that the electoral process is not systematically biased against any participant.

Such is not the case in non-democratic regimes. Indeed, what most obviously makes a system non-democratic is that the bulk of its people have no practical say in who governs them, which makes government by the people impossible. The principal difference between democracies and non-democracies is that only in the former can citizens change their government though a vote in a regularly scheduled election. However, there are five other important distinctions: accountability, participation, pluralism, rule of law, and transparency. Democracies should display all of these features; nevertheless, not even democracies always meet all these criteria fully.

Accountability

In democratic regimes, governments are expected to account for their actions to citizens, the media, the courts, auditors or controllers, and legislatures. This accountability runs vertically, from the government up to the electors who gave it power in the first place, and horizontally, from the government laterally to other parts of the state. Although many non-democratic governments also have those to whom they are accountable, this seldom includes ordinary citizens. Thus, hybrid and authoritarian systems often cannot reliably be controlled by their citizens, and governments can act as if they have no responsibility to their citizens.

Participation

Citizens of democracies have many opportunities to participate in politics. These start with voting and include participation in political parties and movements, and contacting elected officials and the media with questions or comments about public affairs. Although hybrid regimes routinely hold elections and many authoritarian states do as well, these are often votes the government cannot lose. Further, while non-democratic regimes encourage their citizens to join public service organizations, those organizations seldom operate independently of government. Civil society organizations (CSOs), which are groups formed by private individuals or organizations to pursue some public purpose, are also suspect. The conclusion is that non-democratic political systems offer citizens far fewer meaningful opportunities to take part in governing their countries than democracies do.

Pluralism

Pluralism exists where there are large numbers of organizations that actively pursue political objectives free from government control. This ensures that citizens have many choices and a potential ability to influence government decisions should they decide to become active in public affairs. Pluralism, thus, is a necessary feature of democratic government. In non-democratic systems, however, the state works to limit pluralism. Only organizations aligned with the regime, if not controlled by it, are allowed to operate. As a result, the CSOs that are so important in democratic countries—everything from kids' soccer leagues to groups seeking to legalize marijuana—are usually unwelcome in authoritarian or hybrid regimes because they are independent of government. Non-democratic governments are especially opposed to CSOs with foreign links, as is often the case with groups promoting development, and paint them as foreign agents bent on subverting the established order.

Rule of Law

Having a government of laws is one of the principles of the rule of law. It demands that the government must be bound by the same laws as its citizens. But the rule of law goes further to insist that the law be applied impartially to all and plays no favourites. Thus, government interference in the justice system cannot be tolerated. In non-democratic regimes, however, governments are far more able to influence the course of justice, even to dictate the outcome they want. This is politicized justice, not the impartial justice that the rule of law prescribes.

Transparency

A government is transparent to the extent that citizens have easy access to information about not just government decisions but also about how those decisions were made. Transparency ensures that citizens' right to know how their government operates can be exercised effectively. Logically, then, government secrecy should be minimized in a democracy. In non-democratic systems, though, governments limit access to information to an extreme degree. The media are often censored, failed policies are never mentioned, and even basic economic data are reported in distorted form. "What the people don't know won't hurt the government" is the guiding principle.

Although some non-democratic regimes deviate further from democratic standards than others, none attain the democratic threshold. Thus, both hybrid and authoritarian systems are different in kind from democracies, not just in degree. When we examine non-democratic regimes, therefore, we are dealing with political systems whose mode of governing is both unfamiliar and unacceptable to most Canadians.

Although non-democratic political systems differ from democratic ones in significant ways, this does not mean that non-democratic states never look after their citizens; many of the wealthier ones do this job reasonably well. However, because non-democratic governments do not give their citizens a political voice, any benefits the people receive come only because the government decides to award those benefits. Despite these similarities, such regimes take many different shapes and govern in a variety of ways.

AUTHORITARIAN REGIMES

Types of Authoritarian Regimes

The term *authoritarian political system* was coined by Juan Linz (1994) to refer to those non-democratic governments that, unlike totalitarian states, did not attempt to control all facets of life in a country. Today, however, we use the term *hybrid* to refer to a government that gains and keeps power through electoral fraud, corruption, and legal manoeuvres designed to hobble the opposition, reserving *authoritarian* for states that systematically feature absolute rule over the population. Thus, yesterday's totalitarians are grouped with today's authoritarians and are one of the examples of authoritarian rule we shall examine, along with personal dictatorships, party dictatorships, military dictatorships, and theocratic dictatorships. Table 11-2 gives a selection of states with authoritarian regimes. Some, such as Saudi Arabia, are wealthy; Syria and Iran are middle-income states; Laos and the Democratic Republic of Congo are quite poor. Wealth is no protection against authoritarianism.

Authoritarian Regimes: Research
http://dictators.la.psu.edu

TOTALITARIAN SYSTEMS   All dictatorships, indeed all authoritarian regimes, share a common trait: a high level of concentration of political power. Ordinary citizens have no right to select their governors in a free election, let alone influencing the laws that govern them. The distinguishing characteristic of a **totalitarian dictatorship** is that it seeks to control all aspects of life within a country (see Box 11-2 Does Totalitarianism Still Exist?). Benito Mussolini, the founder of Italian fascism, neatly summed up the nature of totalitarianism with this slogan: "All within the state, nothing outside the state, nothing against the state!"

Complete domination was probably always a tyrant's dream, but before the twentieth century it was unrealizable. During the last hundred years, however, advances in transportation and communications have made it possible to approximate total control. Carl Friederich and Zbigniew Brzezinski (1956)

totalitarian dictatorship

A regime that seeks to control all aspects of life within a country.

AUTHORITARIAN	HYBRID
Angola	Armenia
Belarus	Bangladesh
Cuba	Honduras
Democratic Republic of Congo	Mozambique
Iran	Nepal
Kazakhstan	Nicaragua
Laos	Sierra Leone
People's Democratic Republic of Korea (North Korea)	Singapore
Saudi Arabia	Tanzania
Syria	Turkey

Source: Compiled by authors from BTI (2016); EIU (2016); FH (2016); Polity IV (2014)

TABLE 11-2
Contemporary Authoritarian and Hybrid Regimes: Some Examples

BOX 11-2 Does Totalitarianism Still Exist?

In 1979, Jeane Kirkpatrick, an American political scientist who served as her country's ambassador to the United Nations, argued that ordinary authoritarian and totalitarian dictatorships were intrinsically different (Kirkpatrick, 1979). She believed that ordinary authoritarian governments, which she labelled traditional *autocracies*, were less entrenched, made fewer changes, and could be reformed from within. In contrast, totalitarian regimes (which Kirkpatrick called *revolutionary autocracies*) turned their countries upside down but could never be changed from within.

Was Kirkpatrick right? As is so often the case in political science, she was partly right and partly wrong.

The collapse of Eastern European communism a decade after Kirkpatrick's article, followed two years later by the disappearance of the Soviet Union, showed that totalitarianism was not impervious to internal pressures. In fact, attempts to reform communism by Soviet leader Mikhail Gorbachev set the process of change in the Soviet Union in motion.

However, some old-style totalitarian states still exist among the handful of communist systems that remain. Of these, North Korea comes closest to the totalitarian mould, followed (now at greater distance) by Cuba, while Vietnam and China have moved further away from the old model, especially its economic aspects.

identified six traits that characterized the totalitarian dictatorships of the first part of the twentieth century. All had the following characteristics:

1. an official ideology
2. a single mass party usually led by the dictator, and made up of no more than 10 percent of the population
3. a police state that used terror to control the population
4. a nearly complete monopoly by the party over all means of mass communication
5. a similarly complete monopoly by the party over all means of armed combat
6. an economy planned and controlled by the party

Most Important Practitioners The most important practitioners of totalitarian rule were the various fascist and communist movements that reached their highest point between 1920 and 1970. Although they were different in many ways, both communism and fascism sought to unite all people of a country in a common project commanded by an individual leader and a single political party.

Leading the totalitarian states were very powerful, unchecked rulers, dictators such as Benito Mussolini in Italy, Adolf Hitler in Germany, Joseph Stalin in the former Soviet Union, and Mao Zedong in the People's Republic of China. All were able to mobilize their populations and harness them to the needs of the state. As well, they ruled by force and violence. Leading great projects that were supposed to transform society or even remake human nature, totalitarian rulers brooked no interference and wasted no time negotiating with those who opposed them. In this respect, they acted as dictators have always acted. It was their ability to monitor and control the lives of their citizens that made the totalitarians distinctive. Yet all of the totalitarian rulers failed. World War II put an end to Mussolini and Hitler, and while communism in the Soviet Union and China lived on after Stalin and Mao, later rulers generally reduced repression and relaxed, to a limited degree, their control over their people.

Cuba, which Fidel Castro ruled from 1959 until 2006 when illness caused him to cede power to his brother Raúl, is the totalitarian country Canadians know best, because so many of us vacation there. Although the Castros have looked after Cubans by providing free education and health care and ensuring that no one starves, political opponents are repressed, and the Communist Party of Cuba can never be voted from office. In these latter respects, Cuba conforms perfectly to Friederich and Brzezinski's definition. Reforms undertaken since 2006 have increased the freedom of individual Cubans by legalizing the sale of homes and cars, encouraging the development of small family businesses and cooperatives, and no longer requiring an exit permit to travel abroad. In 2015, Cuba and the US restored diplomatic relations. However, censorship is still the rule, human rights continue to be violated, and political repression shows no signs of abating.

Pathological Tyrants   Perhaps the most shockingly bloodthirsty totalitarian ruler of our age was Pol Pot, who terrorized Cambodia from 1975 to 1979 (Kiernan, 2008). He and his Khmer Rouge turned the Southeast Asian country into a killing field, murdering 1.5 million of its roughly 8 million inhabitants.

Pathological tyrants are neither new nor especially uncommon. Nineteenth-century Paraguay produced José Gaspar Rodríguez de Francia, who styled himself as *El Supremo* and shut his country off from the rest of the world for almost thirty years (White, 1978). In the 1970s, the tiny African country of Equatorial Guinea (see Box 11-3 From Pathological Tyrant to Ordinary Personal Dictator: The Sad Case of Equatorial Guinea) had the misfortune to fall under the control of Francisco Macias Nguema, who brutalized and impoverished his nation while persecuting educated individuals (Decalo, 1988).

Emergence from a Vacuum   We should note here that totalitarian states, whether ruled by madmen or shrewd dictators, often grow out of periods of turmoil and societal chaos. It is as if the vacuum caused by breakdown opens the way to those who would exercise total control over their people. This suggests that societies that are able to function effectively are poor targets for totalitarian rulers.

PERSONAL RULERS: AUTOCRATS   Today we encounter two kinds of personal rulers: absolute monarchs and individual dictatorships. These are sometimes called autocrats, because the right to rule is vested totally in one person. This does not mean that there is only one person running the country

BOX 11-3 From Pathological Tyrant to Ordinary Personal Dictator: The Sad Case of Equatorial Guinea

Equatorial Guinea is a very small country in West Africa that was once Spain's only sub-Saharan African colony. When it became independent in 1968, Francisco Macias Nguema became Equatorial Guinea's first president. Two years later, he installed a one-party state and after another two years made himself president for life—pretty routine stuff for a dictator. However, Macias then emerged as a murderous tyrant. Estimates of those killed over a five-year period, 1974–1979, range from a quarter to a third of the population, thus up to 100 000 people. A coup, led by Macias's nephew, Teodoro Obiang Nguema, overthrew the dictator in 1979.

Obiang did not bring Equatorial Guinea democracy. Although his dictatorship is more conventional, it is still brutal and very corrupt, but it is not pathological. In the mid-1990s, oil was discovered in the country, making it the richest state in sub-Saharan Africa. Yet the vast majority of Equatoguineans, now numbering over 800 000, see little of this new wealth, as President Obiang and his family take the lion's share of the benefits. Equatorial Guinea's history shows that not only can dictators emerge from an unsettled political context; they can also leave chaos behind that invites new dictators to replace them.

institutional dictatorship

An undemocratic government controlled by an established political institution. The most common examples are military dictatorships, party dictatorships, and theocratic dictatorships.

absolute monarchy

A political system in which a king or queen has total power, unconstrained by law.

totally alone, but rather that one person has the authority and ability to rule as he or she wishes, unconstrained by law and unaccountable to the public. These systems differ from party, military, and theocratic dictatorships in that the latter three are **institutional dictatorships** in which an institution (party, military, or religious organization) exercises power, and not an individual.

ABSOLUTE MONARCHIES Historically, most countries have been ruled by monarchs. Some contemporary monarchies (such as the British, Dutch, and Spanish) are constitutional, meaning that the monarch is subject to the law like everyone else and has very limited powers. Constitutional monarchs are the symbolic leaders of their countries and do not have an active role in governing. However, some monarchies, such as Saudi Arabia's, are labelled **absolute monarchies** because the monarch has unlimited power. This was the type of system that the French Revolution toppled in 1789. In fact, much of today's thinking about democratic government was first conceived to serve as an antidote to absolutism.

In absolute monarchies, political activity is constrained. Political parties are often prohibited, and there are seldom elections since government positions are filled by royal appointment. If there is a representative assembly, it is more likely to be a council of nobles than an elected body that speaks for the people. There is usually strict censorship, and the liberties of those outside the ruling circle are radically circumscribed.

Given those characteristics, it is no surprise to learn that in the twentieth century, absolute monarchies were often victims of revolution. This fate befell the Russian empire in 1917, the Ethiopian empire in 1974, and the Iranian empire in 1979. However, in none of these cases was the ensuing regime democratic. Rather, absolutism gave way to other forms of dictatorship. It may be that making political activity illegal forces those who want change into clandestine revolutionary movements. If successful, they may use their tightly disciplined organizations to control the state.

PERSONAL DICTATORSHIPS   Just as there are fewer absolute monarchies now than before, so too are **personal dictatorships** harder to find today than they would have been up until 1990. These regimes have a single leader who rules far more according to personal preferences than by following the law. There are two great dangers in this form of government. One is that, as in all dictatorships, there are no institutional constraints on the leader, who leaves power only when he dies or is deposed. This is what happened to Saddam Hussein in Iraq and Muammar Gaddafi in Libya. The disorder that reigned in both Iraq and Libya after their dictators fell is the second hazard: since the man is the regime, his removal often leads to violent conflict among those who have different ideas about a new regime. Nevertheless, Frantz and Ezrow (2011) report that personalist leaders stay in power an average of ten years, longer than their colleagues who head dictatorships built around political parties or the military. The authors argue that this is because in personal dictatorships the elite is loyal only to the dictator, whereas in party or military regimes the elite owes its first loyalty to the institution.

King Salman became king of Saudi Arabia in 2015 after his half-brother King Abdullah died. Western democracies including Canada and the U.S. have continued to support the Saudi monarchs despite their highly repressive rule.

Dpa picture alliance/Alamy Stock Photo

PARTY DICTATORSHIPS   **Party dictatorships** differ from other authoritarian regimes in that political life is controlled by a single party rather than by a lone individual or some other group. The People's Republic of China (PRC) offers the clearest example of a party dictatorship today, as the Communist Party of China (CPC) is the dominant force in that nation's political life, far outweighing any individual leader. In party dictatorships, either only one party has the legal right to exist or, if others do exist, only one party is legally able to exercise power. Sometimes an individual ruler will also command the party in a party dictatorship. This occurred in the Soviet Union under Joseph Stalin, who dominated the Soviet Communist Party between 1927 and his death in 1953, and in the PRC under Mao Zedong who controlled the CPC from 1949 until he died in 1976. As well, dictators can organize their own parties and, once they assume power, outlaw other parties. Benito Mussolini did this with his Fascist party in Italy, and Adolf Hitler did the same with the Nazis in Germany.

One-party states were also very common in Africa from independence, usually in the 1960s, to the early 1990s. Rulers of these African states generally justified their turn to one-party rule in terms of unifying the nation.

personal dictatorship

An undemocratic government dominated by a single individual. Saddam Hussein's Iraq or Muammar Gaddafi's Libya were classic examples of this kind of system.

party dictatorship

An undemocratic political system that is controlled by one party. The most familiar examples are found in communist political systems.

They argued that the best way to build a strong nation out of the many tribes that often coexisted uncomfortably within their countries was to channel all political action through one party. Although this is a logical premise, in practice, eliminating other parties led to dictatorship. Throughout history, most dictatorships of this sort have met violent ends, but since the 1970s more of them are negotiating the conditions of their demise with other political forces. Currently, though, leaders of party dictatorships can look forward to remaining in office for only about five years, although some have lasted much longer (Frantz & Ezrow, 2011).

Somewhat similar to party dictatorships is the form of government we will see in our discussion of hybrid regimes: the **hegemonic party regime**. These governments allow other parties to exist and do not legally exclude them from winning power. However, by manipulating electoral rules and controlling the electoral process from voter registration to counting the votes and announcing the results, the government is sure that it will not lose. Although such systems are non-democratic, they still give citizens more choice than do rigorously one-party states.

MILITARY DICTATORSHIPS In **military dictatorships**, the military provides the country's rulers (Fitch, 1998; Janowitz, 1977). These systems are established in the wake of a military seizure of power, a *coup d'état*. Sometimes military dictatorships are run by committees of a country's armed forces, known as military *juntas*. Most military regimes start with a junta but many are quickly dominated by a single leader. When this happens, the resulting government takes on some of the traits of a personal dictatorship, distinguishing itself mostly by giving the military special benefits. Unlike other dictatorships, however, military governments often leave power of their own volition. It is quite common for the military to oust a civilian government, rule for a few years, and then arrange elections for a new civilian government. Although the military frequently imposes restrictions on who may compete for power, the transition is usually peaceful. However, military rulers often fall to other military leaders. In fact, the rulers of military regimes only remain in office for an average of three years (Frantz & Ezrow, 2011), unless they are able to refashion themselves as personal leaders.

In 2009, a new twist on the role of the military in politics arose in Honduras, where the military overthrew the sitting president but did not assume power. Rather, it handed the government over to a senior politician from a party opposed to the president's. Some argued that this was not a *coup d'état*, since the military did not take power; thus, the action was legal particularly because the military was acting on a warrant issued by the Supreme Court. Others believed that the fact that an armed overthrow of a properly elected president did not produce a military dictatorship did nothing to make the overthrow legal and proper. If nothing else, the episode showed that the military can still play a critical role in shaping its country's politics.

---

hegemonic party regime

A political system in which opposition parties exist and compete for power but cannot win because government control over the electoral system assures that the ruling party does not lose.

---

military dictatorship

An undemocratic government run by the military.

"The people of this country are going to catch on to this thing called democracy . . . and if they don't we'll make them!"
Tami Thirlwell

BLENDED DICTATORSHIPS Dictatorships frequently exhibit more than one form of rule. For example, from 1959 to 2006, the system that prevailed in Cuba combined Fidel Castro's personal rule with that of the Communist Party. In fact, the blend of personal and party dictatorship was common in Communist-led regimes. Among the best known examples are Joseph Stalin in the Soviet Union (1927–1953), Tito (Josip Broz) in Yugoslavia (1943–1980), Mao Zedong in the People's Republic of China (1949–1976), and Enver Hoxa in Albania (1944–1985).

Military dictatorships sometimes show this same tendency. For example, General Augusto Pinochet eventually dominated the military government that ruled Chile from 1973 to 1989, just as General Ibrahim Babangida was master of Nigeria's military government from 1985 to 1993, when General Sani Abacha replaced him, ruling until 1998. Sometimes, however, there emerges from a military junta a figure who becomes a personal dictator. This describes General Alfredo Stroessner, who governed Paraguay from 1954 to 1989, and Jean-Bédel Bokassa, ruler of the Central African Republic from 1966 to 1977 before changing the country's name to the Central African Empire and declaring himself emperor in 1977; he was deposed in 1979.

THEOCRATIC DICTATORSHIPS A **theocratic dictatorship** is run by religious elites (theocracy is government in the name of God or by priests).

theocratic dictatorship

An undemocratic state run by religious elites.

Iran is the best current example of a theocratic state (see Box 11-4 Theocracy in Iran). Until overthrown in 2001 by US-led forces that included Canada, the Taliban government in Afghanistan was the most extreme theocratic dictatorship of modern times. Basing its governing philosophy on a radical reading of the Qur'an, the Taliban government was infamous for eliminating virtually all rights for women. Both the Iranian and Taliban regimes emerged when a preceding secular authoritarian state was overthrown. Beginning in 2015, ISIS, the Islamic State in Syria and Iraq, joined this list, although at the time of writing it was unclear how long ISIS would control the territory it captured.

In an authoritarian state, it is common and usually legal for elites to disregard the public's wishes. Such systems often use force with impunity when challenged by their citizens. The fact that in cases like Iran the authorities believe they are acting morally—indeed, in accordance with God's will—may serve only to strengthen their resolve and make movement toward more rights for more people even harder.

Although Islam is the faith underlying almost all of today's theocracies, other religions have been the basis for theocratic rule. North America produced one in the seventeenth-century Massachusetts Bay Colony, which was founded and run by the Puritans, a Protestant group that had come to the new world to pursue their view of a divinely ordained society. As is the case with any religious dictator, the Puritans declared that no one had the right to sin and were zealous in their pursuit of those who violated the colony's rigid moral codes (Parrington, 1987). Immigration and the establishment of religious tolerance in neighbouring colonies ended the Puritans' experiment. Thus, dictatorships based on religion can become more democratic political systems.

Iran's Supreme Leader Ayatollah Ali Khamenei greets a crowd on June 4, 2011. Although voters elect a president, political power in Iran's theocracy rests ultimately with this religious leader.

ZUMA Press, Inc./Alamy

BOX 11-4   Theocracy in Iran

Iran's seventy million people have had very little experience with democracy. Only briefly under the Mossadegh government* was there respite from authoritarianism.

Although the 1979 Iranian Revolution promised greater freedom after overthrowing the increasingly repressive and autocratic monarchy of the Shah, it soon instituted a theocratic system, an Islamic Republic, headed by the religious leader Ayatollah Ruhollah Khomeini. Best known in the West for its uncompromising application of law based on religious doctrine, Iran's political system has also relied on the country's armed forces, the Revolutionary Guards, and a volunteer paramilitary force, the Basij (Persian for "mobilization"), to ensure compliance.

By 1997, however, there were signs of change. Iranians elected Muhammad Khatami, a moderate cleric committed to reform, president of Iran. The reformers were fought at every turn by conservatives who supported a theocratic dictatorship, but nevertheless made significant gains. The Majlis (legislative) elections of 2000 produced a pro-reform majority, and Khatami himself was re-elected in 2001 with a huge majority. However, Khatami and his allies in the Majlis were not Iran's ultimate authority. That rested in the hands of a religious leader, Ayatollah Ali Khamenei, Iran's "Supreme Leader." The Supreme Leader is chosen by an elected Council of Experts, all of whom are clerics. Among his other roles, the Supreme Leader is commander-in-chief of the armed forces and the police, head of the state television and radio company, and the country's top jurist.

In 2003, university students led Iranians into the streets in a call for freedom and democracy. Their demonstrations were broken up not just by the police, but also by vigilantes who used clubs and chains. Then, before legislative elections in 2003, the Guardian Council (a twelve-member chamber, half of whom are appointed by the Supreme Leader and half by the Majlis, with absolute veto powers) struck four thousand reformist candidates from the lists. The remaining reformers boycotted the vote. The conservative candidates, approved by the Guardian Council, won in a landslide. In the 2005 presidential elections, hardliners won again, as Mahmoud Ahmadinejad took power after a convincing win in a runoff election.

Running for re-election in 2009 against Mir-Hossein Mousavi, President Ahmadinejad faced what many predicted would be a close race. When the results were in, though, they showed a twenty-nine-point landslide victory for the sitting president. With university students assuming an active role, Iranians then took to the streets. Through more than a week of protests, Iranians denounced what they saw as electoral fraud. The government responded with force, causing at least 36 deaths. In the end, President Ahmadinejad was declared re-elected (BBC, 2010).

Hassan Rouhani, usually described as a "moderate cleric," was elected president in 2013. Moderates and reformers who supported Rouhani won about 42 percent of the legislative seats in 2016 and with the support of a number of independents generally have a legislative majority. The "hardliners" opposed to reforms won only about 30 percent of the seats. Moderate clerics won about 59 percent of the seats on the Council of Experts. The success of the moderates and reformers was remarkable given that nearly half of those seeking to be legislative candidates and four-fifths of those seeking to be elected to the Council of Experts (including all women) were not allowed to run by the Guardian Council.

Although there is a substantial desire for change, Iran is still more of a theocracy than a democracy.

---

*The Mossadegh government was overthrown in 1953 by a coup engineered by the British government and the US Central Intelligence Agency after the British Anglo-American Oil Company was nationalized by the Iranian government.

How Authoritarians Govern

Obviously, it is harder to study the politics of authoritarian states than democratic ones. We have already observed that authoritarian systems operate less transparently, impose strict limits on what the media can report, and are generally unwilling to reveal much about their operations. Nevertheless, political scientists have increasingly begun analyzing just how non-democratic governments govern. As a result, it is now possible to get a better grasp on the politics of authoritarian regimes.

Given the variety of non-democratic regimes, it follows that no two will govern in exactly the same way. For example, some will have normal democratic governmental institutions—elections, legislatures, and parties—but they will be only for show. Others, however, will actually use them to govern, but not as they are used in democracies. And a few will not use them at all. Similarly, some authoritarian regimes rely heavily on coercion to maintain order, but others count more on co-optation, gaining people's compliance by offering them material benefits —which of course democracies do, too.

Just as individual democratic systems differ from one another, so too do the different classes of authoritarian states. Institutional dictatorships do not operate exactly as do **autocracies**. Military regimes do not function precisely as do party dictatorships. And both are easily distinguishable from theocracies. Finally, absolute monarchies do not face the same challenges as personal dictatorships and consequently will use different institutions of government.

autocracy

Rule by one person with unlimited power.

The Institutions They Use

All governments work through institutions. These may include established practices such as elections, and specifically created structures such as legislatures. However, without actually examining those institutions, it is impossible to know how they work. In general, when Canadians hear a reference to the political institutions of authoritarian regimes, we think first of the secret police, labour camps, and propaganda ministries. If we see a dictatorship that has more than one party, holds elections, and convenes a legislature, we assume that these institutions are window dressing. Although that is true in some cases, it does not apply universally.

To understand why authoritarian regimes, which do not put power on the line, would even think about using the institutions of democratic government, we need to remember this: authoritarian rulers fall far more often to movements mounted by elites within their regimes than to opponents from the outside (Geddes, 2006; Gandhi, 2007; Frantz & Ezrow, 2011). This does not mean that dictators need not worry about the majority who are excluded from power—just that in many cases they have more to fear from the enemy within. Thus, the familiar institutions of democracy can be used in non-democratic regimes to make it harder to oust the ruler.

Courts Courts are found in all political systems, from the most open and democratic to the most oppressively authoritarian. They apply the law, so every political system has to have them. In democracies, we demand that courts be independent of the executive and the legislature so that their decisions are not influenced by partisan considerations.

In authoritarian systems, the range of judicial independence is set by the executive. The methods used to control courts include punishing judges who rendered decisions that displeased the regimes, usually transferring those judges to unattractive places; setting up parallel courts to handle cases the regime found critically important; and encouraging judicial self-restraint, having the judges police themselves (Ginsburg and Moustafa, 2007; Helmke and Rosenbluth, 2009). Yet courts can be very helpful to authoritarians. They can be used to secure property rights, thus assuring investors their money is safe. Similarly they can be used to punish low-level corruption and bureaucratic arbitrariness, making the regime appear fair and concerned about its citizens' welfare.

Parties When we think of political parties and authoritarian regimes what usually comes to mind is the one-party state, especially when the party is the official party and the president's personal political machine. Geddes (2006) refers to these as support parties whose purpose is to ensure that the president stays in power. However, in some cases authoritarian regimes permit other parties to exist, thereby creating a **licenced opposition**. These parties can run for office and even win legislative seats, raising their profile and giving them a chance to promote their agenda. However, they will never be permitted to win power, either because only the official party may govern or because elections are controlled by the government and "the one who counts the votes wins."

licenced opposition

Opposition parties that are allowed to exist, contest elections, and win legislative seats, but that can never take power.

Why would an authoritarian leader ever allow other parties to exist? In part, it lets the regime co-opt opponents with relatively high-profile political posts, thereby giving them a stake in the system. As well, it burnishes the claims of the authoritarian country to be democratic. Having opponents contest elections also helps a non-democratic government in two other ways. First, the campaign lets the government connect with its supporters and gives it an occasion to spend money on public projects. Second, because the government controls the electoral machinery, it knows it will win by a large margin, which tells possible dissidents within the government ranks that, if they defect, they have no hope of winning (Magaloni, 2006; Kratsev & Holmes, 2012).

Legislatures As with parties, the idea of a legislature in an authoritarian regime conjures up images of grim-faced legislators, all members of the official party, called to the capital for a week to listen to their leader recite the regime's achievements. They then return home to the tasks the party assigns them. Yet where there is a licenced opposition, the sessions last longer, and because there are opposition parties, there is actually debate. Just as dictators need not permit opposition parties to exist, neither do they have to give them a forum in the legislature. Similarly, it seems illogical for the leader of an opposition party to allow her followers to participate in a legislature where they will never win a vote. Yet both sides can profit from the arrangement.

Jennifer Gandhi (2007) has analyzed both legislatures and parties in authoritarian regimes. She argues that these institutions help dictators deal with basic problems of governing, thereby helping them neutralize threats to their rule. Legislatures do this by providing a place where the opponents of the regime can make their arguments under controlled conditions, which lets the regime cede some points to its opponents, keeping them within the system. For their part, the regime's opponents get occasional amendments to legislation and, more importantly, material benefits for their supporters. As in a democracy, these benefits are sometimes small, perhaps helping people solve problems with their pensions, and sometimes larger, such as finally getting a bridge repaired.

Elections We have seen that authoritarian rulers allow others to compete in elections whose outcome is predetermined in order to show the party's colours, connect with voters, spend money, and keep potential foes within the regime's party in line. In addition, holding even minimally competitive elections makes an authoritarian government look far more legitimate to the outside world, certainly well beyond what the obviously rigged, one-candidate **plebiscites** that give the dictator 99.73 percent of the vote can provide. Yet even the guaranteed losers get something from such elections. They, too, usually receive some funding so they can run, get more publicity that they otherwise would, and they stay alive as a potentially real option for a few more years.

Democratic institutions thus have real roles to play in authoritarian regimes. To be sure, these are not the roles they assume in democracies. Knowing this makes us aware that there is more to democracy than a set of machinery, important though that is.

HYBRID REGIMES

The political systems that are neither clearly democratic nor unmistakably authoritarian go by a number of different names. This middle range of the democratic–authoritarian continuum could simply be labelled semi-democratic or semi-authoritarian; yet while both terms are commonly used to describe individual regimes, neither is often applied to the class as a whole. It is important to remember that, even though these regimes are more open and less repressive than authoritarians, they cannot be classed as democratic. Further, hybrid regimes can maintain their blend of democratic and non-democratic rule for a long time: they are not necessarily evolving into either democracies or dictatorships.

plebiscite

A vote in which the entire electorate is asked to approve or reject a specific question; for example, whether the current president should be elected president for life.

The list of examples of hybrid regimes presented in Table 11-2 shows that these regimes can be found in all parts of the world and can be found in different economic settings. Four on the list (Bangladesh, Mozambique, Nepal, and Tanzania) are poor; four (Armenia, Honduras, Nicaragua, and Turkey) are middle-income states. Singapore is a high-income state; in fact, its annual per capita income of US$ 56 000 is higher than Canada's US$ 50 000 (World Bank, 2016a). Thus, like both democracies and authoritarians, both rich and poor countries also produce semi-democratic regimes.

What Makes a Hybrid a Hybrid?

A hybrid regime demonstrates some level of pluralism, perhaps allowing the private sector or organized religion some freedom from state interference. It might also permit some essentially free media outlets to function. Similarly, hybrid systems could tolerate more political activity by their opponents, even letting them take a minor role in governing. Yet even if hybrids have moved some distance from the most obvious authoritarian systems, they cannot be called democracies.

There are a number of areas where a hybrid can fail to reach democratic standards. The judicial system may lack independence, which allows government to use the courts to harass its opponents or to legitimate government decisions. Similarly, there may be restrictions on media freedom that make it difficult for the views opposed to the government's to reach the public. Further, rules governing elections can exclude parties or candidates a government does not want to run. However, deciding when these deficiencies push a political system out of the democratic class and into the hybrid category (or expel it from among the hybrids to rest with the authoritarians) is complicated as the boundaries between regimes are quite fuzzy.

Political science has long known that regimes exist that combine democratic and authoritarian aspects. These systems have gone be several names, usually semi-democracies or pseudo-democracies. However, it is only recently that these not-quite democracies began receiving systematic attention. Between 1974 and the end of the twentieth century, many authoritarian states embraced democracy. Among them were what had been the Soviet Union and the entire Soviet Bloc; long-standing Western European dictatorships, such as Portugal and Spain; military dictatorships in Latin America, Africa, and Asia, for example, Chile, Nigeria, and Indonesia. Analysts expected these democracies to persist and prosper, and that soon the great majority of the world's people would live in democracies.

However, as the 1990s progressed, it became clear that numerous new democracies were not getting more democratic, but rather stalling or even going backward. This "de-democratization" seldom led to full authoritarianism. Validimir Putin's Russia stands out as an exception that has tended to move in the direction of full authoritarianism.

To describe what was happening, political scientists searched for new names, among them defective democracies, illiberal democracies, and electoral authoritarians. By 2002, the label "hybrid" (Diamond, 2002) was being applied to them, and the governments that fell into this "grey zone" between democracies and dictatorships (Carothers, 2002) came into better focus. By 2015, depending on the publication being consulted, the number of hybrid regimes ranged from a low of 37 (22 percent of all states) (Economist Intelligence Unit, 2015), to a high of 59 (30 percent of all states) (Freedom House, 2016a).

This is an important class of political systems, and there are three points we must examine to understand hybrid regimes better. First, how did they develop? Second, how do they operate? Third, what makes this class of governments a regime?

How Hybrids Developed

There are three distinct ways that hybrid regimes can come into being (Morlino, 2008). Some began as authoritarian states, and although they are no longer dictatorships, they never became democracies. Nepal is an example. Others were democratic, but have restricted the scope of democracy significantly, even if not enough to be deemed authoritarian. Nicaragua fits here. Finally, there are cases, such as Tanzania and Singapore, where the political system that developed post-independence always blended democratic and authoritarian elements.

How Hybrids Govern

In the cases of Nicaragua and Singapore (see Box 11-5 Two Very Different Hybrid Regimes: Nicaragua and Singapore), and probably in most others as well, it is an array of attributes that leads to their classification as hybrids—neither fully democratic nor totally authoritarian. Politicized courts and at least a strong suspicion of systematic electoral malfeasance are among the traits most frequently associated with hybrid regimes. In the final analysis, it is the fact that a government has built a political system that leaves its citizens some degree of personal freedom while remaining effectively unbeatable that puts it in this intermediate category.

It is the electoral longevity of governments in hybrid regimes that has led political scientists to focus on what are called semi-free elections (Schleder, 2006; Brownlee, 2007; Levitsky & Way, 2010). In a typical hybrid regime, elections are held regularly. There is competition among parties, and opposition parties have some freedom to criticize government and mount campaigns. The media are free enough to report reasonably accurately on current affairs. What do not exist are the periodic winners and losers that Przeworski (1991) asserts is the hallmark of democracy. Citizens in hybrid regimes can vote

BOX 11-5 Two Very Different Hybrid Regimes: Nicaragua and Singapore

Compared on socioeconomic criteria, Nicaragua and Singapore have little in common. The former is a typical developing country that lives off its natural resources and has a per capita income of US$ 2000 per year. Singapore has one of the world's most sophisticated economies, and the average Singaporean's per capita income is over US$ 56 000 yearly. Politically, though, both are hybrid regimes, with some democratic features but not enough to enter the ranks of democracies.

Singapore became independent in 1965. Since that time, one party, the People's Action Party (PAP), has won every election; in fact, counting pre-independence elections, it has been undefeated since 1959. In most of those elections, it took every seat and garnered over 75 percent of the vote. Its worst showing was 2011, when it lost six of 82 seats and won 60 percent of the vote; in 2015, it captured 70 percent of the vote giving it 83 of the 89 seats. Understandably, there have been charges of electoral manipulation. However, since beyond its electoral domination the PAP controls most of the media and the courts, those charges have not been upheld. Singapore is thus conventionally classed as a hybrid because the state's influence over the courts and media, when coupled with the PAP's unbroken electoral success, leaves citizens with few controls on the government.

Nicaragua has been independent since 1821. During that time it has known decades of civil wars, revolutions, and dictatorships. After the Sandinista Revolution (1979) brought the Sandinista National Liberation Front (FSLN) to power, the country moved toward stability and democracy, holding its first free and fair elections with universal suffrage in 1984, losing power itself in 1990. Things looked promising until 2000, when the two largest parties signed a power-sharing pact that sought to exclude all other parties from power. The situation worsened after the FSLN, the party that started Nicaragua on a democratic path, returned to power in 2006. Municipal elections in 2008 and 2012 brought credible charges of fraud, as did national elections in 2011. Further, in 2009, a Sandinista-dominated court declared that a constitutional provision prohibiting immediate presidential re-election did not apply to fellow-Sandinista, President Daniel Ortega. Nicaragua therefore enters the hybrid ranks due to its partisan courts and growing indications of electoral manipulation. Nevertheless, Nicaragua, unlike Singapore, has relatively free media.

Although neither Singapore nor Nicaragua meets the threshold standards for democracy, neither country can be called authoritarian. Political opponents do exist and have some ability to act, and the authorities in both countries generally limit the use of violence. However, the lack of judicial freedom in both nations undermines the rule of law and removes a check on government action.

against the government but they cannot defeat it; thus, elections are semi-free. Clearly, this better than having no voice at all, but it is far from what Canadians think of as democracy.

Of course, there are cases even in democracies where a single political party has a long, uninterrupted stay in power. For example, Social Democrats governed Sweden from 1936 to 1976, the Liberal Democratic Party governed Japan from 1955 to 1993, and the so-called solid South in the United States voted overwhelmingly for the Democrats from 1876 to the mid-1960s and since then has supported the Republicans similarly strongly. In all these cases,

dominant-party system

A political system where one party holds power for an extended period of time by winning free and fair elections.

hegemonic party system

A political system where one party holds power for an extended period of time by winning fraudulent elections.

the government won free elections. These are called **dominant-party systems** (Sartori, 1976). Where governments stay in office due to their control of the electoral process, there is a **hegemonic party system** (Sartori, 1976). The best example of a hegemonic party system was found in Mexico, where the Institutional Revolutionary Party held the presidency from 1929 until 2000.

Why Hybrid Political Systems Constitute a Regime

Hybrid political systems should be treated as a separate class of regime for two reasons. The first is that they exhibit political institutions and practices not found in either democratic or authoritarian systems. Hybrids are less pluralistic, open, and free than democracies, but more so than authoritarian regimes. The second reason is that hybrid systems are durable: Tanzania's dates from 1962 and Singapore's from 1965. However, this does not mean that a particular hybrid regime cannot become either fully democratic or completely authoritarian.

✓• SUMMARY AND CONCLUSION

In the early 1970s, political systems that were not democratic were found in 70 percent of the nations of the world. In 2016, non-democratic regimes still governed slightly over half the world's countries. All of these non-democratic governments share two characteristics:

1. All restrict the right to determine what constitutes the common good to a restricted number of people. Thus, in non-democratic systems the common good is less what is good for everyone than what the rulers believe is good. (Skeptics will say that the same thing happens in democracies, because elites set the agenda there as well.)

2. Non-democratic governments are more likely to use coercion as a normal governing instrument than are democracies. This happens because a government that is unelected and unaccountable does not fear the judgment of its citizens. Therefore, it does not need to convince them that a particular action is good for the country; it is enough to declare it so and punish those who object. In a democracy, persuasion and consultation are government's best and most useful tools. In a non-democratic state,

although a government can try to persuade its people, coercion is easier and more effective, at least in the short term.

We can sum up the differences between democratic and non-democratic governments in this way: Democracy aims to be rule by the people. Non-democratic governments aim only to rule the people.

Non-democratic regimes continue to exist because they offer political elites security, and some of them provide their citizens with acceptable public services. What these regimes do not and cannot do is give citizens the rights, freedoms, and opportunities to govern themselves that all democracies make available. It is also important to remember that not all non-democratic regimes are the same. Some (the totalitarians) are extremely repressive. Although the vast majority of authoritarian regimes seriously limit people's freedom, they do not violate their citizens' rights as completely and systematically as totalitarian regimes. Hybrid regimes, even if they cannot meet minimum democratic standards, tolerate more dissent and exercise less control than any authoritarian regime.

✓• KEY TERMS

DISCUSSION QUESTIONS

1. Why might a political elite prefer to govern through a non-democratic system? Is it just fear of losing power? Could there be a defensible reason for rejecting democracy?

2. Non-democratic regimes appear effectively impregnable, yet sometimes they become more democratic or even fully democratic. Why do you think this might happen? How do you think this might happen?

3. Do you think it makes more sense to divide the world's political system cleanly into two parts, democratic versus undemocratic, than it does to arrange them along a scale from most democratic, though hybrid systems, to most authoritarian? Why?

FURTHER READING

Brooker, P. (2009). *Non-democratic regimes*. London: Palgrave Macmillan.

Diamond, L. & Plattner, M., eds. (2015) *Democracy in decline?* Baltimore: Johns Hopkins University Press.

Ezrow, N. & Frantz, E. (2011). *Dictators and dictatorships: Understanding authoritarian regimes and their leaders*. New York: Continuum Publishing.

Linz, J. (2000). *Totalitarian and authoritarian regimes*. Boulder, CO: Lynne Rienner Publishers.

Newell, W. (2016). *Tyrants*. New York: Cambridge University Press.

12 Constitutions, Courts, and Laws

When Kevin Bourassa and Joe Varnell exchanged wedding vows in Toronto's Metropolitan Community Church in 2001, attendees included Ontario's NDP leader and journalists from around the world. Outside, protesters wore devil masks.   Kevin Frayer/The Canadian Press

After reading this chapter, you should be able to:

1. explain the significance of a constitution and constitutional government
2. describe the major characteristics of the Canadian constitution
3. outline the provisions of the Canadian Charter of Rights and Freedoms
4. discuss the political importance of the courts and the methods used to select judges
5. explain the difference between common law and codified law
6. discuss the significance of international law

When two same-sex couples, Kevin Bourassa and Joe Varnell and Elaine and Anne Vautour, exchanged wedding vows in Toronto's Metropolitan Community Church on January 14, 2001, Ontario's NDP leader attended, along with journalists from around the world. Governor General Adrienne Clarkson sent a congratulatory telegram. Outside, protestors wore devil masks.

The Ontario government refused to register the wedding licences, and a legal battle over same-sex marriage ensued. Within a few years, courts in several provinces ruled that the traditional legal definition of marriage—a union of one man and one woman—was discriminatory and violated the equality rights provisions of the Charter of Rights and Freedoms in Canada's constitution. The marriages were officially registered on June 11, 2003, and since then many gay and lesbian couples have been legally married. However, former Alberta Premier Ralph Klein indicated that, if necessary, he would use the "notwithstanding clause," a clause in the Charter that allows the passing of legislation that infringes on certain rights, in order to prevent the legalization of same-sex marriages in Alberta.

In 1999, the Liberals supported a Reform party motion in the House of Commons upholding the traditional definition of marriage. However, following the provincial court decisions, Liberal Prime Minister Jean Chrétien decided to introduce legislation to define marriage as involving two persons. Calgary's Catholic bishop said that Chrétien risked burning in hell, and the Pope reminded Catholic politicians of their obligation to vote according to their faith. Upon becoming prime minister, Paul Martin tried to downplay the issue, hoping that a decision could be delayed until after an election. Toward the end of the 2004 election campaign, however, Martin was facing a possible Liberal defeat and decided to use the issue to attack the Conservatives. The Conservatives,

Martin argued, would take away people's rights by using the Charter's "notwithstanding clause." Conservative leader Stephen Harper said that he opposed same-sex marriage and, if his party formed the government, he would hold a free vote (one in which MPs were not expected to vote with their party) in the House of Commons to decide the issue. Although he avoided the question of whether the "notwithstanding clause" should be used to protect a ban on same-sex marriages from court challenges, other Conservatives were more forthright. MP Randy White proclaimed, "To heck with the courts . . . the politicians make the laws" (Hume, 2004).

The Civil Marriage Act, which makes same-sex marriages legal in all parts of Canada, was passed by Parliament in 2005. The Conservative government elected in 2006 reopened the issue through a motion in the House of Commons asking the government to introduce legislation that would restore the traditional definition of marriage. The motion was defeated 175–123. As a result, the question of whether the Conservatives would try to use the "notwithstanding clause" to overrule the interpretation of the Charter by the courts that legalized same-sex marriages was avoided.

The issue of same-sex marriage raised questions about how rights should be protected. Should the courts or legislative bodies have the final say in determining how general constitutional rights such as equality rights should be applied to particular issues?

INTRODUCTION

Liberal democracy is based on the perspective that the power and scope of government should be limited, that government should abide by the rule of law, and that the rights of the people should be protected from arbitrary actions by government. In other words, liberal democracy is characterized not only by government elected by the people, but also by **constitutional government**, that is, a government that consistently acts in accordance with established fundamental rules and principles. In this chapter, we focus on the basic features of the Canadian constitution and examine the legal system that plays a key role in upholding the rights and freedoms that are an important part of the constitution.

WHAT IS A CONSTITUTION?

A **constitution** establishes the fundamental rules and principles by which a state is governed. It determines which institutions have the authority to make laws and governing decisions and the relationships among those institutions. A constitution also lays out the basic relationship between government and the people, including the rights and freedoms of the people.

Almost all countries today with the exception of the United Kingdom (see Box 12-1 The British Constitution) and New Zealand have a **codified constitution**; that is, a formal constitutional document or set of documents that establishes the major constitutional provisions. Generally, the provisions of a codified constitution are legally superior to laws passed by a country's legislative bodies. Ordinary laws are expected to be consistent with the constitution.

Codified constitutions typically do not provide a complete and detailed description of the governing system. For example, Canada's formal constitution does not mention the position of prime minister even though that person is the central figure in government. **Constitutional conventions**—fundamental principles that are consistently followed even though they are not contained in a legal document and are not generally enforceable in the courts—are very important in determining how the governing system operates. In addition, judicial interpretations of the formal constitution are important in determining the meaning of constitutional provisions. Finally, some important aspects of the governing system (such as the laws concerning elections) are often established in ordinary legislation rather than in the formal constitution.

The United States (1787) and France (1789) pioneered the use of a formal, written, codified constitution. As Heather MacIvor (2006) points out, those who developed the American constitution believed that legitimate authority should be based on the consent of the governed. A written constitution would limit the power of government and allow the courts to ensure that government acted in accordance with the will of the people that was expressed in the constitution. However, the assumption that a written constitution necessarily reflects the will of the people, rather than the views of those who drafted it, can be questioned.

constitutional government

A government that consistently acts in accordance with established fundamental rules and principles.

constitution

The fundamental rules and principles by which a state is governed.

codified constitution

A constitution whose major provisions are set out in a formal constitutional document or a set of constitutional documents.

constitutional conventions

Fundamental principles that are consistently followed even though they are not contained in a legal document and are not generally enforceable in the courts.

Canadian Constitutional Documents: A Legal History
www.solon.org/Constitutions/ Canada/English

Constitution Finder
http://confinder.richmond.edu

BOX 12-1   The British Constitution

Although the United Kingdom is generally considered to have one of the oldest constitutional governments, it is often described as having an unwritten constitution. Much of the British constitution consists of constitutional conventions. For example, by convention, the British monarch will always give the assent needed for a bill (proposed legislation) to become an act (also known as a statute) if a majority in Parliament has passed it.

The British constitution is not entirely unwritten, and thus it is more accurately described as an uncodified constitution. A number of important statutes have been passed by the British Parliament concerning various aspects of the system of government. For example, the Bill of Rights (1689) limited the power of the monarch by requiring that any new taxes be approved by Parliament, guaranteeing free speech in Parliament, and preventing the monarch from interfering with the law. The Act of Settlement (1701) established the independence of the judiciary and provided rules concerning who could become the monarch. More recently, the Scotland Act (1998) established a Parliament for Scotland, the Constitutional Reform Act (2005) provided for the creation of the Supreme Court of the United Kingdom, the Constitutional Reform and

Governance Act (2010) contained various provisions to increase the accountability and transparency of the government, and the Succession to the Crown Act (2013) ended gender bias and disqualification for marrying a Roman Catholic in royal succession. Despite the importance of these acts, they can be changed by an ordinary Act of Parliament, as a basic principle of the British system is that Parliament cannot bind a future Parliament. Some of the written decisions of judges and commentaries of learned scholars could also be considered part of the British constitution.

Some praise the British constitution for its flexibility. Others argue that it would be desirable to establish a codified constitution that is superior to ordinary legislation, would more clearly establish democratic principles, and would provide stronger guarantees of individual rights and freedoms. Despite some important constitutional reforms in recent times that have changed the nature of the British system of government, there has been no serious effort by British governments to codify the constitution (Flinders, 2010). Nevertheless, British law is expected to be consistent with European Union law. Even after the UK leaves the EU, it will still be subject to the rulings of the European Court of Human Rights that is not a part of the EU.

The Canadian Constitution

The Canadian constitution can be considered a combination of a variety of elements.

The **Constitution Act, 1867** (originally known as the British North America Act), is the core, written element of the constitution. This Act of the United Kingdom Parliament established Canada by uniting the colonies of Canada (Ontario and Quebec), Nova Scotia, and New Brunswick. It also set out many of the features of Canada's system of governing, including the basic features of parliament and the federal system. Over the years, there have been a number of amendments and proposed amendments to the Constitution Act (see Figure 12-1). As well, various other British statutes and orders-in-council (Cabinet decisions) and acts of the Canadian Parliament by which other provinces and territories joined Canada are part of the formal Canadian constitution.

Constitution Act, 1867

An Act of the United Kingdom Parliament that established Canada by uniting the colonies of Canada (Ontario and Quebec), Nova Scotia, and New Brunswick. It also set out many of the features of Canada's system of governing.

FIGURE 12-1
Canadian Constitutional Timeline

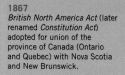

1867
British North America Act (later renamed *Constitution Act*) adopted for union of the province of Canada (Ontario and Quebec) with Nova Scotia and New Brunswick.

1870
Province of Manitoba established.

1905
Provinces of Saskatchewan and Alberta created.

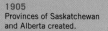

1926
Imperial Conference proclaims Canada and other British dominions as "autonomous."

1871
British Columbia joins Canada.

1873
Prince Edward Island joins Canada.

1927
Attempts begin to find a formula to allow the constitution to be amended in Canada.

Constitution Act, 1982

The Act that made the constitution fully Canadian, added the Charter of Rights and Freedoms to the constitution, and established procedures for amending the constitution.

The **Constitution Act, 1982,** made the constitution a fully Canadian document,[1] made it clear that the formal constitution is the supreme law of Canada, and specifically indicated which documents are to be considered part of the codified constitution. As discussed below, it also added the Charter of Rights and Freedoms to the formal constitution and established procedures for amending the constitution.

There are also legislative statutes, such as the Canada Elections Act, that can be considered constitutional because of their fundamental importance even though they can be changed by an Act of Parliament.

Constitutional conventions, many of which were inherited from Britain, establish important principles that determine the functioning of the system of governing. For example, the convention that the prime minister and Cabinet can remain in office only if they have the confidence (support) of a majority of the members in the House of Commons is a fundamental principle underlying Canada's system of government.

Judicial bodies such as the Supreme Court of Canada have made many important decisions that determine how the constitution is interpreted. For

---

[1]Technically the Constitution Act, 1982, is a schedule attached to the Canada Act, 1982, passed by the UK Parliament that terminated any power of the UK Parliament to legislate for Canada.

1931
Statute of Westminster confirms that Canada is a sovereign country.

1960–1966
Quebec governments seek constitutional changes.

1976
Parti Québécois elected.

1982
Constitution Act, 1982, adopted making the constitution fully amendable in Canada and adding the Charter of Rights and Freedoms to the *Constitution Act.*

1990
Meech Lake Accord fails to pass in Newfoundland and Manitoba legislatures.

1995
Quebec referendum on sovereignty narrowly defeated.

1940   1950   1960   1970   1980   1990   2000

1949
Most aspects of constitution can be amended in Canada. Supreme Court of Canada replaces the Judicial Committee of the British Privy Council as the highest court of appeal. Newfoundland joins Canada.

1967–1971
Constitutional negotiations end in failure.

1980
Quebec government request for a mandate to negotiate sovereignty-association defeated in a Quebec referendum.

1987
Prime minister and premiers reach agreement on the Meech Lake Accord.

1992
Prime minister, premiers, and Aboriginal leaders reach agreement on Charlottetown Accord. Accord defeated in a national referendum.

2000
Clarity Act setting out conditions for a province to become independent passed by Parliament.

example, judicial bodies have had a major role in interpreting the division of law-making powers between the national and provincial legislatures, establishing the rights of Aboriginal peoples, and applying the provisions of the Charter of Rights and Freedoms.

In 1982, Queen Elizabeth II signed the documents that made the constitution entirely Canadian, watched by Prime Minister Pierre Elliott Trudeau (seated).
Stf-Ron Poling/The Canadian Press

CONSTITUTIONAL PROVISIONS

We can analyze constitutions in terms of four basic elements (Newton & Van Deth, 2010):

1. A preamble
2. Provisions concerning the institutions of government, including the procedures for passing laws
3. Provisions establishing the rights and freedoms of the population
4. Procedures for amending (changing) the constitution

Preamble

Many formal constitutions begin with a statement concerning the basic values and goals of the country. For example, the preamble to the American Constitution (1787) proclaims

> We the People of the United States, in Order to form a more perfect Union, establish Justice, insure domestic Tranquility, provide for the common defence, promote the general Welfare, and secure the Blessings of Liberty to ourselves and our Posterity, do ordain and establish this Constitution for the United States of America.

The preamble to the Canadian constitution (1867) is more mundane:

> Whereas the Provinces of Canada, Nova Scotia, and New Brunswick have expressed their Desire to be federally united into One Dominion under the Crown of the United Kingdom of Great Britain and Ireland, with a Constitution similar in Principle to that of the United Kingdom . . . such a Union would conduce to the Welfare of the Provinces and promote the Interests of the British Empire.

The German Basic Law (1949) refers to "the determination to promote world peace as an equal partner in a united Europe," while the French constitution (1958, as amended) affirms the "Rights of Man," the "principles of national sovereignty," and "the rights and duties as defined in the Charter for the Environment." Among the aims of the South African constitution (1996) are to "heal the divisions of the past and establish a society based on democratic values, social justice and fundamental human rights."

Governing Institutions

constitutional monarchy

A system of governing in which the monarch acts as official head of state but is strictly limited in power by the constitution.

Constitutions establish the basic organization and legal responsibilities of various governing institutions.

In Canada, as in the United Kingdom and other countries with a **constitutional monarchy**, executive authority is formally held by the monarch (with this formal authority exercised in Canada by the governor general and, at the provincial level, lieutenant-governors). Governments act in the name of the

Crown. However, by constitutional convention, the governor general acts on the advice of the prime minister and Cabinet except in certain exceptional circumstances. Thus, the monarch's power is strictly limited by the constitution. In Canada, and other democratic countries, legislative (law-making) authority rests primarily with an elected representative body. However, parliamentary and presidential systems differ in the constitutional relationship between the executive and legislature. In parliamentary systems, there is a close relationship between the executive (prime minister and Cabinet) and the legislature. The power of the executive is dependent on maintaining the support of a majority in the legislature. In presidential systems, the president is not required to have the support of Congress (the legislative branch) to remain in office. In most parliamentary and presidential democratic systems, judicial institutions are expected to be independent of both executive and legislative institutions in order to uphold the law in a fair, impartial, and nonpartisan manner.

Constitutions in a number of countries also establish the authority and institutions of different levels of government. In countries with federal systems (such as Canada, the United States, and Australia), the constitution divides much of the authority to make laws between the national and provincial or state levels of government.

Rights and Freedoms

Nearly all constitutions contain provisions concerning the rights and freedoms of individuals. In the United States, for example, the Bill of Rights, a set of ten amendments to the constitution, was adopted in 1791. As a result, American governments are prohibited from passing laws that infringe upon such matters as freedom of religion, speech, and association and the right to a fair trial. In addition, constitutions usually establish a variety of political rights, including the right of all citizens to vote and seek public office, and provide protection against discrimination based on a variety of characteristics such as gender, race, and religion. However in many non-democratic countries these rights are not protected in practice even if they are established in the constitution and international agreements.

Some modern constitutions also require government to take action to ensure that all persons have various economic, social, and cultural rights so that they can enjoy a basic standard of living and quality of life (see Box 12-2 Economic, Social, and Cultural Rights). More than 100 countries have also established a constitutional right to a healthy environment (Boyd, 2011). Although Canada's constitution makes no mention of environmental rights, Quebec's Charter of Human Rights and Freedoms includes the right to "live in a healthful environment in which biodiversity is preserved."

PROTECTING RIGHTS IN CANADA The original Canadian constitution, the Constitution Act, 1867, did not explicitly protect rights and freedoms, other than the right to use English or French in Parliament, the Quebec legislature, and federal and Quebec courts, as well as the right of denominational

BOX 12-2 Economic, Social, and Cultural Rights

Based on the 1948 United Nations Universal Declaration of Human Rights, 18 international covenants have been adopted by the General Assembly of the United Nations. The International Covenant on Civil and Political Rights (1965) has been ratified by 168 countries, including Canada and the United States. The International Covenant on Economic, Social, and Cultural Rights (1966) has been ratified by 164 countries, including Canada, but not the United States.

The economic, social, and cultural rights include the right to adequate food, clothing and shelter, education, physical and mental health, and work. However, given the obstacles to achieving these goals, particularly in developing countries, the Covenant requires government to use the "maximum of its available resources, with a view to achieve progressively the full realization of the rights." Some countries, such as South Africa, have included these rights in their constitutions. In Canada, however, the set of proposed constitutional amendments known as the Charlottetown Accord (1992), which included some of these rights in a social charter, failed to pass.

International covenants are considered to be legally binding on the countries that ratify them. However there is no international enforcement mechanism. Some countries have added declarations and reservations to their ratification. For example Saudi Arabia and some other Islamic states have declared that their acceptance only applies if a Covenant does not contradict Islamic law.

While some people view binding, constitutional commitments to be desirable so that governments are required to ensure that all persons have access to what is needed for a life of dignity, others argue that governments should be able to determine their own budgetary priorities and the level of services they provide.

Charter of Rights and Freedoms

As part of the Constitution Act, 1982, the Charter protects a variety of rights and freedoms. It is superior to ordinary legislation, explicitly allows the courts to invalidate legislation, and applies to the actions of all governments and organizations under the control of government.

United Nations Human Rights Fact Sheets
**www.ohchr.org/EN/
PublicationsResourcesPages/
FactSheets.aspx**

Canadian Civil Liberties Association
www.ccla.org

schools to receive public funding in some provinces. Instead, following British practice, it was assumed that Parliament and provincial legislatures would not infringe upon traditional liberties and that judicial bodies would, where possible, interpret laws in a manner consistent with those liberties.

The tradition of respecting rights and freedoms was generally followed. However, there were important exceptions, particularly the extensive abuse and mistreatment of Aboriginal peoples and the failure of governments to respect their rights. As well, Canadian citizens of Japanese descent were forcibly relocated from British Columbia during and after World War II and their property and possessions sold without their consent.

Beginning with Saskatchewan in 1947, the federal and all provincial governments eventually adopted Bills of Rights, although these did not have the weight of a constitutional provision. In 1982, the **Charter of Rights and Freedoms** was added to Canada's formal, written constitution. The Charter is superior to ordinary legislation, and thus all legislation is expected to be consistent with its provisions. It explicitly allows the courts to invalidate legislation that is inconsistent with the Charter, and it applies to the actions of all governments and organizations under the control of government.[2]

---

[2]Human rights codes adopted by provincial and national governments provide for a number of human rights, including protection against various forms of discrimination by private employers and other organizations and individuals. These codes are expected to be consistent with the Charter.

The basic provisions of the Canadian Charter of Rights and Freedoms include the following:

- *Fundamental freedoms* (Section 2) protect freedom of conscience and religion, and freedom of opinion and expression, including freedom of the media, freedom of peaceful assembly, and freedom of association.
- *Democratic rights* (Sections 3 to 5) include the right of all citizens to vote and hold elected office. The maximum term of Parliament and provincial legislatures is limited to five years.
- *Mobility rights* (Section 6) include the right to move and to pursue a livelihood in any province. However, provinces are allowed to adopt provincial preference policies that improve the conditions of socially or economically disadvantaged individuals if the province has a below-average rate of employment.
- A variety of *legal rights* (Sections 7 to 14), including the right to life, liberty, and security of the person, the right to be secure against unreasonable search or arbitrary detention, the right to a trial within a reasonable period of time, the right to be presumed innocent until proven guilty, and the right not to be subject to any cruel and unusual punishment.
- The *equality rights* clause (Section 15) provides that every person is equal under the law and has the right to the equal protection and equal benefit of the law without discrimination on such grounds as race, origin, colour, religion, sex, age, or mental or physical disability. However, *affirmative action* laws or programs designed to help disadvantaged individuals or groups are permitted.
- *Language rights* (Sections 16 to 23) include the declaration that English and French are the official languages of Canada and New Brunswick and are given equal status in the operations of the Canadian and New Brunswick governments. Canadian citizens whose mother tongue is either English or French have the right to have their children educated in their own language where numbers warrant. In Quebec, this right only applies to parents who received their schooling in Canada.

In general, the Charter includes quite a comprehensive set of individual rights and freedoms. Unlike the American Bill of Rights, equality rights and some provisions relating to group rights and affirmative action are included. Section 25 guarantees that the Charter does not diminish the rights of Aboriginal peoples (including treaty rights and rights established by land claims agreements past, present, and future). Section 27 requires that "the Charter shall be interpreted in a manner consistent with the preservation and enhancement of the multicultural heritage of Canada."

LIMITS TO RIGHTS AND FREEDOMS Rights and freedoms are not absolute. Many countries have laws that prohibit the possession, production, and distribution of pornography, prohibit the expression of hatred directed at various groups, and place limits on advertising directed at children. Although certain limitations to freedoms are necessary to avoid harm to other people, the question of how far governments should go in limiting freedoms is often controversial. Section 1 of the Canadian Charter of Rights and Freedoms explicitly allows for laws to place "reasonable limits" on rights and freedoms, provided that the limits can be "demonstrably justified in a free and democratic society." Using the **reasonable limits clause**, the Supreme Court of Canada has upheld laws prohibiting hate literature and possession of child pornography as reasonable limits on freedom of expression.

In the United States, the Supreme Court upheld the conviction in 1919 of the Socialist Party secretary for distributing flyers urging opposition to the military draft in World War I. The Court ruled that there was a "clear and present danger" in times of war that justified restrictions of freedom of speech. However, in 1969 the US Supreme Court struck down the conviction of a Ku Klux Klan leader who had given a speech calling for revenge against "niggers" and Jews arguing that the constitutional right to freedom of speech could not be restricted unless "advocacy is directed to inciting or producing imminent lawless action and is likely to incite or produce such action" (*Brandenburg v. Ohio* 395 U.S. 444).

Constitutional rights and freedoms have been challenged in recent years in many countries by concerns about terrorism, as discussed in Box 12-3 Terrorism and Rights.

reasonable limits clause

A provision in the Charter of Rights and Freedoms that allows for "reasonable limits" to be placed on rights and freedoms, provided that the limits can be "demonstrably justified in a free and democratic society."

Canadian Charter of Rights and Freedoms
http://laws.justice.gc.ca/eng/Const/Const_index.html

The US constitution states: "No person shall be deprived of life, liberty, and property without due process of the law." Thus far, killings by drone approved by the President without due process of the law have only occurred outside the U.S. They have included a few Americans located in foreign countries and who are believed to be terrorists.

Tami Thirlwell

BOX 12-3   Terrorism and Rights

In the wake of the terrorist attacks, the governments of many democratic countries have taken strong measures to deal with terrorism. Some of these measures have been criticized for violating the rule of law and individual rights and freedoms. As part of the American "war against terrorism," several hundred foreigners, including juveniles, were captured after al-Qaeda's attack on the United States and the subsequent conflict in Afghanistan. They were held for very lengthy periods of time at Guantánamo Bay, a US military base leased from Cuba since 1903 where American law does not apply, without being charged. Prisoners were denied access to their families and to legal counsel and subjected to very harsh treatment. Although Obama promised to close Guantánamo within a year when he ran for president in 2008, this did not occur. As of September 2016, 61 prisoners still remained at Guantánamo, 57 of whom have been held for over 10 years, the majority without charge or trial (Human Rights First, 2016).

Canada's Anti-Terrorism Act adopted in 2001 provided stiff penalties for terrorist activities. As well, individuals suspected of involvement in terrorism could be held for 72 hours without a charge being laid, and imprisoned for up to 12 months if they did not abide by certain restrictive conditions. Non-citizens could be held indefinitely without charge based on secret evidence unless they decided to return immediately to their home countries. This provision was struck down by the Supreme Court of Canada in 2007. The Combatting Terrorism Act (2013) allowed the courts to compel witnesses to provide information about possible acts of terrorism, limited the freedom of those suspected of engaging in terrorist activities, and sentenced those leaving the country to engage in terrorist activity or harbouring a person involved in terrorism to a lengthy prison term.

In October 2014, a Canadian inspired by Islamic extremism rammed a car killing one soldier and injuring another. Two days later, another Canadian convert to Islam shot and killed a soldier at the War Memorial in Ottawa and then invaded Parliament before being killed. In response, a new Anti-Terrorism Act (Bill C-51) was passed allowing the Canadian Security Intelligence Service (CSIS) to take any action that it considers reasonable to "reduce . . . threats to the security of Canada". This includes breaking laws and violating the Charter of Rights and Freedoms provided that there has been judicial permission based on a secret hearing in which only the government can present its case. It also made it a serious criminal offence to advocate or promote "terrorism in general," facilitated the sharing of information with foreign agencies, and allowed telecom companies to voluntarily provide information about their customers (Forcese & Roach, 2015). While the Liberal party supported the Conservative legislation, the Liberals promised in the 2015 election campaign to amend the legislation to balance security with protection of rights and freedoms.

Some argue that the threat of terrorism justifies extraordinary measures; others argue that terrorism should be fought without substantial changes to the rights and freedoms of liberal democracies.

OVERRIDING THE CHARTER: THE NOTWITHSTANDING CLAUSE   The Canadian Charter of Rights and Freedoms was opposed by some premiers who argued that Parliament or provincial legislatures rather than the courts should have the final say in determining the appropriate extent of rights and freedoms. As a compromise, Section 33 of the Charter allows Parliament or a provincial legislature to override some

Terrorism and the rule of law: several hundred foreigners were held for very lengthy periods of time at Guantánamo Bay (a US military base on land perpetually leased from Cuba in 1903) without being charged. Allegations of ill treatment and torture of prisoners later surfaced.

Shane T. McCoy/U.S. Navy/Getty Images News/Getty Images

rights by using the **notwithstanding clause** (see Table 12-1). This involves Parliament or a provincial legislature explicitly declaring that a particular law shall operate *notwithstanding* the provisions of the Charter. Such a declaration is only effective for five years, although it can be re-enacted as often as is desired. Because of the public's strong support for the rights and freedoms listed in the Charter, this clause has been rarely used. The only significant use was by the Quebec legislature in 1988 when passing a law that did not permit languages other than French on signs outside stores. However, this controversial use of the notwithstanding clause was not renewed in 1993. Instead, a new law required that French be given a prominent position on signs in Quebec was adopted without using the clause.

notwithstanding clause

A provision in the Charter of Rights and Freedoms that allows a legislative body to explicitly declare that a particular law (related to some parts of the Charter) shall operate *notwithstanding* the provisions of the Charter. Such a declaration is only effective for five years, although it can be re-enacted as often as is desired.

constitutional amendment

A formal change to the constitution.

Amending the Constitution

Constitutional amendments are needed from time to time because of changing circumstances and the changing values of a country's citizens. Experiences with the constitution may also lead to a desire to improve it. However, to try to ensure that a government does not change the constitution to gain excessive powers or to take away constitutionally protected rights, most countries require a higher level of support to change their formal, written constitution than is needed to pass or change an ordinary law. For example, amendments to the American constitution must be proposed by a two-thirds majority in each of the two Houses of Congress. Three-quarters of the states must ratify the proposal.[3] Only twenty-seven amendments to the American constitution have been passed in more than 200 years. Some countries (such as Sweden, Denmark, and the Netherlands) require that amendments be passed by parliamentary bodies twice—once before and once after an election. Other countries

TABLE 12-1

The Charter and the Notwithstanding Clause

PROVISIONS THAT CANNOT BE OVERRIDDEN	NOTWITHSTANDING CLAUSE APPLIES TO
Democratic rights	Fundamental freedoms
Mobility rights	Legal rights
Language rights	Equality rights
Male–female equality rights	

[3]Alternatively a national convention requested by two-thirds of the states could propose constitutional changes and conventions held in three-quarters of the states could ratify these changes, but this procedure has very rarely been used. Presidential approval is not required for amendments.

(including Australia,[4] Switzerland, and Japan) require approval in a referendum as well as by legislative bodies (Rasch & Congleton, 2006).

AMENDING CANADA'S CONSTITUTION Some aspects of the Canadian constitution can be changed without any procedural difficulties. The unwritten aspects of the Canadian constitution—conventions and judicial interpretations—evolve over time. Ordinary laws that are of constitutional significance (such as the Canada Elections Act) can be changed by the adoption of a new law by a simple majority in Parliament. The procedures adopted in 1982 for amending the Constitution Act are more complex:

- A few provisions of the Constitution Act, such as the offices of the monarch, governor general, and lieutenant-governors, and the composition of the Supreme Court of Canada, are only amendable by the resolution of a majority in Parliament[5] and in all of the provincial legislatures.
- Most of the Constitution Act (including the division of law-making authority between Parliament and provincial legislatures) can be changed with the agreement of majorities in the House of Commons and the Senate and majorities in at least two-thirds of the provincial legislatures, provided those legislatures represent provinces containing at least one-half of the population of all the provinces.[6] A province has the right to "opt out" of a constitutional amendment that reduces the powers of its legislature and receive "reasonable compensation" if it relates to education or other cultural matters.
- Although a referendum is not required to approve constitutional changes, the use of a referendum in 1992 to seek approval for a major package of changes suggests that there is a political expectation that a referendum be held to approve major changes. British Columbia and Alberta require that a referendum be held before their legislatures approve an amendment to the Canadian constitution.
- Changes to constitutional provisions that affect only certain provinces require the approval of Parliament and the affected provincial legislatures.

Major amendments to the formal constitution have proven difficult to achieve. The Constitution Act, 1982 was passed over the strenuous objections

---

[4]The referendum to approve constitutional changes in Australia requires support by a national majority and majorities in a majority of states.

[5]A majority in each of the chambers of Parliament (that is, the House of Commons and the Senate) is normally needed for any amendments to the constitution. However, if the Senate does not pass the resolution for the amendment, after one hundred and eighty days the House of Commons can repass the resolution, in which case the approval of the Senate is not needed for the amendment.

[6]Although this is still the procedure in the Constitution Act, the Canadian Parliament passed legislation in 1996 requiring that proposed constitutional changes introduced into the Canadian Parliament must also have the support of the legislatures of Ontario, Quebec, British Columbia, the Prairie provinces (in effect, Alberta plus either Saskatchewan or Manitoba), and the Atlantic provinces (at least two provinces containing at least one-half of the region's population).

of the Quebec government and some Aboriginal leaders and groups. An attempt to win the support of Quebec for the Constitution Act, 1982 met with failure when a package of constitutional changes known as the **Meech Lake Accord** failed to win the approval of the Newfoundland and Manitoba legislatures within the required time frame in 1990. Although the Meech Lake Accord initially had the support of the prime minister and all ten premiers, it aroused strong opposition, particularly to the clause recognizing Quebec as a "distinct society," in the rest of Canada. A second attempt, the **Charlottetown Accord** (1992), gained the support of the prime minister, premiers, territorial leaders, and national Aboriginal leaders for a package of constitutional changes that included recognition of the inherent right of Aboriginals to self-government and major changes to the Senate. However, the Charlottetown Accord was defeated in a referendum, with 55 percent of Canadians rejecting it.

Overall, the different views on the nature of Canada held by many English-speaking Canadians, French-speaking Quebecers, and Aboriginal peoples have made major changes to Canada's formal constitution very contentious. With a high level of agreement needed for constitutional changes, it is not surprising that major changes have been difficult to achieve.

JUDICIAL REVIEW

In some countries (including Japan, Australia, Italy, and India), the courts have the authority to strike down legislation or governmental actions that are deemed to be in violation of the constitution. Even though the power of **judicial review** is not explicitly stated in the American constitution, the Supreme Court assumed this power by its ruling in *Marbury v. Madison* (1803) that "Congress cannot pass laws that are contrary to the Constitution and it is the role of the federal courts to interpret what the Constitution permits." Likewise in Canada, although the Constitution Act, 1867 did not explicitly include the power of judicial review, judicial bodies early on assumed this role in ruling on disputes concerning the distribution of law-making authority between Parliament and provincial legislatures. The importance of judicial review was enhanced by the Charter of Rights and Freedoms and by Section 52 of the Constitution Act, 1982, which states that the constitution is "the supreme law of Canada" and that "any law that is inconsistent with the Constitution is, to the extent of the inconsistency, of no force or effect."

In many countries (including Germany, Austria, France, and Chile), judicial review is carried out by a special constitutional court rather than by the regular court system. Some countries (including Belgium, the Netherlands, and Switzerland) do not provide for judicial review or have only a weak version of it (Lane & Ersson, 2000; Newton & Van Deth, 2010). Rather than determining whether legislation is constitutional, the courts in these countries may interpret laws in ways that emphasize individual rights and procedural fairness.

In the United Kingdom, the principle of **parliamentary sovereignty** (also known as parliamentary supremacy) means that Parliament is the supreme

Meech Lake Accord

A 1987 package of proposed constitutional changes that was not passed. It contained controversial provisions, including the recognition of Quebec as a "distinct society."

Charlottetown Accord

A 1992 package of proposed constitutional changes, including recognition of the inherent right of Aboriginals to self-government and major changes to the Senate. It was defeated in a referendum.

judicial review

The authority of the courts to strike down legislation or governmental actions that the courts deem to be in violation of the constitution.

parliamentary sovereignty

A basic principle of the British system of governing, recognizing Parliament as the supreme law-making body such that the courts cannot invalidate an Act of Parliament.

law-making body and the courts cannot invalidate an Act of Parliament. However, the United Kingdom is expected to abide by the rules and regulations of the European Union as long as it is a member. In addition, the courts can declare an Act of Parliament as incompatible with the Human Rights Act (1998) which is based on the European Convention of Human Rights[7]. The courts will try to interpret an Act of Parliament to make it consistent with the Human Rights Act, but a declaration of incompatibility does not invalidate an Act.

Even in countries where judicial review is available, there is considerable variation in the degree to which the courts are active in invalidating legislation and government actions that are inconsistent with the constitution. The United States is often viewed as the best example of **judicial activism**. For example, in the 1930s, the Supreme Court overturned a number of laws that had been passed as part of President Roosevelt's "New Deal" to address the problems created by Great Depression. The US Supreme Court also played a major role in ending racial segregation (which it had earlier upheld) by invalidating state laws that prevented black students from attending white schools, overturning state laws that made interracial marriages illegal, and ordering that children be bused from one neighbourhood to another to try to achieve racial integration in public schools. Its decision in *Roe v. Wade* (1973) disallowed restrictive abortion laws that infringed upon constitutional rights.

In Canada, the Judicial Committee of the Privy Council (a panel of judges primarily from the British House of Lords) was the highest court of appeal for many matters until 1949. It had an important effect on the evolution of Canada's federal system, particularly by striking down a number of federal laws that it viewed as infringing upon provincial legislative authority. After the Charter of Rights and Freedoms was adopted in 1982, the Supreme Court of Canada became quite active in invalidating laws and policies that the court viewed as inconsistent with the Charter. For example, in 1988 the Supreme Court struck down a law that made abortion a criminal offence unless authorized by a hospital committee, ruling that the law violated the Charter right to "security of the person" because a delay in treatment increased the risk to a woman's health. A subsequent attempt to pass a new law specifying the conditions under which abortion would be allowed failed to be approved by Parliament. Similarly, the courts have struck down various laws that discriminate against gays and lesbians by interpreting the equality rights provision in the Charter so as to prohibit discrimination on the basis of sexual orientation, even though sexual orientation is not explicitly mentioned in the Charter. As discussed in Box 12-4 Is Judicial Activism Desirable?, there has been considerable controversy about the role of judicial activism in Canada's courts.

judicial activism

The term used when the courts are active in invalidating legislation and government actions that are inconsistent with the constitution.

---

[7]The European Convention is an international treaty established by the 47 member states of the Council of Europe. The Council is not a European Union institution.

BOX 12-4   Is Judicial Activism Desirable?

Some commentators have argued that judicial activism has made Canadian courts too powerful. Instead of the elected representatives of the people making decisions about controversial issues, appointed judges who are unaccountable have, in effect, made important decisions concerning issues such as abortion, same-sex marriage, and the legalization of the medical use of marijuana. Because governments have been very reluctant to use the Charter's "notwithstanding clause," there is no check on what some view as the excessive activism of the courts (Morton, 2003). As well, the courts (unlike governments) generally do not have the capability to monitor and assess the consequences of their decisions.

Other commentators argue that, by actively using the Charter, the courts have helped to protect the rights of minorities. When it adopted the Charter of Rights and Freedoms, Canada established itself as a true constitutional democracy in which an independent judiciary sets limits to the power of government (Potter, 2003). The courts are more likely to be concerned about the rights of unpopular minorities than elected officials, who may be pressured by majority opinion.

In assessing each argument, it should be noted that the courts have been more active in invalidating legislation at some points in time and more deferential to the wishes of legislative bodies at other points in time, depending on the issues involved and the judges who are hearing the cases. As well, governments and legislative bodies have sometimes preferred to leave controversial moral issues to the courts to decide.

Although some European countries allow their constitutional courts to review legislation before it becomes law, Canadian and American courts generally only consider the validity of laws when faced with a particular case. Given the costs of pursuing cases through the court system, many laws and government actions are not reviewed by the courts. The Canadian government will occasionally refer a proposed law to the Supreme Court of Canada (and provincial governments to the highest court in their province) for an advisory opinion, as the Canadian government did concerning same-sex marriage. As well, governments may try to ensure that proposed legislation is "Charter-proof" to avoid the possibility that it will be struck down if a case comes before the courts. In fact, the justice minister has a legal obligation to report to Parliament if proposed legislation is likely to be inconsistent with the Charter, although this obligation has often been ignored (Canadian Civil Liberties Association, 2016).

The Independence of the Judiciary

To ensure that the rule of law is upheld, the judicial system should be independent of government and other influences. Where a court system is not free from political interference, governments and their agents can intimidate the population, corruption may be widespread, and the principle that all persons should be treated fairly and equally by the law is likely to be undermined.

To protect their independence, judges in Canada and many other constitutional democracies are given a high level of job security, such that they cannot be removed from their position by the government. Federally appointed judges in Canada retain their positions until age seventy-five. Removal can occur only through a resolution passed by a majority in both the House of Commons and the Senate. This action is taken only after the Canadian Judicial Council, which is composed of the provincial chief justices and associate chief justices, conducts an inquiry.

In addition, it is considered improper for politicians or government officials to try to influence a judge (for example, by calling a judge to discuss a case). Judges are expected to refrain from political activity once appointed to the bench.

Selection Process

Although judges are supposed to be completely non-political and non-partisan once appointed, the selection of judges can be controversial because government leaders will likely select judges who share their ideological perspective.

In Canada, the authority to recommend Supreme Court of Canada judges rests with the Cabinet, although in practice the choice is up to the prime minister after what has been a largely secretive consultation process. Those chosen must have been a judge of a provincial superior court or a member of the bar for at least ten years. Three of the nine Supreme Court judges must be from Quebec's appeal or superior court or among the members of the Quebec bar. In 2004, Prime Minister Paul Martin established a parliamentary advisory committee to provide a confidential unranked short list of three candidates from which the prime minister would make the choice. Prime Minister Stephen Harper added an element of transparency by having a parliamentary committee ask questions of the chosen candidate in a televised hearing. However disputes between the Harper and the opposition parties resulted in three Supreme Court judges being appointed without a selection committee and a parliamentary hearing. The prime minister is also responsible for recommending the appointment of the chief justices and associate chief justices of each of the provincial superior courts while the federal minister of justice makes recommendations to the Cabinet for other federally appointed judges.[8] The attorney general of a province (a Cabinet minister) makes recommendations to the provincial Cabinet for appointment to the provincial courts.

In the United States, the president nominates persons to the Supreme Court and nominates all other federal judges. They face hearings conducted

---

[8]An eight-member judicial advisory committee in each province makes a recommendation from among lawyers and judges.

Beverely McLachlin was appointed Chief Justice of the Supreme Court of Canada in 2000. She is the first woman to hold this position, and is the long-serving Chief Justice.

Supreme Court of Canada

by the Senate Judiciary Committee before the Senate decides whether to confirm the nomination by a majority vote. Some of these hearings have involved extensive investigations into the beliefs and even the personal lives of the nominees. The president's nominees are usually confirmed by the Senate although the Senate has rejected some nominees.[9] US Supreme Court judges can hold their position for life, as there is no mandatory retirement age.

In more than three-quarters of American states, judges are elected by voters rather than appointed and are subject to re-election at regular intervals. While this provides for some democratic accountability of judges, it also may reduce the willingness of judges to act fairly and impartially when the public is incensed about a particular crime or issue. As well, the reliance of judges on campaign contributions to get elected or re-elected can raise questions about their impartiality.

In Canada, all federally appointed judges and most provincially appointed judges must have at least 10 years of experience as a judge or lawyer. In the United States, there are no formal qualifications for Supreme Court judges (although many have had distinguished legal careers). In Germany (and some other Western European countries), judges are selected (based on examinations) after completing law school and receive specialized training before beginning their judicial careers; however, the members of Germany's Constitutional Court are elected by the two legislative bodies for a fixed twelve-year term. In many European countries, a judicial appointments commission (often consisting of judges, lawyers, and parliamentary appointees) is responsible for recommending promotion to higher levels of the court system.

In recent times, to varying extents, efforts in Canada have been made to appoint judges with more diverse characteristics than in the past. With the retirement of Justice Thomas Cromwell in September 2016, four of the eight Supreme Court of Canada judges were female, including Chief Justice Beverley McLachlin. A new independent advisory board was established by Prime Minister Trudeau to prepare a short-list of qualified, bilingual candidates that reflect Canada's diversity. Although candidates from all regions of Canada were recommended to replace Cromwell, Trudeau followed the tradition of having one Supreme Court judge from Atlantic Canada by appointing the well-qualified Newfoundland judge, Malcolm Rowe. No Aboriginal has ever been appointed to the Supreme Court, and there are few Aboriginal or non-white judges in other courts.

---

[9]In March 2016, President Obama nominated the liberally minded Merrick Garland to replace the conservative Antonin Scalin who had died. This would shift the balance in the Court from conservative to liberal. The Republican Senate majority indicated that they would not hold a hearing to assess Garland until a new president was in office in 2017.

Court Systems

Court systems are generally hierarchical in nature, with appeals from lower courts heard in higher courts. Canada can also be described as having a basically unified court system in that the same court system is used for cases involving most laws under federal or provincial jurisdiction. Federally appointed judges are used in all but the lowest (provincial) courts, while provincial governments are responsible for the organization and administration of all courts except the Supreme Court of Canada. Exceptions to this unified court system are the Federal Court, which adjudicates cases related to certain acts of Parliament (including laws related to copyright and patents, and citizenship and immigration), the Tax Court of Canada, and military courts.

The United States has a dual or parallel court system in which the vast majority of cases are tried in state courts. Federal courts deal with federal law, but generally do not hear appeals from state courts unless the death penalty has been imposed. The US Supreme Court hears appeals from the highest level of state courts only if it considers the case to involve substantial constitutional issues, a federal statute, or the actions of a federal official (McKenna, 1990).

Legal Systems

Common law and codified law are the two major legal systems used in most liberal democracies. The common law system originated in the twelfth century as the King's courts in England began to use the "common customs" of the country as the basis for their decisions rather than the traditions of different localities used in the courts presided over by the nobles (Hausegger, Hennigar, & Riddell, 2015). Judges would use precedents (that is, decisions made in previous similar cases) to guide their decisions. Thus, **common law** consists of court judgments that have accumulated over many centuries. Many areas of common law have been superseded by statutory law (that is, law passed by a legislative body); nevertheless, common law continues to be an important component of **private law**; that is, law that deals with the relationships among individuals, groups, and businesses that are primarily of private interest rather than of general public interest.

Codified law (often referred to as a civil code or civil law) involves the adoption of a comprehensive system of principles that judges use to determine the outcome of a particular case. Many systems of codified law have been influenced by the code commissioned by French Emperor Napoleon in 1804 (often referred to as the Napoleonic Code), which was derived from the laws of the Roman Empire as well as sources in French law. The German Civil Code has also influenced the development of the legal systems of a number of countries.

common law

A system of law-based court judgments that have accumulated over many centuries.

private law

Law that deals with the relationships among individuals, groups, and businesses that are primarily of private interest rather than of general public interest.

codified law

A system of law based on the adoption of a comprehensive set of principles that judges use to determine the outcome of a particular case.

Sharia law

Sharia law is based on the Qur'an, the teachings and practices of Mohammed, and Islamic jurisprudence. It deals with private behaviour and beliefs as well as public behaviour and is used to varying extents in many Muslim countries. There are several different versions of Sharia law with Saudi Arabia using a particularly strict version of Sharia enforced, in part, by religious police. Radical Islamic groups including ISIS, Taliban, and Boko Haram have also sought to impose a very strict version of Sharia law. In some countries Sharia law is used in combination with Western legal systems. In the United Kingdom, there are a significant number of Sharia courts or tribunals settling disputes concerning issues such as divorce and inheritance among Muslims. In 2005, the Ontario government banned Sharia arbitration (and that of other religions) because of the unequal treatment of women in Sharia jurisprudence.

Common law is used in England and most of the former British colonies. Codified law (in various versions) is used in most countries in continental Europe and Latin America as well as Japan. In Canada, nine provinces use common law while Quebec uses its own Civil Code. Criminal law is the responsibility of the federal government, with most criminal law compiled in an Act of Parliament known as the Criminal Code. American states also use the common law, although Louisiana's Civil Code is based in part on the Napoleonic Code. Some jurisdictions (including Scotland, South Africa, and Israel) use a mixture of common law and codified law.

International Law

International law is often thought of as very different than the domestic laws that govern behaviour within a country. International law was developed primarily as law related to the relations and disputes between sovereign states rather than law concerning individuals or businesses within states.

Over a period of centuries a large body of international law has developed. A large number of treaties as well as customary practices (such as the immunity of diplomats in foreign countries) have formed the basis of much international law. The International Court of Justice (ICJ; also known as the World Court), an organ of the United Nations, hears cases that countries with a dispute submit to it. Its 15 judges are elected by the General Assembly and Security Council of the United Nations and can only adjudicate disputes if the states concerned have accepted its jurisdiction. Only a small proportion of states have accepted the jurisdiction of the ICJ on all disputes, but many states have agreed to accept ICJ jurisdiction on treaties they have signed (Lowe, 2015). Unlike domestic courts, the ICJ does not generally have the means to enforce its decisions. Economic or military sanctions can only be applied by the Security Council of the United Nations, and are limited to the breach of peace and actions of aggression by states. With each of the five permanent member states of the Security

Council having a veto, it is highly unlikely that sanctions would be applied to these powerful states. In fact, sanctions have never been used to enforce ICJ judgements. Nevertheless, the ICJ has been successful in resolving some disputes. For example, the ICJ settled a dispute between Canada and the US concerning the maritime boundary in the George's Bank area of the Gulf of Maine in 1984.

International law does not only involve relations among states, but increasingly deals with individual human rights as well as international trade and environmental protection. Centuries ago, piracy was considered an international crime with states allowed to prosecute and punish pirates seized on the high seas (Lowe, 2015). After the end of World War II an international military tribunal (for the Nuremberg trials) tried, convicted, and punished Nazi leaders for crimes against humanity. Similarly, international criminal tribunals were established for the former Yugoslavia and for Rwanda in the 1990s. For example, in 2016 the former president of the Bosnian Serb Republic, Radovan Karadžić, was found responsible for the 1995 massacre of at least 6000 Muslim men and boys and sentenced to 40 years of imprisonment. In 2002 the International Criminal Court (ICC) was established in The Hague, Netherlands as a permanent court to deal with the most serious cases involving the perpetrators of genocide, crimes against humanity, and war crimes that have not be prosecuted effectively by a national court. At the time of writing, 124 countries (including Canada) had adopted the Rome Statute, the treaty on which the ICC is based.

There are a number of other international courts and tribunals that deal with issues such as human rights, trade, and investment. For example, the European Court of Human Rights set up by the 47 member states of the Council of Europe has dealt with thousands of allegations by individuals of violation of their civil and political rights. Many free trade agreements establish independent tribunals that can award businesses financial compensation from foreign governments that have acted in a way that could deprive them of profits.

✓• SUMMARY AND CONCLUSION

The basic legal framework for governing is provided by the constitution. Ideally, constitutions reflect a fundamental consensus among citizens about the governing of their country. Where the constitution is widely accepted, the power of those in governing positions becomes legitimate authority as long as constitutional rules and procedures are followed. However, because a constitution has a strong effect on the distribution of political power, the constitution and proposals for constitutional change can be very controversial.

The constitutions of most countries potentially limit the power of government by establishing various rights and freedoms for the population. Most countries in modern times have given the courts the authority to review legislation and government actions to determine whether they are consistent with the constitution. Where the courts are active in exercising that power, judicial review can provide strong protection for rights and freedoms. However, some argue that involving judges in determining the validity of legislation makes the judiciary too powerful and interferes with the principle that the judiciary should be separate from politics. The political significance of the courts makes the process of selecting judges very important.

The protection of rights and freedoms and the promotion of economic, environmental, social, and cultural rights may be considered desirable for the promotion of the common good. A free society in which people do not fear arbitrary action by government, have the right to participate in political life, and are able to enjoy a basic standard of living and quality of life will be more likely to foster the good of all than will a society controlled by a dictatorial government. Some commentators argue that too much emphasis is placed on individual rights in countries such as Canada and the United States without a corresponding concern for the responsibility of individuals to each other and to their community. For example, it can be argued that the right to vote carries with it a responsibility to make an informed judgment about what is good for the community when voting. However, if freedoms are only granted to those who act "responsibly," then the freedoms may be so limited as to be meaningless. Political freedoms allow a diversity of opinions to be expressed so that, through discussion, the best course of action can emerge. Developing a sense of responsibility in all citizens is undoubtedly desirable, but may be best achieved through encouragement and education rather than through legal requirements.

Critics of our "rights culture" also argue that by focusing attention on individual rights, discussion of the common good may be neglected. Going to court to pursue one's rights not only is expensive, and thus more available to the wealthier elements of society, but also detracts from the democratic political activity of trying to convince others that a particular course of action is for the common good. Nevertheless, legal action can be a useful way to ensure that government and public agencies are accountable for their actions.

The courts are important not only in ensuring that people accused of violating the law receive a fair trial, but also in interpreting and reviewing laws and government actions to ensure that they are compatible with the constitution. To ensure that the judicial system works for the common good and protects the rights of individuals and minorities, it should be independent of government, impartial, and fair. However, the methods used to select judges may raise questions about whether the judicial system is completely independent and impartial.

The three major types of legal systems used in the contemporary world are common law, codified law, and sharia law, each of which has various versions. Combinations of these types are present in a number of countries. International law has become increasingly important, in part because of economic globalization and increasing concern about human rights.

✓• KEY TERMS

Charlottetown Accord 290	Constitution Act, 1867 279	Judicial review 290
Charter of Rights and Freedoms 284	Constitution Act, 1982 280	Meech Lake Accord 290
Codified constitution 278	Constitutional amendment 288	Notwithstanding clause 288
Codified law 295	Constitutional conventions 278	Parliamentary sovereignty 290
Common law 295	Constitutional government 278	Private law 295
Constitution 278	Constitutional monarchy 282	Reasonable limits clause 286
	Judicial activism 291	Sharia law 296

DISCUSSION QUESTIONS

1. Should economic, environmental, social, and cultural rights be added to the Canadian Charter of Rights and Freedoms?

2. Should the "notwithstanding clause" be eliminated from the Canadian constitution?

3. Should the rule of law and civil liberties be suspended when a country is faced with terrorist threats?

4. How should judges be chosen?

5. Is judicial activism desirable?

FURTHER READING

Boyd, D.R. (2011). *The environmental rights revolution: A global study of constitutions, human rights and the environment.* Vancouver: UBC Press.

Burrows, J. (2010). *Canada's indigenous constitution.* Toronto: University of Toronto Press.

Dodek, A. (2016). *The Canadian constitution* (2nd ed.). Toronto: Dundurn Press.

Green, I. (2014). *The Charter of Rights and Freedoms: 30+ years of decisions that shape Canadian life.* Toronto: Lorimer.

Hausegger, L., Hennigar, M., & Riddell, T. (2015). *Canadian courts: Law, politics, and process* (2nd ed.). Toronto, ON: Oxford University Press.

Klabbers, J. (2013). *International law.* Cambridge, UK: Cambridge University Press.

Malleson, K., & Russell, P.H. (Eds.). (2006). *Appointing judges in an age of judicial power: Critical perspectives from around the world.* Toronto: University of Toronto Press.

Qvortrup, M. (Ed.) (2013). *The British constitution: Continuity and change.* Oxford, UK: Hart Publishing.

Russell, P. (2004). *Constitutional odyssey* (3rd ed.). Toronto: University of Toronto Press.

13 Multiple Governments

On May 16, 2007, Alex Salmond, leader of a party that is committed to holding a referendum on independence for Scotland, became head of the Scottish government.   David Gordon/Alamy Stock Photo

After reading this chapter, you should be able to:

1. describe and assess unitary, federal, and confederal systems
2. define the meaning of devolution and discuss how it has been applied
3. compare the Canadian federal system to other federal systems
4. outline the basic features of the European Union
5. discuss the significance of local government

On May 16, 2007, Alex Salmond, the leader of the Scottish National Party, which is committed to an independent Scotland within the European Union, was sworn in as First Minister of the Scottish government.

The United Kingdom has often been thought of as a highly centralized country. The principle of parliamentary sovereignty has meant that the British prime minister and Cabinet with the support of the majority party in Parliament has had virtually unlimited powers. For example, although there are many local governments, Prime Minister Margaret Thatcher didn't hesitate to eliminate the Greater London Council in 1986 because she viewed it as too left-wing. Nevertheless, the United Kingdom can be considered a multinational country in which England, Scotland, Wales, and Northern Ireland each retain a distinctive identity. Although political authority has been concentrated in London, some laws and policies have reflected the differences among the component units of the country. For example, Scotland has retained its own legal and educational systems.

As in a number of other countries, there has been a move away from centralized political authority in the United Kingdom in recent times. The rise of nationalism, particularly in Scotland in the 1970s, created pressure for change. The governing Conservative party under Thatcher was perceived as pursuing a centralization of power. This contributed to the Conservative party losing all of its seats in Scotland and Wales. The Labour party, which had considerable support in those areas, adopted the cause of establishing Scottish and Welsh Parliaments. Upon being elected in 1997, the Labour party proceeded to hold a referendum in Scotland and Wales that endorsed the idea of a Parliament for Scotland and an Assembly for Wales. This did not fully satisfy many in Scotland who felt that the powers granted were too limited. Others in the

United Kingdom, however, worried that the creation of Scottish and Welsh governments could eventually lead to the breakup of the United Kingdom.

The Scottish National Party (SNP), committed to pursuing Scottish independence, won 47 of the 129 seats in the Scottish Parliament in 2007 and formed a minority government. The 2011 Scottish election resulted in a majority government for the SNP, which decided to hold a referendum on September 18, 2014 on the question "Should Scotland be an independent country?" The British government announced that it would accept the outcome of the referendum. However, with the majority of Scottish voters favouring greater powers for the Scottish Parliament rather than independence, Salmond faced a difficult task to persuade voters (including those 16 and 17 years old) to vote "yes" in the referendum. In the end, Scottish independence was rejected by 55.3% of voters based on a turnout of 84.6%. Salmond resigned and was replaced by Nicola Sturgeon as SNP leader and Scotland's First Minister.

Sturgeon indicated that that a second referendum on Scottish independence would not likely be held in the near future. Instead until there was clear majority support for independence, the Scottish government would exercise its increased powers within the United Kingdom. Nevertheless, because the majority (62 percent) of Scottish voters favoured remaining within the European Union while the majority in the UK voted to leave the European Union, the Scottish government prepared a draft referendum bill in October 2016 to enable the holding of a second independence referendum. This might be used to try to keep Scotland in the European Union.

In Canada both provincial and the national governments have important powers to make policies that affect our lives. In Scotland, as in Quebec, a significant proportion of the population would like to have their own independent government, while the majority would prefer to have a substantial level of self-government rather than independence. However, a majority in Scotland disagree with the United Kingdom's plan to exit from the European Union.

INTRODUCTION

Virtually every country has more than one government. In addition to the central government, often termed the national government, there are usually a variety of local governments. Many countries also have regional governments or regional administrative bodies. This raises several important questions:

- How do the governments within a country relate to one another?
- Is the central government the supreme authority, or is authority shared between central and regional governments?
- Do different governments within a country co-operate for the common good of the country, or are the relations between governments characterized by conflict and power struggles?

Furthermore, there are not only various governments within a country, but also a variety of international governmental agreements and organizations (such as the North American Free Trade Agreement) that affect the policies of the member states. A particularly important development is that most of the independent countries in Europe have agreed to share some of their sovereign powers with the European Union, which to some extent acts as a **supranational government** (that is, a government above the governments of its member-states).

To understand the relations among governments within a country, a distinction is usually made between unitary systems and federal systems. In a **unitary system**, sovereign authority rests with the central government. In a **federal system**, sovereign authority is divided or shared between the central government and governments representing provinces in Canada and South Africa; states in the United States, India, and Australia; Länder in Germany and Austria; and cantons in Switzerland.

UNITARY SYSTEMS

Many countries have unitary systems of government (see Table 13-1 for examples). The constitutional relationship among different governments is hierarchical, with regional and local governments subordinate to the central government. Even though the central government typically delegates some responsibilities to other levels of government or to regional and local administrative authorities, the central government is generally superior to other governments.

supranational government

Government above the governments of its member-states.

unitary system

A system of governing in which sovereign authority rests with the central government; regional and local governments are subordinate.

federal system

A system of governing in which sovereign authority is divided or shared between the central government and regional governments, with each deriving its authority from the constitution.

BASICALLY UNITARY	BASICALLY FEDERAL
Bangladesh	Argentina
Bolivia	Australia
Chile	Austria
Czech Republic	Belgium
Denmark	Brazil
Finland	Canada
France	Ethiopia
Greece	Germany
Hungary	India
Ireland	Malaysia
Japan	Mexico
Netherlands	Nigeria
New Zealand	Russia
Poland	South Africa
South Korea	Switzerland
Sweden	United States
Turkey	Venezuela

TABLE 13-1
Unitary and Federal Systems

Unitary systems generally provide uniformity across the country in terms of common laws and policies. Regional and local authorities may carry out some of the central government's policies and often have some ability to adopt regulations and develop programs that do not conflict with those of the central government.

Devolution

The governments of some countries with unitary systems have granted some legislative (law-making) powers as well as administrative responsibilities to one or more regional bodies—a process termed **devolution**. For example, France adopted decentralization in 1982 by establishing regional governments with elected assemblies that have significant powers in their region of the country. As discussed in the introductory vignette, the United Kingdom has established regional governments and legislatures for Scotland, Wales, and Northern Ireland, though not for England, which has a large majority of seats in the UK Parliament.[1] These governments are able to legislate on such matters as health, education, law and order, and transportation that have been delegated to them by the British Parliament.

Devolution does not involve sharing sovereignty with regional governments. The Parliament of the United Kingdom could revoke the devolution

devolution

A system of governing in which the central government grants some legislative (law-making) powers as well as administrative responsibilities to one or more regional bodies.

---

[1]A plan to establish a series of regional assemblies in England was scuttled when voters in northeast England defeated a proposal for a regional assembly in 2004.

of powers regardless of the wishes of the regional legislatures. Indeed, the Parliament of the United Kingdom suspended the Parliament of Northern Ireland in 1972 (reinstated in 2007) because of the violent conflicts in that territory. Nevertheless, Scotland has become increasingly self-governing within the United Kingdom, and it is unlikely that the British government would take away the powers that have been granted to the Scottish Parliament.

In some basically unitary countries, certain distinctive regions have extensive autonomy that is, in some cases, constitutionally protected. For example, the former colonies of Hong Kong and Macau are special administrative regions of the People's Republic of China with a degree of autonomy in accordance with a Basic Law providing for "one country, two systems" for at least 50 years. Greenland became self-governing in 2009, although Denmark remains responsible for military protection and foreign policy as well as providing some financial assistance.

Generally, there has been a tendency in recent decades for central governments in unitary systems to devolve powers to regional authorities. In part, devolution has allowed for greater responsiveness to the needs, cultures, and circumstances of different parts of the country and for greater participation of citizens in governing. As well, devolution can be a response to nationalist movements seeking self-government or independence.

FEDERAL SYSTEMS

In a federal system, regional governments—such as provincial governments in Canada and state governments in the United States—are not subordinate to the central (national or federal) government. The federal and provincial

Bitter opponents Protestant Unionist leader Ian Paisley and Catholic Sinn Fein leader Gerry Adams sit together after agreeing on a historic power-sharing agreement that allowed the reopening of the Northern Ireland Assembly in 2007.

Paul Faith/Pool/Reuters

governments each derive their authority from the constitution. Provincial governments cannot be abolished by the central government, nor can the federal government be abolished by provincial governments. Many constitutional changes, particularly those that affect the powers of the two levels of government, require the agreement of both levels of government. Both the central and the regional governments interact directly with those they govern. That is, citizens directly elect representatives to both their provincial legislature and the national Parliament, and the laws and policies of national and provincial governments directly affect the people and territory they govern.

Reasons for Adoption

In some cases, federal systems have been established as a way of creating or holding together large countries. Federal systems have also been adopted to provide regionally based language, ethnic, or cultural groups with a degree of self-government.

The first modern federal system was established in the United States in 1789 when the thirteen states that had fought for their independence from Britain agreed to establish a central government. The founders of the United States believed in the virtues of limited government and wanted the states to continue to be self-governing in many respects (Lyons, Scheb, & Richardson, 1995). As a result, they developed a federal system in which necessary governing powers would be divided between the two levels of government. Subsequently, a variety of other countries (see Table 13-1) have adopted federal systems. At present, about twenty-five countries constituting about 40 percent of the world's population can be considered to have basically federal systems (Watts, 2008).

Canada adopted a federal system because the idea of uniting the British North American colonies that was proposed in the 1860s met with considerable opposition in both Quebec and the Maritimes, where many people feared being dominated by the central government. Maritimers wanted to retain the legislatures they had developed. Quebecers, fearful of the potential consequences of becoming a minority in the new country, wanted to retain control over their own culture.

Division of Powers

Federal systems typically involve a division of powers between national and provincial governments, with the constitution giving some responsibilities to the national government and other responsibilities to provincial governments (see Table 13-2). To varying extents, the constitutions of federal countries also provide for some concurrent policy areas where both levels of government can pass legislation.

It is virtually impossible to divide legislative authority neatly between the national and provincial governments, and thus there is inevitably some overlap

TABLE 13-2 The Constitutional Division of Powers in Canada

SOME AREAS OF LAW-MAKING THAT ARE THE EXCLUSIVE RESPONSIBILITY OF THE PARLIAMENT OF CANADA	SOME AREAS OF LAW-MAKING THAT ARE THE RESPONSIBILITY OF THE PROVINCIAL LEGISLATURES	AREAS IN WHICH BOTH PARLIAMENT AND PROVINCIAL LEGISLATURES HAVE LAW-MAKING AUTHORITY
Regulation of trade and commerce (interprovincial and international)	Management of public lands	Agriculture
Employment insurance	Hospitals	Immigration
Postal service	Municipal institutions	Public pensions
Defence	Education	
Fisheries	Most "local works and undertakings"	
Currency	Laws concerning property rights and the relations among individuals	
Banking	Administration of justice within a province	
Indian affairs	"Generally all Matters of merely local or private nature in the Province"	
Criminal law	Non-renewable natural resources, forest resources, and electrical energy	
Marriage and divorce		
The "peace, order, and good government of Canada"		
Foreign affairs		

in the responsibilities of each level of government. Through their interpretation of constitutional provisions, the courts or other judicial bodies have often played a significant role in determining the powers of each level of government. For example, Parliament's authority by the Constitution Act, 1867 to legislate for the "peace, order, and good government of Canada" has generally been interpreted quite narrowly rather than giving the Canadian government a general power to act in the interests of the country as a whole.

SHARED DECISION MAKING Some federal systems are characterized primarily by shared decision making. For example, in the German federal system, the national Parliament is responsible for legislation in most fields, although this often involves negotiations between the representatives of the national governing coalition parties and the representatives of the Land (state) governments that sit in the upper chamber of Parliament (the Bundesrat). The Land governments are responsible for administering most of the legislation passed by the national Parliament, although much of the actual provision is, in turn, carried out by local governments (Courchene, 2007; Swenden, 2006).

Intergovernmental Relations

In what is often termed **classical or dual federalism**, the federal and provincial or state governments each concern themselves with their own areas of

classical or dual federalism

A version of federalism in which the federal and provincial or state governments each concern themselves with their own areas of constitutional authority without infringing upon the areas of authority of the other level of government.

constitutional authority without infringing upon the areas of authority of the other level of government. Each government is viewed as supreme in its own policy areas. Classical federalism, which in Canada lasted from the mid 1890s until 1939 (with the exception of the period around World War I), involved a low level of interaction and co-operation between the two levels of government.

As the activities of governments expanded, particularly with the development of the modern welfare state, the need to coordinate the policies of the central and provincial governments became more important. Contemporary federal systems typically feature both levels of government involved in many of the same areas of activity, often jointly involved in developing and administering important public services. As well, large amounts of financial resources often need to be transferred from the central to the regional governments to carry out their programs. For example, the Canadian government contributes to the financing of many programs that are the constitutional responsibility of provincial governments, including health care, post-secondary education, and social assistance. Generally, Canadian government transfers to provincial governments for these programs (usually on a per capita basis) are unconditional; that is, the money can be spent as the provincial government sees fit. However, in the case of the Canada Health Transfer, provincial and territorial governments are required to follow the principles of public administration, comprehensiveness, universality, portability, and accessibility in providing basic public health care. In addition, the Canadian government provides unconditional **equalization payments** to the governments of the poorer provinces to assist them in providing services to their residents (as discussed in Box 13-1 Equalization Payments).

equalization payments

Payments made by the federal government to try to ensure that poorer provincial governments are able to provide an equivalent level of services to their populations without resorting to excessive levels of taxation.

CO-OPERATIVE FEDERALISM Modern federal systems usually involve a high degree of interaction between the two levels of government, often described as **co-operative federalism**. In Canada, this interaction primarily involves the executives (prime minister and Cabinet and premiers and their Cabinets) as well as senior officials rather than Parliament and provincial legislatures. However, there are no regularly scheduled meetings between the prime ministers and premiers, Instead meetings are called when desired by the prime minister. Some prime ministers have preferred to meet privately with individual premiers rather than having formal public conferences that can be confrontational.

Despite the substantial level of co-operation between the two levels of government in developing, financing, and administering many programs, this does not necessarily mean that the relationships between the two levels of government are harmonious. There can be serious power struggles if the central government tries to impose national standards on programs run by provincial or state governments. Each level of government typically wants a larger share of total government revenues so that it can provide popular programs and services or reduce taxes. The interests of particular states or provinces may

co-operative federalism

A federal system in which the two levels of government are jointly involved in developing, financing, and administering many government services.

BOX 13-1   Equalization Payments

Most countries, whether unitary or federal, provide some assistance to the poorer regions of their country. In federal systems, particularly those in which provincial governments provide many of the important and costly public services such as health care, education, and social services, the governments of the poorer regions may not be able to afford to provide the same level of services to their citizens without resorting to excessive levels of taxation. Thus, a system of equalization is important for the well-being and unity of the country.

In Canada, a commitment to the principle of equalization to ensure that "provincial governments have sufficient resources to provide reasonably comparable levels of public services at reasonably comparable levels of taxation" was included in the Constitution Act, 1982. The Canadian government provides equalization payments to the governments of the less prosperous provinces to give them the same fiscal capability (ability to raise money through taxes) as an "average" province. No conditions are attached to these payments. In the 2015–2016 fiscal year, equalization payments to six provinces (Prince Edward Island, Nova Scotia, New Brunswick, Quebec, Ontario, and Manitoba) amounted to about $17.3 billion. Changes to the fiscal capacity of provinces (over a three-year period) can result in different provinces being the recipients of equalization. Unlike Australia, however, the needs of different provinces and the costs of providing a standard set of services are not taken into account in the calculation of equalization payments.

In almost all countries, the national government pays for equalization. However, in Germany, the bulk of equalization funding for the poorer Länder (states) comes from the governments of the richer Länder. The United States does not have an equalization system although some federal grants to state governments include larger per capita payments to states with low per capita incomes. Federal grants in the US are generally conditional in that they are earmarked for a specific purpose or require a state adopt a particular policy.

differ from the interests of the country as a whole. The competition between different political parties that may be in control of each level of government can also create tensions in intergovernmental relations.

The Canadian federal system often features considerable conflict between national and provincial governments. A number of provincial governments have resented the "interference" of the national government in areas of provincial authority and have wanted increased powers for provincial governments along with a larger share of tax revenues. Many provincial premiers have found that being strong defenders of provincial interests is useful in winning re-election, even if that means challenging a Canadian government of the same political party. Likewise, some Canadian governments have found it useful to take an adversarial relationship with provincial governments so as to be seen as a strong defender of the national interest. Co-operative federalism is not really all that co-operative!

Attempts to coordinate the activities of the two levels of government typically involve difficult negotiations between the Canadian and provincial governments. Nevertheless, there is considerable collaboration among Canadian governments. For example, collaboration among provincial, territorial, and Canadian ministers of the environment and their officials was formalized with the adoption of the Canada-wide Accord on Environmental Harmonization in 1998.[2]

The American federal system tends to feature less conflict between the national and state governments. With the US Congress, particularly the Senate, playing a major role in representing state interests, there is generally a less competitive and adversarial relationship between the national and state governments (Bakvis & Brown, 2010; Simeon & Radin, 2010).

Regional Representation

In most federal countries, the interests of states or their equivalent are represented in the upper chamber of the national legislature. In some cases (such as the United States, Brazil, and Australia), each state has the same number of representatives in the Senate regardless of population differences. In other countries (including Canada, Germany, and Switzerland), equal representation of each province in the Senate does not exist; however, less populated units receive more representation than they would if representation were in proportion to population. For example, Newfoundland and Labrador has six Senate seats, the same number as British Columbia, while there are in total 24 Senators for the Maritime provinces, the same number as Ontario.

In many countries, the members of the upper chamber are elected by voters in each state. Because of the importance of political parties in most countries, this means that representatives of each state will generally tend to vote in accordance with the national perspective of their party rather than the particular interests of their state. In the United States, however, party discipline is weaker, allowing senators more opportunity to represent the interests of their state. For example, American senators (and representatives) from states with a large coal-mining industry have made it difficult to pass legislation limiting the production, use, and export of coal, the largest source of greenhouse gas emissions. The Canadian Senate (the upper house of Parliament) was intended to represent regional interests. However, its members who hold office until age 75 are appointees of the prime minister.[3] Thus, it has not effectively represented provincial interests. To some extent, provincial interests are represented in the Canadian government through the practice of including persons from all, or almost all, provinces in the Canadian Cabinet. However, the ability of Cabinet ministers to represent provincial interests is limited by Cabinet solidarity and Cabinet secrecy.

---

[2]The Quebec government did not sign the Accord. However, it worked out a co-operation agreement with the Canadian government on environmental assessment.

[3]Prime Minister Justin Trudeau modified the procedure for selecting Senators by appointing an independent committee for each province that recommends a list of persons for vacant Senate seats from which the prime minister can choose. He also removed Liberal Senators from the Liberal caucus, and thus they are not subject to party discipline.

Centralization and Decentralization

There are considerable differences among federal systems in the extent to which governing is decentralized. In some federal systems (such as that of Australia), the national government can be considered the major government, with considerable control over government finances and with the ability to take a leading role in a wide variety of policy areas. The Canadian federal system, on the other hand, can be viewed as quite decentralized, as it features strong provincial governments whose decisions have a major impact on the lives of their residents. Provincial governments in Canada control a larger share of government revenue than in most other federal systems.

The extent to which a federal system is centralized or decentralized is affected not only by the provisions concerning the division of powers in the constitution and how the constitutional division has been interpreted by judicial bodies, but also by various political, social, and economic factors.

Individual countries have moved in the direction of centralization or decentralization depending on the circumstances of a particular time. Despite being established as a decentralized federal system, the central government in the United States has come to play a leading role in American politics, although state governments continue to have important powers. Many Americans look to the central government to solve economic, social, and security problems. The international role of the United States also helps to enhance the power of the central government. At times legislation such as the Homeland Security Act of 2002 and the No Child Left Behind Act, 2001 (increasing central government involvement in public education) has increased federal power, while at other times Republican party control in the Congress has sought to limit the influence of the US government in domestic affairs.

Institute of Intergovernmental Relations
www.queensu.ca/iigr

The Canadian federal system, in contrast to the American system, initially concentrated considerable power in the hands of the Canadian government. However, a number of provincial governments resisted efforts by the federal government to get involved in matters under provincial jurisdiction. Judicial decisions in the late nineteenth and early twentieth centuries contributed to decentralization by interpreting the constitution in ways that limited some of the general powers of the Canadian government. In recent decades, the threat of Quebec independence has helped to move the Canadian federal system further toward decentralization. Other provincial governments have also sought greater powers.

MODERNIZATION AND GLOBALIZATION   In the past, it was often thought that, as countries modernized, they would become more centralized. Regional differences would decline as transportation and communication links tied a country closer together. The increased mobility of people would make ties to a particular place of residence less important. A strong central government would be needed to manage the national economy effectively and to provide a variety of social services to the population. However, in recent

"We can keep dumping in this river for now . . . it will take years until the federal and provincial governments agree on who should legislate a ban."
Tami Thirlwell

decades there has been a tendency in both unitary and federal systems to disperse power from the central government to regional and local governments (Hooghe & Marks, 2001).

Some analysts have suggested that globalization encourages decentralization. as the ability of central government to manage the national economy is reduced (Courchene, 1992). Regions and important cities often develop international and global links. For example, the North American Free Trade Agreement has, to some extent, increased economic links between Canadian provinces and neighbouring American states. However, the impact of globalization appears to be mixed: in some cases, it has encouraged a trend toward centralization, in others toward decentralization, and in still others has had no apparent effect. One set of studies found that the effects of globalization have

BOX 13-2   Asymmetrical Federalism in Canada

In Canada, the question of whether Quebec should be recognized as a distinct society, which could provide a justification for having more areas of legislative authority than the other provincial governments, has been very controversial. For many Canadians outside Quebec, the principle of the equal legal status of the provinces is fundamental. Each provincial government should have the same powers, and Quebec should not have any form of different or special status. More powers for the Quebec government, it is argued, would undermine national unity and lead eventually to Quebec independence. Many French-speaking Quebecers, on the other hand, view the Quebec government as representing one of the major founding peoples of Canada and support

the desire of the Quebec government to lead the social and economic development of the province.

In the words of former Prime Minister Joe Clark, Canada is a "community of communities." From this perspective, "national" communities such as Quebec and First Nations should have the powers needed to protect and develop their cultures (Gagnon, 2010).

Asymmetrical federalism can make a federal system more flexible by responding to the different political cultures and identities of different areas of the country. However, it tends to reduce the uniformity of programs and policies across the country and to increase the complexity of the federal system.

not, at least not yet, been powerful enough to change the balance between centralization and decentralization in various federal systems. Changes in the direction of centralization or decentralization appear to be affected more by domestic factors than by external factors such as globalization (Lazar, Telford, & Watts, 2003).

Asymmetrical Federalism

In some federal systems, such as the United States, there is uniformity among state governments in that each has the same legislative powers. In others, such as India, Malaysia, and Belgium, some regional governments have a greater degree of self-government than other regional governments, a system described as **asymmetrical federalism** (Watts, 2008). In some cases, the constitution establishes different powers for different regional governments (as discussed in Box 13-2 Asymmetrical Federalism in Canada). In other cases, the constitution allows regional governments to opt in or opt out of national programs, thus creating asymmetry when some, but not all, regional governments take advantage of that opportunity.[4]

The Canadian federal system has some asymmetrical elements. The Constitution Act, 1867 provided for a different system of private (civil) law for Quebec. When the Canada Pension Plan was established in 1965, Quebec alone exercised the right of provincial governments to control pensions by setting

asymmetrical federalism

A version of federalism in which some provincial or state governments have a greater degree of self-government than others.

---

[4]Many unitary systems also feature asymmetry in that certain regional governments have more powers than others. Devolution to some regional governments in the United Kingdom is a form of asymmetry.

up the Quebec Pension Plan. Through an agreement between the Quebec and Canadian governments, Quebec established a Parental Insurance Plan in 2006 to provide different maternity, paternity, parental, and adoption benefits than are available through the federal Employment Insurance program in the rest of Canada.

Community Self-Government

A federal system usually involves a division of authority between the central government and a number of regional governments that represent particular geographical areas. However, a federal system can also involve linguistic, ethnic, or religious communities that have a degree of self-government. For example, the federal system in Belgium involves three communities (corresponding to the Dutch-, French-, and German-speaking groups) that are responsible for linguistic and cultural matters, as well as three regional governments. In Canada, the gradual movement toward Aboriginal self-government may eventually result in a "third order" of governments, with substantial authority based on membership in particular Aboriginal nations. Treaty and land claim settlements in recent decades have provided some Aboriginal nations (such as the Nisga'a in B.C. and the Nunatsiavut government in Labrador) with quite extensive constitutionally protected governing authority. However, given their small populations and economic weaknesses, it may be difficult for many First Nations to fully exercise their potential powers.

ASSESSING UNITARY AND FEDERAL SYSTEMS

Benefits of the Unitary System

There are several reasons why a unitary system might be the best way to provide for the common good, such as the following:

- The governing authorities may be more likely to work for the common good of the whole country, as there are no strong subnational governments promoting the particular interests of their region at the expense of the country as a whole.
- National unity may be promoted because greater attention is likely to be given to national issues and problems. In a federal system, provincial governments may find it politically advantageous to highlight and exaggerate regional grievances so that they can be perceived by voters as defenders of their province.
- The central government can be more easily held accountable by citizens as it cannot easily shift blame for problems to other governments.
- People will be more likely to have the same level of government services available in all regions. Uniform standards for education, health care,

and environmental quality are likely to be adopted. Thus, all persons may feel that they are equal citizens of the country.

- Greater efficiencies in governing are possible. With a central government in control, policies can be consistently directed toward certain objectives without different governments pursuing different and possibly inconsistent goals. Costly duplication of services by different governments may be avoided. Total administrative costs will likely be lower if many of the activities of government are centralized.
- People may find it easier to have their professional, technical, and educational qualifications recognized, find employment, and conduct business in different parts of the country.

Benefits of the Federal System

Federal systems also have a variety of positive features:

- Provincial or state governments may be more sensitive to the needs and desires of people in particular areas of the country. The flexibility of a federal system enables provincial governments to adopt policies that reflect the circumstances of their region and the values of the people in that region.
- Less populated and remote areas of the country might be ignored in a unitary system, but can find a voice in their own provincial government.
- Citizens may find it easier to participate in the policy-making process in their own province than in the processes of a distant central government.
- A federal system allows for greater diversity than does a unitary state. Minorities that are concentrated within a particular province can use their provincial government to develop their culture. For example, the French language and culture in Canada has been preserved and developed in part because of the powers of the Quebec government. In this case, a group that is a minority in the country as a whole constitutes a large majority in a particular province and thus is able to achieve a degree of self-government.
- A federal system helps to limit the concentration of power. Consistent with the ideal of liberal democracy, a federal system places constitutional limits on the powers of each government. Competition between central and provincial governments may serve to check the power of each level of government.
- A federal system can allow for experimentation with different policies and approaches by different governments. For example, the government of Saskatchewan initiated the system of free medical care that was subsequently adopted by other provinces and then turned into a nationwide program funded, to some extent, by the Canadian government and administered by provincial governments.

CONFEDERAL SYSTEMS

Independent states generally retain their sovereignty when they interact with each other on the international stage. In some cases, however, sovereign states have agreed to delegate some of their authority to a joint government with limited authority while retaining their sovereignty. In this arrangement, known as a **confederal system**, the institutions of the confederation only have those powers that have been delegated to them by the governments of the sovereign states. Because the member-states retain their sovereignty, they could withdraw from the confederation without necessarily seeking the approval of other member-states. In a pure confederal system, the institutions

The Louise Weiss Building in Strasbourg, France, is the official location of the European Parliament.
3000ad/Shutterstock

of the confederation do not interact with citizens directly. Instead, they rely on the governments of the member-states to implement the agreements (Swenden, 2006). As well, unlike in federal systems, citizens do not directly elect a confederal government; instead, it consists of representatives of the governments of the member-states.

Confederal systems are not very common.[5] Switzerland, until 1848, was a confederation of cantons. A loose German confederation of 39 states existed between 1815 and 1866. The Haudenosaunee (Iroquois Six Nations) also established a basically confederal system. After the War of Independence, the independent American states established a confederal system in 1781. The Congress of the United States (controlled by representatives of state governments) had very limited powers, and there was no head of government or head of state for the country. Congress could declare war and conduct foreign relations, but it did not have the power to levy taxes or prevent states from levying tariffs on goods coming in from other American states. Within a few years, agreement was reached to establish a federal system to create "a more perfect union" of the states.[6] In the contemporary world, Benelux (Belgium, Netherlands, and Luxembourg) and the Caribbean Community (consisting of 15 member-states and 5 associate members) might be considered to be basically confederations.

confederal system

A system of governing in which sovereign states have agreed to delegate some of their authority to a joint government with limited authority while retaining their sovereignty.

---

[5]Although the formation of Canada in 1867 is often described as Confederation, Canada has never had a confederal system. Likewise, Switzerland is officially named the Swiss Confederation, but it has a federal system of governing.

[6]During the American Civil War (1861–65), the southern states that seceded from the union formed the Confederate States (also known as the Confederacy).

THE EUROPEAN UNION

European Union (EU)

An economic and political union of many European countries that have pooled some of their sovereignty.

The **European Union** (EU) is an economic and political union of 28 European countries (as of September 2016) that have pooled some of their sovereignty. Although the EU is not a state, it has features that are typical of confederal and federal systems.

The origins of the EU can be traced to the desire of the United States to see Western European states co-operate and strengthen themselves against the threat represented by the Soviet Union as well as the commitment of some European leaders to avoid the repetition of the wars that had devastated the continent. France, in particular, was concerned about the resurgence of a powerful Germany. In 1951, six countries formed the European Coal and Steel Community to manage these materials that are important for warfare. This was followed in 1957 by the establishment of the **European common market** known as the European Economic Community, which also developed common agricultural and fisheries policies and a regional development program to aid the poorer member-states.

European common market

A stage in the process of economic integration in which the member states remove all duties on trade with one another (as in a free trade area), adopt a common external tariff on trade with other countries (as in a customs union), and allow for the free movement of people from one member state to another.

In 1992, the Treaty on European Union (often referred to as the Maastricht Treaty) proclaimed the goal of "creating an ever closer union among the peoples of Europe" based on "respect for human dignity, liberty, democracy, equality, the rule of law, and human rights." Since 1992, sixteen more countries have joined the EU.[7] This has made the EU, with a population of about 508 million as of 2016 and a gross national product of about US$ 18.5 trillion, the world's largest economy. In 2009, the member-states unanimously ratified the Treaty of Lisbon that increased the power of the European Parliament and the transparency of EU governing institutions.

Europa: Gateway to the European Union
http://europa.eu/index_en.htm

Key Features

A key feature of the EU is the establishment of a single market which means EU regulations provide that persons, goods, services, and capital can move freely throughout the Union[8] while a common customs tariff is placed on goods originating outside the EU. Citizens of the EU have the right to work, set up businesses, and reside in any member country.

---

[7]There are also five official candidate members and three potential members. The often lengthy process of being admitted to the EU involves meeting all EU conditions including having a stable democracy and the rule of law, a free market economy, and bringing national legislation in line with all EU legislation. Controversy has developed about the admission of Turkey (an official candidate) to the EU.

[8]By the Schengen Agreement most of the EU countries (and a few non-EU members) abolished border controls and the need for visas. However, the refugee crisis in 2015 and 2016 resulted in some countries establishing border controls and refusing to accept the quota of refugees determined by the EU.

The official currency of the EU is the euro. As of September 2016, 19 members of the EU had adopted the euro and discontinued the use of their national currency. Other member-states were working toward meeting the requirements to adopt it. However, the UK and Denmark have been exempted from the obligation to adopt the euro, and Swedish voters rejected its use in a referendum. Several countries that are not yet members of the EU (including Montenegro and Kosovo) also use the euro as their currency, and a number of other countries (including various former French colonies) have pegged the value of their own currencies to the euro.

The adoption of the euro, along with the establishment of the European Central Bank to manage monetary policy in the **Eurozone** (countries using the euro), involves requirements that EU member-states implement certain fiscal policies, including a maximum level of government debt and deficit. The euro and the management of the Eurozone have created serious problems for the EU as discussed in Box 13-3 Crisis in the Eurozone.

Eurozone

The countries of the European Union that have adopted the euro as their currency and discontinued the use of their national currencies.

Governing Institutions

Some supporters of the EU hoped that it would evolve into a federal system creating what might be termed the United States of Europe. In the wake of the crisis that began in 2009, however, the atmosphere of public permissive consensus that allowed the growth of the EU in the past (both the deepening of integration and its enlargement to include new members) has turned into considerable skepticism and even outright opposition to a more powerful EU that could become a federal state. The EU is, therefore, likely to retain its current hybrid nature, that is, to continue to be less than a modern, conventional, federal state but much more than an international organization such as the United Nations and the International Monetary Fund or an international agreement such as the North American Free Trade Agreement.

The powers of the EU as specified in the Treaty of Lisbon are classified in terms of three major areas of competence:

1. Exclusive competence of the EU to legislate on such topics as the customs union, competition policy necessary for the internal market, monetary policy for countries using the euro, and the common trading policy.
2. Shared competence allowing member-states to legislate in some policy areas if the EU does not legislate. These areas include the internal market, various aspects of social policy, agriculture and fisheries, environment, consumer protection, transport, energy, freedom, security and justice, and development and humanitarian aid.
3. Support and coordination in areas where member-states have exclusive competence, including health care, education, industry, culture, and tourism.

BOX 13-3   Crisis in the Eurozone

A serious crisis in the Eurozone began in 2009. Governments in Ireland, Spain, Portugal, Italy, Greece, and Cyprus faced huge deficits and debts and sharply declining credit ratings. This resulted in high interest rates for government-backed bonds and serious concerns that these countries might default on their borrowings, as well as concern for the potential failure of major banks. In part, these financial problems were the product of the slowdown of the global economy resulting from the 2007–2008 US financial crisis. The weaker economies of southern European countries were particularly hard hit by the global recession.

The rules of the Eurozone require that the annual government budgetary deficit of each country should not exceed 3 percent of each country's gross domestic product (GDP) and its debt should not exceed 60 percent of its GDP; however, this rule has often been ignored, particularly as countries stimulated their economies in the face of recession and rising unemployment. Government economic mismanagement, corruption, and widespread tax evasion in some countries aggravated the problem. With the adoption of the euro, countries with weak economies could not devalue their currency (for example, by printing more money or equivalent measures) to pay their debts and make their exports more competitive. With the German and north-western European economies functioning reasonably well, the value of the euro (compared to other major currencies) did not drop sufficiently to give a boost to the weaker economies of southern Europe.

To avoid countries defaulting on their debts, losing the ability to finance government, or dropping out of the Eurozone, the European Central Bank and the International Monetary Fund (IMF) provided large amounts of financial assistance. In 2010, the European Financial Stability Facility was created to provide financial assistance to Eurozone countries facing a sovereign (government) debt crisis. Contrary to other financial rescue programs managed by the IMF alone, however, this one did not provide for a restructuring of the sovereign debt owed by the countries in trouble. The reason was to protect German and French banks, which had been the main providers of credit, from debt write-offs lest the crisis spread to the whole Eurozone (Orphanides, 2015). As a consequence, the adoption of strict austerity measures by the countries in debt proved particularly painful, leading to severe cutbacks in government services, soaring unemployment rates reaching over 25 percent (and over 50 percent among young people) in Spain and Greece, and riots and general strikes in several countries. At the same time, in the member states less touched by the crisis and in Germany, the key financial backer of the euro, public discontent with what was perceived to be the subsidization of countries that had mismanaged their economies grew.

The crisis indicated that it is difficult to maintain a common currency given the increasing economic disparities between rich and poor EU countries (Pisani-Ferry, 2013). The imposition of harsh economic policies on the poorer countries by the richer ones (particularly Germany) could undermine the values of equality, solidarity, and co-operation on which the EU was founded (Soros, 2013). For some, the solution lies in moving towards a fuller political union in which there is centralized control over economic policy (Fischer, 2012), but that seems unlikely to happen at least in the near future.

The main decision-making body of the EU, the *Council of the European Union*,[9] is composed of ministers from each of the member-states. Many

---

[9]This should not be confused with the European Council, meetings of the presidents or prime ministers of the member-states to set the general direction and priorities of the EU and select the President of the Council of the European Union.

decisions can be taken by majority vote. However, some important decisions on topics such as taxes (although the EU does not directly tax residents of the EU), social security, foreign policy, and defence policy require unanimous agreement. Governments of the member-states also appoint the *European Commission* that initiates proposals for EU legislation and oversees the implementation of EU policies (either by the EU public service or, more often, by member-states).

The EU is not simply an organization run by the governments of its member-states. Voters in the EU countries every five years directly elect the *European Parliament*. Originally a consultative body, it now generally shares legislative and budgetary powers with the Council of the European Union. It can censure the European Commission and conduct independent inquiries. There is also the *Court of Justice of the European Union* that can make decisions based on EU laws that take precedence over the laws of member-states. Finally, the *European Central Bank* manages the euro and is responsible for the EU's monetary policy.

Despite possessing some important powers, the EU is committed to the basic principle of **subsidiarity**, the idea that decisions and actions should be carried out by the level of governing that is closest to citizens. Thus, the EU should act only on matters that cannot be effectively carried out by national, regional, or local governments.

subsidiarity

The principle that decisions and actions should be carried out, if possible, by the level of governing that is closest to citizens.

Legitimacy

The EU still lacks widespread popular support and legitimacy among the citizens of Europe. National identities continue to be much stronger than a European identity. There is considerable reluctance to transfer more sovereignty from their own country to the EU and resentment when EU laws challenge national laws. The EU is often described as having a "democratic deficit" because its institutions and operations seem remote and inaccessible to ordinary citizens. Voter turnout for European Parliament elections in 2014 was the lowest ever, with only 42.6 percent of eligible voters casting a ballot. Distrust of the EU is particularly evident in Britain where concerns about the influence of Germany and France and the undermining of parliamentary sovereignty is often expressed (see Box 13-4 Brexit: British Exit from the European Union). The rise of nationalistic populist parties in a number of EU countries also presents a serious challenge to the European Union.

Foreign and Defence Policy

On the world scene, the European Community was long considered an "economic giant" but a "political pygmy." In 1969, however, EC member-states set up an informal consultation process to try to coordinate their foreign policies excluding security issues. The Maastricht treaty included a Common Foreign

BOX 13-4 Brexit: British Exit from the European Union

On June 23, 2016, in a United Kingdom referendum, 52% voted to leave the European Union while 48% favoured remaining in the EU. The vote was called by Conservative prime minister David Cameron who was in favour of remaining in the EU. Having received promises that the UK could reduce the amount of benefits for migrant workers in the UK, that Eurozone regulations would not be imposed on the British financial services industry, that the UK would be reimbursed for any British money spent on bailout of debt-ridden Eurozone countries, and that the UK would not be part of an "ever closer union" with other EU members, Cameron thought that the referendum would show that anti-EU sentiment was only held by a minority of British citizens.

However it was not only the right-wing United Kingdom Independence Party (which had obtained 12.6% of the vote in the 2015 British election) that campaigned to leave the EU, but also about one-half of Conservative party MPs. While majorities in Scotland and Northern Ireland voted to remain in the EU, the majority in England voted to leave. Although the majority in London voted to remain the in EU (reflecting its ethnic diversity and the negative implications for its important banking and financial interests), in many other parts of England majorities voted to leave the EU. Only 10 of the 230 Labour MPs favoured "leave," but many of their working-class supporters voted "leave" worried that increased immigration would result in lower wages and could lead to reductions in government social and health programs. More than 70% of young persons (18–24) enjoying the right to live, work, and study in the EU voted "remain," while a large majority of persons over 60 years old voted "leave" with many feeling that increasing immigration undermined English culture and traditions (Helm, 2016).

The immediate result of the referendum was the resignation of prime minister Cameron (with Theresa May, the sole candidate for Conservative leader, becoming prime minister), political challenges to Labour leader Jeremy Corbyn, and a petition signed by more than 4.1 million people for a second referendum (which May rejected) to overturn the surprising "leave" result.

The process of leaving the EU can take up to two years after the UK invokes Article 50 of the Lisbon Treaty. If the UK wants to continue to have full access to the EU's single market, it will likely have to comply with the rules that other non-EU countries, such as Norway, have accepted including free movement of goods, services, capital, and workers in the European Economic Area (Gros, 2016). Even so, there is no guarantee that the legislatures of EU countries would agree to UK's access to the single market.

and Security Policy (CFSP) that not only included "all questions related to the security of the Union" but also looked to "the eventual framing of a common defence policy which might in time lead to a common defence" (The Maastricht Treaty, 1992, p. 8). Nevertheless, the EU could do very little, if anything, to quell the conflicts in Yugoslavia in the 1990s.

In 1998, France and the United Kingdom, which had long disagreed on the issue of giving the EU a military capability, agreed to give the EU "the capacity for autonomous action, backed up by credible military forces, the means to use them and the readiness to do so, in order to respond to international crises." A European Rapid Reaction Force was established to conduct EU-led military operations in response to international crises as well as stabilization and reconstructions missions if NATO as a whole is not involved.[10] The 2007 Lisbon Treaty created a Common Security and Defence Policy (CSDP) along with a High Representative of the Union for Foreign Affairs and Security Policy who heads the European External Action Service (in effect, the EU diplomatic service).

When he was US Secretary of State, Henry Kissinger once lamented that if he wished to call "Europe," he did not know which phone number to call. Today the EU has given itself such a phone number as well as an expeditionary military force, decision-making institutions, command-and-control capabilities, and all the other paraphernalia that are required for mounting military operations abroad. The EU record, however, is still that of a small power. In total the EU has deployed 30 small civilian and military operations, mostly aimed at making a contribution to the reconstruction and stabilization of countries in the Balkans as well as some in the Middle East, Africa (mostly in former French and Belgian colonies), and Asia. Such operations, however, have contributed more to giving the EU a visible international presence than they have to rebuilding international peace and state capacity.

LOCAL GOVERNMENTS

Although attention in political life often focuses on politics and governing at the national and international levels, it is the local communities we live in that are particularly important to our quality of life. The friendliness and safety of our neighbourhoods; the availability of parks, playgrounds, and public places; our ability to commute to work or school within a reasonable period of time; the accessibility of recreational and cultural activities; and the opportunities for involvement in community life are important determinants of our happiness and well-being.

United Cities and Local Governments
www.cities-localgovernments.org

Local (municipal) governments are typically responsible for many of the services that affect the quality of life in our communities, such as water, sewage treatment, garbage disposal, roads, public transportation, fire and police protection, land development and zoning, parks, and recreational facilities.

Local governments in some countries have responsibilities for administering welfare and other social services. Local governments are also involved in promoting the economic development of their communities.

Local governments often only have whatever authority the central government—or, in the case of federal systems, provincial or state governments—decide to delegate to them. Thus, despite their importance, local governments are generally subordinate to higher levels of government. The actual degree of autonomy of local governments may vary over time

---

[10]France and Germany opposed the US-led invasion of Iraq while the UK and a number of other EU countries participated in that war. Germany (unlike the UK and France) did not support military intervention in Libya against the Gaddafi regime in 2011.

depending upon the thinking of the higher levels of government. For example, in Great Britain, which has a long tradition of strong local self-government, both Conservative and Labour governments have moved in recent decades toward greater regulation by the central government. In contrast, France, which has a long tradition of control by the central government, has moved to allow greater autonomy to local and regional communities (Stoker, 2006).

Some countries, including Germany, India, and Switzerland, provide constitutional protection for the powers of local governments. Indeed, Brazil, Venezuela, and South Africa recognize local governments as a distinct "third order of government" alongside the national and state/provincial governments (Watts, 2008, p. 132). In the United States, many state constitutions provide some protection for the powers of municipal governments, with the larger cities often provided with some form of "home rule" that protects their powers and structures from being changed without their consent (Sancton, 2002).

The Canadian Version

Federation of Canadian Municipalities
www.fcm.ca

In Canada, provincial governments have authority over local governments. Indeed, provincial governments can alter the boundaries of municipalities as they see fit. For example, in 1998, the government of Ontario decided to amalgamate the six municipalities of Metropolitan Toronto despite opposition from local political leaders and 73 percent of those who voted in a referendum.

Although local governments in Canada make some important decisions affecting their communities, they generally have to carry out their activities in accordance with the rules and regulations adopted by their provincial government and seek provincial approval for some decisions. Municipal governments often administer some aspects of provincial government policies such as the environment, policing, and building standards. However, many provincial governments have taken over the administration of health, education, and social services that used to be primarily the responsibility of local authorities (Young, 2009).

Local governments in Canada (unlike those in the United States) do not have the authority to raise revenues from income or sales taxes. Instead, they depend largely on property taxes and, to a lesser extent, provincial government grants (which are often tied to conditions or purposes set by the provincial government) and various user fees. Although the Canadian government does not have any direct constitutional authority over local governments, it has contributed to special projects such as the development of public mass transit systems. In 2013, the Canadian government established the Community Improvement Fund (combining the Gas Tax Fund and Goods and Services Tax rebate

The City of Toronto has been seeking greater legislative and financial powers so that it can more effectively carry out its role as a leading force in the national and global economy.
Elenathewise/Fotolia

to municipalities) that is expected to provide more than $32 billion over ten years for community infrastructure including roads, bridges, public transit, water and sewage treatment plants, and recreational facilities. Although this seems like a large amount, it is only a portion of the $171.8 billion that the Federation of Canadian Municipalities (2012) estimated is needed to replace aging municipal infrastructure. More recently, a study found that $141 billion of municipal infrastructure assets are in very poor or poor condition and $247 billion in fair condition. Overall, there has been a decline in the physical condition of local infrastructure since the 1970s and a growing need for better infrastructure (Project Steering Committee, 2016).

As cities have grown, they have sought greater political and financial power. Major cities have become leading forces of national and global economic growth in the knowledge-based economies of the advanced countries. However, they lack sufficient powers and finances to carry out this role effectively (Courchene, 2007). Former Toronto Mayor Mel Lastman suggested that Toronto, which has a greater population than all of the Atlantic provinces plus two of the Prairie provinces combined, should be given provincial government status. Through Ontario's City of Toronto Act, 2006, Canada's largest city has been given broader legislative powers, a greater ability to manage its own financial affairs, and recognition of its right to enter into agreements with the Canadian government.

Complex Governing Authorities

There are often complex sets of governing authorities at the local level. School boards may be responsible for all of the schools in a city, a large region, or even an entire province. Likewise, there may be library boards, police boards, community centre boards, health boards, hospital boards, transit authorities, conservation authorities, parks boards, public utilities commissions, and water and sewage authorities. Such agencies, boards, and commissions are often independent of the municipal government and may service a broader geographical area than a municipal government. This fragmentation of decision-making power at the local level can make it difficult for city politicians and administrators to pursue a coherent set of objectives or respond to the wishes of city residents (Leo & Mulligan, 2006). As well, various local authorities (such as school and hospital boards where they still exist) have been increasingly subject to control by provincial governments rather than by the local community.

Democracy and Local Government

Are local governments more likely than more distant central or provincial governments to foster the participation of citizens? Given the direct effect of local governments on the people they govern, one might expect citizens to be more

CITY	YEAR OF ELECTION	TURNOUT
Toronto	2014	54.7%
Calgary	2013	43.7%
Ottawa	2014	39.9%
Montreal	2013	43.3%
Winnipeg	2014	50.2%
Halifax	2016	31.8%
Saskatoon	2016	40.1%
Vancouver	2014	43.4%
Edmonton	2013	34.5%
Victoria	2014	39.7%

Source: City election websites.

likely to participate at the local level. Indeed, some democratic theorists have argued that democracy at the local level is an essential building block of a democratic political system. It may be easier for citizens at the local level (particularly in smaller cities and towns) to develop connections to other citizens, engage in meaningful discussion, learn about the issues that affect them, and actively participate in political life (McAllister, 2004).

Turnout in local elections, however, is almost always lower than in national or provincial elections. Although this generalization is valid for a variety of countries, the lower level of voting in local elections is particularly evident in Canada (see Table 13-3).

Political parties, which can make voting easier by highlighting issues, presenting different platforms, and mobilizing voters, are not generally involved in local politics in Canada.[11] In some cases, the lack of credible challengers to an incumbent mayor can reduce turnout. Where the Republican and Democratic parties involve themselves in local politics in some American cities, voter turnout is generally higher than in cities that feature non-partisan elections, but still is usually substantially lower than in national and state elections. In Western Europe, higher voter turnout in local elections may reflect the ability of political parties to mobilize voters in local elections on the basis of national political issues and long-standing ideological and social divisions. In these countries there is often not a sharp distinction between national and local politics (Milner, 1997; Morlan, 1984).

The low level of participation in some municipal elections in Canada does not necessarily mean that citizens are uninterested in the decisions that affect their local community. Many cities have active community and neighbourhood organizations involved in improving the quality of life in the city. Issue-oriented

---

[11]Civic parties exist in some cities, including Montreal and Vancouver, and at times the NDP has involved itself in local politics in some cities.

groups and civic movements have attracted considerable support for efforts such as challenging freeway construction that would go through quiet neighbourhoods, preserving the character of neighbourhoods that are threatened by development projects, protecting green spaces, encouraging the development of public transit and bicycle-friendly policies, and promoting the provision of low-cost housing for the poor.

✔• SUMMARY AND CONCLUSION

Almost all countries have multiple governments. The existence of multiple governments adds complexity to political life and makes an understanding of the relationships among governments essential for an understanding of governing processes.

Unitary systems feature a hierarchical relationship among governments, with the central government superior to other governments. Nevertheless, some distinctive parts of the country may be granted a significant level of autonomy, and local or regional authorities may have responsibility for delivering many government services.

Federal systems feature a substantial level of self-government for provinces or their equivalent and, generally, a shared involvement in a number of policy areas between central and provincial governments. Each citizen is directly affected by both national and provincial governments, and citizens elect both national and provincial legislative bodies.

Confederal systems result when sovereign states join together to establish a central governing agency with limited powers delegated from the member-states. The European Union features a unique combination of some confederal and federal features in its evolving system of governing. However it faces serious economic and political challenges.

Although local governments deliver a variety of important services to their communities, they are often restricted in their capabilities because of controls by "higher" levels of government and limited financial resources. Despite the development of many groups seeking to improve the quality of life in their community, local politics (like national politics) often falls short of the democratic ideal of an active, engaged citizenry.

The existence of multiple governments has important political implications. Coordination and co-operation among different governments within a country are important requirements for effective governing. However, power struggles between national and provincial governments, as well as their different interests and values, can make co-operation difficult to achieve, as is often evident in the Canadian federal system. Ensuring that multiple governments work toward the common good and are responsive and accountable to those they govern often presents difficult challenges.

✔• KEY TERMS

Asymmetrical federalism 312
Classical or dual federalism 306
Confederal system 315
Co-operative federalism 307
Devolution 303

Equalization payments 307
European common market 316
European Union (EU) 316
Eurozone 317
Federal system 302

Subsidiarity 319
Supranational government 302
Unitary system 302

DISCUSSION QUESTIONS

1. Do the advantages of a federal system outweigh its disadvantages in Canada? Should other countries such as the United Kingdom adopt a federal system?

2. Why has the Canadian federal system tended to become more decentralized?

3. Should Canada move further in the direction of asymmetrical federalism?

4. Would it be desirable to create a North American Union similar to the European Union?

5. Do you think that local governments should have greater authority?

FURTHER READING

Bakvis, H., & Skogstad, G. (Eds.). (2012). *Canadian federalism: Performance, effectiveness, and legitimacy* (3rd ed.). Don Mills, ON: Oxford University Press.

Bickerton, C. (2016). *The European Union: A Citizen's Guide.* London, UK: Pelican

Cini, M., & Borragan, N.P.-S. (Eds.). (2016). *European Union politics* (5th ed.). Oxford: Oxford University Press.

Deacon, R. (2012). *Devolution in the United Kingdom* (2nd ed.). Edinburgh: Edinburgh University Press.

Gagnon, A.-G. (2013). *The case for multinational federalism: Beyond the all-encompassing nation* (2nd ed.). London and New York: Routledge.

Inwood, G. J. (2013). *Understanding Canadian federalism: An introduction to theory and practice.* Toronto: Pearson Canada.

Sancton, A. (2014). *Canadian local government: An urban perspective.* Don Mills, ON: Oxford University Press.

Tindal, C.R., *et. al.* (2012). *Local government in Canada* (8th ed.). Toronto: Nelson Canada.

Watts, R.L. (2008). *Comparing federal systems* (3rd ed.). Montreal: McGill–Queen's University Press.

14 Parliamentary Systems

On April 27, 2010, the Speaker of Canada's House of Commons, Peter Milliken, ruled that Stephen Harper's Conservative government could be considered to be in contempt of Parliament for refusing to let members of Parliament see documents related to the torture of Afghan detainees that had been handed over to Afghanistan's National Directorate of Security by Canadian military police.   Blair Gable/Reuters

After reading this chapter, you should be able to:

1. outline the basic characteristics of parliamentary systems
2. define the meaning of majority, minority, and coalition governments
3. describe how the prime minister and Cabinet are chosen in Canada
4. discuss whether there is too great a concentration of power in the Canadian governing system
5. examine the organization and functioning of the Canadian Parliament

On April 27, 2010, the Speaker of the Canadian House of Commons, Peter Milliken, ruled that Stephen Harper's Conservative government could be considered to be in contempt of Parliament for refusing to let members of Parliament see documents related to the torture of Afghan detainees who had been handed over to Afghanistan's National Directorate of Security by Canadian military police.

Richard Colvin, a senior Canadian diplomat in Afghanistan, repeatedly sent memos warning senior government and military officials that the torture of prisoners was a common practice. However, his warnings were ignored. In 2007, the Canadian Military Police Complaints Commission started an investigation of the issue. The federal government tried unsuccessfully to prevent the investigation and subsequent hearings and to stop Colvin from testifying. Although military officials denied Colvin's allegations, the Commission had difficulty determining the truth since government censors had redacted (blacked out) most of Colvin's memos and he was forbidden to testify about the redacted material.

In 2009, a special House of Commons committee reported that the government had breached parliamentary privileges by refusing the committee's request for documents. The House of Commons passed a motion ordering the government to release the documents. Although the government tabled thousands of pages of documents, these were heavily redacted and did not comply with the House of Commons order.

In his ruling, Milliken (2010) upheld the centuries-old fundamental right of Parliament to hold the government to account for its actions. However, he gave time for the government to reach a compromise in which the relevant documents would be provided without compromising national security.

Nearly a year later, a majority of members of the House of Commons supported a motion citing the Conservative government's contempt of Parliament for refusing to reveal the true costs of various government budget items. This was the first time in the history of the Commonwealth that a government had been found to be in contempt of Parliament. Nevertheless, in the election that followed, the Conservative government was returned to power with a majority of seats in the House based on 39.6 percent of the votes cast.

In a parliamentary system, the government (the prime minister and Cabinet) is responsible to Parliament, particularly to the elected House of Commons whose support it needs to remain in office. However the ability of the House of Commons to hold the government accountable for its actions can be limited by government secrecy. While some degree of secrecy is necessary in certain situations, a democratic government should be as transparent as possible so that government is accountable to the House of Commons and to the people.

THE DEVELOPMENT OF THE PARLIAMENTARY SYSTEM

The development of the **parliamentary system** is associated with the political history of the United Kingdom. In 1215, English nobles upset with the king's tax increases (which were needed to finance a war with France) forced King John I to sign the Magna Carta. Among its provisions was one that established a council of barons separate from the king and his advisers to approve taxes. It also began the establishment of the rule of law, rather than arbitrary rule by the king, by enabling the courts to order (through a writ of *habeas corpus*) that an imprisoned person be brought before a court for trial and punishment. As the monarch's need for financing continued to increase, knights and local leaders representing the "commons" were invited to what became known as Parliament, which separated into two houses: the House of Lords and the House of Commons. Over time, the convention developed that bills for taxation had to originate in the Commons and that money would only be supplied to the monarch after grievances had been dealt with. After Parliament forced King James II from the throne in the Glorious Revolution, Parliament passed the Bill of Rights (1689), which guaranteed freedom of speech in Parliament, required Parliament's consent for the levying of taxes, and stipulated that the monarch could not make or suspend laws without Parliament's approval. In accepting the Bill of Rights, the new king and queen, William and Mary, swore an oath to govern in accordance with the statutes, laws, and customs of Parliament.

Out of the body of royal officials, known as the Privy Council, that advised the king evolved an inner committee known as the Cabinet. The practice developed that the King's ministers who were responsible for various executive offices would be members of Parliament. The position of prime minister as the chief minister became recognized toward the middle of the eighteenth century. Subsequently, the Cabinet strengthened its position in relation to both the monarch and Parliament by viewing itself as a collective body taking a united stance (Punnett, 1971). A majority of reformers committed to a particular program was elected to the House of Commons in 1831 and the Reform Act (1832) reduced the ability of the monarch to manipulate elections. This led to the development of the principle of **responsible government** (Birch, 1980). This means that the political executive (the prime minister and Cabinet) is accountable to Parliament for its actions and must retain the support of the elected members of the House of Commons to remain in office. Parliament thus not only became the supreme law-making body, but also could make or unmake governments. With the development in the United Kingdom of two disciplined (unified) political parties (Conservatives and Liberals, with Labour later replacing the Liberals as a major party), voters could hold the government accountable by supporting or defeating the governing party in an election. As well, the development of cohesive parties made the House of Commons an

parliamentary system

A system of governing in which there is a close interrelationship between the political executive (prime minister and Cabinet) and Parliament (the legislative or law-making body). The executive is generally composed of members of the House of Commons (the elected parliamentary body) and must maintain the support of the House of Commons.

responsible government

A governing system in which the political executive (the prime minister and Cabinet) is accountable to Parliament for its actions and must retain the support of the elected members of Parliament to remain in office.

The Palace of Westminster, where the Parliament of the United Kingdom meets.

Markus Gann/Shutterstock

Westminster system

A governing system that developed in Britain, featuring single party majority rule, executive dominance of Parliament, and an adversarial relationship between the governing party and the opposition.

The UK Parliament: About Parliament
www.parliament.uk/about/how/

adversarial body where the governing party defended its actions and Her Majesty's Loyal Opposition held the government accountable.

The British parliamentary system, often referred to as the **Westminster system** (because the UK Parliament meets in Westminster Palace), is sometimes characterized as a majoritarian system in which the governing party, if it has a majority of seats in Parliament, is able to ensure that its legislative program will be adopted and implemented. However, a governing party's majority in the House of Commons does not usually reflect the votes of the majority of the electorate because the single member plurality electoral system often converts a minority of votes for one party into a majority of seats. For its supporters, the traditional Westminster system provides efficient and stable government. Due to its simplicity, voters can easily choose to elect or defeat the governing party. However, by heavily concentrating power in the hands of the prime minister and Cabinet, Parliament as a whole is of limited significance in a majority government situation. This may result in different views and interests being ignored.

The Westminster system was exported to other parts of the British Empire. The parliamentary systems of many former British colonies, including Canada, Australia, India, and a number of Caribbean countries, are modelled on the Westminster system (with various modifications). The majority of European countries also have a parliamentary system as do Japan, Turkey, and Israel. Some have a monarch as the formal head of state, while others are republics with a president (or equivalent) having limited powers.

Some countries have adopted more consensus-based, power-sharing parliamentary systems than the Westminster system. In part, this is a result of adopting proportional representation electoral systems that typically lead to coalition governments with a greater balance in power between the executive and the elected legislative body. Arend Lijphart (2012) found that consensus-based democracies tended to be superior on a variety of criteria, including the quality of democracy, provision of welfare, environmental protection, the representation of women, and assistance to poorer countries.

In this chapter, we focus on the Westminster system, particularly as it applies to Canada. Among the modifications of the Westminster system that make the governing of Canada different than that of the United Kingdom are the federal system, the Charter of Rights and Freedoms, and the power of judicial review exercised by the courts.

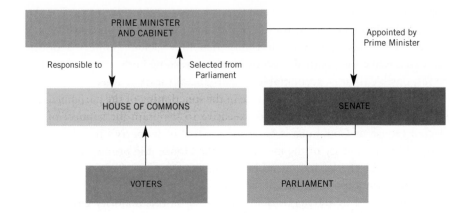

EXECUTIVE–LEGISLATIVE RELATIONS

A basic feature of parliamentary systems is the close interrelationship of Parliament (the legislative body) and the political executive (the prime minister and Cabinet). The members of the political executive are themselves members of Parliament, usually from the House of Commons (see Figure 14-1).

The authority of the government is based on maintaining the confidence of the majority of elected members of Parliament. If the majority passes a non-confidence vote or if the government is defeated on a major legislative proposal (such as the budget) the government is expected to resign. This will normally result in an election, although the head of state (governor-general in Canada) could ask another party leader to try to form a government.[1] Although Canada adopted a fixed election date law, the governor general called an early election requested by the prime minister in 2008.

In the United Kingdom, the Fixed Term Parliamentary Act, 2011 only allows an early election in two circumstances: (1) the government is defeated on an explicit vote of non-confidence and a new government cannot be formed that has the confidence of the House or (2) at least two-thirds of MPs agree to an early election. This reduces the power of the prime minister and Cabinet as ordinary members of the governing party can vote against government legislation knowing that they will not face an early election (Norton, 2016)

Although Parliament has to approve new laws (and changes to existing laws), it is the political executive (prime minister and Cabinet) that proposes almost all of the laws that are passed by Parliament. The political executive also presents the government's spending and taxing plans for Parliament's

---

[1]In several countries (including Germany, Spain, Hungary, Poland, Belgium, and Israel), a non-confidence motion presented by a member of an opposition party can be passed only if a majority is able to agree on another person to be prime minister. This provision, termed a "constructive vote of confidence," makes it less likely that the government will be forced out of office.

approval. As well, the political executive is responsible for overseeing the implementation and administration of the laws passed by Parliament and for making day-to-day governing decisions (that may include military actions). However, while the political executive is the governing body, it is expected to be responsible (that is, accountable) to Parliament for its actions.

Political parties play a crucial role in the functioning of the parliamentary system. The ability of the political executive to maintain the support of the elected House of Commons is based on control of its party's members. If a party elects a majority of the members of the House, the prime minister and Cabinet will be the leading members of the governing party and are almost certain to maintain the support of the House and have most of their legislative initiatives passed by the majority in the House. In this **majority government** situation, the prime minister and Cabinet dominate the House of Commons.

If no single party has elected its members to a majority of seats in the House of Commons, one party may, nevertheless, form a **minority government**. As with a majority government, the prime minister chooses the Cabinet from among his or her party's members of Parliament. To pass legislation, gain approval for government's spending and taxing plans, and avoid being defeated on a vote of non-confidence, the prime minister and Cabinet need to gain the support of one or more other parties (unless one or more opposition parties decide to abstain from voting). This support may be negotiated on an issue-by-issue basis or be part of a general formal or informal agreement.

Alternatively, if no one party has a majority of seats, a **coalition government** consisting of two or more political parties may be formed (see Box 14-1 Coalition Governments). In this situation, there will be negotiations among the coalition partners to determine which Cabinet positions each party will receive and the policies the government will pursue. In some cases, coalitions among parties will be formed before the election such that the winning coalition will form the government. In other cases, the negotiations among parties seeking to form a coalition government occur after the results of an election are known.[2] Shifts in the parties joining or leaving the coalition may also occur without an election being held.

Typically, coalition governments involve parties that are relatively close to each other in ideological terms. In a number of countries, coalition governments are stable such that the coalition remains in office for its full term and is able to govern effectively. This has been the experience of Germany, which has been governed by coalitions since 1949. In some countries, however, coalition governments have been undermined by disputes among the coalition partners.

majority government

The government formed when the prime minister's party has a majority of the members of the House of Commons; thus, a single party forms the government.

minority government

A single party governs, but that party does not have a majority of the members in the House of Commons. Thus, a minority government needs to gain the support of one or more other parties to pass legislation and to stay in office.

coalition government

A government in which two or more political parties jointly govern, sharing the Cabinet positions.

---

[2]In 2013, the second-place German Social Democratic party held a referendum of its members to decide whether to join a coalition government with the Christian Democratic party that won the most seats.

BOX 14-1 Coalition Governments

Coalition governments are the norm in many European parliamentary systems because proportional representation makes majority government very unlikely. However, coalition governments have not been common in many of the Commonwealth countries that have a single member plurality electoral system. The United Kingdom had coalition governments during the exceptional circumstances of the two world wars and the Great Depression.

When the May 2010 UK election resulted in a "hung Parliament" in which no party held a majority of the 650 seats in the House of Commons, the Liberal Democratic party, which had won 57 seats, negotiated with the Conservative party (306 seats) and the Labour party (258 seats) to form a coalition government. After five days, a deal was struck between the Conservatives and Liberal Democrats. In addition to agreeing on a number of policy positions, the Liberal Democrats were appointed to six Cabinet positions (including the party's leader, Nick Clegg, as deputy prime minister) in Conservative Prime Minister David Cameron's government. In the next election (2015) the Conservatives won a slight majority of seats (based on 36.8 percent of the vote) and formed the government without the Liberal Democrats who won only 8 seats.

Although Canada has had 13 minority governments since 1921, its only coalition government was formed during World War I. Prime ministers have preferred minority

government to coalition government in the hope that their party can win a majority in a subsequent election. After the 2008 Canadian election, Stephen Harper formed his second Conservative minority government. Shortly afterward, the government presented a budget update that angered the three opposition parties. Not only did the update fail to stimulate the economy as the world was entering a severe recession, but it also proposed to eliminate the public subsidy provided to political parties. With the government headed for defeat on a motion of non-confidence, the Liberal and New Democratic parties signed an agreement to form a coalition government in which they would share Cabinet positions. The Bloc Québécois promised to support the coalition for 18 months.

Before the non-confidence motion could be voted on, Harper requested that Governor General Michaëlle Jean prorogue Parliament, thereby ending the session without a vote. Jean agreed to the request, and the Conservatives mounted a successful public campaign criticizing the proposed coalition as "undemocratic" and as giving power to "separatists and socialists." Liberal leader Stéphane Dion resigned and Michael Ignatieff was selected as interim Liberal leader. The Liberals subsequently decided not to bring down the government, and the Harper government brought in a budget that increased government spending and temporarily retained the subsidy for political parties.

Former British Conservative prime minister David Cameron speaks about the midterm review of the coalition government on January 7, 2013. He is accompanied by deputy prime minister Nick Clegg, leader of the Liberal Democrats that partnered with the Conservatives in the coalition government.
FACUNDO ARRIZABALAGA/EPA/Newscom

Should Canada Have Its Own Head of State?

In Canada, the British monarch is the official head of state in her role as Queen of Canada. This symbolizes Canada's historic ties to Britain and continuing membership in the Commonwealth, of which the Queen is the ceremonial head.

For some Canadians, the use of a foreign monarch as the formal head of state is an outdated relic of the country's colonial past. There was a sizable protest when the Queen visited Quebec in 1964; subsequent royal visits to Quebec generally have been greeted with indifference. In 2002, Foreign Affairs Minister John Manley suggested that Canada should have an elected head of state. However, the issue was quickly dropped because it was considered too controversial. A poll conducted in 2016 found that 64 percent of Canadians support Queen Elizabeth II as Canada's monarch. However only 46 percent said that they would support her heir, Prince Charles, as Canada's future monarch (Thompson, 2016).

A number of Commonwealth countries including India, Pakistan, and many African countries no longer have the Queen as head of state. Despite opinion polls indicating that a majority of Australians favour ending the monarchy, 55 percent of Australians in a 1999 referendum rejected a constitutional proposal that would have replaced the Queen with a president chosen by Parliament. Some rejected the proposal because they did not favour the method proposed for selecting a president.

Italy, for example, was characterized by political instability, with 61 coalition governments formed after 1945 (although until 1984 all were dominated by the Christian Democratic Party). The establishment of two broad coalitions of parties, one leaning left and the other leaning right, brought greater stability to Italian politics from 1996 until 2012.

The Head of State

In addition to the close interrelationship of the political executive and Parliament, parliamentary systems also differ from presidential systems in having different individuals as head of state and head of government. The **head of state** is an important but largely ceremonial position in a parliamentary system. The head of state carries out a variety of official functions but is expected to be "above" politics and thus is not usually involved in making governing decisions. Having a non-partisan head of state can provide a symbol of unity for a country (see Box 14-2 Should Canada Have Its Own Head of State?). The head of state will not be tarnished by government incompetence or scandal because the head of state is not involved in politics and governing. This provides the legitimacy needed for the head of state to act, if necessary, in some unusual circumstances, to ensure that a legitimate government is in place, or to dismiss a government that is acting unconstitutionally.

In some countries with parliamentary systems, the head of state is a president with a limited term of office. The president may be elected directly by the

head of state

In a parliamentary system, the head of state is an important but largely ceremonial position, but has the responsibility to ensure that a legitimate government is in place.

Commonwealth Parliamentary Association
www.cpahq.org

country's citizens (as, for example, in Austria, Ireland, and Israel) or selected by a vote of members of the national Parliament along with, in some cases, regional representatives (as, for example, in Germany, Greece, and Italy). In a number of countries with parliamentary systems (including the United Kingdom, Sweden, Denmark, Spain, and the Netherlands), a hereditary monarch is the head of state. The powers of the monarch in these democratic countries have been greatly restricted by formal constitutional provisions or "unwritten" constitutional conventions.

The Canadian Governor General

Canadian governments act in the name of the Crown. However, the duties and responsibilities of the monarch have been delegated to the **governor general** at the national level and to **lieutenant-governors** at the provincial level. The governor general and lieutenant-governors are appointed by the monarch on the recommendation of the Canadian prime minister normally for five years (which is sometimes extended for a year or two).

The governor general has the important responsibility of ensuring that a government (prime minister and Cabinet) is in place at all times. Usually, the choice of prime minister is merely a formality. The governor general is expected to choose the leader of the party that has the support of the House of Commons. In the event of the death, retirement, or resignation of the prime minister, the governing political party will recommend a replacement. The governor general must approve all legislation, many appointments, and various executive decisions, such as the ratification of treaties and a declaration of war. However, in these matters, the governor general always acts on the advice of the prime minister and Cabinet (or, for certain matters, the prime minister alone).

The governor general is not entirely powerless. There are some **prerogative powers** (also known as reserve powers)—powers of the monarch that have not been taken away by Parliament—where the governor general in exceptional circumstances can use personal discretion in deciding how to act. These powers include the appointment and dismissal of the prime minister and the **dissolution** of Parliament (termination followed by an election) or **prorogation** of Parliament (ending of a Parliamentary session).[3] If the prime minister violated the constitution or lacked the support of the House of Commons, the governor general could dismiss the prime minister.

The use of the prerogative powers can involve the governor general in political controversies. For example, there was considerable controversy in 2009 when prime minister Harper requested that the governor general prorogue Parliament to give the government time to "recalibrate" its policies.

governor general

The person who carries out the duties and responsibilities of the monarch at the national level in Canada.

lieutenant-governor

The person who carries out the duties and responsibilities of the monarch at the provincial level in Canada.

prerogative powers

Powers of the monarch that have not been taken away by Parliament. These are also known as reserve powers.

dissolution

The termination of Parliament followed by the holding of an election for the House of Commons.

prorogation

The suspension of Parliament and its committees by the governor general at the request of the prime minister. Prorogation (unlike an adjournment) ends a session of Parliament such that the work of committees is ended and bills that have not been passed have to be reintroduced unless Parliament in the next session agrees otherwise.

---

[3]Lieutenant-governors have essentially the same powers and responsibilities at the provincial level.

The opposition parties argued it was an attempt to muzzle the Commons committee that was investigating the detainee transfer issue discussed in the opening vignette.

The Prime Minister and Cabinet

head of government

The person who heads the executive side of government and is usually responsible for choosing the Cabinet. In Canada, the prime minister is the head of the Canadian government, while the heads of provincial governments are known as premiers (in Quebec, *premier ministre*).

In Canada and many Commonwealth countries, the positions and powers of the prime minister and Cabinet are not specified in the formal constitution, but instead are established by convention. The prime minister, who acts as the **head of government**, is normally the leader of the political party that is able to maintain the confidence of the House of Commons either by itself or with the support of other political parties. The prime minister is almost always a member of the House of Commons representing a particular electoral district and thus not directly elected by voters in the country as a whole. Usually, but not always, the prime minister's party elected the most representatives to the House of Commons. After an election, a prime minister usually will resign if his or her party did not win the most seats. The governor general will then choose as prime minister the party leader that is most likely to have the support of a majority of members in the House of Commons.[4] However, if a prime minister thinks his or her party can gain sufficient support from other parties, the prime minister and Cabinet can remain in office until defeated in the House of Commons. In some countries such as Germany, the chancellor (prime minister) is elected by the members of the Bundestag (the equivalent of the Canadian House of Commons). In countries where coalition governments are common, the head of state may hold discussions with various party leaders to determine who has sufficient support to head the government. Regardless of the precise procedure used for selecting the head of government in different countries, the prime minister is usually the leader of one of the largest parties.

Cabinet

The members of the political executive. The Cabinet in a parliamentary system is led by the prime minister, with many or most Cabinet ministers having the responsibility of heading a government department.

executive dominance

A parliamentary system that places considerable power in the hands of the prime minister and Cabinet through their ability to control the House of Commons, particularly in a majority government situation.

The prime minister is responsible for recommending the appointment (and dismissal) of the members of the **Cabinet** as well as determining what Cabinet positions they will hold. In Canada, and many other countries, the selection of Cabinet ministers is a prime ministerial responsibility. Together, the prime minister and Cabinet ministers are the political executive with responsibility for governing. Although the prime minister and Cabinet are expected to be responsible and accountable to Parliament for their actions, in reality the prime minister and Cabinet in Canada and other countries that basically follow the Westminster model normally control the dominant party in the House of Commons. Thus, the parliamentary system is often described as a system of **executive dominance**, as it places considerable power in the hands of the prime minister and Cabinet, particularly in a majority government situation.

---

[4]For example, the Progressive Conservative party won the most seats but less than a majority of seats in the 1985 Ontario election. After the NDP agreed to support a Liberal government (although not establishing a formal coalition), the Liberal leader was appointed premier.

The Prime Minister and Cabinet in Canada

The prime minister is the leading figure within the Canadian Cabinet. The prime minister determines who will be appointed to the Cabinet and what their responsibilities will be. At any time, the prime minister may change the responsibilities of any Cabinet minister or demand a Cabinet minister's resignation. The prime minister is also responsible for organizing the Cabinet including establishing Cabinet committees and choosing their members. The prime minister chairs Cabinet meetings, sets their agenda, and (since votes are not held in the Cabinet) determines the consensus of the Cabinet. Although modern prime ministers do not run a particular government department, they normally play a leading role in foreign affairs and military actions, federal–provincial relations, and constitutional negotiations with provincial governments. In addition the prime minister takes a leading role in defending the government in the House of Commons. The mass media and the public pay far more attention to the prime minister than to any other political figure. Prime ministers make a substantial number of prestigious appointments and so can reward loyal supporters.

A prime minister cannot govern alone. Nevertheless, prime ministers have tended to become less dependent upon their Cabinets for advice. Instead, they provide central direction or, at least, central coordination to the government. To help achieve this, the size, importance, and activities of the offices that provide advice and assistance directly to the prime minister have increased substantially in recent decades. The **Privy Council Office (PCO)**, an administrative structure that is directly responsible to the prime minister, has a central role in organizing the Cabinet and coordinating and directing the activities of government and the public service. It is also very important in providing policy advice to the prime minister. The **Prime Minister's Office (PMO)**, consisting mainly of loyal supporters of the prime minister, not only provides secretarial support such as scheduling appointments and handling correspondence, but also is involved in maintaining the prime minister's power and popularity by providing partisan advice, writing speeches, managing the media, making recommendations concerning patronage appointments, and trying to maintain party unity and loyalty to its leader. Together, the PCO and PMO provide the prime minister with a dedicated source of advice and a capability to direct and coordinate the activities of government. The concentration of power has led some analysts to characterize the governing system in Canada (and various other parliamentary systems such as the United Kingdom and Australia) as **prime ministerial government**, as discussed in Box 14-3 Prime Ministerial Government.

Although some Canadian prime ministers (and premiers) have dominated their Cabinets, it should be kept in mind that some Cabinet ministers (such as the Finance minister) are also very important in government policy making because of the departments they control and their popularity within the party or the country. The power of the Canadian prime minister is also limited by

Privy Council Office (PCO)

An administrative structure that is directly responsible to the Canadian prime minister, has a central role in organizing the Cabinet and coordinating and directing the activities of government, and provides policy advice to the prime minister.

Prime Minister's Office (PMO)

The office that provides support and political advice to the prime minister.

prime ministerial government

The view that the prime minister has become the dominant member of the political executive, rather than "first among equals" in the Cabinet.

BOX 14-3 Prime Ministerial Government

Has Canada has developed a prime ministerial government? Have prime ministers become the equivalent of American presidents in the sense that they are the chief executive, rather than the traditional view that they are "first among equals" in the Cabinet?

In his study of governing in Canada, Donald Savoie (1999, pp. 7, 362) concluded that

> power has shifted to the prime minister and his senior advisers at both the political and public service levels and away from Cabinet and Cabinet Committees. . . . Cabinet has now joined Parliament as an institution being bypassed. . . . The Canadian prime minister has little in the way of institutional check, at least inside government, to inhibit his ability to have his way.

Savoie (2008, p. 16) has also described the governments of both Canada and the United Kingdom as "court governments" in which "effective political power now rests with the prime minister and a small group of carefully selected courtiers."

Others, however, argue that the idea that there has been an almost dictatorial concentration of power in the hands of the prime minister and his senior advisers is a myth. According to Eddie Goldenberg, Prime Minister Jean Chrétien's chief of staff, the prime minister sets the overall tone and priorities of government and makes some critical decisions, but typically leaves the implementation of policy priorities to individual Cabinet ministers and their staff (Goldenberg, 2006). Some prime ministers are more likely to involve themselves as much as possible in all aspects of governing, while others focus on a few key priorities.

Having a powerful prime minister is nothing new in Canadian politics. Sir John A. Macdonald and William Lyon Mackenzie King were more than "first among equals" in their Cabinets, although they had to work with a few important regional "strongmen." However, particularly with the influence of the media, there has been a "presidentialization" of government with the prime minister (and often spouse and children) becoming highly visible public figures. This has certainly been the case with Justin Trudeau and his family who attract national and international attention. No longer can prime ministers walk the streets of Ottawa alone at night, as did Mackenzie King (prime minister from 1921 to 1930 and 1935 to 1948), without being recognized and subjected to intense media scrutiny of their personal life.

the nature of the federal system. Prime ministers often face serious challenges in their relationships with provincial governments and have to compromise to achieve objectives that require the involvement of provincial governments.

The concentration of power in the hands of the prime minister and an inner circle is not unique to Canada. The United Kingdom and other countries that follow the Westminster model have also tended to move from Cabinet government to prime ministerial government (Weller, 1985). Margaret Thatcher, British prime minister from 1979 to 1990, governed with single-minded determination and changed the direction of British politics, overriding opposition within Cabinet and her party's caucus. Eventually, however, she failed to maintain sufficient support of her caucus and resigned when it appeared that she might not win in a leadership contest involving Conservative MPs. Tony Blair, British prime minister from 1997 to 2007, also was a dominant figure within the British government, often ignoring the views of Cabinet and caucus and adopting a presidential style. However, Gordon Brown, Chancellor of the Exchequer (finance minister), had considerable power and independence in determining the economic policies of the government. Brown was able to frustrate Blair's plans to have Britain adopt the euro (the European Union's currency) and was a vocal critic of Blair within the Cabinet (Rhodes, Wanner, & Weller, 2009). Conservative prime minister David Cameron faced opposition from several cabinet ministers (and more than two-fifths of his party's MPs) to his call for the UK to remain in the European Union in a June 2016 referendum. He resigned immediately after the results of the referendum (that the "remain" side lost in a close vote) were announced.

The Cabinet

There are important political considerations that affect the prime minister's choice of Cabinet ministers. Canadian prime ministers devote considerable attention to ensuring that their Cabinets are geographically representative. There is almost always at least one Cabinet minister from each province,[5] with more Cabinet ministers from the provinces with greater populations. The proportion of French Canadians in the Cabinet has tended to be in proportion to their share of Canada's population. There is also an expectation that French Canadians outside Quebec and English-speaking Quebecers will each have their own representative in the Cabinet.

Before 1957, Cabinets were exclusively composed of men of British, Irish, or French ancestry. In recent times, prime ministers have made an effort to appoint more women and persons of different ethnic and racial backgrounds to the Cabinet. In particular, Justin Trudeau's first Cabinet featured 15 women and 15 men along with a significant proportion of persons with different ethnic or racial characteristics.

DEPARTMENTS Many of the activities of government are divided among a number of departments (such as justice, health, and national defence), each of which is headed by a Cabinet minister who is expected to take responsibility for the actions of his or her department.

Because each department is concerned with a particular policy area and the particular set of interests associated with that policy area, there is often some disagreement among the different departments. For example, the Department of Agriculture has had a more favourable view of the use of certain pesticides than the Department of the Environment. Further, each department will typically seek more money and employees for its programs, while the

---

[5]Occasionally Prince Edward Island has not been represented in the Cabinet. Newfoundland and Labrador has been without Cabinet representation twice when voters in that province did not elect any members to the governing Conservative party.

Justin Trudeau's first cabinet featured an equal number of women and men as well as a sizable number of persons with different ethnic or racial characteristics.
Fred Chartrand/Canadian Press Images
Xinhua/Alamy Stock Photo

Treasury Board

A permanent Cabinet committee with its own staff and minister that plays a major role in governing in Canada because of its responsibility for the expenditure and management practices of government.

Cabinet solidarity

The convention in a parliamentary system that each member of the Cabinet is expected to fully support and defend the decisions and actions that Cabinet takes.

Institute on Governance
www.iog.ca

Department of Finance and the **Treasury Board,** a Cabinet committee responsible for the government's expenditures, will normally try to limit spending.

CABINET ORGANIZATION The Cabinet has traditionally been viewed as a body that collectively makes governing decisions. Because each member of the Cabinet is expected to maintain **Cabinet solidarity** (that is, fully support and defend the decisions and actions that Cabinet takes), there is an expectation that the Cabinet as a whole will discuss and deliberate on the key governing decisions. In reality, however, Cabinet members have too little time to fully consider all of the decisions that government makes. Thus, discussion of specific Cabinet decisions is typically done in one of the committees of Cabinet. Some prime ministers have used a select group of Cabinet ministers—the Priorities and Planning Committee chaired by the prime minister—to set the strategic direction of the government and make many decisions on behalf of the Cabinet as a whole. After becoming prime minister, Justin Trudeau established nine Cabinet committees[6] including a committee on Agenda, Results, and Communications that he chaired (along with chairing the Intelligence and Emergency Management Committee). He also specified that the minister of finance and the president of the Treasury Board can participate in all committees.

COORDINATION Although many individual Cabinet ministers are responsible for overseeing a department of government, in recent decades

---

[6]In addition, Trudeau's initial Cabinet included a subcommittee on Canada-US Relations and an ad hoc Committee on Defence Procurement.

considerable attention has been devoted to trying to coordinate the diverse activities of government. In Canada, this coordination and direction for the government is provided by the staff in **central agencies and central departments**. These include the Privy Council Office, the Prime Minister's Office, the Treasury Board Secretariat, and the Finance Department.

POWERS The prime minister and Cabinet are responsible for the executive powers of government. This includes gaining parliamentary approval for government's revenues and expenditures, overseeing relations with provincial and foreign governments, preparing proposals for legislation, issuing a large number of regulations, making a substantial number of important appointments, and overseeing the administrative apparatus of government.

CABINET RESPONSIBILITY The prime minister and Cabinet are accountable for their actions in governing through their responsibility to the House of Commons. Because the prime minister and Cabinet hold their positions only as long as they have the support of the majority of members of the House of Commons, there is an expectation that the Cabinet as a group will defend, explain, and take responsibility for the actions of the government in Parliament. In a majority government situation, it is highly unlikely that the House of Commons would pass a motion of non-confidence in the government or defeat important legislative and financial proposals presented by the Cabinet. Nevertheless, the rules of the House of Commons provide opportunities for the opposition parties to raise questions about and criticisms of the actions and performance of the government. In particular, Canada's daily Question Period provides for lively, if not always informative, exchanges between the opposition and governing parties.

In addition to the **collective responsibility** of the Cabinet to the House of Commons, there is an expectation that individual Cabinet ministers will take responsibility for the actions of the department they administer. If there are problems within a department, opposition party members typically call for the minister to resign from the Cabinet. However, Cabinet ministers in Canada have not resigned for the errors of officials in the departments they administer. Instead, Cabinet ministers may promise to look into a problem and try to rectify it. Ministers are more likely to be asked by the prime minister to resign for personal failings. For example, Labrador MP Peter Penashue resigned from the Cabinet and the House of Commons in 2013 after Elections Canada found that there had been a number of ineligible and improper contributions to his 2011 election campaign. He was unsuccessful in regaining his seat in a subsequent by-election.

SECRECY The accountability of the government is also limited by **Cabinet secrecy**. The Cabinet meets behind closed doors, and Cabinet documents, briefing notes, discussion papers, and other Cabinet-related material termed "Cabinet confidences" normally remain secret for 20 years. Cabinet secrecy

central agencies and central departments

Organizations that provide direction and coordination to government. In Canada, the key central agencies are the Privy Council Office, the Prime Minister's Office, the Treasury Board Secretariat, and the Department of Finance.

collective responsibility

The convention that the Cabinet as a group will defend, explain, and take responsibility for the actions of the government in Parliament.

Cabinet secrecy

The convention that the views expressed in Cabinet remain secret to enable full and frank discussion and maintain Cabinet solidarity.

helps to maintain Cabinet solidarity and ensure that the Cabinet is seen as a united team, regardless of the disagreements that undoubtedly exist among individual Cabinet ministers. Cabinet discussions can be full and frank because participants expect that word of disagreement will not get out to the media or to opposition parties. As well, Cabinet secrecy helps to shield public servants who advise the Cabinet from public criticism (public servants, being politically neutral, do not normally respond to criticisms). However, the principle of Cabinet secrecy can be used to avoid releasing research conducted by the government that would aid in public discussion of an issue and assist the opposition parties and the public in holding the government accountable for its actions. Since 1983, the Access to Information Act has established the right of journalists, interest groups, opposition parties, and the public to obtain government information for a small fee. However, less than 20 percent of requests for information have been met with full and timely disclosure (*CBC News*, 2013). In a number of cases, released information has been heavily redacted (blacked out). The Information Commissioner has complained that she has been unable to assess whether the government has gone beyond the rules to withhold information that should be made public.

In the 2015 election campaign, the Liberal party promised more open government including giving the Information Commissioner the power to order the release of documents that did not involve Cabinet confidences (as is the case in the UK and Australia). This would allow the Commissioner (an officer of parliament) access to Cabinet documents to determine whether or not they could be released in accordance with the provisions of the Access of Information Act. At the time of writing, it was not known to what extent the Liberal government would adopt measures for more open government. The Liberal government did remove the Conservative government's "gag order" that had prevented many government scientists speaking publicly and publishing their research findings, publicly released the mandate letters of newly appointed cabinet ministers, and eliminated most fees for information requests.

Access to Information and Privacy Office
http://justice.gc.ca/eng/trans/ atip-aiprp/

The secretive nature of the Canadian government has extended to the budgetary process, where MPs have often not had sufficient information to analyze the expenditure plans of government that they approve. Although a small Parliamentary Budget Office was established in 2007, it had to go to court in 2012 to get the government to release information about the effect of budget cuts.

Accountability has also been impeded as governments have rushed several-hundred-page budget implementation bills ("omnibus bills") through Parliament. Omnibus bills have included significant changes to dozens of laws (many of which been unrelated to the budget) with little time allocated for examination.[7]

---

[7]In the 2015 election campaign the Liberal party promised to end the practice of using omnibus bills to limit parliamentary review and debate of government proposals. However the opposition parties claimed that the Liberal government's 179-page 2016 budget implementation bill was an omnibus bill.

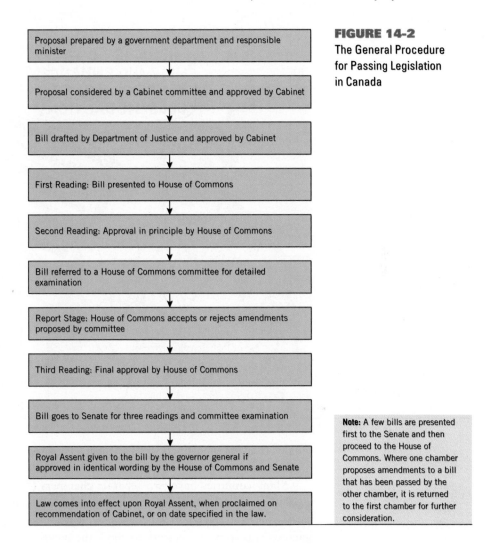

FIGURE 14-2
The General Procedure for Passing Legislation in Canada

Proposal prepared by a government department and responsible minister

↓

Proposal considered by a Cabinet committee and approved by Cabinet

↓

Bill drafted by Department of Justice and approved by Cabinet

↓

First Reading: Bill presented to House of Commons

↓

Second Reading: Approval in principle by House of Commons

↓

Bill referred to a House of Commons committee for detailed examination

↓

Report Stage: House of Commons accepts or rejects amendments proposed by committee

↓

Third Reading: Final approval by House of Commons

↓

Bill goes to Senate for three readings and committee examination

↓

Royal Assent given to the bill by the governor general if approved in identical wording by the House of Commons and Senate

↓

Law comes into effect upon Royal Assent, when proclaimed on recommendation of Cabinet, or on date specified in the law.

Note: A few bills are presented first to the Senate and then proceed to the House of Commons. Where one chamber proposes amendments to a bill that has been passed by the other chamber, it is returned to the first chamber for further consideration.

Parliament

Parliament is responsible for passing laws and approving the spending and taxing plans of government (see Figure 14-2). In addition, Parliament, particularly the House of Commons, is expected to hold the government accountable for its actions. In this regard, Parliament provides a visible forum in which the opposition can criticize the actions or inactions of government and the governing party can defend what it is doing. This not only helps to keep the government "on its toes," but also may help voters to make up their minds as to which party to support in the next election. In addition, although the Cabinet oversees the development of most new laws, Parliament can play a useful role by carefully examining proposed legislation and suggesting modifications of some details of proposed legislation to make it more effective.

Prime Minister Stephen
Harper's "open government."
Tami Thirlwell

The Parliament of Canada
www.parl.gc.ca

Keeping Tabs on Canada's
Parliament
http://openparliament.ca

Finally, individual members of Parliament frequently raise issues and concerns of those they represent.

Many countries have two separate chambers ("houses") involved in the legislative process (termed "bicameral legislatures"). In some cases, this is a carry-over from the non-democratic past, when a body representing privileged interests was seen as necessary to check the power of a body representing the people.[8] For example, the British House of Lords in the past consisted primarily of nobles who inherited their position. Since 1958, the UK prime minister has been able to recommend the appointment of life peers (some of whom are recommended by the House of Lords Appointments Committee). In 1997 the number of those holding hereditary positions was reduced to 92. There are also 26 Church of England archbishops and bishops who sit in the House of Lords.

The House of Lords has grown to about 840 members as prime ministers have rewarded supporters by recommending that they be life peers. There is a general consensus that substantial reform of the House of Lords is needed; the Conservative party favours a mainly elected body while the Labour party and the Liberal Democratic party favour a fully elected second chamber.

---

[8]In most federal systems, the second or upper chamber represents the interests of provinces or states.

The Parliament of Canada consists of two chambers: the House of Commons and the Senate. Provincial legislatures have only a single chamber of elected representatives.

The Canadian House of Commons

The **Canadian House of Commons** is the elected chamber of Parliament, with each member representing a particular electoral district.[9] Representation is by population, with district boundaries drawn after the decennial census so that, in most cases, each member of the House of Commons represents approximately the same number of people. A few large remote areas have substantially fewer voters, and a minimum level of representation from each Atlantic province is constitutionally guaranteed.

On the surface, the House of Commons controls the executive because the prime minister and Cabinet have to maintain the confidence (support) of the House of Commons. If a majority of members of the House of Commons pass a motion of non-confidence in the government, or if a major proposal made by the Cabinet, such as a budget proposal, is defeated, the prime minister must either request that an election be held or resign. However, in reality it is the prime minister and Cabinet who control the House of Commons, particularly in a majority government situation. **Party discipline** is the basic operating principle of the House of Commons (see Box 14-4 Should Party Discipline Be Relaxed?). That is, members of each party normally vote in accordance with the position that the party has adopted in caucus. The prime minister and Cabinet are usually able to convince their party's members in the House of Commons to support them and their legislative proposals. Therefore, as long as their party elected a majority of members to the House of Commons, the prime minister and Cabinet do not have to worry about losing the confidence of the House of Commons. Nevertheless, the opposition parties can sometimes persuade the government to change or withdraw a legislative proposal, particularly if the opposition can mobilize public opinion to its side or if the proposal is not a high priority for the government.

PRIVATE MEMBERS Ordinary members of the House of Commons who are not in the Cabinet (termed **private members**) have generally played a limited role in the development of new legislation. Private members in Canada cannot propose laws that involve the imposition of taxes or the spending of money for a new and distinct purpose without the approval of Cabinet. Although private members propose a large number of bills, only a very small number are passed. However, changes to procedures have provided time for a selected number of these bills to be debated and voted upon. For example, in 2010 the Canadian House of Commons passed a private member's bill,

Canadian House of Commons

The elected chamber of Parliament, with each member representing a particular electoral district.

party discipline

The expectation that members of each party will vote in accordance with the position that the party has adopted in caucus.

private members

Ordinary members of the House of Commons who are not in the Cabinet.

---

[9]This may change if Canada adopts a new electoral system.

BOX 14-4 Should Party Discipline Be Relaxed?

According to political scientist Leslie Seidle, "in the advanced parliamentary democracies, there is nowhere that has heavier, tighter party discipline than the Canadian House of Commons" (cited in Galloway, 2013).

In the United Kingdom it is not unusual for legislative proposals coming from Cabinet to be defeated in the House of Commons even when the governing party has a majority of seats. Votes in the British House of Commons are designated according to three classifications: one-line whip,* in which MPs, including Cabinet ministers, are free from party discipline; two-line whip, in which party members are encouraged and Cabinet ministers are expected to vote in accordance with their party's position; and three-line whip, in which party discipline is imposed on all members. However, the imposition of party discipline is not always successful. For example, in August 2013, a government motion to join the United States in military action against Syria was defeated when 30 Conservative MPs voted against the motion and 31 failed to vote (including some government ministers) despite the imposition of a three-line whip. However, in 2015 airstrikes in Syria supported by the Conservative leader were approved as only 7 Conservative MPs voted against the motion. The Labour party opposed the airstrikes, but 66 of their 218 MPs voted for the airstrikes despite the imposition of the three-line whip by their party leader.

In Canada, there have been only a few free votes for which party discipline has been withdrawn—usually on controversial moral issues such as capital punishment and abortion—so that members can follow their consciences. MPs almost always vote the way their party leader demands; legislative proposals and motions from ordinary MPs usually have little chance of being passed unless supported by the Cabinet, and the party leadership largely controls who will speak and what will be said. However, during the 2015 election campaign the Liberal party promised that all votes would be free votes with the exception of votes to implement their election platform, confidence votes (including the budget), and votes related to the values and protections in the Charter of Rights and Freedom (Liberal Party of Canada, 2015). To what extent this promise to relax party discipline will be fulfilled was not known at the time of writing.

The tightness of party discipline in Canada has often been criticized. Party discipline reduces the significance of ordinary members of Parliament, who are expected to toe the party line. Members may be expected to vote against the wishes or interests of their constituents. Provincial and regional interests may not be adequately represented in Parliament because parties and their leaders may be concerned about the dominant interests of the country as a whole or those areas viewed as crucial to electoral success.

There are, however, some positive features to party discipline. It helps to ensure that the positions taken by different parties are clear. This makes it easier for voters to choose among competing parties and to hold the governing party accountable for its actions. Further, it means that the government can focus on doing what it considers to be for the common good of the whole country (or what's good for their party) without having to satisfy individual members of Parliament seeking special benefits for their constituency in return for their voting support.

*The Whip is the enforcer of party discipline.

the Climate Change Accountability Act (which would set national greenhouse gas emission targets), that was introduced by then NDP MP Bruce Hyer and supported by the three opposition parties. However, it was defeated by the Conservative majority in the Senate. More frequently, ordinary members of Parliament have been successful in making minor modifications to legislation proposed by the Cabinet.

COMMITTEES House of Commons committees, composed of government and opposition party members in proportion to their party's strength in the House of Commons, provide detailed examination of proposed legislation and often suggest modifications to that legislation. As well, they examine the annual estimates of government's proposed spending. At times, they investigate or hold public hearings on particular policy issues, thus making a contribution to the development of new policies.

OPPOSITION The House of Commons is particularly important in providing a public forum for the criticism and defence of the actions of the executive and its legislative proposals. The party with the second-highest number of seats usually is designated as the **official opposition** and leads off the questioning or criticism of government every day that the House is sitting. Other parties with at least 12 seats in the House of Commons have official party status, which, along with other privileges, gives them a budget for hiring research and support staff.

Various opportunities are provided for opposition members to propose **non-confidence motions** in the government. Although non-confidence motions are usually unsuccessful, they provide an opportunity to focus attention on what the opposition parties see as the failings of the governing party.

Although the House of Commons provides a forum for debating proposed legislation, the governing party can put forward a motion of **closure** to limit debate in the House to one day or, more frequently, a time allocation motion to set the amount of time allocated to a bill if an agreement on a timetable for debate cannot be reached with the other parties. Sometimes these limits are used to avoid a **filibuster**, the use of delaying tactics by the opposition. There has been considerable criticism of the excessive use of closure and time allocation to limit debate on important pieces of proposed legislation.

The Canadian Senate

Canada's **Senate** was established, in part, to provide a body of "sober second thought" to check the democratic tendencies of the House of Commons. As well, to allay fears that the House of Commons would be dominated by Ontario and Quebec, the Senate provided for equal regional representation.

Although the government does not need to maintain the confidence of the Senate, legislation needs the approval of the Senate as well as the House of Commons. Only in the case of resolutions to approve constitutional changes can the Canadian House of Commons override the opposition of the Senate.

As in the House of Commons, senators examine legislative proposals and introduce modifications that are, on occasion, accepted by the government and the House of Commons. Legislative proposals that do not involve government spending or taxing can also be introduced in the Senate. Senators usually have been reluctant to block the passage of legislation approved by the House of Commons. However, when Brian Mulroney was prime minister (1984–1993),

House of Commons committees

Committees composed of government and opposition party members in proportion to their party's strength in the House of Commons; they provide detailed examination of proposed legislation and often suggest modifications to that legislation.

official opposition

The party with the second-highest number of seats in the House of Commons; the official opposition leads off the questioning or criticism of government every day that the House is sitting.

non-confidence motion

A motion put forward by opposition members in a legislature expressing a lack of confidence in the government. If passed, the prime minister is expected to either resign or request that an election be held.

closure

A procedure in a legislative body that cuts off debate if approved by a majority vote.

filibuster

The use of various delaying tactics by those opposed to the passage of a particular piece of legislation.

Senate (Canada)

The upper chamber of Parliament, appointed on the recommendation of the prime minister. Senators hold their positions until age 75.

the Liberal majority in the Senate engaged in confrontation with the Progressive Conservative majority in the House of Commons on such important legislation as the Canada–United States Free Trade Agreement and the imposition of the Goods and Services Tax.

Generally, the proceedings in the Senate do not receive much media and public attention. Because of the expertise of many senators, the greater amount of time available for deliberation, and the somewhat less partisan nature of the Senate, this second chamber (particularly through its committees) can make useful suggestions for improving legislative proposals. Over the years, the Senate has also prepared important reports on such topics as poverty, the mass media, science policy, free trade, terrorism, and aging.

REPRESENTATION   There are twenty-four senators from each of Ontario, Quebec, the Maritimes (ten each from Nova Scotia and New Brunswick; four from Prince Edward Island), and the West (six each from Manitoba, Saskatchewan, Alberta, and British Columbia), plus six from Newfoundland and Labrador and one from each of the three territories. However, it is questionable whether senators "represent," in a meaningful way, the province for which they are appointed. In most other countries with federal systems, the upper chamber is elected by the people in each province or state. For example, in the United States and Australia, the Senate is elected with each state having the same number of senators. In Germany, the Bundesrat (upper house) consists of delegates of the Länder (provincial) governments with each Land having four, five, or six votes depending on the size of its population.

APPOINTMENTS   The prime minister recommends the appointment of senators. In the past most appointees have been loyal supporters of the prime minister's party. Senators hold their positions until age 75 and can only be removed from office for failing to attend two consecutive sessions of Parliament, becoming bankrupt, or being convicted of treason, a felony, or other "infamous crime."

SENATE REFORM OR ABOLITION   Reform of the Senate has been a staple of Canadian political discussion for many decades. Some, including the New Democratic Party, argue that the Senate should be abolished. In their view, the ability of an appointed body to reject legislation passed by an elected, representative body is a relic of the non-democratic past. Others, including an Alberta-based movement, have advocated the adoption of a "Triple-E" Senate (one that is elected, effective, and based on an equal number of representatives from each province). While a Triple-E Senate would give a stronger voice to the smaller provinces, critics argue that it could lead to a deadlock as elected senators would be less likely to back off from a confrontation with the House of Commons.[10]

[10]This occurred in Australia in 1975 when the elected Senate refused to approve the funds needed to run the government. In a very controversial decision, the governor general dismissed the prime minister and appointed the opposition party leader as interim prime minister until elections for both houses of Parliament were called.

Former Prime Minister Harper proposed that the prime minister recommend the appointment of elected senators for a single nine-year term. However, the Supreme Court of Canada ruled that this change would require a constitutional amendment supported by the legislatures of at least two-thirds of the provinces. Abolishing the Senate would require the agreement of all the provincial legislatures. Constitutional amendments would be unlikely to gain the required support and thus Harper did not pursue the proposal.

Justin Trudeau removed the Liberal Senators from the Liberal party caucus; thus they became independent Senators. After becoming prime minister, Trudeau appointed non-partisan provincial committees of prominent persons to nominate a group of potential senators. The prime minister then chose those needed to fill Senate vacancies. One of these new appointees, Peter Harder, was named as government representative in the Senate. Although sitting as an independent he could attend Cabinet meetings as his role is to shepherd government legislation through the Senate. Conservative party critics argued that the process of choosing senators remained largely secretive and undemocratic as Senators were not elected.

✓• SUMMARY AND CONCLUSION

Parliamentary systems are often described as having a close interrelationship of legislative and executive powers. Despite the label *parliamentary system*, considerable power rests with the prime minister and Cabinet, particularly in a majority government situation. The role of the ordinary member of Parliament is limited. Although the prime minister and Cabinet must retain the support of the House of Commons, this is largely a formality in a majority government situation. Nevertheless, they are expected to be responsible to the House of Commons for their actions.

The Westminster version of the parliamentary system, in which majority government is the norm, facilitates decisive action by the government. By maintaining tight party discipline, the governing party can act in ways that it believes will be for the good of the country as a whole or, at least, for the re-election of the governing party. It also can facilitate the accountability of the government to the people, as praise or blame for the actions of the government and most of the laws passed by Parliament can be attributed to the governing party.

However, this concentration of power can have negative consequences. A majority government, elected by a minority of voters, may ignore different sections of the population or different viewpoints. Because of strict party discipline, the task of holding the government accountable for its actions rests with the opposition parties in the House of Commons. Although the parliamentary system does provide an opportunity for the opposition parties to question and criticize the prime minister and Cabinet, this does not often lead the government to modify its policies. Further, the secrecy within which government often operates and the large number of activities conducted by modern governments can make it difficult for the opposition parties to investigate the actions of government. Effective access to information legislation; independent officers of Parliament able to scrutinize government spending, pursue public complaints, and ensure that those entrusted with power are acting ethically; an independent judiciary; vigilant media; and an attentive public are also important in trying to ensure that government does not abuse its power.

Parliamentary systems feature collective decision making by the prime minister and Cabinet. Ideally, government decisions are based on discussion and deliberation by Cabinet ministers, most of whom have the expertise of their departments of government to provide them with advice. Power has, however, tended to drift from the Cabinet as a whole to the prime minister and a small group of aides, officials, and ministers at the centre. Prime ministerial government may result in a clear direction for a government run by a decisive leader, but it carries the risk of wrong-headed or insensitive decisions made by the head of government without adequate deliberation among those with different ideas and perspectives.

✓• KEY TERMS

Cabinet 336
Cabinet secrecy 341
Cabinet solidarity 340
Canadian House of Commons 345
Central agencies and central
   departments 341
Closure 347
Coalition government 332
Collective responsibility 341
Dissolution 335
Executive dominance 336
Filibuster 347

Governor general 335
Head of government 336
Head of state 334
House of Commons
   committees 347
Lieutenant-governor 335
Majority government 332
Minority government 332
Non-confidence motion 347
Official opposition 347
Parliamentary system 329
Party discipline 345

Prerogative powers 335
Prime Minister's Office
   (PMO) 337
Prime ministerial government 337
Private members 345
Privy Council Office (PCO) 337
Prorogation 335
Responsible government 329
Senate (Canada) 347
Treasury Board 340
Westminster system 330

✦• DISCUSSION QUESTIONS

1. Should Canada replace the monarchy with an elected head of state?

2. Does the Canadian parliamentary system give too much power to the prime minister?

3. Should party discipline in Parliament be loosened?

4. Is a coalition government preferable to a minority government?

5. Are Trudeau's Senate reforms worthwhile?

6. Is the Westminster system of parliamentary government the best way to achieve the common good?

FURTHER READING

Docherty, D.C. (2005). *Legislatures*. Vancouver: UBC Press.

Lijphart, A. (2008). *Thinking about democracy: Power sharing and majority rule in theory and practice.* New York: Routledge.

Lijphart, A. (2012). *Patterns of democracy: Government forms and performance in thirty-six countries* (2nd ed.). New Haven: Yale University Press.

Loat, A., & MacMillan, M. (2014). *Tragedy in the Commons: Former Members of Parliament speak out about Canada's failing democracy.* Toronto: Random House Canada.

Rhodes, R.A.W., Wanna, J., & Weller, P. (2011). *Comparing Westminster.* Oxford: Oxford University Press.

Russell, P.H., & Sossin, L. (Eds.). (2009). *Parliamentary democracy in crisis.* Toronto: University of Toronto Press.

Savoie, D.J. (2008). *Court government and the collapse of accountability in Canada and the United Kingdom.* Toronto: University of Toronto Press.

Smith, D.E. (2007). *The people's House of Commons: Theories of democracy in contention.* Toronto: University of Toronto Press.

Smith, J. (Ed.). (2009). *The democratic dilemma: Reforming the Canadian Senate.* Montreal: McGill-Queen's University Press.

White, G. (2005). *Cabinets and first ministers.* Vancouver: UBC Press.

15 Presidential and Semi-Presidential Systems

US President Barack Obama speaks to the media on March 1, 2013, following a meeting with House of Representatives Speaker John Boehner after talks failed to avert an automatic $85 billion in arbitrary budget cuts.   Saul Loea/AFP/Getty Images/Newscom

After reading this chapter, you should be able to:

1. outline the basic differences between parliamentary and presidential systems of government
2. discuss the relationship between the president and Congress in the United States
3. examine the strengths and weaknesses of presidential systems
4. explain the basic features of semi-presidential systems

On October 1, 2013, the government of the United States shut down. About 800 000 federal employees were placed on unpaid leave and essential employees were required to continue their work with no guarantee that they would be paid.

The annual funding for the US government by appropriation bills is the responsibility of Congress (although the President can veto these bills). In 2013, Republican Congressman Ted Cruz led a Republican attack on the Patient Protection and Affordable Care Act (often termed "Obamacare"), a key law promoted by Democratic president Barack Obama. The Republicans refused to pass an appropriation bill to fund the government unless major changes were made to the Act. The Republicans were also opposed to an increase in the ceiling for government debt that allowed government to borrow money to pay for authorized expenditures. Without raising the ceiling, the US government might have defaulted on its debt payments on October 17, 2013.

At the last minute on October 16, three-eighths of the House Republicans voted with the Democrats to pass an appropriations bill that allowed the government to reopen. The debt ceiling was lifted.

This was not the first time that the US government was closed because of a conflict between the president and Congress (often called "gridlock"). In 1994, a Republican majority in Congress rejected a budget prepared by Democratic president Bill Clinton because it did not include tax cuts, measures to ensure a balanced budget, and a major reduction in social welfare programs. This resulted in shutdowns lasting a total of 27 days. Presidents Ronald Reagan and George H.W. Bush also faced budgetary conflicts with Congress, but the shutdowns that resulted were very short.

The American Constitution establishes the principle of separation of powers between the president and Congress. Unlike parliamentary systems where there is a close connection between the political executive (prime minister and Cabinet) and the party (or parties) that control Parliament, Congress and the president are largely independent of each other. The increased ideological polarization between the two major American parties (reflecting ideological differences among their supporters) has increased the conflict between the two branches of government (Thurber & Yoshinaka, 2015).

The United States tends to differ from many other countries that have a presidential system. In particular, the power and independence of the Congress in the United States is generally greater than in other presidential systems.

THE PRESIDENTIAL SYSTEM

The **presidential system** of government was developed in the United States. The loose confederation of the thirteen American states created during the War of Independence (1775–1783) reflected the general view that a strong central government would threaten individual liberties and the rights of the individual states. However, a group known as the "federalists" argued that the problems faced by the country—including economic weakness, debts from the war, disagreements among the states, and the difficulty in raising an army to put down a rebellion—made it necessary to create an effective central government. In the view of James Madison, a leading federalist, tyranny could be prevented by separating the power of government into different institutions each independent of the others. On the basis of the assumption that individuals were motivated primarily by self-interest, Madison argued that "ambition must be made to counteract ambition" (*Federalist Papers*, no. 51). In other words, by ensuring that the executive branch (headed by the president), the legislative branch (**Congress**), and the judicial branch were each independent, the ambitions of those in each branch to become more powerful would be checked by those in the other branches who had their own ambition to be powerful. In addition, the power of the American government would be restricted by providing it with a limited range of constitutional powers.

Presidential systems feature a **separation of powers** in which the president and Congress each have separate bases of authority (see Figure 15-1). Unlike a parliamentary system, those holding executive positions cannot be members of the legislative branch. The judicial branch is also considered an independent branch, although its members are recommended for appointment by the president and approved by the Senate. Ideally, the separation of powers creates a system of **checks and balances** that prevents any branch of government or any individual from becoming too powerful.

Unlike the prime minister in a parliamentary system, the president does not need to maintain the support of the legislature to remain in office. Both the president and the members of Congress have fixed terms of office. The president cannot dissolve Congress and order an election in the hope that this will result in a Congress that is more willing to support the executive. Even though

presidential system

A system of governing in which the president and Congress each separately derive their authority from being elected by the people and have a fixed term of office.

Congress

The legislative branch of the American government consisting of the House of Representatives and the Senate.

separation of powers

A basic feature of presidential systems in which the executive, legislative, and judicial branches of government are separate from each other, with each having different personnel and different bases of authority.

checks and balances

A basic principle of the American presidential system in which each of the three branches of government is able to check the actions of the others so that no individual or institution becomes too powerful.

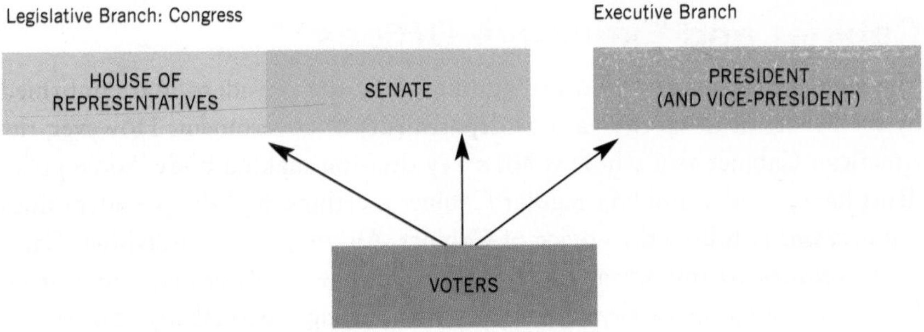

Legislative Branch: Congress   Executive Branch

HOUSE OF REPRESENTATIVES   SENATE   PRESIDENT (AND VICE-PRESIDENT)

VOTERS

FIGURE 15-1

A Simplified Depiction of the American Presidential System

the executive and legislative branches are independent of each other, the passage of legislation and the approval of spending and taxes involve both branches.

Almost all countries in Central and South America as well as some countries in other parts of the world, including Indonesia, the Philippines, Cyprus, Nigeria, Ghana, and Malawi, have adopted a version of the presidential system (Shugart, 2006). However, the presidential system of the United States differs considerably in practice from the presidential systems of other countries. Although all presidential systems feature a separation of executive and legislative powers, the president and the executive branch tends to be dominant in countries other than the United States with presidential systems (Smith, 2011). We will focus primarily on the American presidential system in this chapter.

The President

In a presidential system, the president is both head of state and head of government. That is, the president carries out the ceremonial duties associated with the head of state, but also heads the executive branch of government. As chief executive, the president is commander-in-chief of the armed forces, exercises considerable control over foreign policy, helps to shape domestic policy, and exercises some control over the public (civil) service. Although the president heads the executive branch of government and thus is responsible for the implementation of laws, the president is also involved in the legislative activity of passing laws. Not only are the president and the executive branch active in proposing legislation to Congress, but the president's ability to veto laws passed by Congress (discussed below) means that Congress has to take into account the president's views in passing legislation.

The president of the United States nominates a variety of senior officials and Supreme Court and other federal judges. However, to check the power of the president, many presidential nominations (including Cabinet and senior departmental officials, ambassadors, federal and Supreme Court judges, members of regulatory agencies and advisory boards, and senior military officers) must be approved by the Senate (the upper chamber of Congress). Likewise, although the president has the authority to negotiate treaties, they must be approved by a two-thirds majority in the Senate.

The American President
www.whitehouse.gov

Cabinet and Executive Offices

The Cabinet secretaries who are appointed by the president and confirmed by the Senate head up the various departments of government. However, the American Cabinet as a whole is not a key decision-making body. Some presidents have avoided holding regular Cabinet meetings, and the president does not necessarily follow the advice of Cabinet. Although some individual Cabinet secretaries are important advisers to the president, advice also comes from White House staff, usually individuals with strong personal loyalties to the president. Nevertheless, individual Cabinet secretaries are important in running their departments and drafting proposals and regulations. The president also controls various executive offices (referred to as the Executive Office of the President), including the Office of Management and Budget and the Council of Economic Advisers, which are important sources of advice for the president. Of particular importance is the National Security Council, which plays a central role in national security and foreign policy decisions. The Council is chaired by the president and includes the vice president, the Secretaries of State, Defense, and Treasury, and the chair of the Joint Chiefs of (Military) Staff and the Director of National Intelligence, Various other key persons are also invited to attend the Security Council meetings.

Although Congress is responsible for passing legislation, the president can issue executive orders. For example, President Obama used an executive order to stop the deportation of large numbers of illegal immigrants who were brought to the United States as children. Various presidents have used executive orders to send troops to engage in conflicts in foreign countries. The president can also affect how the laws passed by Congress are implemented and how regulations are applied by appointing the top officials in government agencies who share the president's perspectives.

Presidential Selection and Term

The president, along with a vice-presidential running mate, is elected by the American people. Although voters in the United States choose among the competing presidential candidates, technically they are voting for members of the Electoral College committed to casting their ballot for a particular presidential candidate. A majority of Electoral College votes is needed to elect a president. If no candidate has a majority of Electoral College votes, the president would be elected by the House of Representatives, the lower house of Congress, with each state delegation casting a single vote. Because the United States has a two-party system, this has not occurred since 1824.

Other countries with presidential systems directly elect their president rather than using an electoral college. In many countries a runoff election is held if no candidate has a majority (or, in some countries, a large plurality) of votes. For example, in Argentina a presidential candidate needs at least 45 percent of the vote or 40 percent with a 10 percent lead over the nearest rival to win outright. Otherwise a second round of voting is held between the top two candidates. In 2015 Daniel Scioli obtained 37.08 percent of the vote while Mauricio Macri received 34.15 percent. In the second round Macri won with 51.34 percent of the vote. In Mexico and the Philippines, the candidate with the most votes on a single ballot wins. For example, in the 2012 Mexican election, the winning candidate (Peña Nieto) obtained 38.2 percent of the vote.

Because of concerns that excessive power may accumulate in the hands of a long-serving president, presidential systems limit the amount of time that

BOX 15-1 Presidential Impeachment

Although a number of American presidents have faced impeachment proceedings, no president has ever been removed by this process. Richard Nixon resigned in 1974 before he could be impeached for participating in the cover-up of illegal activities (including the break-in to the Democratic Party offices in Washington's Watergate building). In 1999, Bill Clinton was accused of false testimony and obstructing justice when he stated that he had not had sexual relations (as he defined those "relations") with his intern, Monica Lewinsky, in a deposition to a grand jury. Although a small majority of the House voted to impeach the president, only one-half of senators voted for conviction, and thus Clinton was able to complete his term.

The power of impeachment has been successfully used in several other countries to remove a president, particularly for corruption. For example, President Fernando Collor of Brazil was removed from office in 1992 as a result of allegations by his younger brother that Collor was benefiting from illegal deals engaged in by a friend of the president. The "gifts" from his friend included two ranches, renovations of his apartments in

Brazil and Paris, expensive cars for his children, and cash to various family members. Pressure from the public to impeach the president helped to ensure that representatives in Congress voted to impeach despite attempts by the president's friends to bribe representatives (Kara, 2005). In 2016, Brazil's President Dilma Rousseff was impeached for violating fiscal responsibility laws (by moving funds between different government budgets to maintain social programs). Vice president Michel Temer then became president despite his conviction for violating campaign finance limits that may prevent him from seeking re-election. Temer has also been accused of taking bribes. Indeed many of the legislators who voted for impeachment have also been under investigation for corruption. In 1996, President Ernesto Samper of Colombia was able to survive credible allegations that his presidential campaign was funded by the Cali cocaine cartel. Efforts to impeach him were voted down by Colombia's House of Representatives, which also prohibited further investigations. In this case, the popularity of the president discouraged representatives from voting for impeachment (Hinojosa & Pérez-Liñán, 2005).

presidents can hold the office. For example, Mexico limits its president to a single six-year term. The president of the United States has a fixed term in office of four years and can be elected to a maximum of two terms. Unlike the prime minister in a parliamentary system, the president holds office regardless of the support of Congress. Thus it is not unusual for a president to have a different party affiliation than the majority in one or both chambers of Congress.

IMPEACHMENT Although presidents have a fixed term of office, Congress does have the ability to remove a president who has engaged in illegal behaviour. The process, known as **impeachment**, is difficult and lengthy. In the United States, the president, other top officials, and judges can be removed from office only if convicted of "treason, bribery or other high crimes and misdemeanors." After an investigation by the Judiciary Committee of the House of Representatives, a majority in the House has to pass articles of impeachment stating the offence(s). Then, after holding a trial, a two-thirds majority in the Senate has to reach a guilty verdict in order to remove the president (see Box 15-1 Presidential Impeachment).

impeachment

A process by which a president and other public officials can be removed from office after being accused of criminal behaviour and convicted by a legislative body.

The Vice President

A candidate for vice president in the United States is handpicked by a presidential candidate to serve as an election running mate, sometimes providing balance in the sense of appealing to different regions, appealing to persons with a somewhat different ideological perspective, or having different personal characteristics than the president. For example, Barack Obama chose Joe Biden as his vice presidential candidate partly because Biden's more than 35 years as a Senator offset Obama's limited political experience. Mitt Romney's choice of Paul Ryan in 2012 was likely intended to ensure that strongly conservative voters who thought Romney was too moderate would vote for the Republican team. Hillary Clinton's choice of Virginia Senator Tim Kaine in 2016 was designed to appeal to centrist voters and to try to swing Virginia to the Democrats. Donald Trump's choice of Indiana governor Michael Pence appealed to the social conservative base of the Republican party with Pence's opposition to abortion, gay and lesbian rights, and laws reducing carbon emissions.

The vice president has the constitutional right to preside over the Senate, although does so only occasionally, and can vote only in the case of a tie. Otherwise, the major constitutional role of the vice president is to be available to take over the presidency in case the president dies or is unable to continue in office. In the past, the office of vice president was often ridiculed. President John Adams described it as "the most insignificant office that ever the invention of man contrived," while Vice President John Nance Garner described it as "not worth a bucket of warm piss". Nevertheless, recent vice presidents have provided advice to the president and are members of the important National Security Council; Vice President Richard (Dick) Cheney had a major influence on government policies in George W. Bush's administration. Joe Biden was tasked with overseeing the important economic stimulus package and provided advice on foreign policy to President Obama.

The American Congress

The American Congress is a legislative body composed of two separate chambers:

- The **House of Representatives**, which is elected every two years from districts of approximately equal population size.
- The **Senate**, which is composed of persons elected for six-year terms on a two-per-state basis with one-third of the Senate being elected every two years.

The president does not have the power to dissolve Congress and thus has to live with a Congress that has a different political perspective. Because the president does not need the support of Congress to remain in office, Congress can feel free to reject legislative or budgetary proposals from the president,

House of Representatives

The lower chamber of the American Congress, elected for a two-year term from districts of approximately equal population size.

Senate (United States)

The upper chamber of Congress. Two senators are elected by voters in each state for a six-year term.

knowing that it will not lead to an early election. To protect the independence of Congress, the president and the Cabinet secretaries are not allowed to be members of Congress.

Both the Senate and the House of Representatives are active bodies. Because the Senate is smaller, contains elected representatives of states rather than smaller districts, has a longer term of office, and has the authority to approve treaties and reject presidential nominees, the Senate is considered to be the more important of the two chambers. Many members of the House of Representatives are interested in seeking to become senators when the opportunity arises. Nevertheless, both chambers are active participants in the legislative process. Proposed legislation often contains different provisions when passed by each chamber. A joint conference committee is then established to find a compromise between the two bills. Bills must be passed in identical form in the two chambers before being presented to the president (see Figure 15-2). Revenue bills (those involving taxes and, in practice, government spending) must be initiated in the lower chamber, the House of Representatives, although the Senate can propose amendments.

The American president does not attend Congress except to present the annual State of the Union address. Proposals for legislation must be presented by a member of Congress.[1] Although the executive branch prepares many of the legislative proposals that Congress considers, Congress is very active in modifying or rejecting the executive's proposals. Members of the American Congress have sizable staffs that are often involved in drafting and modifying legislative proposals. Congress is therefore active not only in approving legislation, but also in developing it.

United States House
of Representatives
www.house.gov

United States Senate
www.senate.gov

presidential veto

The ability of the president to prevent the passage of a bill. The president of the United States has the authority to veto laws passed by Congress, although this veto can be overridden by a two-thirds majority in each body of Congress.

PRESIDENTIAL VETO   As a check on the legislative power of Congress, the president has the authority to veto any law passed by Congress. Congress can override the **presidential veto**, but this requires a two-thirds majority in each body of Congress, and thus is quite rare. For example, in 2015 President Obama vetoed an Act passed by both Houses to approve the controversial Keystone XL pipeline that would carry Alberta crude oil to American refineries. An attempt to override the veto failed to get the required two-thirds support. As of July 2016, Obama had vetoed eleven laws passed by Congress since 2009, but none of them were overturned by Congress (Woolley & Peters, 2016).

The US president also has the power to use a "pocket veto." If Congress adjourns after passing the bill and the president does not sign the bill within 10 days, the bill does not become law. Pocket vetoes cannot be overridden by Congress. For example, President Obama used a pocket veto to defeat measures that would scrap the Clean Power Plan, a key climate change initiative to reduce carbon dioxide emissions from power plants (Korte, 2015).

---

[1]In other countries, the president usually has the authority to introduce legislation to Congress and may be able to limit the ability of Congress to amend the proposed legislation.

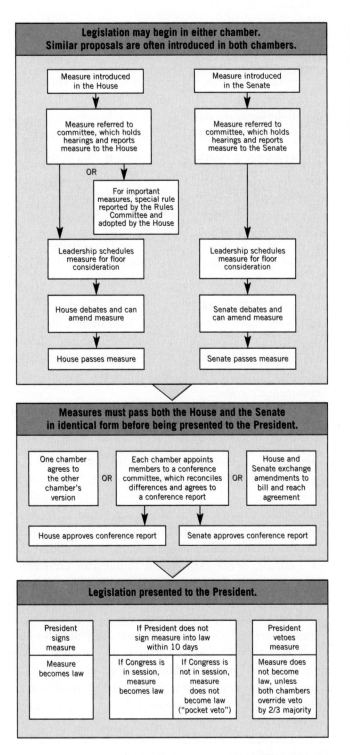

FIGURE 15-2

How a Bill Becomes a Law in the United States

Source: Copyright © 2007 by TheCapitol.Net, Inc. All Rights Reserved. This image, section 8.01 from the Congressional Deskbook, by Michael Koempel and Judy Schneider. www.CongressionalDeskbook.com.

The veto power of the president, although important, has limitations. The American president can only veto a bill in its entirety, rather than approving some aspects and rejecting others.[2] Thus, if Congress is preparing a bill that the president opposes, members of Congress will often include some provisions that the president wants in order to reduce the likelihood of a veto. Even though the president does not use the veto frequently, the anticipation of a veto will often lead Congress to modify its proposals to try to satisfy the president.

CONGRESS'S OVERSIGHT ROLE   An important aspect of the "checks and balances" of the American presidential system is the oversight role of Congress. Federal departments, agencies, programs, operations, and activities can be investigated, monitored, and reviewed by Congress. This includes Congressional hearings, investigations by select Congressional committees, annual reviews of government spending, and requirements that departments and agencies report to Congress (Halchin & Kaiser, 2012). Nevertheless, presidents have invoked "executive privilege" to try to limit oversight of certain activities.

PARTY DISCIPLINE   Party discipline in the American Congress usually is not very tight. There has often been quite a broad spectrum of differing perspectives within each of the two parties represented in Congress. Because the president and Cabinet do not need the support of a majority in Congress to stay in power, there is less pressure to maintain party discipline than in a parliamentary system.

Individual members of the US Congress often vote as they see fit, or in the interests of the state or district they represent, rather than as members of a party team. This means that some members of the president's party may vote against proposals promoted by the president. For example, in the vote on Patient Protection and Affordable Care Act, 2010 ("Obamacare"), thirty-four Democrats in the House of Representatives voted against the bill that was the centrepiece of the president's first term. Conversely, a president faced with a Congress that has a majority of opposing party members has some ability to influence individual members of Congress regardless of their party affiliation. For example, in the early 1980s, Republican President Ronald Reagan was able to get much of his program adopted despite the control of Congress by the Democratic Party. Reagan persuaded some conservative-minded Democrats of the virtues of his proposals. As well, by making his case directly to the American public, he created a favourable climate of opinion for his proposals, thus putting pressure on members of Congress to pass them. Nevertheless, as discussed in in the opening vignette, differences between the president and Congress can potentially lead to **political gridlock**, particularly if Congress is dominated by a political party that has a strongly different perspective than the president.

political gridlock

A situation where necessary legislation is unable to be passed particularly because of tension between the president and one or both chambers of Congress controlled by an opposing political party.

---

[2]In some American states, the governor possesses a line-item veto, allowing the governor to reject parts of the proposed legislation. Some countries give their presidents this powerful tool.

Although party discipline is not as tight in the United States as it is in most parliamentary systems, it should not be concluded that political parties are irrelevant. Members of a party do tend to vote the same way as the other members of their party. The parties in Congress have become more cohesive in the past few decades as the Democrats have become more consistently liberal or centrist and the Republicans more strongly conservative. Nevertheless, some moderate Democrats vote with the Republicans when Republicans present relatively moderate proposals, and some moderate Republicans vote with the Democrats on other issues (Brady & Volden, 2006).

COMMITTEES Congressional committees are a very important aspect of the American Congress. It is in the hundreds of committees and subcommittees of the House and Senate that legislative and expenditure proposals are most thoroughly debated, modified, or discarded. In some cases, legislation is drafted by a congressional committee. The chairs of these powerful committees are chosen by the majority party in the Senate and in the House; the chair is often the party member who has served on that committee the longest. The committee chairs are often quite independent-minded and thus do not always feel the need to adhere to their party's positions.

In general, the passing of legislation in the American system is a very difficult process. There are a large number of obstacles to overcome. Presidents have to use all of their persuasive capabilities and negotiating skills in order to have their proposals accepted. As President George H.W. Bush once said, perhaps with some exaggeration, it was easier to deal with Iraqi dictator Saddam Hussein than with the US Congress. Within Congress, proposed legislation has to pass a variety of hurdles. For example, a committee chair may refuse to allocate time to discuss a bill. In the Senate, filibusters are quite common, as each senator can speak on a proposal for as long as he or she wants. Senators

Despite widespread support for legislation extending background checks for those purchasing guns after the Newtown massacre of 30 young students, a Senate filibuster prevented the majority in the Senate from passing the legislation.
Zhang Chuanshi/Xinhua/Sipa USA/Newscom

are quite willing to use this power to express their opposition to a particular piece of legislation. A motion of cloture to limit debate must be passed by a 60 percent majority. Through the use of a filibuster, 41 of the 100 senators can prevent legislation from coming to a vote. Thus, in most cases, controversial legislation will not likely be voted on in the Senate unless support can be found in both political parties. A supermajority (60 percent) is usually needed to pass legislation. For example, a proposal to extend background checks for those purchasing guns to include online and gun show sales was defeated by a filibuster in the Senate after the 2012 Newtown massacre of 30 young students even though the proposal had bipartisan support, and 54 of the 100 senators, the president, and 80 percent of the public were in favour (Whitesides & Lawder, 2013).

The Balance between Executive and Legislative Powers

Does the presidential system in the United States provide a suitable balance of powers between the executive and legislative branches so that each is able to check the power of the other? At times, the balance has shifted in favour of Congress such that the system might be best described as a congressional system. At other times, the president has been dominant such that some have described the system as having an "imperial presidency," with the president becoming like a powerful monarch. In particular, as the United States became heavily involved militarily around the world and as concerns about national security increased, presidents have tended to assume greater powers, as discussed in Box 15-2 War Powers. Nevertheless, Congress is important in determining the country's domestic policies.

Evaluating the Presidential System

Evaluating governing systems is complex. A variety of criteria can be used, and different people are likely to have different views about which criteria are most important. There is considerable variation in how any particular system of governing operates, not only as a result of different specific constitutional provisions, but also as a result of differences in the party system, the electoral system, and political culture as well as the broader economic and social circumstances and distribution of power that exist in any particular country. There are not only variations in how a particular system operates in particular countries, but also differences over time within a particular country. Further, in evaluating the presidential system, it is important to keep in mind that the United States is the only developed country that has maintained a democratic presidential system for a very lengthy period of time. Nevertheless, we can discuss some potential strengths and weaknesses in the presidential system by comparing it to the parliamentary system.

BOX 15-2 War Powers

On March 18, 2011, President Obama authorized an American missile attack (in conjunction with NATO) on Libyan forces and air defences to protect civilians as Libyan forces advanced towards the rebel stronghold of Benghazi. Several months later, the House of Representatives passed a resolution (268–145) criticizing Obama for the continuing US military role in the Libyan conflict without the consent of Congress.

There is an inherent tension in the American governing system concerning the use of military force. As commander-in-chief of the Armed Forces, the president is responsible for national security. However, it is the constitutional responsibility of Congress to decide whether to declare war and to provide the funds needed by the military. To circumvent the constitutional requirement concerning a declaration of war by Congress, presidents have, on numerous occasions, ordered military actions without a formal declaration of war. In fact, the United States government has not formally declared war since 1942 even though its armed forces has been engaged in many conflicts since then.

For example, in 1964, after two apparent attacks on US naval vessels by North Vietnam, President Lyndon Johnson convinced almost all members of Congress to pass the Gulf of Tonkin Resolution, which authorized the president to take "all necessary actions to protect our Armed Forces." War was never declared. However this Resolution was used to justify sending more than half a million troops to fight in Vietnam and to engage in the secret bombing and invasion of Cambodia to disrupt the supply routes of the Viet Cong guerrillas. As the lengthy conflict continued and the Senate Foreign Relations Committee found that it had been deceived about at least one of the two attacks on American military vessels, strong opposition to the war effort grew among the public and many members of Congress.

With President Richard Nixon discredited by the "Watergate" scandal (the break-in at the Democratic National Committee headquarters in 1972 and the subsequent cover-up by Nixon's aides) and the attempts of his administration to stifle legitimate dissent, Congress decided to restrict the powers of the president by passing the War Powers Act in 1973 overriding President Nixon's veto. The Act asserts that the president may only send armed forces into "hostilities" if Congress has issued a declaration of war, passed specific legislation authorizing the action, or if it involves a national emergency created by an attack on the United States. The president is required to notify Congress when troops are to be sent into foreign combat, and the troops must be brought home within 60 days (or 90 days, if necessary) unless Congress declares war or extends the length of troop involvement. As well, the president is required to answer any questions about the conflict that are raised by Congress and to submit periodic reports. The War Powers Act has been viewed by presidents as an infringement of their executive powers.

As the US bombed ISIS and sent Special Forces to Syria in 2015 and 2016, President Obama justified the action by invoking the Authorization of Use of Military Force passed by Congress in 2001 to fight al-Qaeda in response to its terrorist attack on the United States. He argued that the use of the 2001 authorization was necessary because the Republican majority in the Senate was reluctant to pass a new authorization as it would tie the hands of a new president.

Overall, as Senator Tim Kaine (2014) pointed out, the executive branch has over-reached its authority and Congress has abdicated its responsibility in deciding whether the US should engage in significant armed conflicts.

LEADERSHIP AND DECISIVE ACTION Those who prefer a presidential system often view it as providing strong leadership. The president leads the executive branch of government and is secure in office. Being elected in a national vote, the president can claim to speak for the people of the country as a whole. However, given the independence of Congress, it is difficult for a president to ensure that a coherent set of policies is adopted. Thus, particularly in the American presidential system, decisive action on domestic issues can be difficult to achieve.

In a parliamentary system, the prime minister and Cabinet are capable of decisive action in a majority government situation because of their domination of the legislative branch. However, where no party has a majority, bargaining and negotiating among parties is required to gain majority support for legislative proposals. In some countries, the parliamentary system has been characterized by series of weak and unstable governments because of a highly fragmented party system in which stable coalitions cannot be formed.

DEMOCRATIC ELECTION The presidential system is sometimes viewed as more democratic than the parliamentary system, as the president is elected by the people. Unlike parliamentary systems where voters do not directly choose the prime minister, Americans have an opportunity to vote for the president as well as for the individuals who will represent their state and district in Congress.

REPRESENTATIVENESS Members of Congress have greater independence than members of Parliament to represent the population and interests of their district or state, as they are not as tightly bound by party discipline as is the case in most parliamentary systems. In contrast, the party discipline characteristic of parliamentary systems limits the ability of members of the House of Commons to represent their constituents.

RESPONSIVENESS Individual members of Congress are often very responsive to the voters or important interests in the districts or states they represent. However, the difficulties in passing legislation can make the governing system slow to respond to the wishes of the electorate as a whole. Although the American president may be responsive to the public in order to gain re-election, the term limit means that the president does not have to be responsive to public opinion in the second term. As well, Cabinet secretaries are not elected and may be unresponsive to the public. In parliamentary systems, the prime minister, Cabinet, and the governing party have an incentive to be responsive to the voters to secure re-election and, in a majority government situation, have the capability to respond quickly to the views and demands of the citizenry.

ACCOUNTABILITY The president and Cabinet do not sit in Congress and are not accountable to Congress. Nevertheless, the committees of the US Congress are able to investigate executive actions as part of their "oversight"

American presidents have found ways to avoid the constitutional provision that only Congress has the authority to declare war.
Tami Thirlwell

role to ensure that the executive is acting properly. At times, presidents and other executive officials have claimed "executive privilege" to try to avoid releasing documents and testifying before a congressional committee. The extent of executive privilege has never been clearly established, although the courts have tended to view it as a qualified privilege relevant in certain situations. More generally, the separation of powers allows each branch of government to try to shift blame to the other for any problems, making it difficult for voters to determine who to hold accountable.

A parliamentary system makes government responsible to the House of Commons for its actions. However, in a majority government situation, the governing party normally does not need to worry about maintaining the support of the House of Commons. Nevertheless, because the prime minister and Cabinet actively participate in the House of Commons, the public may have an opportunity to assess the performance of the government through the ongoing verbal exchanges between government and the opposition in the House.

OPENNESS The presidential system tends to be more open than the parliamentary system. Rather than policy choices being made in the secrecy of Cabinet, Congress plays an active and more public role in developing and modifying policy proposals. Policy differences between Congress and the president are often aired publicly. This transparency may facilitate greater public participation in the policy-making process and make the process more inclusive of differing interests and viewpoints. However, the openness of the American political system makes the system more susceptible to influence by groups with specific interests (such as a variety of corporate interests) that may be able to prevent laws for the common good from being passed.

FLEXIBILITY   Presidential systems tend to be less flexible than parliamentary systems (Linz, 1994). The fixed terms of office in presidential systems can make it difficult to resolve impasses between the executive and legislative branches, as an election cannot be held before the end of the term of each elected politician. In parliamentary systems, a government that is unable to retain the confidence of the majority in the House of Commons can be removed from office. Likewise, prime ministers that lose the support of their party or their party's parliamentary caucus can be pressured to step down.

EXPERIENCE   The American presidential system often features "outsiders" being elected. Popular personalities and wealthy individuals are sometimes able to appeal to the public at large even if they do not have a strong connection to a particular party. Although this may bring a fresh perspective to national politics, it means that the president may have very limited experience in national politics and international affairs. For example, although Bill Clinton and George W. Bush had political experience as state governors, neither had experience in national politics before becoming president. Barack Obama served fewer than four years in the US Senate (with part of that time spent campaigning) before being elected president. As well, since a president is unrestricted in the choice of Cabinet secretaries, some of those chosen have had little or no political experience (although they often have considerable expertise). Prime ministers often have extensive political experience, although a few Canadian prime ministers (such as Brian Mulroney and Justin Trudeau) have come to office with little experience as an elected politician. Unlike parliamentary systems, in which a potential prime minister can gain experience and knowledge by serving as leader of an opposition party, presidential systems offer no formal role for losing presidential candidates.[3]

semi-presidential system

A system of governing in which an elected president with a fixed term of office shares executive power with a prime minister and Cabinet who are collectively responsible to an elected legislature.

SEMI-PRESIDENTIAL SYSTEMS

A number of countries have adopted systems of governing involving a mixture of parliamentary and presidential features, which are often referred to as **semi-presidential systems**. Specifically, a semi-presidential system features an elected president with a fixed term of office who shares executive power with

---

[3] An exception is Nicaragua, where the runner-up in the presidential election automatically receives a seat in the National Assembly.

a prime minister and Cabinet who are collectively responsible to an elected legislature (Choudhry & Stacey, 2014).

The term "semi-presidential system" was originally developed by Maurice Duverger (1980) to describe the governing system adopted by France in 1958 (discussed below). Other examples of countries that are frequently described as having semi-presidential systems include Poland, Peru, Romania, Sri Lanka, Tunisia, Taiwan, and Ukraine. Constitutionally, Russia also has a semi-presidential system. However, President Vladimir Putin has exercised tight control over Russia, and thus its governing system differs considerably in practice from the power-sharing characteristic of democratic semi-presidential systems.

In a semi-presidential system, an elected president chooses and appoints (and, in some countries, can dismiss) the prime minister (and, in some countries, Cabinet ministers). As well, the president generally has the power (in some cases with limitations) to dissolve the elected legislature and require that a legislative election be held. The president cannot be removed from office during the fixed term except through an impeachment process. Generally the president can only serve a limited number of terms (two terms in a number of countries). In a semi-presidential system, the president as head of state has a significant role in decision making, but the government (prime minister and Cabinet) which needs to maintain the support of an elected legislature to remain in office, is generally responsible for legislation.

There is considerable variation among semi-presidential systems of different countries. In some, termed "president–parliamentary," the prime minister can be removed from office by either the president or the legislature. In others, termed "premier–presidential," the prime minister and Cabinet can only be removed by a vote of the legislature. The president–parliamentary version may be more likely to lead to confusion and instability as the Cabinet is accountable to two different masters. It can also result in an overly powerful president. The premier–parliamentary version, on the other hand, provides an important incentive for the president to work with the prime minister (thus sharing power) since the president does not have the authority to dismiss the prime minister (Elgie, 2011).

The Semi-Presidential One
www.semipresidentialism.com

France's Semi-Presidential System

From 1871 to 1958, France's parliamentary system did not function well. Governments changed frequently and were often unable to

Based on dissatisfaction with its parliamentary system, France adopted a semi-presidential system in 1958 with wartime leader Charles de Gaulle as president.

Marka/press/Alamy Stock Photo

act effectively. In 1958, French army officers unhappy with the government's efforts against the war of liberation in the French colony of Algeria staged a *coup d'état* in Algiers and threatened to overthrow the French government unless Charles de Gaulle (the leader of the Free French who fought to liberate France from fascist control in World War II) was made president. The president of France invited de Gaulle to take over as prime minister instead. De Gaulle accepted this invitation on the condition that a new constitution providing for a powerful president was adopted. A referendum approving a semi-presidential system was passed by a large margin in 1958. De Gaulle was then chosen president, a position he held until stepping down in 1969.

The French president is elected for a fixed five-year term and can serve a maximum of two terms.[4] The president appoints the prime minister who has the support of the majority party or a coalition of parties that has the majority in the elected National Assembly. The president, with advice from the prime minister, appoints the members of the Council of Ministers (Cabinet) as well as top public, military, and judicial officials. The president chairs the meetings of the Council of Ministers. The broader government including senior and junior ministers (secretaries of state) is headed by the prime minister.

The president does not sit in the National Assembly. The Assembly, elected for a maximum five-year term, can censure the prime minister and Council of Ministers and force them to resign but cannot censure the president or force a presidential election.[5] However, unlike the American presidential system, the French president can dissolve the Assembly and have a new Assembly election conducted (although another election cannot be held for at least one year). The French president cannot veto laws passed by the Assembly but can refer a proposed law back to the Assembly for reconsideration one time and can also refer the law to the Constitutional Court to determine its validity before signing the legislation.

The French president can call national referendums, determine when the National Assembly meets and what its agenda will be, assume emergency powers, and propose constitutional amendments. As well, the president has a leading role in foreign affairs, is responsible for negotiating and ratifying foreign treaties, and is commander-in-chief of the armed forces (Elgie, 2005).

When the Assembly has a majority of members from the same party as the president (or parties that support the president), the president tends to be the dominant figure in the French government. The prime minister, in this situation, is usually someone who has personal loyalty to the president. Although the president does not have the constitutional authority to dismiss a prime minister, presidents have been able to encourage prime ministers of their own

---

[4]Prior to 2007, the president could serve an unlimited number of seven-year terms.

[5]There is also a Senate elected by a very large number of elected officials. Although technically equal in some respects to the Assembly, it generally is less important than the Assembly.

party to resign (in some cases, it has been alleged, by requiring them to sign an undated letter of resignation before taking office).

If the majority in the Assembly represents a party that has a different perspective than the president, the president will find it necessary to choose the leader of that party as prime minister, as the government must have the support of the majority in the Assembly. The president can dissolve the Assembly and call an election, but if the election leads to a similar result, the president will have to live with a government that has a different political perspective. In this situation, termed **cohabitation**, the president shares power with the prime minister and Cabinet. From 1986 to 1988 and 1993 to 1995, Socialist President François Mitterrand shared power with the conservative parties that controlled the Assembly, while from 1997 to 2002, President Jacques Chirac, a conservative, shared power with Socialist Prime Minister Lionel Jospin. In this power-sharing arrangement, the prime minister has a strong ability to determine the domestic policies that will be adopted, regardless of the views of the president (Elgie, 2005). However, the likelihood of cohabitation has been reduced with a change in electoral rules so that the Assembly election is held shortly after the presidential election. In 2002, 2007, and 2012, parties supporting the president won in each following Assembly election. The adoption in recent times of primary elections by the major political parties to choose their presidential candidate could make it difficult for a president who is not supported by ordinary party members to seek a second term.

cohabitation

The sharing of power between the French president and prime minister that occurs when the Assembly is controlled by a party opposed to the president.

✓• SUMMARY AND CONCLUSION

The term *presidential system* can be misleading. The president controls the executive branch of government and serves as both head of state and head of government. However, particularly in the United States, the separation of powers allows each of the three branches of government to check the powers of the other branches. The sharing of powers between the president and Congress usually makes bargaining and compromises between the president and Congress necessary in order to make governing decisions. Therefore, some political scientists have suggested that it would be more accurate to describe the American system of government as a presidential–congressional system rather than a presidential system. To a considerable extent the power of the American president is dependent on the president's ability to persuade the public and individual members of Congress of the merits of a particular policy. As head of state as well as

head of government, a president can successfully claim to speak on behalf of the national interest, as long as the president retains the respect and support of the people. Because individual members of Congress tend to represent state or district interests, it can be difficult for Congress to take coherent action for the common good of the country as a whole.

The American presidential system was the model for the adoption of presidential systems in many countries (for example, most Latin American countries). However, in practice, many presidential systems feature a strong president whose powers are not effectively checked and balanced by a strong and independent Congress.

Semi-presidential systems generally have both an elected president with a fixed term in office and significant powers, and a prime minister and Cabinet that are responsible to an elected legislature (and, in some countries, to the president as well). Because the elected legislature can be dissolved before its term is up, there is somewhat greater flexibility than in a pure presidential system, where both the president and Congress have fixed terms in office. As with all systems of governing, the actual functioning of semi-presidential systems is affected by constitutional provisions, the nature of the political party system, the context within which the governing system was established, and the personalities of the leading political figures (Elgie, 1999).

✔• KEY TERMS

Checks and balances   353
Cohabitation   369
Congress   353
House of Representatives   357

Impeachment   356
Political gridlock   360
Presidential system   353
Presidential veto   358

Semi-presidential system   366
Senate (United States)   357
Separation of powers   353

DISCUSSION QUESTIONS

1. Do you think it would be best for a new democracy to adopt a parliamentary, presidential, or semi-presidential system?

2. What criteria are particularly important in evaluating different systems of governing?

3. Is Canada's parliamentary system preferable to an American-style presidential system?

4. Is there an appropriate balance between legislative and executive power in the United States?

5. Does the semi-presidential system create a hybrid that contains the best or the worst of the parliamentary and presidential systems?

FURTHER READING

Brady, D.W., & Volden, C. (2006). *Revolving gridlock: Politics and policy from Jimmy Carter to George W. Bush* (2nd ed.). Boulder, CO: Westview Press.

Carrier, M. (2016). *Executive politics in semi-presidential regimes: Power distribution and conflicts between presidents and prime ministers.* Lanham, MD: Lexington Books.

Cheibub, J.A. (2007). *Presidentialism, parliamentarism and democracy.* Cambridge: Cambridge University Press.

Elgie, R., (2011). *Semi-presidentialism. Subtypes and democratic performance.* Oxford: Oxford University Press.

Ginsberg, B. (2016). *Presidential government.* New Haven, CT: Yale University Press.

Howell, W.G. (2013). *Thinking about the presidency: The primacy of power.* Princeton, NJ: Princeton University Press.

Smith, R.A. (2014). *The American anomaly. U.S. politics and government in comparative perspective* (3rd ed.). New York: Routledge.

Thurber, J.A. (Ed.) (2013). *Rivals for power: Presidential-Congressional relations* (5th ed.). Latham, MD: Rowman & Littlefield.

16 Public Policy and Public Administration

On April 20, 2010, BP's oil drilling rig exploded in the Gulf of Mexico. For many months, millions of litres of oil a day gushed from the site, causing an ecological disaster.

Gerald Herbert/AP Photo/The Canadian Press

After reading this chapter, you should be able to:

1. discuss whether economic growth should be the leading objective of public policy
2. examine the growth of income inequality and challenges to the welfare state
3. compare the general perspectives on public policy
4. describe the characteristics of bureaucracies
5. evaluate public administration reforms

On April 20, 2010, an oil-drilling rig working for BP, one of the world's largest petroleum companies, exploded in the Gulf of Mexico, killing 11 workers. A blowout preventer on the 1.5 km deep well failed, and for months the leakage of millions of litres of oil a day killed birds, dolphins, and fish and fouled the ecologically sensitive marshes of Louisiana and the coastline of several states.

BP had been granted a "categorical exemption" from the environmental assessment required under the National Environmental Policy Act. BP's application for a drilling permit stated that a spill was "unlikely" and that even if it were to occur it would have "sub-lethal effects on fish and marine mammals." Less than two weeks before the disaster, BP lobbied the US government to broaden the use of categorical exemptions so as to avoid unnecessary paperwork and time delays (Eilperin, 2010).

The disaster in the Gulf raises issues about government regulation of industry. In recent decades, there has been a move to deregulate industry as much as possible. Government regulations are seen by business interests as inefficient and harmful to the competitive free market. In the United States, responsibility for ensuring safety in offshore drilling gradually has been shifting to the oil industry, although various requirements concerning blowout preventers remain. In Canada in 2009, the National Energy Board, which is responsible for regulating the industry, adopted what it termed a "modern, goal-oriented" approach that allows companies to determine what technologies intended to protect the environment are most appropriate for their particular projects (Mayeda, 2010).

Several petroleum companies, including BP, Imperial Oil, and Exxon have oil-drilling licences for the Canadian Arctic's Beaufort Sea. However they have delayed plans to drill in the area and have requested an extension of their licences to drill that expire in 2020. Shell was forced to postpone its Arctic drilling in 2012 due to the grounding of its drill rig off Alaska. A review found that it was not prepared for the extreme conditions in the Arctic and a test of its oil spill containment device failed in the calmer waters off Seattle (Goldenberg, 2013). While a number of petroleum companies seek to tap the resources of the Arctic, a blowout in the fragile Arctic ecosystem would be much more difficult to contain than in the Gulf of Mexico.

In the pursuit of profit and multimillion-dollar bonuses for their executives, corporations may take excessive risks and seek to cut costs by pressuring governments to reduce regulation. This is the case not only in the petroleum industry but also in the financial industry, where excessive risk and greed led to the near collapse of the global economy in 2008. Further, because of their financial clout and lobbying efforts, corporations may be able to gain special privileges (such as exemptions from regulations) that may not come to public attention until a disaster occurs.

Rigid and excessive regulations may be harmful to the economy. However, appropriate and carefully administered government regulations are essential to protect the economy and the environment.

INTRODUCTION

Public policy can be defined as "a course of action or inaction chosen by public authorities to address a given problem or interrelated set of problems" (Pal, 1992, p. 2). In this chapter, we examine some of the major policy issues that are important in pursuing the common good. We also look at how policies are carried out by examining some features of public administration.

public policy

A course of action or inaction chosen by public authorities to address a given problem or interrelated set of problems.

THE GOALS OF PUBLIC POLICY

Safety and Security

A classic argument for the existence of government is the need for personal safety and security. Thomas Hobbes (1588–1670) argued that before the establishment of government people lived in the state of nature that involved a war of "all against all." This resulted in lives that were "solitary, poor, nasty, brutish, and short." Therefore, people quickly contracted to form a government to preserve order. Indeed Hobbes argued that the ruler or the government should have absolute, undivided authority to preserve order and prevent civil war. However, John Locke (1632–1704) had a somewhat different view. He assumed that individuals had been free and equal in the state of nature, but lacked the means to settle disputes. Therefore, through what he termed the "social contract," people agreed to establish government for specific purposes: the protection of life, liberty, and property. Rather than having an all-powerful ruler, government should be limited in its powers, acting as a trustee to protect the rights of the people. People should remove the government, by force if necessary, if it should infringe on the liberties that government was established to protect.

Regardless of whether the assumptions Hobbes and Locke held about the original formation of government are at all accurate, there are countries in the world today, for example, Somalia, South Sudan, Syria, and Yemen, where violent civil wars have been raging and people fear for their lives. However, life under a tyrannical dictator or a totalitarian regime can also be fearful even if there is the semblance of order.

In the majority of countries severe forms of violence are not all that common. For example, in Canada the incidence of intentional homicide in 2014 was 1.45 per 100 000, a decline from its peak of 3.02 in 1975 (Statistics Canada, 2015).[1] In some countries, the rate was much lower (for example Japan 0.3 and Germany 0.7), while the rate in the United States (5.1) and the global average (6.2) were higher in 2013 (United Nations Office on Drugs and Crime, 2014). Honduras had the highest rate at 90.2 per 100 000.

---

[1]Aboriginals were about six times as likely to be homicide victims. A national inquiry was initiated in 2016 into the large number of Aboriginal women and girls who have been murdered or missing since 1980. The homicide rate for Aboriginal males was 10.9 per 100 000 in 2014.

In liberal democracies, we expect that there will be a high level of individual freedom. However, some limitations are needed to ensure safety and security. For example, there is no right to yell "fire" in a crowded theatre if there is no fire. Beyond that, should laws and policies seek to protect vulnerable people from those who promote racism, sexism, and homophobia? Similarly, to what extent should public policies allow for strong action and restrictions on rights and freedoms to deal with threats of violence?

A well-trained police force is very important in providing safety and security. However, in a number of countries, some members of police and military forces contribute to violence. In the United States, for example, there have been some incidents where police shooting those (particularly blacks) who appear to be violating the law have led to riots. In Canada, there have been allegations of severe mistreatment of Aboriginals by some police officers. Large-scale extrajudicial killings by police and military have occurred, at times, in Latin America, Africa, and other parts of the world. Indeed, Rodrigo Duterte (sometimes called "The Punisher"), who was elected president of the Philippines in 2016, boasted about personally killing suspected criminals when he was a mayor, and is alleged to have ordered the killing of more than 3000 drug dealers and users in his first months as president (Holmes, 2016).

Security also involves protecting a country and its people from a foreign attack. Canada has been fortunate in suffering only a small number of casualties from attacks on its territory. Nevertheless, the development of modern military technology means that Canada's geographical isolation would no longer provide protection if a major world war or terrorist action were to occur. In Canada, as elsewhere, defence policy along with foreign policy can be of great importance in pursuing a more peaceful world.

In addition, a variety of public policies are needed to ensure the safety of food, medicines, and consumer products, workplaces, roads, bridges, buildings, and vehicles. As well, welfare state policies (discussed in this chapter) play an important part in providing a sense of security by reducing fears about the consequences of losing one's job or being unable to support one's family.

Economic Prosperity

In *The Wealth of Nations* (1776) Scottish philosopher Adam Smith argued that individuals pursuing their own interests increase the wealth of a country through the "invisible hand of the marketplace." Based on this perspective, it is often claimed that a free-market economy along with free trade leads to economic prosperity both within a country and in the world as a whole.

A **capitalist economic system** is one in which most businesses are privately owned and seek profit through the production and sale of goods and services in a basically free market (Bowles, 2012). However, few, if any, countries in the contemporary world could be considered to have a pure free-market

capitalist economic system

A system in which most businesses are privately owned and seek profit through the production and sale of goods and services in the market.

economy with very little government control of business and the market. There is considerable variation in capitalist economic systems (Hall & Sockice, 2001). Some countries such as the United States, Canada, Britain, Australia, and New Zealand can be described as having basically liberal capitalist economies in which businesses are relatively free to act in the marketplace as they see fit. Somewhat different are the "coordinated market economies" of Germany, Scandinavia, and Japan where there is greater cooperation among different businesses. This may also involve cooperation between corporation executives and their employees, for example, worker participation in business decision making; provision by businesses of vocational training for their workers; and collaboration between business and government on research and development (Bronk, 2000; Hancké, 2009).

In theory, a capitalist system with a minimum of government involvement in the economy results in the maximum wealth of a country. Competition among different firms provides strong incentives to produce goods that people want as cheaply as possible thereby benefiting consumers. However, the reality tends to be more complex. Competition is not always strong. For example, if one firm is successful in marketing its product, other firms may find that producing the product is unprofitable and cease production. The successful firm is then in a powerful position to raise its price particularly if the start-up costs for other companies to produce that product are high. As well, a substantial proportion of a corporation's revenues and profits often go to the top executives and the board of directors. Indeed, as some of the largest American banks and financial institutions were failing in 2008 due to huge mistakes, some executives continued to receive hundreds of millions of dollars each year while the US government spent many billions to bailout these institutions. The justification provided by the government for the bailout was that these corporations were "too big to fail" meaning that their failure could result in crashing the economy.

In addition to ensuring that competition is maintained in the marketplace, governments need to develop public policies to ensure that consumers have the information they need to make informed choices. Public policies are also needed to ensure that workers are treated fairly, that workplaces are safe, and that hiring practices are not discriminatory. More generally, the contribution of some political scientists to the study of public policy is to go beyond the analysis of economic efficiency to consider questions of accountability, legitimacy, feasibility, the distribution of power (Atkinson, 2013), and the implications for the pursuit of social justice.

Public policies are also important in ensuring that the overall economy functions smoothly. Economic activity tends to go through cycles of expansion and contraction. During the Great Depression of the 1930s, when business investment collapsed and unemployment rates skyrocketed, British economist John Maynard Keynes (1883–1946) developed the idea that government could smooth out the ups and downs of the free-market economy.

Keynesian economic policies

The idea that government can smooth out the ups and downs of the free-market economy by stimulating the economy when private business investment is low and cooling down the economy when excessive investment is creating inflation.

Keynesian economic policies involve the government stimulating the economy (by spending money and/or reducing taxes) when private business investment is low and cooling down the economy (by reducing spending and/or raising taxes) when excessive investment is creating inflation. As well, because the poor tend to spend rather than save their money, government programs that put money into the hands of the poor can help to ensure that there is sufficient demand for the goods and services that business can supply. This in turn can result in full or nearly full employment. In general, Keynesian economic policies reflect the view that government can have a positive role in ensuring the smooth functioning of the free-market capitalist system without directly intervening in business decisions.

Keynesian economic policies were adopted by most of the advanced capitalist countries during and after World War II. They were successful in providing three decades of sustained growth and prosperity. However, Keynesian economic policies fell out of favour among economists and government policymakers in the mid-1970s when economies suffered from a simultaneous combination of inflation and economic stagnation ("stagflation"). In their place, neoliberal ideas that viewed the market as efficient and self-regulating became influential. Cutting taxes, reducing regulation, and reducing government spending were seen as the key to economic growth.

In particular, influential American economist Milton Friedman (1912–2006) argued that government should have a balanced budget; that is, government spending should not exceed its revenues each year. This means that government spending will be reduced in recessionary times as tax revenues decline. However, introducing strict government austerity measures during a recession can drive the economy deeper into economic decline. Likewise, tax cuts will not stimulate economic growth unless business and consumers are confident that the economy is healthy.

Friedman also argued that the role of government in the economy should be substantially reduced. With less regulation and lower taxes, there would be greater incentives for investment and production. Economic problems would be resolved by the free market rather than by government. However, the idea that the free market by itself can solve serious economic problems may be wishful thinking as discussed in Box 16-1 The Impact of the Financial Crisis of 2007–2009.

Inequality in Income and Wealth

In many countries, including Canada and the United States, inequality in income and wealth has been increasing, particularly as top corporate executives have awarded themselves very high compensation while the wages of their employees have often stagnated. Indeed the average CEO of the largest US corporations in 2012 received total earnings 354 times that of an

BOX 16-1 The Impact of the Financial Crisis of 2007–2009

The financial crisis of 2007–2009 was caused, to a very considerable extent, by the lack of adequate regulation of major financial institutions in the United States and Europe. This led to an expensive bailout of banks and financial institutions, major government spending programs, and exceptionally low (even negative in some countries) interest rates to provide economic stimulus. In 2010, as the government of Greece was about to default on its loans and several other European countries faced huge government deficits and debts, the European Union along with the International Monetary Fund and the European Central Bank put together a loan facility of about one trillion dollars to assist governments in financial troubles and prevent a collapse of the euro. As German Chancellor Angela Merkl told the German Parliament:

> "The lack of rules and limits can make behavior in financial markets driven purely by the profit motive destructive and lead to an existential threat to financial stability in Europe and even the world. . . . The market alone won't correct these mistakes." (quoted in Leonard, 2010)

The conditions for receiving loans involved the imposition of austerity programs including major cuts to public programs and to the employment, wages, and pensions of public servants. However, the severe austerity programs in some countries led to unrest and very high youth unemployment rates. Years later, the effects of the austerity programs were still being felt.

Here's a tax tip kid: try not to pay them! I don't and maybe one day you too can buy yourself a waterfront villa!
Tami Thirlwell

average employee. By comparison the ratio in 1965 was 20:1(Kiatpongsan & Norton, 2014). The 100 highest paid CEOs in Canada received an average of $8.96 million in 2014, 184 times that of the average Canadian worker (MacKenzie, 2016).

There has been a growing gap between the wealthiest top 1 percent and the 99 percent of the population of many countries and the world as a whole. Indeed, the wealth of the wealthiest 62 persons is now equal to the total wealth of the bottom 50 percent of the world's population (Oxfam, 2016). Some of the super-rich have hidden their money in tax havens such as Jersey, Isle of Man, Cayman Islands, Bermuda, Panama, Switzerland, and Hong Kong to avoid taxes. One study found that this hidden wealth amounted to at least US$ 7.6 trillion (Zucman, 2015). Oxfam (2016) claims that African countries lose US$ 14 billion a year in tax revenue through the transfer of money to tax havens. This would be "enough to pay for healthcare that would save the lives of four million children and employ enough teachers to get every African child into school."

In 2016 thousands of documents leaked from a law firm in Panama provided information on 214 448 offshore accounts. Some of the accounts involved the proceeds of crime and corruption. Others were legal transactions to maintain privacy and avoid taxes in the home country. World leaders named in the Panama Papers included the prime minister of Iceland who then resigned, the prime minister of Pakistan, the king of Saudi Arabia, and about $2 billion in the hands of Russian President Putin's associates. In Canada, the offshore transfer of funds was estimated to result in tax losses to the Canadian government of $6 to $7.8 billion per year (Gribb & Oved, 2016).

Not only has the share of income going to the "super-rich" increased in recent decades, but also the bottom two-fifths of the population have not shared in economic growth and, in some countries, have seen their real income (income after taking into account the effects of inflation) decline (OECD, 2015). In Canada, income inequality has increased in the past two decades. The share of total national income going to the low and middle income groups decreased while the top 1 percent increased their share of income (Conference Board of Canada, 2016). The United States has one of the highest proportions of income going to the top 1 percent and one of the highest poverty rates among the developed countries (Atkinson, 2015).

The outsourcing of production to low-wage countries and an increase in temporary and part-time employment has resulted in the loss of many well-paid jobs. Public policies to encourage more on-the-job training, ensure that high quality education is available to all, improve the provision of child care, and increase the minimum wage could improve the position of the less well-off and improve the quality of the workforce.

Globalization (including free trade) has, to some extent, reduced inequalities between countries while increasing inequalities within countries. Workers in Canada and, particularly, the United States have faced a decline in high-paying jobs because of foreign competition (and changes in manufacturing processes) while top corporate executives, the wealthy, and some highly educated professionals have generally benefited from free trade (Milanovic, 2016). However, political scientists Hacker and Pierson (2010) argue that the rich have become richer in the United States primarily because of government policies that aid the rich rather than because of globalization, trade, and technological changes.

It has often been thought that income inequality provides an important incentive for individuals to pursue education, work hard, and to save and invest. However, a study by the International Monetary Fund concluded that "equality appears to be an important ingredient in promoting and sustaining growth." Without adequate finances, many people will rely on borrowing money, which can lead to a financial crisis if there is a high level of debt that cannot be repaid. As well, severe inequality may lead to heightened political conflict which discourages investment (Conference Board of Canada, 2016).

Overall, economic prosperity does not necessarily improve the quality of life of the people of a country. The accessibility of health care, good education, social and recreational activities, a clean environment, and safe communities are also very important. A high level of inequality in income and wealth can undermine social cohesion and the common good.

Free Trade and Investment Protection Agreements

The pursuit of free-trade agreements is an important aspect of the economic policies of many countries, including Canada. Free trade is viewed as increasing the wealth of nations by encouraging businesses to produce goods and services on which they have a comparative advantage such that they can sell those products in the global market. Consumers can benefit by having a choice of a wider range of goods that are available at lower prices because of greater competition. However, labour interests are usually critical of unrestricted free trade because global competition can pressure businesses to reduce the wages and benefits of their workers or to move production to countries where the costs of production are lowest. In effect, free trade tends to increase the power of large multinational corporations.

Free trade agreements are often very lengthy and complex documents that governments have usually negotiated with the participation of business representatives. Indeed, major free-trade agreements, such as the North American Free Trade Agreement (NAFTA), EU-Canada Comprehensive Economic and Trade Agreement (CETA), Transatlantic Trade and Investment Partnership (TTIP), Trade in Services Agreement (TiSA), and the proposed

Trans-Pacific Partnership (TPP) contain many provisions that go beyond free trade.[2] Typically, this involves extending protection of intellectual property (including pharmaceutical patents and copyrights) along with special arrangements for certain agricultural products, public services, and cultural products. The major free-trade agreements have been the subject of considerable controversy because they can substantially affect a country's economy. Some changes can negatively affect many workers, farmers, and small businesses. During the 2016 US presidential election campaign, both Clinton and Trump promised to kill the Trans-Pacific Partnership, and Trump talked about tearing up NAFTA. The Transatlantic Partnership was also under attack by politicians in both the United States and Europe.

NAFTA also provides for an investor-state dispute resolution mechanism that allows foreign companies to sue governments that they claim are harming their investments through expropriation or actions that affect "the company's future profitability or opportunities for growth" (Boyd, 2003, p. 257). Decisions are made in a private tribunal that can require that a government pay very large amounts of compensation to the foreign company. Similarly, the Canadian government has negotiated a number of foreign investment promotion and protection agreements (FIPAs) with about 50 countries. Particularly controversial is the Canada-China FIPA adopted in 2014 by the Canadian Cabinet without parliamentary debate or scrutiny. This gives Chinese corporations (including China's many government -owned corporations) operating in Canada the right to challenge any law or regulation passed by any level of government that threatens their profitability, with independent arbitrators deciding on compensation. The agreement lasts a minimum of 15 years. Even if cancelled, claims can be pursued for an additional 16 years. Critics claim that the FIPA threatens Canadian and provincial laws and regulations concerning environmental protection, natural resource conservation, labour rights, and Aboriginal treaties, as these could be challenged by Chinese resource investments in Canada (Van Harten, 2015). The Conservative government that promoted the FIPA viewed it as a way to attract more foreign investment.

Social Policy

In the past, people were expected to be self-reliant. The failure to provide for oneself and one's family was often viewed as a result of personal irresponsibility

---

[2]Canada, the United States, and Mexico are members of NAFTA, which came into effect in 1994, The TPP, signed in 2016, is an agreement involving 12 countries (including Canada, the United States, and Japan) accounting for about two-fifths of the world's economic output. CETA, signed in 2014, is an agreement between Canada and the European Union; the TTIP is an agreement between the United States and the European Union. TiSA involves 50 countries including Canada, the United States, and the European Union. Canada has also adopted a substantial number of agreements with individual countries. At the time of writing, the TPP and CETA had not been ratified and the TTIP and TiSA were still being negotiated.

rather than a general failure of the economy. This view was challenged during the Great Depression of the 1930s, when millions of people were unable to find work. Private charities and local governments had difficulty dealing with the problems faced by the needy. The successful mobilization of society and the economy by governments for World War II increased the capabilities of governments and created more positive attitudes toward an active role for government. There were expectations that governments should take responsibility for the well-being of returning soldiers and the families of those who had sacrificed their lives. As well, the threat of communism and the growing strength of labour and socialist parties in the 1940s and 1950s created a political climate favourable to the development (or expansion) of the **welfare state**. This includes government programs to provide income assistance for those facing hardships caused by old age, disabilities, poverty, and unemployment. It also involves ensuring that reasonable levels of education, health care, and housing are available to everyone.

The welfare state has been the subject of considerable debate in recent decades, as discussed in Box 16-2 Criticism of the Welfare State. Some have suggested that providing a guaranteed basic annual income not conditional on a means test or commitment to work would provide a simpler way to assist the poor while avoiding the stigma of traditional welfare programs (Segal, 2008; Martin, 2011). For example, in 2003 the government of Brazil established a citizen's right to a basic income and has been gradually implementing this right particularly through its Bolsa Familia. The debit card given to the female head of the household (averaging $65 a month) is conditional on sending children to school and having them vaccinated. The program has been successful in reducing poverty, improving health, and boosting the overall economy, and has been adopted by a number of other countries and a few US cities (Tepperman, 2016).

welfare state

A state in which government ensures that all people have a decent standard of living and are provided protection from hardships resulting from circumstances such as unemployment, sickness, disability, and old age.

Basic Income Earth Network
www.basicincome.org

The Quality of Individual and Community Life

The policies adopted by government play an important role in improving the general quality of life. Public health care systems have helped to increase life expectancy and are generally less costly than private profit-oriented health insurance systems. Historically, health care was generally provided by doctors for those who could pay for their services and by religious and charitable organizations that ran many hospitals with some assistance from governments. In the UK, a comprehensive health care system (the National Health Service) funded by taxes was established by the Labour government in 1948. Premier T.C. (Tommy) Douglas's CCF government brought universal access to hospital services to Saskatchewan in 1957, and universal access to physician services in 1962 despite a 23-day strike by doctors who opposed the plan. National hospital insurance was adopted in 1957 while the Medical Care Act, 1966 provided for other medical services. Medicare was implemented by all provinces by 1971.

BOX 16-2   Criticism of the Welfare State

Critics view the welfare state as substantially increasing the tax burden that people face and contributing to government deficits and debt. Increases in government spending and borrowing can crowd out private investment and activity. The welfare state interferes with the "discipline" of the marketplace, particularly by reducing the incentive for people to work. Instead, the welfare state encourages people to become dependent on government and less likely to take responsibility for their own lives.

Are these criticisms of the welfare state valid? Government provision of basic health care, education, and various social services has contributed to the high quality of life enjoyed by most Canadians. Welfare-state programs do not necessarily reduce the competitiveness of an economy. It can allow people to take greater risks, such as finding new jobs, knowing that they have security to fall back on. As well, various social programs help people to adjust as economies change in response to globalization. In the contemporary knowledge-based economies of advanced countries, an efficient welfare state combined with major government investments in education, health, culture, and research can help develop a highly productive workforce (Castells, 2004). A study conducted for the International Monetary Fund found that lower levels of inequality tended to be associated with long-term economic growth (Berg & Ostry, 2011).

Welfare-state programs contributed to the long period of social peace and economic growth in the decades after World War II by helping to achieve a compromise between the demands of workers and the pursuit of profit by business. Welfare-state policies may help to legitimate the free-market capitalist system in the eyes of the public by removing some of the harshness of the economic system. Nevertheless, welfare-state programs have faced serious cuts in many countries in part due to economic challenges and the rising costs of health and social programs. In addition, the influential ideology of neoliberalism has emphasized the importance of economic growth rather than other values such as social justice, equality, and fairness (Brown, 2015).

The Canadian government in recent decades has substantially reduced the proportion of unemployed persons who are eligible to collect employment insurance. Some provincial governments have reduced social assistance payments and required that the able-bodied work for their social assistance payments. The United States has had one of the weakest welfare-state programs of the developed countries (as well as low minimum wages) due, in part, to the weakness of its labour unions. In 1996, the US government adopted a policy limiting welfare to a maximum of five years in one's lifetime (and some states put stricter limits on receiving welfare cheques). In 2013, US medicare benefits for seniors and some young persons with disabilities were scheduled to be cut by 2 percent each year.

Although Canadians are generally proud of their health care system there are some important problems. A substantial number of Canadians are unable to find a family doctor. Although some operations can usually be obtained in a reasonable time, wait times for other procedures and for seeing specialists can be very long. Emergency rooms are often insufficiently staffed and a number of hospitals are in need of repair or replacement. Canada's medical technology tends to lag behind that of some Western European countries, particularly in electronic record-keeping and the communication of test results (Simpson, 2012).

Despite the adoption of public health care, the health of Canadians is still affected by inequalities. Paying for expensive prescription drugs can be very difficult, particularly for those without health care plans. Many Aboriginal communities, particularly in northern Canada, lack adequate medical care, psychological care (to deal with high levels of suicide, violence, and drug and alcohol abuse), and proper nutrition. Along with a high incidence of poverty, disease, and infant mortality, the life expectancy of Aboriginals is about five to seven years less than that of non-Aboriginals (Assembly of First Nations, 2011).

While nearly all of the developed countries now have publicly funded medical care systems, the United States has faced serious obstacles in moving toward universal access to medical care even though the largely private medical care system is more costly than the public systems of other countries. The controversial Patient Protection and Affordable Care Act, 2010, (often called "Obamacare") included a requirement that businesses with 50 or more employees provide health insurance to their workers. The Affordable Care Act includes both public and private plans rather than a single-payer public system. Although the proportion of Americans without health care coverage has been substantially reduced, "Obamacare" faces ongoing legal and political challenges. As well, the increasing cost of buying health care insurance and the complexity of the system have made it unpopular among a significant part of the population.

The provision of parks, recreational facilities, and public meeting places can increase health and happiness as well as creating a sense of community. A high level of government-subsidized education is important not only for creating a skilled workforce and increasing prosperity, but also for promoting a more active, knowledgeable, and informed citizenry. The provision of good public transit and intelligent urban planning can reduce aggravating commuting times, improve air quality, and enhance city life.

Government can also be involved in combating discrimination against various groups including women; racial, ethnic, and religious minorities; immigrants; the disabled; and those with different sexual orientations. Pay equity laws, affirmative action programs, subsidized child care, recognition of the rights and cultures of Indigenous peoples, and assistance to immigrants are some of the ways that governments can try to promote a more harmonious and just society.

Environmental Quality

Protecting the natural environment and substantially reducing greenhouse gas emissions can be considered the most serious long-term challenge facing the world. Effective government policies are necessary because corporations are usually reluctant to take costly measures to limit their impact on the environment. Indeed, large energy corporations are continuing their search for new sources of fossil fuels while trying to present a positive image by participating in some renewable energy projects. It is also unlikely that the public as a whole will voluntarily reduce their environmental impact. For example, a British study found that a majority of people (especially the young and well-educated) believe that human-induced climate change is occurring and favour policies to mitigate climate change; however, even climate-change believers appeared reluctant to modify their behaviour, for example by reducing their travel (Johnston & Deeming, 2016).

Many governments have been unwilling to take determined and effective action, despite overwhelming scientific evidence that the increasing concentrations of greenhouse gases in the atmosphere pose a lethal threat to humanity within a few decades. The effects of climate change are already having serious consequences such as more frequent and severe famines, flooding, and forest fires. However, with fossil-fuel industries employing large numbers of people and providing much government revenue, moving away from a petroleum-based economy will be very difficult. For example, the oil industry in Alberta employed over 133 000 persons in 2014 and provided $5.2 billion in royalties to the Alberta government.

While governments have committed to substantially reducing greenhouse gases over the coming decades, the policies that are needed to achieve that objective often involve costly and unpopular measures. Indeed, consumption of fossil fuels has continued to increase (Institute for Energy Research, 2015). Nevertheless, some countries (for example, Denmark) have been able to largely replace fossil fuels with renewable energy sources for electricity generation.

Balancing the Different Goals of Public Policy

Developing a set of policies that will accomplish a variety of goals such as those discussed above is a difficult task. For example, growth in gross domestic product (GDP) is often used as the leading measure of successful public policy. With the world's population continuing to increase and poorer countries trying to meet the needs of their population, economic growth is generally viewed as necessary to maintain or improve the quality of life. However, if the benefits of economic growth are pocketed mainly by those who are already wealthy thereby increasing inequality, the result may be increased political conflict and dissatisfaction among those who do not share in the increased prosperity. Further, economic growth can contribute to environmental degradation. While economic growth may bring short-term benefits, these benefits may be outweighed by the long-term costs; however, political realities may lead politicians to focus on winning the next election rather than the long-term effects of the policies adopted.

There are various efforts to develop indicators of the quality of life as well as indicators of environmental quality to achieve a more balanced indication of progress toward a variety of goals. The king of the tiny Himalayan country of Bhutan introduced the idea of gross national happiness (GNH) in 1972. This has been measured in that country by a survey of its citizens on a variety of subjects including health and wealth, community vitality, and emotional balance. A number of countries and communities in recent years conducted have their own surveys of happiness or well-being. A World Happiness Report, based on surveys from 2012–2014, found that Switzerland, Iceland, Denmark, Norway, and Canada were the top five countries while Afghanistan, Rwanda, and Syria were among the least happy with Togo the least happy (Helliwell, Layard, & Sachs, 2015). It remains to be seen whether measures of the quality of life will have a significant effect on public policy decisions.

World Happiness Report 2015
http://worldhappiness.report/
wp-content/uploads/
sites/2/2015/04/WHR15.pdf

ANALYZING PUBLIC POLICY

Analyzing government's choice of public policies involves looking at the broad set of forces that set the context for public policy and examining the details of the processes that led to the adoption of specific policies. Among the general influences on public policy are the ideas and ideologies that affect how the various individuals and groups involved in policy making decide what problems to address, how those problems are defined, and the general patterns of policies in that political community. Very important as well is the distribution of power and the ways in which different groups attempt to influence public policy. Developing public policy is not only a process through which government officials try to determine which policy is "best" in some technical way, but also a political process that reflects the contending ideas and interests of various groups in society and those in governing institutions.

General Perspectives

There are various general perspectives concerning the policy-making process and the outcomes of the process in democratic countries. Each of the approaches gives a different answer to why government acts the way it does and who tends to benefit from public policies (Brooks, 1998).

The **pluralist perspective** views public policies in liberal democracies as the outcome of competition among a wide variety of organized groups that seek to protect and promote the interests of their members. Some groups are more influential than others on particular issues, but no group has a dominant influence on a wide range of policies. Business interests have many resources that they can use to exert influence, but other groups and interests also have resources they can use to influence policy if they use those resources skilfully (Graefe, 2007). Governments are not systematically biased in favour of any particular group or interest. Instead governments try to develop policies that satisfy a wide variety of groups.

pluralist perspective

A perspective that views public policies as the outcome of competition among a wide variety of organized groups that seek to protect and promote the interests of their members, with no group having a dominant influence.

public choice theory

A perspective based on the assumption that all political actors are rationally attempting to maximize their own individual interests or preferences.

neo-Marxist theory

A perspective that views politics as reflecting the conflicts that result from the way society is organized to produce goods. Public policies in a capitalist society will reflect the unequal power relations between the dominant capitalist forces and the subordinate working class.

state-centred theory

A perspective that views public policies as reflecting, to a considerable extent, the preferences and priorities of those in important positions of authority within various state institutions.

Public choice theory assumes that all individuals involved in politics (including politicians, government employees, interest group leaders, and voters) are rationally attempting to maximize their own individual interests or preferences. Politicians wanting to maximize their power by winning elections will adopt policy positions preferred by the majority of voters or those voters who are crucial to the outcome of an election. This can lead to excessive government spending as politicians compete with one another for votes by making expensive promises. As well, public servants encourage the adoption of policies that expand the activities of government to increase their own status and chances for promotion.

Neo-Marxist theory views politics as reflecting the conflicts that result from the way society is organized to produce goods and services. Government policies generally reflect the unequal power relations between the dominant capitalist forces and the subordinate working class.[3] Economic globalization further enhances the dominance of capitalist interests and increases the pressure for policies that favour capitalist interests based on the argument that such policies are needed if a country is to be competitive in the global economy (Graefe, 2007).

State-centred theory views public policies as reflecting, to a considerable extent, the preferences and priorities of those in important positions of authority within various state institutions. Disputes over policies can arise out of the struggles and conflicts within and among different state institutions. State officials have considerable autonomy from social forces and an ability to gain support for the policies they prefer. The state-centred perspective tends to view senior public servants as being of particular importance because of their permanence and expertise.

Overall, none of the general theoretical approaches, while useful, seems to fully account for the general patterns of public policy. Other factors including ideas and ideologies, the organization and workings of government institutions, financial circumstances, partisan political competition, and the ways in which policy problems are defined and discussed are also important. Nevertheless, Gilens and Page (2014; 2016) in what they acknowledge is a tentative and preliminary study, found that "economic elites and organized groups representing business interest have substantial independent impacts on U.S. government policy, while mass-based interest groups and average citizens have little or no independent influence" (2014, p. 565). This conclusion may reflect the strong political power of big business interests in the United States.

The International Dimension

Public policy is a product not only of influences and decision-making processes within a country; globalization, international institutions, and international

---

[3]Some contemporary neo-Marxists extend this analysis to argue that capitalism also creates relations of inequality among individuals based on gender, race, ethnicity, and sexual orientation.

agreements are increasingly important in affecting public policy. For example, the meetings of the heads of government of the countries with the largest economies (the G7/G8 and the G20) play an important role, particularly in trying to coordinate policies to manage the global economy. Likewise, international financial institutions such as the International Monetary Fund use their financial power and influence to affect the policies of many countries.

International agreements play an increasingly important role in affecting the policies adopted by individual countries. International environmental agreements, for example, committed governments to adopt policies to phase out the use of ozone-depleting chemicals and prohibit trade in products made from endangered species.

PUBLIC ADMINISTRATION

How should the many policies, programs, and services of government be carried out? Over the past century, governments have developed large administrative structures staffed primarily by permanent employees (termed public or civil servants) to carry out these activities and to provide advice concerning policies and programs to the political executive.

Bureaucratic Organization

The origins of bureaucratic organization can be traced back about two thousand years when Chinese emperors began to choose public servants for life-long careers based on merit and virtue. In the sixth century CE a system of rigorous written exams in knowledge of Confucian thought, poetry, and literature was adopted to choose many public servants. The mandarinate, as they came to be known, has often had a powerful influence on the governing of China.

In 1764, the French philosopher Baron de Grimm developed the term **bureaucracy** to describe rule by offices and officials—a new form of government that he considered undesirable (Albrow, 1970). As discussed in Box 16-3 Bureaucratic Organization: A Threat to Democracy, some consider bureaucracy to be a threat to democracy.

Given the complex nature of many governing tasks, a specialized form of organization based on public servants with a high level of professional expertise is needed for effective modern governing. Instead of government employees being hired largely on the basis of political patronage (that is, based on ties to the governing party), hiring and promotion since the early twentieth century in Canada has been based primarily on merit (such as qualifications and competitive examinations).

REPRESENTATIVE BUREAUCRACY Staffing the public service strictly based on merit can make the public service unrepresentative of the characteristics of the society as a whole. An emphasis on formal qualifications,

bureaucracy

An organization in which people are hired and promoted based on their qualifications and merit, work is organized in terms of specialized positions, detailed rules and procedures are followed by all members of the organization, and there is a hierarchical chain of command so that those at the top can direct and supervise large numbers of people.

BOX 16-3 Bureaucratic Organization: A Threat to Democracy?

The organization of the modern public service is often termed a bureaucracy (a term that literally means "rule by offices"). In the view of Max Weber (1958), bureaucratic organizations are a key characteristic of modern societies, reflecting the capitalist system's concern with efficiency and the use of legal–rational forms of rule in modern political systems. Weber characterized a bureaucratic organization as one in which people are hired and promoted based on their qualifications and merit, work is organized in terms of specialized positions (offices), detailed rules and procedures are followed by all members of the organization, and there is a hierarchical chain of command so that those at the top can direct and supervise large numbers of people. These characteristics can make bureaucratic organizations efficient, although their adherence to rules and regulations can also result in these organizations being inflexible and impersonal. Indeed, the emphasis on hierarchy and discipline in modern military organizations and the factory as well as in the government bureaucracy were viewed by Weber as having dehumanizing effects on modern society.

Weber was concerned that powerful bureaucratic organizations controlled by senior officials would dominate the governments of modern societies thereby limiting the democratic ideal of rule by the people (Heywood, 2002). However, while the government bureaucracy has considerable potential power because of its permanence and expertise, elected political leaders often also draw upon other sources of advice and do not always rely on the bureaucracy to carry out government programs. Those governments that have a firm sense of their goals and priorities can direct the bureaucracy on key issues rather than be directed by the bureaucracy.

representative bureaucracy

A bureaucracy that reflects the characteristics of society, particularly by trying to ensure that all levels of the public service have a proportion of women and various disadvantaged minority groups similar to that of the population as a whole.

Public Service Commission of Canada
www.psc-cfp.gc.ca

deputy minister

The executive head of a department of government appointed by the prime minister in consultation with the Clerk of the Privy Council Office. The deputy minister runs the department with oversight by the Cabinet minister who is the political head of the department.

such as university degrees and scores on public service examinations, may result in hiring practices that favour people from some parts of society more than others. In Canada efforts began in the 1960s to increase the relatively small proportion of French-speaking persons in the public service in order to create a public service that could operate in both official languages and increase French Quebecers' attachment to the Canadian government. Since then, efforts have been made to create a more **representative bureaucracy** by establishing targets for hiring and promoting more women, Aboriginals, visible minorities, and persons with disabilities. Likewise, beginning in the 1970s, the United States adopted affirmative action policies to create a representative bureaucracy to ensure full representation of women and racial minorities at all levels of the civil service (Watkins-Hayes, 2010).

Politics and Administration

Public administration is often thought of in terms of the carrying out of the policies adopted by the government. In Canada, each department of government is headed by a Cabinet minister who is expected to oversee and take responsibility for the actions of the department. The day-to-day running of a department is in the hands of a **deputy minister**, usually a senior public servant appointed by the prime minister in consultation with the Clerk (head) of the Privy Council Office. The Privy Council Office, under the direction of the prime minister, also plays a major role in coordinating and directing the work of the deputy ministers and senior public servants.

Because public servants are an important source of information, analysis, and advice for Cabinet ministers, they often play an important role in the policy-making process. It is sometimes said that an important duty of public servants is to "speak truth to power." Based on their expertise and non-partisanship, the advice that public servants give to Cabinet ministers in confidence is expected to be based on their objective analysis of what is in the long-term good of the country. In turn, Cabinet ministers are expected to take responsibility for the decisions of Cabinet (which may reflect short-term partisan interests) rather than publicly blaming public servants for the advice that was given in private.

The large majority of public service activity involves the implementation of laws and policies. Once a law is passed by Parliament or a policy adopted, it is typically the public servants within a particular department that are involved in recommending how implementation is going to be conducted. Likewise, the regulations needed to determine how the law is to be applied are often drafted by public servants and then approved by Cabinet.

However, the prime minister and Cabinet ministers do not always provide the direction, financial resources, and public service staff needed to put a policy into effect. For example, Canada's Oceans Act (1966), the United Nations Fish Stocks Agreement (ratified by Canada in 1999), and Canada's Sustainable Fisheries Framework (2009) established the precautionary approach to fisheries conservation and sustainability; however, as of April 2016, there had been limited progress in implementing these objectives. In part, budget cuts to the science branch of the Department of Fisheries and Oceans meant that public service managers did not have the advice needed for sustainable management. As well the responsibility of Fisheries ministers to oversee policy implementation may have been subject to pressure from the fishing industry that would be affected by cuts to the allowable catch (Hutchings, Peterman, & VanderZwaag, 2016).

A tension exists between the duty of public servants to carry out the wishes of the government of the day and their duty to the public interest.[4] The duty to the public interest requires some degree of independence from the political executive in order to ensure that government is acting in accordance with the rule of law and to speak out against wrongdoing by the government including actions that jeopardize the life, health, and safety of the public (Sossin, 2005). Various jurisdictions have adopted "whistleblower" legislation to try to protect public servants who speak out against illegal or harmful policies.

---

[4]Technically in Canada this is a duty to the Crown, which symbolically represents the public interest.

Criticisms of the Government Bureaucracy

The government bureaucracy has come under considerable criticism in recent decades for several reasons:

- Bureaucratic organization is often viewed as slow moving, rigid, and inflexible rather than efficient.
- The commitment of public servants to the public interest is sometimes questioned.
- Users of government services sometimes receive insufficient attention and respect.

In particular, public choice theory, based on the assumption that individuals pursue their own self-interest, asserts that public servants seek to expand the programs and expenditures of government so as to enhance their own position, privileges, and power. The effect, compounded by the efforts of government to try to satisfy the demands of a variety of interest groups, is that government has become much larger than necessary. This, it is argued, has stifled the growth of the more dynamic and efficient private sector.

Concerns about administrative inefficiencies, the stifling of entrepreneurial initiatives by government "red tape," and excessive rules and regulations have led many governments to undertake major reforms of their administrative structures and practices. These changes include shrinking the size of government, privatizing state-owned enterprises, contracting out the delivery of some services to private businesses, establishing public-private partnerships, reducing business regulation, and focusing on being competitive in the global marketplace. Such changes often reflect the ideology of neoliberalism.

New Public Management

new public management

The adoption of the practices of private business in the administrative activities of government.

The adoption of the practices of private business is a major feature of what is termed **new public management**, an idea that has influenced changes to government administration in many countries since the 1980s. In particular, this approach emphasizes efficiency by reducing the size of the public service, providing performance incentives to employees, and encouraging competition to provide public services between private and public organizations so that services are provided at the lowest cost. Instead of the hierarchical structure and rules and procedures of the traditional bureaucracy, the emphasis is on decentralized structures in which managers have the autonomy to make managerial decisions and to create a leaner, more flexible operation. Further, like private business, the focus should be on satisfying the customers of public services. Finally, advocates of new public management are often critical of the leading role of the public service in providing policy advice to government.

ALTERNATIVE SERVICE DELIVERY   One aspect of the new public management is the development of new methods of delivering government programs, termed **alternative service delivery**. This may involve establishing government service agencies that have considerable autonomy from the normal departmental structures and rules, for example, Passport Canada, Canada Revenue Agency, Canadian Food Inspection Agency, and Parks Canada. Some agencies are expected to be self-financing.

Another form of alternative service delivery involves establishing partnerships with business, other levels of government, and voluntary organizations to deliver services. Alternative service delivery can also involve contracting out government activities to private business or to groups of former public servants. This approach is particularly common in the United States, where private businesses have been contracted not only by a number of cities to manage garbage collection and road maintenance, but also by state and national governments to run prisons and carry out a variety of military functions. Indeed, employees hired by private contractors far outnumbered the US troops they worked alongside in Afghanistan in 2008 and 2009 (Cole, 2009). President Obama complained that private defence contractors were often being paid for services that were not performed. Further, when local citizens were killed or injured by contract employees, it caused problems for American relations with the Afghanistan government and those who had supported that government.

PROBLEMS   A key problem with the efforts to make government more businesslike is that there are inherent differences between government and business. In particular, the goals of government are more complex than the simple bottom line of profitability that drives business activity. According to Donald Savoie "efforts to make the public sector look like the private sector have been misguided, are costly to taxpayers, and entailed a profoundly negative effect on the public service as an institution" (2013, p. 12).

The idea that the role of the public service in developing policies should be reduced is also controversial. Based on its experience in administering programs, the public service is able to provide useful advice in developing new policies and modifying existing ones. Further, a knowledgeable, professional public service protected by a high level of job security may be more likely to provide honest, forthright advice than consulting firms and partisan advisers who may tend to tell Cabinet ministers what they want to hear (Savoie, 2003).

The adoption of private-sector methods does not necessarily lead to the most desirable results. Focusing on efficiency and competitiveness may undermine the sense of public service that has been developed among the employees of government in countries such as Canada and the United Kingdom. Privatized services are not always better managed than government-run services. For example, the Ontario government conducted a performance review of a

alternative service delivery

New methods of delivering government programs, such as the establishment of government service agencies that have considerable autonomy from the normal departmental structures and rules and the establishment of partnerships with business, other levels of government, and voluntary organizations to deliver services.

"Wouldn't it be great if government no longer ran the parks?"
Tami Thirlwell

large maximum security prison whose operations had been contracted out to a major American prison management corporation. It found that an equivalent government-run prison had better security and health care and reduced repeat offender rates. Thus, the government decided to take over the running of the prison (*CBC News*, 2006).

Finally, the idea that much of the work of the public service should be done by autonomous agencies, each responsible for a particular program, has been questioned. In looking at new public management in Britain and New Zealand, analysts have found that this approach made it more difficult for governments to deal with complex problems that require coordination among a variety of departments and agencies (Aucoin, 2002). In New Zealand, the pioneer in the adoption of new public management, the establishment of 300 separate agencies increased administrative costs and made coordination of public services difficult. Since 1996, New Zealand governments have stopped pursuing radical market-oriented changes in public administration and instead gradually reasserted government control of various public functions (Dunleavy et al., 2006).

✓• SUMMARY AND CONCLUSION

Governing, ideally, involves pursuing and balancing a variety of crucial policy goals to promote the common good. Many important problems such as climate change, economic development, inequality, and social justice can only be thoroughly addressed by public policy (Savoie, 2015). However, public policy in Canada and the United States has often focused on pursuing economic growth while increased inequality, social welfare needs, and serious environmental problems have tended to receive less attention by governments.

The policies adopted by governments are typically the result of complex processes involving a variety of different political actors. Interest groups, social movements, businesses, political parties, think tanks, and journalists seek to influence the choice of issues that will be the subject of policy making, as well as trying to affect how policy makers think about those issues. In addition, policy making is increasingly affected by forces beyond the state, including international organizations and agreements and the global economy.

Policy making is not simply a matter of problem solving or trying to determine the best policy to achieve the common good. Rather, it is a matter of choice in which resources are limited and the goals and objectives of those interested or involved in policy making differ and cannot easily be weighed against each other. In other words, the public policy process is a political process in which different goals, interests, and values are involved (Simeon, 1976). The policies that are adopted and implemented do not necessarily reflect the common good, but rather may reflect the political interests of the government, the perspectives of those involved in the policy process, and the ability of various groups and individuals to exert influence. When issues that affect the economy are being considered, business interests typically have a strong ability to influence public policy.

The idea that the government bureaucracy is dedicated to the public interest has been challenged by those who contend that public servants pursue their own interests by seeking to expand the activities of government. The public service has also been criticized as being too rule-bound, slow to act, and inefficient. Attempts have been made to adopt a more businesslike approach to administration through the techniques of the new public management. Providing greater autonomy and flexibility for administrative managers may be useful in reducing inefficiency and cutting red tape. However, a strong, professional public service is important in the effort to pursue the common good of a political community. Good public administration involves the fair, equal, and efficient delivery of services, and the provision of quality, impartial, and expert advice to government.

✓• KEY TERMS

Alternative service delivery   391
Bureaucracy   387
Capitalist economic system   374
Deputy minister   388
Keynesian economic policies   376

Neo-Marxist theory   386
New public management   390
Pluralist perspective   385
Public choice theory   386
Public policy   373

Representative bureaucracy   388
State-centred theory   386
Welfare state   381

DISCUSSION QUESTIONS

1. Should economic growth be the primary public policy goal?

2. Which of the general perspectives is most applicable to understanding public policy?

3. Is greater public participation in the policy process desirable?

4. Is bureaucratic organization undesirable? Is it a threat to democracy?

5. What are the advantages and disadvantages of new public management reforms?

FURTHER READING

Adolini, J.R., & Blake, C.H. (2010). *Comparing public policies: Issues and choices in industrialized societies* (2nd ed.). Washington, DC: CQ Press.

Bowles, P. (2012). *Capitalism* (2nd ed.). London, UK: Taylor & Francis.

Dodds, A. (2013). *Comparative public policy.* Houndmills, UK: Palgrave Macmillan.

Inwood, G.J. (2011). *Understanding Canadian public administration: An introduction to theory and practice* (4th ed.). Toronto: Pearson Education Canada.

Milanovic, B. (2016). *Global inequality: A new approach for the age of globalization.* Cambridge, MA: Belknap Press.

Miljan, L. (2012). *Public policy in Canada: An introduction* (6th ed.). Don Mills, ON: Oxford University Press.

Osborne, D., & Gaebler, T. (1992). *Reinventing government: How the entrepreneurial spirit is transforming the public sector.* Reading, MA: Addison-Wesley.

Pal, L.A. (2013). *Beyond policy analysis: Public issue management in turbulent times* (5th ed.). Scarborough, ON: Nelson.

Savoie, D.J. (2015). *What is government good at? A Canadian answer.* Montreal: McGill-Queen's University Press.

Stiglitz, J.E. (2012). *The price of inequality: How today's divided society endangers our future.* New York: Norton.

Wilkinson, R. & Pickett, K. (2009). *The spirit level: Why more equal societies almost always do better.* London: Allen Lane.

17 Politics and Development in the World's Poorer Countries

Singapore's skyline. Singapore, a country with a hybrid political system, is one of Asia's miracle economies.   Leungchopan/Fotolia

After reading this chapter, you should be able to:

1. identify the terms that are used to depict the poorer countries
2. outline the extent of global inequality
3. discuss the meaning of development and the different development strategies
4. evaluate Canada's foreign-aid policies
5. examine the political problems of the Third World

Economic miracles: Will China and India join Singapore, South Korea, and Taiwan as success stories?

It seems that whenever a country has several consecutive years of strong economic growth, at least 5 percent annually, it is dubbed a miracle economy. Most of these quickly return to normal when their boom ends. Still, there are genuine miracle economies, ones that grow fast over a long period and also consolidate that growth, restructure their economies, and become developed countries. The second half of the twentieth century saw three economic miracles, all in Asia: Singapore, South Korea (the Republic of Korea, ROK), and Taiwan (the Republic of China, ROC). All started off among the world's poor and ended up among the developed rich.

The twenty-first century's contributions to the list of economic miracles are the People's Republic of China (PRC, usually just called China or Beijing, after the capital) and India. Neither ranks among the rich, but both attained mid-level per capita incomes (India is in the lower-middle band, China the upper-middle) and built economies with many sectors as modern as anyone's. Since 2013, though, both are growing more slowly, suggesting either that they are now restructuring their economies or are encountering the **middle-income trap**, and will show less dramatic gains in the future.

When thinking about these miracle economies, there are two points that are important to political science. One is the economic policies behind their spectacular growth. Although we know that what worked in one country may not work in another, it is still essential to understand what programs have produced economic miracles. The other point is whether a particular political system has been especially successful in building economic miracles.

These economic success stories range from the communist China government, which nevertheless embraced the basic values and logic of capitalism, to India, which comes closest to a free-enterprise economy. In between, Singapore, South Korea, and Taiwan operate a "governed market."

Democratic countries are not always the most likely homes to economic miracles. The People's Republic of China, an authoritarian single-party dictatorship, demonstrates that a democratic political system is not necessary for rapid economic growth. Further, although both South Korea and Taiwan have been democracies since 1987, they began their economic ascents under dictatorships, and Singapore remains a semi-democratic, semi-authoritarian hybrid system. Of the five countries with miracle economies only India has remained democratic throughout its dramatic economic rise.

THE DEVELOPMENT GAP

About one-fourth of the world's people live in high-income countries like Canada and the United States. The rest have a per capita income that is much less than that of Canada (see Table 17-1). Canadian governments have trouble funding all of the services that people need, so the situation is obviously worse where far less money per person is available to fund education, health care, roads, and other important services. We live in a world where the average income of each of the 1.4 billion people living in high-income countries is 61 times that of each of the 622 million people living in low-income countries, although the difference falls to 25.5 times greater if we use **purchasing power parity (PPP)** adjusted income figures (World Bank, 2016b). Is it meaningful to talk about achieving the common good in the poorest countries? Should Canadians be concerned about the problem of global inequality? How can poor countries develop?

Social scientists have applied a variety of names to the world's poor countries. Among them have been **Third World**, developing, less developed, **underdeveloped**, and the **South** (terms discussed in Box 17-1 Evolution of the Term *Third World*). Political science generally prefers Third World (Green & Luehrmann, 2011; Handelman, 2012) but uses all of the terms noted earlier. Whatever the name, it is the mix of economic and social characteristics of poor states combined with how their political systems function that draws the attention of political scientists, policy makers, and the politically informed public in the wealthy (or developed) countries of what some call the **North**.

WHAT IS DEVELOPMENT?

Terms such as **developing countries**, *less developed countries*, or *underdeveloped countries* are often used to describe Third World countries, but they raise several questions: What exactly does "development" mean? In what ways are poorer countries "less developed" than the richer countries? Are the poorer countries "developing"? Does that mean that they will become just like the richer "developed" countries?

---

middle-income trap

A condition in which a country with a middle-level annual per capita income (roughly US$ 1200 – US $13 000) cannot grow to the level of the wealthy (>US$ 13 000).

purchasing power parity (PPP)

A measure of per capita income that shows the purchasing power of an income, instead of its worth at current exchange rates.

Third World

Less developed countries.

underdeveloped countries

A term often used to describe Third World countries.

South

Less developed, poorer countries.

North

The rich, developed countries.

developing countries

Countries that have not reached the same level of development as the richer, advanced countries.

INCOME GROUP	ANNUAL INCOME RANGE	WORLD'S INCOME	WORLD'S POPULATION
High	> US$ 12 736	67.8%	19.2%
Upper Middle	US$ 4125–12 376	24.3%	32.5%
Lower Middle	US$ 1045–4125	8.6%	39.7%
Low	< US$ 1045	0.5%	8.6%
Canada	US$ 51 630	2.3%	0.05%
	(average annual income)		

TABLE 17-1
The Wealth of the World*

Source: Calculated from World Bank, *Data 2016.* [http://data.worldbank.org/country]) Washington: The World Bank.

BOX 17-1　Evolution of the Term *Third World*

Various names have been developed over the years to refer to the world's poorest countries.

The *Third World* was political scientists' first choice. It was introduced in the late 1940s to distinguish the then small number of independent countries in Africa, Asia, and Latin America from the blocs linked to the two great powers of the day: the United States and the Soviet Union. The United States and its allies (for example, Canada) formed the First World and the Soviet Union and its allies (for example, Bulgaria) were termed the Second World. The rest were the "Third World." Although many of these countries later banded together to form the Non-Aligned Movement, the Third World soon came to symbolize poverty and political instability instead of an independent foreign policy.

The *South* is another label political scientists have used. This emphasizes the fact that most poor countries lie in the tropics, to the south of the rich states of the northern hemisphere. Of course, the name is not literally accurate, because the southern hemisphere includes developed countries such as Australia and New Zealand.

Underdeveloped, developing, and *less developed* are variations on a final theme used to categorize the poor states of the world. The focus here is the low levels of economic well-being that characterize these countries. Nevertheless, there is the implicit assumption that development is possible and that eventually every country will meet its citizens' needs.

These countries tend to be new democracies, if they are democratic at all. These labels are applied to nations in all of Latin America and the Caribbean; Africa; the Middle East, except Israel (although some of the oil-producing states like Saudi Arabia and Qatar have high per capita incomes); and Asia, except Japan, the People's Republic of China, Singapore, Taiwan (Republic of China), and South Korea. The last three states were considered Third World countries until the 1980s but now all are high-income states.

gross domestic product (GDP)

The market value of goods and services produced in a country, excluding transactions with other countries.

development

A condition that involves the satisfaction of the basic needs of all of the people as well as the means for them to live fulfilling and productive lives based on the creation of a more diversified, sophisticated, and sustainable economy.

The less developed countries are often compared to the more developed countries in terms of per capita **gross domestic product (GDP)** (the amount of goods and services produced) and in terms of average incomes (see Table 17-1). Such measures are available for nearly all countries and give us a sense of the economic disparities between rich and poor nations. If countries increase their GDP, we can say that economic growth is occurring. Economic growth, however, does not always result in **development**. For example, economic growth need not reduce poverty. Indeed, in some cases, increased poverty has accompanied increased growth (United Nations Development Programme [UNDP], 2003). Because of the great inequalities in wealth and power in many less-developed countries, additional wealth often ends up in the pockets of the rich. New oil wells, mines, factories, stores, and dams may result in the dislocation of peasant farmers, urban workers, and Indigenous peoples, reducing their ability to eke out a living. The distinction between growth and development is discussed further in Box 17-2 Development versus Growth.

Development may be thought of in terms of three goals:

1. Satisfying the basic needs of everyone, such as food, housing, clothing, and clean water, as well as the creating the means to live fulfilling and productive lives through education, health care, employment, and

BOX 17-2   Development versus Growth

Imagine living in a country whose economy is based on mining diamonds.

If we mine and sell more diamonds, the economy's GDP will *grow*. But the country has not necessarily developed. Increased diamond mining might simply let the mine owners buy more imported luxury items or invest their profits abroad. However, processing the diamonds into jewellery or using the profits from diamond mining to develop new industries would lead to a more broadly based economy that would rely less on one commodity. It would also encourage people to develop more skills.

Generally, if more of the profits from increased mining activity remained in the country to buy locally produced goods and services, the economic *development* of the country would rise. Likewise, if government used increased tax revenues to improve roads, schools, and health care, there would be a stronger foundation for future development.

security against severe hardships. For example, the World Bank aims to eliminate extreme poverty, defined as subsisting on less than US$ 1.90 per day, and reduce ordinary poverty, defined as living on less than US$ 3.10 daily (World Bank, 2015). This will require improving the status of women. Improving the status of women, especially ensuring that young women receive an education, tends to result in a healthier population, slower population growth, and a more skilled workforce.

2. Building a more diversified and sophisticated economy. This requires moving from an economy centred on the production of unprocessed natural resources to one that turns those resources into finished goods. As well, it requires developing the scientific, technological, and managerial capabilities needed to compete with the developed countries. Further, it requires moving from being a supplier of low-cost labour to multinational corporations based in the rich countries to developing local entrepreneurial capacity and the banking, legal, and other services needed to support domestic businesses.

3. Creating environmentally sustainable development. Economic growth has often come through unrestrained exploitation of natural resources. Indiscriminate logging and fishing may bring short-term economic growth, but harm long-term development. One of the major dilemmas of development is that industrialization and increased wealth often create a heavy burden on the environment. Although the rich countries use a high proportion of the world's resources and produce a substantial share of global pollution, increases in the wealth in heavily populated Third World countries have the potential to place great stresses on the world's environment. For example, shifting from bicycles to cars as a major means of transportation creates serious problems of congestion and air pollution in many Third World cities and also contributes to global climate change. From an environmental perspective, Third World economic growth that brings consumption levels like those of the richer countries would be unsustainable.

Center for Global Development
www.cgdev.org

Measuring Development

Rather than simply measuring a country's wealth, the United Nations Development Programme uses an index based on education, life expectancy, and per capita gross national income (GNI) to get a broader picture of how well countries are doing in their pursuit of development (see Table 17-2). On this **Human Development Index (HDI)**, rankings do not always correspond exactly to GDP.

human development index (HDI)

An annual index for most countries, calculated by the United Nations Development Programme and based on educational attainment, life expectancy, and per capita gross national income (GNI).

Cuba, for instance, ranks forty-seven places higher on the HDI than it does on GNI. This indicates that Cuba produces very good human development results for its level of economic activity. At the other extreme, Equatorial Guinea, a small African oil-producing state, has an HDI level 84 places below its income rank. I It has a high national income that has not produced benefits for its people.[1]

The good news is that, however it is measured, development has clearly occurred throughout the Third World. Life expectancy has increased substantially, literacy rates and school enrolment at all levels have jumped (with gender parity in African primary schools), there is greater representation of women in decision-making, and a substantial reduction in poverty (Sirleaf, 2015).

However, these figures hide disturbing facts. Although only 13 percent of the population of the developing world (down from one-half in 1980) qualifies as "extremely poor" (living on US$ 1.90 or less per day) about 900 million people still fall into that category (World Bank, 2015). Further, some parts of the world fare worse than others. In sub-Saharan Africa, the percentage of the population living in extreme poverty is 43 percent, down from 57 percent in 1990. In India, the proportion is 21 percent; it was 60 percent in 1981 (World Bank, 2015). China has seen even greater improvement, with those living in extreme poverty falling from

TABLE 17-2
Human Development Index, Selected Countries, 2014

HDI RANK	COUNTRY	INCOME PER CAPITA (GNI) (PPP US$)	EXPECTED YEARS OF SCHOOLING	LIFE EXPECTANCY (YEARS)	INCOME RANK (GNI) MINUS HDI RANK*
1	Norway	64 992	12.6	81.6	5
2	Australia	42 261	13.0	82.4	17
9	Canada	42 155	15.9	82.0	11
67	Cuba	7 301	13.8	79.4	47
90	China (PRC)	12 547	13.1	75.8	−7
130	India	5 497	11.7	68.0	−4
138	Equatorial Guinea	21 056	9.0	57.6	−84
163	Haiti	1 669	4.9	62.8	4
188	Niger	908	5.4	61.4	−5

Notes: Income per capita is calculated in terms of purchasing power parity.

*A positive figure indicates that the HDI rank is higher than the per capita income (GNI) rank.

Source: Adapted from United Nations Development Programme, *Human Development Report 2015*, http://hdr.undp.org/en/reports/global/hdr2015/download/.

---

[1]The HDI says nothing about a country's political system. Both Cuba and Equatorial Guinea are dictatorships. The difference in their HDI levels shows clearly that not all dictatorships are the same.

Run-down one-room housing is very common in Ethiopia. Depicted here: Harar, a city in eastern Ethiopia.

Eric Mintz

84 percent in 1981 to 11 percent in 2010 (World Bank, 2015). India and China thus show that miracle economies can raise the living standards of the poorest.

Certain regions have made great strides. Fifty years ago the countries of Southeast and East Asia were extremely poor, with a short life expectancy and high levels of illiteracy and infant mortality. From China to Thailand, however, conditions are much improved. In fact, aside from North Korea, the region's experience demonstrates that development is not just possible, but can be achieved in a generation.

However, just as there are development success stories, there are also failures. In 2000, the UN set eight Millennium Development Goals (MDG) to be achieved by 2015: (1) eradicate extreme poverty and hunger; (2) achieve universal primary education; (3) empower women and advance gender equality; (4) reduce child mortality; (5) improve maternal health; (6) combat HIV/AIDS, malaria, and other diseases; (7) ensure environmental stability; (8) develop a global partnership for development (UNMDG, 2005). Progress was made on all measures, but only one goal was fully realized: equal primary school for boys and girls, part of Goal 3 (UNMDG, 2015). In 2016, the United Nations announced a set of seventeen sustainable development goals to be met by 2030 (UNSDG 2016).[2]

Overall, living standards throughout the poor world have improved over the past 50 years, and some countries have reached the ranks of developed

---

[2]The seventeen goals are no poverty; zero hunger; good health; quality education; gender equality; clean water and sanitation; renewable energy; good jobs and economic growth; innovation and infrastructure; reduced inequalities; sustainable cities and communities; responsible consumption; climate action; life below water; life on land; peace and justice; partnership for the goals.

BOX 17-3   Three Development Scenarios

There are cases of failed development and reversed development as well as successful development.

1. *Failed development.* When the Belgian Congo became independent in 1960, it was very ill-prepared and there were few well-educated Congolese to exercise power. The new country was immediately plunged into civil war, with the Americans backing one faction and the Soviets another. The eventual winner of the conflict was Joseph Mobutu, who later changed his name to Mobutu Sese Seko and the country's name to Zaire. From 1965 to 1997, he exercised dictatorial rule, becoming Africa's most corrupt leader. From 1996 to 2003, as many as 5 million people died as a result of two wars in the Congo that involved many African countries.

   Things did not improve for the Congolese after Laurent Kabila ousted Mobutu and renamed the country the Democratic Republic of the Congo (DR-Congo). In 2001, Kabila was assassinated. His son, Joseph Kabila, then seized power, but in 2006 won the country's first-ever multiparty election and was re-elected in 2011. Fighting began anew in 2008, and was marked by the apparently systematic rape of thousands of women and girls by both DR-Congo soldiers and their enemies (York, 2010). In 2013, a peace deal was signed although fighting and rapes have continued to plague eastern Congo. In September 2016, violent protests broke out after the country's Electoral Commission postponed the scheduled November presidential election. Although Kabila is required to step down in 2016 having served the maximum two terms, he announced that he will remain in office until 2018. The country's seventy-three million inhabitants have annual per capita incomes of only US$380, but their land is rich in natural resources. The Congolese, however, need peace and stability to benefit from their gold, silver, and oil in their homeland.

2. *Reversed development.* Early in the twentieth century, Argentina had a per capita income similar to Canada's. In 2015, it was less than 30 percent of ours. Argentina is a big country, with forty-three million well-educated people. It has significant natural resources (agricultural and mineral), a once large but now declining manufacturing base, and modern service industries. However, between 1930 and 1983 the country was almost always ruled by dictatorships, all of which pursued bad policies. Since 1983, the country has been democratic, but this has not solved its problems. In December 2001, Argentina's economy nearly collapsed and sparked a political crisis that saw five presidents governing within two weeks. By 2006, it had recovered much of the lost ground and enjoyed several years of prosperity due to foreign demand for its agricultural exports. By 2012, though, the export boom had stalled, inflation had risen, and Argentines again faced hard economic times. Argentina shows the importance of having stable democratic politics and sustainable economic policies.

3. *Successful development.* South Korea (officially, the Republic of Korea) is a developed country today with a population of thirty-eight million. At its founding in 1946, the country's prospects were poor. Formerly a Japanese colony, Korea was divided into a communist north (the Korean Democratic Republic) and a non-communist south. Over the next four decades, while North Korea stagnated, South Korea prospered by using a form of government-managed capitalism (Wade, 1990) Until 1988, South Korea was ruled by a series of dictatorships, most of them military. It is now a stable, economically developed democracy.

nations. However, there are states where earlier movement toward development reversed and others where development simply has not occurred. Box 17-3 Three Development Scenarios presents some cases of successful and failed development.

HOW CAN COUNTRIES DEVELOP?

Finding the best way to develop means answering two questions, one political and one economic. The political question asks if development comes faster under democracies or under authoritarian systems. The economic question wants to know if market-centred or state-directed policies work better.

Politics and Development

Since the 1950s, political scientists have debated whether it is easier for a country to develop economically and socially under a democracy—with constitutional government, free elections, open opposition, and extensive rights and freedoms for everyone—or by using an authoritarian model—few rights for citizens, unaccountable government, and limited possibilities to criticize and oppose government. Those who favour the authoritarian alternative point to South Korea and the Republic of China (Taiwan), which did not democratize until after they had developed; the People's Republic of China and Vietnam, both of which are growing rapidly richer under single-party dictatorships; and Singapore (the second-richest country in Asia after Japan), which remains a hybrid regime (a mixture of democratic and non-democratic rule). Proponents of the democratic option cite India's rapid growth; the economic success of such small democracies as Botswana, Costa Rica, Mauritius, and Uruguay; and the woeful economic records of the vast majority of the world's dictatorships.

Arguing that authoritarian governments are best suited to direct development means stressing that authoritarians do not depend on popular support and so can take decisions the majority would not accept. Authoritarians supposedly can base economic decisions solely on economic principles. This happened in the cases noted earlier. However, authoritarians can also use government to enrich themselves, leaving the economy in ruins.

Moreover, democracy's record in building strong economies is quite impressive. Among the countries that were democratic by the standards of their day when they developed were Canada, Australia, the United States, and much of Northern Europe. A government that has to face the people has to provide the people with an economy that lets them prosper. Unfortunately, many governments in the Third World have achieved neither democracy nor prosperity.

Economic Policy for Development

Research by the British economist Ha-Joon Chang (2003) reveals that, of all the countries that we count as "developed," only the Netherlands and Switzerland even remotely followed a free-market model to do so. However, most of the advice that the Third World gets from international agencies (such

free-market economic model

An economic model that emphasizes private enterprise and significantly limits the economic role of the state.

statist economic model

An economic policy that gives government a significant role in directing a country's economy.

modernization theory

A development model that views the traditional values, practices, and institutions of Third World countries as the basic cause of underdevelopment. To develop, poor countries should change their cultural outlook, social structure, economic organization, and political system based on the model of the advanced Western societies.

dependency theory

Dependency theory argues that underdevelopment results from unequal power relations between the centre (dominant capitalist countries) and the periphery (poor, dependent countries).

Washington Consensus

A series of policies put together by the International Monetary Fund and the World Bank that encourage developing countries to generate more revenue for debt repayment by cutting government expenditures to balance their budgets, selling off government-owned enterprises (privatization), and fully opening their countries to foreign goods and investments.

as the International Monetary Fund or the World Bank) and from many economists argues that government involvement in the economy is undesirable and only the **free-market economic model**, free trade, and unrestricted foreign investment leads to prosperity. However, of the countries that have developed most successfully since 1950, all but India have used a **statist economic model**, and even India never fully subscribed to free-market orthodoxy. Examining both market and statist models will show these principles in practice.

MARKET MODELS There have been two major free-market models. The first, **modernization theory**, was important from about 1950 to 1970. It argued that poor countries had to change their traditional values, institutions, and practices in order to develop. Change could be achieved by copying the ways of developed countries, especially the United States, beginning with their economic policies by bringing in the most modern firms from abroad. That would set in motion a process that would break down old social orders and lead to democratic government, as well as produce more wealth.

Unfortunately, expectations were not fulfilled. Foreign firms came but had less impact on local life than expected. Thus social change was less thoroughgoing, elites retained power, and democracy was stifled. And economic growth was less than promised. Theorists (Cardoso & Falletto, 1979; Frank, 1979) responded with a non-market model: **dependency theory**. It saw underdevelopment as a result of unequal power relations between the centre (dominant capitalist countries) and the periphery (poor, dependent countries). Although dependency theory was right about the unequal power of rich and poor countries, it offered little in the way of concrete suggestions for improvement, besides turning to socialism. The market model then re-emerged as the Washington Consensus.

The Washington Consensus In the 1980s, when many poor countries encountered grave foreign-debt problems, another free-market solution was adopted: the **Washington Consensus**, so called because it involved the United States Treasury (finance department) and two **international financial institutions (IFIs)** headquartered in Washington: the International Monetary Fund and the World Bank. This was therefore another plan that originated in the wealthy countries.

The Washington Consensus called for poor countries to generate more revenue for debt repayment by cutting government expenditures, including social programs. Austerity thus formed the core of **structural adjustment programs (SAPs)**. Administered by IFIs, SAPs offered governments loans at low interest rates ("soft loans") if their countries enacted the Washington Consensus programs. A country that refused could find itself without access to credit because private banks do not lend to clients, even sovereign states, that cannot or do not pay their debts. Without such loans, countries could not import such necessary items as spare parts for cars and trucks, since exporters want to be paid in a major international currency, normally US dollars.

Like modernization theory before it, the Washington Consensus model was a disappointment. No economic miracles resulted, although some countries reoriented their economies, and cuts to social programs resulted in rising levels of poverty in many nations. This has led some to conclude that these market models are more about protecting the wealthy countries of the North (for example, by ensuring that countries do not default on their loans and destabilize the global banking system) than developing the South. Although the World Bank and the International Monetary Fund are mandated to assist the poorer countries, control of these organizations rests with the governments of the rich countries, who have a majority of the votes. Overall, free-market approaches have not been spectacularly successful in achieving development.

STATIST APPROACHES There are two classes of state-directed development approaches: socialist and capitalist. The latter has been more successful and has the best record of actually producing development.

Socialist Models Many development models have been labelled "socialist." Some were Marxist and based on the experience of the Soviet Union, while others were built around a democratic socialism. Like the free-market models, a few had some success, but others failed badly. As well, like the free-market experiments, many of these socialist models came from the outside and did not fit local conditions.

This model originated in the Soviet Union after the Bolshevik Revolution of 1917. It featured collectivized agriculture, a focus on heavy industry, and the use of central planning. This approach turned a semi-industrialized Russia into a highly industrialized Soviet Union, a country that from 1945 to 1991 was, along with the United States, a military superpower. However, the Soviet model had significant limitations that kept living standards fairly low in the Soviet bloc (the Soviet Union and its European satellites: Bulgaria, the former Czechoslovakia, East Germany, Hungary, Poland, and Romania). This model was also exported to Cuba, Vietnam, Laos, North Korea, and China. Although it did not produce superlative results anywhere, it usually ensured that people had access to education, reasonable health care, and basic housing. Socialist development in communist-led countries did, however, produce catastrophic failures. In China, the "Great Leap Forward" (1958–1961) involving industrialization and collectivization resulted in a famine that caused tens of millions of deaths. A brutal struggle for ideological purity during the "Cultural Revolution" (1966–1969) that included the purging of government officials, the closing of schools, and transfer of urban

international financial institution (IFI)

An organization that has some ability to affect the global economic system; for example, the International Monetary Fund and the World Bank.

structural adjustment program (SAP)

A program administered by international financial institutions, which offers loans at very low interest rates to governments facing problems paying their debt on the condition that they adopt the programs endorsed by the Washington Consensus.

youth to the countryside resulted in millions of deaths and severe damage to the economy. North Korea has suffered famine and continues to have difficulty feeding its population. Instead its leader focuses on its military and the development of nuclear weapons.

Democratic socialist development has a better record. Its economic results generally beat the centrally planned systems, and its social results were often better than those achieved by the free-market model. An interesting example of this system is the Indian state of Kerala. The state boasts high levels of literacy and health care and has promoted women's rights. Kerala's success began with the election in 1957 of the Communist Party of India (Marxist), or CP(M), a democratic party despite its name. Since then, power has shifted between the CP(M) or the coalition it led, and the Indian National Congress Party or the coalition it led. Though not wealthy, Kerala's per capita income is among the top third of Indian states (Statistics Times, 2015).

import substitution industrialization

A model of economic development in which a country establishes high tariffs to protect businesses setting up to manufacture goods that replace imports.

tariffs

Taxes on exports.

State-Directed Capitalist Models   Two development policies, **import substitution industrialization (ISI)** and the Asian model, were conceived in poor countries. ISI was widely adopted in Latin America and Africa and worked well for several decades. The Asian model is indigenous to East Asia and has registered some spectacular successes since the 1970s.

ISI sought to industrialize countries by setting up businesses to produce manufactured goods that a country already imported. Governments protected these firms with high **tariffs**—taxes on imports—in order to diversify their countries' economies. For a while, from the 1940s to about 1970, ISI worked well in countries such as Mexico, Brazil, and Argentina. However, it eventually failed because of problems inherent in the policy. Countries applying ISI did build new industries, but these industries never flourished because they kept making expensive goods of poor quality. If governments talked about reducing tariffs to force these firms to become more efficient, their owners warned of foreign takeovers, and their workers staged demonstrations to protect their jobs. Governments got the message and backed down.

export-led industrialization (ELI)

A model of economic development with a capitalist system in which government and the biggest businesses co-operate to develop export industries. Government influences investments, provides incentives for exports, and can decide whether firms are allowed to export products.

Another practical approach to development is **export-led industrialization (ELI)**, whose best-known example is the Asian model because Asian countries have used it most effectively. It is newer than ISI, but has had a longer run of success, only encountering difficulties after about 50 very good years.

Sometimes called "the governed economy" (Wade, 1990), the Asian model aims to build the strongest economy possible in the shortest time possible. Japan did this twice: in the nineteenth century when it first industrialized, and then when it rebuilt after World War II. South Korea and Taiwan followed Japan's lead to develop rapidly and defend themselves against their communist neighbours (North Korea and the People's Republic of China, respectively) when US aid was reduced in the 1970s. Other countries that have followed this path more or less successfully include Singapore, Malaysia, Thailand, Indonesia, and more recently and spectacularly, the People's Republic of China.

Although the system is capitalist, it sees government and the biggest businesses work closely together. Government influences investments and provides incentives for exports. Further, parts of the domestic economy are typically protected from foreign competition. As well, by keeping the value of their currency artificially low and by paying very low wages (often by suppressing unions and not enforcing labour laws), the newly industrialized countries can sell goods at very low prices (Martin & Schumann, 1997).

The Asian model has two striking features:

1. *It works with both non-democratic and democratic governments.* South Korea, Taiwan, and Indonesia were all dictatorships when they began their spectacular development, but now have democratic governments.
2. *It has worked best in Asia.* Some say this is due to cultural factors (called Asian values) including a strong work ethic, thrift, discipline, and an emphasis on social cohesion rather than individualism. Others argue that the countries that followed this had governments that were able economic managers who chose the right policies, such as emphasizing education. Finally, some commentators hold that the Asian model has not spread because the international trade rules now in place discriminate against countries that use government to build their economies.

Relatives identify the bodies of those who died when a nine-storey building in Savar, Bangladesh collapsed on April 25, 2013, killing over 1000 people. Most of the victims were women working in the very unsafe facility for $38 a month to produce clothing for export to the rich countries.
Palash khan/Alamy Stock Photo

Both ISI and the Asian model worked well for a while in some countries. This suggests that there is no single formula for development. Intuitively, this makes sense: Canada did not follow the same path to development as the United States or Britain, yet all became developed democracies. Nevertheless, the search for the magic bullet continues, with many now looking to China and India.

TWO "MIRACLE ECONOMIES": INDIA AND THE PEOPLE'S REPUBLIC OF CHINA

Miracle economies grow very quickly (greater than 5 percent annually) for an extended period (at least five years). The Asian model produced economic miracles in Japan, South Korea, Taiwan, Singapore, and to some extent Malaysia during the last third of the twentieth century. In the twenty-first century, the miracle economies are the People's Republic of China (PRC) and India.

What most interests us about the PRC and India is their political systems. The PRC is the first communist state to embrace capitalist economics. Like other Communist party states, power in China is concentrated in the central government, which allows Beijing to direct development. India, on the other hand, has been democratic since becoming independent in 1947. Moreover, it is a federation, so authority is divided between the centre and the states. Therefore, the federal government in New Delhi cannot assume a role that parallels Beijing's.

The People's Republic of China

From the Communist Revolution in 1949 until 1978, the PRC's economic performance was poor. Mao Zedong's revolutionary government began with a drive to build heavy industry, but two highly disruptive political movements launched by Mao himself, the Great Leap Forward (1958–1962) and the Cultural Revolution (1967–1976), set development back substantially. It was only in 1978, two years after Mao died, that Deng Xiaoping (de facto Chinese leader) began to limit the role of communist ideology in economic policy. This led quickly to a return to private agriculture, legalizing private businesses, and allowing foreign firms to invest in the PRC and establish their businesses there. Since 1990 the PRC's economy has grown at approximately 9 percent annually. Between 1990 and 2015, annual per capita income rose from US$ 351 to an estimated US$ 7250 (World Bank, 2015), a twenty-fold increase.

The PRC accomplished this by emphasizing export-led growth, the keystone of the Asian model. China also follows the Asian model by using

China seeks African resources to fuel its rapid economic growth.

Tami Thirlwell

BOX 17-4   Chinese Foreign Policy

The People's Republic of China (PRC) is not only the world's most populous country with one of the world's fastest-growing economies, but also a nuclear power, thus automatically a significant foreign-policy actor. Although Beijing's military power is important, it is the role that the PRC plays in the developing world that is really eye-catching.

The PRC has been particularly active in Africa. It is interested in the continent's raw materials, which the PRC needs to fuel its economy. Beijing offers generous development assistance to African nations. Blessed with ample international reserves (the foreign currency and gold a country holds), the PRC can offer concessional (very low-interest) loans with easy repayment schedules. The PRC has stressed financing infrastructure projects, such as roads, energy development, and ports. Unlike the practice of developed democracies, such as Canada,

Sweden, or the United States, the PRC does not set political conditions on its development assistance, giving it access to countries like Zimbabwe or Sudan, which Ottawa or Washington would scorn (Brautigam, 2009; Rotberg, 2008).

Similar patterns of trade and aid also characterize the PRC's relations with both Southeast Asia and Latin America (Roett & Paz, 2008; Sutter, 2008). Once again, Beijing's principal interest is securing access to natural resources, and its development assistance focuses on infrastructure, which is necessary to ensure that those resources reach China easily. The PRC clearly pumps a great deal of money into the economies of nations that export natural resources. Yet this just reconfirms the role of many African, Latin American, and Southeast Asian states as just suppliers of raw materials to more developed countries.

---

a powerful undemocratic state. The PRC departs from the model by having a communist government; the Communist Party of China is the architect of the PRC's capitalist economic miracle. Beijing's experience has been copied by another Asian communist state, Vietnam. Vietnam's economy is estimated to be 16 times bigger in 2009 than it was in 1990, and the annual per capita income for Vietnam's 92 million people has risen from US$ 98 to US$ 2170 (International Monetary Fund, 2015). Communists are skilful capitalists!

China's large, rapidly growing economy affects its foreign policy, as it seeks natural resources needed for its industrial development (Box 17-4 Chinese Foreign Policy).

India

India's population of 1.33 billion is only slightly smaller than the PRC's. However, its recent history and the nature of its economic miracle are very different. First, India has chosen its leaders, both federal and state, through democratic elections since independence in 1947. Although Indian politics exhibits high levels of both corruption (Quah, 2008) and political violence between religious groups and castes (Basu & Roy, 2007), it is unquestionably the world's largest democracy.

India started its "miraculous" growth when it began to move away from a **protectionist economic policy** in 1991. A series of reforms cut red tape,

protectionist economic policy

An economic policy that uses high tariffs to ensure that domestic firms have an edge when competing with foreign companies. Import substitution industrialization is an example.

encouraged foreign investment, and abolished government monopolies in many areas. The results have been impressive. International Monetary Fund estimates indicate that India's economy is almost five times larger in 2014 than it was in 1990 and that per capita income has risen to US$ 1688 from US$ 362 (Kushnir Macroeconomics, 2016). Although Indian governments, federal and state, still play a significant role in the economy, especially in infrastructure development (for example, roads and airports), the country's experience offers another path for countries trying to overcome poverty.

India differs from the PRC in that its economic takeoff was powered by services and not manufactured goods. In particular, India has thrived due to its huge pool of well-educated, English-speaking information technology (IT) personnel. Many North American firms shifted much of their IT work to India to take advantage of the far lower wages there. However, although services may be the engine driving Indian prosperity, this may not be enough to benefit the 70 to 75 percent of Indians who live in villages, many without clean water, electricity, or paved roads. Labour-intensive manufacturing, the option chosen by other Asian model countries to build their economies, can lift many people out of extreme poverty.

Taken together, the Chinese and Indian examples demonstrate that development can be achieved by both authoritarian and democratic governments, through policies that depend more or less on the free market, and through manufacturing or services. For all of their differences, however, both of these successful examples of development work within a basically capitalist framework. Although both countries are growing rapidly, we must remember that the PRC and India still have high levels of poverty. Even in the better-off PRC, 11.2 percent of the people live on less than US$ 1.90 a day; in India the figure is 27.2 percent (World Bank, 2015). Even miracle economies face challenges.

FOREIGN AID

official development assistance (ODA)

Aid to the poorer countries given by the governments of the richer countries.

Official Development Assistance (ODA), foreign aid, refers to resources given by the governments of rich countries to promote economic and social development in poor countries. It consists of grants and low-interest loans. ODA is not charity (although disaster relief and humanitarian assistance frequently have altruistic motives) but part of foreign policy. Among the things it finances are infrastructure projects, gender equality programs, democracy promotion, and debt relief, all aiming to both help the recipient and advance the donor's foreign policy objectives. Sometimes, ODA specifies that the recipient must spend a portion of the aid in the donor country. This is called "tied aid" and was used by Canada until 2008.

Canada gives less aid than many Canadians think it does. In 1969, former Canadian Prime Minister Lester Pearson proposed that the wealthy countries dedicate 0.7 percent of their gross national income (GNI) to foreign aid. This goal has been accepted by the richer countries[3] and adopted by the United Nations. However, only a few countries (including Sweden, Norway, Denmark, and the Netherlands) have met or exceeded this goal. Canadian governments state their commitment to that goal, but in reality, assistance as a proportion of GNI has declined, reaching 0.24 percent of GNI in 2014. However, in 2015 it increased to 0.28 percent (OECD, 2016). Supporters of ODA point to increased literacy, longer life expectancies, and greater opportunities throughout the poor world. Jeffery Sachs (2005), an economist who supports increased aid, argues that without significant external assistance many countries will be unable to break free from what he calls "the poverty trap" and attain a measure of economic prosperity.

Critics, however, note that 900 million people, some 13 percent of the world's population, subsist on US$ 1.90 or less per day, so ODA is not working well. William Easterly (2006), another economist, criticizes ODA programs for being paternalistic and unaccountable. He advocates giving groups of poor people, not countries, development vouchers that they could use to contract the services of any aid agency or **non-governmental organization (NGO)**.

Economists Abhijit Banerjee and Esther Duflo (2011) offer a third alternative. They criticize both Sachs and Easterly for taking stands based on one big idea and not allowing any exceptions. Banerjee and Duflo ask what works (or doesn't) and why. They do not offer sweeping panaceas but rather carefully examined analyses of particular cases. Their objective is to accumulate evidence that will let both Third World governments and donors choose the best response to a particular problem of development.

> **non-governmental organization (NGO)**
>
> A private organization that often delivers public services but is independent of government. NGOs have been very active in international development activities.

Economic Discrimination

Seen from the South, the reluctance of the rich countries to open their markets fully to the Third World and to accept fair global trading rules is at least as important as economic assistance. Canada, like other wealthy countries, talks about free trade and levelling the international economic playing field. But when trading with poor countries, wealthy countries find ways to discriminate against the products that poor countries produce more cheaply, primarily foodstuffs and textiles, in order to protect their own producers. As well, the richer countries subsidize many exports, giving them a competitive advantage over Third World products; however, we insist that Third World countries must not protect their producers from our products. We can do this because we are stronger, and the poorer countries need to trade with us so desperately that they often accept an unfair deal.

---

[3]The People's Republic of China has also become a major provider of ODA to Africa (Provost & Harris, 2013).

Trade Pacts

There are numerous trade agreements involving both rich and poor countries. As of 2016 one hundred and sixty-four countries are members of the World Trade Organization (WTO), an international organization dealing with the rules of trade between countries. It is the only international economic organization that does not assign member countries votes based on the size of their economies. There are also many regional free-trade agreements such as the North American Free Trade Agreement and bilateral agreements such as the Canada–Chile Free Trade Agreement.

Free-trade agreements establish binding trade rules and sometimes set up impartial panels to settle trade disputes. In theory, this helps weaker countries, as the stronger countries can be constrained by the rules. The products of the poor countries can potentially gain access to the markets of the world's developed countries without facing discriminatory tariffs and quotas.

However, many poor countries argue that trade agreements are biased against them and do not lead to fair trade. For example, agriculture is the major economic activity in many less developed countries, with a large proportion of the population often engaged in farming. However, rich countries provide about US$ 1 billion a day in subsidies to their own farmers. Agricultural products are then exported at very low prices, making it difficult for farmers in poorer countries to sell their products. Because poor countries are dependent on access to the markets of rich countries, they are vulnerable to pressure to accept rules that may be more beneficial to the rich countries. The WTO, whose task is to facilitate international trade, has had trouble addressing the issue of rich country agricultural subsidies.

POLITICS IN THE THIRD WORLD

Few Third World countries have effective democratic systems. Politics in most of these states has been characterized by instability, military rule, violence, and corruption. These traits have contributed to the problems of development. Although many less developed countries made **democratic transitions** between 1980 and 2000, only a minority has succeeded in forming stable **consolidated democracies**. In 2016, "de-democratization" in some countries is evident.

In one sense, politics in the Third World is no different from politics anywhere. People want to control the state, to make rules that they think are good, and to enforce those rules as they think best. However, Third World politics diverges from politics in consolidated democracies, such as Canada, in three important ways:

1. Liberal democracies have been rare in the Third World.
2. Third World countries have weak governmental institutions.
3. Violence plays a much bigger part in Third World politics than in developed, consolidated democracies.

democratic transition

A process of change involving abandoning authoritarian government for democratic rule.

consolidated democracies

Countries with democratic governments that are stable, well accepted by both ordinary citizens and political elites, and unlikely to be overthrown.

Few Liberal Democracies

Had we looked at the governments of the Third World in 1980, we would have found only a handful of liberal democracies where the rule of law is respected, rights and freedoms are protected, and citizens have a voice in governing. These would have included India, Botswana, Costa Rica, and Barbados. There were also countries that were semi-democracies or marginal cases, such as Singapore and Sri Lanka, but most Third World countries would not have been considered democratic in 1980. Now, 65 of the 125 countries that Freedom House (2016b) identifies as electoral democracies (countries that choose their leaders through free elections) are developing nations. Since the overall sample of countries examined by Freedom House includes 137 states that can be considered developing nations, nearly half of them can be called democratic.

Transitions from authoritarian, non-democratic governments in many countries led to democratically elected ones. However, it takes more than dismantling an authoritarian state and holding elections to build a strong, stable democracy. A number of countries have the form but not the substance of democracy. There are often few institutional limits on the executive's power. Once elected, a president or prime minister can often govern without restraint until the next election.

Weak Institutions

Strong, **personalistic leaders** have historically dominated politics in poor countries. Almost always men, they are called *caudillos* in Latin America, *big men* in Africa, and *bosses* just about everywhere. Giving one leader too much power can be a problem anywhere, even in the United States (Schlesinger, 1973), Britain (Weir & Beetham, 1999), and Canada (Simpson, 2001). Consolidated democracies, however, generally have counterweights to executive power that seldom exist in new democracies.

These counterweights include **political institutions** inside and outside of government, such as legislatures, courts, the public service, the media, organized interests, political parties, and groups independent of government. Democracies need to have both sets of institutions working well. Having strong political institutions lessens the risk that one person, group, or organization will become too powerful in two different ways. A multiplicity of robust institutions disperses power among many centres, each having some ability to counter the actions of the others. Further, having several powerful institutions in a political system gives citizens more chances to present their views to government.

Almost all countries have at least one strong governmental institution: the executive. In Canada, the executive refers to the prime minister or premier, the Cabinet, and the public service. In much of the Third World, however, the president or prime minister monopolizes executive power. Hence, there is little

personalistic leader

A political leader whose claim to rule is based on some presumed inherent personal qualities. It also signals a government in which all important decisions are made by the leader according to the leader's wishes.

political institutions

Behavioural patterns or established organizations associated with politics and governing.

accountability, and corruption is often a serious problem. Political corruption exists in all countries. However, poor countries appear especially vulnerable to this problem. Why?

In part, poor countries are vulnerable to corruption due to weak political institutions that cannot protect the public. Corruption is also a sign that politics is a winner-take-all game, with no place left for opponents. Making matters worse is a failure of legitimacy. Citizens do not trust government because government concentrates control in the hands of those who are already powerful. Governments then rule through force or fraud, and opponents use force to try to change the government. Although this oversimplifies the situation, it gives a sense of the dynamics that produce political violence in the Third World.

The Role of Force and Violence

Violence has always characterized politics in the developing world (as it once did everywhere). Even Third World nations with long histories of democratic rule, such as Costa Rica, experienced coups, revolutions, and insurgencies in the past. Other democracies, such as Jamaica and India, still have a lot of political violence, especially during election campaigns. And the non-democratic countries face even graver challenges, as violence is often a standard instrument of rule.

Evidence of political violence and its devastating effects exists in several sub-Saharan African states. Rwanda and Burundi have been racked by ethnic warfare that spilled over their borders and affected neighbouring states. One of those neighbours, the Democratic Republic of Congo, has also been the scene of violent conflict. Governments in Sierra Leone, Liberia, and Somalia have collapsed at times, leaving their citizens to be plundered and murdered by marauding armed bands. In the Middle East, Iraq, Syria, and Yemen have been wracked by violence. Development is obviously impossible in these settings. Why, though, has violence been so common throughout the Third World?

coup d'état

A forcible overthrow of government by the military.

CHANGING TIMES   The main agent of political violence in the Third World has been a politically active military. Recently, however, those militaries have taken a less prominent role, resulting in fewer **coups d'état** (forcible overthrows of government by the military). Militaries in poor countries have long been politicized; that is, they have regularly taken clear political stances, occasionally seizing power. They have done this because they have the guns, but also because they are commonly the best organized institution in a country, with the highest concentration of technically skilled, well-trained personnel. Accordingly, when civilian politicians were corrupt or incompetent, or have gone against the military's wishes, the soldiers stepped in and took over (see Box 17-5 Military Coups).

BOX 17-5 Military Coups

Military takeovers of government do not just happen. Studies of coups and how they work help us understand this phenomenon (Farcau, 1994; Fitch, 1977; Luttwak, 1969).

- First, the army will almost certainly be involved because, of all the armed services, it has the armed troops, tanks, and other armour that are needed to topple a government. The air force can strafe buildings and opposing troops, while the navy can shell shorelines and block harbours, but the army secures the area.
- Second, although some coups have been led by sergeants and generals, many coups are led by majors and colonels because they directly command large numbers of soldiers.

- Third, coups succeed or fail based on whether key figures oppose or support them. For example, an attempted coup failed in Spain in 1981 because the king opposed it publicly, causing military commanders to fall in line behind him.
- Fourth, successful coups capture not only government leaders, but also the communications media. When a coup succeeds, it often forms a governing committee or junta (a Spanish word meaning "board" or "committee"). The junta contains all of the key players in coups.
- Finally, some coups are bloodless, because they are essentially unopposed, but others spur civil wars or lead to cruel dictatorships.

Through the 1980s, it seemed that there was no general solution to the problem of politically active militaries. However, the wave of democratic transitions that began then has coincided with a sharp fall in the frequency of coups. This may reflect a heightened democratic consciousness among soldiers, but there are several other plausible explanations.

One is that citizens in many countries have become dissatisfied with military governments. This is especially true of four South American countries (Argentina, Brazil, Chile, and Uruguay) that saw particularly brutal and long-lasting military regimes in the late twentieth century. Another is that militaries around the world have recognized their nearly uniform failure as governors. Militaries can impose order and throw out inept rulers, but with only a handful of exceptions they have not presided over extended periods of development. Finally, the international community no longer tolerates military governments. International financial institutions now are very reluctant to make loans to military regimes and often demand that civilian governments cut military budgets to qualify for loans.

Coups, however, still occur: Honduras had one in 2009, Mali in 2012, the Central African Republic in 2013, and Thailand in 2014. The military remains a political actor and there will likely always be some military regimes, although fewer than before.

Coups in the World, 1950–Present
http://www.jonathanmpowell.com/ coup-detat-dataset.html

PUTTING PROBLEMS INTO PERSPECTIVE Why do the political conditions just described affect the Third World? The fact that today's wealthy democracies have pasts as unsavoury and unpromising as what we find in today's developing world tells us that improvement is possible. We often forget that democratization—in its social and economic manifestations of less rigid class barriers and a more equal distribution of wealth as well as in its political form—has been under way for more than 200 years in the historic democracies of northwestern Europe and North America. To expect Africa, Asia, and Latin America to cover the same distance in a decade or even a generation is unrealistic. Nevertheless, ever more countries are offering their citizens increasingly accountable, honest, and efficient governments. This signifies progress toward building states that can pursue the common good.

We must recognize, however, that poverty makes good government difficult. In poor countries, controlling the state may offer the surest road to wealth. Where that is the case, keeping the power to govern may seem too important to risk by holding elections, allowing a free press, and encouraging citizens to participate actively in politics. Such conditions also work against building strong state institutions other than the presidency and the security forces because strong organizations can become independent and work toward the common good instead of the ruler's interests. In addition, poor countries often have difficulty in establishing an honest, efficient, and knowledgeable staff for government and its agencies. Because government may not pay adequate salaries, public servants may look to other sources of income, such as soliciting bribes or holding multiple jobs, to make a decent living.

IDRC—International Development Research Centre
http://www.idrc.ca/EN/Pages/default.aspx

Foreign Intervention

The political problems that many Third World countries face are not all of their own making. To a considerable extent, they are a product of a history of domination and exploitation.[4]

The control and colonization of most of the world by European powers often left Third World countries ill-prepared for governing after becoming independent. In a number of cases, the boundaries of the new countries made little sense, as they combined groups of people of different ancestries, cultures, languages, and religions. To make matters worse, the imperial powers frequently stimulated ethnic divisions within their colonies as part of a divide-and-rule strategy. In other cases, the descendants of the European colonists tried to maintain their economic and political power after independence against the challenges of Indigenous peoples.

POST-INDEPENDENCE   Although most of the Third World was able to achieve independence in the decades following World War II, this did not end

---

[4]Domination and exploitation have been associated not only with Western powers. Imperialism, colonization, slavery, forced religious conversion, and the massacre of conquered peoples have been carried out at various times by the powerful, whether Western or non-Western.

foreign intervention in their affairs. During the Cold War, the Western and Soviet blocs struggled to gain the support of Third World governments. This involved not only giving their supporters economic and military aid, but also overthrowing unfriendly governments; supporting repressive regimes, revolutionary movements, and terrorist groups; and even encouraging wars among Third World countries.

The end of the Cold War reduced these negative forms of foreign intervention that disrupted the political development of Third World countries. However, concerns about international terrorism, the rise of radical Islamism, the security of oil supplies, and the international trade in illegal drugs keep powerful countries intervening in the politics of the Third World.

Recently, another apparently more benign form of political intervention has emerged: humanitarian intervention in failed states. *Failed states* are those that no longer have the capacity to maintain order. This is not a new phenomenon, but we have only recently given it a name. Examples of failed states in recent years include Sierra Leone, Liberia, Somalia, and Haiti. In all of these cases, troops from several countries were dispatched under United Nations authority to restore order. One hundred years ago, either the disorder in a country whose government had ceased functioning would have been ignored or, more likely, a powerful state such as Britain, France, or the United States would have taken over.[5]

Fragile states index
http://library.fundforpeace.org/fsi

---

[5]Foreign military invention has also been used occasionally to protect part of a population that is severely threatened by its own government or security forces. This "responsibility to protect" has been controversial, particularly when such intervention has not been authorized by the United Nations Security Council.

✔• SUMMARY AND CONCLUSION

Although there have been improvements in living standards throughout much of the Third World, particularly in the newly industrialized countries of East Asia, income inequalities between the richest and the poorest countries continue to increase. Almost a billion people in the developing world live in extreme poverty with incomes of less than US $1.90 a day. This is down from 1.9 billion, one-half of the total population in the developing world, in 1981 (World Bank, 2015). Feeding growing populations, creating employment, and providing housing and other services to those who have flocked to the slums of congested cities pose difficult challenges for many countries.

The problems of the world's poorest states are everyone's problems. A world of great wealth for some and grinding poverty for others is, potentially, a very unstable place. Political violence in Third World countries is not just local, but can affect people in all countries. Poverty, unemployment, or violence in underdeveloped countries leads to migration, legal or illegal, to the richer countries. Environmental problems, such as the destruction of rainforests to achieve rapid economic growth, affect the ecosystems of the world as a whole.

We do not fully understand how countries develop successfully. There does not seem to be a single, universally applicable route to solving the economic, social, and political problems of underdevelopment. We know that some policies have worked for a while but that none has fully delivered on its promises. Adopting the free-market policies of the United States and other rich Western countries has not generally been very successful. In the past, the adoption of the state socialist approach of the Soviet Union failed. Although several Asian countries have achieved high rates of economic growth through export-led industrialization, it is unclear whether this approach can be replicated successfully elsewhere or, indeed, if the successes of some Asian countries can be maintained.

Development is a political and social issue as well as an economic one; thus, abstract economic theories need to be qualified by an understanding of the political, social, and cultural realities of particular underdeveloped countries. Political problems such as corruption, wars, instability, ineffective government administration, and poorly regulated economic activity create serious obstacles to development. Political institutions, both governmental and non-governmental, need to be strengthened and reformed to involve the people in the process of development, to hold government accountable for its actions, and to ensure that sound policies are designed and implemented. The development of Third World countries can also be promoted by pressuring various international institutions to provide fairer opportunities for countries that are weak and poor. Social and cultural changes such as improving the status of women and encouraging the involvement of local communities in the development process can be very helpful.

Overall, the poorer countries face difficult problems in seeking the common good of their citizens. With limited wealth, it is difficult to meet even the most basic needs of the population. Governments often lack the resources needed for effective governing. The great inequalities found in many poor countries let the wealthy wield enormous political power, which hinders needed reforms. Further, underdeveloped countries face not only internal problems, but also problems resulting from global inequities in power. The poorer countries have faced domination and exploitation by the powerful wealthy countries, whether through imperialism or the global economic system. Various forms of assistance to the poorer countries are often insufficient to overcome the challenges they face.

In sum, if we want to achieve the common good of humanity, addressing global imbalances in economic and political power as well as providing meaningful assistance to developing countries is necessary. A key problem is that governments and citizens typically are concerned primarily with the good of their own countries.

✓• KEY TERMS

Consolidated democracies 412

Coup d'état 414

Democratic transition 412

Dependency theory 404

Developing countries 397

Development 398

Export-led industrialization (ELI) 406

Free-market economic model 404

Gross domestic product (GDP) 398

Human Development Index (HDI) 400

Import substitution industrialization (ISI) 406

International financial institution (IFI) 405

Middle-income trap 397

Modernization theory 404

Non-governmental organization (NGO) 411

North 397

Official Development Assistance (ODA) 410

Personalistic leader 413

Political institutions 413

Protectionist economic policy 409

Purchasing power parity (PPP) 397

South 397

Statist economic model 404

Structural adjustment program (SAP) 405

Tariff 406

Third World 397

Underdeveloped countries 397

Washington Consensus 404

❖ DISCUSSION QUESTIONS

1. Why is global inequality so severe?

2. What should a poor country do to develop?

3. Why have some countries in the Third World prospered while others remain poor?

4. Should wealthy countries provide greater assistance to poor countries?

5. Should developed countries help less developed countries to become consolidated democracies?

6. Should poor countries have to meet certain standards of transparency and accountability before they can receive official development assistance?

FURTHER READING

Anderson, R., Seibert, R., & Wagner, J. (2011). *Politics and change in the Middle East* (10th ed.).New York: Routledge.

Banerjee, A. & Duflo, E. (2011). *Poor economics: A radical rethinking of the way to fight global poverty.* New York: Public Affairs.

Brautigam, D. (2009). *The dragon's gift: The real story of China in Africa.* New York: Oxford University Press.

Charlton, E. (2009). *Comparing Asian politics: India, China, and Japan* (3rd ed.). Boulder, CO: Westview Press.

Close, D. (2016). *Latin American politics: An introduction* (2nd ed.). Toronto: University of Toronto Press.

Collier, P. (2009). *Wars, guns and votes: Democracy in dangerous places.* New York: HarperCollins.

De Rivero, O. (2013). *The myth of development: Non-viable economies and the crisis of civilization* (2nd ed.). London, UK: Zed Books.

Green, D., & Luehrmann, L. (2011). *Comparative politics of the third world: Linking concepts and cases* (3rd ed.). Boulder, CO: Lynne Rienner Publishers.

Handelman, H. (2012). *The challenge of third world development* (7th ed.). Upper Saddle River, NJ: Pearson/Prentice-Hall.

Huntington, S. (1968). *Political order in changing societies.* Boston: MIT Press.

Hyden, G. (2006). *African politics in comparative perspective.* New York: Cambridge University Press.

Kapstein, E., & Converse, N. (2008). *The fate of young democracies.* New York: Cambridge University Press.

Seligson, M., & Passe-Smith, J. (Eds.). (2014). *Development and underdevelopment: The political economy of global inequality* (5th ed.). Boulder, CO: Lynne Rienner Publishers.

Sen, A. (1999). *Development as freedom.* New York: Knopf.

Thomson, A. (2010). *An introduction to African politics* (3rd ed.). London, UK: Routledge.

Tsai, K. (2015). *Capitalism without democracy: The private sector in contemporary China*: Version 2 Ithaca, NY: Cornell University Press.

United Nations Development Programme. *Human development report.* www.undp.org/content/dam/undp/library/corporate/HDR/2013GlobalHDR/English/HDR2013%20Report%20English.pdf[annual].

United Nations Conference on Trade and Development. *The least developed countries report.* www.unctad.org/ldcr [biennial].

World Bank. *World development report.* http://wdronline.worldbank.org [annual].

The international conflict known as the turbot war broke out in March 1995. The Canadian Coast Guard seized the Spanish trawler Estai on the Grand Banks off Newfoundland, accusing it of contravening measures to conserve fish stocks.   Fred Chartrand/The Canadian Press

After reading this chapter, you should be able to:

1. discuss the differences between national politics and international politics
2. explain the differences between various theoretical approaches to the study of international politics
3. analyze contemporary international political issues and states' foreign policy decisions
4. assess the chances of international peace and the possibilities of order and governance at the global level

The international conflict known as the turbot war broke out on March 9, 1995, when the Canadian Coast Guard seized a Spanish trawler, the *Estai*, on the Grand Banks off Newfoundland, accusing it of contravening measures to conserve fish stocks.

The Grand Banks used to be one of the richest and most popular fishing grounds in the world. By the 1970s, it became clear that unless rigorous fisheries conservation measures were adopted, its fish stocks would collapse. On January 1, 1977, Canada declared a 200-nautical mile exclusive economic zone and imposed strict controls on fishing inside the zone. However, about 10 percent of the Grand Banks is beyond the limits of Canada's economic zone. In 1979, the conservation of the fish stocks outside the 200-nautical mile limit became the responsibility of an international governmental organization, the Northwest Atlantic Fisheries Organization (NAFO). In February 1995, NAFO announced its allocation decision for the total allowable catch for turbot for 1995, with a breakdown for Canada, the European Union (EU), and other countries that left the EU dissatisfied. Since NAFO procedures so allow, the EU unilaterally set itself a higher quota.

In May 1994, following the collapse of the cod stocks and the belated adoption of a moratorium, the Canadian government decided to search, and if necessary seize, any foreign vessels suspected of fishing in violation of conservation measures. Following the EU decision to set its own quota, the Canadian government called for a turbot fishing moratorium of 60 days to which the EU refused to adhere. On March 9, 1995, the Canadian government seized the Spanish trawler *Estai* in international waters and accused it of fishing with nets smaller than those permitted under NAFO's conservation mea-

sures and of purposely misreporting its fish landings. Seizing a foreign vessel in international waters meant acting against international norms but, given the inability of NAFO to enforce its own quota and conservation measures, Canadian decision makers felt that ignoring international law was the only way to safeguard the turbot stocks and to protect its interests as a user of those stocks. The Spanish government accused Canada of piracy and brought the case before the International Court of Justice (ICJ) in The Hague. Eventually, however, both countries dropped their charges.

A similar incident occurred in May 2004 when the Canadian Coast Guard boarded two Portuguese vessels and gathered evidence of their illegal fishing. According to Article 18 of the NAFO Convention, however, prosecution of vessels suspected of illegal fishing is the responsibility of the flag state acting on the basis of evidence gathered by inspectors upon boarding. In this case, the Portuguese authorities considered the evidence gathered by Canada to be insufficient and did not take legal action against the two vessels.

These two episodes exemplify the predicament in which states find themselves in international politics, namely whether to entrust the defence of their interests to international organizations with limited enforcement abilities or to rely on themselves, which might at times require acting against international law and using force. This chapter examines politics at the global level, that is, politics *among* states as opposed to *within* states.

INTERNATIONAL POLITICS AND GOVERNANCE

There is a major difference between national politics (politics within one state) and international politics (politics among states). States are entities composed of a population, a government, and a territory. They are sovereign, meaning that their governments have the final authority to make and enforce rules on the population living within their territorial boundaries. The world as a whole does not have such a central authority. There is no world government; states live in a world characterized by **international anarchy**.

This means that the organization of authority within the world is not hierarchical as within a state. The world has as many authorities as there are sovereign states—almost two hundred of them. The fact that the world is anarchic does not mean, however, that there are no rules in relations among states. Rules do exist. They are based on customary practices as well as agreements (called international treaties) negotiated and signed by states directly or negotiated and agreed upon within the framework of international governmental organizations. These are associations of sovereign states created to facilitate co-operation among them about specific issues. International rules also derive from interpretations of existing international law provided by international courts.

Because the world is anarchic, though, there is no certain mechanism to enforce international rules. An individual who breaks the law within a state will, more often than not, be apprehended by police, tried in a court of law, and punished. A state that chooses to ignore international rules either because it interprets them in a different way than other states or simply because it is in its interest to do so will often escape punishment. Citizens of a state cannot claim that the state's rules do not apply to them or refuse to appear in court if summoned. A state, however, can refuse to be bound by some rules by choosing not to sign the treaty establishing them. A state may also refuse to submit to a court when accused of violating international law. The International Court of Justice (ICJ), which has the task of settling disputes among states, has no compulsory jurisdiction. This means that the ICJ cannot summon a state to appear before its fifteen judges who sit in The Hague in the Netherlands unless that state has voluntarily agreed to recognize the jurisdiction of the court and submit itself to its judgment.

Although the world as a whole does not have a government, it can be said to have **global governance**, which can be defined as the process whereby a number of different actors (mainly states and international governmental and non-governmental organizations) act in competition and co-operation to provide a certain degree of order and predictability to relations among states.

international anarchy

The absence of a central authority to make and enforce rules upon states in the international system.

International Court of Justice
www.icj-cij.org

global governance

The process whereby a number of different actors act to provide a certain degree of order and predictability to relations among states.

All scholars of international politics agree in defining the world as anarchic, in the sense that it lacks a central authority. They also agree in recognizing that, anarchy notwithstanding, a certain degree of governance exists. When it comes to assessing the significance of anarchy, identifying its consequences, and making policy suggestions, however, scholars divide themselves into a number of different schools. This chapter focuses primarily on the two major schools: realism and liberal–internationalism.[1]

REALISM

The realist school assumes that, since the world is anarchic, states find themselves in the same predicament as that of individuals in the state of nature before the establishment of government imagined by English philosopher Thomas Hobbes (1588–1679). According to Hobbes, life in the state of nature was "solitary, poor, nasty, brutish, and short" (1651/1968, p. 186). States in the international system, like individuals in the state of nature, have to fend for themselves in a competitive and dangerous environment.

Realism also assumes that the main objective of states is their own security, understood primarily as the defence of their territorial borders, form of government, and type of economic system, as well as the protection of their population from external threats. This objective is the core of what is usually called the **national interest**, which realists view as the most important common good that governments pursue when conducting foreign policy—that is, when acting in relation to other states or actors outside their national territories.

For realists, the pursuit of the national interest is a central and constant feature of the foreign policy of any state, regardless of changes of governments or political leaders. So, at least in regard to the quest for national security, realists tend to regard each state as a unitary actor that makes decisions as if it were a single person, even if decisions are made by different individuals and institutions acting on behalf of the state.

If states have to rely only on themselves for their security, it follows that they must seek to preserve and increase their power. Power—that is, the ability of a state to get its way in the international arena when its interests or preferences clash with those of other states—derives from a variety of resources or capabilities. These may be tangible and measurable, such as economic and military resources, or intangible and unquantifiable, such as ideological and cultural resources. The European Union, for instance,

realism

An approach to the study of international politics that assumes that, because the international system is anarchic, security is the major preoccupation of states. Peace rests primarily on deterrence, and the possibility of international governance is limited because states are reluctant to put constraints on their sovereignty.

national interest

The goals a state pursues in the conduct of its foreign policy. The term is multi-faceted and, besides the quest for power and security, includes goals ranging from the pursuit of economic growth and wealth to the preservation and expansion of national culture.

---

[1]The most prominent representatives of the realist school are Carr (1939/2001), Morgenthau (1948), Waltz (1979), and Gilpin (1981). The works of Keohane and Nye (1977) and Keohane (1984) have shaped the liberal–internationalist school. For an overview of all theoretical approaches, see Sterling-Folker (2006).

believes that its security and that of its member-states depends primarily on its ability to attract other states to copy its own political, economic, and social model. Thus, its security strategy calls for "spreading good governance, supporting social and political reform, dealing with corruption and abuse of power, establishing the rule of law and protecting human rights" (European Council, 2003). Tangible resources or capabilities are usually defined as constituting hard power, whereas intangible resources are usually referred to as soft power. Both are important.

Since all states are sovereign, they are equal from a legal point of view. Equal in law, however, does not mean equal in fact. Some states have more power capabilities than others. This means, as first pointed out by the Greek historian Thucydides some 2400 years ago, that "the strong do what they have the power to do and the weak accept what they have to accept" (Thucydides, 1972, p. 4). According to the realist school,[2] a world divided into sovereign states constitutes an **international system**. How power is distributed among states affects the way the system works, that is, how states within the system tend to relate to one another (see Box 18-1 Power Distribution in the Classroom and at the Pub).

The modern international system dates from the treaties of Münster and Osnabrück signed in 1648. They are collectively known as the Peace of Westphalia and hence the system is sometimes referred to as the Westphalian system. The treaties put an end to the so-called wars of religion that had devastated Europe since the Protestant Reformation of 1517. Even more importantly, it recognized and incorporated the concept of state sovereignty, which had been developed by the French jurist Jean Bodin (1503–1596). Since then, sovereign states have been the major units of the international system. The distribution of power among the states in the system has undergone changes, however.

We distinguish among different types of international systems based on how power is distributed among states. Because each concentration of power is called a **pole**, we talk about multipolar, bipolar, and unipolar international systems.

international system

A concept referring to both the most important international actors (states and international governmental organizations) and the pattern of interactions among them. The latter depends primarily on how power is distributed among states.

pole

A concentration of power in the international system. It could be a state or an alliance of states.

---

[2]To be more precise, one should make a distinction between two trends within the realist school. Traditional or classical realism looked at the behaviour of states in the international system the way Hobbes speculated about the behaviour of individuals in a state of nature. The most representative work of this phase is Morgenthau (1948). Later, a group of scholars, called neo-realists, focused on examining the dynamics of different types of international systems and their impact on the behaviour of states. Their most representative work is Waltz ((1979). More recently, the two trends have come together in a new approach, known as "neoclassical realism," which regards the behaviour of states in the international system as being the result of the complex interaction of systemic, state-, and individual-level variables. For an example of such an approach, see Rose (1998), Toje & Kunz (2012), and Lobell, Ripsman, & Taliaferro (2009).

BOX 18-1 Power Distribution in the Classroom and at the Pub

A university class—a group of students and their lecturer—can be regarded as a type of system. Its components or units in this case are not states but individuals. When these individuals move out of their normal classroom environment, say to a local pub, the distribution of power among them will change.

When the class meets in a classroom, power is concentrated in one individual, the lecturer, while the students are in a subordinate position. When they meet at the pub, their behaviour will change. Most likely it will be much less formal and predictable than in the classroom.

In a classroom, the lecturer will speak most of the time and occasionally call upon students who signal their desire to speak. While some students will listen attentively, others will let their minds wander or even fall asleep. In the pub, the lecturer will no longer shape the interaction between himself or herself and the students and among the students themselves. Some students might continue debating the topic that occupied them in

class, but they will be more willing to express their views and will not ask formal permission from the lecturer to intervene in the conversation. Others will strike up side conversations, maybe on a different topic.

Because the distribution of power among them has changed, the behaviour of the components of the system changes. Outside the classroom, power is no longer concentrated in one individual, the lecturer, but is equally distributed among all components of the system— students and lecturer. In the pub, the lecturer no longer has any official authority over students and consequently their behaviour is no longer constrained in the same way as in the classroom. The same thing happens in the international system. The range and type of foreign policy actions that states can prudently pursue in an international system in which power is more or less equally distributed will be much larger, and less predictable, than those they can pursue in a system in which power is concentrated in two states, for instance.

Multipolarity

From the Peace of Westphalia until World War II, the international system was **multipolar**, meaning that it contained at least four, and sometimes more than four, major poles.[3]

Great powers in a multipolar system tend to maintain what is called a **balance of power**; that is, they tend to behave in such a way as to prevent the emergence of one of them as a dominant power. On one hand, a great power must try to preserve or even increase its power in order to guarantee its security. On the other hand, it must be careful not to be perceived by other great powers as representing a threat to them because in such a case it would eventually face a confrontation with them. Great powers thus face what is called a **security dilemma**: they need power to feel secure, but the

multipolar system

A type of international system dominated by four or more great powers. The other states in the system play only a marginal role.

balance of power

A situation in which no great power is dominant in the global system.

security dilemma

The dilemma that arises when states need power to feel secure, but their accumulation of power might undermine rather than increase their security if it leads other states to feel that they are in danger and form an alliance to meet the perceived threat.

---

[3]Note that scholars do not regard a tripolar system, of which there is no historical example, as a type of multipolar system. The reason is that the policy of balancing, which is the central characteristic of a multipolar system, would be difficult to pursue since two states could ally and prevail on the third. A tripolar system is therefore considered a distinct type and inherently unstable.

BOX 18-2 Anatomy of Alliances

Alliances in the realist perspective are not based on friendship or a commonality of ideology or views, but on interest. In other words, alliances are formed whenever they are needed to meet a common threat. There are two main characteristics of alliances:

1. To be effective as a mechanism to balance power, they must not be permanent but be able to shift according to needs.

2. If war becomes necessary to prevent one great power from becoming dominant, the defeated great power is not eliminated from the map, but simply cut down to size and reinstated in the system so that it can participate in the formation of any new alliance that may become necessary to maintain a balance of power in the system. For instance, this is how European powers dealt with France after they had defeated Napoleon at the beginning of the nineteenth century.

accumulation of power might undermine rather than increase their security if it leads other great powers to feel in danger and form an alliance to meet the perceived threat.

Power, in fact, can be augmented not only through an increase in capabilities, but also through the formation of alliances. Indeed, in a multipolar system, the formation of alliances plays a key role in the maintenance of a balance of power (see Box 18-2 Anatomy of Alliances).

Bipolarity

The distribution of power in the international system may change. This can occur when some great powers are unable to continue producing the power resources and capabilities needed to sustain their position in the system, or when changes in technology such as the development of the nuclear bomb lead to the rise of new powers. At the end of World War II, the international system that had been multipolar since its inception became **bipolar**. The United States and the Soviet Union emerged as rival superpowers, so called because of their formidable nuclear arsenals, which no other state could match.

Their rivalry was undoubtedly compounded by the differences in their economic and political regimes—the United States was a liberal democracy with a free-market economy whereas the Soviet Union had a communist dictatorship with a command economy (an economy under the total control of the state). Realists, however, argue that in a bipolar system the two superpowers are bound to compete with one another regardless of their political–economic characteristics. The other states in the system will fall within the sphere of influence of one or the other of the two superpowers, and thus two opposing blocs will be formed. Some states might be able

bipolarity

A type of international system in which two superpowers compete with one another. The other states in the system fall within the sphere of influence of one or the other of the two superpowers.

The devastation of Hiroshima, Japan, by an American atomic bomb in 1945 helped to end the Second World War. Subsequently, the international system became bipolar as the United States and the Soviet Union became rival superpowers with formidable nuclear arsenals that could destroy each other and their allies.
Library of Congress, Prints and Photographs Division Washington, DC [LC-USZ62-134192]

to remain non-aligned, but competition between the two superpowers and their respective blocs is the defining characteristic of a bipolar system and will overshadow all other issues. Each superpower will try to keep the other in check and at the same time try to increase its own power. Each will also try to recruit new members to its respective bloc, while trying to prevent others from joining the rival one.

In the past, the rivalries between Sparta and Athens in the ancient Greek city-state system and between Rome and Carthage ended in a direct military confrontation and the defeat (and, in the case of Carthage, destruction) of one of the two rivals. This was not the case with the confrontation between the United States and the Soviet Union, which is why the period between 1946 and 1989 is known as the Cold War. Realists argue that the two superpowers did not clash militarily because of the presence of nuclear weapons. As Robert Oppenheimer, one of the scientists who worked on the development of the atomic bomb in the United States, put it, the two superpowers were like two scorpions in a bottle—if one attacked the other, it must do so at the price of its own destruction (Oppenheimer, 1953, p. 529). While avoiding direct military confrontation, however, the two superpowers did fight each other by proxy. Military confrontation took place between some of their client states and even within one state that they were both trying to bring to their respective bloc, in the form of a civil war.

Unipolarity

unipolarity

An international system with a single
superpower.

The economic collapse of the Soviet Union and its subsequent political disinte-
gration at the beginning of the 1990s left the United States as sole superpower
and transformed the system from bipolar to **unipolar**. Given its overwhelming military superiority and economic size, currently at least, no other state is
capable of matching the United States in terms of overall power capabilities
(see Box 18-3 Toward a Theory of Unipolarity).

The Limits of International Co-operation

**international
governmental
organization (IGO)**

An organization created by states to
facilitate co-operation among them.

Realists recognize that during the twentieth century, **international governmental organizations (IGOs)** have come to play an increasingly visible and important role in the international system. They also recognize that IGOs can, and
often do, constrain the action of states.

**United Nations
(UN)**

An international governmental organization representing almost all of the
world's states.

Iraq, for instance, did not get away with its invasion and forced annexa-
tion of Kuwait in August 1990. Acting through its Security Council, the **United
Nations (UN)** (see Box 18-4 The United Nations), the most visible and ambi-
tious among IGOs, immediately called for Iraq's withdrawal (Security Council
Resolution 660 of August 2, 1990). Since Iraq ignored this and subsequent
resolutions, the Security Council, through Resolution 678 of November 29,
1990, called for Iraq's ousting by inviting member-states "to use all necessary
means" (a euphemism for military force). Based on this resolution, a number
of countries led by the United States assembled a military coalition, defeated
Iraq in the 1991 Gulf War, and forced it to withdraw from Kuwait. What
happened to Iraq, however, could not happen to any of the five permanent
members of the Security Council, without whose vote no resolution could be
approved. It would also be unlikely to happen to any state that is a close ally
of any of the permanent five.

Realists also underline the fact that the UN is not a supranational body.
Its members are sovereign states, and the respect of state sovereignty is one of
the core principles on which the UN is based. The UN, in the realist view, is
simply a multilateral political arena that states have set up and in which they
pursue their national interests, as they do in bilateral relations. Inevitably,
therefore, the big powers enjoy as privileged a position within the UN as they
do outside it.

United Nations
www.un.org

IGOS AS TOOLS AND ARENAS   Realists point out that IGOs usually
have been set up through the initiative of big powers. Their institutional structure and the way they work reflect the distribution of power in the international system, or at least the distribution that existed when they were founded.
This means that the big powers occupy a key position and play a key role
in the functioning of the organization. Thus, for example, the so-called Big
Five, victors in World War II (the United States, the Soviet Union, the United
Kingdom, China, and France), gave themselves permanent seats on the UN

International Monetary Fund
www.imf.org

BOX 18-3 Toward a Theory of Unipolarity

The evaluation of "capabilities" deemed to be indicators of power leaves no doubt as to the singular position of the United States. On the military side, US defence spending is close to half of global military expenditure and its defence research and development budget equals about three-quarters of the total defence expenditures of China, the country most often indicated as its main future rival. The United States is also the only country capable of projecting its military power anywhere in the world and thus commands the commons (sea, space, and air). On the economic front, the United States is still the largest economy (in nominal GDP) in the world. The European Union and China follow very closely behind but their GDP per capita is only three-quarters (less without the UK in the EU) and one-tenth, respectively, of that of the United States. Capabilities notwithstanding, the most important question is whether or not the United States is willing to assume the global responsibilities that go with its position in the system (Monteiro, 2014). So far, one could say that the United States has been willing to play such a role, although at times it has acted with more reluctance than it exhibited, for instance, during the bipolar confrontation. On the one hand, a sole superpower has the ability to act unilaterally (that is, without the formal approval of international organizations and even in defiance of international law) to enforce its vision of a global order. On the other hand, it has an incentive to build as vast a consensus as possible around its choices and exercise power through persuasion and with the approval of relevant international organizations so that its actions are perceived as legitimate by other states in the system. In other words, the sole superpower must act as much as possible as a **hegemon**. The repeated use of coercion might solve problems in the short run, but in the longer run it might invite the formation of a countervailing bloc and thus erode its position in the system as well as its security. It seems highly unlikely that France, Germany, Russia, and China, for instance, would be able to form a lasting coalition capable of rivalling the United States. Yet their collective attempt to hold the United States back from intervening in Iraq in the winter of 2002–2003, although unsuccessful, provides an example of how a countervailing bloc might originate.

Some observers have argued that the unipolarity is fleeting and bound to eventually morph into multipolarity, first because, in the absence of another great power to check its actions, the United States will weaken itself by overextending itself internationally, and second, because power asymmetry will lead other states to try to strengthen their positions in order to balance against the US (Waltz, 2000). So far, however, nothing of the sort has happened. The attention of the EU, for instance, is devoted primarily to its internal problems with only occasional and fleeting looks paid to its eastern and southern neighborhoods. China's efforts are primarily focused on keeping up its economic growth, which is essential for the Communist party to maintain its grip on power (Gurtov, 2013). Russia is only a poor copy of the former Soviet Union and capable of playing a limited role primarily in its "near abroad." The challenge to US supremacy is therefore more likely to come by the strengthening of isolationist feelings at home than by its overextension abroad or the challenges mounted by other powers.

Security Council as well as the ability to block any of its resolutions through a veto. In the International Monetary Fund, each country has a number of votes proportional to the reserve funds it has contributed, which means that, in May 2016, the United States had 831 395 votes, corresponding to 16.66 percent of the total number of votes, while the microstate of Palau had 1484 votes, corresponding to 0.03 percent.

hegemon

A superpower that exercises power primarily through leadership and persuasion and thus creates a large consensus around its actions.

BOX 18-4   The United Nations

The name United Nations was first used during World War II in the so-called Declaration by United Nations of January 1, 1942, when representatives of 26 countries pledged their willingness to continue fighting together against the Axis powers (Germany, Japan, Italy, and their allies).

In 1945, representatives of 50 countries met in San Francisco at the United Nations Conference on International Organization to draw up the United Nations Charter. The Charter, which is the international treaty that established the UN, was signed on June 26, 1945, and its ratification completed by October 24, 1945. The forerunner and model on which the United Nations was based was the League of Nations, an organization conceived in similar circumstances during World War I and established in 1919 to promote international co-operation and to achieve peace and security.

The principal organs of the UN are:

- *The General Assembly*, which seats the permanent diplomatic representatives of all UN member states (193 as of May 2016). The General Assembly can debate any topic that falls within the provisions of the Charter. Each member has one vote. Its decisions, called General Assembly Resolutions, have no legally binding force for member-states. They simply carry the weight of that body's opinion on major international issues and, since the General Assembly is the nearest thing the world has to a global Parliament, perhaps can also be said to carry the moral authority of the world community. The "perhaps" seems necessary since, according to Freedom House (2016a), in 2016 only 86 UN member-states (corresponding to 44.5 percent of the total) are full-fledged democracies (representing 40 percent of the world's population); therefore, the views of a majority of UN member-states cannot necessarily be considered to represent the views of a majority of the world's people.

United Nations Headquarters, Manhattan, New York City
Tom-Hanisch/Fotolia

- *The Security Council*, which is the body responsible for peace and security issues. It is supposed to identify aggressors and situations that represent a threat to peace and decide on enforcement measures. It has fifteen members, five of which are permanent (the United States, Russia, China, the United Kingdom, and France). The other ten rotating members are selected for a two-year period. A Security Council resolution needs nine votes, including those of the five permanent members or their abstention, to be approved. This means that any of the permanent five can block a resolution and with it the activity of the Security Council. Security Council resolutions are binding on all UN members, but this does not mean that they can always be enforced. In case of non-compliance on the part of the state to which the resolution is addressed, in fact, enforcement depends on the willingness of other UN members to heed the provisions of the resolution, which might also mean readiness to put some of their military forces at the UN's disposal.

- *The Secretariat,* which is the administrative organ of the organization. As of 2016, it had about 44 000 staff members around the world headed by the secretary-general, who is elected for a five-year renewable term by the General Assembly and the Security Council.

According to the realists, IGOs are best regarded as tools that big powers create in order to help them fulfill their responsibilities for the maintenance of order in the international system. The role of IGOs is primarily to help foster international consensus, and so provide legitimacy for an order that inevitably reflects more closely the interests and preferences of the big powers than those of other states in the system.

IGOs, once formed, might impose some constraints on the big powers, but such constraints are largely self-imposed. Even in the current unipolar system, the United States prefers to act either with the approval of the UN or at least with the political support of a coalition of allies. Realists, however, focus on the fact that, when states perceive that a certain action is necessary for their own security, they will act—if they have the power to do so—even without UN approval, as the United States arguably did in the spring of 2003 in regard to Iraq.

These cases might be infrequent but, according to realists, they prove that, in the final analysis, states are the main players in the system, not least because they have a monopoly on the use of force. The UN might authorize the use of coercion (whether in the form of economic sanctions or military intervention) against one of its members, but the UN has no ability to enforce its own resolutions and depends on the willingness of its member-states to do so. According to realists, therefore, states work with IGOs when it is in their interest to do so, but do not delegate responsibility for their own security to the UN or any other IGOs.

War and Peace in the International System

Realists view competition and rivalry, and hence conflict, as the normal mode of interaction among states. The fact that the international system is anarchic means that there is no authority capable of taming conflict and that consequently conflict can easily lead to war. To maintain peace, one cannot replace competition and rivalry with co-operation and friendship or eliminate anarchy through the creation of a central authority in the system. For realists, the problem is how to make sure that competition and rivalry stop short of war. Their solution is to make war too costly an option for a would-be aggressor. It follows that peace can be attained only through strength. Wolves cannot be turned into lambs, but they can be deterred from attacking if it is made clear to them that they cannot possibly prevail.

MAINTAINING PEACE IN MULTIPOLAR AND BIPOLAR SYSTEMS What keeps peace in a multipolar system is the relatively equal distribution of power among its "great powers" that deters any of them from taking aggressive action. If one great power increases its power capabilities and begins to be perceived as a threat by the other great powers, an alliance will be formed between two or more of the latter to counter the would-be aggressor. In other words, formation of flexible alliances keeps a balance of power among the great powers and hence maintains peace in the system.

The balance of terror, also known as the doctrine of mutual assured destruction (MAD), kept peace during the Cold War, or to be more precise, prevented a direct military confrontation between the United States and the Soviet Union. The two contenders had accumulated such vast arsenals of nuclear weapons that neither had an incentive to launch an attack since the initiator could not hope to survive a retaliatory strike from the adversary. War would mean mutual assured destruction, no matter who initiated it.

The knowledge that peace rested only on the balance of terror or mutual assured destruction led the two states to sign the 1972 Anti-Ballistic Missile (ABM) Treaty, which purposely limited to two (later reduced to one) the number of strategic defence systems each country could deploy. Since ABM systems were supposed to neutralize incoming missiles while still in the air, it was thought that their deployment would destabilize the balance of terror and hence increase the probabilities of a nuclear exchange. The superpower that would succeed first in protecting all of its territory with such systems might in fact be tempted to launch an initial strike in the hope of being able to withstand the retaliatory one and escape from the exchange relatively unscathed.[4] The signing of the treaty was an implicit acknowledgment that maintaining peace did not depend on the simple desire for it—because in this case the two superpowers could have agreed to disarm completely. Peace rested instead on tying one's hands or, to put it differently, resisting any temptation one might have to resort to war by eliminating all advantages one might derive from an attack.

Global Security Institute
www.gsinstitute.org

Bulletin of the Atomic Scientists
www.thebulletin.org

---

[4]The United States has continued to work on the technology needed for ABM systems and intends to deploy a National Missile Defence (NMD) designed to protect its territory and that of its allies from the threat represented by the missiles of the so-called "rogue" states, mainly North Korea and Iran.

The United States tries to persuade the UN Security Council to participate in the latest war.

Tami Thirlwell

MAINTAINING PEACE IN A UNIPOLAR SYSTEM   It is more difficult to analyze how peace can be maintained in a unipolar system since such a system has been around for less than three decades, and hence there are few data on which to base any conclusion. It would appear, however, that in a unipolar system the sole superpower confronts a rather difficult task. On one hand, it has primary responsibility for maintaining stability and order in the international system. On the other hand, any initiative the superpower takes for this purpose risks being perceived by other actors as nothing but the blatant pursuit of its national interests and hence as an aggressive action.

The UN, for instance, could hardly undertake any military operation with respect to breaches of the peace, threats to the peace, or acts of aggression (the so-called Chapter 7 operations) if it could not rely on the willingness of the United States to provide its military forces for such operations. This means, however, that the United States has to be involved in all activities executing mandates under Chapter 7 of the UN Charter. As the United States also desires to retain command and control of its own troops in such operations, the impression is inevitably given that these interventions are not the duly authorized execution of a UN mandate but American wars.

The 1950–53 Korean War and the 1991 Gulf War are often thought of as American wars and not as UN-mandated interventions. When the UN mandate is acknowledged, the suggestion is often made that the United States coerced and cajoled the members of the UN Security Council to obtain its authorization in order to legitimize an intervention it was ready to undertake unilaterally. Things are even worse, of course, when the sole superpower takes initiatives without a very clear UN authorization, as was the case in 2003 when the United States and some of its allies invaded Iraq.

The provisional conclusion seems to be that, in a unipolar system, peace depends not only on the willingness of the superpower to intervene to maintain stability and order, but also on its ability to forge consensus around such order and the actions it undertakes to maintain it. In other words, a superpower in a unipolar system must act as a hegemon. Without willing partners and eager followers, **hegemony** deteriorates into domination and a dominant power invites the formation of countervailing alliances, which leads to turbulence and war.

hegemony or hegemonic system

A type of unipolar system in which the superpower exercises power primarily through leadership and persuasion and thus creates a large consensus around its actions.

The Realist School and the Limits of Governance

Realists are skeptical about the possibility of global governance. They regard it at best as limited and based on the ability and willingness of big powers to take the lead in shaping and providing it. There are two reasons for such skepticism:

1. Realists focus primarily on the issue of security, which they assume to be the central concern of sovereign states and therefore unlikely to be completely delegated to any IGO, the UN included.
2. States are generally unwilling to put constraints on their sovereignty. Hence, the international system might change in terms of its distribution of power among states, but it is unlikely to change in terms of its organization of authority. In other words, the system is likely to remain anarchic.

For realists, therefore, the possibility of global governance depends on the ability of bigger powers (whether many, two, or one) to develop suitable rules and institutions. Even though such rules and institutions would likely confer privileges on the bigger powers, global governance to be acceptable would require that lesser powers accept their legitimacy. For realists, in other words, global governance means at best the benign rule of hegemons.

liberal–internationalism

An approach to the study of international politics that assumes that increased cultural and social connections as well as economic interdependence are leading to the emergence of a global civil society in which co-operation, the rule of law, and peace are valued and global governance is spreading both functionally and geographically.

LIBERAL–INTERNATIONALISM

The liberal–internationalist school has a less sombre view of the consequences of international anarchy and is more optimistic about the possibilities of global governance. **Liberal–internationalism** differs from realism in a number of ways (see also Table 18-1):

- Liberal–internationalists believe that, while states might still be the most important actors in the international arena, they are not the only

	REALISM	LIBERAL–INTERNATIONALISM
Key actors	States	States, IGOs, INGOs, groups, individuals
View of the state	Unitary actor, power seeking, moved by national interest	Network of different actors, competing national interests
View of the international system	Anarchic	Interdependence of actors, international society
Views on peace	Attainable through strength, deterrence, balance of power	Attainable through law
Views on possibility of international governance	Weak; provided by hegemonic powers	Strong; governance is spreading fast

TABLE 18-1
Major Differences between Realism and Liberal–Internationalism

ones. Other actors, such as IGOs; **international non-governmental organizations** (INGOs)—examples include Greenpeace and Amnesty International;[5] specific state institutions such as parliaments and bureaucracies; societal groups; multinational corporations (MNCs); and even individuals, play an important role.

- For liberal–internationalists, states and societies interact in many different issue areas—political, economic, social, and cultural. Each of these issue areas affects the others, and none is dominant all of the time. For this reason, liberal–internationalists tend to speak of international relations (conceived of as a vast array of interactions between states and societies) as opposed to simply international politics (which suggests primarily power relations). Hence, national security, although important, cannot be examined in isolation.
- Liberal–internationalists regard states as a network of different actors—individuals, socio-economic groups, and governmental institutions and departments—each with different interests, priorities, and preferences. These actors interact with similar actors across national borders on many different issue areas, each of which is of primary importance to some actors and of lesser importance to others. Unlike realists, liberal–internationalists do not believe that there is a constant overarching national interest. Instead, there are many different, shifting, and competing national interests. Thus, even if everyone might agree on the primacy of national security (that is, the need to defend one's state from external threats), disagreements will inevitably occur concerning the means that should be used to defend oneself from such

international non-governmental organization (INGO)

An international organization whose members are not states but rather representatives of civil society.

---

[5]INGOs are distinguished from IGOs because they are established and controlled by individuals and/or groups in civil society rather than by national governments.

threats. Therefore, how a state behaves on the international scene is always the result of a bargaining process among competing domestic groups and institutions.

An International Society in the Making

Liberal–internationalists agree with realists that the world is made up of sovereign states and that there is no authority above them. They disagree, however, on the question of how significant anarchy is for the functioning of the international system and the behaviour of its members. According to them, the principle of sovereignty, which has traditionally regulated interstate relations, is constantly evolving.

The idea has recently gained ground, for instance, that sovereign states have a responsibility to protect their own citizens from avoidable catastrophes as well as to guarantee their enjoyment of human rights. When states are unwilling or unable to do so, that responsibility must be borne by the international community as a whole. Thus, under certain circumstances it is appropriate for the United Nations or another IGO, a coalition of states, or even a single state to take action—including military action—against another state in order to protect the latter's population or part of it. This is, of course, an important limitation on state sovereignty.

INTERDEPENDENCE Liberal–internationalists also point out that the range of international interactions is so vast and its reach so deep that all actors in the international system are interdependent—that is, each is affected by the actions of others. The interdependence of actors, the fact that all of them face an increasing number of common challenges, such as environmental degradation, increasing global population, climate change, and the immediacy of global communication and travel, are slowly leading, according to liberal–internationalists, to the development of a common identity, a sense of "we-ness" on planet Earth.

For all of these reasons, liberal–internationalists think that the international system is not an almost immutable structure constraining the behaviour of its units, but an evolving one. The international system does constrain the behaviour of its units, but the units—states, groups, and individuals—are constantly modifying the system itself through their own ideas and actions. The increasing number and relevance of INGOs, moreover, is evidence of the rapid emergence of a vibrant global civil society, which will eventually give birth to a global and democratic political society. Thus, for liberal–internationalists the world is more than a system of independent sovereign states. It is also an **international or global society** in the making.

international or global society

The idea that the increasing number and importance of international interactions and the rising degree of interdependence is creating a global common identity and leading to the development of a global society.

Why States Co-Operate

Liberal–internationalists point out that, although there are occasional exceptions, states usually comply with international law even in the absence of a central authority capable of enforcing it. They do so for two reasons:

1. States prefer to do what is considered right and moral because they do not wish to lose prestige in international public opinion.
2. Even more importantly, states have learned over time that it is in their interest to abide by international law because it is preferable to live in an ordered and predictable world rather than in a lawless, uncertain, and dangerous one.

Order and predictability allow states not to have to worry too much about the behaviour of other states, since it can be assumed that their behaviour will fall within the parameters allowed by the law.

JOINING IGOS   The desire to reduce uncertainty in interstate relations has pushed states to establish and join an increasing number of IGOs. Although IGOs can rarely enforce rules on states unwilling to abide by them, they are useful because they provide a context in which it is easier for states to co-operate with one another. That is, they can help to find a mutually satisfying adjustment in situations of conflicting interests or preferences.

Membership in IGOs does not weaken state sovereignty; it simply provides a different context in which to exercise it. More precisely, the context provided by IGOs reduces the costs of negotiating agreements by providing clear rules, better information, and opportunities for compromises and side payments through issue linkages. When different issues are on the table, states are more willing to make concessions on some if, at the same time, they get what they want on others. Membership in IGOs also improves the chances of voluntary compliance since the costs of defection (or non-compliance), in terms of reputation and credibility, are higher than they would be in a bilateral relationship. This explains why smaller powers like Canada value membership in IGOs more than big powers do. Their sovereignty is enhanced because they gain more voice and hence influence, especially when acting in concert, than they would have in bilateral relationships with bigger powers.

The argument of liberal–internationalists is undoubtedly very convincing when applied to the technical and even economic issue areas of international relations (Keohane, 1984). For example, an effective **international regime**—defined as a set of principles, norms, and procedures that regulates (usually, but not necessarily, through IGOs) international activity in a

international regime

A set of principles, norms, and treaties, usually but not necessarily centred around an IGO, that regulates international activity in a specific issue area.

BOX 18-5 The World Trade Organization

Based in Geneva, Switzerland, the World Trade Organization (WTO) is the international organization charged with managing trade relations among its 164 members (as of July 2016). At the same time, the WTO promotes free trade through the progressive dismantling of tariff and non-tariff barriers, provides a forum for governments to negotiate trade agreements, and provides a place and mechanism for them to settle trade disputes.

The WTO was established in 1995, but its origins date back to 1947 when 23 states negotiated a General Agreement on Tariffs and Trade (GATT) aimed at overcoming economic nationalism, which was perceived as one of the factors responsible for the outbreak of World War II, and promoting freer international trade. To this end, GATT sponsored a series of trade negotiations called "rounds" that reduced tariffs and non-tariff barriers and increased the total value of world merchandise trade from $53 billion in 1948 to $18 494 billion in 2015. At the end of the last successful round—the Uruguay round—the WTO was formed.

The latest round of trade negotiations—the Doha round, launched in November 2001—tackled trade in services and agricultural products, particularly the issue of subsidies that hurt the less developed countries. It is on this issue, however, that talks stalled in 2008. Trade liberalization is supposed to take place according to the principle of the "most favoured nation," which means that concessions granted to one WTO member must be extended to all other members. Exceptions exist,

however, in the case of regional free-trade areas and in favour of less developed countries. Trade liberalization, moreover, can also be suspended when domestic industries face severe injury.

The WTO's top-level decision-making body is the Ministerial Conference, which is formed by member-states' ministers of international trade and meets at least once every two years. Day-to-day operations are conducted by the heads of national delegations, which meet as the General Council. Each member-state has the right to have one representative on the Council, whose work is supported by a Secretariat with 634 regular staff members (as of 2015) headed by a Director General.

An important innovation of the WTO as compared with GATT is its dispute-resolution mechanism. It provides fixed timetables for the various steps in the procedure, which means that any dispute is solved in a maximum of 15 months. Disputes are submitted to the General Council, which then selects a panel to hear the dispute and submit a report for adoption. The procedure is repeated if there is an appeal of the first report. What is new with respect to the old GATT procedure is that disputes cannot be prolonged indefinitely and no party to a dispute can block or veto the adoption of a report. Now, a report can be blocked only if every WTO member agrees to do so. The procedure has changed, in other words, from negative to positive consensus and, as a result, the international trade regime has been strengthened.

World Trade Organization
www.wto.org

specific issue area—exists in the area of telecommunications. International trade also has an increasingly effective regime centred on the World Trade Organization (see Box 18-5 The World Trade Organization). Indeed, as interdependence has increased, so have the need for IGOs and international regimes and the eagerness of states to form them. The proliferation of IGOs and international regimes reinforces the habit of co-operation, and this, according to liberal–internationalists, bodes well for an increasingly peaceful future (Brown, 1995).

The Problem of Security and the Search for Peace

Unlike realists, who think that, ultimately, states can rely only on self-help for their security, liberal–internationalists believe that states can and should rely on IGOs and law. For them, state security is better achieved through a collective approach. The principle of **collective security** posits that states pledge to intervene on behalf of a member whose security is threatened by the aggressive actions of another state.

The UN is first and foremost a collective security organization, as was its predecessor, the League of Nations. The principle of collective security is consistent with the realist reliance on deterrence to discourage aggression and maintain peace. If states can be certain that aggression will be punished by collective action, they will refrain from engaging in aggressive behaviour.

For a system of collective security to work, however, one must assume that participating members can always agree on establishing who the aggressor is when two states come to blows. Unfortunately, this is not always easy since states, much like individuals, are more likely to listen sympathetically to the arguments of friends than to those of foes. For collective security to work, one must also assume that participating members are always ready and willing to act against the aggressor. The historical record on this point is not too comforting. When Japan invaded Manchuria and Italy conquered Ethiopia in the 1930s, members of the League of Nations did not make good on their promise to intervene. Thus, the system of collective security effectively collapsed, leading to further aggression by Germany against Czechoslovakia and Poland and, in the end, to World War II.

Things did not fare any better with the UN Security Council during the Cold War, since the ideological and political rivalry between the United States and the Soviet Union effectively paralyzed the Council until the end of the Cold War. Only two acts of international aggression met with a collective response by the UN between 1945 and 1991:

- *The intervention against North Korea for its invasion of South Korea in 1950.* The UN was able to intervene only because, at the time, the Soviet Union was boycotting the meetings of the Security Council to protest the fact that Taiwan (the Republic of China) and not the People's Republic of China had a seat at the UN. Had the Soviet Union been present, it would certainly have vetoed an intervention against its North Korean ally.
- *The 1991 intervention against Iraq following its invasion of Kuwait.* The end of the Cold War rekindled liberal–internationalist hopes that the UN could finally fulfill its collective security responsibility, but these hopes did not last very long.

collective security

The principle that all members of the collectivity of states (or simply a number of them) are jointly responsible for the security of each of them and therefore pledge to intervene on behalf of a member whose security is threatened by the aggressive actions of another state.

As the debate over what to do with Iraq's protracted defiance of the disarmament terms imposed by UN Security Council Resolution 687 at the end of the 1991 Gulf War showed, disagreements among Security Council members resurfaced almost immediately and manifested themselves dramatically during the period immediately preceding the 2003 intervention against Saddam Hussein's regime. Such disagreements were due partly to the ambiguity of the evidence available to decide whether Iraq represented an immediate threat to regional and world peace, and partly to the desire of some permanent members of the Security Council—France and Russia, in particular—to try to constrain the range of action of the United States, the superpower.

Reducing the Likelihood of War: The Role of Economic Interdependence

Some liberal–internationalists believe that, as a method of solving interstate conflicts, war is losing legitimacy, just as the duel has lost legitimacy as a way of solving interpersonal disputes (Mueller, 1989). Indeed, states formally renounced recourse to war for the solution of international controversies and as an instrument of national policy in 1928 when they signed the General Treaty for the Renunciation of War (better known as the Briand-Kellogg Pact, from the names of the French and American foreign ministers instrumental in negotiating it). The treaty had little practical effect but was significant at the level of ideas since it indicated a rapidly changing attitude toward state-sanctioned violence. Liberal–internationalists argue that interests, rather than just sensibilities, are changing. The high degree of economic interdependence that characterizes liberal democratic states has made war a very costly mechanism to solve disputes because it entails economic disruptions, both commercial and financial, and hence economic costs for most warring states.

For example, France and Germany went to war three times in less than a century, but war between the two countries—or any two European countries, for that matter—would be unlikely today given their high degree of economic interdependence. Indeed, economic interdependence has also led to the building of a network of common political institutions (the countries belonging to the European Union being those that have gone the farthest in this direction), which has made war an even more remote possibility.

Some liberals argue that the European Union (see Chapter 13) represents an example of a **postmodern state**—that is, a state in which the meaning and practice of sovereignty have been redefined since tools of governance are shared, foreign and domestic policies have become inextricably intertwined, and security is no longer based on control of borders and deterrence (Cooper, 2000). The idea is that the example of the European Union could be

European Union
http://europa.eu

postmodern state

A state in which the meaning and practice of sovereignty have been redefined since tools of governance are shared, foreign and domestic policies have become inextricably intertwined, and security is no longer based on control of borders and deterrence.
----

replicated in other parts of the world, until the entire world would become a postmodern state.

Given also the traditional liberal idea—whose origins go back to the German philosopher Immanuel Kant (1724–1804)—that states with liberal democratic governments are less likely than states with other types of government to wage war against one another, liberal–internationalists believe that international peace can be promoted by fostering the development of free-market economies and democratic institutions around the world. Such a policy, however, if not pursued subtly and carefully, might lead, at least in some parts of the world, to resentment and resistance, and thus end up triggering, rather than preventing, disorders and even military hostilities.

The Liberal–Internationalist Promise of Governance

Liberal–internationalists are more optimistic than realists about the possibility of global governance. The world, they argue, does not resemble Hobbes's mythical state of nature. It also appears to be increasingly acquiring the features of a global civil society, as evidenced by a growing network of connections across national boundaries (Lipschutz, 2000).

These connections, which have traditionally linked organized groups, now involve single individuals thanks to the World Wide Web. One can see the slow but nevertheless sure emergence of a global consciousness that is increasingly bringing challenges to and slowly eroding the traditional primacy of the sovereign states. To be sure, the world does not yet have a central authority—and it might never have one. Yet it exhibits an increasing number of functional areas (for example, telecommunications or international trade) in which the rule of law prevails. Such a trend, moreover, is self-reinforcing and hence unlikely to be reversed.

OTHER THEORETICAL APPROACHES

Besides realism and liberal–internationalism, other theoretical approaches to the study of international politics include the radical and the constructivist approaches.[6] Largely drawing inspiration from the writings of Karl Marx, radical approaches share some characteristics with realism but also differ from it in significant ways. Radicals regard social classes and particularly transnational economic elites as the key actors in international politics. For radicals, states are simply agents acting in the interests of these elites and the

---

[6]On radicalism, see Cox (1987) and Wallerstein (2011); on constructivism, see Wendt (1999) and Zehfuss (2002). There is also a feminist approach to the study of international relations; see, for instance, Enloe (1989) and Sylvester (1994).

most significant feature of the international system is its capitalist structure. The radical view is that the international system is organized hierarchically between a developed, exploiting core and an economically exploited and dependent periphery.

For realists, the existing international order reflects more closely the interests and preferences of the big power; for radicals the existing order serves the interests of transnational economic elites. The difference between the two approaches is that, whereas realists limit themselves to describing the existing order and regard it as an inescapable feature of how international politics works, radicals denounce the existing order as inequitable and oppressive and argue that it should be changed. Unlike liberal–internationalists who regard liberal democracy as a carrier of peace, radicals argue the opposite. Radicals believe that the free-market capitalist economy is exactly what causes conflict and war, both nationally and internationally. For radicals, therefore, the possibility of global governance and the promotion of the common good rest upon overcoming the current liberal–capitalist system.

While radicals consider international politics as driven primarily by economic interests, constructivists regard international politics as the result of ideas and norms, especially those of the social and political elites. The national interest is not determined by the fact that the international system is anarchic (realism) or results from the competing interests of domestic groups (liberal–internationalism), nor is it merely economic (radicalism). National interests are instead "constructed" by social and political elites and are based on their "identities"—that is, their beliefs about what is worth pursuing (values) and how it should be pursued (norms). Indeed, constructivists argue that power in international politics is based primarily on, and derives from, ideas and not material structures; as Wendt (1999, p.6) put it, "Anarchy is what states make of it." Consequently, constructivists argue that the behaviour of actors in the international system changes, sometimes even very quickly, as a result of interactions and socialization. It also follows that, given the increasing degree of international interactions brought about by economic globalization and the strength and attraction of liberal democratic ideas, the international system is constantly evolving. Most constructivists hold robust expectations about the eventual emergence of a reliable system of global governance for at least three reasons. First, since World War II, European states have rejected power politics and instead developed a system of widely shared norms. Second, these states have been relatively successful in projecting this new system in their immediate neighbourhood (Central and Eastern Europe). Third, these developments are expected to be replicated in other parts of the world. Overall, the major contribution of the constructivist approach—so far, at least—seems to be reminding students of international politics that ideas, norms, and culture are not simply dependent variables, but can play a significant and independent role.

THEORETICAL APPROACHES: AN EVALUATION

It should be remembered that all of these theoretical approaches are lenses that analysts put on to help make sense of international political events. Each approach yields different pictures or tells different stories, and each is suited to make sense of some time period or issue area better than others. Thus, the realist approach is certainly very effective in explaining the working of the international system from its birth to the beginning of the twentieth century, while the liberal–internationalist approach yields a better picture of the evolution of the international system from the beginning of the twentieth century until today. Realism is perhaps more effective in explaining security relations while liberal–internationalism seems more convincing when applied to state relations in economic issue areas. Some academics spend considerable time and energy to promote the superiority of their preferred approach over all others, often forgetting that approaches are essentially working tools and are more complementary than mutually exclusive.[7]

State Behaviour in the Real World

Theoretical approaches only offer an explanation of how the international system as a whole works and of how states tend to behave in it over time. These approaches, however, do not explain how states make specific foreign policy decisions nor do government decision makers follow the policy suggestions offered by these theoretical approaches. Decision makers make choices to promote what they perceive to be the "national interest" (or "common good"). In doing so, they often have to try to reconcile a number of potentially conflicting objectives such as bolstering, or at least not endangering, national security; enhancing national economic prosperity; being perceived, both internationally and nationally, as doing what is right; and, last but not least, making sure that their choices do not negatively affect their likelihood of being re-elected. Thus, to explain a state's foreign policy decision at a specific point in time, one needs to open the so-called black box, that is, to examine the complex processes by which decisions are made within states. In other words, one needs to move beyond the assumptions that the state is rational and unitary (realism) or rational and made up of different actors (liberal–internationalism) and examine in more detail how actors—individuals, groups, and governmental institutions—interact to arrive at specific decisions (see, for instance, Box 18-6 The US Decision to Intervene in Iraq).

The study of foreign policy decisions involves examining variables at different levels of analysis. At the individual level, it examines the preferences of

---

[7] On theoretical debates in international relations see, for instance, Ashworth (2002).

BOX 18-6   The US Decision to Intervene in Iraq

Iraq's protracted failure to comply fully with the disarmament terms imposed by UN Security Council Resolution 687 at the end of the 1991 Gulf War (caused by Iraq's invasion of Kuwait in 1990) was met throughout the 1990s by a policy of containment centred on the imposition of economic sanctions. The only military acts were the destruction of some targets that represented a threat to US and UK planes enforcing two UN designated no-fly zones protecting the Kurdish and Shia Muslim populations that had in the past been the victims of attacks from Saddam Hussein's regime. In October 1998, President Bill Clinton signed the "Iraq Liberation Act," which committed the United States to regime change in Iraq. The act explicitly excluded the use of the US military to achieve its stated objective and therefore, except for the provision of financial and military aid to anti-Saddam groups, it did not lead to any major change in the existing policy, which continued also during the first few months of the Bush presidency. The al-Qaeda terrorist attack of September 11, 2001, although not involving Iraq, changed policy thinking in Washington. The Bush administration concluded that Iraq's defiance needed a more resolute response, a military one if necessary (Pollack, 2002).

The official rationale provided for this change of policy was that the world could not risk Iraq retaining chemical or biological weapons given Saddam Hussein's past willingness to use them against his enemies both at home and abroad. To those critics who argued that the Iraq threat did not appear so imminent as to justify preemptive military action, the Bush administration answered that the concept of "imminent threat" needed to be modified to take into account "the capabilities and objectives of today's adversaries." Prudence, in other words, called for action before rogue states or terrorists could use weapons of mass destruction (WMD).

The rationale for action, however, was not entirely based on (realist) security considerations. It also rested on a good dose of (liberal–internationalist) interventionism.

The Bush administration, in fact, also argued that the replacement of Saddam Hussein's dictatorship with a liberal democratic regime would bring similar changes in other countries in the region and thus promote peace regionally and internationally. The administration justified the intervention even in "humanitarian" terms. However, this argument was used sparingly since the Iraqi regime had committed its worst atrocities against Kurds and Shia Muslim groups between 1987 and 1991.

Before September 11, 2001, it would have been difficult to convince the American public that a military intervention to topple Saddam Hussein was required for national security. After September 11, however, all that was needed was to emphasize the possibility that Saddam's WMD might be passed on to, or simply fall into the hands of, Islamic terrorists. The intelligence supporting such dire predictions was dubious at best and revolved primarily around the fact that Saddam Hussein was impeding the work of UN weapons inspectors. What was not known at the time was that Saddam Hussein, who feared his domestic and regional enemies (Iran in particular) more than he feared the United States, had deliberately chosen to leave doubts about his complete disarmament. Saddam underestimated the probability that the United States would invade Iraq and was convinced that, should it happen, all he needed was to resist a few days before Western public opinion would mobilize and press for a withdrawal (Kohn, 2003; Battle, 2009). Before the policy change could be implemented, its supporters in the Bush administration had to overcome the skepticism of the State Department and of some members of the military who argued that the reconstruction of Iraq along democratic lines required a bigger allocation of financial and human resources than senior people in the administration seemed to think necessary (Wallack, 2006). Before the military invasion took place, the United States tried to obtain an explicit UN approval. When this failed, it moved to the second-best option, that is, building a large political alliance—the so-called "coalition of the willing". The United States argued that military action was justified by previous UN Security Council resolutions, particularly Resolution 687 of April 3, 1991, which made the Gulf War cease-fire conditional on Iraqi compliance with the inspection and dismantling of its chemical and biological weapons, and Resolution 1154 of March 2, 1998 which warned Iraq of "severest consequences" for continued violation of the terms indicated in Resolution 687 (Prados and Katzman, 2002).

key decision makers—for example, presidents or prime ministers and foreign ministers—as expressed, for instance, in official government documents, and it explores the process by which they are formed. These preferences, whether initiatives or responses to other states' actions, pass various tests and go through a number of stages before becoming foreign policy decisions or choices.

At the systemic level, foreign policy choices must be consistent with the structure of the international system. Prudent foreign policy choices must fall within a range whose boundaries depend on the distribution of power in the system and the place the state in question occupies in it. Thus, during the Cold War, a satellite of the Soviet Union or of the United States could not reasonably and safely pursue a foreign policy objective that was perceived as damaging to the interests of the superpower in whose sphere it orbited. In 1956, Hungary found this out to its cost after it announced its decision to withdraw from the Warsaw Pact[8]—the collective security agreement that bound the Soviet camp states together—and embrace neutrality.

At the national level, three factors influence the formulation of foreign policy choices. The first is capabilities: the implementation of foreign policy choices cannot require more power capabilities than the state can marshal. There is little practical use in establishing the objective, as Canada did when Lloyd Axworthy held the position of minister of foreign affairs, of promoting "human security," even if understood not in its widest sense of general improvement of the quality-of-life conditions experienced by individuals worldwide but only in the more limited sense of protection of civilians during civil conflicts (Axworthy, 2003). Canada does not have the power capabilities to improve "human security" worldwide in either of those two ways; it could at best only bring attention to such issues. The second factor is political: foreign policy choices must enjoy domestic consensus (Hanrieder, 1967) and hence be perceived as consistent with national identity and effective in promoting the country's national interest, however the latter might be defined. In parliamentary systems, such as the Canadian one, these policy choices must enjoy the support of the governing party (or parties) and at least a permissive

---

[8]A revolt initiated by a student protest led to the formation of a new government that favoured neutrality. The Soviet Union crushed the revolt and installed a harsh new pro-Soviet government.

attitude among the public at large. The third factor is the role of civil servants. Governments may change as a result of an election, and the prime minister may change the Cabinet minister(s) responsible for foreign policy. Thus, to a considerable extent, governments rely on career professionals in the Foreign Affairs Department (now termed Global Affairs Canada) to process incoming information, formulate policy options, and implement policy. Long careers in the department lead to the accumulation of what Hill (2003, p. 77) has called "institutional memory" that acts as a constraint on the preferences politicians might have. Finally, before they become foreign policy decisions, preferences must also go through a complex policy process whose institutional characteristics depend on the type of political system of the country in question. In general, it can be said that the more liberal democratic, and hence open, the political system is, the more likely it is that the original preferences are adjusted and modified during the policy-making process. For all of these reasons, a democratic country's foreign policy has a built-in bias in favour of continuity. A new foreign policy is likely to emerge only in the wake of a major change in the structure of the international system and/or in the country's capabilities, two events that happen rarely.

✓• SUMMARY AND CONCLUSION

This chapter has examined the difference between national politics and international politics: the fact that the respect of rules at the international level depends more on voluntary compliance on the part of states than on enforcement. It has also examined the differences between various theoretical approaches to the study of international politics, focusing in particular on realism and liberal–internationalism.

Realists argue that the fact that states are sovereign makes the international system anarchic and hence very similar to Hobbes's state of nature. In such a world, security, which is the major preoccupation of states, depends on self-help and hence on power. Peace depends on deterrence, namely making it clear to potential aggressors that the costs of aggression outweigh the potential benefits. Because states are jealous of their sovereignty, the possibilities of international governance are limited.

Liberal–internationalists argue that although the world is still politically organized in states, each of whose governments claims to be the ultimate authority over its

territory and population, increased cultural and social connections and economic interdependence are leading to the emergence of a global civil society—one that values co-operation, the rule of law, and peace. A world political federation might never emerge, but international governance is spreading both functionally and geographically.

Overall, international politics raises difficult issues for the pursuit of the common good. Given the problems that the world faces (such as war, global climate change, global inequality, international terrorism, and the protection of basic human rights), it would be desirable for the common good to be considered, at least in part, in terms of the common good of humanity or of the entire planet.

However, the realist perspective alerts us to the continuing importance of national interests. The common good of humanity can, at best, be achieved only to a limited degree in an anarchic world. In contrast, liberal–internationalists have a more optimistic outlook on achieving the common good. In their view, the development of international organizations and agreements, along with increased interaction among the peoples of the world in areas such as trade and communications and the spread of democracy, make progress toward a more peaceful and prosperous world possible. But international organizations and trade agreements do not necessarily lead to the global common good, as they may reflect the interests of the powerful. As well, international governmental organizations are often not particularly democratic. Achieving the global common good, therefore, presents us with difficult challenges.

KEY TERMS

Balance of power   425
Bipolarity   426
Collective security   439
Global governance   422
Hegemon   429
Hegemony or hegemonic
   system   434
International anarchy   422

International governmental
   organization (IGO)   428
International non-governmental
   organization (INGO)   435
International or global society   436
International regime   437
International system   424
Liberal–internationalism   434

Multipolar system   425
National interest   423
Pole   424
Postmodern state   440
Realism   423
Security dilemma   425
Unipolarity   428
United Nations (UN)   428

◆ DISCUSSION QUESTIONS

1. What are the major differences between the realist and liberal–international approaches to the study of world politics? What are the implications for policy suggestions?

2. What are the policy options and the dilemmas a state confronts in trying to guarantee its own security?

3. Can the United Nations be considered a world government? How significant is the lack of a central authority in world politics?

4. Is a peaceful world a realistic objective? How might a more peaceful world be achieved?

FURTHER READING

Baylis, J., Smith, S., & Owens, P. (Eds.). (2011). *The globalization of world politics: An introduction to international relations* (5th ed.). Oxford: Oxford University Press.

Baylis, J., Wirts, J., & Gray, C.S. (Eds.). (2013). *Strategy in the contemporary world: An introduction to strategic studies* (4th ed.). Oxford: Oxford University Press.

Gurtov, M. (2013). *Will this be China's century? A skeptic's view.* Boulder: Lynne Rienner.

Jackson, R., & Sørensen, G. (2013). *Introduction to international relations: Theories and approaches* (5th ed.). Oxford: Oxford University Press.

Kennedy, P. (1987). *The rise and fall of the great powers: Economic change and military conflict from 1500 to 2000.* New York: Vintage Books.

Lobell, S., Ripsman, N. & Taliaferro, J. (Eds.). (2009). *Neoclassical realism, the state, and foreign policy.* Cambridge: Cambridge University Press.

Monteiro, N.P. (2014). *Theory of unipolar politics.* Cambridge: Cambridge University Press.

Ravenhill, J. (Ed.). (2007). *Global political economy* (2nd ed.). Oxford: Oxford University Press.

Toje, A. and Kunz, B. (Eds.). (2012). *Neoclassical realism in European politics: Bringing power back in.* Manchester: Manchester University Press.

Absolute monarchy   A political system in which a king or queen has total power, unconstrained by law.

Alternative service delivery   New methods of delivering government programs, such as the establishment of government service agencies that have considerable autonomy from the normal departmental structures and rules and the establishment of partnerships with business, other levels of government, and voluntary organizations to deliver services.

Anarchism   An ideology that views the state as the key source of oppression and seeks to replace the state with a system based on voluntary co-operation.

Anthropocentrism   The focus on human well-being that is at the centre of most political thought.

Asymmetrical federalism   A version of federalism in which some provincial or state governments have a greater degree of self-government than others.

Authoritarian regimes   Non-democratic governing systems that feature absolute rule over the population. People are prevented from choosing their government and influencing its decisions.

Authority   The right to exercise power.

Autocracy   Rule by one person with unlimited power.

Balance of power   A situation in which no state is dominant in the global system.

Binational or multinational states   States whose populations are composed of two or more nations.

Bipolarity   A type of international system in which two superpowers compete with one another. The other states in the system fall within the sphere of influence of one or the other of the two superpowers.

Brokerage party   A party that attempts to find compromises to accommodate a variety of interests (particularly regional and ethnic/cultural divisions) so as to try to build broad support across the country in a non-ideological manner.

Bureaucracy   An organization in which people are hired and promoted based on their qualifications and merit, work is organized in terms of specialized positions, detailed rules and procedures are followed by all members of the organization, and there is a hierarchical chain of command so that those at the top can direct and supervise large numbers of people.

Cabinet secrecy   The convention that the views expressed in Cabinet remain secret to enable full and frank discussion and maintain Cabinet solidarity.

Cabinet solidarity   The convention in a parliamentary system that each member of the Cabinet is expected to fully support and defend the decisions and actions that Cabinet takes.

Cabinet   The members of the political executive. The Cabinet in a parliamentary system is led by the prime minister, with many or most Cabinet ministers having the responsibility of heading a government department.

Cadre party   A loosely organized party usually established by members of a legislative body with the support of local notables. Cadre parties are concerned primarily with electing members of the party to legislative bodies, rather than with building a strong, centralized, membership-based organization outside of the legislature.

Canadian House of Commons   The elected chamber of Parliament, with each member representing a particular electoral district.

Capitalist economic system   A system in which most businesses are privately owned and seek profit through the production and sale of goods and services in the market.

Charismatic authority   Authority based on the perception that a leader has extraordinary or supernatural qualities.

Charlottetown Accord   A 1992 package of proposed constitutional changes, including recognition of the inherent right of Aboriginals to self-government and major changes to the Senate. It was defeated in a referendum.

Charter of Rights and Freedoms   As part of the Constitution Act, 1982, the Charter protects a variety of rights and freedoms. It is superior to ordinary legislation, explicitly allows the courts to invalidate legislation, and applies to the actions of all governments and organizations under the control of government.

Checks and balances   A basic principle of the American presidential system in which each of the three branches of government is able to check the actions of the others so that no individual or institution becomes too powerful.

Citizens' initiatives   A procedure that gives citizens the right, by obtaining a sizable number of signatures on a petition, to have a proposition that they have drafted put to a vote by the electorate for approval.

Citizens' jury   A group of randomly selected persons that deliberate about and make recommendations concerning particular issues.

Citizenship   The idea that a country's permanent residents are full members of the political community with certain duties and rights.

Civic culture   A mixture of subject and participant political roles among the general population.

Civic nationalism   Nationalism based on the shared political values and political history of those who are citizens of a country.

Civil disobedience   Deliberate lawbreaking that accepts punishment by state authorities as part of the action.

Civil society   The voluntary groups and organizations that are not controlled by the state.

Classical liberalism   A form of liberalism that views government has having the limited purposes of protecting life, liberty, and property.

Classical or dual federalism   A version of federalism in which the federal and provincial or state governments each concern themselves with their own areas of constitutional authority without infringing upon the areas of authority of the other level of government.

Cleavage   A social division that involves those associated with each grouping having a distinct collective identity and distinct interests that can lead to the development of organizations such as political parties that reflect the different sides of the social division.

Closure   A procedure in a legislative body that cuts off debate if approved by a majority vote.

Co-operative federalism   A federal system in which the two levels of government are jointly involved in developing, financing, and administering many government services.

Coalition government   A government in which two or more political parties jointly govern, sharing the Cabinet positions.

Codified constitution   A constitution whose major provisions are set out in a formal constitutional document or a set of constitutional documents.

Codified law   A system of law based on the adoption of a comprehensive set of principles that judges use to determine the outcome of a particular case.

Cohabitation   The sharing of power between the French president and prime minister that occurs when the Assembly is controlled by a party opposed to the president.

Collective responsibility   The convention that the Cabinet as a group will defend, explain, and take responsibility for the actions of the government in Parliament.

Collective security   The principle that all members of the collectivity of states (or simply a number of them) are jointly responsible for the security of each of them and therefore pledge to intervene on behalf of a member whose security is threatened by the aggressive actions of another state.

Common good   What is good for the entire political community.

Common law   A system of law-based court judgments that have accumulated over many centuries.

Communism   A system in which private property has been replaced by collective or communal ownership and everyone is free to take from society what they need.

Confederal system   A system of governing in which sovereign states have agreed to delegate some of their authority to a joint government with limited authority while retaining their sovereignty.

Congress   The legislative branch of the American government consisting of the House of Representatives and the Senate.

Conservatism   A perspective or ideology that emphasizes the values of order, stability, respect for authority, and tradition, based on a view that humans are inherently imperfect, with a limited capacity to reason.

Consolidated democracies   Countries with democratic governments that are stable, well accepted by both ordinary citizens and political elites, and unlikely to be overthrown.

Constitution Act, 1867   An Act of the United Kingdom Parliament that established Canada by uniting the colonies of Canada (Ontario and Quebec), Nova Scotia, and New Brunswick. It also set out many of the features of Canada's system of governing.

Constitution Act, 1982   The Act that made the constitution fully Canadian, added the Charter of Rights and Freedoms to the constitution, and established procedures for amending the constitution.

Constitution   The fundamental rules and principles by which a state is governed.

Constitutional amendment   A formal change to the constitution.

Constitutional conventions   Fundamental principles that are consistently followed even though they are not contained in a legal document and are not generally enforceable in the courts.

Constitutional government   A government that consistently acts in accordance with established fundamental rules and principles.

Constitutional monarchy   A system of governing in which the monarch acts as official head of state but is strictly limited in power by the constitution.

Contentious politics   The usually disruptive, direct, and highly conflictive ways that people advance their claims on elites, authorities, and opponents, ranging from peaceful political protest to wars and other lethal conflicts.

Corporate state   A system associated with fascist Italy in which business and labour work harmoniously to achieve goals established by the state to advance the good of the nation.

Counter-insurgency   A blend of military and political action taken by a government to defeat an insurgency. The tactics are usually described as a mixture of repression and reform.

Coup d'état   A forcible overthrow of government by the military.

Deep ecology   An environmentalist perspective that views anthropocentrism as the fundamental cause of environmental degradation and advocates the cultivation of an environmental consciousness and a sense of oneness with the world that recognizes the unity of humans, plants, animals, and the Earth.

Deliberative democracy   A political system in which decisions are made based on discussion by citizens rather than by elected representatives alone.

Democracy   Rule by the people.

Democratic deficit   The substantial level of public dissatisfaction with the performance of democratic governments and politicians exhibited in declining levels of voter turnout, low levels of trust and confidence in government and politicians, increased protest activity, and a feeling that ordinary people have little influence on government.

Democratic socialism   The perspective that socialism should be achieved by democratic rather than revolutionary means and that a socialist society should be democratic in nature with political rights and freedoms respected.

Democratic transition   A process of change involving abandoning authoritarian government for democratic rule.

Dependency theory   Dependency theory argues that underdevelopment results from unequal power relations between the centre (dominant capitalist countries) and the periphery (poor, dependent countries).

Deputy minister The executive head of a department of government appointed by the prime minister in consultation with the Clerk of the Privy Council Office. The deputy minister runs the department with oversight by the Cabinet minister who is the political head of the department.

Developing countries Countries that have not reached the same level of development as the richer, advanced countries.

Development A condition that involves the satisfaction of the basic needs of all of the people as well as the means for them to live fulfilling and productive lives based on the creation of a more diversified, sophisticated, and sustainable economy.

Devolution A system of governing in which the central government grants some legislative (law-making) powers as well as administrative responsibilities to one or more regional bodies.

Direct democracy A system in which citizens themselves make the governing decisions.

Dissolution The termination of Parliament followed by the holding of an election for the House of Commons.

Dominant-party system A political system where one party holds power for an extended period of time by winning free and fair elections.

Ecocentrism The view that nature has intrinsic value and should not be valued only in terms of its use for human beings.

Ecofeminism A combination of environmentalism and feminism that views male dominance as the basic cause of the degradation of the Earth.

Electoral College A body that elects the president of the United States. Members of the Electoral College from each state are expected to vote for the presidential candidate who has won the most votes in their state.

Electoral system The system used to translate the votes that people cast into the composition of the legislature and the selection of the government.

Electoral–professional party A political party whose dominant concern is winning elections and that relies on professional experts to market the party to voters.

Empirical analysis Analysis that involves explaining various aspects of politics, particularly by using careful observation and comparison to develop generalizations and testable theories.

Enlightenment An intellectual movement that developed in the mid-eighteenth century, emphasizing the power of human reason to understand and improve the world.

Environmentalism A perspective based on the idea that humanity needs to change its relationship to nature so as to protect the natural environment and ensure that it can sustain all forms of life.

Equalization payments Payments made by the federal government to try to ensure that poorer provincial governments are able to provide an equivalent level of services to their populations without resorting to excessive levels of taxation.

Ethnic nationalism Nationalism based on common ancestry along with the cultural traditions and language associated with a particular ethnic group.

European common market A stage in the process of economic integration in which the member states remove all duties on trade with one another (as in a free trade area), adopt a common external tariff on trade with other countries (as in a customs union), and allow for the free movement of people from one member state to another.

European Union (EU) An economic and political union of many European countries that have pooled some of their sovereignty.

Eurozone The countries of the European Union that have adopted the euro as their currency and discontinued the use of their national currency.

Executive dominance A parliamentary system that places considerable power in the hands of the prime minister and Cabinet through their ability to control the House of Commons, particularly in a majority government situation.

Export-led industrialization (ELI) A model of economic development with a capitalist system in which government and the biggest businesses co-operate to develop export industries. Government influences investments, provides incentives for exports, and can decide whether firms are allowed to export products.

Failed state A state that is unable to enforce laws, maintain order, protect the lives of citizens, and provide basic services.

Fascism An ideology that combines an aggressive form of nationalism with a strong belief in the naturalness of inequality and opposition to both liberal democracy and communism.

Federal system A system of governing in which sovereign authority is divided or shared between the central government and regional governments, with each deriving its authority from the constitution.

Feminism A perspective that views society as patriarchal and seeks to achieve full independence and equality for women.

Filibuster The use of various delaying tactics by those opposed to the passage of a particular piece of legislation.

Framing Selecting and highlighting some facets of events or issues, and making connections among them so as to promote a particular interpretation, evaluation, and/or solution.

Free-rider problem A problem with voluntary collective action that results because an individual can enjoy the benefits of group action without contributing.

Free-market economic model An economic model that emphasizes private enterprise and significantly limits the economic role of the state.

Free-market environmentalism The perspective that holds that guarantees of the rights of private property and a free-market economy are crucial to environmental protection.

Fundamentalism The revival of strict religious beliefs seeking to promote the fundamental principles of the faith, including the belief that sacred scriptures are the word of God, and should be strictly followed in all areas of life.

Generational effect The effect on attitudes and behaviour of the views of different generations that persist throughout the life cycle.

Gerrymander The manipulation of the division of the country into electoral districts so as to benefit a particular party.

Global governance   The process whereby a number of different actors act to provide a certain degree of order and predictability to relations among states.

Globalization   The processes that are increasing the interconnectedness of the world.

Governance   The making and implementing of decisions often with the involvement of state and non-state organizations.

Government   The set of institutions that makes decisions and oversees their implementation on behalf of the state for a particular period of time.

Governor general   The person who carries out the duties and responsibilities of the monarch at the national level in Canada.

Gross domestic product (GDP)   The market value of goods and services produced in a country, excluding transactions with other countries.

Guerrilla warfare   A form of highly political warfare built around lightly armed irregulars who oppose a government and use hit-and-run tactics and political work to take power.

Head of government   The person who heads the executive side of government and is usually responsible for choosing the Cabinet. In Canada, the prime minister is the head of the Canadian government, while the heads of provincial governments are known as premiers (in Quebec, premier ministre).

Head of state   In a parliamentary system, the head of state is an important but largely ceremonial position, but has the responsibility to ensure that a legitimate government is in place.

Hegemon   A superpower that exercises power primarily through leadership and persuasion and thus creates a large consensus around its actions.

Hegemonic party regime   A political system in which opposition parties exist and compete for power but cannot win because government control over the electoral system assures that the ruling party does not lose.

Hegemonic-party system   A political system where one party holds power for an extended period of time by winning fraudulent elections.

Hegemony or hegemonic system   A type of unipolar system in which the superpower exercises power primarily through leadership and persuasion and thus creates a large consensus around its actions.

Historical materialism   The view that historical development and the dynamics of society and politics can be understood in terms of the way society is organized to produce material goods.

Holocaust   The systematic extermination of six million European Jews by the Nazis during World War II.

House of Commons committees   Committees composed of government and opposition party members in proportion to their party's strength in the House of Commons; they provide detailed examination of proposed legislation and often suggest modifications to that legislation.

House of Representatives   The lower chamber of the American Congress, elected for a two-year term from districts of approximately equal population size.

Human development index (HDI)   An annual index for most countries, calculated by the United Nations Development Programme and based on educational attainment, life expectancy, and per capita gross national income (GNI).

Hybrid regimes   Governing systems that are a mixture of democratic and non-democratic rule. Hybrid governments typically gain and keep power through electoral fraud, corruption, and legal manoeuvers.

Impeachment   A process by which a president and other public officials can be removed from office after being accused of criminal behaviour and convicted by a legislative body.

Import substitution industrialization   A model of economic development in which a country establishes high tariffs to protect businesses setting up to manufacture goods that replace imports.

Individualist perspective   A perspective that views human beings as acting primarily in accordance with their own interests.

Infotainment   The merging of information and entertainment in news and public affairs programming of the mass media, particularly television.

Inside strategies   Strategies in which interest group leaders develop close contacts with key decision makers in government and the public service in order to influence public policies.

Institutional dictatorship   An undemocratic government controlled by an established political institution. The most common examples are military dictatorships, party dictatorships, and theocratic dictatorships.

Institutionalized interest group   A group that has developed a formal organization, including such features as a well-established membership base, paid professional staff, permanent offices, and the capability to keep its members and the public aware of its views and activities.

Insurgency   A rebellion or revolt, especially one employing the tools of guerrilla warfare.

Interest group   An organization that pursues the common interests of groups of people, particularly by trying to influence the development, adoption, and implementation of public policies.

International anarchy   The absence of a central authority to make and enforce rules upon states in the international system.

International financial institution (IFI)   An organization that has some ability to affect the global economic system; for example, the International Monetary Fund and the World Bank.

International governmental organization (IGO)   An organization created by states to facilitate co-operation among them.

International non-governmental organization (INGO)   An international organization whose members are not states but rather representatives of civil society.

International or global society   The idea that the increasing number and importance of international interactions and the rising degree of interdependence is creating a global common identity and leading to the development of a global society.

International regime   A set of principles, norms, and treaties, usually but not necessarily centred around an IGO, that regulates international activity in a specific issue area.

International system A concept referring to both the most important international actors (states and international governmental organizations) and the pattern of interactions among them. The latter depends primarily on how power is distributed among actors.

Iron law of oligarchy A generalization that claims that all organizations, even those that appear democratic, inevitably become dominated by a small group of leaders.

Islamism The revival of Islam based on a strict, literal interpretation of the Qur'an and a belief that public and private life should be governed by the sharia (Islamic law).

Issue-oriented interest group An interest group that spontaneously develops to express the views of people on a particular issue, concern, or grievance.

Judicial activism The term used when the courts are active in invalidating legislation and government actions that are inconsistent with the constitution.

Judicial review The authority of the courts to strike down legislation or governmental actions that the courts deem to be in violation of the constitution.

Keynesian economic policies The idea that government can smooth out the ups and downs of the free-market economy by stimulating the economy when private business investment is low and cooling down the economy when excessive investment is creating inflation.

Laissez-faire economic system A system in which privately owned businesses, workers, and consumers freely interact in the marketplace without government interference.

Left The general ideological position associated with advocacy of greater social and economic equality, laws based on universal human rights rather than traditional morality, and opposition to state support for religious institutions.

Legal–rational authority The right to rule based on legal rules and procedures rather than on the personal qualities or characteristics of the rulers.

Legislature An institution whose responsibilities include the approval of legislation and the raising and spending of funds by the government.

Legitimacy Acceptance by the members of a political community that those in positions of authority have the right to govern.

Leninism The version of Marxism that includes the belief that the capitalist system can be overthrown only by force, by means of a tightly disciplined party controlled by a revolutionary vanguard.

Liberal democracy A political system that combines the liberal ideas of limited government, individual freedom, and the rule of law with a democratic system of governing based on the election of representatives.

Liberal–internationalism An approach to the study of international politics that assumes that increased cultural and social connections as well as economic interdependence are leading to the emergence of a global civil society in which co-operation, the rule of law, and peace are valued and global governance is spreading both functionally and geographically.

Liberation Freeing the human potential that has been stifled by the organization and values of society.

Libertarian perspective on the mass media The idea that if the mass media are free from government control and regulation, individuals will be able to obtain and assess the information and ideas they want.

Licenced opposition Opposition parties that are allowed to exist, contest elections, and win legislative seats, but that can never take power.

Lieutenant-governor The person who carries out the duties and responsibilities of the monarch at the provincial level in Canada.

Life-cycle effect The effect of one's age on one's attitudes and behaviour. As people grow older, their attitudes and behaviours may change due to changing circumstances (such as education, marriage, employment, and retirement) related to age.

Lobbying An effort to persuade those involved in making and implementing public policies to adopt and implement policies or decisions favoured by an individual, business, or group particularly through direct personal contact.

Majority government The government formed when the prime minister's party has a majority of the members of the House of Commons; thus, a single party forms the government.

Marginalization Exclusion from the mainstream.

Mass party A party that draws its support from a regular dues-paying membership and features a strong party organization outside of the legislature.

Meech Lake Accord A 1987 package of proposed constitutional changes that was not passed. It contained controversial provisions, including the recognition of Quebec as a "distinct society."

Middle-income trap A condition in which a country with a middle-level annual per capita income (roughly US$ 1200 - US $13 000) cannot grow to the level of the wealthy (>US$ 13 000).

Military dictatorship An undemocratic government run by the military.

Minority government A single party governs, but that party does not have a majority of the members in the House of Commons. Thus, a minority government needs to gain the support of one or more other parties to pass legislation and to stay in office.

Mixed member proportional (MMP) system An electoral system in which some legislators are elected to represent particular electoral districts based on gaining the most votes in that district, while others are elected based on the popular vote received by their party.

Modernization theory A development model that views the traditional values, practices, and institutions of Third World countries as the basic cause of underdevelopment. To develop, poor countries should change their cultural outlook, social structure, economic organization, and political system based on the model of the advanced Western societies.

Multiparty system A political party system featuring several parties that are significant actors in the competition for political power.

Multipolar system A type of international system dominated by four or more great powers. The other states in the system play only a marginal role.

Nation-state A sovereign state based on people living in a country who share a sense of common identity as members of a particular nation.

Nation A group of people who share a sense of common identity and who typically believe they should be self-governing within their homeland.

National interest The goals a state pursues in the conduct of its foreign policy. The term is multi-faceted and, besides the quest for power and security, includes goals ranging from the pursuit of economic growth and wealth to the preservation and expansion of national culture.

National self-determination The idea that nations should have the right to determine their political status, including choosing to have their own sovereign state.

Nationalism The idea that the nation-state is the best form of political community, that a nation should have its own self-governing state, and that the interests, culture, and values of the nation should be promoted.

Nazism A version of fascism associated with Adolf Hitler, the Nazi leader of Germany, emphasizing racial conflict and the superiority of the "Aryan race."

Neo-corporatism A political system in which the state actively collaborates with selected major interests (particularly the national organizations of business and labour) to seek a consensus concerning the country's major economic and social policies.

Neo-fascism A revival of some of the characteristics of fascism in contemporary times including ethnic nationalism, opposition to immigrants who have different racial or religious characteristics, and support for a populist leader who will take decisive action to strengthen the nation.

Neo-liberalism A perspective based on a strong belief in the free marketplace and opposition to government intervention in the economy.

Neo-Marxist theory A perspective that views politics as reflecting the conflicts that result from the way society is organized to produce goods. Public policies in a capitalist society will reflect the unequal power relations between the dominant capitalist forces and subordinate groups.

New public management The adoption of the practices of private business in the administrative activities of government.

New Right A perspective that combines, in various ways, the promotion of free-market capitalism and limited government and traditional cultural and moral values.

New style of citizen politics A set of changes including greater citizen activism, the questioning of authority, the development of new political parties and new social movements, the raising of new types of issues, and the development of more liberal social values.

News management The controlling and shaping of the presentation of news in order to affect the public's evaluation of news stories.

Non-confidence motion A motion put forward by opposition members in a legislature expressing a lack of confidence in the government. If passed, the prime minister is expected to either resign or request that an election be held.

Non-governmental organization (NGO) A private organization that often delivers public services but is independent of government. NGOs have been very active in international development activities.

Normative analysis Analysis that includes examining ideas about how the community should be governed and what values should be pursued through politics.

North The rich, developed countries.

Notwithstanding clause A provision in the Charter of Rights and Freedoms that allows a legislative body to explicitly declare that a particular law (related to some parts of the Charter) shall operate notwithstanding the provisions of the Charter. Such a declaration is only effective for five years, although it can be re-enacted as often as is desired.

Official development assistance (ODA) Aid to the poorer countries given by the governments of the richer countries.

Official multiculturalism The policy of recognizing the cultural diversity of the country and providing encouragement and support for those of different cultures to help them retain and foster their cultures and traditions.

Official opposition The party with the second-highest number of seats in the House of Commons; the official opposition leads off the questioning or criticism of government every day that the House is sitting.

One-party dominant system A party system in which a single party rules for long periods of time and the opposition parties are not likely to gain the support needed to successfully challenge the dominant party for control of the government.

Outside strategies Strategies in which interest group leaders appeal to the public for support and mobilize members in order to put pressure on decision makers concerning public policies.

Parliamentary sovereignty A basic principle of the British system of governing, recognizing Parliament as the supreme law-making body such that the courts cannot invalidate an Act of Parliament.

Parliamentary system A system of governing in which there is a close interrelationship between the political executive (prime minister and Cabinet) and Parliament (the legislative or law-making body). The executive is generally composed of members of the House of Commons (the elected parliamentary body) and must maintain the support of the House of Commons.

Party convention A meeting of delegates from party constituency associations as well as the party's legislators and party officials.

Party dictatorship An undemocratic political system that is controlled by one party. The most familiar examples are found in communist political systems.

Party discipline The expectation that members of each party will vote in accordance with the position that the party has adopted in caucus.

Party identification A long-term attachment to a particular political party.

Patriarchy A system in which power is in the hands of men and many aspects of women's lives are controlled by men.

Personal dictatorship An undemocratic government dominated by a single individual. Saddam Hussein's Iraq or Muammar Gaddafi's Libya were classic examples of this kind of system.

Personalistic leader   A political leader whose claim to rule is based on some presumed inherent personal qualities. It also signals a government in which all important decisions are made by the leader according to the leader's wishes.

Personalistic party   A party dominated by a powerful leader combined with a weak party organization that follows the wishes of the leader.

Plebiscitary democracy   A form of democracy in which citizens have greater control than in representative democracy through the use of such devices as referendums, citizens' initiatives, and recall elections.

Plebiscite   A vote in which the entire electorate is asked to approve or reject a specific question; for example, whether the current president should be elected president for life.

Pluralist perspective   A perspective that views public policies as the outcome of competition among a wide variety of organized groups that seek to protect and promote the interests of their members, with no group having a dominant influence.

Pluralist system   A political system in which a large number of groups representing a wide variety of interests are able to influence the decisions of government. Government tries to satisfy as many groups as possible, and no group has a dominant influence on government.

Pole   A concentration of power in the international system. It could be a state or an alliance of states.

Political agenda   The issues that are considered important and given priority in political deliberations.

Political conflict   A state of opposition, usually involving groups and the state, over something government is doing or proposes to do.

Political culture   The fundamental political values, beliefs, and orientations that are widely held within a political community.

Political efficacy   The attitude that individuals can have an impact on political decisions and that government is responsive to what people want.

Political gridlock   A situation where necessary legislation is unable to be passed particularly because of tension between the president and one or both Houses of Congress controlled by an opposing political party.

Political ideology   A package of interrelated ideas and beliefs about government, society, the economy, and human nature that inspire and affect political action. Each ideology provides a different perspective that is used to understand and evaluate how the world actually works. Most ideologies also provide a vision of what the world should be like and propose a means of political action to achieve their objectives.

Political institutions   Behavioural patterns or established organizations associated with politics and governing.

Political opportunity structures (POS)   The openings that political institutions and processes offer to or withhold from movements.

Political party   An organization that has a central role in the competition for political power in legislative bodies and in governing.

Political protest   Oppositional political action that takes place outside formal channels, generally seeking to have government make significant changes in its policies.

Political science   The systematic study of politics.

Political socialization   The processes by which the values, attitudes, and beliefs of the political culture are transmitted to members of the political community.

Political violence   The use of physical force with a political objective.

Politics   Activity related to influencing, making, or implementing collective decisions for a political community.

Populism   A perspective that advocates putting power in the hands of the people rather than the elites who control politics and society.

Postmaterialist theory   A theory that modern societies are undergoing a fundamental change in value priorities because generations that grew up in the relative security and affluence of the Western world since World War II are more likely to give priority to postmaterialist values than to materialist values.

Postmaterialist values   Non-materialist values such as freedom of expression, participation, concern about the quality of life, and appreciation of a more beautiful environment.

Postmodern state   A state in which the meaning and practice of sovereignty have been redefined since tools of governance are shared, foreign and domestic policies have become inextricably intertwined, and security is no longer based on control of borders and deterrence.

Power   The ability to achieve an objective by influencing the behaviour of others, particularly to get them to do what they would not have otherwise done.

Preferential ballot   An electoral system in which voters rank candidates in order of preference. If no candidate has a majority of first preferences, the candidate with the least votes is dropped, and the second preferences of those who voted for that candidate are added to the votes of other candidates. This process continues until one candidate has a majority.

Prerogative powers   Powers of the monarch that have not been taken away by Parliament. These are also known as reserve powers.

Presidential system   A system of governing in which the president and Congress each separately derive their authority from being elected by the people and have a fixed term of office.

Presidential veto   The ability of the president to prevent the passage of a bill. The president of the United States has the authority to veto laws passed by Congress, although this veto can be overridden by a two-thirds majority in each body of Congress.

Primary election   An election in which citizens select the candidates for the party they support prior to the general election.

Prime Minister's Office (PMO)   The office that provides support and political advice to the prime minister.

Prime ministerial government   The view that the prime minister has become the dominant member of the political executive, rather than "first among equals" in the Cabinet.

Private law   Law that deals with the relationships among individuals, groups, and businesses that are primarily of private interest rather than of general public interest.

Private members   Ordinary members of the House of Commons who are not in the Cabinet.

Privy Council Office (PCO)   An administrative structure that is directly responsible to the Canadian prime minister, has a central role in organizing the Cabinet and coordinating and directing the activities of government, and provides policy advice to the prime minister.

Programmatic party   A party that has a distinct ideological perspective or a coherent set of policy goals that are consistently followed over time.

Proportional representation (PR) system   An electoral system in which the proportion of seats a party receives in the legislature reflects the proportion of votes it has obtained.

Prorogation   The suspension of Parliament and its committees by the governor general at the request of the prime minister. Prorogation (unlike an adjournment) ends a session of Parliament such that the work of committees is ended and bills that have not been passed have to be reintroduced unless Parliament in the next session agrees otherwise.

Protectionist economic policy   An economic policy that uses high tariffs to ensure that domestic firms have an edge when competing with foreign companies. Import substitution industrialization is an example.

Public choice theory   A perspective based on the assumption that all political actors are rationally attempting to maximize their own individual interests or preferences.

Public interest group   A group that seeks to achieve goals that the group views as being for the good of the community as a whole rather than providing specific benefits for its members.

Public policy   A course of action or inaction chosen by public authorities to address a given problem or interrelated set of problems.

Purchasing power parity (PPP)   A measure of per capita income that shows the purchasing power of an income, instead of its worth at current exchange rates.

Radical feminism   A version of feminism that views society as based on the oppression of women and seeks to liberate women through the fundamental transformation of social institutions, values, and personal relationships.

Radical Islamism   The perspective often associated with those seeking to purge "degenerate" foreign elements from Muslim society and establish a "pure" Islamic state based strictly on the sharia (Islamic law).

Reactionary   A conservative who favours a return to the values and institutions of the past.

Realism   An approach to the study of international politics that assumes that, because the international system is anarchic, security is the major preoccupation of states. Peace rests primarily on deterrence, and the possibility of international governance is limited because states are reluctant to put constraints on their sovereignty.

Reasonable limits clause   A provision in the Charter of Rights and Freedoms that allows for "reasonable limits" to be placed on rights and freedoms, provided that the limits can be "demonstrably justified in a free and democratic society."

Recall   A procedure that allows citizens to remove representatives from office. By gaining a sufficient number of signa-

tures on a petition, citizens can require that their representative seek re-election before the representative's term is over.

Referendum   A vote by citizens on a particular issue or law.

Reform environmentalism   A perspective that views the solution to environmental problems primarily in terms of better science, technology, and environmental management.

Reform liberalism   A version of liberalism that combines support for individual freedom with a belief that government action may be needed to help remove obstacles to individual development.

Regime violence   Political violence used by a government against its citizens, generally as a way to repress dissent and keep order.

Regime   The broadest class of political system, it encompasses the bases of the system's legitimacy; how and to whom government is accountable; who has access to and influence with government; how government, civil society, and private citizens interact; and what its governmental institutions are. Examples include democracy, dictatorship, and monarchy.

Representative bureaucracy   A bureaucracy that reflects the characteristics of society, particularly by trying to ensure that all levels of the public service have a proportion of women and various disadvantaged minority groups similar to that of the population as a whole.

Representative democracy   A form of democracy in which citizens elect representatives to the legislature to make decisions on their behalf.

Responsible government   A governing system in which the political executive (the prime minister and Cabinet) is accountable to Parliament for its actions and must retain the support of the elected members of Parliament to remain in office.

Revolution   The use of violence to overthrow a government, especially when the overthrow is followed by rapid, thoroughgoing social, economic, and political restructuring.

Right   The general ideological position associated with opposition to imposing greater social and economic equality and with maintaining traditional (usually religious-based) moral values and institutions.

Rule of law   The idea that people should be subject to known, predictable, and impartial rules of conduct, rather than to the arbitrary orders of particular individuals. Both the rulers and the ruled should be equally subject to the law.

Runoff election   An election held if no candidate receives a majority of votes; generally, only the top two candidates appear on the ballot to ensure that the winning candidate has a majority of the votes cast.

Secessionist   A person who favours separation of a territory from an existing state.

Secular humanism   The view that ethical principles and moral standards can be developed through human reason.

Security dilemma   The dilemma that arises when states need power to feel secure, but their accumulation of power might undermine rather than increase their security if it leads other states to feel that they are in danger and form an alliance to meet the perceived threat.

Segregation   The legal separation of blacks and whites, particularly in the southern United States.

Selective incentive   A particular benefit that is made available to members of an interest group but is not available to the public as a whole.

Self-interest group   An interest group whose primary objective is to promote the interests of the group and its members and to seek benefits that are primarily or exclusively for its members.

Semi-presidential system   A system of governing in which an elected president with a fixed term of office shares executive power with a prime minister and Cabinet who are collectively responsible to an elected legislature.

Senate (Canada)   The upper chamber of Parliament, appointed on the recommendation of the prime minister. Senators hold their positions until age 75.

Senate (United States)   The upper chamber of Congress. Two senators are elected by voters in each state for a six-year term.

Separation of powers   A basic feature of presidential systems in which the executive, legislative, and judicial branches of government are separate from each other, with each having different personnel and different bases of authority.

Sharia law   A system of law based on the Quran, the teachings and practices of Mohammed, and Islamic jurisprudence.

Single member plurality (SMP) system   An electoral system in which voters in each electoral district elect a single representative to the legislature. The candidate with the most votes is elected, even if that candidate did not receive the majority of votes.

Single transferable vote (STV) system   An electoral system in which voters mark their preferences for candidates in a multimember electoral district. Candidates who receive a certain proportion of the vote are declared elected. The second preference of a voter that is surplus to what that winning candidate need is then transferred to that voter's second preference candidate. The process is continued until all seats in the district are filled.

Social conservatism   A version of conservatism that advocates public policies based on traditional moral and religious values including opposition to abortion, same-sex marriage, pre-marital sex, and euthanasia.

Social Darwinism   The use of Darwin's theory of evolution to argue that competition and conflict allow humanity to evolve through the "survival of the fittest."

Social ecology   A perspective that views social, economic, and political relationships of hierarchy and domination as the cause of both human and environmental problems.

Social movement   A network of groups and individuals that seeks major social and political changes, particularly by acting outside of established political institutions.

Social revolution   A revolution that changes not just who governs but also how a state is organized and how its society and economy are structured.

Socialism   An ideological perspective based on the view that human beings are basically social in nature and that the capitalist system undermines the cooperative and community-oriented nature of humanity. Socialism advocates the establishment of an egalitarian society.

Socialist feminism   A version of feminism that views women as oppressed by both the male-dominated character of society and the capitalist system. The liberation of women is connected to the transformation of capitalism into a more co-operative and egalitarian socialist system.

South   Less developed, poorer countries.

Sovereignty   The principle that states are the highest authority for their population and territory and are not subject to any external authority.

State-centred theory   A perspective that views public policies as reflecting, to a considerable extent, the preferences and priorities of those in important positions of authority within various state institutions.

State   An independent, self-governing political community whose governing institutions have the capability to make rules that are binding on the population residing within a particular territory.

Statist economic model   An economic policy that gives government a significant role in directing a country's economy.

Structural adjustment program (SAP)   A program administered by international financial institutions, which offers loans at very low interest rates to governments facing problems paying their debt on the condition that they adopt the programs endorsed by the Washington Consensus.

Subsidiarity   The principle that decisions and actions should be carried out, if possible, by the level of governing that is closest to citizens.

Suicide terrorism   A form of terrorist violence in which the attacker's object is to kill herself or himself as well as the target.

Supranational government   Government above the governments of its member-states.

Sustainability   Maintaining the integrity of ecosystems by ensuring that renewable resources are not being used at a rate that exceeds the ability of ecosystems to regenerate them, developing renewable substitutes to replace the consumption of non-renewable resources, and ensuring that the emission of pollutants does not exceed the ability of the ecosystem to handle them without damage.

Sustainable development   Meeting the needs of the present without compromising the ability of future generations to meet their own needs; it involves development to ensure that the needs of the poor are fulfilled and protecting the environment for the well-being of future generations.

Tariffs   Taxes on exports.

Terrorism   The deliberate use of violence designed to induce fear in a population in order to achieve a political objective.

Theocratic dictatorship   An undemocratic state run by religious elites.

Third World   Less developed countries.

Totalitarian dictatorship   A regime that seeks to control all aspects of life within a country.

Traditional authority   Authority based on customs that establish the right of certain persons to rule.

Transparency   Government's obligation to provide timely access to information and to operate visibly so that it can be held accountable for its actions.

Treasury Board   A permanent Cabinet committee with its own staff and minister that plays a major role in governing in

Canada because of its responsibility for the expenditure and management practices of government.

Two-party system A party system in which two major parties contend to control the government.

Underdeveloped countries A term often used to describe Third World countries.

Unipolarity An international system with a single superpower.

Unitary system A system of governing in which sovereign authority rests with the central government; regional and local governments are subordinate.

United Nations (UN) An international governmental organization representing almost all of the world's states.

Universal suffrage The right of all adult citizens to vote regardless of such characteristics as gender, ethnicity, wealth, or education.

Valence issues Issues on which the contending parties differ as to which party is most competent to deal with a problem rather than clearly taking different positions as to what should be done.

Washington Consensus A series of policies put together by the International Monetary Fund and the World Bank that encourage developing countries to generate more revenue for debt repayment by cutting government expenditures to balance their budgets, selling off government-owned enterprises (privatization), and fully opening their countries to foreign goods and investments.

Welfare state A state in which government ensures that all people have a decent standard of living and are provided protection from hardships resulting from circumstances such as unemployment, sickness, disability, and old age.

Westminster system A governing system that developed in Britain, featuring single party majority rule, executive dominance of Parliament, and an adversarial relationship between the governing party and the opposition.

REFERENCES

Abramowitz, A. & Saunders, K.L. (2006). Explaining the bases of partisanship in the American electorate. Social identity vs ideology. *Political Research Quarterly, 59*(2), 175–187.

Adams, I. (2001). *Political ideology today* (2nd ed.). Manchester, UK: Manchester University Press.

Adams, J., & Merrill, S. (2005). Candidate policy platforms andelectoral outcomes: The three faces of policy representation. *European Journal of Political Research, 44*, 881–896.

Adams, M. (2015, December 9). Why Canada, U.S. diverge on Syrian refugees. *The Globe and Mail.* Retrieved from http://www.theglobeandmail.com/opinion/distinct-societies-why-canada-us-diverge-on-syrian-refugees/article27652245/

Albrow, M. (1970). *Bureaucracy.* London: Macmillan.

Allan, J. (2014). *Democracy in decline. Steps in the wrong direction.* Montreal: McGill-Queen's University Press.

Almond, G.A., Appleby, R.S., & Sivan, E. (2003). *Strong religions: The rise of fundamentalism around the world.* Chicago: University of Chicago Press.

Almond, G., & Verba, S. (1963). *The civic culture: Political attitudes and democracy in five nations.* Princeton, NJ: Princeton University Press.

Alterman, E. (2003). *What liberal media? The truth about bias and the news.* New York: Basic Books.

Americas Barometer, Canada 2014 Final Report. Retrieved from: http://www.vanderbilt.edu/lapop/canada/Canada-2014-Report_120414_W.pdf

Anderson, B. (2001). *Imagined communities: Reflections on the origin and spread of nationalism* (revised ed.). London: Verso.

Anderson, T.L., & Leal, D.R. (2001). *Free market environmentalism* (revised ed.). Houndmills, Basingstoke, Hampshire, UK: Palgrave Macmillan.

Anderson, T.L. & Leal, D.R. (Eds). (2015). *Free Market environmentalism for the next generation.* New York, NY: Palgrave Macmillan.

Andersen, V.N. & Hansen, K.M. (2007). How deliberation makes better citizens. The Danish Deliberative Poll on the euro. *European Journal of Political Research 46*(4), 531–556.

ANES Guide to Public Opinion and Electoral Behavior. (n.d.) Retrieved from www.electionstudies.org/nesguide/nesguide.htm

Ansolabehere, S., Iyengar, S., Simon, A., & Valentino, N. (1997). Does attack advertising demobilize the electorate? In S. Iyengar & R. Reeves (Eds.), *Do the media govern? Politicians, voters, and reporters in America* (pp. 195–207). Thousand Oaks, CA: Sage Publications.

Arrow, K., et al. (1995). Economic growth, carrying capacity and the environment. *Science, 268*(5210), 520–521.

Ashworth, L. (2002). "Did the Realist-Idealist great debate really happen? A revisionist history of International relations," *International Relations, 16*(1), 33–51.

Assembly of First Nations (2011). Fact Sheet Quality of Life of First Nations, June 2011. Retrieved from www.afn.ca/uploads/files/factsheets/quality_of_life_final_fe.pdf

Atkinson, A.B. (2015). *Inequality.* Cambridge, MA: Harvard University Press.

Atkinson, M.M. (2013). Policy, politics and political science. *Canadian Journal of Political Science, 46*(4), 751–772.

Aucoin, P. (2002). Beyond the "new" public management reform in Canada: Catching the next wave? In C. Dunn (Ed.), *The handbook of Canadian public administration* (pp. 37–52). Don Mills, ON: Oxford University Press.

Axworthy, L. (2003). *Navigating a new world: Canada's global future.* Toronto: Alfred A. Knopf.

Babbie, E. (1995). *The practice of social research* (7th ed.). Belmont, CA: Wadsworth Publishing Company.

Bachrach, P. & Baratz, M. (1962). The two faces of power. *American Political Science Review, 56*, 947–952.

Baer, D., Curtis, J., & Grabb, E. (2001). Has voluntary association activity declined? Cross-national analysis for fifteen countries. *Canadian Review of Sociology and Anthropology, 38*, 249–272.

Bakvis, H. & Brown, D. (2010). Policy coordination in federal systems: Comparing intergovernmental processes and outcomes in Canada and the United States. *Publius, 40*(3), 484–507.

Baldini, G., & Papalardo, A. (2009). *Elections, electoral systems and volatile voters.* New York: Palgrave Macmillan.

Ball, T., & Dagger, R. (2004). *Political ideologies and the democratic ideal* (5th ed.). New York: Pearson Longman.

Banerjee, A. & Duflo, E. (2011). *Poor Economics: A Radical Rethinking of the Way to Fight Global Poverty.* New York: Public Affairs.

Barber, B. (1995). *Jihad vs. McWorld: How globalization and tribalism are reshaping the world.* New York: Ballantine.

Barnard, F.M. (2001). *Democratic legitimacy: Plural values and political power.* Montreal: McGill-Queen's University Press.

Basu, A., & Roy, S. (Eds.). (2007). *Violence and democracy in India.* Calcutta, India: Seagull Books.

Battle, J. (2009). Saddam Hussein Talks to the FBI: Twenty Interviews and Five Conversations with "High Value Detainee # 1" in 2004. The National Security Archive, http://nsarchive.gwu.edu/NSAEBB/NSAEBB279/

Baum, L. (2012a). Presidential ad war tops 1M airings. Retrieved from www.mediaproject.wesleyan.edu/2012/11/02/presidential-ad-war-tops-1m-airings/

Baum, L. (2012b). 2012 shatters 2004 and 2008 records for total ads aired. Retrieved from www.mediaproject. wesleyan.edu/2012/10/24/2012-shatters-2004-and-2008-records-for-total-ads-aired

BBC News. (2009). Ethiopia imposes aid agency curbs. Retrieved from www.news.bbc.co.uk/2/hi/7814145.stm

BBC. (2010). Iran crisis. Retrieved February 10, 2010, from http://news.bbc.co.uk/2/hi/in_depth/middle_east/2009/iran/default.stm

Beckerman, W. (1992). Economic growth and the environment: Whose growth? Whose environment? *World Development, 20*, 481–496.

Beckett, I. (2001). *Modern insurgencies and counter-insurgencies: Guerrillas and their opponents since 1750.* London, UK: Routledge.

Bell, D. (1998). The end of ideology revisited. *Government and Opposition, 23*, 131–150; 321–328.

Bell, D.V.J. (2004). Political culture in Canada. In M. Whittington & G. Williams (Eds.), *Canadian politics in the 21st century* (6th ed.). Toronto: Nelson.

Benedicto, J. (2004). Cultural structures and political life: The cultural matrix of democracy in Spain. *European Journal of Political Research, 43*(3), 287–307.

Berg, A.G., & Ostry, J.D. (2011). Inequality and unsustainable growth: Two sides of the same coin. Retrieved from www.imf.org/external/pubs/ff/sdn/2011/sdn1108.pdf

Berry, M.J. & Bickers, K.N. (2013). Forecasting the 2012 election with state level economic indicators: A post-mortem. *PS: Political Science and Politics 46*(1, January).

Birch, A.H. (1971). *Representation.* London: Pall Mall Press.

Birch, A.H. (1980). *The British system of government* (4th ed.). London: George Allen & Unwin.

Bittner, A. (2011). *Platform or personality. The role of party leaders in elections.* Oxford: Oxford University Press.

Bittner, A. & Koop, R. (Eds.). (2013). *Parties, elections and the future of Canadian politics.* Vancouver: UBC Press.

Blais, A. (2011). Political leaders and democratic elections. In Aarts, K., Blais, A., & Schmitt, H. (Eds.) *Political leaders and democratic elections.* Oxford, UK: Oxford University Press, pp. 1–10.

Blais, A., Gidengil, E., Dobryznska, A., Nevitte, N., & Nadeau, R. (2003). Does the local candidate matter? Candidate effects in the Canadian election of 2000. *Canadian Journal of Political Science, 36*, 657–664.

Blais, A., Gidengil, E., Nadeau, R, & Nevitte, N. (2002). *Anatomy of a Liberal victory: Making sense of the vote in the 2000 Canadian election.* Peterborough, ON: Broadview.

Blais, A, Gidengil, E., Nevitte, N., & Nadeau, R. (2004). Where does turnout decline come from? *European Journal of Political Research, 43*, 221–236.

Blais, A., & Massicotte, L. (2002). Electoral systems. In L. LeDuc, R.G. Niemi, & P. Norris (Eds.), *Comparing democracies 2: New challenges in the study of elections and voting* (pp. 40–69). London: Sage.

Blais, A., Massicotte, L., & Dobrzynska, A. (2003). *Why is election turnout higher in some countries than others?* Retrieved May 26, 2004, from www.elections.ca

Boatright, R.G. (2009). Campaign finance in the 2008 election. In J.M. Box-Steffensmeier & S.E. Schier (Eds.), *The American elections of 2008.* Lanham, MD: Rowman & Littlefield.

Bookchin, M. (1980). *Towards an ecological society.* Montreal: Black Rose.

Bosso, C.J. (2005). *Environment, Inc.: From grassroots to beltway.* Lawrence, KS: University Press of Kansas.

Bowles, P. (2012). *Capitalism* (2nd ed.). London: Taylor & Francis.

Boyd, D.R. (2003). *Unnatural law: Rethinking Canadian environmental law and policy.* Vancouver: UBC Press.

Boyd, D.R. (2011). *The environmental rights revolution. A global study of constitutions, human rights and the environment.* Vancouver: UBC Press.

Bradshaw, L. (1991). Political rule, prudence and the "woman question" in Aristotle. *Canadian Journal of Political Science, 24*(3), 557–573.

Brady, D.W., & Volden, C. (2006). *Revolving gridlock: Politics and policy from Jimmy Carter to George W. Bush* (2nd ed.). Boulder, CO: Westview Press.

Brauer, J. (2013). The US Firearms industry: Production and supply. Retrieved from http://www.smallarmssurvey.org/about-us/highlights/highlight-wp14.html

Braun, S., & Gillum, J. (2012). 2012 presidential election cost hits $2 billion. Retrieved from www.huffingtonpost.com/2012/12/06/2012-presidential-election-cost_n_2254138.html

Brautigam, D. (2009). *The dragon's gift: The real story of China in Africa.* New York: Oxford University Press.

Brinton, C. (1965). *The anatomy of a revolution.* New York: Vintage.

Broadbent, E. (2001). Social democracy—The way ahead. Conference on the future of social democracy in Canada. Retrieved August 26, 2006, from www.misc-iecm.mcgill.ca/socdem/ebeng.htm

Brodie, J., & Jenson, J. (1988). *Crisis, challenge and change: Party and class in Canada revisited.* Ottawa: Carleton University Press.

Brooks, S. (1998). *Public policy in Canada* (3rd. ed.). Toronto: Oxford University Press.

Bronk, R. (2000). Which model of capitalism? *OECD Observer, 221*(22), 12–15. Retrieved from www.oecdobserver.org/news/archivestory.php/.../Which_model_of_capitalism_html

Brown, S. (1995). *New forces, old forces and the future of world politics.* New York: HarperCollins.

Brown, W. (2015). *Undoing the demos: Neoliberalism's stealth revolution.* New York: Zone Books.

Brownlee, J. (2007). *Authoritarianism in an age of democratization.* New York: Cambridge University Press.

Brownmiller, S. (1975). *Against our will: Men, women and rape.* New York: Simon & Schuster.

Bryson, V. (2003). *Feminist political theory: An introduction* (2nd ed.). Houndmills, Basingstoke, Hampshire, UK: Palgrave Macmillan.

Budge, I., Keman, H., McDonald, M.D., & Pennings, P. (2012). *Organizing democratic choice. Party representation over time.* Oxford: Oxford University Press.

Burke, E. (1955). *Reflections on the revolution in France.* (T.H.D. Mahoney, Ed.). Indianapolis, IN: The Liberal Arts Press. (Original work published in 1790.)

Cairns, A.C. (2000). *Citizens plus: Aboriginal peoples and the Canadian state.* Vancouver: UBC Press.

Canadian Broadcasting Corporation. (2004). *CBC/Radio Canada pre-election poll*. Retrieved May 26, 2004, from www.cbc.ca/canadavotes/thepolls/democracypoll.htm

Canadian Civil Liberties Association. (2016). #Charter First. Retrieved from ccla.org/campaigns/charterfirst.

Canadian Opinion Research Archive (n.d.). Retrieved from www.queensu.ca/cora/trends

Cardoso, F.H., & Falletto, E. (1979). *Dependency and development in Latin America*. Berkeley: University of California Press.

Carothers, T. (2002). The end of the transition paradigm. *Journal of Democracy*, 13(1), 5–22.

Carr, E.H. (1939/2001). *The twenty years' crisis: 1919–39: An introduction to international relations*. New York: Harper and Row.

Carty, R.K. (2013). Has brokerage politics ended? Canadian parties in the new century. In Bittner, A. & Koop, R. (Eds.), *Parties, elections and the future of Canadian politics*. Vancouver: UBC Press.

Castells, M. (2004). *The information age: Economy, society and culture. Volume II: The power of identity* (2nd ed.). Malden, MA: Blackwell.

Castle, B. (1987). *Sylvia and Cristabel Pankhurst*. New York: Penguin Books.

Caul, M.L., & Gray, M.M. (2000). From platform declarations to policy outcomes: Changing party profiles and partisan influence over policy. In R.J. Dalton & M.P. Wattenberg (Eds.), *Parties without partisans: Political change in advanced industrial democracies* (pp. 208–237). Oxford: Oxford University Press.

CBC News (2006, November 10). Ontario to take back control of private super-jail. Retrieved from www.cbc.ca/news/canada/toronto/story/2006/11/10/private-jail.html

CBC News (2013, February 9). "Feds 'not the most transparent,' says information commissioner." Retrieved from www.cbc.ca/news/canada/story/2013/02/09/access-information-legault.html

Chang, H.-J. (2003). *Kicking away the ladder: Development strategy in historical perspective*. London: Anthem Press.

Choudhry, S. & Stacey, R. (2014). *Semi-presidentialism as power sharing: Constitutional reform after the Arab Spring*. Centre for Constitutional Transitions at NYU School of Law and IDEA. Available at http://constitutionaltransitions.org/publications/semi-presidentialism-as-power-sharing/

Clark, S.D., Grayson, J.P., & Grayson, L. (1976). General introduction: The nature of social movements. In S.D. Clark, J.P. Grayson, & L.M. Grayson (Eds.), *Prophecy and protest: Social movements in twentieth-century Canada* (pp. 1–38). Toronto: Gage.

Clarke, H.D., Kornberg, A., & Scotto, T.S. (2009a). *Making political choices: Canada and the United States*. Toronto: University of Toronto Press.

Clarke, H.D., Kornberg, A., & Scotto, T.S. (2009b). None of the above: Voters in the 2008 federal election. In J.H. Pammett & C. Dornan (Eds), *The Canadian federal election of 2008*. Toronto: Dundurn Press.

Clarke, H.D., Reiffler, J., Scotto, T.J., & Stewart, M.C. (2016). It's spring again. Voting in the 2015 federal election. In J. H. Pammett & C. Dornan, *The Canadian federal election of 2015*. (pp. 275–304).Toronto: Dundurn Press.

Clarke, H.D., Scotto, T.J., Reifler, J., & Kornberg, A. (2011). Winners and losers: Voters in the 2011 federal election. In J.H. Pammett & C. Dornan (Eds.), *The Canadian federal election of 2011*. Toronto: Dundurn.

Cleverdon, C.L. (1974). *The woman suffrage movement in Canada* (2nd ed.). Toronto: University of Toronto Press.

Close, D., & Mintz, E. (2005). State sponsorship and community environmental groups: The Atlantic coastal action program in Newfoundland. *American Review of Canadian Studies*, 35(4), 621–639.

CNBC (2015). The world's biggest sovereign wealth funds. www.cnbc.com/2015/07/17/the-worlds-biggest-sovereign-wealth-funds.

CNBC (2015, July 17). World's biggest sovereign wealth funds. Retrieved from: http://www.cnbc.com/2015/07/17/the-worlds-biggest-sovereign-wealth-funds.html.

Cochrane, C. (2010). Left/right ideology and Canadian politics. Canadian Journal of Political Science 43,3 (Sept.), pp. 583–605.

Cockburn, P. (2015). *The rise of the new Islamic state: ISIS and the Sunni revolution*. London: Verso.

Code, L. (1988). Feminist theory. In S. Burt, L. Code, & L. Dorney (Eds.), *Changing patterns: Women in Canada*. Toronto: McClelland & Stewart.

Cole, A. (2009, August 22). Afghanistan Contractors Outnumber Troops. *The Wall Street Journal*. Retrieved from http://www.wsj.com/articles/SB125089638739950599

Conference Board of Canada. (2016). How Canada Performs. Retrieved from www.conferenceboard.ca/hcp/hot-topics/caninequality.aspx

Consumer Education Foundation. (2009). Sold out: How Wall Street and Washington betrayed Americans. Retrieved from www.wallstreetwatch.org/reports/sold_out.pdf

Cook, D. (2005). *Understanding jihad*. Berkeley, CA: University of California Press.

Coombes, C. (2003). *Terrorism in the twenty-first century* (3rd ed.). Upper Saddle River, NJ: Prentice-Hall.

Cooper, R. (2000). *The post-modern state and world order*. London: Foreign Policy Centre.

Coupland, R. (1964). *The British anti-slavery movement*. London: Frank Cass.

Courchene, T.J. (1992). *Rearrangements: The Courchene papers*. Oakville, ON: Mosaic Press.

Courchene, T.J. (2007). Global futures for Canada's global cities. *Policy Matters*, 8(2).

Cox, R.W. (1987). *Production, power, and world order: Social forces in the making of history*. New York: Columbia University Press.

Crick, B. (1993). *In defence of politics* (4th American ed.). Chicago: University of Chicago Press.

Cross, W. (2004). *Political parties*. Vancouver: UBC Press.

Croteau, D. (1998). *Examining the "liberal media" claim: Journalists' views on politics, economic policy, and media coverage*. Retrieved November 15, 2003, from www.fair.org/reports/journalist-survey.html

Crozier, M., Huntington, S.P., & Watanuki, J. (1975). *The crisis of democracy*. New York: New York University Press.

Curran, J. & Aalberg, T. (Eds.) (2012). *How media informs democracy: A comparative approach*. New York: Routledge.

Dahl, R.A. (1961). Who governs? *Democracy and power in an American city*. New Haven: Yale University Press.

Dahl, R.A. (1984). *Modern political analysis* (4th ed.). Englewood Cliffs, NJ: Prentice-Hall.

Dale, D. (2012, June 29). In Greece, anti-immigrant Golden Dawn party rides wave of xenophobia. *Toronto Star*.

Dalton, R.J. (2000). The decline of party identifications. In R.J. Dalton & M.P. Wattenberg (Eds.), *Parties without partisans: Political change in advanced industrial democracies* (pp. 19–36). Oxford: Oxford University Press.

Dalton, R.J. (2006). *Citizen politics: Public opinion and political parties in advanced industrial democracies* (4th ed.). Washington, DC: CQ Press.

Dalton, R.J., Farrell, D.M., & McAllister, I. (2011). *Political parties and democratic linkage. How parties organize democracy*. Oxford: Oxford University Press.

Dalton, R.J., & Wattenburg, M.P. (2000). Partisan change and the democratic process. In R.J. Dalton & M.P. Wattenberg (Eds.), *Parties with partisans: Political change in advanced industrial democracies* (pp. 261–285). Oxford: Oxford University Press.

Dalton, R.J. & Welzel, C. (Eds.) (2014). *The civic culture transformed. From allegiant to assertive citizens*. New York: Cambridge University Press.

Decalo, S. (1988). *Psychoses of power: African personal dictatorships*. Boulder, CO: Westview Press.

Devall, B., & Sessions, G. (1998). Deep ecology. In D. VanDeVeer & C. Pierce (Eds.), *The environmental ethics and policy book: Philosophy, ecology, economics* (2nd ed.) (pp. 221–226). Belmont, CA: Wadsworth.

DeWeil, B. (2000). *Democracy: A history of ideas*. Vancouver: UBC Press.

Diamond, L. (2002). Thinking about hybrid regimes. *Journal of Democracy*. 13(2), 21–35.

Dickinson, E. (2011). The first wikileaks revolutions? *Foreign Policy* (January 13). Retrieved from http://wikileaks.foreignpolicy.com/posts/2011/01/13/wikileaks_and_the_tunisia_protests?sms_ss=twitter&at_xt=4d2fb0630bc13672,0

Dietz, T., Ostrom, E., & Stern, P.C. (2003). "The struggle to govern the commons." *Science*, 302 (5652), pp. 1907–1912.

Dinas, E. (October, 2014). Why does the apple fall far from the tree? How early political socialization prompts parent-child dissimilarity. *British Journal of Political Science* 44(4), 827–852.

Dobson, A. (2007). *Green political thought* (4th ed.). New York: Routledge.

Domhoff, G.W. (2009). *Who rules America? Challenges to corporate and class dominance*. New York: McGraw-Hill.

Doust, J.J. & Bol, D. (2016). *Strategic voting*. Retrieved from: electoraldemocracy.com/strategic voting-2099

Drutman, L. (2015). *The business of America is lobbying: How corporations became politicized and politics became more corporate*. New York: Oxford University Press.

Dryzek, J.S. & Dunleavy, P. (2009). *Theories of the democratic state*. Houndmills, UK: Palgrave Macmillan.

Dunleavy, P., *et al.* (2006). New public management is dead—long live digital-era governance. *Journal of Public Administration Research and Theory*, 16(3), 467–494.

Duverger, M. (1964). *Political parties: Their organization and activity in the modern state* (3rd ed.). London: Methuen.

Duverger, M. (1980). A new political system model: semi-presidential government. *European Journal of Political Research 8*(2), 165–87.

Dyer, G. (2008). *Climate wars*. Toronto: Random House.

Easterly, W. (2006). *The white man's burden*. New York, Penguin.

Easton, D. (1953). *The political system: An enquiry into the state of political science*. New York: Knopf.

Eatwell, R. (1995). *Fascism: A history*. New York: Penguin Books.

Eckersley, R. (1992). *Environmentalism and political theory: Towards an ecocentric approach*. Albany, NY: State University of New York Press.

The Economist. (2010, June 3). Reaching for a longer spoon. Retrieved from http://www.economist.com/node/16274145

Economist Intelligence Unit. 2015. Democracy Index. www.eiu.com/democracy2015

Ehrenreich, B., & English, D. (1979). *For her own good: 150 years of the experts' advice to women*. New York: Anchor Press.

Eilperin, J. (2010, May 5). U.S. exempted BP's Gulf of Mexico drilling from environmental impact study. *Washington Post*. Retrieved from www.washingtonpost.com/wp-dyn/content/article/2010/05/04/AR2010050404118.html

Eisenhower, D. (1961). Farewell Address. Available at http://avalon.law.yale.edu/20th_century/eisenhower001.asp

Ekospolitics.com. (2015). Retrieved from http://www.ekospolitics.com/index.php/2015/10/deadlock-broken-liberals-surging/

Elections Canada Online. (n.d.). Estimation of voter turnout by age group and gender for the 2011 federal election. Retrieved from http://www.elections.ca/content.aspx?section=res&dir=rec/part/estim/41ge&document=report41&lang=e

Elections Canada (1997). A history of the vote in Canada. Retrieved from www.elections.ca

Elections Canada (2012). Estimation of voter turnout by age group and gender at the 2011 federal general election. Retrieved from www.elections.ca

Elections Canada (n.d.). Report on the evaluations of the 41st general election of May 2, 2001. Retrieved from www.elections.ca

Elgie, R. (1999). Semi-presidentialism and comparative institutional engineering. In R. Elgie (Ed.), *Semi-presidentialism in Europe*. Oxford: Oxford University Press.

Elgie, R. (2005). The political executive. In A. Cole, P. Le Galès, & J. Levy (Eds.), *Developments in French politics 3*. Houndmills, Basingstoke, Hampshire, UK: Palgrave Macmillan.

Elgie, R. (2011). *Semi-presidentialism. Subtypes and democratic performance*. Oxford: Oxford University Press.

Elkins, D.J. (1993). *Manipulation and consent: How voters and leaders manage complexity*. Vancouver: UBC Press.

Elster, J. (1998). *Deliberative democracy*. Cambridge: Cambridge University Press.

Englehart, T & Greenwald, G. (2014). *Shadow government: Surveillance, secret wars, and the global security state in a single superpower*. Chicago: Harymarket Books.

Enloe, C. (1989). *Bananas, beaches and bases: Making feminist sense of international relations*. London: Pandora.

Entman, R.M. (2004). *Projections of power: Framing news, public opinion, and U.S. foreign policy*. Chicago: University of Chicago Press.

European Council. (2003). *A secure Europe in a better world: European security strategy.* Retrieved August 15, 2007, from www.consilium.europa.eu/uedocs/cmsUpload/78367.pdf

Fallin, A., Grana, R., & Glantz, S.A. (2013). 'To quarterback behind the scenes, third party efforts': the tobacco industry and the Tea Party. Retrieved from www.tobaccocontrol.bmj.com/content/early/2013/02/20/tobaccocontrol-2012-050815.full

Farcau, B.W. (1994). *The coup: Tactics in the seizure of power.* Westport, CT: Praeger.

Federation of Canadian Municipalities. (2012). Canadian infrastructure report card: Volume 1: 2012 municipal roads and water systems. Retrieved from http://fcm.ca/Documents/reports/Canadian _Infrastructure_Report_Card_EN.pdf

Ferguson, N. (2011). *Civilization, the West and the rest.* London: Allen Lane.

Ferguson, Y.H., & Mansbach, R.W. (2012). *Globalization. The return of borders to a borderless world?* New York: Routledge.

Fischer, J. (2012, December 31) Europe's New Year's Irresolution. Retrieved from www.project-syndicate.org/commentary/europe-s-worsening-crisis-in-2013-by-joschka-fischer

Fitch, J.S. (1977). *The military coup d'etat as a political process.* Baltimore, MD: Johns Hopkins University Press.

Fitch, S. (1998). *The armed forces and democracy in Latin America.* Baltimore, MD: Johns Hopkins University Press.

Flinders, M. (2010). Bagehot smiling: Gordon Brown's "new constitution" and the revolution that did not happen. *Political Quarterly, 81*(1), 57–73.

Forcese, C. & Roach, K. (2015). Bill C-51: the good, the Bad . . . and the Truly Ugly. Retrieved from: https://thewalrus.ca/bill-c-51-the-good-the-bad-and-the-truly-ugly/

Fournier, P. (2002). The uninformed Canadian voter. In J. Everitt & B. O'Neill (Eds.), *Citizen politics: Research and theory in Canadian political behaviour* (pp. 92–109). Don Mills, ON: Oxford University Press.

Fournier, P., Cutler, F., Soroka, S. & Stolle, D. (2011). *The 2011 Canadian Election Study.* Retrieved from www.queensu.ca/cora/ces.html

Fowler, E.F., Franz, M.M., & Ridout, T.N. (2016). *Political Advertising in the United States.* Boulder, CO: Westview Press.

Francoli, M., Greenberg, J., & Waddell, C. (2011). The campaign in the digital media. In Pammett, J.H. & Dornan, C. (Eds.), *The Canadian federal election of 2011.* Toronto: Dundurn.

Frank, A.G. (1979). *Dependent accumulation and underdevelopment.* New York: Monthly Review Press.

Frantz, G.T. & Ezrow, T.M. (2011). *The politics of dictatorship: Institutions and outcomes in authoritarian regimes.* Boulder, CO: Lynne Riemer.

Freedom House. (2016a). *Freedom in the world 2016.* Retrieved from https://freedomhouse.org/report/freedom-world/freedom-world-2016

Freedom House. (2016b). *Freedom in the world, 2016.* https://freedomhouse.org/report-types/freedom-world

Friedan, B. (1963). *The Feminine Mystique.* New York: W.W. Norton.

Friederich, C., & Brzezinski, Z. (1956). *Totalitarian dictatorship and democracy.* Cambridge, MA: Harvard University Press.

Friedman, T. (2005). *The world is flat: A brief history of the twenty-first century.* New York: Farrar, Straus and Giroux.

Fukuyama, F. (1989). The end of history? *The National Interest, 16,* 3–18.

Fukuyama, F. (1992). *The end of history and the last man.* New York: Free Press.

Gagnon, A.-G. (2010). *The case for multinational federalism: Beyond the all-encompassing nation.* New York: Routledge.

Galloway, G. (2013, February 7). "Is Canada's party discipline the strictest in the world? Experts say yes." *The Globe and Mail.*

Gambone, M.D. (2001). *Capturing the Revolution: The United States, Central America, and Nicaragua, 1961–1972.* Westport, CT: Praeger Publishers.

Gandhi, J. (2007). *Political institutions under dictatorship.* New York: Cambridge University Press.

Ganuza, E. & Baiocchi, G. (2012). The Power of Ambiguity: How Participatory Budgeting Travels the Globe. Journal of Public Deliberation, 8(2). Available at http://www.publicdeliberation.net/jpd/vol8/iss2/art8.

Geddes, B. (2006). *Why parties and elections in authoritarian regimes?* Revised version of paper presented to the American Political Science Association.

Gibbins, R., & Youngman, L. (1996). *Mindscapes: Political ideologies towards the 21st century.* Toronto: McGraw-Hill Ryerson.

Gidengil, E., Blais, A., Nadeau, R., & Nevitte, N. (2003). Women to the left? Gender differences in political beliefs and policy preferences. In M. Tremblay & L. Trimble (eds.). *Women and electoral politics in Canada* (pp. 140–159). Don Mills, ON: Oxford University Press.

Gidengil, E., Fournier, P., Everitt, J., Nevitte, N., & Blais, A. (2009). The anatomy of a Liberal defeat. Paper prepared for the annual meeting of the Canadian Political Science Association, May 2009. Retrieved from http://ces-eec.mcgill.ca/publications.html

Gidengil, E., Nevitte, N., Blais, A., Everitt, J., & Fournier, P. (2012*). Dominance & Decline. Making sense of recent Canadian elections.* Toronto: University of Toronto Press.

Gillens, M. & Page, B.I. (2014). Testing theories of American politics: Elites, interest groups and the average citizen. *Perspectives on Politics, 121*(3), 564–581. Retrieved from https://scholar.princeton.edu/sites/default/files/mgilens/files/gilens_and_page_2014_-testing_theories_of_american_politics.doc.pdf

Gillens, M. & Page, B.I. (2016, May 23). Critics argue with our analysis of U.S. political inequality: Here are 5 ways they are wrong. *Washington Post.* Retrieved from https://www.washingtonpost.com/news/monkey-cage/wp/2016/05/23/critics-challenge-our-portrait-of-americas-political-inequality-heres-5-ways-they-are-wrong/?wpmm=1&wpisrc=nl_cage

Gilley, B. (2006). The meaning and measurement of state legitimacy: Results for 72 countries. *European Journal of Political Research, 45,* 499–525.

Gilpin, R. (1981). *War and change in world politics.* Cambridge, UK: Cambridge University Press.

Ginsburg, T. & Moustafa, T. (2007). *Rule by law: The politics of courts in authoritarian regimes.* New York: Cambridge University Press.

Global Footprint Network (n.d.) Retrieved from www.footprintnetwork.org

Global Footprint Network (2015). World Footprint. Retrieved from: http://www.footprintnetwork.org/en/index.php/GFN/page/world_footprint/

Goldenberg, E. (2006). *The way it works.* Toronto: McClelland & Stewart.

Goldenberg, S. (2013, March 15). Shell barred from return to drill for oil in Arctic without overhaul. *The Guardian.* Retrieved from www.guardian.co.uk/business/2013/mar/15/shell-barred-drill-oil-arctic

Goldstone, J. (1995). Predicting revolution: Why we could and (and should) have foreseen the revolutions of 1989–1991 in the U.S.S.R. and Eastern Europe. In N. Keddie (Ed.), *Debating revolution* (pp. 39–64). New York: New York University Press.

Grabb, E.C., & Curtis, J. (2005). *Regions apart: The four societies of Canada and the United States.* Toronto: Oxford University Press.

Graefe, P. (2007). Political economy and Canadian public policy. In M. Orsini & M. Smith (Eds.), *Critical policy studies.* Vancouver: UBC Press.

Grant, H. (2001). *The vestibule of hell: Why left and right have never made sense in politics and life.* Toronto: Stoddart.

Green, D., & Luehrmann, L. (2003). *Comparative politics of the Third World.* Boulder, CO: Lynne Rienner.

Grenier, É. (2015). Éric Grenier's poll tracker. *CBC News.* Canada Votes. Retrieved from http:/www.cbc.ca/news2/interactives/poll tracker/2015

Gret, M. (2005). *The Porto Alegre experiment: Learning lessons for better democracy.* London, UK: Zed Books.

Gribb, R. & Oved, M.C. (2016, April 15). How offshore banking is costing Canada billions of dollars a year. *Toronto Star.* Retrieved from https://www.thestar.com/news/world/2016/04/04/how-offshore-tax-havens-are-costing-canada-billions-of-dollars-a-year.html

Griffin, M. (2010). *Modernism and fascism. The sense of a beginning under Mussolini and Hitler.* New York: Palgrave Macmillan.

Gros, D. (2016, July 7). Britain's moment of truth. *Project Syndicate.* Retrieved from https://www.project-syndicate.org/commentary/brexit-norway-model-by-daniel-gros-2016–07

The *Guardian* (2016, January 10). Catalan independence back on track as new leader is sworn in. Retrieved from http://www.theguardian.com/world/2016/jan/10/catalan-independence-back-on-track-as-new-leader-is-sworn-in.

The *Guardian* (2016, July 27). Separatist movement in Catalonia steps up battle with Madrid.. Retrieved from: https://www.theguardian.com/world/2016/jul/27/catalonia-independence-spain-democratic-mandate

Gunther, R., & Diamond, L. (2001). Types and functions of parties. In L. Diamond & R. Gunther (Eds.), *Political parties and democracy.* Baltimore, MD: Johns Hopkins University Press.

Gurr, T.R. (1970). *Why men rebel.* Princeton, NJ: Princeton University Press.

Gurtov, M. (2013). *Will this be China's century? A skeptic's view.* Boulder: Lynne Rienner.

Habermas, J. (1975). *Legitimation crisis* (T. McCarthy, Trans.). Boston: Beacon Press. (Original work published 1973).

Hacker, J.S. & Pierson, P. (2010). *Winner-take-all politics: How Washington made the rich richer—and turned its back on the middle class.* New York: Simon & Schuster.

Hackett, R.A., & Zhao, Y. (1998). *Sustaining democracy? Journalism and the politics of objectivity.* Toronto: Garamond Press.

Halchin, L.E., & Kaiser, F.M. (2012). *Congressional oversight.* Congressional Research Service. Retrieved from www.crs.gov

Hall, P.A. & Sockice, D. (Eds.). (2001). *Varieties of capitalism: The institutional foundations of comparative advantage.* Oxford, UK: Oxford University Press.

Hallowell, J.H., & Porter, J.M. (1997). *Political philosophy: The search for humanity and order.* Scarborough, ON: Prentice Hall Canada.

Hancké, B. (Ed.). (2009). *Debating varieties of capitalism: A reader.* Oxford: Oxford University Press.

Handelman, H. (2012). *The challenge of Third World development.* (7th ed.) Upper Saddle River, NJ: Pearson/Prentice-Hall.

Hanrieder, W.F. (1967). "Compatibility and consensus: a proposal for the conceptual linkage of external and internal dimensions of foreign policy," *American Political Science Review, 61*(4), 971–82.

Hardin, G. (1968, December 13). The tragedy of the commons. *Science, 162,* 1243–1248.

Hardin, G. (1974). Lifeboat ethics: The case against helping the poor. *Psychology Today,* September.

Harty, S., & Murphy, M. (2005). *In defence of multinational citizenship.* Vancouver and Toronto: UBC Press.

Hartz, L. (1964). *The founding of new societies.* Toronto: Longmans.

Hausegger, L., Hennigar, M., & Riddell, T. (2015). *Canadian courts: Law, politics, and process.* (2nd ed.) Toronto , ON: Oxford University Press.

Hay, C. (2002). *Political analysis: A critical introduction.* New York: Palgrave.

Heberle, R. (1951). *Social movements.* New York: Appleton, Century, Crofts.

Heilbroner, R. (1974). An *inquiry into the human prospect.* New York: W.W. Norton.

Helliwell, J.F., Layard, R., & Sachs, J. (Eds.). *World Happiness Report 2015.* Retrieved from http://worldhappiness.report/wp-content/uploads/sites/2/2015/04/WHR15.pdf

Helm, T. (2016, July 2). Poll reveals young remain voters reduced to tears by Brexit result. *The Guardian.* Retrieved from http://www.theguardian.com/politics/2016/jul/02/brexit-referendum-voters-survey

Helmke, G. & Rosenbluth, F. (2009). Regimes and the rule of law: Judicial independence in comparative perspective. *Annual Review of Political Science, 12,* 345–66.

Herbert, D. (2013, February 28). More than 550 notices of claim have been filed in the Love Canal lawsuit. *The Buffalo News.*

Heywood, A. (2002). *Politics* (2nd ed.). Houndmills, Basingstoke, Hampshire, UK: Palgrave.

Heywood, A. (2003). *Political ideologies: An introduction* (3rd ed.). Houndmills, Basingstoke, Hampshire, UK: Palgrave.

Hill, C. (2003). *The changing politics of foreign policy.* New York: Palgrave.

Hinojosa, V.J., & Pérez-Liñán, A. (2005). Presidential impeachment and the politics of survival: The case of Colombia. In J.C. Baumgarner & N. Kada (Eds.), *Checking executive power: Presidential impeachment in comparative perspective.* Westport, CT: Praeger.

Hobbes, T. (1651/1968). *Leviathan.* C.B. Macpherson (Ed.). Harmondsworth, UK: Penguin.

Hoffman, B. (2004). *Insurgency and counterinsurgency in Iraq.* RAND Corporation Occasional Paper OP-127. Santa Monica, CA: Rand Corporation; www.rand.org/pubs/occasional_papers/2005/RAND_OP127.pdf

Holmes, O. (2016, September 15). Philippines president ordered murders and killed official, claims hitman. *The Guardian.* Retrieved from https://www.theguardian.com/world/2016/sep/15/philippines-president-drug-dealers-rodrigo-duterte-extrajudicial-killings-crocodile

Hooghe, L., & Marks, G. (2001). *Multi-level governance and European integration.* Boulder, CO: Rowman and Littlefield.

Horowitz, G. (1966). Conservatism, liberalism and socialism in Canada: An interpretation. *Canadian Journal of Economics and Political Science, 32*(2), 143–171.

Huang, R. (2015). The Islamic State as an ordinary insurgency. *POMEPS Studies, 15,* 13–16.

Human Rights First. (2016). https://www.humanrightsfirst.org/sites/default/files/gtmo-by-the-numbers.pdf

Hume, M. (2004, July 12). For whistle blower, it got personal. *The Globe and Mail,* A4.

Huntington, S.P. (1957). Conservatism as an Ideology. *American Political Science Review, 51*(2), 459.

Huntington, S.P. (1993). The clash of civilizations? *Foreign Affairs, 72*(3), 22–49.

Huntington, S.P. (1996). *The clash of civilizations and the remaking of world order.* New York: Simon & Schuster.

Hutchings, J.A., Perterman, R.M., VanderZwaag, D.L. (2016. April). Sustainability of Canadian fisheries requires bold political leadership. *Policy Options.* Retrieved from http://policyoptions.irpp.org/magazines/april-2016/sustainability-of-canadian-fisheries-requires-bold-political-leadership/

Inglehart, R.I. (1977). *The silent revolution: Changing values and political styles among Western publics.* Princeton, NJ: Princeton University Press.

Inglehart, R.I. (1990). *Culture shift in advanced industrial society.* Princeton, NJ: Princeton University Press.

Inglehart, R.I., & Welzel, C. (2005). *Modernization, cultural change and democracy: The human development sequence.* New York: Cambridge University Press.

Initiative and Referendum Institute, 2014. http://www.iandrinstitute.org/docs/BW%202014-2%20Election%20results%20(v1)%202014-11-04.pdf

Institute for Energy Research. 2015. Global consumption of fossil fuels continues to increase. Retrieved from http://instituteforenergyresearch.org/analysis/global-consumption-of-fossil-fuels-continues-to-increase/

International Institute for Democracy and Electoral Assistance. (2007a). *Global database of quotas for women.* Retrieved July 10, 2007, from www.quotaproject.org/system.cfm

International Monetary Fund. (2015). *World Economic Outlook Database 2015.* http://www.imf.org/external/pubs/ft/weo/2015/02/weodata/index.aspx.

Inter-Parliamentary Union (2016). Women in National Parliaments. Retrieved from: www.ipu.org/wmn-e/world.htm

Ipsos MORI. (2010). How Britain voted in 2010. Retrieved from www.ipsos-mori.com/researchpublications/researcharchive/poll.aspx?oItemId=2613&view=wide

Ipsos MORI. (2015). How Britain voted in 2015. https://www.ipsos-mori.com/researchpublications/researcharchive/3575/How-Britain-voted-in-2015.aspx?view=wide

Ipsos MORI. (2015). *How Britain voted in 2015.* Retrieved from: https://www.ipsos-mori.com/researchpublications/researcharchive/3575/How-Britain-voted-in-2015.aspx?view=wide

Ipsos Reid/Dominion Institute. (2007). *National citizenship exam: 10 year benchmark study.* Retrieved July 12, 2007, from www.dominion.ca/Dominion_Institute_Press_Release_Mock_Exam.pdf

Jacques, M. (2012). *When China rules the world. The end of the Western World and the birth of a new global order.* (2nd ed.). London: Penguin.

Jamieson, K.H. (1992). *Dirty politics: Deception, distraction, democracy.* New York: Oxford University Press.

Jang, B. & Marotte, B. (2013, May 21). Boreal forest talks break down. *The Globe and Mail.*

Janowitz, M. (1977). *Military institutions and coercion in the developing nations.* Chicago: University of Chicago Press.

Jeffrey, B. "The disappearing Liberals: Caught in the crossfire. In J. H. Pammett & C. Dornan, (Eds.). *The Canadian federal election of 2011* (pp. 45–76). Toronto: Dundur.

Jennings, M.K. (1984). The intergenerational transfer of political ideologies in eight Western nations. *European Journal of Political Research, 12,* 261–276.

Jennings, M.K., & Niemi, R.G. (1968). The transmission of political values from parent to child. *American Political Science Review, 62,* 169–184.

Jennings, M.K., & Niemi, R.G. (1981). *Generations and politics: A panel study of young adults and their parents.* Princeton, NJ: Princeton University Press.

Joes, A. (1992). *Modern guerrilla insurgency.* Westport, CT: Praeger Publishers.

Joes, A. (2004). *Resisting rebellion: The history and politics of counterinsurgency.* Lexington, KY: University of Kentucky Press.

Johnson, S. (2009, May). The quiet coup. *The Atlantic.* Retrieved from http://www.theatlantic.com/magazine/archive/2009/05/the-quiet-coup/307364/

Johnston, R. & Deeming, C. (2016). British political values, attitudes to climate change change, and travel behaviour. *Policy and Politics, 44*(2), 191–213.

Kaine, T. (2014). Obama must get Congress's backing for the fight against ISIS. Retrieved from http://www.nytimes.com/2014/09/16/opinion/obama-must-get-congress-backing-for-the-fight-against-isis.html?_r=0

Kara, N. (2005). Impeachment as punishment for corruption? The cases of Brazil and Venezuela. In J.C. Baumgarner & N. Kada (Eds.), *Checking executive power: Presidential impeachment in comparative perspective.* Westport, CT: Praeger.

Karreth, J., Polk, J.T. & Allen, C.S. (2013). Catch-all or catch and release? The electoral consequences of Social Democratic parties' march to the middle in Western Europe. *Comparative Political Studies, 46*(7), 791–822.

Katz, R.S., & Mair, P. (1995). Changing models of party organization and party democracy: The emergence of the cartel party. *Party Politics, 1,* 5–28.

Keating, M. (1996). *Nations against the state: The new politics of nationalism in Quebec, Catalonia and Scotland.* Houndmills, Basingstoke, Hampshire, UK: Macmillan.

Keddie, N. (1995). Can revolutions be predicted; Can their causes be understood? In N. Keddie (Ed.), *Debating revolution* (pp. 1–26). New York: New York University Press.

Kent, A. (1996). *Risk and redemption: Surviving the network news wars.* Toronto: Penguin Books Canada.

Keohane, R.O. (1984). *After hegemony: Cooperation and discord in the world political economy.* Princeton, NJ: Princeton University Press.

Keohane, R.O., & Nye, J.S. (1977). *Power and interdependence: World politics in transition.* Boston: Little, Brown.

Kiernan, B. (2008). *The Pol Pot regime: race, power, and genocide in Cambodia under the Khmer Rouge, 1975–79* (3rd ed.). New Haven: Yale University Press.

Kiatpongsan, C. & Norton, M.I. (2014). How much (more) should CEOs make: A universal desire for more equal pay. *Perspectives on Psychological Science, 9*(6), 587–593.

Kirchheimer, O. (1966). The transformation of West European party systems. In J. LaPalombara & M. Weiner (Eds.), *Political parties and political development* (pp. 177–200). Princeton, NJ: Princeton University Press.

Kirkpatrick, J. (1979). Dictatorships and double standards. *Commentary, 68*(5), 34–45.

Kitschelt, H. (1986). Political opportunity structures and political protest: Anti-nuclear movements in four democracies. *British Journal of Political Science, 16*(1) 57–79.

Klein, N. (2015). *This changes everything. Capitalism vs the climate.* Toronto: Vintage Canada.

Kohn, D. (2003). Transcript: Saddam Hussein's interview. http://www.cbsnews.com/news/transcript-saddam-hussein-interview-pt-1/

Koopmans, R. (2015). "Religious fundamentalism and hostility against out-groups: A comparison of Muslims and Christians in Western Europe." *Journal of Ethnic and Migration Studies, 41*(1), 33–57.

Korte, G. (2015). Using pocket vetoes, Obama rebuffs GOP attempts to kill Clean Power Plan. *USA Today.* Retrieved from http://www.usatoday.com/story/news/politics/2015/12/19/obama-pocket-veto-clean-power-plan-climate-change/77619582/

Korten, D.C. (1996). *When corporations rule the world.* West Hartford, CT: Kumarian Press.

Kostadinova, T. & Levitt, B. (2014). Towards a theory of personalist parties: Concept formation and theory building. *Politics and Policy, 4*(2), 490–512.

Krasny, R. (2012, November 22). New Mitt Romney attack ad called 'deceitful' by Obama campaign. *National Post.*

Kratsev, I, and Holmes, S. (2012). An Autopsy of Managed Democracy. *Journal of Democracy,* 22.3, 33–45.

Kushnir Macroeconomics. (2016). Gross domestic product (GDP); India; 1970–2014. http://www.kushnirs.org/macroeconomics_/en/india__gdp.html

Lane, J.-E., & Ersson, S. (2000). *The new institutional politics: Performance and outcomes.* London, UK: Routledge.

Laquer, W. (1977). *Guerrilla: A historical and critical study.* London, UK: Weidenfeld and Nicolson.

Lau, R., Sigelman, L., Heldman, C., & Babbitt, P. (1999). The effects of negative political advertisements: A meta-analytic assessment. *American Political Science Review, 93,* 851–875.

Laycock, D.H. (2002). *The new right and democracy in Canada: Understanding Reform and the Canadian Alliance.* Don Mills, ON: Oxford University Press.

Lazar, H., Telford, H., & Watts, R. (2003). Divergent trajectories: The impact of global and regional integration on federal systems. In H. lazar, H. Telford, & R. Watts (Eds.), *The impact of global and regional integration on federal systems.* Montreal & Kingston: McGill-Queen's University Press.

LeDuc, L. & Pammett, J.H. (2011). The evolution of the Harper dynasty. In J.J. Pammett & C. Dornan (Eds.). *The Canadian federal election of 2011.* Toronto: Dundurn.

Leftwich, A. (1983). *Redefining politics: People, resources and power.* London and New York: Methuen.

Leggett, W. (2007). British social democracy beyond new Labour: Entrenching a progressive consensus. *British Journal of Politics and International Relations, 9,* 346–364.

Leo, C., & Mulligan, S. (2006). City politics: Globalization and community democracy. In J. Grace & B. Sheldreck (Eds.), *Canadian politics: Democracy and dissent.* Toronto: Pearson Education.

Leonard, A. (2010). Germany's blitzkrieg against short-sellers. *Salon.* Retrieved from http://www.salon.com/2010/05/19/the_german_blitzkrieg_against_short_sellers

Levitsky, S., & Way, L.A. (2010). *Competitive authoritarianism: Hybrid regimes after the Cold War.* New York: Cambridge University Press.

Lewin, L. (1991). *Self-interest and public interest in Western politics* (D. Lavery, Trans.). Oxford: Oxford University Press.

Lewis, B. (2004). *The crisis of Islam. Holy war and unholy terror.* New York: Random House.

Lewis-Beck, M.S. & Whiffen, G.D. (2013). Economics and elections: Effects deep and wide. *Electoral Studies, 32*(3), 393–395.

Liberal Party of Canada (2013). National rules for the selection of candidates for the Liberal Party of Canada, 2013. Retrieved from https://www.liberal.ca/files/2014/01/national-nomination-rules.pdf

Liberal Party of Canada (2015). *Liberal Party Platform* (2015). https://www.liberal.ca/realchange/free-votes/

Lijphart, A. (2012). *Patterns of democracy: Government forms and performance in thirty-six countries* (2nd ed.). New Haven, CT: Yale University Press.

Lilleker, D.G. & Jackson, N.A. (2011). *Political campaigning, elections and the internet. Comparing the US, UK, France and Germany.* London: Routledge.

Lindblom, C.E. (1977). *Politics and markets: The world's political-economic systems.* New York: Basic Books.

Linz, J. (1994). Presidential or parliamentary democracy: Does it make a difference? In J.J. Linz & A. Valenzuela (Eds.), *The failure of presidential democracy: Vol. 1. Comparative perspectives* (pp. 3–87). Baltimore, MD: John Hopkins University Press.

Lipschutz, R.D. (2000). *After authority: War, peace and global politics in the 21st century.* Albany, NY: State University of New York Press.

Lipset, S.M. (1950). *Agrarian socialism*. Berkeley, CA: University of California Press.

Lipset, S.M. (1990). *Continental divide: The values and institutions of the United States and Canada*. New York: Routledge.

Lipset, S.M., & Rokkan, S. (1967). Cleavage structures, party systems and voter alignments: An introduction. In S.M. Lipset & S. Rokkan (Eds.), *Party systems and voter alignments: Cross-national perspectives*. New York: Free Press.

Lipsky, R. (1968). Protest as a political resource. *American Political Science Review*, 62(4), 1144–1158.

Liptak, A. (2010, January 21). Justices, 5–4, reject corporate spending limit. Retrieved from www.nytimes.com/2010/01/22/us/politics/22scotus.html

Lobe, J. (2002, September 27). The arrogance of power. *Foreign Policy in Focus*.

Lobell, S., Ripsman, N. and Taliaferro, J. (Eds.). (2009). *Neoclassical Realism, the State, and Foreign Policy*. Cambridge: Cambridge University Press.

Lofgren, M. (2016). *The deep state. The fall of the constitution and the rise of a shadow government*. New York: Penguin.

Lowe, V. (2015).*International law: A very short introduction*. Oxford: Oxford University Press.

Lukes, S. (1974). *Power: A radical view*. London: Macmillan.

Luttwak, E. (1969). *Coup d'etat*. New York: Alfred A. Knopf.

Lutz, M.A. (1999). *Economics for the common good: Two centuries of social economic thought in the humanist tradition*. New York: Routledge.

Lyons, W., Scheb, J.M., & Richardson, L.E. (1995). *American government: Politics and political culture*. St. Paul, MN: West Publishing.

Maastricht Treaty (1992). Retrieved from www.eurotreaties.com/maastrichteu.pdf

MacIvor, H. (2006). *Canadian politics and government in the Charter era*. Toronto: Thomson Nelson.

MacKenzie, H. (2016). Staying power, CEO pay in Canada. Retrieved from https://www.policyalternatives.ca/ceo2016

Macpherson, C.B. (1954). *Democracy in Alberta*. Toronto: University of Toronto Press.

Macpherson, C.B. (1965). *The real world of democracy*. Toronto: University of Toronto Press.

Macpherson, C.B. (1980). *Burke*. Toronto: Oxford University Press.

Magaloni, B. (2006). *Voting for autocracy: Hegemonic party survival and its demise in Mexico*. New York: Cambridge University Press.

Mahoney, C. (2008). *Brussels versus the Beltway: Advocacy in the United States and the European Union*. Washington, DC: Georgetown University Press.

Mahoney, C., & Baumgartner, F. (2008). Converging perspectives on interest group research in Europe and America. *West European Politics, 31*(6), 1253–1273.

Makin, K. (2005, January 29). Politician's promises not set in stone, court says. *The Globe and Mail*. Retrieved from http://www.theglobeandmail.com/news/national/politicians-promises-not-set-in-stone-court-says/article1114002/

Mann, M. (2004). *Fascists*. New York: Cambridge University Press.

Marshall, K. (2011). Paid and unpaid work over three generations. Perspectives on labour and income. Statistics Canada. Retrieved from www.statcan.gc.ca/pub/75-001-x/75-001-x2012001-eng.htm

Martell, L. (1994). *Ecology and society: An introduction*. Amherst, MA: University of Massachusetts Press.

Martin, H.-P., & Schumann, H. (1997). *The global trap: Globalization and the assault on democracy and prosperity*. Montreal: Black Rose Books.

Martin, M. (2011). International perspectives on guaranteed annual income programs. *Queen's Policy Review* 2(1).

Martinez-Arboleda, A. (2015). Podemos, the 15M indignados movement and the radical left in Spain. New Politics. Retrieved from newpol.org/context/podemos-15m-indignados-movement-and-radical-left-spain

Mascaro, L. (2016, March 20). Donald Trump's campaign might break apart the tea party. *Los Angeles Times*. Retrieved from http://www.latimes.com/politics/la-na-trump-tea-party-divide-20160318-story.html

Mayeda, A. (2010, May 12). Canadian offshore drilling regulations relaxed last year. *The Western Star*.

McAllister, M.L. (2004). *Governing ourselves: The politics of local communities*. Vancouver, BC: UBC Press.

McDevitt, M. & Chaffee, S. (2002). From top-down to trickle-up influence. Revisiting assumptions about the family in political socialization. *Political Communication 19*(3), 281–301

McFarland, J. (2013, February 19). Women's slow climb to the top in corporate Canada. *The Globe and Mail*.

McGovern (2007). The emergence of the modern state. In E. Cudworth, T. Hall, & J. McGovern (Eds.). *The modern state. Theories and ideologies* (pp. 20–36). Edinburgh: Edinburgh University Press.

McKenna, G. (1990). *The drama of democracy: American government and politics*. Guilford, CT: Dushkin Publishing.

McLeod, G. (2014). Forex market size: A traders advantage. *Daily FX*. Retrieved from https://www4.dailyfx.com/forex/education/trading_tips/daily_trading_lesson/2014/01/24/FX_Market_Size.html

Meyer, J. (2016, February 27). Forget Trump - 'Dark money' from Koch brothers is shaping Republican party. Retrieved from http://www.cbc.ca/news/world/koch-brothers-dark-money-republican-party-1.3466477

Milanovic, B. (2016). *Global inequality. A new approach for the age of globalization*. Cambridge, MA: Belknap Press.

Miljan, L.A., & Cooper, B. (2003). *Hidden agendas: How journalists influence the news*. Vancouver: UBC Press.

Mill, J.S. (1912). *On liberty. Representative government. The subjection of women. Three essays*. London: Oxford University Press. (Originally published in 1859.)

Miller, W.L., & Niemi, R.G. (2002). Voting: Choice, conditioning, and constraint. In L. LeDuc, R.G. Niemi, & P. Norris (Eds.), *Comparing democracies 2: New challenges in the study of elections and voting* (pp. 169–188). London: Sage.

Millett, K. (1985). *Sexual politics*. London: Virago.

Milliken, P. (2010, April 27). Ruling on the question of privilege. *House of Commons Debates (Hansard)*.

Milner, H. (1997). Electoral systems, integrated institutions and turnout in local and national elections: Canada in comparative perspective. *Canadian Journal of Political Science, 30*(1, March), 89–106.

Milner, H. (2002). *Civic literacy: How informed citizens make democracy work*. Hanover, NH: University Press of New England.

Milton-Edwards, B. (2005). *Islamic fundamentalism since 1945*. London, UK: Routledge.

Mintz, E. (1993). Two generations: The political attitudes of high school students and their parents. *International Journal of Canadian Studies*, (special issue), 59–71.

Mitchell, K. (2003). Educating the national citizen in neoliberal times: From the multicultural self to the strategic cosmopolitan. *Transactions of the Institute of British Geographers, 28*(4), 387–403.

Mittelstaedt, M. (2010, May 17). Canada's long-time adversaries posed to announce peace pact, switch to partnership model. *The Globe and Mail*. Retrieved from www.theglobeandmail.com/report-on-business/loggers-environmentalists-reach-truce/article1571684.

Monteiro, N.P. (2014). *Theory of Unipolar Politics*, Cambridge: Cambridge University Press.

Montpetit, É. (2004). Governance and interest group activities. In J. Bickerton and A-G. Gagnon (Eds.), *Canadian politics* (4th ed.). Peterborough, ON: Broadview Press.

More, T. (2004). Utopia. In T. Ball & R. Dagger (Eds.), *Ideals and ideologies: A reader* (5th ed.). New York: Pearson Longman. (Original work published in 1516.)

Morgan, R. (1977). *Going too far: The personal chronicle of a feminist*. New York: Random House.

Morgenthau, H.J. (1948). *Politics among nations: The struggle for power and peace*. New York: Knopf.

Morlan, R.L. (1984). Municipal vs. national election voter turnout: Europe and the United States. *Political Science Quarterly, 99*, 457–70.

Morlino, L. (2008). Hybrid regimes or regimes in transition? *Working Paper 70*. Madrid: FRIDE. www.plataformademocratica.org/Publicacoes/4618_Cached.pdf

Morozov, E. (2011). *Net delusion: the dark side of internet freedom*. New York: Public Affairs.

Morton, F.L. (2003). Can judicial supremacy be stopped? *Policy Options, 24*(9), 25–99.

Morton, W.L. (1950). *The Progressive Party in Canada*. Toronto: University of Toronto Press

Mueller, J. (1989). *Retreat from doomsday: The obsolescence of major war*. New York: Basic Books.

Naess, A., & Sessions, G. (1993). The deep ecology platform. In B. Devall (Ed.), *Clearcut: The tragedy of industrial forestry*. San Francisco: Sierra Book Club & Earth Island Press.

National Oceanic and Atmospheric Administration (2015), Earth Systems Research Laboratory. Retrieved from: http://www.esrl.noaa.gov/gmd/ccgg/trends/2015

Needler, M.C. (1996). *Identity, interest, and ideology: An introduction to politics*. Westport, CT: Praeger.

Nelson, B.R. (2006). *The making of the modern state: A theoretical evolution*. New York: Palgrave Macmillan.

Neocleous, M. (1997). *Fascism*. Minneapolis, MN: University of Minnesota Press.

Nevitte, N. (1996). *The decline of deference: Canadian value change in cross-national perspective*. Peterborough, ON: Broadview Press.

New York Times. (2008, November 5). Election results 2008. Retrieved from http://elections.nytimes.com/2008/results/president/national-exit-polls.htm

Newton, K., & Van Deth, J.W. (2010). *Foundations of comparative politics: Democracies of the modern world* (2nd ed.). Cambridge: Cambridge University Press.

Niemi, R.G. & Hepburn, M.A. (1995). The rebirth of political socialization. *Perspectives on Political Science, 24*(1), 7–16.

Norris, P. (2000). *A virtuous circle: Political communications in postindustrial societies*. Cambridge, UK: Cambridge University Press, 2000.

Norris, P. (2002). Campaign communications. In L. LeDuc, R.G. Niemi, & P. Norris (Eds.), *Comparing democracies 2: New challenges in the study of elections and voting* (pp. 127–147). London, UK: Sage.

Norris, P. (2011). *Democratic deficit: Critical citizens revisited*. Cambridge: Cambridge University Press.

Norris, P. & Inglehart, R. (2002). *Islam and the West: Testing the clash of civilizations thesis*. Retrieved from: http://www.hks.harvard.edu/fs/pnorris/Acrobat/Clash%20of%20Civilization.pdf

Norton, P. (2016). The Fixed Term Parliament Act and votes of confidence. *Parliamentary Affairs, 69*, 3–18.

Nozick, R. (1974). *Anarchy, State and Utopia*. New York: Basic Books.

Nye, J.S., JR. (2004). *Soft power: The means to success in world politics*. New York: Public Affairs.

Oakeshott, M. (1991). On Being Conservative. In *Rationalism in Politics and Other Essays (*pp. 407–437). Indianapolis, Indiana: Liberty Fund.

Obama, B. (2006). *The audacity of hope: Thoughts on reclaiming the American dream*. New York: Vintage Books.

OECD. (2015). *In it together. Why less inequality benefits all*. Retrieved from HYPERLINK "http://www.oecd/els/" www.oecd/els/OECD2015-In-It-together

OECD. (2016). *Net ODA: Trends in volume as a share of GNI, 1999–2015*. http://www.oecd.org/dac/canada.htm

Office of the Commissioner of Lobbying of Canada. (2015). *Annual Report 2014–15*. Retrieved from lobbycanada.gc.ca.

Olson, M. (1965). *The logic of collective action: Public goods and the theory of groups*. Cambridge, MA: Harvard University Press.

O'Neill, B. (2002). Sugar and spice? Political culture and the political behaviour of Canadian women. In J. Everitt & B. O'Neill (eds.). *Citizen politics: Research and theory in Canadian political behaviour* (pp. 40–55). Don Mills, ON: Oxford University Press.

O'Neill, B. & Thomas, M. (2016). "Because It's 2015": Gender and the 2015 Federal Election. In J. H. Pammett & C. Dornan, *The Canadian federal election of 2015*. pp. 275–304. Toronto: Dundurn Press.

Opp, K.-D. (1989). *The rationality of political protest*. Boulder, CO: Westview Press.

Oppenheimer, J.R. (1953). Atomic weapons and American policy. *Foreign Affairs, 31*(4), 525–535.

Orphanides, A. (2015). The Euro Area crisis five years after the original sin. http://papers.ssrn.com/sol3/papers.cfm?abstract_id=2676103

Ostrom, E. (2000). *Governing the commons: The evolution of institutions for collective action*. New York: Cambridge University Press.

Owen, D. (2009). The campaign and the media. In J.M. Box-Steffensmeier & S.E. Schier (Eds.), *The American elections of 2008*. Lanham, MD: Rowman & Littlefield.

Oxfam. (2016). *210 Oxfam briefing paper*. Retrieved from: bp210-economy-one-percent-tax-havens-180116-en-pdf

Oxley, Z. (2012). More sources, better informed public? New media and political knowledge. In R.L. Fox & J.M. Ramos (Eds.), *iPolitics: Citizens, elections and governing in the new media era*. New York: Cambridge University Press.

Page, K. (2015). *Unaccountable: Truth and lies on Parliament Hill*. Toronto: Penguin.

Pal, L.A. (1992). *Public policy analysis: An introduction* (2nd ed.). Scarborough, ON: Nelson Canada.

Pal, L.A. (1993). *Interests of state: The politics of language, multiculturalism and feminism in Canada*. Montreal: McGill–Queen's University Press.

Palmer, D. (1994). *Shining Path of Peru*. New York: St. Martin's Press.

Pammett, J.H., & LeDuc, L. (2003). *Explaining the turnout decline in Canadian federal elections: A new survey of non-voters*. Retrieved May 26, 2004, from www.elections.ca

Panebianco, A. (1988). *Political parties: Organization and power*. Cambridge, UK: Cambridge University Press.

Parrington, V. (1987). *Main currents in American thought* (Vols. 1–2). Norman, OK: University of Oklahoma Press.

Pape, R.A. (2005). *Dying to win: The strategic logic of suicide terrorism*. New York: Random House.

Parenti, M. (1970). Power and pluralism: A view from the bottom. *Journal of Politics, 32*(3), 501–530.

Pew Research Center for the People and the Press (2012). Party affiliation and election polls. Retrieved from www.people-press.org/2012/08/03/party-affiliation-and-election-polls/

Pharr, S., Putnam, R.D., & Dalton, R.J. (2000). A quarter century of declining confidence. *Journal of Democracy, 11*(2), 5–25.

Pierson, C. (2011). *The modern state* (3rd ed.). London: Routledge.

Pisani-Ferry, J. (2013, March1). The euro's house divided. Retrieved from www.project-syndicate.org/commentary/the-eurozone-s-persistent-regional-disparities-by-jean-pisani-ferry

Pischedda, C. (2015, August 27). A provocative article says the Islamic State is a mystery. Here's why that's wrong. *Washington Post*. Retrieved August 27, 2015, from https://www.washingtonpost.com/blogs/monkey-cage/wp/2015/08/27/the-islamic-state-is-no-mystery

Plasser, F., with Plasser, G. (2002). *Global political campaigning: A worldwide analysis of campaign professionals and their practices*. Westport, CT: Praeger.

Poguntke, T. (2014). Towards a new party system. The vanishing hold of the catch-all parties in Germany. *Party Politics, 20*(6), 950–64.

Pollack, K.M. (2002). *The threatening storm: The case for invading Iraq*. New York: Random House.

Potter, S.V. (2003). Judging the judiciary: The rule of law in the age of the Charter. *Policy Options, 24*(9), 34–38.

Prados, A.B and Katzman, K. (2002, February 20). Iraq-U.S. Confrontation. Washington D.C.: The Library of Congress, Congressional Research Services. http://fpc.state.gov/documents/organization/9043.pdf

Pross, A.P. (1993). *Group politics and public policies* (2nd ed.). Toronto: Oxford University Press.

Project Steering Committee. (2016). *Canadian infrastructure report card*. Retrieved from http://www.canadainfrastructure.ca/downloads/Canadian_Infrastructure_Report_2016.pdf

Provost, C. & Harris, R. (2013, April 29). China commits billions in aid to Africa as part of charm offensive. *The Guardian*.

Przeworski, A. (1991). *Democracy and the Market: Political andEconomic Reforms in Eastern Europe and Latin America*. Cambridge, UK: Cambridge University Press.

Przeworski, A. (2009). Conquered or granted? A history of suffrage extension. *British Journal of Political Science 39*(2), 291–321.

Punnett, R.M. (1971). *British politics and government* (2nd ed.). London: Heinemann Educational Books.

Putnam, R. (1993). *Making democracy work: Civic traditions in modern Italy*. Princeton, NJ: Princeton University Press.

Putnam, R. (2000). *Bowling alone: The collapse and revival of American community*. New York: Simon & Schuster.

Quah, J.S.T. (2008). Curbing corruption in India: An impossible dream? *Asian Journal of Political Science, 16*(3), 240–259.

Rasch. B.E., & Congleton, R.D. (2006). Amendment procedures and constitutional stability. In R.D. Congleton & B. Swedenborg (Eds.), *Democratic constitutional design and public policy: Analysis and evidence*. Cambridge, MA: MIT Press.

Rawls, J. (1999). *A Theory of Justice* (revised ed.). Cambridge, MA: Belknap Press.

Rees, W., & Wackernagel, M. (1996). *Our ecological footprint: Reducing human impact on earth*. Gabriola Island, BC: New Society Publishers.

Resnick, P. (1997). *Twenty-first century democracy*. Montreal: McGill-Queen's University Press.

Rhodes, R.A.W., Wanner, J., & Weller, P. (2009). *Comparing Westminster*. Oxford: Oxford University Press.

Rihoux, B., & Frankland, E.G. (2008). Conclusion: The metamorphosis of amateur-activist newborns into professional-activist centaurs. In E.G. Frankland, P. Lucardie, & B. Rihoux (Eds.), *Green parties in transition: The end of grass-roots democracy?* (pp. 250–287). Farnham, UK: Ashgate Publishing.

Ritzer, G. (2012). *The McDonaldization of society* (7th ed.). Thousand Oaks, CA: Sage Publications.

Rochlin, J. (2003). *Vanguard revolutionaries in Latin America: Peru, Colombia, Mexico*. Boulder, CO: Lynne Reinner Publishers.

Rodrick, D. (2011). *The globalization paradox. Democracy and the future of the world economy*. New York: W.W. Norton.

Roett, R., & Paz, G. (Eds.). (2008). *China's expansion into the western hemisphere*. Washington, DC: Brookings Institution Press.

Rose, G. (1998). "Neoclassical Realism and Theories of Foreign Policy," *World Politics, 51*(1), 144–72.

Rotberg, R. (Ed.). (2008). *China into Africa: Trade, aid, and influence*. Washington, DC: Brookings Institution Press.

Rothkopf, D. (2008). *The global power elite and the world they are making*. New York: Farrar, Straus & Giroux

Rothkopf, D. (2009). *Superclass: The global power elite and the world they are making*. Toronto: Penguin Canada.

Rothkopf, D. (2012). *Power, Inc. The epic rivalry between big business and government*. New York: Farrar, Straus & Giroux.

Rousseau, J.-J. (1968). *The social contract* (M. Cranston, Trans.). Harmondsworth, UK: Penguin. (Original work published in 1762).

Sabato, L. (1992). *Feeding frenzy: How attack journalism has transformed American politics*. New York: Free Press.

Sachs, J.D. (2005). *The End of poverty. Economic possibilities for our time*. New York: Penguin.

Samara Canada (2014). Lightweights. Political participation beyond the ballot box. Retrieved from http://www.samaracanada.com/docs/default-document-library/samara_lightweights.pdf

Samara Canada (2015). Democracy 360. Talk. Act. Lead. Retrieved from: http://www.inm.qc.ca/Centre_doc/2014_Samara_Democracy_360.pdf

Sancton, A. (2002). Municipalities, cities, and globalization: Implications for Canadian federalism. In H. Bakvis & G. Skogstad (Eds.), *Canadian federalism: Performance, effectiveness, and legitimacy* (pp. 261–277). Don Mills, ON: Oxford University Press.

Sartori, G. (1976). *Parties and party systems*. New York: Cambridge University Press.

Savoie, D.J. (1999). *Governing from the centre: The concentration of power in Canadian politics*. Toronto: University of Toronto Press.

Savoie, D.J. (2003). *Breaking the bargain: Public servants, ministers and Parliament*. Toronto: University of Toronto Press.

Savoie, D.J. (2008). *Court government and the collapse of accountability in Canada and the United Kingdom*. Toronto: University of Toronto Press.

Savoie, D.J. (2013). *Whatever happened to the music teacher: How government decides and why*. Montreal: McGill-Queen's University Press.

Savoie, D.J. (2015). *What is government good at? A Canadian answer*. Montreal: McGill-Queen's University Press.

Scarrow, S.E., Webb, P., & Farrell, D.M. (2000). From social integration to electoral contestation: The changing distribution of power within political parties. In R.J. Dalton & M.P. Wattenberg (Eds.), *Parties without partisans: Political change in advanced industrial democracies* (pp. 129–153). Oxford: Oxford University Press.

Schattschneider, E.E. (1942/1977). *Party government*. Westport, CT: Greenwood Press.

Schleder, A. (2006). *Electoral authoritarianism: The dynamics of unfree competition*. Boulder, CO: Lynne Riemmer.

Schlesinger, A.E. (1973). *The imperial presidency*. Boston: Houghton Mifflin.

Schumacher, E.F. (1973). *Small is beautiful: A study of economics as if people mattered*. London: Sphere Books.

Segal, H. (2008). Guaranteed annual income: Why Milton Friedman and Bob Stanfield were right. *Policy Options*. April.

Shaiko, R.G. (1999). *Voices and echoes for the environment: Public interest representation in the 1990s and beyond*. New York: Columbia University Press.

Shub, D. (1966). *Lenin: A biography*. Baltimore, MD: Penguin Books.

Shugart, M.S. (2006). Comparative executive-legislative relations. In R.A.W. Rhodes, S.A. Binder, & B.A. Rockman (Eds.), *The Oxford handbook of political institutions*. Oxford: Oxford University Press.

Siaroff, A. (2009a). Comparing political regimes: A thematic introduction to comparative politics (2nd ed.). Toronto: University of Toronto Press.

Siaroff, A. (2009b). The decline of political participation: An empirical overview of voter turnout and party membership. In J. DeBardeleben & J.H. Pammeett (Eds.), *Activating the citizen: Dilemmas of participation in Europe and Canada*. New York: Palgrave Macmillan.

Simeon, R. (1976). Studying public policy. *Canadian Journal of Political Science, 9*(3), 548–580.

Simeon, R. & Radin, B.A. (2010). Reflections on comparing federalisms: Canada and the United States. *Publius, 40*(3), 357–365.

Simpson, J. (2001). *The friendly dictatorship*. Toronto: McClelland & Stewart.

Simpson, J. (2012). *Chronic Condition. Why Canada's health-care system needs to be dragged into the 21st century*. Toronto: Allen Lane.

Sirleaf, E.J. (2015). *25 years of human development, an African perspective*. http://hdr.undp.org/en/content/25-years-human-development-african-perspective

Skocpol, T. (1979). *States and social revolutions: A comparative analysis of France, Russia, and China*. New York: Cambridge University Press.

Small Arms Survey, 2007. http://www.smallarmssurvey.org/fileadmin/docs/A-Yearbook/2007/en/Small-Arms-Survey-2007-Chapter-02-annexe-4-EN.pdf

Smith, A. (1759/2010). *The theory of moral sentiments*. New York: Penguin Classics.

Smith, A. (1776/1993). *The Wealth of Nations*. Cambridge, Indianapolis: Hackett Publishing.

Smith, G., & Wales, C. (2000). Citizens' juries and deliberative democracy. *Political Studies 48*(1, March), 51–65.

Smith, R. A. (2011). *The American anomaly. U.S. politics and government in comparative perspective* (2nd ed.). New York: Routledge.

Sniderman, P.M., Fletcher, J.F., Russell, P.H., & Tetlock, P. (1996). *The clash of rights: Liberty, equality, and legitimacy in pluralist democracy*. New Haven: Yale University Press.

Solomon, S., Plattner, G-K., Knutti, R. & Friedlingstein, P. (2009). Irreversible climate change due to carbon dioxide emissions. *Proceedings of the National Academy of Sciences of the United States of America (PNAS), 106*(6), 1704–1709.

Soroka, S., Cutler, F., Stolle, D., & Fournier, P. (2011). Capturing change (and stability) in the 2011 campaign. *Policy Options*, (June–July), 70–77.

Soros, G. (2013, April 13). Europe's crisis of values. Retrieved from www.project-syndicate.org/commentary/the-existential-crisis-of-the-european-union-by-george-soros

Sossin, L. (2005). Speaking truth to power? The search for bureaucratic independence in Canada. *University of Toronto Law Journal 55*(1), 1–59.

Sovereign Wealth Fund Institute (2016). Retrieved from www.swfinstitute.org/fund-rankings

Specht, C. (2013, February 9). $113 million Love Canal lawsuit: Is history repeating itself? *The Buffalo News.*

Spector, N. (2009, August 27). More harmonizing than harmonized. *The Globe and Mail.*

Statistics Canada (2011). Reasons for not voting among those that did not vote, by sex and by age group, May 2011 federal election. Retrieved from www.statcan.gc.ca/daily-quotidien/110705/dq110705a-eng.htm

Statistics Canada. (2015). Homicide in Canada, 2014. *The Daily.* Retrieved from http://www.statcan.gc.ca/daily-quotidien/151125/dq151125a-eng.htm

Statistics Times. (2015). Indian states by gdp per capita. http://statisticstimes.com/economy/gdp-capita-of-indian-states.php

Steinmo, S., (2010). *The evolution of modern states: Sweden, Japan, and the United States.* New York: Cambridge University Press.

Stern, D.I. (2004). The rise and fall of the environmental Kutznets curve. *World Development, 32*(8), 1419–1439.

Stern, J., and Berger, J.M. (2015). *ISIS: The state of terror.* New York: Ecco Press.

Sterling-Folker, J. (Ed.). (2006). *Making sense of international relations theory.* Boulder, CO: Lynne Rienner.

Stoker, G. (2006). Comparative local governance. In R.A.W. Rhodes, S.A. Binder, & B.A. Rockman (Eds.), *The Oxford handbook of political Institutions.* Oxford: Oxford University Press.

Sunderlin, W.D. (2003). *Ideology, social theory, and the environment.* Lanham, MD: Rowman & Littlefield.

Suny, R.G. (2006). Nationalism, nation making and the postcolonial states of Asia, Africa, and Eurasia. In L. Barrington (Ed.) *Making and protecting the nation in postcolonial and postcommunist states.* Ann Arbor, MI: University of Michigan Press.

Sutherland, C. (2012). *Nationalism in the twenty-first century.* Houndmills, UK: Palgrave Macmillan.

Sutter, R.G. (2008). *Chinese foreign relations: Power and policy since the Cold War.* Lanham, MD: Rowman & Littlefield.

Swenden, W. (2006). *Federalism and regionalism in Western Europe: A comparative and thematic analysis.* Houndmills, Basingstoke, Hampshire, UK: Palgrave Macmillan.

Sylvester, C. (1994). *Feminist theory and international relations in a postmodern era.* New York: Cambridge University Press.

Talbot, D. (2015). *The devil's chessboard: Allen Dulles, the CIA, and the rise of America's secret government.* New York: HarperCollins.

Tarrow, S. (1999). *Power in movement: Social movements and contentious politics.* Cambridge, UK: Cambridge University Press.

Tepperman, J. (2016). Brazil's antipoverty breakthrough. The surprising success of Bolsa Familia. *Foreign Affairs,* January/February, 2016.

The Responsibility to Protect. International Commission on Intervention and State Sovereignty https://web.archive.org/web/20070731161527/http://www.iciss-ciise.gc.ca/report2-en.asp

Thompson, D. (1984). *The Chartists.* New York: Pantheon.

Thompson, N. (2016, April 16). Canadians like the Queen but her heir? Not so much. Canadian Press. Retrieved from http://www.theglobeandmail.com/news/national/canadians-like-the-queen-but-her-heir-not-so-much-surveysays/article29658118/

Thucydides (1972). *History of the Peleponnesian war.* London: Penguin.

Thurber, T.R. & Yoshinaka, A. (2015). (Eds.). *American gridlock. The sources, character, and impact of political polarization.* New York: Cambridge University Press.

Tilly, C., & Tarrow, S. (2007). *Contentious politics.* Boulder, CO: Paradigm Publishers.

Toje, A. and Kunz, B. (Eds.). (2012). *Neoclassical Realism in European Politics: Bringing Power Back In.* Manchester: Manchester University Press.

Trudeau, P.-E. (1993). *Memoirs.* Toronto: McClelland & Stewart.

UNDP [United Nations Development Programme]. (1995, 2002, 2003, 2010). *Human development report, 1995, 2002, 2003, 2010.* New York: Oxford University Press.

United Nations Office on Drugs and Crime (2014). *Global study on homicide.* https://www.unodc.org/documents/gsh/pdfs/2014_GLOBAL_HOMICIDE_BOOK_web.pdf

UNMDG (2005). *MDG Info 2005.* http://www.un.org/millenniumgoals/bkgd.shtml

UNMDG (2015). *UN Millennium Development Goals.* Retrieved from: http://www.un.org/millenniumgoals/2015_MDG_Report/pdf/MDG%202015%20rev%20(July%201).pdf

UNSDG (2016). *UN Sustainable Development Goals.* Retrieved from: http://www.un.org/sustainabledevelopment/sustainable-development-goals/

US Army. (2006). *Counterinsurgency.* Field Manual 3–24. Washington: Department of the Army. Available at http://usacac.army.mil/cac/repository/materials/coin-fm3-24.pdf

Van Harten, G. (2015). *Sold down the Yangtze: Canada's lopsided investment deal with China.* Toronto: Lorimer.

Verba, S., Nie, N., & Kim, J.O. (1978). *Participation and political equality.* New York: Cambridge University Press.

Veseth, M. (2010). *Globaloney 2.0. The crash of 2008 and the future of globalization* (2nd ed.). Lanham, MD: Rowman and Littlefield.

Wade, R. (1990). *Governing the market.* Princeton, NJ: Princeton University Press.

Wallack, M. (2006). From compellence to pre-emption: Kosovo and Iraq as U.S. responses to contested hegemony. In O. Croci & A. Verdun (Eds.), *The transatlantic divide: Foreign and security policies in the Atlantic Alliance from Kosovo to Iraq* (pp. 109–125). Manchester, UK: Manchester University Press.

Wallerstein, I. (2011) *The modern world system*, Volumes I–IV. Berkeley, CA: University of California Press.

Waltz, K.N. (1979). *Theory of international politics*. Reading, MA: Addison-Wesley.

Monteiro, N.P. (2014). *Theory of Unipolar Politics*, Cambridge: Cambridge University Press.

Ware, A. (1987). *Political parties: Electoral change and structural response*. Oxford: Basil Blackwell.

Warren, M. (2002). Deliberative democracy. In A. Carter & G. Stokes (Eds.), *Democratic theory today: Challenges for the 21st century* (pp. 173–202). Cambridge, UK: Polity Press.

Watkins-Hayes, C. (2010). Human services as "race work"? Historical lessons and contemporary challenges of black providers. In Y. Hasenfeld (Ed.), *Human services as complex organizations* (2nd ed.). Thousand Oaks, CA: Sage Publications.

Watts, J. (2016, May 23). Brazil minister ousted after secret tape reveals plot to topple President Rousseff. *The Guardian*. Retrieved from https://www.theguardian.com/world/2016/may/23/brazil-dilma-rousseff-plot-secret-phone-transcript-impeachment

Watts, R.L. (2008). *Comparing federal systems* (3rd ed.). Montreal & Kingston: McGill-Queen's University Press.

Weale, A. (1992). *The new politics of pollution*. Manchester, UK: Manchester University Press.

Weber, E. (1976). *Peasants into Frenchmen: The modernization of rural France, 1870–1914*. Stanford, CA: Stanford University.

Weber, M. (1958). In H.H. Gerth & C.W. Mills (Eds. & Trans.), *Max Weber: Essays in sociology*. New York: Oxford University Press.

Weber, M. (1970). In H.H. Gerth & C. Wright Mills (Eds. & Trans*.). From Max Weber: Essays in sociology*. London: Routledge and Kegan Paul.

Weir, S., & Beetham, D. (1999). *Political power and democratic control in Britain*. London: Routledge.

Weller, P. (1985). *First among equals: Prime ministers in Westminster systems*. Sydney: George Allen & Unwin.

Welzel, C. (2011). The Asian values thesis revisited. Evidence from the World Values Survey. *Japanese Journal of Political Science, 12*(1), 1–31.

Wendt, A. (1999). *Social theory of international politics*. Cambridge, UK: Cambridge University Press, 1999.

Wheaton, B., & Z. Kavan (1992). *The Velvet Revolution: Czechoslovakia, 1988–1991*. Boulder, CO: Westview Press.

Whitaker, R. (1997). Canadian politics at the end of the millennium: Old dreams, new nightmares. In D. Taras & B. Rasporich (Eds.), *A passion for identity: An introduction to Canadian studies* (3rd ed.) (pp. 119–137). Toronto: ITP Nelson.

White, R. (1978). *Paraguay's autonomous revolution: 1810–1840*. Albuquerque, NM: University of New Mexico Press.

Whitesides, J., & Lawder, D. (2013, April 17). 'A shameful day' says Obama as Senate rejects gun control measure. *The Globe and Mail*.

Wilson, J. (2002). Continuity and change in the Canadian environmental movement: Assessing the effects of institutionalization. In D.L. VanNijnatten & R. Boardman (Eds.), *Canadian environmental policy: Context and cases*. Don Mills, ON: Oxford University Press.

Wolf, M. (2001). Will the nation-state survive globalization? *Foreign Affairs, 80*(1), 178–190.

Wolin, S.S. (1960). *Politics and Vision: Continuity and innovation in Western political thought*. Boston: Little, Brown.

Woolley, J. & Peters, G. (2016). *The American Presidency Project*. Retrieved from http://www.presidency.ucsb.edu/index.php

World Bank. (2015). *Poverty: Overview*. http://www.worldbank.org/en/topic/poverty/overview

World Bank. (2016a). Data. GDP per capita (current US$). Retrieved from http://data.worldbank.org/indicator/NY.GDP.PCAP.CD

World Bank. (2016b). Updated income classifications. http://data.worldbank.org/news/2015-country-classifications

World Commission on Environment and Development. (1987). *Our common future*. Oxford: Oxford University Press.

World Population Clock (n.d.). Retrieved January 30, 2016 from: www.worldometers.info/world-population

World Values Survey. *Fifth Wave, 2005–2008*. Retrieved from www.worldvaluessurvey.org

World Values Survey. *Sixth Wave, 2010–2014*. Retrieved from www.worldvaluessurvey.org

World Wildlife Fund. "Canadians must choose environment and economy for strong future." *Living Planet Report, 2014*. Retrieved from http://www.wwf.ca/newsroom/reports/living_planet_report_2014.cfm

World Vision. (2016, April 11). Syria refugee crisis FAQ. How the war is affecting children. Retrieved from https://www.worldvision.org/wv/news/Syria-war-refugee-crisis-FAQ

York, G. (2010, March 27). The war that won't end. *The Globe and Mail*, F1, F6–F7.

Young, L., & Everitt, J. (2004). *Advocacy groups*. Vancouver: UBC Press.

Young, R. (2009). Conclusion. In A. Sancton & R. Young (Eds.). *Foundations of governance: Municipal government in Canada's provinces*. Toronto: University of Toronto Press.

Zehfuss, M. (2002). *Constructivism in international relations: The politics of reality*. Cambridge, UK: Cambridge University Press.

Zucman, G. (2015). *The hidden wealth of nations. The scourge of tax havens*. Chicago: University of Chicago Press.